CAMBRIDGE
EDUCATIONAL SERVICES®

AMERICA'S PREMIERE TESTING READINESS PROGRAM

Essential Skills

Required for College and Career Readiness

STUDENT TEXT

ACT® • PLAN® • EXPLORE® • SAT • PSAT/NMSQT • WorkKeys® • GRE® • GMAT® • LSAT® • GED® • TASC™ • HiSET™ • ITBS • MCAT® • PRAXIS® • Stanford
EOC and State Tests • Data Services • Classroom Texts • Teacher Curriculum • Professional Development • Web Courses • Question Writing • Online Services
CollegePrep™ • Guidance Services • Motivation/Admissions Workshops • Learning Styles • Career Interest Inventory
Non-Negotiable Skills™ • Essential Skills • Cambridge Ignite™ eBooks

The above-cited marks are the property of their respective owners.

Our Mission: Progress Through Partnership

Cambridge Educational Services partners with educators who share the significant mission of educational advancement for all students. By partnering together, we can best achieve our common goals: to build skills, raise test scores, enhance curriculum, and support instruction. A leading innovator in education for over twenty years, Cambridge is the nation's premiere provider of school-based test preparation and supplemental curriculum services.

Cambridge Publishing, Inc.
www.CambridgeEd.com

© 1994, 1995, 1996, 1997, 2000, 2003, 2004, 2005, 2009, 2010, 2011, 2014 by Cambridge Publishing, Inc.
All rights reserved. First edition 1994
Twelfth edition 2014

Printed in the United States of America
17 16 15 14   1 2 3 4 5

ISBN-13: 978-1-58894-194-7

MIX
From responsible sources
FSC® C099992
www.fsc.org

TABLE OF CONTENTS

Intermediate 389

Advanced 511

SCIENCE SKILLS REVIEW 667

Basic 671

Intermediate 711

Advanced 751

ANSWER KEY 799

HOW TO USE THIS BOOK

This text contains skills review lessons and items that will enable you to do three things: (1) review material that you may have forgotten; (2) learn material that you may never have learned; and (3) master the skills required to answer the more difficult multiple-choice items on standardized tests.

This book is divided into four chapters:

- English and Writing Skills Review

- Reading Skills Review

- Math Skills Review

- Science Skills Review

Each chapter contains three levels: Basic, Intermediate, and Advanced. The book is organized in a grid system, working left to right in the grid within each level. For example, the Math Skills Review is organized according to this grid:

	Basic Manipulations	Statistics and Data Presentations	Number Concepts	Algebraic Expressions, Equations, and Inequalities	Graphical Representations	Plane Figures	Measurement	Functions
Basic								
Intermediate								
Advanced								

Each cell in the grid represents one or more specific skills. For example, the first cell in the Basic level, Basic Manipulations, includes the following skills:

- Perform simple one-operation calculations, such as addition, subtraction, multiplication, and division, using whole numbers and decimals.

- Perform simple conversions such as inches to feet or minutes to hours.

- Solve simple one-step and two-step arithmetic problems involving whole numbers, fractions, decimals, and percents.

Each skill is introduced with a brief lesson and examples. Then the skill is tested through an exercise.

English and Writing
Skills Review

Course Concept Outline

I. Basic (p. 5)

A. Organization and Coherence (p. 5)

1. Logical Connections (p. 5; Exercise 1, Items #1–20, pp. 6–8)
2. Writing Accessible Paragraphs (p. 9; Exercise 2, Items #21–35, pp. 10–17)

B. Word Choice (p. 18)

1. Economy of Words (p. 18; Exercise 3, Items #36–50, pp. 20–22)
   a) Avoid Awkward Sentences
   b) Eliminate Needless Repetition
   c) Eliminate Informal Usage
2. Revising for Clarity (p. 23; Exercise 4, Items #51–70, pp. 24–26)

C. Sentence Structure and Formation (p. 27)

1. Write in Complete Sentences (p. 27; Exercise 5, Items #71–90, pp. 29–32)
2. Verb Tense (p. 32; Exercise 6, Items #91–110, pp. 34–35)

D. Conventions of Usage (p. 36)

1. Ensure Agreement (p. 36; Exercise 7, Items #111–130, pp. 40–42)
   a) Principal Parts of Verbs
   b) Subject-Verb Agreement
   c) Adjective Forms
   d) Pronoun Antecedent Agreement
2. Idiomatic Wording (p. 43; Exercise 8, Items #131–180, pp. 46–48)
   a) Wrong Preposition
   b) Frequently Confused Word Pairs

week 1

	Organization and Coherence (ORG)	Word Choice (WC)	Sentence Structure and Formation (SSF)	Conventions of Usage (COU)	Punctuation (COP)
Basic	Use conjunctive adverbs and adverbial phrases to show time. Add a new sentence.	Correct awkward wording, eliminate needless repetition, and eliminate informal usage. Revise vague nouns and pronouns.	Use conjunctions and punctuation to eliminate fragments and join clauses. Use appropriate verb tense.	Use correct verb and adjective forms; ensure subject-verb and pronoun-antecedent agreement. Choose idiomatic wording (correct prepositions and commonly confused word pairs).	Delete gratuitous commas. Use commas correctly in common situations.
Intermediate	Use conjunctive adverbs and adverbial phrases to show logical connections. Reorder sentences; add an introductory/ transitional/ conclusionary sentence.	Simplify redundant phrasings. Identify and correct ambiguous pronoun references. Conform elements to overall style and tone.	Correct disturbances in sentence structure and flow (fragments, dangling modifiers, etc.) Maintain consistent verb tense and pronoun person.	Ensure subject-verb agreement and pronoun-antecedent agreement in more complex sentences. Use correct prepositions.	Eliminate unnecessary commas. Use commas for parenthetical phrases.
Advanced	Use conjunctive adverbs or phrases and other transitions to signal the appropriate logical connection between ideas. Create well-developed paragraphs and essays.	Eliminate needless verbiage created by seemingly sophisticated phrasings. Correct vague, wordy, and clumsy phrasings of seemingly sophisticated sentences.	Use conjunctions, punctuation, and verb forms to avoid problematic sentence structures (run-ons, comma splices, fragments, etc.). Maintain consistent and logical use of verb tense and pronoun person throughout a paragraph or essay. Manage lengthy, complex sentences by ensuring structural integrity and logical flow.	Correctly use reflexive, relative, and possessive pronouns. Ensure subject-verb agreement in complex sentences.	Use commas correctly for appositives, asides, nonessential (nonrestrictive) clauses, and other parenthetical remarks. Correctly use apostrophes. Use semicolons to join independent clauses. Use colons to introduce elaboration, explanation, or illustration.

BASIC | Organization and Coherence

Logical Connections

A ***conjunctive adverb*** is a combination of a conjunction and an adverb. Like a conjunction ("and," "but," "since," "while," etc.), it joins clauses or sentences. And like an adverb ("carelessly," "gladly," "peacefully," "slowly," etc.), it modifies a verb.

The most important functions of conjunctive adverbs are to show a connection between clauses or sentences and to help explain how the ideas expressed are connected to each other in terms of order or sequence.

Examples:

In a deep-water start, a water skier in a sitting position allows the boat to pull him up out of the water, <u>then</u> he rises to a standing position.

George made waffles for breakfast. <u>At the same time</u>, he told us about his recent trip to Oregon.

In these examples the conjunctive adverb and adverbial phrase join two clauses or sentences and tells you the order or sequence of the events.

EXERCISE 1

DIRECTIONS: In each of the following items, a word or phrase is underlined. Following each sentence or sentences are alternative suggestions for rewriting the underlined part. If you think the original is correct, choose NO CHANGE. Otherwise, choose the best alternative. Answers are on page 800.

1. We need to gather about four cups of spinach from the garden. At the same time, we will purchase the rest of the ingredients.

   A. NO CHANGE
   B. Once
   C. Later
   D. Sometimes

2. Two hundred people were standing in line for tickets when the booth opened; then, only 30 people were left.

   F. NO CHANGE
   G. before
   H. later
   J. more

3. The weather was gloomy and cold all morning. At first, the sun came out, and the temperature rose significantly.

   A. NO CHANGE
   B. Meanwhile
   C. At last
   D. Before then

4. Bill Clinton was president from 1993 to 2001. Afterward, he stayed in the public eye and supported his wife's political ambitions, including her bid to become President in 2008.

   F. NO CHANGE
   G. At long last
   H. Before long
   J. Until then

5. Flawless skin does not last forever. Then it will lose its elasticity and start to droop and wrinkle.

   A. NO CHANGE
   B. Eventually
   C. Next
   D. Afterward

6. After waiting for an hour in the rain, the sun once came out, and we were able to play.

   F. NO CHANGE
   G. at last
   H. so far
   J. until then

7. Once called Siam, this exotic Asian country is now known as Thailand.

   A. NO CHANGE
   B. beforehand
   C. afterwards
   D. still

8. When we bought our house, a number of repairs needed to be made before we could move in. Fortunately, our contractor was able to fix everything. <u>So next</u>, we can move in and enjoy our new home.

   F. NO CHANGE
   G. So now
   H. In the beginning
   J. So then

9. The school's talent show will have many more acts this year. <u>At the time of</u> the opening act performed by the emcee, there will be a dance performance, a singing group, and a comedy skit.

   A. NO CHANGE
   B. Once
   C. Then
   D. Following

10. Every Halloween we look forward to handing out candy to trick-or-treaters. We usually get about twenty to thirty visitors, but I remember that <u>for a year</u> we only got a handful.

   F. NO CHANGE
   G. year in and year out
   H. yearly
   J. one year

11. At the beginning of the teacher's strike, it appeared as though the Board of Education was not willing to negotiate with the teachers union. But the Board of Education <u>next</u> gave in to the strikers' demands for higher wages and gave them a five percent salary increase.

   A. NO CHANGE
   B. first
   C. eventually
   D. occasionally

12. Before Orville and Wilbur Wright invented the airplane, humans could only dream of flying. <u>Today</u>, we hardly give a thought to how remarkable it is to be transported above the clouds.

   F. NO CHANGE
   G. Following that
   H. After a while
   J. Over the years

13. After you put the dry pasta in the pot of boiling water, wait for it to reboil. <u>At that point</u>, set the timer for the number of minutes recommended on the package.

   A. NO CHANGE
   B. Originally
   C. Lastly
   D. Again

14. Eighth graders can apply to multiple high schools before the deadline in December. However, they won't find out which ones have accepted them <u>during</u> late spring.

    F. NO CHANGE
    G. after
    H. until
    J. next

15. We lost all electrical power at 9:00 p.m. last Monday. It wasn't restored until <u>the following</u> afternoon.

    A. NO CHANGE
    B. one
    C. later
    D. tomorrow

16. Carol Moseley Braun was the first African American woman elected to serve as a US Senator, representing the state of Illinois. <u>Immediately,</u> after a lengthy period of anonymity, she ran for mayor of Chicago, but received only nine percent of the vote.

    F. NO CHANGE
    G. Years later
    H. Before
    J. Instead

17. Corn originated <u>first</u> in the Americas and was brought to Europe by Christopher Columbus. It quickly became an important food source throughout the European continent as well as parts of Africa and Asia.

    A. NO CHANGE
    B. before
    C. afterwards
    D. one time

18. For many years Willis Tower, formerly known as the Sears Tower, was the tallest building in the world. <u>Sometimes,</u> it is not even in the top ten.

    F. NO CHANGE
    G. In time
    H. At last
    J. Today

19. Until she wrote the first book of the Harry Potter series, J.K. Rowling was an impoverished single mother; she <u>subsequently</u> became one of the wealthiest individuals in the United Kingdom.

    A. NO CHANGE
    B. instead
    C. always
    D. by then

20. Lead was a common ingredient in paint sold in the US for many decades. <u>Later,</u> it was discovered to be toxic and is no longer used.

    F. NO CHANGE
    G. Now
    H. After all
    J. Besides

Writing Accessible Paragraphs

One of the most important features of a properly written paragraph is **coherence**. A paragraph has coherence when the relationship among the ideas is readily apparent and the progression from one sentence to the next is easy for the reader to follow.

Good writers use several techniques to achieve coherence in their paragraphs. First, good writers make extensive use of conjunctive adverbs and other transitional words and phrases such as "nevertheless," "however," and "on the other hand."

Example:

The National Agricultural Statistics Service considered five factors in significantly reducing the Agricultural Chemical Usage data program. <u>However</u>, the agency did not consult program users in its decision making or gauge the potential impact of the program's cutback. Users <u>subsequently</u> told us they disagreed with the decision factors because they perceived the factors to be irrelevant or misapplied to the program.

Second, good writers arrange the sentences to reflect an order of ideas. For example, the sentences in a paragraph that tell a story are most often arranged in chronological order, while a paragraph that is descriptive of a person or place might be organized spatially.

Other common forms of paragraph organization include arranging ideas from least to greatest importance (or vice versa), developing contrasting ideas (on the one hand, on the other hand), and illustration (generalization). The scheme chosen by a writer will depend in large part on the topic discussed, but whatever the topic, the organization of the paragraph should be readily apparent to the reader by the order of the ideas presented.

Finally, the order of sentences in a paragraph is supported and reinforced by a variety of transitional devices such as pronouns, repetition, transitional words and phrases, and parallel structures.

EXERCISE 2

DIRECTIONS: In each of the following items, a new sentence is provided. Choose the best placement of the new sentence out of the four answer choices provided. Answers are on page 800.

Questions 21–22

[1]

[1] There are two kinds of diabetes that can happen at any age. [2] In type 1 diabetes, the body makes little or no insulin. [3] This type of diabetes develops most often in children and young adults. [4] In type 2 diabetes, the body makes insulin, but doesn't use it the right way. [5] It is the most common kind of diabetes. [6] Your chance of getting type 2 diabetes is higher if you are overweight, inactive, or have a family history of diabetes.

[2]

[1] Diabetes can affect many parts of your body. [2] It is important to keep type 2 diabetes under control. [3] Over time it can cause problems like heart disease, stroke, kidney disease, blindness, nerve damage, and circulation problems that may lead to amputation.

21. The writer wishes to add the following sentence to Paragraph 1:

    You may have heard it called adult-onset diabetes.

    The best place for this sentence is:

    A. before sentence 1.
    B. after sentence 1.
    C. after sentence 5.
    D. after sentence 6.

22. The writer wishes to add the following sentence to Paragraph 2:

    People with type 2 diabetes also have a greater risk for Alzheimer's disease.

    The best place for this sentence is:

    F. before sentence 1.
    G. after sentence 1.
    H. after sentence 2.
    J. after sentence 3.

Questions 23–24

[1]

[1] Early American colonists used English, Spanish, and French money while they were under English rule. [2] However, in 1775, when the Revolutionary War became inevitable, the Continental Congress authorized the issuance of currency to finance the conflict. [3] Paul Revere designed the first plates used to engrave this money, known as "Continental Currency." [4] These notes were redeemable in Spanish milled dollars.

[2]

[1] After the US Constitution was ratified, Congress passed the "Mint Act" of April 2, 1792, which established the coinage system of the United States and the dollar as the principal unit of currency. [2] The first US coins were struck in 1793 at the Philadelphia Mint and presented to Martha Washington. [3] In 1861, Congress authorized the United States Treasury to issue paper money.

23. The writer realizes that an interesting fact was omitted from Paragraph 1 and intends to add the following sentence:

The depreciation of this currency gave rise to the phrase "not worth a Continental."

The sentence should be placed:

A. before sentence 1.
B. after sentence 1.
C. after sentence 2.
D. after sentence 4.

24. The writer intends to add the following sentence to Paragraph 2:

By this Act, the US became the first country in the world to adopt the decimal system for currency.

The sentence should be placed:

F. before sentence 1.
G. after sentence 1.
H. after sentence 2.
J. after sentence 3.

Questions 25–26

[1]

[1] An injury and illness prevention program is a proactive process to help employers find and fix workplace hazards before workers are hurt. [2] We know these programs can be effective at reducing injuries, illnesses, and fatalities. [3] Not only do these employers experience dramatic decreases in workplace injuries, but they often report a transformed workplace culture that can lead to higher productivity, reduced turnover, and greater employee satisfaction. [4] In addition, these employers achieve compliance with existing regulations and experience many of the financial benefits of a safer and healthier workplace.

[2]

[1] Employers across the United States have implemented injury and illness prevention programs, and many jurisdictions, in the United States and abroad, currently require or encourage implementation of these programs. [2] Currently, 34 US states have established laws or regulations designed to encourage injury and illness prevention programs, including 15 states with mandatory regulations for all or some employers. [3] Other states have created financial incentives for employers to implement such programs.

25. The writer wishes to add the following sentence to Paragraph 1:

Many workplaces have already adopted such programs.

The sentence would best be placed:

A. before sentence 1.
B. after sentence 2.
C. after sentence 3.
D. after sentence 4.

26. The writer wishes to add the following sentence to Paragraph 2:

In some instances this involves providing reductions in workers' compensation insurance premiums.

The sentence would best be placed:

F. before sentence 1.
G. after sentence 1.
H. after sentence 2.
J. after sentence 3.

Question 27

[1] The likelihood that you and your family will survive a house fire depends as much on having a working smoke detector and an exit strategy as on a well-trained fire department. [2] We must have the tools and plans in place to survive, at least for a period of time, no matter where we are when an emergency happens. [3] Just like having a working smoke detector, preparing for the unexpected makes sense.

27. The writer wishes to add the following sentence to the paragraph:

    The same is true for surviving a terrorist attack or other emergency.

    The sentence would best be placed:

    A. before sentence 1.
    B. after sentence 1.
    C. after sentence 2.
    D. after sentence 3.

Question 28

[1] Today the Secret Service's primary investigative mission is to safeguard the payment and financial systems of the United States. [2] Since 1984, the Secret Service's investigative responsibilities have expanded to include crimes such as financial institution fraud, computer and telecommunications fraud, false identification documents, electronic funds transfers, and money laundering. [3] To combat these crimes, the Secret Service has adopted a proactive approach that utilizes advanced technologies.

28. The writer wishes to add the following sentence to the paragraph:

    Historically, this has been accomplished through the enforcement of counterfeiting statutes to preserve the integrity of United States currency, coin, and financial obligations.

    The sentence would best be placed:

    F. before sentence 1.
    G. after sentence 1.
    H. after sentence 2.
    J. after sentence 3.

Question 29

[1] These air pollutants are found all over the United States. [2] They are particle pollution, ground-level ozone, carbon monoxide, sulfur oxides, nitrogen oxides, and lead. [3] These pollutants can harm your health and the environment. [4] Of the six pollutants, particle pollution and ground-level ozone are the most widespread health threats.

29. The writer intends to add the following sentence to the paragraph:

    The Clean Air Act requires the EPA to set National Air Quality Standards for six common air pollutants.

    The sentence should be placed:

    A. before sentence 1.
    B. after sentence 1.
    C. after sentence 2.
    D. after sentence 3.

Question 30

[1] The average American family uses more than 300 gallons of water per day at home. [2] Outdoor water use accounts for 30 percent of household use on average, but can be much higher in drier parts of the country and in more water-intensive landscapes. [3] For example, the arid West has some of the highest per capita residential water use because of landscape irrigation.

30. The writer intends to add the following sentence to the paragraph:

    On average, 70 percent of this use occurs indoors.

    The sentence should be placed:

    F. before sentence 1.
    G. after sentence 1.
    H. after sentence 2.
    J. after sentence 3.

Question 31

[1] Ancient healers had little understanding of how various potions worked their magic, but we know much more today. [2] Some pharmacologists study how our bodies work, while others study the chemical properties of medicines. [3] Still others investigate the physical and behavioral effects that medicines have on the body. [4] Since medicines work in so many different ways in so many different organs of the body, pharmacology research touches just about every area of biomedicine.

31. The writer intends to add the following sentence to the paragraph:

    For thousands of years, people have used nature as the source for medicines to treat their symptoms.

    The sentence should be placed:

    A. before sentence 1.
    B. after sentence 1.
    C. after sentence 2.
    D. after sentence 3.

Question 32

[1] In 1846, a dentist publicly demonstrated that ether would put patients to sleep during surgery, and the practice began to spread. [2] Doctors soaked a sponge or a cloth with ether and had patients breathe in the fumes through an inhaler. [3] The fumes knocked the person out, but there was no way to control the amount inhaled. [4] To make matters worse, ether is highly flammable, and a spark in the operating room could cause a dangerous explosion. [5] Despite the problems with ether, its use enabled surgeons to perform internal procedures that would have been too painful or complicated to conduct on conscious patients.

32. The writer intends to add the following sentence to the paragraph:

    If patients inhaled too little, they could wake up and flail about in pain; if they inhaled too much, they might never wake.

    The sentence should be placed:

    F. after sentence 1.
    G. after sentence 3.
    H. after sentence 4.
    J. after sentence 5.

Question 33

[1] During the night of September 13, 1814, the British fleet bombarded Fort McHenry at the harbor in Baltimore, Maryland. [2] Francis Scott Key, a 34-year-old lawyer-poet, watched the attack from the deck of a British prisoner-exchange ship. [3] As the battle ceased on the following morning, Key turned his telescope to the fort and saw that the American flag was still waving. [4] The sight so inspired him that he pulled a letter from his pocket and began to write the poem which eventually was adopted as the national anthem of the United States, "The Star-Spangled Banner."

33. The writer plans to add the following sentence to the paragraph:

He had gone to seek the release of a friend but was refused permission to go ashore until after the attack had been made.

The sentence should be placed:

A. after sentence 1.
B. after sentence 2.
C. after sentence 3.
D. after sentence 4.

Question 34

[1] Thanksgiving Day is celebrated on the fourth Thursday in November. [2] It is traced back to 1621, when Pilgrims held a three-day feast to celebrate a bountiful harvest. [3] The Thanksgiving feast became a national tradition and almost always includes some of the foods served at the first feast: roasted turkey, cranberry sauce, potatoes, and pumpkin pie.

34. The writer intends to add the following sentence to the paragraph:

Many regard this event as the nation's first Thanksgiving.

The sentence should be placed:

F. before sentence 1.
G. after sentence 1.
H. after sentence 2.
J. after sentence 3.

Question 35

[1] Scammers have adopted the practice of Caller ID spoofing to obtain personal information from consumers. [2] In this fraud, someone calls you using a false name and phone number on the Caller ID screen. [3] During the call, the scammer describes an urgent scenario, such as the cancellation of an account. [4] If you provide the sensitive information, the scammer can use it to steal your identity or to access your bank accounts.

35. The writer intends to add the following sentence to the paragraph:

The caller may say that you can avoid the cancellation if you provide your bank account or credit card number to pay the company.

The sentence should be placed:

A. after sentence 1.
B. after sentence 2.
C. after sentence 3.
D. after sentence 4.

Word Choice

Economy of Words

Avoid Awkward Sentences

In order for sentences to be clear and concise, one should eliminate unnecessary or redundant words and phrases. Using the passive voice can add to the wordiness of a sentence, so using the active voice is a more efficient way to get your point across. The active voice just means that the subject of the sentence performs the action expressed in the verb.

Correct awkward wording, eliminate needless repetition, and eliminate informal usage.

BASIC
INTERMEDIATE
ADVANCED

Examples:

The ball was thrown by me. ✗

I threw the ball. ✓

> As we see in this example, the active voice creates a shorter, more concise sentence than the passive voice.

A sentence may be grammatically and logically correct but still be awkward.

Examples:

We left town on October 1st, which was a month after the hurricane which hit on September 1st. ✗

We left town a month after the September 1st hurricane. ✓

Eliminate Needless Repetition

Sometimes, a sentence will be incorrect because it is needlessly wordy.

Examples:

It was an hour after sunrise in the early morning when I went for a run. ✗

I went for a run an hour after sunrise. ✓

I went for a run in the early morning. ✓

> "An hour after sunrise" implies that it is early in the morning, so either one of these phrases is sufficient to adequately express the time of day.

Eliminate Informal Usage

Most of us speak two different versions of English. We know instinctively the difference between "proper" English, the English that we use in a formal setting, and "improper" English, the everyday English that we use with our friends in less formal settings.

When you write, you need to be attentive that you don't cross the line from the realm of formal English into that of everyday English. Slang expressions such as "gross" (to mean "disgusting" rather than "large" or "unrefined"), "sick" (to mean "amazing" or "hard to believe" rather than "ill"), and "totally" (to mean "very" rather than "completely") are informal usage.

Example:

After swimming in the pool, we found some beach chairs and <u>caught some rays</u>.

A. NO CHANGE
B. toasted ourselves
C. got some sun
D. laid in the sun

The correct answer is (D). "Caught some rays" is slang for sitting in the sun, probably with the intention of getting a tan. There is nothing wrong with "caught some rays" in and of itself. In fact, it is a clever turn of phrase. But it is slang and doesn't belong in formal writing. (B) and (C) are also informal usages.

EXERCISE 3

DIRECTIONS: In each of the following items, a word or phrase is underlined. Following each sentence or sentences are alternative suggestions for rewriting the underlined part. If you think the original is correct, choose NO CHANGE. Otherwise, choose the best alternative. Answers are on page 800.

36. Brian is traveling to Ireland this summer, when <u>the small village where his mother was born will be visited</u>.

    F. NO CHANGE
    G. the small village where his mother had been born will be visited
    H. he will visit the small village where his mother was born
    J. there will be a visit to the small village where his mother was born

37. <u>Marinated in oil and spices, we grilled the skewered vegetables</u> until they were tender and ready to eat.

    A. NO CHANGE
    B. The skewered vegetables were marinated in oil and spices by us, grilling them
    C. We marinated the skewered vegetables in oil and spices, and grilled them
    D. Marinated by us in oil and spices, we grilled the vegetables

38. Although she had done poorly on the exam, Maria was able to raise her grade <u>when completing an essay for extra credit</u>.

    F. NO CHANGE
    G. when an essay she completed for extra credit
    H. from the essay completed for extra credit
    J. by completing an essay for extra credit

39. Stuart does not like to shop, so I doubt <u>that even he will give us</u> a trinket for Christmas.

    A. NO CHANGE
    B. even that he will give us
    C. that he will give us even
    D. that he even will give us

40. <u>The supervisor congratulated the workers on successfully completing the project in the conference room during the morning meeting.</u>

    F. NO CHANGE
    G. During the morning meeting, the supervisor congratulated the workers on successfully completing the project in the conference room.
    H. The supervisor in the conference room during the morning meeting congratulated the workers on successfully completing the project.
    J. In the conference room during the morning meeting, the supervisor congratulated the workers on successfully completing the project.

41. <u>Because of the fact that</u> the deadline had passed, the student was unable to apply for the scholarship.

    A. NO CHANGE
    B. Because
    C. That
    D. The fact that

42. When I found out that the subject of Sarah's research paper was the same as mine, I feared they would be <u>too much alike and similar</u>, but at least her style of writing is completely different than mine.

    F. NO CHANGE
    G. very alike and similar
    H. too similar
    J. too much similarity

43. In the lawsuit, the <u>former employee alleged and claimed</u> that she was discriminated against during her employment with the company.

    A. NO CHANGE
    B. employee who formerly alleged and claimed
    C. former employee alleged
    D. former employee allegedly claimed

44. Flannery O'Connor <u>authored</u> many short stories that featured southern settings and grotesque characters.

    F. NO CHANGE
    G. wrote and authored
    H. was the writer who authored
    J. authored as the writer

45. Group homes are typically <u>private residences where children who cannot live with their families or people with disabilities live</u>.

    A. NO CHANGE
    B. private residences for living with children without families or people with disabilities
    C. living private residences for children who cannot live with their families or people with disabilities
    D. private residences for people with disabilities or children who cannot live with their families

46. Based on the criminal's abnormal behavior and incoherent statements, the court-ordered psychiatrist concluded that he was <u>a real psycho</u>.

    F. NO CHANGE
    G. wacko
    H. completely mental
    J. a very disturbed individual

47. When I learned my sister had borrowed my car without asking, I <u>became extremely angry</u>.

    A. NO CHANGE
    B. lit into her
    C. blew a fuse
    D. snapped

48. Robert may be <u>a real smart kid</u>, but he never seems to turn in his work on time.

    F. NO CHANGE
    G. such a genius
    H. very intelligent
    J. a brainiac

49. I am not exactly sure what our neighbor does for a living, but I know that he is <u>some kind of big shot</u> in the corporate world.

    A. NO CHANGE
    B. a big cheese
    C. a very important person
    D. on the up and up

50. The couple got into a fight in the middle of the restaurant, and the woman <u>split</u> without even touching her food.

    F. NO CHANGE
    G. booked it
    H. left abruptly
    J. blew him off

Revising for Clarity

Nouns and pronouns can introduce ambiguity into a sentence. You can avoid this problem by making sure that your nouns mean what you intend and your pronouns clearly refer to some other noun or some other pronoun (the intended antecedent).

Revise vague nouns and pronouns.

BASIC
INTERMEDIATE
ADVANCED

Example:

The performance includes dances by ten students; they were created over a six-month period.

> As written, it is not clear whether the dances were created over a six-month period or the students were. The ambiguity can be corrected by eliminating the "they":

The performance includes dances by ten students. The dances were created over a six-month period.

Or:

The performance includes dances created by ten students over a six-month period.

Example:

Visitors cannot place items on any grave site except their own.

> The sentence seems to say that no one may put items on any grave except the grave that the person himself or herself is buried in, and that would be impossible. The sentence can be revised:

Visitors cannot place items on any grave site except those of loved ones.

EXERCISE 4

DIRECTIONS: In each of the following items, a word or phrase is underlined. Following each sentence or sentences are alternative suggestions for rewriting the underlined part. If you think the original is correct, choose NO CHANGE. Otherwise, choose the best alternative. Answers are on page 800.

51. The electrician determined that the electrical wiring had not been installed correctly in the basement, so to correct <u>it</u>, he removed all the wiring and started over from scratch.

A. NO CHANGE
B. them
C. the problem
D. these

52. The teacher plans to buy ten new reading books because of the addition of five new students and the deterioration of <u>some others</u>.

F. NO CHANGE
G. some of the books
H. some of them
J. others

53. Because cleaning products could accidentally be swallowed by young children, it is important to keep <u>them</u> locked securely in a cabinet.

A. NO CHANGE
B. some
C. these products
D. some of them

54. Rachel was very excited about her new bubble gum machine, but when she put it on the counter, <u>it</u> broke, and her mother had to buy another.

F. NO CHANGE
G. the bubble gum
H. the counter
J. the machine

55. The announcement stated <u>that there is a new swimming class for adults who like to swim but don't know it</u>.

A. NO CHANGE
B. that there is a new swimming class for adults who don't know it but like to swim
C. that there is a new swimming class for adults who like to swim
D. that there is a new swimming class for adults who don't know it

56. The police officer received a plaque for his bravery as well as a reward, but he was too modest to display <u>it</u> on his wall.

F. NO CHANGE
G. them
H. the plaque
J. the reward

57. Karen's mother and father died when she was a young child, and <u>it made growing up</u> extremely hard.

    A. NO CHANGE
    B. growing up made it
    C. growing up as an orphan was
    D. they made growing up

58. Having no sense of humor is my top reason for rejecting a potential suitor, but I rarely meet anyone <u>who has it</u>.

    F. NO CHANGE
    G. having it
    H. with it
    J. who is funny

59. The medication can have harmful side effects such as dizziness, and <u>this</u> is described in detail on the prescription's insert.

    A. NO CHANGE
    B. that
    C. this harm
    D. this risk

60. The researcher modified his data to show a positive outcome, and <u>this</u> prevented the results from being replicated.

    F. NO CHANGE
    G. it
    H. this modification
    J. this outcome

61. The jewelry display was protected by an alarm so that <u>it</u> wouldn't get stolen.

    A. NO CHANGE
    B. the display
    C. the jewelry
    D. the alarm

62. After making the pasta on the stove, cover the pot with a lid so that <u>it</u> stays warm.

    F. NO CHANGE
    G. the lid
    H. the pasta
    J. the stove

63. Therapists recommend open communication and active listening to minimize tension <u>and it can cause</u> arguments.

    A. NO CHANGE
    B. that can cause
    C. that are caused by
    D. because it can cause

64. The food spilled in the car, so we had to throw <u>it</u> away.

    F. NO CHANGE
    G. the spillage
    H. the car
    J. the food

65. The children sold lemonade and cookies to customers all day but eventually ran out of <u>them</u>.

    A. NO CHANGE
    B. customers
    C. items to sell
    D. all of them

66. When she took the train home from work on Friday, <u>it</u> was late.

    F. NO CHANGE
    G. the day
    H. her work
    J. the train

67. The pain Marcia felt from her knee surgery last week did not go away, so pain medication was prescribed to alleviate <u>it</u>.

    A. NO CHANGE
    B. the discomfort
    C. the surgery
    D. the knee

68. The office manager plans to purchase five new computers due to the addition of three new hires and the breakdown of <u>two others</u>.

    F. NO CHANGE
    G. two other computers
    H. the others
    J. two more

69. Because radiation could be harmful to a growing child, any exposure to <u>it</u> must be limited.

    A. NO CHANGE
    B. a child
    C. radiation
    D. them

70. As soon as I put my cat, Fluffy, down on the floor of the living room, <u>it</u> ran away as fast as it could.

    F. NO CHANGE
    G. the room
    H. the floor
    J. the cat

Sentence Structure and Formation

Write in Complete Sentences

A **sentence fragment** is a group of words that begins with a capital letter and ends with a period, but lacks a main verb and/or a subject. Therefore, a fragment is an incomplete thought. A **run-on sentence**, which occurs when two or more independent clauses are joined incorrectly, is another common sentence construction error.

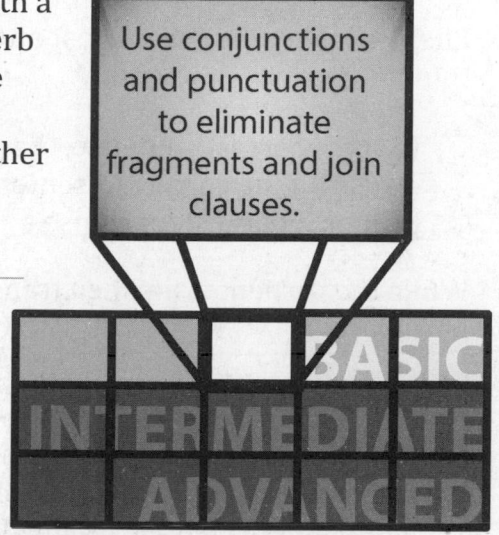

Use conjunctions and punctuation to eliminate fragments and join clauses.

Examples:

The regulation permitting camping in the state forest but not within 100 feet of a lake or stream. ✘

Flights leaving the West Coast and the Midwest were delayed. Because of severe thunderstorms in the east. ✘

While the carpenter finished framing the door, and the locksmith installed the hardware. ✘

I love to bake I would bake every day if I had the time. ✘

If you are editing your own work and find that you have written a sentence fragment or a run-on sentence, you have a lot of flexibility in how you eliminate the error. However, on a multiple-choice test, your options are limited. Typically, you have three choices for fixing a sentence fragment:

> ### METHODS FOR FIXING SENTENCE FRAGMENTS
>
> 1. Change a verb form so that it becomes a main verb.
>
> 2. Combine the fragment with a true independent clause (sentence).
>
> 3. Convert a dependent clause into an independent clause.

Examples:

The regulation permitting camping in the state forest but not within 100 feet of a lake or stream. ✘

The regulation permits camping in the state forest but not within 100 feet of a lake or stream. ✓

    In the incorrect sentence, "permitting" is not a main verb.

Flights leaving the West Coast and the Midwest were delayed. Because of severe thunderstorms in the east. ✘

Flights leaving the West Coast and the Midwest were delayed because of severe thunderstorms in the east. ✓

    In the incorrect sentence, "because" introduces a dependent, not an independent, clause. In the corrected sentence, the fragment is joined as a dependent clause to a proper independent clause.

While the carpenter finished framing the door, and the locksmith installed the hardware. ✘

The carpenter finished framing the door, and the locksmith installed the hardware. ✓

    In the incorrect sentence, "while" makes the word group a dependent clause. In the corrected sentence, eliminating the "while" lets the word group stand as two independent clauses, each with its own main verb.

Typically, you have four options to fix a run-on sentence:

METHODS FOR FIXING RUN-ON SENTENCES

1. Use a period to separate the independent clauses into their own sentences.

2. Insert a semicolon between the independent clauses.

3. Use a comma and a coordinating conjunction.

4. Use a subordinating conjunction.

Example:

I love to bake I would bake every day if I had the time. ✗

I love to bake. I would bake every day if I had the time. ✓

I love to bake; I would bake every day if I had the time. ✓

I love to bake, and I would bake every day if I had the time. ✓

Because I love to bake, I would bake every day if I had the time. ✓

In the incorrect sentence, the two independent clauses are joined incorrectly. One way to correct this error is to use punctuation to separate the clauses (a period or a semicolon). Another way is to use a comma and a coordinating conjunction (in this case, "and" is the coordinating conjunction). A subordinating conjunction (in this case, "because") can also be used to create a dependent and independent clause instead of two independent clauses.

EXERCISE 5

DIRECTIONS: In each of the following items, a word or phrase is underlined. Following each sentence or sentences are alternative suggestions for rewriting the underlined part. If you think the original is correct, choose NO CHANGE. Otherwise, choose the best alternative. Answers are on page 800.

71. <u>During the time that I was in the hospital. I read</u> every one of the Sherlock Holmes stories.

   A. NO CHANGE
   B. During the time that I was in the hospital, reading
   C. During the time that I was in the hospital, I read
   D. During the time of being in the hospital. I read

72. A city ordinance <u>prohibiting the construction of any structure that is</u> taller than the statue of Minerva, the Roman Goddess of Wisdom, on the dome of City Hall.

   F. NO CHANGE
   G. which prohibits the construction of any structure that is
   H. that prohibits the construction of any structure that is
   J. prohibits the construction of any structure that is

73. Because the low-lying land was very <u>marshy and the construction of a complex system of drainage ditches was</u> necessary before construction could begin.

A. NO CHANGE
B. marshy with the construction of a complex system of drainage ditches
C. marshy, the construction of a complex system of drainage ditches being
D. marshy, the construction of a complex system of drainage ditches was

74. The loud noise from the sensitive alarm on the car <u>parked in front of the building making</u> it difficult for the audience to understand the speaker.

F. NO CHANGE
G. that was parked in front of the building making
H. which parked in front of the building making
J. parked in front of the building made

75. <u>Calling Wyoming the "Equality State," and</u> women were permitted to vote in the territory as early as 1869.

A. NO CHANGE
B. Called Wyoming the "Equality State," and
C. Calling Wyoming the "Equality State," because
D. Wyoming is called the "Equality State" because

76. I went to the amusement park with my <u>brother. Who</u> had never been on a Ferris wheel before.

F. NO CHANGE
G. brother. Those who
H. brother that
J. brother, who

77. The children ran towards the ice cream <u>truck. Waving</u> their arms to get the driver's attention.

A. NO CHANGE
B. truck, and waving
C. truck, waving
D. truck, but waved

78. Schools want to have state-of-the-art <u>technology, many</u> have no way of paying for it.

F. NO CHANGE
G. technology many
H. technology since many
J. technology, but many

79. Carol lives with her roommate in an <u>apartment, which they</u> are planning to redecorate it next month.

A. NO CHANGE
B. apartment, they
C. apartment. They
D. apartment but they

80. Our itinerary was full of activities that would last all <u>day this worried</u> me since I tire easily.

F. NO CHANGE
G. day, this worried
H. day, this worrying
J. day, which worried

81. Most children get a balanced <u>diet, some</u> need to take vitamin supplements to get all the nutrition they need.

   A. NO CHANGE
   B diet some
   C. diet, but some
   D. diet, if some

82. When my daughter said she wasn't feeling well, we decided to postpone our <u>trip; we</u> didn't want to leave until she felt better.

   F. NO CHANGE
   G. trip so we
   H. trip, so that we
   J. trip, we

83. Before the Europeans came, smallpox did not exist in <u>America, following</u> the Europeans' arrival it spread quickly among the Native American populations.

   A. NO CHANGE
   B. America following
   C. America, but following
   D. America, and following

84. Our exterminator has done a good job of spraying the entire outside perimeter of the <u>house. Stopping all bugs</u> from entering through cracks and crevices.

   F. NO CHANGE
   G. house, bugs are stopped
   H. house, stopping all bugs
   J. house. The stopping of all bugs

85. Children across the country are getting the message to eat <u>healthier, they are eating more fruit, vegetables, and whole grains</u> than ever before.

   A. NO CHANGE
   B. healthier; they are eating more fruit, vegetables, and whole grains
   C. healthier; their eating of fruit, vegetables, and whole grains is more
   D. healthier, but they are eating more fruit, vegetables, and whole grains

86. We forgot to close the <u>door, the cat</u> got out.

   F. NO CHANGE
   G door, but the cat
   H. door, and the cat
   J. door and, the cat

87. Her father took her to <u>school, her mother</u> picked her up.

   A. NO CHANGE
   B. school, and her mother
   C. school and; her mother
   D. school and her mother

88. Because the waiter at the restaurant mixed up our <u>order. Our</u> food was delayed.

   F. NO CHANGE
   G. order our
   H. order, our
   J. order, and

89. The health club offers many <u>amenities. Such as</u> a pool, spa, and fitness classes.

    A. NO CHANGE
    B. amenities
    C. amenities, such as
    D. amenities. Like

90. Unless I get to school on <u>time. I</u> will be marked as tardy.

    F. NO CHANGE
    G. time, and I
    H. time, but I
    J. time, I

Verb Tense

The tense of a verb indicates whether the action or condition described by the verb belongs to the present, to the past, or to the future.

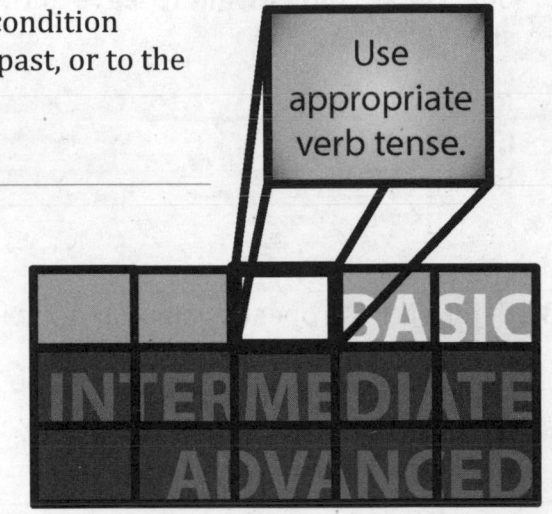

Examples:

Present Tense:

    deliver, learn, open, respond

Past Tense:

    delivered, learned, opened, responded

Future Tense:

    will deliver, will learn, will open, will respond

A problem of logical expression is poor choice of verb tense. The **verb tenses** in a correctly written sentence accurately reflect the **sequence** and/or **logic** of events described. The following examples contain verb tense errors:

Examples:

As soon as Linda finished writing her dissertation, she <u>will take</u> a well-earned vacation in Paris. ✗

> This first example is incorrect because the initial verb phrase ("As soon as Linda finished") describes an action that was entirely completed in the past; however, the subsequent verb phrase ("she will take") makes it sound as if that first action had not been completed and was instead ongoing. Depending on whether Linda has already completed the dissertation, the sentence could be corrected in one of two ways:

As soon as Linda finishes writing her dissertation, she <u>will take</u> a well-earned vacation in Paris. ✓

As soon as Linda finished writing her dissertation, she <u>took</u> a well-earned vacation in Paris. ✓

The first corrected version states that neither event has yet occurred and that the writing will precede the vacation. The second corrected version states that both events are completed and that the writing preceded the vacation. Here is another example:

A recent study shows that many mothers return to the labor force after their children <u>left</u> home. ✗

In this second example, the verb "left" is incorrect because the verb "return" describes a present, on-going action. The sentence can be corrected by making it clear that "children leaving home" is also a present, on-going phenomenon:

A recent study shows that many mothers return to the labor force after their children <u>leave</u> home. ✓

A recent study shows that many mothers return to the labor force after their children <u>have left</u> home. ✓

Either sentence is acceptable since both make it clear that leaving home is not a completed past action but an ongoing phenomenon.

WATCH FOR SHIFTING VERB TENSES

Make sure that verb tenses properly reflect the sequence, as well as the duration, of any action described in the sentence.

Example:

Charles came to town last week and <u>goes</u> to a resort where he <u>rests</u> for three days. ✗

Charles came to town last week and <u>went</u> to a resort where he <u>rested</u> for three days. ✓

EXERCISE 6

DIRECTIONS: In each of the following items, a word or phrase is omitted. Following each sentence are suggestions for completing the sentence. Choose the word or phrase that best completes the sentence. Answers are on page 800.

91. A gentleman is ____ to see you.

    A. comes
    B. came
    C. come
    D. coming

92. Bill was ____ to telephone you last night.

    F. to suppose
    G. supposed
    H. suppose
    J. supposing

93. My friend has ____ to get impatient.

    A. to begin
    B. began
    C. begin
    D. begun

94. He has ____ a serious cold.

    F. catched
    G. caught
    H. catch
    J. catching

95. He could ____ before large groups if he were asked.

    A. sing
    B. sang
    C. sung
    D. singed

96. She has ____ before large groups several times.

    F. sing
    G. sang
    H. sung
    J. singed

97. They have already ____ to the theater.

    A. go
    B. goes
    C. going
    D. gone

98. He has ____ me excellent advice.

    F. give
    G. gave
    H. gived
    J. given

99. He is ____ to his parents.

    A. to devote
    B. devote
    C. devoted
    D. devoting

100. The engineer has designed and ____ his own home.

    F. to build
    G. builds
    H. built
    J. had built

101. He ____ as he ran onto the stage following the clown and the magician.

    A. to laugh
    B. laughing
    C. laughed
    D. had laughed

102. She ____ the high-jump so well at trials that she is going to the Olympics this summer.

    F. had jumped
    G. to jump
    H. jumping
    J. jumped

103. It ____ that she continued to blame me even after she knew it wasn't my fault.

    A. hurt
    B. hurts
    C. has hurt
    D. hurting

104. The man ____ the murder occur if he had really been on that street corner when he said he was.

    F. see
    G. sees
    H. would have saw
    J. would have seen

105. The child ____ everywhere now that she is able to stand up by herself.

    A. to walk
    B. walks
    C. walked
    D. walking

106. Tomorrow morning, Sam ____ his sister.

    F. was calling
    G. called
    H. calling
    J. will call

107. After she had completed her investigation, the state trooper ____ her report.

    A. was writing
    B. wrote
    C. has written
    D. will write

108. When I was growing up, we ____ every summer at my grandmother's home in the country.

    F. spend
    G. will spend
    H. were spending
    J. spent

109. Whenever we get a craving for a late night snack, we ____ a pizza.

    A. order
    B. ordered
    C. had ordered
    D. have ordered

110. For years now, John ____ his milk at the corner grocery.

    F. buys
    G. will buy
    H. has bought
    J. bought

Conventions of Usage

Ensure Agreement

Principal Parts of Verbs

The *principal parts* of verbs are the infinitive or present tense, the past tense, and the past participle. Most verbs are called regular verbs because the past tense and the past participle are formed by adding "-d" or "-ed" to the infinitive or present tense form:

Use correct verb and adjective forms; ensure subject-verb and pronoun-antecedent agreement.

Examples:

Present Tense:

    borrow, dare, guard, miss, staple

Past Tense:

    borrowed, dared, guarded, missed, stapled

Past Participle:

    borrowed, dared, guarded, missed, stapled

Some verbs, however, do not follow the usual rule. They are called irregular verbs.

PRINCIPAL PARTS OF COMMON IRREGULAR VERBS

Present	Past	Past Participle	Present	Past	Past Participle
arise	arose	arisen	drink	drank	drunk
be	was, were	been	drive	drove	driven
bear	bore	borne	eat	ate	eaten
become	became	become	fall	fell	fallen
begin	began	begun	feed	fed	fed
blow	blew	blown	feel	felt	felt
break	broke	broken	fight	fought	fought
bring	brought	brought	find	found	found
build	built	built	fly	flew	flown
buy	bought	bought	forget	forgot	forgotten
catch	caught	caught	forgive	forgave	forgiven
choose	chose	chosen	freeze	froze	frozen
come	came	come	get	got	gotten
cut	cut	cut	give	gave	given
do	did	done	go	went	gone
draw	drew	drawn	grow	grew	grown

Present	Past	Past Participle	Present	Past	Past Participle
hang (a person)	hanged	hanged	shoot	shot	shot
hang (an object)	hung	hung	shrink	shrank, shrunk	shrunk, shrunken
hear	heard	heard	slay	slew	slain
hide	hid	hidden	sleep	slept	slept
hold	held	held	slide	slid	slid
hurt	hurt	hurt	speak	spoke	spoken
keep	kept	kept	spend	spent	spent
know	knew	known	spin	spun	spun
lay	laid	laid	spring	sprang, sprung	sprung
lead	led	led	stand	stood	stood
leave	left	left	steal	stole	stolen
lend	lent	lent	sting	stung	stung
lie	lay	lain	swear	swore	sworn
light	lit, lighted	lit, lighted	swing	swung	swung
lose	lost	lost	swim	swam	swum
make	made	made	take	took	taken
meet	met	met	teach	taught	taught
read	read	read	tear	tore	torn
ride	rode	ridden	tell	told	told
ring	rang	rung	think	thought	thought
rise	rose	risen	throw	threw	thrown
run	ran	run	wake	waked, woke	waked, woken
see	saw	seen	wear	wore	worn
send	sent	sent	weave	weaved, wove	woven
sew	sewed	sewn	win	won	won
shake	shook	shaken	wring	wrung	wrung
sit	sat	sat	write	wrote	written

Subject-Verb Agreement

One common grammatical error is lack of agreement between subject and verb. If the subject is singular, it must take a singular verb. If the subject is plural, it must take a plural verb.

Examples:

The books <u>is</u> on the shelf. ✗

The books <u>are</u> on the shelf. ✓

My dog <u>eat</u> twice a day and <u>sleep</u> inside. ✗

My dog <u>eats</u> twice a day and <u>sleeps</u> inside. ✓

Adjective Forms

Adjectives have three forms: the simple, the comparative, and the superlative. The simple form is used to attribute a characteristic to a noun by modifying it.

Examples:

The <u>blue</u> book is on the shelf.

The book is on the <u>top</u> shelf.

When two things are compared, the comparative form of the adjective should be used. The comparative is generally formed in one of two ways:

RULES FOR COMPARISONS BETWEEN TWO OBJECTS

1. Two objects can be compared by adding "-er" to the adjective.

or

2. Two objects can be compared by placing "more" before the adjective.

Examples:

She is <u>more busier</u> than her sister. ✘

She is <u>busier</u> than her sister. ✓

She is <u>more busy</u> than her sister. ✓

Jeremy is <u>more wiser</u> than we know. ✘

Jeremy is <u>wiser</u> than we know. ✓

Jeremy is <u>more wise</u> than we know. ✓

If three or more things are being compared, the superlative form of the adjective is used. The superlative is generally formed in one of two ways:

RULES FOR COMPARISONS AMONG THREE OR MORE OBJECTS

1. Three or more objects can be compared by adding "-est" to the adjective.

or

2. Three or more objects can be compared by placing "most" before the adjective.

Examples:

Mary is the <u>shorter</u> of all of her friends. ✗

Mary is the <u>shortest</u> of all of her friends. ✓

Of all the books, this one is the <u>more</u> difficult. ✗

Of all the books, this one is the <u>most</u> difficult. ✓

This is the <u>most sharpest</u> knife I have. ✗

This is the <u>sharpest</u> knife I have. ✓

Some comparative and superlative modifiers require changing the words themselves. A few of these irregular comparisons are given below. Whenever you are in doubt about the comparative forms of any adjective or adverb, consult your dictionary.

MODIFIERS THAT DO CHANGE

Simple	*Comparative*	*Superlative*
good	better	best
well	better	best
bad (evil, ill)	worse	worst
badly	worse	worst
far	farther, further	farthest, furthest
late	later	latest, last
little	less, lesser	least
many, much	more	most

Pronoun-Antecedent Agreement

A pronoun must agree with its antecedent. Consider the following example:

Example:

Historically, the college dean was also a professor, but today <u>they</u> are usually administrators. ✗

> In the example, "they" must refer to "dean," but "dean" is singular and "they" is plural. The sentence can be corrected in one of two ways: by changing the first clause to the plural or by changing the second clause to the singular.

Historically, college deans were also professors, but today they are usually administrators. ✓

Historically, the college dean was also a professor, but today the dean is usually an administrator. ✓

WATCH FOR PRONOUN-ANTECEDENT AGREEMENT

If the antecedent is singular, the pronoun must be singular; if the antecedent is plural, the pronoun must be plural.

Finally, it is incorrect to use different forms of the same pronoun to refer to an antecedent. This error results in the sentence having different antecedents and therefore a *shifting subject*.

EXERCISE 7

DIRECTIONS: In each of the following items, a word or phrase is underlined. Following each sentence or sentences are alternative suggestions for rewriting the underlined part. If you think the original is correct, choose NO CHANGE. Otherwise, choose the best alternative. Answers are on page 800.

111. As soon as we got home, the snow <u>begun</u> to fall.

    A. NO CHANGE
    B. beginned
    C. began
    D. begint

112. The water balloon <u>busted</u> open as it hit the ground.

    F. NO CHANGE
    G. burst
    H. bust
    J. bursted

113. It was so cold last night, even the lake <u>froze</u>.

    A. NO CHANGE
    B. freezed
    C. freeze
    D. frozed

114. We <u>heared</u> their voices through the door but couldn't understand most of what they were saying.

    F. NO CHANGE
    G. hear
    H. heard
    J. hearred

115. I hadn't seen Rudy since he was a toddler, and couldn't believe how much he'd <u>grew</u>.

    A. NO CHANGE
    B. growt
    C. growed
    D. grown

116. My mom <u>hung</u> that picture on the wall yesterday.

    F. NO CHANGE
    G. hanged
    H. hungen
    J. hang

117. The spider <u>spun</u> its web so close to the entrance that I almost walked right into it.

    A. NO CHANGE
    B. spinned
    C. span
    D. spunned

118. The <u>worst</u> moment of my life was finding out that she had left.

    F. NO CHANGE
    G. badder
    H. baddest
    J. worser

119. <u>The most difficultest</u> task was saved for last.

    A. NO CHANGE
    B. The difficultest
    C. The most difficult
    D. The difficulter

120. I still think the <u>best</u> book of the series is *Twilight*.

    F. NO CHANGE
    G. most better
    H. better
    J. more better

121. I am <u>most certain</u> that our luck will change.

    A. NO CHANGE
    B. most certain
    C. certainest
    D. more certain

122. She received a <u>higher</u> grade in biology than Penelope.

    F. NO CHANGE
    G. highest
    H. more higher
    J. most high

123. My cousin is <u>more taller</u> than my aunt.

    A. NO CHANGE
    B. most tallest
    C. more tallest
    D. taller

124. My dog is the <u>smarter</u> dog in the neighborhood.

    F. NO CHANGE
    G. more smart
    H. smartest
    J. most smartest

125. The stores in the mall <u>opens</u> at 10:00 a.m.

    A. NO CHANGE
    B. is open
    C. open
    D. is opening

126. Many of Taylor Swift's songs <u>is</u> about her experiences as a teenager and young adult.

    F. NO CHANGE
    G. has been
    H. are
    J. was

127. As Otto von Bismarck said, "Even in a declaration of war, <u>one observe</u> the rules of politeness."

    A. NO CHANGE
    B. one observes
    C. they observes
    D. people observes

128. My children used to fill the house, and I miss <u>it</u> greatly.

    F. NO CHANGE
    G. of them
    H. they
    J. them

129. The school is overcrowded and lacks air conditioning, but <u>they have</u> excellent teachers.

    A. NO CHANGE
    B. it is
    C. they had
    D. it has

130. Even though there have been numerous returns and complaints, the company stands by the quality of <u>their merchandise</u>.

    F. NO CHANGE
    G. them
    H. its merchandise
    J. their merchandises

Idiomatic Wording

Wrong Preposition

In standard written English, only certain prepositions can be used with certain verbs. As a result of daily conversation and writing in standard written English, you have an idea of which prepositions and verbs can be used together.

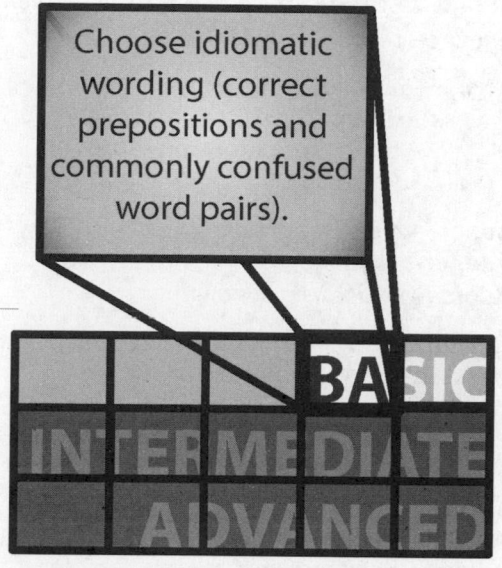

Choose idiomatic wording (correct prepositions and commonly confused word pairs).

Example:

I asked him repeatedly if he was from <u>about</u> here, but he never answered me. ✗

> The phrase "was from about here" is incorrect. From daily conversation, you should recognize the correct phrase: "he was from *around* here."

Frequently Confused Word Pairs

Some sentences are incorrect because they include words that fail to convey the author's intended meaning. An author sometimes makes this mistake because the wrong word and the correct word are actually quite similar.

CONFUSING WORD GROUPS

accept—*to receive*, or *to agree to something*
except—*to exclude* or *excluding*

access—*availability*, or *to get at*
excess—*state of surpassing specified limits*
(noun), or *more than usual*
(adjective)

adapt—*to adjust or change*
adept—*skillful*
adopt—*to take as one's own*

advantage—*a superior position*
benefit—*a favor conferred or earned*

adverse—*unfavorable*
averse—*having a feeling of repugnance or dislike*

advice—*counsel, opinion* (noun)
advise—*to offer advice* (verb)

affect—*to influence* (verb)
effect—*to cause or bring about* (verb), or *a result* (noun)

all ready—*everybody or everything ready*
already—*previously*

all together—*everybody or everything together*
altogether—*completely*

allude—*to make a reference to*
elude—*to escape from*

allusion—*an indirect reference*
illusion—*an erroneous concept or perception*

alongside of—*side by side with*
alongside—*parallel to the side*

among—*a term used with more than two persons or things*
between—*a term used with two persons or things*

ante—a prefix meaning *before*
anti—a prefix meaning *against*

build—*to erect, construct* (verb), or *the physical makeup of a person* (noun)
built—the past tense of *build*

capital—*place of government*, or *wealth*, or in the case of letters, *the uppercase form*
capitol—*building that houses legislatures*

click—*a short, sharp sound*
clique—*a group of people who are exclusive*

cloth—*fabric or material*
clothe—*to put on clothes, to dress*

coarse—*vulgar*, or *harsh*
course—*a path*, or *a plan of study*

complement—*a completing part*
compliment—*an expression of praise or admiration*

conscience—*the ability to recognize the difference between right and wrong*
conscious—*aware*

desert (DEZZ-ert)—*an arid area*
desert (di-ZERT)—*abandon*, or *a reward or punishment*
dessert—*a sweet course or dish served after the end of a meal*

disburse—*to pay out*
disperse—*to scatter, distribute widely*

discomfit—*to upset*
discomfort—*lack of ease*

dual—*double*
duel—*a contest between two persons or groups*

emigrate—*to leave a country*
immigrate—*to enter a country*

eminent—*of high rank, prominent, outstanding*
imminent—*about to occur, impending*

epitaph—*an inscription on a tombstone or monument*
epithet—*a term used to describe or characterize the nature of a person or thing*

expend—*to use up*
expand—*to spread out*

faze—*to worry or disturb*
phase—*an aspect*

CONFUSING WORD GROUPS

formally—*in a formal way*
formerly—*at an earlier time*

fort (fort)—*a fortified place*
forte (FOR-tay)—*a strong point*
forte (FOR-tay)—*a musical term that means loudly*

idle—*unemployed or unoccupied*
idol—*image or object of worship*

in—indicates *inclusion or location*, or *motion within limits*
into—*motion toward one place from another*

incidence—*to the extent* or *frequency of an occurrence*
incidents—*occurrences, events*

it's—the contraction of *it is*, or the contraction of *it has*
its—possessive pronoun meaning *belonging to it*

knew—the past tense of *know*
new—*of recent origin*

know—*to have knowledge or understanding*
no—a negative used to express *denial or refusal*

later—*after a certain time*
latter—*the second of two*

lay—*to put*
lie—*to recline*

lightening—*making less heavy*
lightning—*electric discharge in the atmosphere*, or *moving with great speed*

loose—*not fastened or restrained*, or *not tight-fitting*
lose—*to mislay, to be unable to keep*, or *to be defeated*

moral—*good or ethical* (adjective), or *a lesson to be drawn* (noun)
morale—*spirit*

passed—the past tense of *to pass*
past—*just preceding or an earlier time*, or *in a direction going close to and then beyond*

personal—used to describe *an individual's character, conduct, or private affairs*
personnel—*an organized body of individuals*

precede—*to come before*
proceed—*to go ahead*

principal—*chief or main* (adjective), *a leader*, or *a sum of money* (noun)
principle—*a fundamental truth or belief*

raise—*to lift, to erect*
raze—*to tear down*
rise—*to increase in value*, or *to get up or move from a lower to a higher position*

seem—*to appear*
seen—the past participle of *see*

set—*to place something down* (mainly)
sit—*to seat oneself* (mainly)

stationary—*standing still*
stationery—*writing material*

suppose—*to assume or guess*
supposed—past tense and past participle of *suppose*
supposed—*ought to or should* (followed by *to*)

than—used to express *comparison*
then—used to express *time*, or *a result or consequence*

their—*relating to or belonging to certain people*
there—*in or at that location or place*
they're—*contraction of "they are"*

use—*to employ or put into service*
used—past tense and the past participle of *to use*
used—*in the habit of or accustomed to* (followed by *to*)
used—an adjective meaning *not new*

weather—*atmospheric conditions*
whether—*introduces a choice* (*whether* should not be preceded by *of* or *as to*)

your—a possessive showing *ownership*
you're—the contraction of *you are*

EXERCISE 8

DIRECTIONS: In each of the following items, a word or phrase is omitted. Two words or phrases are provided to complete the sentence. Choose the word or phrase that best completes the sentence. Answers are on page 801.

131. He is the (principal, principle) backer of the play.

132. I hope your company will (accept, except) our offer.

133. We hope to have good (weather, whether) when we are on vacation.

134. Put the rabbit back (in, into) the hat.

135. The attorney will (advice, advise) you of your rights.

136. She is far taller (than, then) I imagined.

137. Are they (all ready, already) to go?

138. She answered the letter on shocking pink (stationary, stationery).

139. What is the (affect, effect) you are trying to achieve?

140. I want to (set, sit) next to my grandfather.

141. He's going to (lay, lie) down for a nap.

142. I'm (all together, altogether) tired of his excuses.

143. He saluted when the flag (passed, past) by.

144. I'd like another portion of (desert, dessert).

145. Try not to (loose, lose) your good reputation.

146. How much will the final examination (effect, affect) my grade?

147. What is it (you're, your) trying to suggest?

148. She's not (use, used) to such cold weather.

149. The cost of the coat will (raise, rise) again.

150. You are (suppose, supposed) to be home at six o'clock.

151. Her cat ran straight for (its, it's) bowl of food.

152. Are you (conscience, conscious) of what you are doing?

153. It will (seen, seem) that we are afraid of snakes.

154. His essays are filled with literary (allusions, illusions).

155. This wine will be a good (complement, compliment) to the meal.

156. It's (later, latter) than you think!

157. My cousin has a swimmer's (build, built).

158. I never (knew, new) him before today.

159. She asked her a (personal, personnel) question about her family.

160. The golf (coarse, course) was very crowded.

161. The costume was made from old (cloth, clothe) napkins.

162. The ball carrier was trying to (allude, elude) the tacklers.

163. There are (know, no) more exhibitions planned.

164. I will wait for you in the (ante, anti) room.

165. Her (moral, morale) is very low.

166. Begin the sentence with a (capital, capitol) letter.

167. The fact that he nearly had an accident did not even (faze, phase) him.

168. He earns royalties in (access, excess) of a million dollars a year.

169. Now, may we (precede, proceed) with the debate?

170. Her (fort, forte) is writing lyrics for musical comedy.

171. They wondered how they were going to (disburse, disperse) the huge crowd.

172. Everyone was dressed (formally, formerly) for the dinner party.

173. I am not (adverse, averse) to continuing the discussion at another time.

174. Can something be done to diminish the (incidence, incidents) of influenza in that area?

175. "Seeing the film in class will serve a (dual, duel) purpose," he explained.

176. I'm not sure I want to (expand, expend) so much energy on that project.

177. Imagine my (discomfit, discomfort) when my ex-girlfriend showed up at the party too!

178. He was a famous matinee (idle, idol) many years ago.

179. When did they (emigrate, immigrate) from New York to Paris?

180. I think she is part of a (click, clique) of snobs.

Punctuation

Correct Comma Usage

Commas help to make sentences clearer by giving the reader signals or directions. As a general rule, commas often appear where a speaker would naturally slow down or pause.

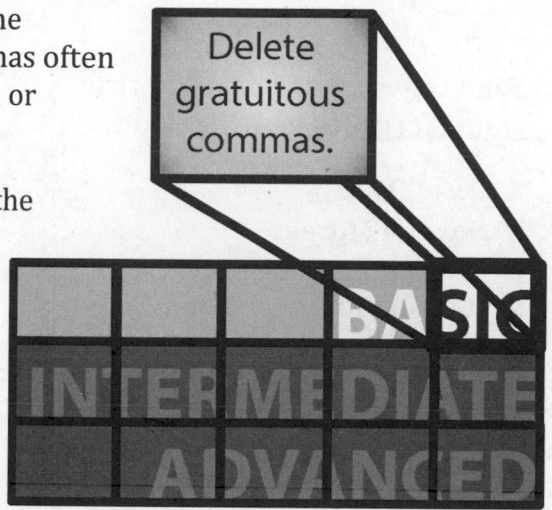

> *Spoken:* The men cooked the meat [pause] and the women prepared the salad.

> *Written:* The men cooked the meat, and the women prepared the salad.

The "speaking" test for commas can be helpful, but sometimes we talk quickly or unclearly. Therefore, it is important to learn the rules for using commas.

In a series of three or more elements, use commas to separate the elements.

> The ice cream contains *sugar, cream, milk, vanilla,* and *chocolate.*

Use a comma before the conjunctions *and, but, or,* or *nor* when one of these words is used to join main clauses. (Note: As you will see in the Intermediate and Advanced levels, there are other conjunctions that also require the use of a comma.)

> April and Jim had a great time on their *date, and Jim* hoped to see April again.

Do not use a comma to separate the subject from its verb.

> The cruise *ship, arrived* at its destination one hour early. ✗

> The cruise *ship arrived* at its destination one hour early. ✓

Do not use a comma to separate the verb from the rest of the sentence.

> Rebecca *called, her friend* to find out what had happened. ✗

> Rebecca *called her friend* to find out what had happened. ✓

EXERCISE 9

DIRECTIONS *(Items #181–195)*: In each of the following items, a word or phrase is underlined. Following each sentence or sentences are alternative suggestions for rewriting the underlined part. If you think the original is correct, choose NO CHANGE. Otherwise, choose the best alternative. Answers are on page 801.

181. Sometimes when I was in a rush, I would forget to lock the door.

   A. NO CHANGE
   B. I would, forget
   C. I would forget
   D. I would forget,

182. My sister got a new bike and rides it almost every day.

   F. NO CHANGE
   G. bike, and rides it
   H. bike and rides, it
   J. bike and, rides it

183. Chocolate chip cookies contain, brown sugar, white sugar, flour, butter, eggs, baking powder, salt, vanilla, and chocolate chips.

   A. NO CHANGE
   B. contain, brown sugar
   C. contain brown sugar,
   D. contain brown, sugar,

184. The mayor visited the site of the new stadium.

   F. NO CHANGE
   G. mayor, visited the site
   H. mayor visited, the site
   J. mayor visited the site,

185. My brother's chores are to clean up, his room and take out the garbage.

   A. NO CHANGE
   B. to clean, up his room
   C. to clean up his room
   D. to clean up his room,

186. Our daily activities at camp included horseback riding, swimming, canoeing, and archery.

   F. NO CHANGE
   G. camp, included horseback riding,
   H. camp included horseback, riding,
   K. camp included, horseback riding,

187. When we got to the airport, we had to get our boarding passes, go through security, and walk to our gate.

   A. NO CHANGE
   B. get, our boarding passes, go through security, and walk
   C. get our boarding passes, go through security and walk,
   D. get our boarding passes go through security and walk

188. Not only is Jack a math whiz, he also <u>excels at, science, social studies, and</u> writing.

F. NO CHANGE
G. excels, at science, social studies and
H. excels at science, social studies, and
J. excels at science, social, studies, and

189. The plane <u>flew faster and higher</u> to get out of the storm as quickly as possible.

A. NO CHANGE
B. flew, faster, and higher
C. flew, faster and higher
D. flew faster, and higher

190. Every autumn I <u>plant a few tulip and daffodil bulbs</u> with the hope that they will bloom in the spring.

F. NO CHANGE
G. a few tulip, and daffodil bulbs
H. a few tulip and, daffodil bulbs
J. plant, a few tulip and daffodil bulbs

191. I eat potatoes all the time and in a variety of <u>ways including, baked, boiled, mashed, and</u> fried.

A. NO CHANGE
B. ways, including baked boiled mashed and
C. ways, including baked, boiled, mashed, and
D. ways, including, baked, boiled, mashed, and

192. I like to get exercise <u>by running, biking, or playing</u> tennis.

F. NO CHANGE
G. by running, biking, or playing,
H. by running biking or playing
J. by, running, biking, or playing

193. The three art classes offered at the school <u>are painting sculpting and drawing</u>.

A. NO CHANGE
B. are painting, sculpting, and drawing
C. are painting sculpting and, drawing
D. are, painting, sculpting, and drawing

194. Most P.T.A. meetings are <u>well-organized, informative and, fun</u> to attend.

F. NO CHANGE
G. well-organized, informative, and, fun
H. well-organized, informative, and fun
J. well-organized informative and fun

195. The rattlesnake <u>is, one of</u> the most venomous snakes in the world.

A. NO CHANGE
B. is one, of
C. is one of
D. is, one, of

DIRECTIONS *(Items #196–200)*: Each of the following sentences contains a single error. The error is underlined and lettered. Choose the one underlined portion that must be changed to produce a correct sentence. In choosing answers, follow the conventions of standard written English. Answers are on page 801.

196. As a boy growing up on a farm,

Robert <u>learned, how to</u> milk <u>cows,</u>
             F   G

<u>feed</u> <u>chickens, gather</u> <u>eggs, and</u> ride
G   H   J

horses.

197. The interior decorator suggested

redesigning the dining <u>room, the</u>
                            A

living <u>room, and</u> the <u>master bedroom,</u>
         B   C

<u>but</u> the owners <u>decided, they</u> couldn't
C   D

afford it.

198. The hotel <u>offers, a</u> fitness <u>room, a</u>
                 F   G

swimming <u>pool, room</u> <u>service, and</u>
            H   J

free HBO.

199. During <u>lunchtime, students</u> can stay
                 A

in the <u>lunchroom go</u> <u>outside, or</u> go to
         B   C

the <u>library, but</u> they cannot leave
      D

school property.

200. The doctor explained that if the

disease is left <u>untreated, it</u> could
                  F

cause <u>lethargy, weight</u> <u>gain hair</u> <u>loss,</u>
         G   H   J

<u>and</u> memory impairment.
J

Use Commas for Clarity

In the previous section, you learned how commas are used to separate three or more items in a series and used before conjunctions that join main clauses (p. 49). Commas are also used for clarity. Commas are used to signal the end of introductory material, mark the end of a dependent clause at the beginning of a sentence, indicate a shift to a quotation, clarify the meaning of a sentence, and to set off parenthetical phrases (this skill is covered in the Intermediate level on page 116).

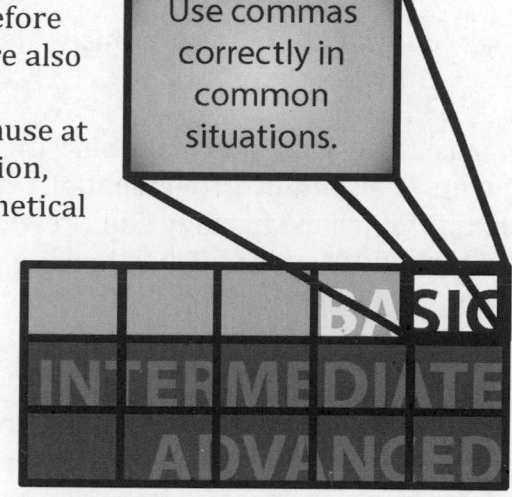

Commas make a writer's meaning clearer to a reader, especially when the writer adds additional words or phrases to introduce a sentence. A comma is needed to signal the end of introductory phrases or clauses.

Example:

With sweat pouring down her face the boxer stepped back into the ring. ✗

With sweat pouring down her face, the boxer stepped back into the ring. ✓

> The comma here marks the end of the introductory phrase that modifies the "boxer." The comma is important because it tells the reader that he or she has reached the end of the introductory modifier and is about to start reading the main part of the sentence.

Commas can also be used to mark the end of a dependent clause at the beginning of a sentence.

Example:

When I visit my cousins in the country we always go swimming in a nearby creek that has a tire swing hanging in a tree. ✗

When I visit my cousins in the country, we always go swimming in a nearby creek that has a tire swing hanging in a tree. ✓

> The sentence above begins with a dependent clause introduced by a subordinating conjunction. The comma marks the end of the dependent clause and the beginning of the independent clause (main part of the sentence).

A comma is also used to introduce quotations into a sentence.

Example:

As Martin Luther King, Jr. once said "Faith is taking the first step even when you can't see the whole staircase." ✗

As Martin Luther King, Jr. once said, "Faith is taking the first step even when you can't see the whole staircase." ✓

Commas are also used to make sure the meaning of a sentence is clear. Some modifying elements of a sentence are essential, restricting the meaning of a term, and some are non-essential, which means they don't restrict the meaning of the term. Non-essential elements are set off with commas. The following examples show how commas can change the meaning of a sentence:

Examples:

The banks that closed yesterday are in serious financial trouble. (Some banks closed yesterday, and those banks are in trouble.) (Essential)

The banks, which closed yesterday, are in serious financial trouble. (All banks closed yesterday, and all banks are in trouble.) (Non-essential)

Inside the people were dancing. ✗

Inside, the people were dancing. ✓

After all crime must be punished. ✗

After all, crime must be punished. ✓

If you read the last two examples aloud, you will hear how a natural pause suggests where a comma should be inserted. When you read these sentences aloud you will typically hear a pause between those words or phrases and the rest of the sentence. This practice of listening for a pause is not infallible. However, it is the best practice when all other rules governing use of the comma seem to fail.

USE COMMAS FOR CLARITY

1. Use a comma if the sentence might be subject to different interpretations without it.

2. Use a comma if a pause would make the sentence clearer and easier to read.

EXERCISE 10

DIRECTIONS: In each of the following items, a word or phrase is underlined. Following each sentence or sentences are alternative suggestions for rewriting the underlined portion. If you think the original is correct, choose NO CHANGE. Otherwise, choose the best alternative. Answers are on page 801.

201. The three-toed box turtle is highly adaptive and perhaps, the only box turtle that can live happily in an indoor enclosure.

A. NO CHANGE
B. The three-toed box turtle is highly adaptive and perhaps the only box turtle, that can live happily in an indoor enclosure.
C. The three-toed box turtle is highly adaptive and, perhaps the only box turtle that can live happily in an indoor enclosure.
D. The three-toed box turtle is highly adaptive and perhaps the only box turtle that can live happily in an indoor enclosure.

202. Tides are caused by the gravitational forces exerted by the moon, the sun, and the rotation, of the earth.

F. NO CHANGE
G. exerted, by the moon, the sun and the rotation of
H. exerted by the moon, the sun, and the rotation of
J. exerted by, the moon, the sun, and the rotation of

203. When a honey bee stings a person it leaves behind not only the stinger, but also part of its abdomen, digestive tract, muscles, and nerves.

A. NO CHANGE
B. person, it leaves behind not only the stinger but
C. person it leaves behind not only the stinger but
D. person, it leaves behind not only the stinger, but

204. Items to be recycled should be placed in a recycle bin or brought to a collection center where they are sorted and cleaned.

F. NO CHANGE
G. center, where they are sorted, and
H. center, where they are sorted and
J. center where, they are sorted and

205. Though the new cars of today may be sold by American companies such as Ford many of their parts are made in foreign countries such as Mexico.

A. NO CHANGE
B. Ford, many of their parts, are
C. Ford many of their parts, are
D. Ford, many of their parts are

206. Even though men and <u>women have equal rights under the law in America, that is not the case, in</u> many other parts of the world.

   F. NO CHANGE
   G. women have equal rights, under the law in America, that is not the case in
   H. women have equal rights under the law in America, that is not the case in
   J. women have equal rights under the law, in America, that is not the case in

207. Breast milk has been proven to be the best source of nutrition for <u>infants providing essential vitamins, proteins, enzymes, and fatty acids</u> that resist infection.

   A. NO CHANGE
   B. infants, providing, essential vitamins, proteins, enzymes, and fatty acids
   C. infants providing, essential vitamins, proteins, enzymes, and fatty acids
   D. infants, providing essential vitamins, proteins, enzymes, and fatty acids

208. The continent with the highest number of orphans is <u>Asia, but the continent with the highest proportion of orphans is</u> Africa.

   F. NO CHANGE
   G. Asia but the continent with the highest proportion of orphans is
   H. Asia, but the continent with the highest proportion of orphans, is
   J. Asia, but the continent, with the highest proportion of orphans is

209. The average life span for indoor male cats is <u>twelve to fourteen years while female cats usually live</u> one to two years longer.

   A. NO CHANGE
   B. twelve to fourteen years, while female cats, usually, live
   C. twelve to fourteen years while, female cats usually live
   D. twelve to fourteen years, while female cats usually live

210. Trying to obtain as <u>much information as possible the investigators interviewed hundreds of witnesses and scrutinized</u> all of the evidence.

   F. NO CHANGE
   G. much information as possible, the investigators interviewed hundreds of witnesses and scrutinized
   H. much information as possible, the investigators interviewed hundreds of witnesses and, scrutinized
   J. much information as possible the investigators interviewed hundreds of witnesses, and scrutinized

211. In the painting *The Persistence of Memory* by Salvador <u>Dalí, the melting clocks are believed by some to symbolize the distortion of time while</u> in a dream state.

A. NO CHANGE
B. Dalí the melting clocks are believed by some to symbolize the distortion of time while
C. Dalí, the melting clocks are believed, by some, to symbolize the distortion of time while
D. Dalí, the melting clocks are believed by some to symbolize the distortion of time, while

212. <u>As the leader, and moral center of the Catholic Church, the Pope is revered around the globe.</u>

F. NO CHANGE
G. As the leader, and moral center, of the Catholic Church, the Pope is revered around the globe.
H. As the leader and moral center of the Catholic Church, the Pope is revered around the globe.
J. As the leader, and moral center of the Catholic Church the Pope is revered around the globe.

213. <u>Due to the influence of the sun's gravitational pull Earth travels</u> in an elliptical orbit around the sun.

A. NO CHANGE
B. Due to the influence, of the sun's gravitational pull, Earth travels
C. Due to the influence of the sun's gravitational pull, Earth, travels
D. Due to the influence of the sun's gravitational pull, Earth travels

214. As Jimi Hendrix said, "<u>When the power of love overcomes the love of power, the world</u> will know peace."

F. NO CHANGE
G. when the power of love, overcomes the love of power, the world
H. when the power of love overcomes the love of power the world
J. when the power of love overcomes, the love of power, the world

215. <u>When viewed from the moon our beautiful planet looks almost like a marble.</u>

A. NO CHANGE
B. When viewed from the moon, our beautiful planet looks almost like a marble.
C. When viewed from the moon, our beautiful planet, looks almost like a marble.
D. When viewed, from the moon, our beautiful planet looks almost like a marble.

216. <u>As one of the most disturbing pieces of art of all time, Edvard Munch's *The Scream,* can</u> give one nightmares.

F. NO CHANGE
G. As one of the most disturbing pieces of art of all time Edvard Munch's, *The Scream*, can
H. As one of the most disturbing pieces of art of all time, Edvard Munch's *The Scream* can
J. As one of the most disturbing pieces of art, of all time, Edvard Munch's *The Scream* can

217. William Shakespeare's actual <u>date of birth is unknown but he was baptized on</u> April 26, 1564.

A. NO CHANGE
B. date of birth is unknown but, he was baptized on
C. date of birth is unknown, but he was baptized on
D. date of birth is unknown, but he was baptized, on

218. Around one hundred new television pilots are made <u>each year but only about one-third of them get picked up by the networks and</u> make it to air.

F. NO CHANGE
G. each year, but only about one-third of them get picked up by the networks, and
H. each year but only about one-third of them get picked up, by the networks and
J. each year, but only about one-third of them get picked up by the networks and

219. Many <u>people assume that the most common language spoken in the world is English or Spanish, but it</u> is actually Mandarin.

A. NO CHANGE
B. people assume, that the most common language spoken in the world is English or Spanish, but it
C. people assume that the most common language spoken in the world is English or Spanish but, it
D. people assume that the most common language spoken in the world is English, or Spanish, but it

220. <u>Writing a book can take an enormous amount of time and trying to get it published can take even longer.</u>

F. NO CHANGE
G. Writing a book can take an enormous amount of time and trying to get it published, can take even longer.
H. Writing a book can take an enormous amount of time, and trying to get it published can take even longer.
J. Writing a book, can take an enormous amount of time, and trying to get it published can take even longer.

INTERMEDIATE | Organization and Coherence

Logical Connections

A conjunctive adverb is part conjunction and part adverb. Like a conjunction, it joins ideas. And like an adverb, it modifies a verb.

Some conjunctive adverbs show sequence and time:

Use conjunctive adverbs and adverbial phrases to show logical connections.

> The conference was a great success, but <u>afterward</u> we faced the enormous task of cleaning up after several hundred guests.

> Jordyn went to the store to get the ingredients for the cake. <u>In the meantime</u>, I set out all the baking supplies and pre-heated the oven.

Other conjunctive adverbs of this sort are "again," "before," "finally," "just as," "next," "now," and "then."

Some conjunctive adverbs show cause-and-effect connections:

> The blizzard coated everything in sight with a heavy layer of snow. <u>As a result</u>, some of the power lines snapped and several buildings were without power for hours.

> Justin failed to attend soccer practice yesterday. <u>Consequently</u>, he will not start in tonight's game.

Other conjunctive adverbs of this sort are "thus," "hence," and "so."

Conjunctive adverbs also express logical connections:

> Tabby is a cat, and all cats are mammals. <u>Therefore</u>, Tabby is a mammal.

> The City Council passed an ordinance requiring that sidewalks be free of any obstacles. <u>Accordingly</u>, property owners must now blow leaves away from the walks.

In each of the previous examples, the conjunctive adverb shows a logical relationship between the ideas expressed in the sentences.

When you write, choose conjunctive adverbs that are appropriate to the statement you are making.

Examples:

Tabby is a cat, and all cats are mammals. <u>Afterward</u>, Tabby is a mammal. ✖

Tabby is a cat, and all cats are mammals. <u>In the meantime</u>, Tabby is a mammal. ✖

Tabby is a cat, and all cats are mammals. <u>After all</u>, Tabby is a mammal. ✖

Tabby is a cat, and all cats are mammals. <u>Therefore</u>, Tabby is a mammal. ✓

Only the fourth sentence pair makes sense.

EXERCISE 1

DIRECTIONS: In each of the following items, a word or phrase is underlined. Following each sentence or sentences are alternatives for rewriting the underlined part. If you think the original is correct, choose NO CHANGE. Otherwise, choose the best alternative. Answers are on page 802.

1. I was afraid the soccer team was going to run out of steam at the end of the game. <u>However</u>, they managed to catch a second wind and claimed a last-minute victory.

   A. NO CHANGE
   B. Similarly
   C. Just as
   D. Indeed

2. If it doesn't rain, the picnic will be held at one o'clock on Sunday. <u>Undoubtedly</u>, it will be postponed until the following week.

   F. NO CHANGE
   G. Besides
   H. Otherwise
   J. Perhaps

3. This was an unusually hot summer, and many farmers were worried about their crops wilting in the heat; <u>in fact</u>, most of the farmers managed to meet their yearly quota of produce.

   A. NO CHANGE
   B. as a result
   C. indeed
   D. nonetheless

4. If we drive to school and then ride the bus to the game, the total trip will take an hour and a half. <u>Likewise</u>, if we drive straight to the game from my house, the trip will take an hour and a half. Either way, we will arrive on time.

   F. NO CHANGE
   G. However
   H. In fact
   J. At last

5. I like shopping at the health food
    store better than the regular grocery
    store because its food is better.
    <u>Nevertheless</u>, the produce at the
    health food store is the freshest in
    town.

    A. NO CHANGE
    B. As a result
    C. Specifically
    D. Equally

6. Many animals have trouble
    distinguishing between certain
    colors; <u>consequently</u>, for a person
    who is color blind, it is nearly
    impossible to tell the difference
    between certain colors, such as red
    and green.

    F. NO CHANGE
    G. on the other hand
    H. similarly
    J. yet

7. In recent years, the number of
    students attending postsecondary
    schools has been increasing. <u>For
    example</u>, the percentage increase in
    the number of students age 25 and
    over has been larger than the
    percentage increase in the number of
    younger students, and this pattern is
    expected to continue.

    A. NO CHANGE
    B. Moreover
    C. Rather
    D. So

8. On a hot summer day, I like to drink a
    glass of ice-cold lemonade. <u>In
    contrast</u>, my sister likes a glass of
    sweet iced tea.

    F. NO CHANGE
    G. In fact
    H. For example
    J. Likewise

9. Our small dining room was barely
    able to seat our entire family for
    Thanksgiving dinner. <u>Further</u>, we
    squeezed in a few extra guests who
    had no family with which to celebrate
    the holiday.

    A. NO CHANGE
    B. Rather
    C. However
    D. Certainly

10. The lunch menu for today will not
    include spaghetti and meatballs. <u>As a
    result</u>, it will include hamburgers and
    French fries.

    F. NO CHANGE
    G. Yet
    H. Instead
    J. Besides

11. <u>Besides</u> the minor mishap during the
    first act of the play, Tom continued
    his performance. By the time the final
    curtain call came, the applause from
    the crowd was nearly deafening.

    A. NO CHANGE
    B. Despite
    C. In contrast to
    D. Equally to

12. The principal will be out of town on business on Thursday; <u>accordingly</u>, the vice principal will assume the duties of principal until the principal returns.

   F. NO CHANGE
   G. on the other hand
   H. surprisingly
   J. finally

13. The volleyball team is hoping to raise $750 through the bowl-a-thon fundraiser. They would be delighted, <u>to be sure</u>, with even $500.

   A. NO CHANGE
   B. instead
   C. however
   D. by the way

14. After Bethany Hamilton was attacked by a shark and tragically lost her left arm, many believed she would never surf again; <u>after all</u>, her accident only strengthened her resolve to prove that she could be the best.

   F. NO CHANGE
   G. as a result
   H. therefore
   J. yet

15. There are some who advocate the use of marijuana for medicinal purposes, citing its potential to treat symptoms associated with such deadly diseases as cancer and HIV/AIDS; <u>on the other hand</u>, the fact that marijuana has also been associated with many serious negative health effects makes its use as a medicinal drug risky, at best.

   A. NO CHANGE
   B. instead
   C. rather
   D. hence

16. The first two books in the trilogy were given very positive reviews in all the magazines and newspapers. <u>By contrast</u>, the final book was also given favorable reviews.

   F. NO CHANGE
   G. Similarly
   H. That is
   J. Besides

17. In fast-pitch softball, a batter may receive up to three strikes and four balls during her turn at bat. <u>Indeed</u>, in slow-pitch softball, a batter may only receive up to two strikes and three balls at bat.

   A. NO CHANGE
   B. Hence
   C. Therefore
   D. Conversely

18. Corals are sessile, which means that they permanently attach themselves to the ocean floor, essentially "taking root" like most plants do. Corals are animals, though, because they do not make their own food, as plants do. Any structure that we call "a coral" is, <u>rather</u>, made up of hundreds to thousands of tiny coral creatures called polyps.

F. NO CHANGE
G. by comparison
H. yet
J. in fact

19. Most of the students at West High prefer English over science; <u>however,</u> of those that prefer English over science, 70 percent said they prefer math over English.

A. NO CHANGE
B. instead
C. rather
D. consequently

20. Smog, which is a form of air pollution, has been known to cause adverse health effects in humans, <u>undoubtedly</u> respiratory disease and the risk of certain birth defects, although the latter has not been widely studied.

F. NO CHANGE
G. such as
H. despite
J. instead

Writing Accessible Paragraphs

Paragraph development is an important writing skill that you must learn and practice. Without proper organization, a paragraph is nothing more than several sentences tossed together, like a salad. Consider the example below:

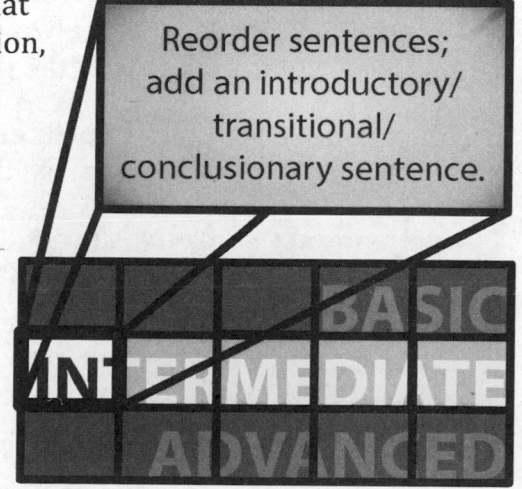

Reorder sentences; add an introductory/ transitional/ conclusionary sentence.

Example:

[1] Courts had ruled this way in the past. [2] They had lived with their owner, an army surgeon, at Fort Snelling, then in the free Territory of Wisconsin. [3] However, what appeared to be a straightforward lawsuit between two private parties became an 11-year legal struggle that

culminated in one of the most notorious decisions ever issued by the United States Supreme Court. [4] The Scotts' freedom could be established on the grounds that they had been held in bondage for extended periods in a free territory and were then returned to a slave state. [5] In 1846, a slave named Dred Scott and his wife, Harriet, sued for their freedom in a St. Louis city court. [6] The odds were in their favor.

> As it's written, the paragraph doesn't really make sense. The first sentence mentions courts having ruled "this way" in the past, and the second sentence uses the pronoun "they," but it is unclear what "this way" and "they" refer to. And that's only the beginning of the confusion. While it's certainly possible to unscramble the sentences and figure out the gist of the paragraph after reading it, the objective of a good paragraph should be to make the story, argument, or information as clear and coherent as possible from the very beginning right through the end. There are some techniques that can help you achieve this, such as arranging ideas in order and using transitional devices.

Notice the difference in readability in the same paragraph below, with the sentences arranged according to the order of ideas:

> [1] In 1846, a slave named Dred Scott and his wife, Harriet, sued for their freedom in a St. Louis city court. [2] The odds were in their favor. [3] They had lived with their owner, an army surgeon, at Fort Snelling, then in the free Territory of Wisconsin. [4] The Scotts' freedom could be established on the grounds that they had been held in bondage for extended periods in a free territory and were then returned to a slave state. [5] Courts had ruled this way in the past. [6] However, what appeared to be a straightforward lawsuit between two private parties became an 11-year legal struggle that culminated in one of the most notorious decisions ever issued by the United States Supreme Court.

The techniques for writing a good passage are the same as those for writing a good paragraph. Organization and clarity are key. Three types of sentences are essential for writing good passages:

Introductory sentences give readers an idea of what to expect in a paragraph or passage. Sometimes, but not always, an introductory sentence may actually include a statement of the main idea of the paragraph, or even the entire passage.

Transitional sentences appear either at the end of one paragraph, or the beginning of the next, and highlight, or clarify, the relationship between the two paragraphs.

Conclusionary sentences provide a clear and concise summary of the paragraph or passage and include a restatement of the main point.

Let's take another look at the paragraph above, which is actually part of a longer passage:

[1]

[1] In 1846, a slave named Dred Scott and his wife, Harriet, sued for their freedom in a St. Louis city court. [2] The odds were in their favor. [3] They had lived with their owner, an army surgeon, at Fort Snelling, then in the free Territory of Wisconsin. [4] The Scotts' freedom could be established on the grounds that they had been held in bondage for extended periods in a free territory and were then returned to a slave state. [5] Courts had ruled this way in the past. [6] However, what appeared to be a straightforward lawsuit between two private parties became an 11-year legal struggle that culminated in one of the most notorious decisions ever issued by the United States Supreme Court.

[2]

[7] On its way to the United States Supreme Court, the Dred Scott case grew in scope and significance as slavery became the single most explosive issue in American politics. [8] By the time the case reached the high court, it had come to have enormous political implications for the entire nation.

[3]

[9] On March 6, 1857, Chief Justice Roger B. Taney read the majority opinion of the Court, which stated that slaves were not citizens of the United States and, therefore, could not expect any protection from the federal government or the courts. [10] The opinion also stated that Congress had no authority to ban slavery from a federal territory. [11] This decision moved the nation a step closer to civil war.

[4]

[12] The decision of *Scott v. Sanford*, considered by legal scholars to be the worst ever rendered by the United States Supreme Court, was overturned by the 13th and 14th amendments to the Constitution, which abolished slavery and declared all persons born in the United States to be citizens of the United States.

> The very first sentence in the passage *introduces* the topic of the passage and gives readers a good idea of what is to come: a discussion about a slave family's struggle for freedom. The final sentence in paragraph 1 makes the *transition* from a story about one slave family to a lawsuit with national repercussions. It becomes clear in paragraphs 2 and 3 that the result of this initially private lawsuit became a major factor in moving the US toward civil war. And finally, paragraph 4 *concludes* the passage with a summary of the main point: the *Scott v. Sanford* decision was and is unconstitutional, defying one of the very beliefs our nation was founded upon—that all men are created equal. The ideas in the passage are clearly organized, and the passage also makes use of transitional devices such as pronouns and transitional words like "however" and "by the time."

EXERCISE 2

DIRECTIONS: In each of the following items, a new sentence is provided or the item asks about the best order to rearrange the original sentences. Choose the best placement of the new sentence or the best order of the sentences from the four choices provided. Answers are on page 802.

Questions 21–26 refer to the following passage.

[1]

[1] George Washington Carver was always interested in plants. [2] When he was a child, he was known as the "plant doctor." [3] He had a secret garden where he grew all kinds of plants. [4] People would ask him for advice when they had sick plants.

[2]

[5] Later, when he was teaching at Tuskegee Institute, he put his plant skills to good use. [6] Many people in the South had been growing only cotton on their land. [7] Eventually, cotton would no longer grow on this land. [8] This was especially bad for poor African American farmers, who relied on selling cotton to support themselves. [9] Carver was dedicated to helping those farmers, so he came up with a plan.

[3]

[10] Carver knew that certain plants put nutrients back into the soil, and one of those plants is the peanut. [11] Peanuts are also a source of protein. [12] Carver thought that if those farmers planted peanuts, the plants would help restore their soil, provide food for their animals, and provide protein for their families—quite a plant! [13] In 1896, peanuts were not even recognized as a crop in the United States, but Carver would help change that.

[4]

[14] Carver told farmers to rotate their crops: plant cotton one year, then the next year plant peanuts and other soil-restoring plants, like peas and sweet potatoes. [15] It worked! [16] The peanut plants grew and added enough nutrients to the soil so cotton grew the next year. [17] Again, Carver had a plan.

[5]

[18] Carver invented all kinds of things made out of peanuts. [19] He wrote down more than 300 uses for peanuts, including peanut milk, peanut paper, and peanut soap. [20] Carver thought that if farmers started making things out of peanuts, they'd have to buy fewer things and would be more self-sufficient. [21] Although not many of Carver's peanut products were ever mass-produced, he did help spread the word about peanuts.

[6]

[22] As time went on, peanuts became more and more popular. [23] And by 1940, peanuts had become one of the top six crops in the US. [24] By 1920, there were enough peanut farmers to form the United Peanut Association of America (UPAA), and in 1921, the UPAA asked Carver to speak to the US Congress about the many uses for peanuts. [25] Soon the whole country had heard of George Washington Carver, the Peanut Man!

21. Suppose you wanted to add this sentence to paragraph 1:

Sometimes he'd take their plants to his garden and nurse them back to health.

Where would be the *best* place to insert the sentence?

A. After sentence 1
B. After sentence 2
C. After sentence 3
D. After sentence 4

22. Suppose you wanted to add this sentence to paragraph 2:

Cotton plants use most of the nutrients in the soil (nutrients provide nourishment to plants), so the soil becomes "worn out" after a few years.

Where would be the *best* place to insert the sentence?

F. After sentence 5
G. After sentence 6
H. After sentence 7
J. After sentence 8

23. In paragraph 3, what would be the best order in which to arrange the sentences?

A. 10, 11, 12, 13 (NO CHANGE)
B. 10, 13, 12, 11
C. 13, 10, 12, 11
D. 13, 11, 12, 10

24. Suppose you wanted to add this sentence to paragraph 4:

Now the farmers had lots of peanuts— too many for their families and animals—and no place to sell the extras.

Where would be the *best* place to insert the sentence?

F. After sentence 14
G. After sentence 15
H. After sentence 16
J. After sentence 17

25. Suppose you wanted to add this sentence to paragraph 5:

And if other people started making things out of peanuts, they would want to buy the extra peanuts, so the farmers would make more money.

Where would be the *best* place to insert the sentence?

A. After sentence 18
B. After sentence 19
C. After sentence 20
D. After sentence 21

26. In paragraph 6, what would be the best order in which to arrange the sentences?

F. 22, 23, 24, 25 (NO CHANGE)
G. 22, 24, 25, 23
H. 25, 22, 23, 24
J. 25, 23, 22, 24

Questions 27–30 refer to the following passage.

[1]

(27) <u>After World War II, General George Marshall served for a time as the US Secretary of Defense.</u> Why? Marshall was a problem-solver, so his superiors wanted him to plan the battles, not fight them. Marshall's final chance for glory came at a key moment during World War II. At that time, Marshall was overseeing the war effort from his desk in Washington DC.

[2]

(28) <u>Marshall had originally wanted to schedule Operation Overlord one year earlier.</u> Operation Overlord would be the turning point of the war. What an honor it would be to lead it! When the time came to choose the commander, President Franklin Delano Roosevelt called Marshall into his office. Roosevelt was ready to reward Marshall for his long service in Washington. **(29)** <u>He asked Marshall if he wanted the job.</u>

[3]

Certainly, Marshall wanted to lead the Allied invasion, but he told the president that it was up to him. The president should make his decision based on what was good for the country, he added, not what was good for Marshall. So what did the president do? He chose General Dwight Eisenhower to command D-Day and sent Marshall back to his desk. **(30)** <u>After the war, Marshall resigned his position as army Chief of Staff.</u>

27. Assuming that all of the following statements are true, which provides the best introduction to paragraph 1?

   A. NO CHANGE
   B. General George Marshall dreamed of being a war hero, but throughout his career, he was usually assigned to the desk.
   C. General George Marshall helped formulate the "Marshall Plan" for rebuilding Europe after World War II.
   D. General George Marshall served the US army in the Philippines during World War I.

28. Assuming that all of the following statements are true, which provides the best introduction to paragraph 2?

   F. NO CHANGE
   G. After World War II, Marshall served for a time as the US Secretary of Defense.
   H. Towards the end of World War II, Marshall coordinated Allied operations in both Europe and the Pacific.
   J. For more than a year, Marshall and his generals had been planning the secret Allied invasion of France.

29. Assuming that all of the following statements are true, which provides the best transition to paragraph 3?

A. NO CHANGE
B. The president appointed George Marshall to the office of Secretary of State.
C. Marshall was given the Nobel Peace Prize for his plan to rebuild Europe after the war.
D. George Marshall was promoted to five-star rank as General of the Army.

30. Assuming that all of the following statements are true, which provides the best conclusion to paragraph 3?

F. NO CHANGE
G. Some of Marshall's ideas and, at times, his ability to choose competent commanders for battle were questionable.
H. Marshall's planning skills were so important the president told Marshall, "I feel I could not sleep at night with you out of the country."
J. During World War II Marshall served as the Army Chief of Staff.

Questions 31–35 refer to the following passage.

[1]

(31) Naturally occurring large areas of hydrothermal resources are called geothermal reservoirs. So, geothermal energy is heat from within the earth. We can recover this heat as steam or hot water and use it to heat buildings or generate electricity. **(32)** Industrial applications of geothermal energy include food dehydration, gold mining, and milk pasteurizing.

[2]

(33) Geothermal energy is generated in the earth's core. Temperatures hotter than the sun's surface are continuously produced inside the earth by the slow decay of radioactive particles, a process that happens in all rocks. The earth has a number of different layers. The core itself has two layers: a solid iron core and an outer core made of very hot melted rock, called magma. The mantle surrounds the core and is about 1,800 miles thick. It is made up of magma and rock. The crust is the outermost layer of the earth, the land that forms the continents and ocean floors. It can be 3 to 5 miles thick under the oceans and 15 to 35 miles thick beneath the continents.

[3]

The earth's crust is broken into pieces called plates. Magma comes close to the earth's surface near the edges of these plates. This is where volcanoes occur. The lava that erupts from volcanoes is partly magma. Deep underground, the rocks and water absorb the heat from this magma. **(34)** Geothermal wells are one to two miles deep.

[4]

People around the world use geothermal energy to heat their homes and to produce electricity by digging deep wells and pumping the heated underground water or steam to the surface. We can also make use of the stable temperatures near the surface of the earth to heat and cool buildings. **(35)** <u>Because geothermal energy has almost no negative impact on the environment and is relatively reliable and cost effective, it is a good source of renewable energy that the US should consider using more of.</u>

31. Assuming that all of the following statements are true, which provides the best introduction to paragraph 1?

A. NO CHANGE
B. Most of the geothermal activity in the world occurs in an area called the Ring of Fire.
C. The word geothermal comes from the Greek words *geo* (earth) and *therme* (heat).
D. Geothermal energy sometimes finds its way to the surface in the form of volcanoes, hot springs, and geysers.

32. Assuming that all of the following statements are true, which provides the best transition to paragraph 2?

F. NO CHANGE
G. Most of the geothermal power plants in the United States are located in the western states and Hawaii, where geothermal energy resources are close to the surface.
H. There have been direct uses of hot water as an energy source since ancient times.
J. Geothermal energy is a renewable energy source because the heat is continuously produced inside the earth.

33. Assuming that all of the following statements are true, which provides the best introduction to paragraph 2?

A. NO CHANGE
B. Geologists use various methods to look for geothermal reservoirs.
C. Geothermal heat pumps use the earth's constant temperatures to heat and cool buildings.
D. We can use these resources by drilling wells into the earth and piping the steam or hot water to the surface.

34. Assuming that all of the following statements are true, which provides the best transition to paragraph 4?

F. NO CHANGE
G. The temperature of the rocks and water gets hotter and hotter as you go deeper underground.
H. The United States leads the world in electricity generation with geothermal power.
J. Geothermal features in national parks, such as geysers and fumaroles in Yellowstone National Park, are protected by law to prevent them from being disturbed.

35. Assuming that all of the following statements are true, which provides the best conclusion to paragraph 4?

A. NO CHANGE
B. According to the US Environmental Protection Agency (EPA), geothermal heat pumps are the most energy efficient, environmentally clean, and cost effective systems for temperature control.
C. In recent years, the US Department of Energy and the EPA have partnered with industry to promote the use of geothermal heat pumps.
D. Direct use and heating applications have almost no negative impact on the environment.

Questions 36–40 refer to the following passage.

[1]

(36) <u>President Dwight D. Eisenhower signed the Federal-Aid Highway Act into law in 1956.</u> The movement behind the construction of a transcontinental superhighway started in the 1930s when President Franklin D. Roosevelt expressed interest in the construction of a network of toll superhighways that would provide more jobs for people in need of work during the Great Depression. The resulting legislation was the Federal-Aid Highway Act of 1938, which directed the chief of the Bureau of Public Roads (BPR) to study the feasibility of a six-route toll network. But with America on the verge of joining the war in Europe, the time for a massive highway program had not arrived. At the end of the war, the Federal-Aid Highway Act of 1944 funded highway improvements and established major new ground by authorizing and designating the construction of 40,000 miles of a "National System of Interstate Highways." **(37)**

[2]

It's clear that there were several highway acts passed before the 1956 act, which finally got the ball rolling. Eisenhower had first realized the value of good highways in 1919, when he participated in the US Army's first transcontinental motor convoy from Washington DC, to San Francisco. Again, during World War II, Eisenhower saw the German advantage that resulted from their autobahn highway network, and he also noted the enhanced mobility of the Allies, on those same highways, when they fought their way into Germany. These experiences significantly shaped Eisenhower's views on highways and their role in national defense. During his State of the Union Address on January 7, 1954, Eisenhower made it clear that he was ready to turn his attention to the nation's highway problems. **(38)** <u>He considered it important to "protect the vital interest of every citizen in a safe and adequate highway system."</u>

[3]

(39) <u>The struggle to create an adequate Interstate Highway System began early in the twentieth century.</u> The main controversy over the highway construction was the apportionment of the funding between the federal government and the states. Undaunted, Eisenhower renewed his call for a "modern, interstate highway system" in his 1956 State of the Union Address. Within a few months, after considerable debate and amendment in the Congress, The Federal-Aid Highway Act of 1956 emerged from the House-Senate conference committee. In the act, the interstate system was expanded to 41,000 miles, and, to construct the network, $25 billion was authorized for fiscal years 1957 through 1969. During his recovery from a minor illness, Eisenhower signed the bill into law at Walter Reed Army Medical Center on the 29th of June. **(40)** <u>The Interstate Highway System ended up taking almost three times as long and over four times as much to construct as initially thought.</u>

36. Assuming that all of the following statements are true, which provides the best introduction to paragraph 1?

    F. NO CHANGE
    G. It was the largest public works project in American history up to that point.
    H. Thirty-five years after it was signed into law, the original portion of the Interstate Highway System was completed.
    J. Popularly known as the National Interstate and Defense Highways Act of 1956, the Federal-Aid Highway Act of 1956 established an interstate highway system in the United States.

37. Assuming that all of the following statements are true, which sentence provides the best transition to paragraph 2 and should be added to the end of paragraph 1?

    A. Construction of the interstate system moved slowly.
    B. Although other presidents had tried before, Eisenhower was the only president successful in creating the Interstate Highway.
    C. When President Dwight D. Eisenhower took office in January 1953, however, the states had only completed 6,500 miles of the system improvements.
    D. But this act required individual states to fund 50 percent of the cost.

38. Assuming that all of the following statements are true, which provides the best transition to paragraph 3?

F. NO CHANGE
G. He informed the nation that in order for progress to be made to overcome inadequacies in the Interstate Highway System, the federal gas tax would remain at 2 cents per gallon.
H. He vowed that when the Commission on Intergovernmental Relations completed its study of the present system of financing highway construction, he would submit it for consideration by the Congress and the governors of the states.
J. He considered it an honor to recommend measures to advance the security, prosperity, and well-being of the American people.

39. Assuming that all of the following statements are true, which provides the best introduction to paragraph 3?

A. NO CHANGE
B. Between 1954 and 1956, there were several failed attempts to pass a national highway bill through the Congress.
C. The Highway Trust Fund handled the majority of the funds for the construction of the Interstate Highway System.
D. The states were required to pay part of the cost of the Interstate Highway System.

40. Assuming that all of the following statements are true, which provides the best conclusion to paragraph 3?

F. NO CHANGE
G. There are now several toll roads included in the Interstate Highway System.
H. The Interstate Highway System improved the mobility of military troops across the country.
J. Because of the 1956 law, and the subsequent Highway Act of 1958, the pattern of community development in America was fundamentally altered and was henceforth based on the automobile.

Word Choice

Be Concise

If you open any book on writing, you will find a unit with a title such as "Conciseness," "Word Economy," or some similar phrasing. Such a unit will stress the importance of eliminating unnecessary words or phrases. After all, no one wants to waste time reading paragraph after paragraph of unnecessary words, phrases, or sentences. Avoiding excessive wordiness, however, also means eliminating needless redundancy within individual sentences.

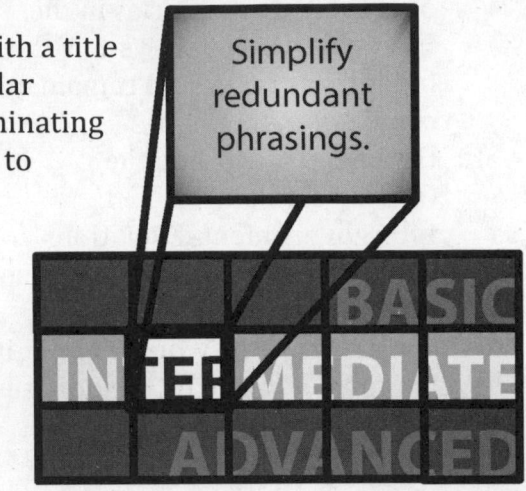

Simplify redundant phrasings.

ELIMINATE UNNECESSARY VERBIAGE

Be aware of the issue and recognize instances of needless repetition when you come across them.

Example:

I enjoy listening to the piano that my cousin uses to play music.

A piano, by definition, is an instrument that plays music, so the verbiage "uses to play music" is redundant. The sentence can be made shorter and more direct:

I enjoy listening to my cousin play the piano.

Example:

<u>On the first Tuesday of every month, I attend our monthly book club meeting</u> where we discuss both the virtues and the shortcomings of our book of choice.

A. NO CHANGE
B. On the first Tuesday of every month, I attend our book club meeting
C. On the first Tuesday of every month, our book club meets for its monthly meeting
D. Our monthly book club gathers on the first Tuesday of every month for a meeting

The correct answer is (B). "Monthly" means "once a month," so there is no need for both "monthly" and "the first Tuesday of every month."

EXERCISE 3

DIRECTION: In each of the following items, a word or phrase is underlined. Following each sentence or sentences are alternatives for rewriting the underlined part. If you think the original is correct, choose NO CHANGE. Otherwise, choose the best alternative. Answers are on page 802.

41. Sir Arthur Conan Doyle <u>wrote and authored</u> the famous fictional stories about detective Sherlock Holmes.

    A. NO CHANGE
    B. was the author who wrote
    C. was the writer who authored
    D. was the author of

42. The mayor <u>unsuccessfully attempted and tried</u> to persuade the town council of the benefit of building a new hotel to accommodate the increasing number of tourists.

    F. NO CHANGE
    G. attempted unsuccessfully
    H. attempted unsuccessfully and tried
    J. tried and attempted unsuccessfully

43. Wool is the fiber in the hair of sheep and goats <u>that for centuries has been woven into material made from it</u> by peoples throughout the world.

    A. NO CHANGE
    B. that for centuries has been woven into material
    C. for centuries that has been woven into material made from it
    D. that has been woven into material made from it for centuries

44. "Ave Maria" is one of Schubert's <u>most popular and well-liked</u> compositions.

    F. NO CHANGE
    G. most well-liked of all his popular
    H. most popular and well-liked of all his
    J. most popular

45. My brother <u>cut the high grass that he mowed</u> in the backyard before grabbing his ball and glove and heading to the baseball field.

   A. NO CHANGE
   B. mowed the high grass
   C. mowed the high grass by cutting it
   D. cut the high grass which he mowed

46. Some of the sounds that dogs can hear have frequencies too high to be <u>audibly heard</u> by the human ear.

   F. NO CHANGE
   G. audible and heard
   H. capable of being heard
   J. heard

47. <u>When my miniature dachshund was adopted as a puppy, he was very small.</u>

   A. NO CHANGE
   B. When my miniature dachshund was very small, he was adopted as a puppy.
   C. My miniature dachshund was a puppy when I adopted him.
   D. A miniature dachshund was adopted as a puppy when he was very small.

48. We will continue to use the oil that has been discovered in the Gulf for fuel <u>until the supply is exhausted</u>.

   F. NO CHANGE
   G. until the supply is exhausted or used up
   H. so long as the supply is not exhausted or used up
   J. while supplies last and are not exhausted

49. One of the largest and longest battles <u>that took place during the Civil War occurred at Gettysburg, Pennsylvania</u>, in July of 1863, and lasted three days.

   A. NO CHANGE
   B. that took place in Gettysburg, Pennsylvania, occurred during the Civil War
   C. of the Civil War took place at Gettysburg, Pennsylvania
   D. of the Civil War that took place in Gettysburg, Pennsylvania, during the Civil War occurred

50. Teal is a <u>shade of blue-green hued color</u> that was first introduced into the English language in the early 1900s.

   F. NO CHANGE
   G. blue-green color
   H. color of blue-green hue
   J. shade and hue of blue-green color

51. <u>The lady's joy and delight at the discovery of the long-lost diamond cannot be put into words.</u>

   A. NO CHANGE
   B. The lady's joy at the discovery of the long-lost diamond cannot be put into words.
   C. The lady's joy and delight, which cannot be put into words, was because of the discovery of the long-lost diamond.
   D. The discovery of the long-lost diamond brought the lady joy and delight which cannot be put into words.

52. The children decorated their art projects using objects such as leaves, pine cones, and acorns <u>from their nature walk</u>.

   F. NO CHANGE
   G. from their nature walk out in the natural environment
   H. that they acquired from the natural surroundings of nature
   J. obtained from the ecosystem of nature

53. My grandmother can weave <u>the most fascinating fictional fantasy</u> of anyone I've ever heard.

   A. NO CHANGE
   B. the most fascinating fantasy
   C. the fictional fantasy that's the most fascinating
   D. the fictionally most fascinating fantasy

54. <u>Despite the frigid coldness of the arctic climate</u>, seals and polar bears survive quite happily in Alaska.

   F. NO CHANGE
   G. Although the arctic climate is cold and frigid
   H. Despite the arctic climate
   J. Given the cold, frigid climate of the arctic

55. Although cricket may appear to be a sport very similar to baseball, there are several differences, one of which is that players must use a flat bat <u>specifically designed for the game of cricket</u>.

   A. NO CHANGE
   B. specifically designed for the game of cricket in particular
   C. specifically designed in particular for the game of cricket
   D. designed specifically for the game of cricket in particular

56. The women's rights movement took a step forward in 1880 <u>with the formation of the National American Woman Suffrage Association that was established in that year</u>.

   F. NO CHANGE
   G. in that year with the formation of the National American Woman Suffrage Association
   H. with the formation of the National American Woman Suffrage Association
   J. with the formation of the National American Woman Suffrage Association established in that year

57. Ponies <u>distinguish themselves by being different</u> from horses by their size and other physical characteristics, as well as their temperament.

   A. NO CHANGE
   B. are distinguished by being different
   C. are distinguished
   D. distinguish themselves differently

58. Cinnamon is a spice <u>that comes from the inner bark of certain trees from which the spice is made</u>.

   F. NO CHANGE
   G. coming from the inner bark of certain trees that it is made from
   H. that comes from the inner bark of certain trees
   J. from the inner bark of certain trees which it is made of

59. Although the bananas you're used to eating are usually between 5 and 8 inches in length, bananas can range <u>in size</u> from 2 to 12 inches in length and from ¾ to 2 inches in width.

   A. NO CHANGE
   B. in their size
   C. in sizes
   D. OMIT the underlined phrase.

60. Mint, a strongly scented herb, <u>has a distinct flavor that is unique</u> from any other herb.

   F. NO CHANGE
   G. is distinguished by being different
   H. has a unique flavor that distinguishes it
   J. is distinguished differently

Precise Pronoun Use

A ***pronoun*** is a word that takes the place of a noun, so a properly used pronoun will have an ***antecedent*** (also called a ***referent***). This is the word the pronoun replaces. The antecedent of a pronoun must be made clear from the structure of the sentence.

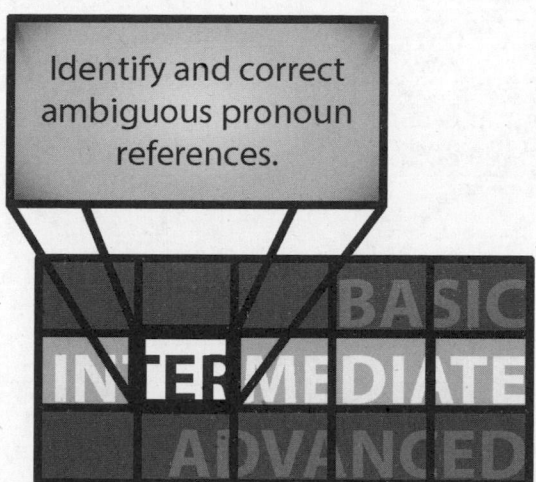

Examples:

Edward's father died before <u>he</u> reached his twentieth birthday, so <u>he</u> never finished his education. ✗

In 1980, the University Council voted to rescind Provision 3, <u>which</u> made it easier for some students to graduate. ✗

In the first example, it is not clear whether the father died before he reached the age of 20 or before Edward reached the age of 20. Furthermore, it is not clear whose education remained unfinished. Similarly, in the second example, the antecedent of "which" is not clear. "Which" may refer to Provision 3 or it may refer to the University Council's vote to rescind Provision 3.

WATCH FOR UNCLEAR ANTECEDENTS

The antecedent of a pronoun must be clearly identified by the structure of the sentence.

Example:

The letter is on the desk <u>that</u> we received yesterday. ✗

The letter <u>that</u> we received yesterday is on the desk. ✓

Beware that the impersonal use of "it," "they," and "you" tends to produce vague, wordy sentences.

Examples:

In the manual, <u>it</u> says to make three copies. ✗

The manual says to make three copies. ✓

<u>They</u> predict we are in for a cold, wet winter. ✗

The almanac predicts a cold, wet winter. ✓

EXERCISE 4

DIRECTIONS: In each of the following items, a word or phrase is underlined. Following each sentence or sentences are alternatives for rewriting the underlined part. If you think the original is correct, choose NO CHANGE. Otherwise, choose the best alternative. Answers are on page 802.

61. The most frequently advanced justifications for rising physicians' fees <u>is they pay increasing malpractice insurance premiums and invest</u> in costly equipment.

  A. NO CHANGE
  B. are they pay increasing malpractice insurance premiums and invest
  C. are that physicians pay increasing malpractice insurance premiums and that they invest
  D. is increasing malpractice insurance premiums and investing

62. Financial statements often relegate to footnotes expenditures such as negotiated settlements with terminated executives because <u>they are not recurring events</u>.

  F. NO CHANGE
  G. they are not a recurring event
  H. it is not a recurring event
  J. such settlements are not recurring events

63. Though an engineering genius, Edison's questionable business decisions include claiming engineering breakthroughs that had not yet happened, distributing slanderous pamphlets about his competitors, and, perhaps most embarrassing of all, <u>he championed direct current over alternating current even though it</u> could not be transmitted over long distances.

  A. NO CHANGE
  B. he championed direct current over alternating current even though direct current
  C. championing direct current over alternating current even though it
  D. championing direct current over alternating current even though direct current

64. After determining that the former CEO, Raoul Simpson, was aware that financial records had been falsified, the board of directors refused to pay $8.7 million of a $15 million severance package, which Simpson has vowed to fight in court.

F. NO CHANGE
G. package that Simpson has vowed to fight in court
H. package, a decision that Simpson has vowed to fight in court
J. package, a court fight by Simpson being vowed

65. French Impressionism had a decided and extended effect on American painting in the decades around the beginning of the twentieth century; it is clearly seen in the works of Americans such as Edward Willis Redfield, John Singer Sargent, and Cecilia Beaux.

A. NO CHANGE
B. this effect is clearly seen in the works of Americans such as
C. as is clearly seen in the works of such Americans as
D. clearly seen in the works of such Americans as

66. The actual votes cast by incumbents can provide voters with a more accurate picture of their attitudes than the speeches they make while campaigning for reelection.

F. NO CHANGE
G. the attitudes of incumbents than the speeches they make
H. the attitudes of incumbents than do the speeches they make
J. the attitudes of incumbents than do the speeches

67. With the writing of *Huckleberry Finn*, it marked the first time that the American vernacular was used in a novel.

A. NO CHANGE
B. Marking the first time that the American vernacular was used in a novel was *Huckleberry Finn.*
C. The writing of *Huckleberry Finn*, a novel, was the first time that the American vernacular was used.
D. The writing of *Huckleberry Finn* marked the first time that the American vernacular was used in a novel.

68. Although today it is cost-effective to make perfumes with synthetic ingredients, <u>they used to make the classic fragrances from flowers only</u> and other natural essences.

F. NO CHANGE
G. the classic fragrances used to be made only from flowers
H. the classic fragrances used to be made by them only from flowers
J. the classic fragrances used to be made from flowers only

69. Approximately 20,000 meteors enter the earth's atmosphere every day, <u>but very few of them reach the earth's surface on the grounds that they</u> are consumed by frictional heat long before they reach the earth.

A. NO CHANGE
B. but very few of them reach the earth's surface because most
C. but very few of them reach the earth's surface because they
D. with very few of them reaching the earth's surface on account of they

70. In the past few years, significant changes have taken place in the organization of our <u>economy that will profoundly affect the character of our labor unions as well as influencing</u> consumer and industrial life.

F. NO CHANGE
G. economy that will profoundly affect the character of our labor unions as well as influence
H. economy; these changes will profoundly affect the character of our labor unions and influence
J. economy, and that will profoundly affect the character of our labor unions as well as influence

71. <u>The delivery in large volume of certain welfare services is costly because of the large number of public contract employees necessary to ensure it is timely.</u>

A. NO CHANGE
B. The delivery of a large volume of certain welfare services are costly because a large number of public contract employees that this requires.
C. The delivery in large volume of certain welfare services is costly because of the large number of public contract employees necessary to ensure a timely delivery.
D. The delivery of certain welfare services in large volume is costly on account of the large numbers of public contract employees that is necessary for it.

72. The fictional ship on the television situation comedy *Gilligan's Island* was named the *Minow*, not *Minnow*, after the head of the Federal Communications Commission who, in 1961, <u>called it</u> a "vast wasteland."

F. NO CHANGE
G. calling it
H. called television
J. called them

73. Ballet dancers warm up before each performance by doing a series of pliés and stretching <u>exercises, and it reduces</u> the chance of injury.

A. NO CHANGE
B. exercises, reducing
C. exercises; the routine reduces
D. exercises, so the routine reduces

74. It is reported that some native tribes used to eat the livers of their slain <u>enemies which they believed allowed them to ingest their courage</u>.

F. NO CHANGE
G. enemies which they believed allowed them to ingest their enemies' courage
H. enemies which would, they believed, allow them to ingest their enemies' courage
J. enemies, a process they believed allowed them to ingest the courage of their enemies

75. Certain infections are <u>made up by both viral and bacterial elements which makes</u> treatment of these infections difficult.

A. NO CHANGE
B. composed by viral as well as bacterial elements and they make
C. composed of both viral and bacterial elements which make
D. composed of both viral and bacterial elements; this combination makes

Use Appropriate Style and Tone

Slang and other informal usages do not belong in a formal essay that you write for a school assignment, but you already knew that. So avoiding such usage is a rule of good writing that is both easy and difficult to follow.

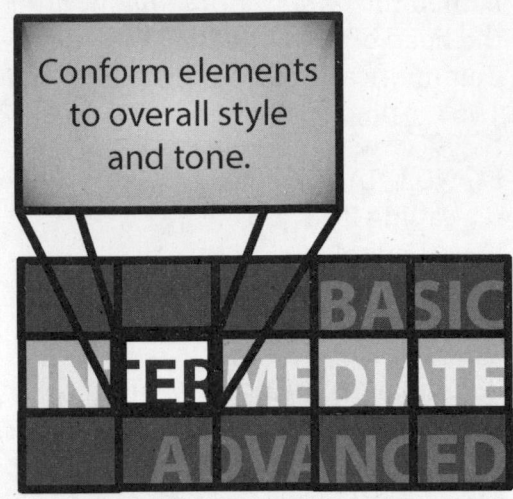

In one sense, the rule is easy because you don't have to memorize anything. There is no lengthy master list of words and phrases that don't belong in a formal essay. Instead, there is just the general rule that you should use the language of standard written English in your writing assignments.

On the other hand, you have to be attentive not to let unacceptable words and phrases slip into your writing. This can be difficult because those everyday sayings are so familiar and comfortable to use that they slip out of the pen (or off the fingers on the keyboard) so naturally that we don't notice. Then you wind up with sentences such as:

> I got hooked on a nerdy TV show and was so overwhelmed by all the scientific formulas they were working with that I thought my head would actually explode. ✘

> That new 3D action movie is just out of this world! ✘

The language is very expressive, but it doesn't belong in a formal document.

USE FORMAL LANGUAGE FOR FORMAL WRITING

Be sure that the overall tone and style of your writing fits the context in which you are writing (e.g., a formal essay for a school assignment).

EXERCISE 5

DIRECTIONS: In each of the following items, a word or phrase is underlined. Following each sentence or sentences are alternatives for rewriting the underlined part. If you think the original is correct, choose NO CHANGE. Otherwise, choose the best alternative. Answers are on page 802.

76. The prospect of hooking a 40-inch Northern pike, fighting to get him to the boat, and finally snagging him with the net really <u>psyches</u> a fisherman.

   F. NO CHANGE
   G. amps up
   H. excites
   J. revs up

77. When you are finished cooking and baking, the kitchen needs to be left spotless, so roll up your sleeves, grab some supplies, and <u>go to it</u>.

   A. NO CHANGE
   B. go to town
   C. get started on it
   D. clean it thoroughly

78. The professor caught her students <u>in la-la land</u> when she announced that there would be a pop quiz right in the middle of her lecture.

   F. NO CHANGE
   G. unawares
   H. asleep at the switch
   J. napping

79. After a busy day exploring the sights, sounds, and smells of the tropical island, the tourists returned to the cruise ship and gathered in the spacious dining room to <u>dig into some fancy cuisine</u>.

   A. NO CHANGE
   B. wolf down a meal
   C. get something to eat
   D. chow down

80. In an interview conducted for the school paper, the science teacher, Mr. Brown, revealed that his favorite pastime is simply <u>vegging out</u> at home with his family.

   F. NO CHANGE
   G. spending time
   H. hanging out
   J. chilling

81. The United States Postal Service functions as a vital communications link in all fifty states, <u>toting</u> letters and packages to hundreds of thousands of locations each year.

   A. NO CHANGE
   B. gunning
   C. schlepping
   D. transporting

82. Sally likes to shop at high-quality discount stores because there she can find fashionable, yet relatively <u>inexpensive</u> clothing for her growing family.

   F. NO CHANGE
   G. cheap-o
   H. dirt cheap
   J. dime-a-dozen

83. By the middle of the race, it looked as though the crowd favorite had fallen too far behind to overcome her late start, but as she approached the finish line, she drew strength from the crowd's cheering, and <u>it was all good</u>.

   A. NO CHANGE
   B. everything was fine
   C. it was all okay
   D. she was successful

84. The bank implemented additional security measures in all of its branches, requiring tellers to take special classes and introducing new technology to <u>put the kibosh on counterfeiting</u>.

   F. NO CHANGE
   G. stop bogus bills
   H. prevent counterfeiting
   J. prevent the making of funny money

85. Eliot Ness, a federal law enforcement agent during Prohibition, is most remembered for his efforts to <u>arrest</u> Al Capone.

   A. NO CHANGE
   B. nail
   C. bust
   D. collar

86. When the head coach signaled his kicker to perform an on-side kick in the first quarter, many fans booed, but it turned out to be a <u>gutsy move</u> that won the game.

   F. NO CHANGE
   G. can-do choice
   H. bold decision
   J. get-down plan

87. The junior class had a great idea for a homecoming float, but when they realized the excessive cost of the endeavor, the plans were <u>nixed</u>.

   A. NO CHANGE
   B. axed
   C. dropped
   D. canned

88. The jury <u>used a fine-tooth comb on</u> all of the evidence before concluding that the accused offender was innocent.

   F. NO CHANGE
   G. gave the third degree to
   H. used a magnifying glass on
   J. carefully examined

89. Kevin excels in most academic subjects, but <u>grammar-wise he is a less-than-stellar student who once received</u> a C in English.

   A. NO CHANGE
   B. he is a mediocre grammar student who once received
   C. his grammar ability is so-so, and he once received
   D. he isn't much as a grammar student, once receiving

90. With the passage of the Volstead Act in 1919, Prohibition agents began hunting down the bootleggers who were <u>making big bucks</u> by smuggling liquor into the United States from Canada and Europe.

   F. NO CHANGE
   G. growing enormously rich
   H. raking in the dough
   J. rolling in the green

Sentence Structure and Formation

Avoiding Sentence Errors

Fragments and Logically Defective Sentences

A common error in English writing is the failure to include both a main subject and a main verb in a word grouping that otherwise includes all the features of a sentence, such as initial capitalization and end punctuation. The result is not truly a complete sentence but a fragment masquerading as a sentence. A writer may also include a main subject and verb but fail to connect one or more elements to one of these two basic structural elements. The result is a sentence that has one or more elements with no logical connection to the others.

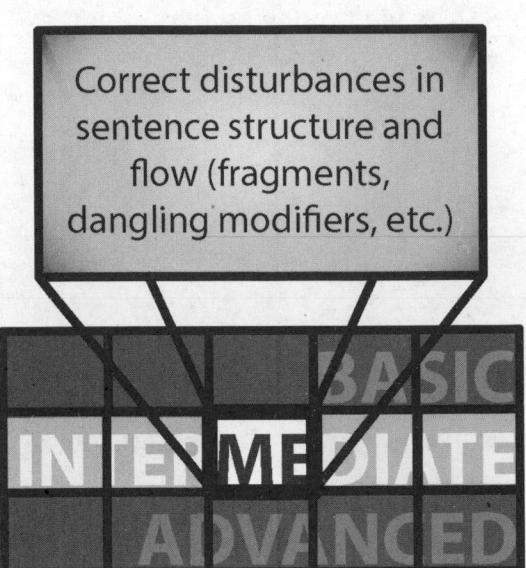

Correct disturbances in sentence structure and flow (fragments, dangling modifiers, etc.)

Example:

Intent on getting her children out the door for school, Mrs. Smith serving them breakfast, making their lunches, handing them their coats, and kissing them goodbye, finally dropping into a kitchen chair where she promptly fell asleep. ✗

In the example, main verbs have been replaced with participles, so the result is a sentence fragment.

Fragments and Relative Pronouns

When a sentence includes a relative clause, the clause must be introduced by a relative pronoun in order to create a complete sentence.

Example:

Thunder, which is the sound caused by lightning, can help determine how far away a lightning strike occurred. ✓

In this example, the subject is further described by a relative clause introduced by the relative pronoun "which."

Misplaced Modifiers

One error of logical expression that is made all too frequently involves misplaced modifiers. A modifier should be as close as possible to what it modifies. If a modifier is too distant from what it is supposed to modify, it can modify the wrong part of the sentence. The misplaced modifier creates some of the most humorous sentences ever formed in the English language.

Examples:

Belching smoke and sparks, the engineer leaned out of the window of the cab as the train sped past small towns on the way to a distant destination. ✗

Skewered on a long spit, mouth stuffed with an apple, and slathered in a sweet-and-sour sauce, the chef cooked the whole pig over a bed of coals on the beach for several hours. ✗

The problem with the two example sentences is the dangling modifier. In each case, the introductory modifier seems to modify the first significant noun or pronoun that follows. Thus:

"Belching smoke and sparks" seems to modify "engineer."

"Skewered...," "mouth stuffed...," and "slathered..." seems to modify "chef."

The way to correct each of the errors is rewrite the sentence so that the modifier is closer to the word it is intended to modify.

> **WATCH FOR MISPLACED MODIFIERS**
>
> Watch for sentences with ambiguous or incorrect modification. A modifier should be as close as possible to the word or phrase it's supposed to modify.

Examples:

I bought a piano from an old lady with intricate carvings. ✗

I bought a piano with intricate carvings from an old lady. ✓

The word "only" can also cause confusion depending on how it's placed in a sentence.

Examples:

<u>Only</u> he kissed her. ✓

He <u>only</u> kissed her. ✓

He kissed <u>only</u> her. ✓

> All of these sentences are logically possible. However, each sentence has a different meaning simply because the word "only" is placed differently in each one.

Finally, participial phrases can create confusion if they're improperly placed.

Examples:

Answering the doorbell, the cake remained in the oven. ✗

Answering the doorbell, we forgot to take the cake from the oven. ✓

> As with previous examples, we can correct the sentence by moving the modifier (i.e., the participial phrase) as close as possible to what it's supposed to modify.

Faulty Parallelism

In general, ideas that are parallel in meaning, such as elements of a series, should be expressed using parallel (matching) grammatical forms. For example:

The activities at summer camp should appeal to Joe, who likes <u>to water-ski</u>, <u>rock-climb</u>, and <u>zip-lining</u>. ✗

The activities at summer camp should appeal to Joe, who likes <u>water-skiing</u>, <u>rock-climbing</u>, and <u>to zip-line</u>. ✗

The activities at summer camp should appeal to Joe, who likes <u>water-skiing</u>, <u>rock-climbing</u>, and <u>zip-lining</u>. ✓

Writers must also use parallel grammatical forms in lists featuring nouns, prepositions, and other parts of speech. Phrases, including modifiers, should also be parallel.

Examples:

Service dogs are trained to help people with disabilities, and the dogs can do such things as pulling a wheelchair, retrieving a telephone, and to perform rescue work. ✗

Service dogs are trained to help people with disabilities, and the dogs can do such things as pulling a wheelchair, retrieving a telephone, and performing rescue work. ✓

Genna is a singer, a dancer, and she can play the flute. ✗

Genna is a singer, a dancer, and a flautist. ✓

EXERCISE 6

91. Written in almost total isolation from
    A
    the world, Emily Dickinson spoke of
    A   B
    love and death in her poems.
         C   D

92. Being highly qualified for the
    F
    position, the bank president will
    F   G
    conduct a final interview with the
    G
    new candidate tomorrow, after which
                                H
    he will make her a job offer.
    J

93. In broken English, the police officer
    A
    patiently listened to the tourist ask
    for directions to Radio City Music
    Hall after which she motioned the
         B   C
    tourist and his family into the squad
    car and drove them to their
                   D
    destination.

94. Following the recent crash of the
    F
    stock market, Peter bought a book on
    F   G
    portfolio management in order to
                        H
    learn methods to protect his
    H
    investments from a well-known
                   J
    investment banker.
    J

95. Although a person may always
    represent himself in a judicial
             A
    proceeding, licensed lawyers only
                                B
    may represent others in such
                  C   D
    proceedings for a fee.

96. Puritans such as William Bradford
    displaying the courage and piety
    F
    needed to survive in the New
    G
    World, a world both promising and
                  H
    threatening which offered unique
                J
    challenges to their faith.

DIRECTIONS (Items #97–105): In each of the following items, a word or phrase is underlined. Following each sentence or sentences are alternatives for rewriting the underlined part. If you think the original is correct, choose NO CHANGE. Otherwise, choose the best alternative. Answers are on page 802.

97. The child prodigy was such a maestro on the piano that his teacher <u>joking that</u> the child should start giving her lessons!

    A. NO CHANGE
    B. joked that
    C. having joked that
    D. joke that

98. The woman who played Glinda in the original Broadway production of the <u>musical *Wicked*, Kristin Chenoweth</u>.

    F. NO CHANGE
    G. musical *Wicked* Kristin Chenoweth
    H. musical *Wicked,* played by Kristin Chenoweth
    J. musical *Wicked* was Kristin Chenoweth

99. With their teeth brushed, their pajamas on, and <u>leaving the crying puppy</u> with a hot water bottle and an old t-shirt with the scent of its mother, the children headed up to bed.

    A. NO CHANGE
    B. crying and leaving the puppy
    C. the crying puppy left
    D. leaving the puppy crying

100. The old love letters that were discovered after the elderly couple had passed away said something about the couple's hopes and dreams, little about their fears, and a lot about <u>the way they were committed</u> to one another.

    F. NO CHANGE
    G. their commitment
    H. their committing
    J. committing themselves

101. One very interesting word in the English language is <u>kakorrhaphiophobia, which is</u> the fear of failure.

    A. NO CHANGE
    B. kakorrhaphiophobia is
    C. kakorrhaphiophobia, is
    D. kakorrhaphiophobia, which

102. If the definition of a fish is a cold-blooded vertebrate that breathes with gills and has scales and fins, then whales <u>not being fish, because whales are</u> warm-blooded, breathe oxygen from the air, and have hair.

    F. NO CHANGE
    G. are not fish, because whales are
    H. not being fish, because whales, being
    J. not fish, because whales are

103. <u>Driving across the Great Plains, herds of cattle and occasionally horses can be seen, lazing away the day or galloping across the open fields.</u>

    A. NO CHANGE
    B. Driving across the Great Plains, lazing the day away, or galloping across the open fields, herds of cattle and occasionally horses can be seen.
    C. Driving across the Great Plains, one can see lazing the day away or galloping across the open fields, herds of cattle and occasionally horses.
    D. As you drive across the Great Plains, you can see herds of cattle and occasionally horses lazing the day away or galloping across the open fields.

104. According to Mr. Jones, the burglar was a stealthy individual, <u>crept</u> into the house and managed to steal a valuable coin collection and disappear before Mr. Jones knew anything was wrong.

    F. NO CHANGE
    G. creeping
    H. but crept
    J. who crept

105. Marissa, who was the leader of the group, could not write the final report because she became ill and had to be hospitalized, but the group, now led by Doug, <u>completing</u> the report just in time.

    A. NO CHANGE
    B. completed
    C. to complete
    D. having completed

Verb Tense and Pronoun Person

You learned about principal parts of verbs, including irregular verbs, in the Basic level of this book (p. 36). In this lesson, you will continue building on what you already know and learn about a few more complicated verb tenses.

The Perfect Tenses

Use the ***present perfect*** for an action begun in the past and extended to the present.

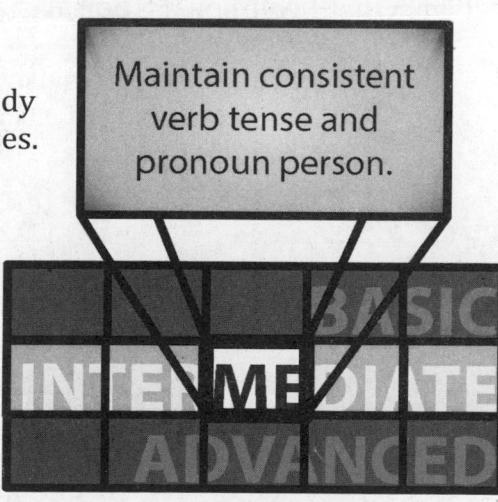

Maintain consistent verb tense and pronoun person.

Example:

I am glad you are here at last; <u>I have waited</u> an hour for you to arrive. ✓

    In this case, "I waited" would be incorrect. The action "have waited" (present perfect) began in the past and extended to the present.

Use the *past perfect* for an action begun and completed in the past before some other past action.

Example:

The foreman asked what <u>had happened</u> to my eye. ✓

> In this case, "happened" would be incorrect. The action "asked" and the action "had happened" (past perfect) are used because one action (regarding the speaker's eye) is "more past" than the other action (the foreman's asking).

Use the *future perfect* for an action begun at any time and completed in the future. When there are two future actions, the action completed first is expressed in the future perfect tense.

Example:

When I reach Chicago tonight, my uncle <u>will have left</u> for Los Angeles. ✓

> The action "will have left" is going to take place before the action "reach," although both actions will occur in the future.

The Subjunctive Mood

The *subjunctive* is used to express a wish, a command, a supposition, or a condition that is contrary to fact. The subjunctive is very important in other languages, but only a few remnants survive in English. The most important forms of the subjunctive are the use of "were" in place of "was" and the use of "be" in place of "am" in clauses requiring the subjunctive.

Example:

I wish that I <u>were</u> on a tropical island lying on the beach. ✓

> In this sentence, "were" is used rather than "was" in order to express the subjunctive (contrary to fact) idea that the speaker is not lying on the beach of a tropical island.

Example:

The teacher required that all reports <u>be</u> typed. ✓

> In this example "be" is used rather than "are" because the teacher wishes or commands that the reports be typed.

Shifting Verb Tenses

Make sure that verb tenses properly reflect the sequence, as well as the duration, of any action described in the sentence.

Examples:

Charles came to town last week and <u>goes</u> to a resort where he <u>rests</u> for three days. ✗

Charles came to town last week and <u>went</u> to a resort where he <u>rested</u> for three days. ✓

Joan came home last week and <u>goes</u> to her summer cottage where she <u>spends</u> the last weekend of her vacation. ✗

Joan came home last week and <u>went</u> to her summer cottage where she <u>spent</u> the last weekend of her vacation. ✓

Pronouns Must Have Proper Case

A pronoun must agree with its antecedent in case, number, and person. The pronoun's function in a sentence determines which case should be used. You should be familiar with the following three categories of pronoun case: nominative (or subjective), objective, and possessive.

TYPES OF PRONOUN CASE

1. *Nominative* (*subjective*) case pronouns are used as subjects of sentences.

2. *Objective* case pronouns are used as objects: direct objects, indirect objects, and objects of prepositions.

3. *Possessive* case pronouns are used to show possession. Use a possessive pronoun preceding a gerund. A gerund is the "-ing" form of a verb that is used as a noun.

The following examples illustrate correct usage of pronoun case:

Examples:

Nominative:

<u>I</u> thought <u>he</u> would like the gift <u>we</u> bought. ✓

Objective:

The choice for the part is between Bob and <u>me</u>. ✓ (The object pronoun <u>me</u> follows the preposition <u>between</u>.)

Possessive:

Do you mind <u>my</u> using your computer? ✓ (The possessive pronoun <u>my</u> precedes the gerund <u>using</u>.)

EXAMPLES OF PRONOUN CASE		1st Person	2nd Person	3rd Person
Nominative Case	Singular: Plural:	I we	you you	he, she, it they
Objective Case	Singular: Plural:	me us	you you	him, her, it them
Possessive Case	Singular: Plural:	my our	your your	his, her, its their

The following are additional examples of the **nominative**, or subjective, pronoun case:

Examples:

John and <u>him</u> were chosen. ✗

John and <u>he</u> were chosen. ✓

"He" is the subject of the verb; we certainly would not say that "him" was chosen.

He is as witty as <u>her</u>. ✗

He is as witty as <u>she</u>. ✓

"She" is the subject of the verb, even though the verb ("is") has been omitted from the end of the sentence; we certainly would not say that "her" is witty.

The following are additional examples of the **objective** pronoun case:

Examples:

They accused Tom and <u>he</u> of stealing. ✗

They accused Tom and <u>him</u> of stealing. ✓

"Him" is the object of the verb "accused"; they accused "him," not "he."

The tickets were given to Bill and <u>I</u>. ✗

The tickets were given to Bill and <u>me</u>. ✓

"Me" is the object of "to"; the tickets were given to "me," not to "I."

Finally, personal pronouns that express ownership never require an apostrophe. Also, a pronoun that precedes a gerund ("-ing" verb form used as a noun) is usually the possessive case.

Examples:

This book is <u>your's</u>, not <u>her's</u>. ✗

This book is <u>yours</u>, not <u>hers</u>. ✓

He rejoiced at <u>him</u> going to the party. ✗

He rejoiced at <u>his</u> going to the party. ✓

EXERCISE 7

DIRECTIONS (*Items #106–113*): Each of the following sentences contains a single error. The error is underlined and lettered. Choose the one underlined portion that must be changed to produce a correct sentence. In choosing answers, follow the conventions of standard written English. Answers are on page 802.

106. The whale had been <u>laying</u> on the
F
beach for over two hours before the

rescue teams <u>were able to begin</u>
G
<u>moving</u> it <u>back into</u> the water.
H   J

107. After he <u>had learned</u> <u>of</u> her suicide,
A   B
he <u>drunk</u> all of the poison <u>from the</u>
C   D
<u>vial</u>.
D

108. The <u>newly</u> <u>purchased</u> picture was
F   G
<u>hanged</u> on the back wall <u>nearest</u> the
H   J
bay window.

109. The <u>opening scene</u> of the film was a
A
<u>grainy, black-and-white</u> shot of an
B
empty town square <u>in which an</u>
C
outlaw was <u>hung</u>.
D

110. The woman to <u>whom</u> I take my
     F

clothes <u>for tailoring</u> has <u>adjusting</u> the
     G**H**

hem on this skirt <u>perfectly</u>.
     J

111. <u>Due</u> to the <u>extremely warm</u> weather
     A**B**

this winter, the water has not <u>froze</u>
     C

on the pond <u>sufficiently</u>.
     D

112. <u>Rather</u> than <u>declaring</u> bankruptcy, he
     F**G**

<u>applied</u> for a loan, and the bank
H

<u>loaned</u> him the money.
J

113. <u>After struggling with the problem</u> for
     A

most of the afternoon, he finally

<u>flinged</u> the papers <u>on</u> the desk and
B**C**

<u>ran out of the room</u>.
     D

DIRECTIONS (Items #114–125): In each of the following items, a word or phrase is underlined. Following each sentence or sentences are alternatives for rewriting the underlined part. If you think the original is correct, choose NO CHANGE. Otherwise, choose the best alternative. Answers are on page 802.

---

114. Major power failures in the United States are rare; but <u>when one occurred, the results included widespread economic damage, serious inconvenience for millions, and human life was endangered</u>.

   F. NO CHANGE
   G. when they occurred, the results included widespread economic damage, serious inconvenience for millions, and human life was endangered
   H. when one occurs, the result includes widespread economic damage, serious inconvenience for millions, and threat to human life
   J. when they occur, the results include widespread economic damage, serious inconvenience for millions, and threat to human life

115. Men's tailored clothing sales have been stagnant in recent years as consumers <u>assembled business casual wardrobes, replacing</u> suits with budget khakis and knit shirts.

   A. NO CHANGE
   B. have assembled business casual wardrobes, replacing
   C. have assembled business casual wardrobes and replacing
   D. had assembled business casual wardrobes, replacing

116. Curare has little effect when ingested, but few people are known to recover from its effects when the poison is introduced directly into the bloodstream.

   F. NO CHANGE
   G. but few people are known to have recovered from its effects
   H. but its effects are known to allow few people to recover
   J. and few people are known to recover from its effects

117. Although Beverly Sills never achieved superstar status in Europe or at the Metropolitan Opera, yet she was singing major roles at the City Opera during 20 years.

   A. NO CHANGE
   B. she did sing major roles at the City Opera during 20 years
   C. she sang major roles at the City Opera for 20 years
   D. but she sang major roles at the City Opera for 20 years

118. The earliest texts in cuneiform script are about 5,000 years old, having antedated the use of the first alphabets by some 1,500 years.

   F. NO CHANGE
   G. old, having antedated the invention
   H. old, antedating the use
   J. old and antedate the invention

119. Queen Elizabeth I was a student of classical languages, and it was her who insisted that Greek and Latin were spoken at court.

   A. NO CHANGE
   B. it was she that insisted on the speaking of Greek and Latin at court
   C. it was she who insisted that Greek and Latin be spoken at court
   D. she insisted that, at court, Greek and Latin were spoken

120. All of the students except George and she intend to order the newest edition of the textbook.

   F. NO CHANGE
   G. her intends to order
   H. she intends to order
   J. her intend to order

121. The paintings of Gustav Klimt are different from those of the painters he inspired who were more interested in exploring the unconscious than him.

   A. NO CHANGE
   B. from those of the painters he inspired being more interested in the exploration of the unconscious than he
   C. from those of the painters he inspired who were more interested in exploring the unconscious than his
   D. from those of the painters he inspired who were more interested in exploring the unconscious than he

122. The men and women of the jury filed slowly out of the courtroom, <u>each occupied with their own thoughts</u>.

    F. NO CHANGE
    G. each occupied with his or her own thoughts
    H. each occupying their own thoughts
    J. occupying each of his or her own thoughts

123. Sally scoffed at the other cheerleaders because <u>she felt they weren't as talented as her</u>.

    A. NO CHANGE
    B. she, feeling they weren't as talented as her
    C. she felt they weren't as talented as she
    D. she feels they weren't as talented as she is

124. <u>The opposing team tried to prevent him getting to the end zone, but failed.</u>

    F. NO CHANGE
    G. The opposing team, trying to prevent him getting to the end zone, but failed.
    H. The opposing team tried to prevent his from getting to the end zone, but failed.
    J. The opposing team tried to prevent his getting to the end zone, but failed.

125. <u>Us boys are going to camp out in the backyard</u>, but first we have to set up the tent.

    A. NO CHANGE
    B. We boys are going to camp out in the backyard
    C. Us boys, we're going to camp out in the backyard
    D. Us boys, camping out in the backyard

Conventions of Usage

...uring Agreement

As you know, a subject must always agree with its verb.

Example:

The <u>professor</u> <u>were traveling</u> in Europe when she received notice of her promotion. ✘

The <u>professor</u> <u>was traveling</u> in Europe when she received notice of her promotion. ✓

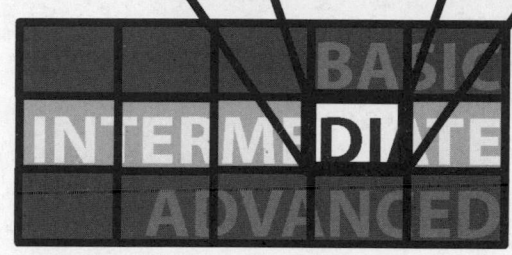

> In the example, it's easy to see that the singular subject, "professor," requires a singular verb, "was traveling." However, in complex sentences, problems of subject-verb agreement can be more difficult to spot.

Examples:

Star <u>performers</u> in the movies or on television usually <u>earns</u> substantial income from royalties. ✘

One school of thought maintains that the federal <u>deficit</u>, not exorbitant corporate profits or excessively high wages, <u>cause</u> most of the inflation we are now experiencing. ✘

A recent survey shows that a <u>household</u> in which both the wife and the husband are pursuing careers <u>stand</u> a better chance of surviving intact than one in which only the husband works. ✘

> In each of these three sentences, the subject and verb do not agree: "performers…earns," "deficit…cause," and "household…stand." However, the errors may not be immediately evident because of the intervening material. In the first sentence, the subject is separated from the verb by prepositional phrases. In the second sentence, the subject and the verb are separated by a parenthetical expression. In the third sentence, a clause intervenes between the subject and the verb.

The plausibility of the incorrect verb choice, and therefore the chance that the error will go unnoticed, is strengthened when there is a word or phrase near the verb that might be mistaken for the subject: "television…earns," "profits and wages…cause," and "careers...stand." If the first word of each of these pairs had been the subject, then there would have been no failure of agreement.

ENSURE SUBJECT-VERB AGREEMENT

Watch for problems of subject-verb agreement, especially in complex sentences where the subject and the verb are separated by intervening material.

Just as a subject must always agree with its verb, so a pronoun must always agree with its antecedent (referent) in both number and person.

Examples:

Although a police officer used to be a symbol of authority, today <u>they</u> receive little respect from most people. ✗

After three years of college education, a person should be allowed to apply to graduate school, because by that time <u>you</u> are ready to choose a profession. ✗

> In the first example, "they" refers to "police officer," which is singular. The best way to correct it is to replace "they" with "he or she." In the second example, "you" refers to "person." But "you" is a second-person pronoun and "person" requires a third-person pronoun. The sentence is corrected by changing "you are" to "one is." This last error is called the error of shifting subject.

PRONOUN-ANTECEDENT AGREEMENT

When analyzing sentences, make sure that a pronoun not only has a referent, but that the pronoun and its antecedent agree in both number and person.

EXERCISE 8

DIRECTIONS (*Items #126–141*): In each of the following items, a word or phrase is underlined. Following each sentence or sentences are alternatives for rewriting the underlined part. If you think the original is correct, choose NO CHANGE. Otherwise, choose the best alternative. Answers are on page 802.

126. My brother, along with several of his friends, <u>were not in</u> school on Monday because he and his friends all contracted a case of poison ivy during a weekend camping trip.

    F. NO CHANGE
    G. was not being in
    H. were not from
    J. was not in

127. The outbreak of an epidemic <u>pose a grave threat</u> to the societies of Third World countries where sanitation is poor and healthcare is limited.

    A. NO CHANGE
    B. pose grave threats
    C. poses a grave threat
    D. posing a grave threat

128. The goal of academic classes <u>is knowledge</u> and understanding, not simply the memorization and regurgitation of facts.

    F. NO CHANGE
    G. is to know
    H. are for knowledge
    J. are to know

129. After he was seriously injured in an accident, one of the athlete's greatest ambitions <u>were to help</u> other athletes with similar injuries overcome their pain and bitterness and rebuild their lives.

    A. NO CHANGE
    B. were helping to
    C. being to help
    D. was to help

130. One of the judge's most important character traits <u>are his courage</u> in the face of the unpopularity of his positions, positions that seem to him to be morally mandated.

    F. NO CHANGE
    G. is his courage
    H. are his courages
    J. being his courage

131. On April 15, 1947, twenty-seven-year-old Jackie Robinson from Cairo, Georgia, hailed as a hero by many young African American boys, <u>were the first</u> African American to play in Major League Baseball.

    A. NO CHANGE
    B. was becoming the first
    C. was the first
    D. first were

132. Towns such as New Orleans, Louisiana, <u>were hit hard</u> by Hurricane Katrina, but the resilient citizens soon began to rebuild their homes and their lives.

    F. NO CHANGE
    G. was hit hard
    H. hardly was hit
    J. hardly were hit

133. The air has never felt so crisp, the snow has never looked so white, and the moon in the night <u>sky shine</u> down with a brilliant glow.

    A. NO CHANGE
    B. sky shining
    C. skies shine
    D. sky shines

134. A quick look at the young intern with his wide eyes, pursed lips, and sweaty forehead <u>reveal</u> that he is actually quite nervous about his first day on the job.

    F. NO CHANGE
    G. to reveal
    H. are revealing
    J. reveals

135. When we went on a sailing expedition, provisions for the day's outing on the water <u>was</u> a picnic lunch in an ice chest and a large container with drinking water.

    A. NO CHANGE
    B. were
    C. being
    D. was being

136. The company's actual earnings <u>for the last quarter is substantially below that</u> reported on the pro forma statement that included the cost of a special category of restricted sales only in obscure footnotes.

    F. NO CHANGE
    G. during the last quarter is substantially below that
    H. for the last quarter are substantial but below that
    J. for the last quarter are substantially below those

137. Most department stores offer customers the option <u>that you may exchange your</u> purchases within ten days.

    A. NO CHANGE
    B. to exchange your
    C. of exchanging your
    D. of exchanging

138. Many physicists think that at some time in the next century <u>we will not only discover life in other galaxies but will also communicate with them</u>.

    F. NO CHANGE
    G. we will discover not only life in other galaxies, but be able to communicate with those
    H. we will not only discover life in other galaxies, but also be able to communicate with it
    J. that not only will we be able to discover life in other galaxies but be able to communicate to them as well

139. All of the students except Kyle and <u>she plans on reading</u> the new book.

    A. NO CHANGE
    B. her plans on reading
    C. her plans to read
    D. her plan to read

140. Fluoride helps protect a child's teeth while the teeth grow, <u>but it is unharmful to their bodies.</u>

    F. NO CHANGE
    G. and it is unharmful to their bodies
    H. and it is not harmful to his or her body
    J. and it is not harmful to the bodies

141. The power of Benton's best paintings comes from <u>one's ability</u> to transform seemingly mundane subjects into something grand.

    A. NO CHANGE
    B. the ability by him
    C. his ability
    D. one ability

DIRECTIONS (*Items #142–145*): Each of the following sentences contains a single error. The error is underlined and lettered. Choose the one underlined portion that must be changed to produce a correct sentence. In choosing answers, follow the conventions of standard written English. Answers are on page 803.

---

142. A recent study <u>indicates</u> that the
                  F

    average person <u>ignores</u> most
                 G

    commercial advertising and <u>does not</u>
                                H

    <u>buy</u> products <u>because of them</u>.
     H   J

143. Charles Dickens <u>wrote</u> about the
                A

    <u>horrifying</u> conditions in the English
     B

    boarding schools when <u>he visited</u>
                      C

    the schools on one <u>of their</u> trips to
                  D

    Yorkshire.

144. During <u>the war</u>, there were many
            F

    people in the Polish countryside <u>that</u>
                              G

    sheltered <u>those</u> who <u>had escaped</u>
           H   J

    from concentration camps.

145. <u>Given the evidence</u> of the existence of
              A

    a complicated system of

    communication <u>used by whales,</u> it is
                      B

    <u>necessary to</u> acknowledge <u>its</u>
       C   D

    intelligence.

Preposition Use

A *preposition* is a word that shows a relationship between another word, usually a noun or pronoun, and some other idea in a sentence.

Use correct prepositions.

Example:

The voice <u>of</u> the singer reverberated <u>off</u> the walls <u>of</u> the concert hall.

Sometimes, a word can be used incorrectly and lead to a construction that is non-idiomatic or not acceptable standard written English.

Example:

The techniques of empirical observation in the social sciences are different <u>than</u> those in the physical sciences. ✗

> The above example is wrong because "different than" is a non-idiomatic expression. The correct idiomatic expression is "different from": "The techniques of empirical observation in the social sciences are different <u>from</u> those in the physical sciences."

> ### USE CORRECT PREPOSITIONS
>
> Choose words that create meaningful phrases that are acceptable in standard written English.

Ending Sentences with Prepositions

One of the pseudo-principles of good grammar that is often repeated is, "Do not end a sentence with a preposition." We call this a pseudo-principle because it sounds official, but there is really no good reason to worry about trying not to end a sentence with a preposition, aside from the possibility of ending a question with a gratuitous "at":

Where is Jimmy <u>at</u>?

Where is Jimmy?

It is difficult to end a sentence with a preposition other than one that is a necessary part of a phrasal verb:

If you don't know the meaning of the word, then you should look it <u>up</u>.

Not only is this sentence grammatically acceptable, but it would also be practically impossible to contrive a sentence that would move the ending preposition:

If you don't know the meaning of the word, then <u>up</u> you should look it.

The point is that you should keep this principle in perspective. If you can reasonably avoid ending a sentence with a preposition, then do so; but if you can't, leave the sentence as it is and move on.

Prepositions That Present Special Problems

except/besides

Except and *besides* have related meanings and so one is sometimes used incorrectly in place of the other. *Except* means "but not." *Besides* means "in addition to." The following examples show the correct usage:

Examples:

Everyone on the team <u>except</u> Jill and Beth will be starting in tonight's softball game.

<u>Besides</u> Jill and Beth, only Therese will be sitting on the bench instead of playing in tonight's softball game.

by/until

By and *until* are another pair that are sometimes confused. *By* means "not later than." *Until* means "before." An assignment due *by* Tuesday means it can be turned in on Tuesday or before. An assignment due *until* Tuesday means that it must be turned in on Monday or before.

Examples:

I will be at work <u>until</u> dinnertime.

<u>By</u> dinnertime, I will be home from work.

between/among

Simply stated, you should use *between* to distinguish between exactly two options and *among* to distinguish between three or more options:

Examples:

The donated books will be divided equally <u>between</u> the two schools.

The donated books will be divided equally <u>among</u> the three schools.

EXERCISE 9

DIRECTIONS: In each of the following items, a word or phrase is underlined. Following each sentence or sentences are alternatives for rewriting the underlined part. If you think the original is correct, choose NO CHANGE. Otherwise, choose the best alternative. Answers are on page 803.

146. He has not yet taken advantage <u>off</u> the sale.

  F. NO CHANGE
  G. of
  H. from
  J. OMIT the underlined portion.

147. The teacher broke the news <u>to</u> the student.

  A. NO CHANGE
  B. too
  C. two
  D. OMIT the underlined portion.

148. Due to decreased sales, the workers were laid <u>off</u> by the company.

  F. NO CHANGE
  G. of
  H. down
  J. OMIT the underlined portion.

149. The manager promised to look <u>in to</u> the customer's complaint.

  A. NO CHANGE
  B. into
  C. unto
  D. OMIT the underlined portion.

150. The lawyer voiced his objection <u>on</u> the recount of the votes.

  F. NO CHANGE
  G. to
  H. about
  J. OMIT the underlined portion.

151. The office will open sometime <u>in</u> a half-hour.

  A. NO CHANGE
  B. within
  C. inside
  D. OMIT the underlined portion.

152. There are many students waiting <u>on</u> the instructor during her office hours.

  F. NO CHANGE
  G. for
  H. to
  J. OMIT the underlined portion.

153. Please save energy by turning <u>of</u> the lights before you leave the house.

  A. NO CHANGE
  B. off
  C. in
  D. OMIT the underlined portion.

154. The dancers swung <u>in</u> motion when the music started.

    F. NO CHANGE
    G. in to
    H. into
    J. OMIT the underlined portion.

155. I work at the bank <u>in</u> the corner of Main and Packard.

    A. NO CHANGE
    B. on
    C. around
    D. OMIT the underlined portion.

156. He took it <u>up on</u> himself to schedule the meeting.

    F. NO CHANGE
    G. on
    H. upon
    J. OMIT the underlined portion.

157. Ralph had difficulty getting to sleep <u>till</u> very late.

    A. NO CHANGE
    B. up to
    C. until
    D. OMIT the underlined portion.

158. This class is different <u>than</u> the other.

    F. NO CHANGE
    G. of
    H. from
    J. OMIT the underlined portion.

159. During the performance, Jackie was far more interested <u>by</u> the sets and costumes than in the actual play itself.

    A. NO CHANGE
    B. for
    C. with
    D. in

160. There is a major difference <u>with</u> saying you will do something and actually doing it; the difference is action.

    F. NO CHANGE
    G. among
    H. between
    J. about

161. The number of children living <u>with</u> the streets in the United States decreased in the latter part of the nineteenth century with the establishment of hundreds of orphanages.

    A. NO CHANGE
    B. at
    C. on
    D. for

162. Michael Jordan began his athletic career when he was young <u>despite</u> playing a variety of sports including baseball, football, and basketball, but basketball emerged as his sport of choice when he was in high school.

    F. NO CHANGE
    G. by means of
    H. during
    J. by

163. <u>By</u> embracing human perception and experience rather than the rules of academic painting, Claude Monet developed a new style of art that came to be known as "Impressionism."

   A. NO CHANGE
   B. Into
   C. Across from
   D. Inside

164. Initially, computers were so large they filled an entire room, but <u>until</u> the development of the transistor, and subsequently the microchip, the computer's size was drastically reduced.

   F. NO CHANGE
   G. in
   H. with
   J. besides

165. Where are you going <u>to</u>?

   A. NO CHANGE
   B. from
   C. in
   D. OMIT the underlined portion.

Punctuation

Comma Usage

The comma in writing corresponds to a brief pause in speech. The purpose of the pause is to help the listener understand the logical structure of the sentence. So the pauses that bracket a parenthetical expression, as indicated by commas in writing, show that the parenthetical expression is not essential to the main body of the sentence (we'll deal more with this in the next section). Pauses and commas also indicate the separations between the elements in a series, and they also show the point at which two independent clauses are tied together and therefore separate from one another. Commas and pauses serve similar functions and are important for clear communication. However, when commas are over-used, or used incorrectly, they can be just as troublesome as missing commas.

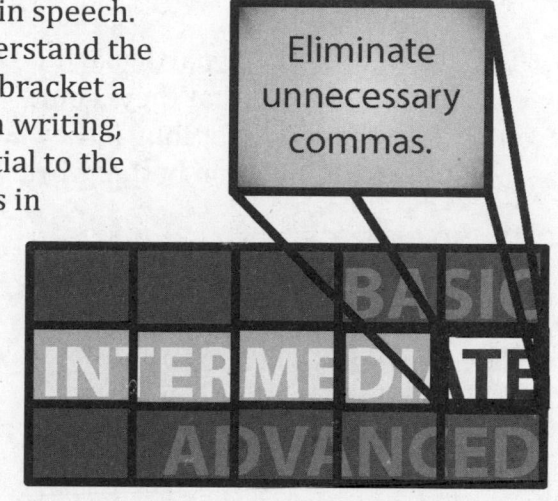

Eliminate unnecessary commas.

WHEN SHOULD COMMAS NOT BE USED?

1. DO NOT use a comma to separate a subject from its verb or a verb from what follows.

2. DO NOT use commas to set off a restrictive or necessary clause or phrase. For example, do not write "The dog, that was barking, bothered me."

3. DO NOT use a comma in place of a conjunction.

Examples:

The flight from Denver, arrived just three minutes before the flight from San Francisco. ✗

The flight from Denver arrived, just three minutes before the flight from San Francisco. ✗

The flight from Denver arrived just three minutes before the flight from San Francisco. ✓

The cookies, in the oven, smell so good! ✗

The cookies in the oven smell so good! ✓

EXERCISE 10

DIRECTIONS: In each of the following items, a word or phrase is underlined. Following each sentence or sentences are alternatives for rewriting the underlined part. If you think the original is correct, choose NO CHANGE. Otherwise, choose the best alternative. Answers are on page 803.

166. The company <u>warned particularly, indolent employees</u> that they would not retain their jobs for long if they did not start to perform better work.

    F. NO CHANGE
    G. warned, particularly indolent employees
    H. warned particularly indolent employees,
    J. warned particularly indolent employees

167. After the school had been quickly and successfully evacuated, the <u>principal revealed, that the fire alarm</u> had only been a drill.

    A. NO CHANGE
    B. principal revealed that, the fire alarm
    C. principal revealed that the fire alarm
    D. principal revealed that the fire alarm,

168. The FBI did not yet <u>know, however, that their informant</u> had been discovered by the enemy.

    F. NO CHANGE
    G. know however that their informant
    H. know, however that their informant
    J. know however that their informant,

169. The specialist whom I have been seeing <u>feels, that there is</u> a very good chance my condition may be reversed.

    A. NO CHANGE
    B. feels that there is
    C. feels that, there is
    D. feel that there is,

170. Michael mowed the lawn and took out the trash but <u>forgot, to take out</u> the recycling.

    F. NO CHANGE
    G. forgot to take out,
    H. forgot to take out
    J. forgot to, take out

ENGLISH AND WRITING | INTERMEDIATE • 113

171. Jane <u>prefers, on the other hand, to spend</u> her time indoors reading books and doing crafts.

   A. NO CHANGE
   B. prefers, on the other hand to spend
   C. prefers on the other hand, to spend
   D. prefers, on the other hand, to spend,

172. In the make-believe world, <u>foods, such as cake,</u> cookies, and candy had the same nutritional value as fruits, vegetables, and grains.

   F. NO CHANGE
   G. foods such as, cake,
   H. foods, such as cake
   J. foods such as cake,

173. As more and more homes are equipped with air conditioners, the increased demand for energy <u>is likely to strain</u> the capacity of the city's power stations and may result in power grid failure.

   A. NO CHANGE
   B. is likely, to strain
   C. is, likely, to strain
   D. is likely to strain,

174. Studies <u>show, that more than half</u> of automobile accidents occur within 5 miles from home.

   F. NO CHANGE
   G. show that more than half
   H. show that, more than half,
   J. show that, more than half

175. The police have <u>determined that, the prisoner was acting independently</u> when he attempted to rob the city bank.

   A. NO CHANGE
   B. determined that the prisoner, was acting independently
   C. determined, that the prisoner was acting independently,
   D. determined that the prisoner was acting independently

176. <u>The platypus is a unique mammal, that has a bill, like a duck, a tail, like a beaver, and feet, like an otter.</u>

   F. NO CHANGE
   G. The platypus is a unique, mammal that has a bill like a duck, a tail like a beaver, and feet like an otter.
   H. The platypus is a unique mammal that has a bill like a duck, a tail like a beaver, and feet like an otter.
   J. The platypus, is a unique mammal that, has a bill like a duck a tail like a beaver and feet like an otter.

177. When they leave earth's atmosphere, rockets forsake the gravitational force that the <u>earth exerts, on all objects and that</u> is why astronauts in space float.

   A. NO CHANGE
   B. earth, exerts on all objects, that
   C earth exerts on all objects, and that
   D. earth, exerts on all, objects and that

178. <u>With its tiny body and rapidly beating wings, the hummingbird, is</u> the only species of bird that can fly backwards.

F. NO CHANGE
G. With its tiny body and rapidly, beating wings, the hummingbird, is
H. With its tiny body and rapidly beating wings, the hummingbird is
J. With its tiny body and rapidly beating wings the hummingbird is

179. Non-governmental organizations such as Doctors Without Borders provide essential services in areas where there is no effectively functionary governmental <u>authority, no outside government cares</u> to intervene.

A. NO CHANGE
B. authority, and, no outside government cares
C. authority and no outside government cares
D. authority, no outside government, cares

180. The proliferation or spread of nuclear weapons has been a problem for <u>years one that will require a coordinated solution</u>.

F. NO CHANGE
G. years, and one that will require a coordinated solution
H. years, and one that, will require a coordinated solution
J. years, is one that will require a coordinated, solution

181. <u>Water has many unique properties, one of which, is that it is not subject to the usual laws of expansion, and contraction that occur in most substances when they are exposed to temperature changes.</u>

A. NO CHANGE
B. Water has many unique properties, one of which is that it is not subject to the usual laws of expansion and contraction that occur in most substances when they are exposed to temperature changes.
C. Water has many unique properties, one of which is that, it is not subject to the usual laws of expansion and contraction that occur in most substances, when they are exposed to temperature changes.
D. Water has many unique properties one of which, is that it is not subject to the usual laws of expansion, and contraction, that occur in most substances when they are exposed to temperature changes.

182. Trying to reproduce the world as exactly as possible, early Renaissance artists conducted intensive studies of <u>nature, steeped themselves</u> in the classical art of antiquity.

F. NO CHANGE
G. nature, and steeped themselves,
H. nature and steeped, themselves
J. nature and steeped themselves

183. During the crisis, the <u>calm demeanor of the emergency responders contrasted, sharply</u> with the intense panic of the victims and bystanders.

A. NO CHANGE
B. calm demeanor of the emergency responders contrasted sharply
C. the calm demeanor, of the emergency responders, contrasted sharply
D. calm demeanor of the emergency responders contrasted sharply,

184. <u>A leader of the civil rights movement, Dr. Martin Luther King, Jr. championed the belief set forth in the Declaration of Independence that all men are created equal.</u>

F. NO CHANGE
G. A leader of the civil rights movement, Dr. Martin Luther King, Jr. championed, the belief set forth in the Declaration of Independence, that all men are created equal.
H. A leader of the civil rights movement, Dr. Martin Luther King, Jr. championed the belief, set forth in the Declaration of Independence that all men, are created equal.
J. A leader of the civil rights movement, Dr. Martin Luther King, Jr., championed the belief set forth in the Declaration of Independence that, all men are created equal.

185. <u>Due in part to the need for women workers, while the men were fighting in World War II, the</u> percentage of women in the workforce increased exponentially during the twentieth century.

A. NO CHANGE
B. Due in part to the need for women workers while the men were fighting in World War II the
C. Due in part to the need for women workers while the men were fighting in World War II, the
D. Due in part, to the need for women workers while the men were fighting, in World War II the

Commas and Parenthetical Phrases

In the previous section, you learned when *not* to use commas. But commas must be used to set off certain phrases and elements that interrupt the natural flow of a sentence.

Parenthetical expressions are words that interrupt the flow of the sentence without changing the meaning of the sentence. Examples include "however," "though," "for instance," "by the way," "to tell the truth," "believe me," "it appears to me," "I am sure," and "as a matter of fact."

> Use commas for parenthetical phrases.
>
> BASIC
> INTERMEDIATE
> ADVANCED

Examples:

The announcer, <u>it appears to me</u>, mispronounced the quarterback's name when he introduced the starting lineup. ✓

Esther, <u>by the way</u>, has made a full recovery after falling out of a pear tree last week. ✓

Read a sentence aloud to determine if commas should be used to set off a parenthetical expression. If you pause before and after the parenthetical expression, use commas to set it off. In general, if material can be omitted without changing the meaning of the main clause, the material is non-restrictive and should be set off by commas.

EXERCISE 11

DIRECTIONS: In each of the following items, a word or phrase is underlined. Following each sentence or sentences are alternatives for rewriting the underlined part. If you think the original is correct, choose NO CHANGE. Otherwise, choose the best alternative. Answers are on page 803.

186. The newly founded medical <u>college, with its state-of-the-art technology is predicted</u> to become the greatest pioneer in cancer research in this decade.

   F. NO CHANGE
   G. college with its state-of-the-art technology is predicted
   H. college with its state-of-the-art technology, is predicted
   J. college, with its state-of-the-art technology, is predicted

187. A handful of students were selected to help manage <u>events, like the annual science fair and the school play, in order to prepare them</u> for future leadership positions.

   A. NO CHANGE
   B. events like the annual science fair and the school play, in order to prepare them
   C. events, like the annual science fair and the school play in order to prepare them
   D. events, like the annual science fair and the school play in order to prepare them,

188. The book's recommendations regarding daily <u>exercise based on studies that used a control group unrepresentative of the general population, were</u> highly unusual and proved harmful to the health of some individuals.

   F. NO CHANGE
   G. exercise based on studies that used a control group unrepresentative of the general population were
   H. exercise, based on studies that used a control group unrepresentative of the general population, were
   J. exercise based on studies, that used a control group unrepresentative of the general population, were

189. Some individuals are very outgoing and energetic, while <u>others, sometimes labeled as introverts,</u> exhibit more reserved, solitary behavior.

   A. NO CHANGE
   B. others, sometimes, labeled as introverts
   C. others sometimes, labeled as introverts,
   D. others, sometimes labeled as introverts

190. One of the first discovered man-made <u>elements, einsteinium, is named</u> after Albert Einstein and is extremely radioactive and considered dangerous to health.

    F. NO CHANGE
    G. elements einsteinium, is named
    H. elements, einsteinium, named
    J. elements einsteinium is named

191. <u>DDT, a once popular insecticide was banned</u> from agricultural use in 1972 because of concerns about negative environmental impacts.

    A. NO CHANGE
    B. DDT, a once popular insecticide, was banned
    C. DDT a once popular, insecticide was banned
    D. DDT, a once popular insecticide was banned,

192. <u>Today nearly 50 years since the passage of the Civil Rights Act that outlawed major forms of discrimination in the US</u> there is a diverse number of races, genders, and religions represented in Congress.

    F. NO CHANGE
    G. Today, nearly 50 years since, the passage of the Civil Rights Act that outlawed major forms of discrimination in the US
    H. Today, nearly 50 years since the passage of the Civil Rights Act that outlawed major forms of discrimination in the US,
    J. Today, nearly 50 years since the passage of the Civil Rights Act, that outlawed major forms of discrimination in the US

193. The role of a United States <u>Marshal a federal law enforcement officer</u> is extremely important and quite diverse, including fugitive and prisoner operations, judicial security, and witness protection.

    A. NO CHANGE
    B. Marshal a federal law enforcement officer,
    C. Marshal, a federal law enforcement officer
    D. Marshal, a federal law enforcement officer,

194. The new <u>disc called a blu-ray, is named for the blue laser</u> used to read the disc that allows information to be stored at a greater density and therefore played back in higher definition.

F. NO CHANGE
G. disc, called a blu-ray, is named for the blue laser
H. disc, called a blu-ray is named for the blue laser,
J. disc called a blu-ray, is named for the blue laser,

195. Both male and female gymnasts perform bar routines which undoubtedly include <u>"giants," a skill in which, the gymnast rotates his or her flat body 360 degrees around the bar.</u>

A. NO CHANGE
B. "giants" a skill in which the gymnast rotates his or her flat body 360 degrees around the bar
C. "giants" a skill in which the gymnast rotates his or her flat body, 360 degrees around the bar
D. "giants," a skill in which the gymnast rotates his or her flat body 360 degrees around the bar

196. <u>Emily Dickinson, an introverted young woman,</u> wrote well over a thousand poems in her lifetime.

F. NO CHANGE
G. Emily Dickinson an introverted young woman
H. Emily Dickinson, an introverted, young woman
J. Emily Dickinson an introverted young, woman

197. Nearly 100 million tons of <u>fish, caught by commercial fishing boats and recreational fishermen,</u> are harvested from the sea each year.

A. NO CHANGE
B. fish caught by commercial fishing boats and recreational fishermen
C. fish caught by commercial fishing boats and recreational fishermen,
D. fish, caught by, commercial fishing boats and recreational fishermen

198. <u>Babe Ruth a famous baseball player, set several records</u> during his career in the Major Leagues.

F. NO CHANGE
G. Babe Ruth, a famous baseball player, set several records
H. Babe Ruth, a famous baseball player set several records
J. Babe Ruth a famous baseball player who set several records

199. Jonah, who accounted for nearly 60 percent of our team's total points for the season was unanimously voted the MVP.

    A. NO CHANGE

    B. Jonah, who accounted for nearly 60 percent of our team's total points for the season, was unanimously voted the MVP.

    C. Jonah, who accounted, for nearly 60 percent of our team's total points for the season was unanimously voted the MVP.

    D. Jonah who accounted for nearly 60 percent of our team's total points for the season was unanimously voted the MVP.

200. While some migratory birds fly hundreds of miles each year chickens, rarely use their wings to fly more than a few feet at a time.

    F. NO CHANGE

    G. While some, migratory birds fly hundreds of miles each year, chickens rarely use their wings to fly more than a few feet at a time.

    H. While some migratory birds fly hundreds of miles each year, chickens rarely use their wings to fly more than a few feet at a time.

    J. While some migratory birds fly hundreds of miles, each year chickens rarely use their wings to fly more than a few feet at a time.

ADVANCED | Organization and Coherence

Logical Connections

Conjunctive adverbs and similar transitions can be used to signal sequence, causal connections, and logical relationships. The Basic (p. 5) and Intermediate (p. 59) levels of this topic review the first two uses; here we cover the third.

Logical relationships are the most abstract of the three types, and certain words and phrases are particularly well-suited to this purpose:

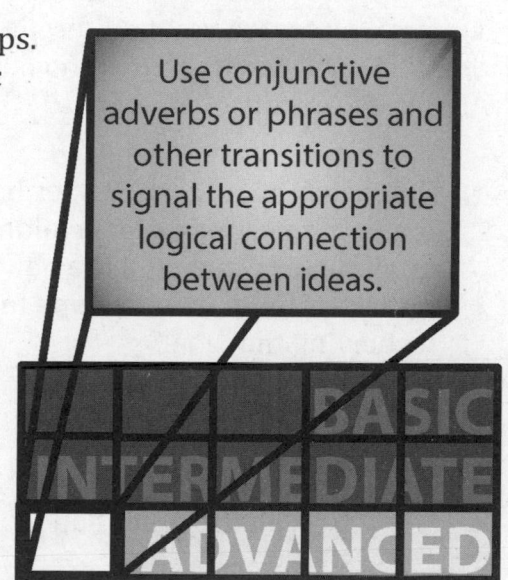

Use conjunctive adverbs or phrases and other transitions to signal the appropriate logical connection between ideas.

Common Logical Connectivity		
accordingly	for instance	moreover
additionally	further	namely
also	furthermore	nonetheless
anyway	however	on the contrary
as a result	in fact	on the other hand
certainly	incidentally	otherwise
consequently	indeed	thereafter
conversely	instead	therefore
finally	likewise	thus
for example	meanwhile	undoubtedly

Examples:

Walking the plank, a form of murder practiced by pirates, is often thought to be a fiction inspired by cinema; <u>however</u>, maritime records from as early as the seventeenth century document actual cases of walking the plank.

When Kennedy proposed the Peace Corps, he expected that volunteers would make a real difference in the lives of those served. <u>Moreover</u>, he hoped that providing this new form of assistance would help to change negative attitudes about America.

The proposal allocated stimulus money for "shovel ready" projects—<u>for example</u>, bridge and road repair. <u>However</u>, very few of the projects were started in time to have an appreciable effect on the economy.

The Democrats have traditionally been considered the party of peace. The Republicans, on the other hand, are thought of as promoting military solutions to political problems. In reality, as many wars have begun under Democratic administrations as under Republican ones.

EXERCISE 1

DIRECTIONS: In each of the following items, a word or phrase is underlined. Following each sentence or sentences are alternative suggestions for rewriting the underlined part. If you think the original is correct, choose NO CHANGE. Otherwise, choose the best alternative. Answers are on page 803.

1. International relief agencies have been trying to eradicate childhood malaria for years, and the new vaccine offers the best hope for achieving that goal.

   A. NO CHANGE
   B. years; however,
   C. years; conversely,
   D. years; on the other hand,

2. The cookbook included instructions for cooking the mac-and-cheese casserole in a microwave oven; a conventional oven, however, produces a nice brown crust that most people really enjoy.

   F. NO CHANGE
   G. accordingly
   H. moreover
   J. by the way

3. Many critics prefer Picasso's more mature works painted after the move to Montparnasse; Professor Gide and her followers, indeed, focus on the earlier canvasses painted in the studio in Montmartre.

   A. NO CHANGE
   B. nonetheless
   C. on the other hand
   D. in fact

4. The possibility of the earth's being struck by a giant asteroid of the sort depicted in science fiction movies is remote; otherwise, the devastating effects from such a collision make it imprudent to overlook the possibility.

   F. NO CHANGE
   G. thus
   H. therefore
   J. nevertheless

5. The bird population of Ecuador is the most diverse in all of South America; <u>in fact</u>, there are up to fifteen hundred different species of birds in a region no bigger than the state of Texas.

   A. NO CHANGE
   B. conversely
   C. as a result
   D. however

6. There is a great deal of anecdotal evidence from sufferers of skin conditions about the healing powers of aloe vera; <u>therefore</u>, these claims have not been supported by scientific research.

   F. NO CHANGE
   G. however
   H. as a result
   J. so

7. Recent scientific studies on weight loss pills show that they do little to block the absorption of fat and so have virtually no beneficial health effects; they can, <u>additionally</u>, actually undermine health by decreasing the body's ability to properly absorb nutrients and protein.

   A. NO CHANGE
   B. especially
   C. otherwise
   D. on the contrary

8. The mayor hopes to obtain a state grant for the construction of a new park; the county, <u>consequently</u>, would like state funding for a new boat ramp in the southern basin of the lake.

   F. NO CHANGE
   G. likewise
   H. to be sure
   J. henceforth

9. Studies show that children who are exposed to reading at an early age can increase their vocabularies significantly faster; <u>therefore</u>, parents who want their children to succeed should introduce them to reading as early as possible.

   A. NO CHANGE
   B. however
   C. on the other hand
   D. instead

10. An elitist approach to taxation oftentimes leads to further gaps between rich and poor; <u>instead</u>, tax cuts that favor top earners reduce government funds needed to support social services upon which the bottom earners depend.

    F. NO CHANGE
    G. consequently
    H. in particular
    J. in comparison

11. Chicago has seen an increase in the consumption of coffee drinks such as lattes and macchiatos by young professionals; <u>instead</u>, this same group is drinking fewer sugar-sweetened soft drinks.

A. NO CHANGE
B. on the other hand
C. moreover
D. further

12. Halloween is generally celebrated as a secular holiday with no particular religious significance attached to the practice of costuming or asking for sweet treats; <u>so</u> it has its roots in paganism and is considered by some religious groups to be blasphemous.

F. NO CHANGE
G. indeed,
H. consequently,
D. nevertheless,

13. On the day that the leader of the revolution triumphantly entered the capital city, tens of thousands cheered; elsewhere, <u>however</u>, in the remote mountains, loyalists who had overnight become rebels, plotted the overthrow of the man who they feared would become a dictator.

A. NO CHANGE
B. in effect
C. by happenstance
D. besides

14. Musicians hope that their songs will become popular so they will reap substantial financial rewards; <u>accordingly</u>, great popularity increases the likelihood that music will be pirated and the musician will earn nothing for his or her efforts.

F. NO CHANGE
G. on the other hand
H. that is
J. additionally

15. With the airport closed due to weather, we were prepared to extend our stay another day. Unfortunately, there were no rooms available at the inn. <u>Instead</u>, the innkeeper, with whom we had become quite friendly over the course of our three-week stay, offered to put us up for the night at her home.

A. NO CHANGE
B. In effect
C. Furthermore
D. Conversely

16. All blues notes are flatter than expected, classically speaking. This flatness may take several forms. <u>On the one hand</u>, it may be a quarter-tone adjustment but the flattening may be full semitone—as it must be on keyboard instruments.

F. NO CHANGE
G. In reality
H. Therefore
J. In essence

17. There is a common misconception that the encroachment of human settlement on previously wooded areas has suppressed the deer population. <u>In retrospect</u>, herds have grown because the suburban environment provides the kind of open land that deer prefer.

    A. NO CHANGE
    B. In effect
    C. In reality
    D. In lieu of

18. Belgian children were educated in both French and Flemish while children in colonies governed by Belgium learned only French as their primary language, often at the expense of their native dialects. <u>Conversely</u>, Belgian domestic policies preserved the cultural heritage of the Belgians while destroying that of the peoples they had colonized.

    F. NO CHANGE
    G. On the other hand
    H. In short
    J. While

19. According to a psychological study, people are less likely to lie in the morning than in the afternoon. The researchers theorize that when people are energetic and ready for challenges, they are willing to fight harder and longer to defend their moral principles. In the afternoon, when they are fatigued and feel overwhelmed, they lie out of desperation. An employer should, <u>accordingly</u>, schedule job interviews in the morning when he or she is more likely to get candid answers from job candidates.

    A. NO CHANGE
    B. in fact
    C. on the other hand
    D. conversely

20. The zoning variance requested by Soccer Unlimited would allow the company to construct additional playing fields, which would generate more revenue for the town. <u>Besides</u>, the land right now is used only for pasturing the dairy cows of the family that would sell it to the company, so no residents would be affected.

    F. NO CHANGE
    G. Instead
    H. Therefore
    J. As a result

Writing Accessible Paragraphs

One of the most important features of a properly written paragraph is *coherence*. A paragraph has coherence when the relationship among the ideas is readily apparent and the progression from one sentence to the next is easy for the reader to follow.

Good writers use several techniques to achieve coherence in their paragraphs. First, good writers arrange the sentences to reflect an order of ideas. For example, the sentences in a paragraph that tells a story are most often arranged in chronological order, while a paragraph that is descriptive of a person or place might be organized spatially.

Other common forms of paragraph organization include arranging ideas from least to greatest importance (or vice versa), developing contrasting ideas (on the one hand, on the other hand), and illustration (generalization). The scheme chosen by a writer will depend in large part on the topic discussed, but whatever the topic, the organization of the paragraph should be readily apparent to the reader in the order of the ideas presented.

Moreover, the order of sentences in a paragraph is supported and reinforced by a variety of transitional devices such as pronouns, repetition, transitional words and phrases, and parallel structures.

Finally, a writer may choose to add an introductory sentence or a conclusionary one, or even both, to the paragraph.

All of these different techniques work together to produce paragraphs and essays that are coherent and easily understandable to the reader.

EXERCISE 2

DIRECTIONS: The paragraphs below are followed by one or more items based on its content. Answer the item on the basis of what is stated or implied in the passage. Answers are on page 803.

Questions 21–24

[1]

[1]The year that Christopher Columbus crossed the Atlantic, a cartographer in Lisbon drew an amazing map detailing the coasts of Europe, the Mediterranean, the Black Sea, and western Africa. [2]Unlike previous rough outlines, the map marks a technical milestone with the rendering of its large coastline. [3]Drawn entirely by hand, the contours of this map are instantly identifiable.

[2]

[4]Portugal was drawn as a brick and North Africa as a block. [5]Our Portuguese cartographer, however, was sketching sinuous coastlines, undulating rivers, and irregular boundaries. [6]At the time, most European geographers were following the tradition from the first century CE. [7]How did the mapmakers' usual world of straight lines, sharp angles, and the occasional perfectly symmetrical circle become transformed into extravagantly complex curves that so accurately reflected the underlying reality?

[3]

[8]We know almost nothing about the man who created this masterpiece; we only have a declaration of authorship in the customary form: "Jorge de Aguiar made me in Lisbon in the year of our Lord Jesus Christ 1492." [9]Other Portuguese maps from this era proclaim their designer in the same fashion, for example, "Pedro Reinel made me," the map thus speaking for itself and its maker. [10]This small inscription of authorship contains all the certain knowledge we have of the mapmaker.

[4]

[11]Beyond that location, scholars have identified two possible sets of relatives. [12]The first connection links him to Portuguese voyages. [13]Two different men surnamed Aguiar commanded eastward-bound ships; one foundered off the coast of Africa in 1502, and the other successfully sailed to India in 1508. [14]The surname Aguiar also appears frequently in lists of Sephardim—Iberian Jews who were forced by the Inquisition to convert or leave, first Spain in 1492 and then Portugal in 1497. [15]Neither source, however, provides much information as to the personal identity of the mapmaker.

[5]

[16]Other mysteries include how an obscure Portuguese map came to encompass so much of the world previously unknown. [17]And how was the mapmaker able to render to scale geographic shapes that until then had been rendered only as icons? [18]No scratches, notes, or palimpsests appear, only the map itself. [19]Nor have any written instructions for building a map been found.

21. The writer wishes to add the following sentence to the first paragraph to dramatize the accuracy of the map:

   In fact, when placed atop a modern map, the outlines of Europe and Africa look the way they do on a contemporary map.

   The sentence should be placed:

   A. before sentence 1.
   B. after sentence 1.
   C. after sentence 2.
   D. after sentence 3.

22. Which of the following represents the most logical order for the sentences of paragraph 2?

   F. 5, 6, 4, 7
   G. 6, 4, 5, 7
   H. 6, 5, 4, 7
   J. 7, 5, 4, 7

23. Which of the following sentences would provide the best introduction to paragraph 4?

   A. The most revealing aspect of the declaration is the surname Aguiar, which is the name of a town in northern Portugal near the River Douro.
   B. In 1755, Lisbon was destroyed by two earthquakes that struck not more than 90 minutes apart and triggered tsunamis, one with waves more than 60 feet high.
   C. Starting in the 1420s, voyages sponsored by Prince Henry, who was nicknamed "The Navigator," were launched with specific directions to collect information for maps.
   D. Portuguese sailors began exploring the coast of Africa in 1419, and over the following decades created a commercial network that brought Portugal great wealth.

24. Which of the following, when added to the final paragraph, would be the best conclusion for the passage?

   F. Perhaps Aguiar the mapmaker was one of those who was forced by the Inquisition to convert to Christianity.
   G. In the history of mapping, we know astonishingly little about this important moment.
   H. The Aguiar map is not really that unusual when one considers that others of the period were signed in similar fashion.
   J. It can reasonably be conjectured that Jorge de Aguiar learned about Africa as a sailor aboard a Portuguese ship sailing the coast of Africa.

Question 25

[1] In your bathroom, you probably have rubbing alcohol, self-adhesive bandage strips, ointment, and other small items that make up a basic first aid kit, but a more complete first aid kit including rolled sterile bandages, non-latex gloves, tweezers, and other items, as well as a first aid manual, may be crucial in the case of injury. [2]The same level of preparedness is also important in case of a home fire. [3]The likelihood that you and your family will survive a house fire depends as much on having a working smoke detector and an exit strategy as on a well-trained fire department. [4] In your car, you should have an emergency kit that includes flares, jumper cables, a flashlight, and similar items.

25. Which of the following, if added following sentence 4, would make the best concluding statement?

   A. Most hardware and home improvement stores offer a variety of emergency lights with backup power supplies.
   B. An inexpensive cell phone with an extra battery is a sensible addition to any emergency kit.
   C. Whatever the emergency, until help arrives, you're the first responder, so be prepared.
   D. More than 1,000 "savable" lives are lost in this country each year because of inefficiencies in response times.

Question 26

[1]The caller may say that you can avoid the cancellation if you provide your bank account or credit card number to pay the company. [2]Telephone scammers are now using techniques developed for use on the web to obtain sensitive personal and financial information. [3]The scammer uses spoofing apps to mimic businesses and government agencies to make the call seem genuine. [4]In this fraud, someone calls you using a false name and phone number on the Caller ID screen. [5]During the call, the scammer describes an urgent scenario, such as the cancellation of an account. [6]If you provide the sensitive information, it can be used to steal your identity or to access your bank accounts.

26. Which of the following represents the most logical ordering of the sentences of the paragraph above?

   F. 2, 4, 3, 5, 1, 6
   G. 2, 1, 3, 4, 6, 5
   H. 3, 5, 2, 4, 1, 6
   J. 5, 6, 4, 2, 3, 1

Question 27

[1]However, because lesions resemble those seen in allergic meningoencephalitis, GME is thought to have an immune-mediated cause. [2]The cause of GME is not certain and is known only to be noninfectious. [3]Cerebrospinal fluid analysis typically shows a large number of white blood cells, but a definitive diagnosis can only be made postmortem. [4]The accepted treatment is the administration of immunosuppressive drugs, though there is evidence that radiation therapy may be effective in some cases. [5]Granulomatous meningoencephalitis, or GME, is an inflammatory disease of the central nervous system of dogs.

27. Which of the following provides the most logical arrangement of the sentences of the paragraph above?

A. 2, 1, 3, 4, 5
B. 4, 3, 2, 1, 5
C. 5, 1, 2, 4, 3
D. 5, 2, 1, 3, 4

Question 28

[1]Appalachia's economy, once highly dependent on mining, forestry, agriculture, chemical industries, and heavy industry, has recently become more diversified to include a variety of manufacturing and service industries. [2]In 1965, one in three Appalachians lived in poverty. [3]In contrast, over the 2007–2011 period, the region's poverty rate was 16.1 percent.

28. Assuming that each of the following is factually true, which would make the best introductory sentence for the paragraph?

F. The Appalachian region is a large, geographically diverse area of the United States covering all or parts of several states.
G. While Appalachia has made great economic strides, more can be done to raise the quality of life for those living in the region.
H. The Appalachian Mountains run from northern Alabama to southern New York.
J. For years, residents of Appalachia have been stereotyped as hillbillies and moonshiners.

Questions 29–30

[1]

[1]Moreover, the camps furnished the migrants with a safe space in which to practice their culture and rekindle a sense of community. [2]The camps were intended to resolve poor sanitation and public health problems, as well as to mitigate the burden placed on state and local infrastructures. [3]The Arvin Migratory Labor Camp in California was the first federally operated camp opened by the government in 1937.

[2]

[4]Although each camp had a small staff of administrators, much of the responsibility for daily operations and governance was delegated to the campers themselves. [5]Civil activities were carried out through camp councils and camp courts. [6]Distribution of funds, activity regulation, and elections were all overseen by camp residents.

[3]

[7]When they were not working or looking for work, or tending to the civil and domestic operations of the camp, migrant workers found time to engage in recreational activities. [8]The camps included recreation halls, where they would play board games such as checkers, and a library for reading. [9]Of greatest importance were the large halls for entertainment. [10]Music-making permeated camp life and provided a focus for communal life.

29. Which of the following is the best order for the sentences in paragraph 1?

A. 1, 2, 3
B. 2, 3, 1
C. 2, 1, 3
D. 3, 2, 1

30. Which of the following is the most logical sequence for the sentences in paragraph 3?

F. 7, 8, 9, 10 (NO CHANGE)
G. 7, 9, 8, 10
H. 9, 8, 10, 7
J. 9, 10, 8, 7

Word Choice

Revising for Precision

Sometimes, a sentence will be incorrect because it is needlessly wordy.

Examples:

The protracted discussion over what route to take continued for a long time. ✗

The discussion over what route to take continued for a long time. ✓

First and foremost, one of the primary objectives of the proposal is chiefly to ensure and guarantee with certainty the academic freedom of students. ✗

One of the primary objectives of the proposal is to ensure the academic freedom of students. ✓

> Eliminate needless verbiage created by seemingly sophisticated phrasings.
>
> BASIC INTERMEDIATE ADVANCED

In the first example, "protracted" is unnecessary because it means "to continue for a long time." In the second example, "First and foremost" is unnecessary, because a "primary" objective indicates that it is of top (foremost) priority. The adverb "chiefly" is unnecessary because a "primary objective" is a chief concern. Likewise, "ensure" is unnecessary because it has the same meaning as "guarantee," as does the phrase "with certainty."

Redundancies and other unnecessary verbiage are more difficult to spot in sentences like these that use such seemingly sophisticated phrasing. But, in fact, such sentences often sacrifice clarity and conciseness for the sake of sounding urbane.

EXERCISE 3

DIRECTIONS: In each of the following items, a word or phrase is underlined. Following each sentence or sentences are alternative suggestions for rewriting the underlined part. If you think the original is correct, choose NO CHANGE. Otherwise, choose the best alternative. Answers are on page 803.

31. The staff will <u>convene together</u> in the conference room at twelve o'clock noon to hear a presentation about office security.

   A. NO CHANGE
   B. convene
   C. get together to convene
   D. convene as a group

32. Alan Lerner and Fritz Lowe were a musical team responsible for some of Broadway's most successful musicals, including *My Fair Lady* and *Camelot*; <u>Lerner was the lyricist who wrote the words and Lowe composed the music</u>.

   F. NO CHANGE
   G. Lerner was the writer who wrote the lyrics and Lowe was the composer who wrote the music
   H. Lerner wrote the lyrics and Lowe composed the music
   J. As the lyricist, Lerner wrote the words while Lowe created the music

33. Kevin has been accepted by the nation's top engineering school, but his family lacks <u>the monetary funds</u> to pay for it.

   A. NO CHANGE
   B. monetary funds, sufficient
   C. the money
   D. the pecuniary funds

34. The recent change in bank policy is <u>beneficially helpful</u> because it assists struggling and low-income families with purchasing a home.

   F. NO CHANGE
   G. beneficial
   H. helpfully providing benefits
   J. providing helpful benefits

35. In the play *Arsenic and Old Lace*, two spinster sisters take to murdering lonely old men with <u>the highly poisonous and toxic element arsenic mixed with wine</u>.

   A. NO CHANGE
   B. arsenic and wine, a highly poisonous element
   C. toxic arsenic, a highly poisonous element mixed with wine
   D. the highly poisonous element arsenic mixed with wine

36. Shortly after Joanna graduated from law school, she received <u>an offer of a position of employment to work</u> at a prestigious law firm, an offer she eagerly accepted.

   F. NO CHANGE
   G. an offer of employment to work
   H. an offer of employment
   J. an employment offer to be

37. <u>During the time of the great dot-com bubble, the stock price of one Internet company rose by an astonishing 3,000 percent from the initial public offering to peak at the highest point two days later</u>, after which the price plummeted to the point at which the stock was virtually worthless.

A. NO CHANGE
B. At the time of the great dot-com bubble, the stock price of one particular Internet company rose by an astonishing 3,000 percent from the initial public offering to peak at the highest point two days later
C. During the great dot-com bubble, the stock price of one Internet company rose by an astonishing 3,000 percent from the initial public offering to a peak two days later
D. During the great dot-com bubble, the stock price of one Internet company rose by an astonishingly large 3,000 percent from the initial public offering until two days later a peak at the highest point was reached

38. The city sought an injunction in federal court after the union <u>threatened a paralyzing shutdown of the transit system</u> during the bitter contract dispute over wages and benefits.

F. NO CHANGE
G. threatened a paralyzing shutdown that would close the transit system
H. threatened to close the transit system with a paralyzing shutdown
J. made threats to the effect that there would be a paralyzing shutdown of the transit system

39. <u>The young toddler was more interested in the colorful illustrated drawings</u> than she was in the story her mother was reading.

A. NO CHANGE
B. The toddler was more interested in the colorful illustrations
C. The toddler was more interested in the colorfully illustrated drawings
D. The child was interested in the illustrated drawings, more so

40. <u>When he was initially introduced to the president of the company for the first time</u>, the young business school graduate was uneasy; but now he is quite comfortable in his role as an executive liaison.

F. NO CHANGE
G. Upon his initial introduction to the president of the company for the first time
H. Initially meeting the president of the company for the first time upon his introduction
J. When he was initially introduced to the president of the company

41. The campaign for a new gymnasium to be added to the high school was a <u>collaboration of the joint cooperative efforts</u> of the basketball team's players, its coaches, and parents of the players, and the successful achievement of their goal was celebrated by the entire school.

A. NO CHANGE
B. collaborative effort stemming from the joint cooperation
C. cooperative effort of the collaboration of
D. collaboration

42. I read in the newspaper that a family from our town <u>received an anonymous donation of money from an unidentified donor</u> after their home was completely destroyed in a fire.

F. NO CHANGE
G. received an anonymous donation of money
H. received a donation of money from an unidentified, anonymous donor
J. was given an anonymous sum of money by a donor who was not identified

43. After the medical examiner made a preliminary finding that the cause of death was accidental drowning, <u>the body of the deceased was transported</u> to the morgue.

A. NO CHANGE
B. the body was transported
C. the body of the deceased individual was taken
D. the deceased individual's body was transported

44. The <u>longing desire for an experience of untamed nature can be traced</u> to a small group of aesthetes living in eighteenth-century Europe, for whom the awesome power of the sea provided powerful emotional stimulation.

F. NO CHANGE
G. longing for an experience of wildly untamed nature can be traced
H. desire for an experience of nature, untamed and wild, can be traced back
J. longing for an experience of untamed nature can be traced

45. Representational and figurative art <u>has fallen into disfavor and is out of fashion</u> in contemporary art circles; a century ago—and going back to at least the Renaissance—skillful modeling of the human figure was necessary for any artist's success.

A. NO CHANGE
B. is out of fashion
C. is out of fashion and disfavored
D. has fallen out of fashion into disfavor

Avoid Awkward Sentences

A sentence may be grammatically and logically correct but still be awkward.

Examples:

The giant condor has the capability of spreading its wings up to 25 feet. ✗

The giant condor has a wingspan of up to 25 feet. ✓

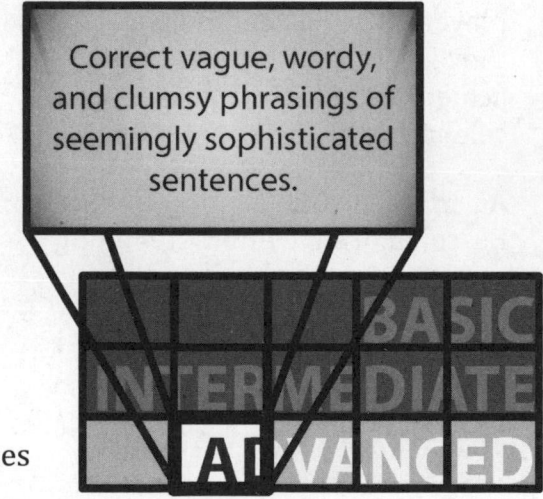

Correct vague, wordy, and clumsy phrasings of seemingly sophisticated sentences.

Although most students would benefit from further study of the sciences, doing so is frightening to most of them in that science courses are more difficult than liberal arts courses. ✗

Although most students would benefit from further study of the sciences, most of them are afraid to take science courses because they are more difficult than liberal arts courses. ✓

Given that the Incas lacked the wheel, the buildings at Machu Picchu are more astonishing than any Greek temples that are comparable as an achievement. ✗

Given that the Incas lacked the wheel, the buildings at Machu Picchu are more astonishing than any comparable Greek temple. ✓

In each pair of sentences above, the second is more direct and clearer.

EXERCISE 4

DIRECTIONS: In each of the following items, a word or phrase is underlined. Following each sentence or sentences are alternative suggestions for rewriting the underlined part. If you think the original is correct, choose NO CHANGE. Otherwise, choose the best alternative. Answers are on page 803.

46. A new president is chosen in the general election held at the beginning of November but will not assume presidential duties until January 20, <u>a date being nearly two-and-a-half months after the election</u>.

   F. NO CHANGE
   G. nearly two-and-a-half months after the election
   H. nearly two-and-a-half months further than the election of November
   J. a date and time being nearly two-and-a-half months following the November election

47. There is nothing <u>to distinguish our small town from any other small town</u> with a single traffic light, one school building, and a lone tavern.

   A. NO CHANGE
   B. making our small town the most unique one
   C. that makes our small town the highly distinguished small town
   D. distinguishably noticeable about our small town

48. <u>There is a very good reason to get your college applications in early which is the fact that</u> there are thousands of other students vying for a limited number of positions and scholarships.

   F. NO CHANGE
   G. There is a very good factual reason for getting your college applications in early which is
   H. Getting your college applications in early is very important for the reason that
   J. You should get your college applications in early because

49. The work of the art forger was of such fine quality that it was hard to distinguish the forgeries from the <u>paintings that are identifiable as the original works of art</u>.

   A. NO CHANGE
   B. originals
   C. identifiably original paintings
   D. paintings identified as originals

50. Leslie has always wanted to perform on stage, but <u>at the mere thought of actually doing it she becomes increasingly so nervous</u> that she will never even audition.

   F. NO CHANGE
   G. the merely thinking of really doing so makes her increasingly nervous so
   H. the mere thought of it increasingly makes her so nervous
   J. the mere thought of performing makes her so nervous

51. Employees <u>in attendance at the staff meeting gave voice to many problematic concerns</u> but were unable to offer any specific solutions.

   A. NO CHANGE
   B. in attendance at the staff meeting voiced many problematic concerns
   C. at the staff meeting gave voice to many concerns
   D. in attendance voiced their problematic concerns

52. The sustained decline in sales makes it doubtful <u>if the company's viability can continue to survive</u>.

   F. NO CHANGE
   G. whether the company can continue to survive in its present viability
   H. that the company can continue to survive
   J. that the company is survivable

53. One of the thrills of bird-watching is catching a fleeting glimpse of <u>a very rare specimen including, but not limited to, the Northern Bobwhite or</u> the Red-shouldered Hawk.

   A. NO CHANGE
   B. a very rare specimen such as the Northern Bobwhite or
   C. a very rare specimen such as the Northern Bobwhite and
   D. very rare specimens not limited to the Northern Bobwhite or

54. The gift certificate for a hot-air balloon ride gives the recipient the option <u>that, should you choose to do so, you may exchange the certificate</u> for cash.

   F. NO CHANGE
   G. that, if you so choose, the certificate may be exchanged
   H. of exchanging the certificate
   J. of your exchanging the certificate

55. The parties have an agreement in principle, <u>and because of it</u> does not mean that they cannot commence doing business immediately.

   A. NO CHANGE
   B. and because of a lack of it
   C. therefore no signed contract
   D. but the lack of a signed contract

56. Both Henry Miller and Ernest Hemingway were Americans but lived in <u>another country, which was France, when they wrote their novels</u>.

    F. NO CHANGE
    G. France, which is another country, when they wrote their novels
    H. another country, namely France, when writing novels
    J. France when they wrote their novels

57. The resurgence of the honeybee in the area has increased pollination of apple blossoms which, when coupled with near-perfect growing conditions over the past couple of years, has <u>produced records of apple harvests</u>.

    A. NO CHANGE
    B. harvested nearly record apples
    C. resulted in records of harvests for apples
    D. produced record apple harvests

58. Because of its harsh winters, Chicago has <u>more of a population of migrating birds than any other</u> major US city.

    F. NO CHANGE
    G. a higher population of migrating birds than another
    H. higher a population of migrating birds every other
    J. a greater population of migrating birds than any other

59. Many of the painters who were inspired by Gustav Klimt were <u>more interested in the exploration of the unconscious than him</u>.

    A. NO CHANGE
    B. interested more about the exploration of the unconscious than him
    C. more interested by exploration of the unconscious than him
    D. more interested in exploring the unconscious than he was

60. Stockholm syndrome refers to the Kreditbanken robbery in Stockholm, Sweden, in 1973 in which several <u>captivated bank employees held hostage</u> in the vault eventually began to have positive feelings toward their captors even to the point of defending their actions.

    F. NO CHANGE
    G. captured bank employees held hostage
    H. bank employees held hostage
    J. banking employees held hostage

Sentence Structure and Formation

Using Sentence-Combining Techniques to Solve Structural Problems

As you already learned, the basic building block of all English writing is the sentence, a word group with a subject and a main (conjugated) verb.

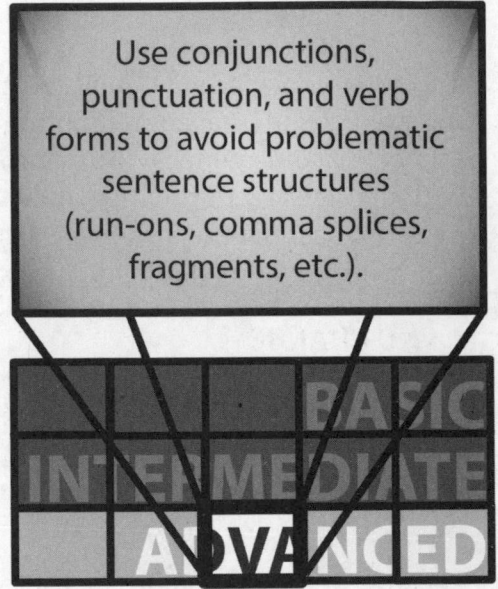

Use conjunctions, punctuation, and verb forms to avoid problematic sentence structures (run-ons, comma splices, fragments, etc.).

Example:

Eleanor asked the barista for a caramel macchiato. The barista misunderstood and prepared a latte instead.

> Here we have two acceptable English sentences, each with a subject and verb. The juxtaposition of the two short sentences, however, is not particularly pleasing to the ear, so the writer might wish to combine them into a single, longer sentence:

Eleanor asked the barista for a caramel macchiato, but the barista misunderstood and prepared a latte instead.

Though Eleanor asked the barista for a caramel macchiato, the barista misunderstood and prepared a latte instead.

Misinterpreting Eleanor's request for a caramel macchiato, the barista prepared a latte instead.

> All of these variations are correct, and one is not necessarily better than or preferable to another. Everything depends on what the writer is trying to accomplish.

These and similar techniques are useful for combining elementary clauses to create more sophisticated prose. They can also be employed to solve various structural problems such as run-on sentences, comma splices, and fragments.

A run-on sentence is a sentence that combines two or more clauses without any device to signal to the reader where one ends and another begins:

Example:

My sister is a vegetarian I was somewhat skeptical about having the family Thanksgiving meal at her home but my first bite of the absolutely delicious squash casserole dispelled any doubts I might have had about a vegetarian Thanksgiving.

Here you have three independent clauses jammed together, one after the other, with nothing to indicate where one ends and the other begins. The problem, however, is easily solved with punctuation and conjunctions:

My sister is a vegetarian, so I was somewhat skeptical about having the family Thanksgiving meal at her home; but my first bite of the absolutely delicious squash casserole dispelled any doubts I might have had about a vegetarian Thanksgiving.

The following rules will help to make sure that you use the techniques correctly:

- You cannot join two independent clauses using just a comma. The result is called a comma splice:

  Patrice was born in Belgium, he grew up in the United States. ✘

  A comma splice can be easily corrected by inserting a suitable coordinating conjunction:

  Patrice was born in Belgium, but he grew up in the United States. ✓

  Patrice was born in Belgium, and he grew up in the United States. ✓

Either version is correct grammatically, and the choice between them depends on the writer's intent.

- You can join two independent clauses with a semicolon:

  The coach signaled from the sidelines that the offense should run either a screen pass or the quarterback option; Terry kept the ball on the option and ran for a first down.

- You can also use a semicolon before an independent clause introduced by a conjunction:

  The coach signaled from the sidelines that the offense should run either a screen pass or the quarterback option; and Terry kept the ball on the option and ran for a first down.

While this approach is technically correct, most writers would use a semicolon only when one or both independent clauses are divided by commas or other punctuation in order to make clear to the reader the main dividing point of the sentence:

The coach signaled from the sidelines that the offense should run either a screen pass or the quarterback option, the team's signature play; and Terry kept the ball on the option and ran for a first down, effectively putting the game out of reach of the other team.

In this example, the independent clauses have elements marked by commas, so the use of a conjunction with the semicolon to signal the juncture between the two independent clauses is a good idea.

Punctuation and conjunctions are useful for eliminating sentence fragments.

Example:

Physicists have discovered that Islamic artists as far back as the fifteenth century were using the concept of quasicrystalline geometry. Symmetrical polygonal shapes in patterns that can be extended indefinitely without repetition.

The problem here is that the second word group lacks a main verb, so it is a fragment rather than a sentence. ("Can be extended" is the verb of a noun clause introduced by "that," not the verb of a main clause.) The problem can be solved by incorporating the fragment into the first word group, which is a complete sentence:

Physicists have discovered that Islamic artists as far back as the fifteenth century were using the concept of quasicrystalline geometry, symmetrical polygonal shapes in patterns that can be extended indefinitely without repetition.

This change incorporates the fragment into an independent clause as an appositive phrase.

Example:

Introducing the young dancer Antonio Gades, who would go on to make a series of important flamenco films including *Boda de Sangre* and *Carmen*. *Los Tarantos* starred Amaya, whose explosive, raw-edged danger made her a pivotal figure in the New York flamenco scene.

The first word group here is a fragment. The verb "would go on" belongs to the relative clause introduced by "who," so the group lacks a main verb. The problem can be corrected by incorporating the participle phrase into the independent clause:

Introducing the young dancer Antonio Gades, who would go on to make a series of important flamenco films including *Boda de Sangre* and *Carmen*, *Los Tarantos* starred Amaya, whose explosive, raw-edged danger made her a pivotal figure in the New York flamenco scene.

Now "introducing" is the beginning of a participle phrase that modifies *Los Tarantos*, the film.

Clauses can also be combined by creating relative clauses.

Example:

My family is traveling to Kauai. Kauai is geologically the oldest of the Hawaiian Islands.

My family is traveling to Kauai, which is geologically the oldest of the Hawaiian Islands.

The two independent clauses can be combined by making the second sentence a relative clause introduced by the relative pronoun "which."

EXERCISE 5

DIRECTIONS: In each of the following items, a word or phrase is underlined. Following each sentence or sentences are alternative suggestions for rewriting the underlined part. If you think the original is correct, choose NO CHANGE. Otherwise, choose the best alternative. Answers are on page 803.

61. Characterized by vibrant colors and bold <u>shapes. Postmodern</u> art drew inspiration from artists such as Cezanne but reacted against the pastel indistinctness of the Impressionist canvasses.

    A. NO CHANGE
    B. shapes, postmodern
    C. shapes; postmodern
    D. shapes and postmodern

62. During the home-canning process, special canning jars are packed with prepared <u>food and self-sealing lids fitted on them, the jars</u> submerged in boiling water for at least ten to twenty minutes, depending on the size.

    F. NO CHANGE
    G. food, and self-sealing lids fitted on them. The jars
    H. food, self-sealing lids fitted on them, the jars are
    J. food, self-sealing lids fitted on them, and the jars

63. After waiting in line for hours in the bitter cold of Black Friday morning, Scott and Eddie finally made it into the store and over to the electronics department <u>at 6:03. Just</u> moments after the last sale-priced TV was claimed by the customer who had been standing in line in front of them.

    A. NO CHANGE
    B. at 6:03, just
    C. at 6:03, it was just
    D. at 6:03. The time being just

64. Football is an exciting game to watch, particularly when your team of choice is on <u>offense, but basketball is</u> my favorite sport because of the non-stop action.

    F. NO CHANGE
    G. offense basketball
    H. offense. Basketball being
    J. offense, but basketball being

65. I returned home late and had to park my car on the <u>street. Sometime</u> during the night, a thief broke one of my car windows and stole the stereo.

A. NO CHANGE
B. street sometime
C. street, sometime
D. street and sometime

66. Because many diseases and insects cause serious damage to crops, special legislation has been passed to provide for the inspection and quarantine of imported <u>plants; to</u> enforce the laws, inspectors are placed at ports of entry to prevent smugglers from bringing in plants that might be dangerous.

F. NO CHANGE
G. plants to
H. plants, to
J. plants and to

67. Each year, millions participate in the sport of showing dogs in formal <u>competitions. During which</u> the animals are judged on traits such as conformation, appearance, and temperament.

A. NO CHANGE
B. competitions, during which
C. competitions which
D. competitions. Which

68. The Iditarod, the annual sled-dog race starting in Anchorage, passing through the town of Iditarod, and finishing in Nome, began in the 1970s as a commemoration of the 1925 emergency medical <u>relay, it also serves</u> as acknowledgment of the heritage of Eskimos and Athabascans, who taught whites how to survive Alaskan winters.

F. NO CHANGE
G. relay; it also serves
H. relay it also serves
J. relay. Serving

69. Introduced in Paris in 1910 and taking the shape of stars, flames, arrows, trees, and almost any other <u>theme, real or imagined. Neon</u> signs have enticed shoppers and visitors to all manner of establishments for decades.

A NO CHANGE
B. theme, real or imagined neon
C. theme. Real or imagined, neon
D. theme, real or imagined, neon

70. A hostess who staged lavish parties during the Revolution and insisted on formality and decorum for these military <u>balls. Lucy</u> Knox dominated the social scene of the Federalist period.

F. NO CHANGE
G. balls; Lucy
H. balls, Lucy
J. balls Lucy

Maintain Consistent Tense and Pronoun Person

You know that consistency within a sentence is important. Your verb tenses must reflect the logic of the sentence, and pronoun use must be consistent.

Examples:

In this region, stubborn, weathered cattle graze, watched by the stubborn, weathered people who <u>made</u> their homes in this hardened land. ✗

In this region, stubborn, weathered cattle graze, watched by the stubborn, weathered people who <u>make</u> their homes in this hardened land. ✓

The steely resolve inspired by the harsh conditions can be seen in the carved faces of the <u>people as she clutches</u> an infant in her arms while balancing a bundle on her head. ✗

> Maintain consistent and logical use of verb tense and pronoun person throughout a paragraph or essay.

The steely resolve inspired by the harsh conditions can be seen in the carved faces of the <u>people; one clutches</u> an infant in her arms while balancing a bundle on her head. ✓

The same requirement applies to paragraphs and to entire passages. A passage written in the present tense should have present tense verbs throughout; a passage about multiple subjects should maintain plural pronouns throughout. If verbs and pronouns change tense or person without an appropriate transition, the reader will have problems.

Examples:

When she was a girl, my grandmother helped her mother preserve fruits and vegetables to eat during the winter months. Early in the morning, she <u>harvests</u> the produce from the orchard
₁
and the garden. Then, she would spend the rest of the morning washing and cutting up the fruits and vegetables. In the

1. A. NO CHANGE
   B. harvested
   C. is harvesting
   D. will harvest

(B) The passage is written in the past tense, so this verb too needs to be in the past tense.

afternoon, she and my great-grandmother prepared the wide-mouthed canning jars that <u>will preserve</u>
₂

2. F. NO CHANGE
G. would preserve
H. had preserved
J. are preserving

(G) Again, the verb should be some form of a past tense, and "would preserve" is used to show continuous or repetitive past events.

<u>it</u> through the winter.
₃

3. A. NO CHANGE
B. them
C. the food
D. those

(C) "It" is singular while "fruits and vegetables" is plural. The error can be corrected by eliminating the ambiguous pronoun and using a noun instead.

<u>You had to sterilize the jars</u> in boiling
₄
water so that no bacteria remained to spoil the food inside the sealed jars.

4. F. NO CHANGE
G. The jars sterilized
H. Boiling water sterilized the jar
J. The jars had to be sterilized

(J) The point of view used by the writer is the third person. "You" is second person. The underlined portion needs to be changed so that the subject of the sentence is in the third person.

<u>They were then</u> stored on the pantry
₅
shelves to be opened for mealtime on cold, wintry evenings.

5. A. NO CHANGE
B. It would then be stored
C. Then there was storage
D. Then they were stored

(A) Here "they" refers to "jars," so the original is correct.

EXERCISE 6

DIRECTIONS: In each of the following items, a word or phrase is underlined. Following each sentence or sentences are alternative suggestions for rewriting the underlined part. If you think the original is correct, choose NO CHANGE. Otherwise, choose the best alternative. Answers are on page 803.

Questions 71–80

The founding of the Peace Corps is one of President John F. Kennedy's most enduring legacies. Yet <u>it got its start</u> 71

in a fortuitous and unexpected moment. Kennedy arrived late to speak to students at the University of Michigan and found himself thronged by a crowd of 10,000 students at two o'clock in the morning. Speaking extemporaneously, the presidential candidate

<u>challenges</u> American youth to devote a part of their 72

lives to living and working in Asia, Africa, and Latin America. Would students back his effort to form a Peace Corps?

The response was affirmative and immediate. Within weeks, students organized a petition drive and gathered 1,000 signatures in support of the idea. Several hundred others pledged to serve. Enthusiastic letters poured into Democratic headquarters.

<u>The response was</u> crucial to Kennedy's decision to make 73

the founding of a Peace Corps a priority. Since then, more than 200,000 citizens of all ages and backgrounds have worked in over 130 countries throughout the world as volunteers in such fields as health, teaching, agriculture, urban planning, skilled trades, forestry, sanitation, and technology.

By 1960, two bills were introduced in Congress that were the direct forerunners of the Peace Corps. Representative Henry S. Reuss of Wisconsin proposed that the government study the idea, and Senator Hubert

71. A. NO CHANGE
B. it gets its start
C. they got their start
D. they got their starts

72. F. NO CHANGE
G. is challenging
H. challenged
J. had challenged

73. A. NO CHANGE
B. They were
C. It was
D. They are

Humphrey of Minnesota asked for the establishment of a Peace Corps itself. These bills

will not likely pass Congress at the time, but
   74

74. F. NO CHANGE
   G. are not likely passing
   H. are not likely to pass
   J. were not likely to pass

it caught the attention of then-Senator Kennedy for
  75

several important reasons.

75. A. NO CHANGE
   B. it catches
   C. they caught
   D. they catch

Kennedy foresaw a "New Frontier" inspired by
    76

Roosevelt's New Deal.

76. F. NO CHANGE
   G. foresees
   H. had foresawn
   J. would foresee

It would fight poverty, help cities, and expand
77

governmental benefits to a wide array of Americans. In foreign affairs, Kennedy was also more of an activist than his predecessor. He viewed the presidency as "the vital center of action in our whole scheme of government." Concerned by what was then perceived as the global threat of communism, Kennedy looked for creative as well as military solutions to counteract

77. A. NO CHANGE
   B. They
   C. Someone
   D. One

them. He was eager to revitalize America's program
  78

of economic aid and to counter negative images of the "Ugly American" and Yankee imperialism. He believed that sending idealistic Americans abroad to work at the

78. F. NO CHANGE
   G. those
   H. that
   J. it

grass-roots level would spread goodwill into the Third
        79

World and help stem the growth of communism there.

79. A. NO CHANGE
   B. spread
   C. spreads
   D. will spread

Kennedy lost no time in actualizing his dream for a Peace Corps. He issued an executive order establishing the Peace Corps within the State Department using funds from mutual security appropriations. Robert Shriver, as head of the new agency, assured its success by his fervent idealism and his willingness to improvise and take action. But to have permanency and eventual

autonomy, the Peace Corps <u>has to be</u> approved and
                              80
funded by Congress. In September 1961, the 87th
Congress passed Public Law 87-293 establishing a Peace
Corps. By this time, because of Kennedy's executive
order and Shriver's leadership, Peace Corps volunteers
were already in the field.

80. F. NO CHANGE
G. had to be
H. was to be
J. was

Managing Complex Sentences

Complex sentences are characteristic of sophisticated writing. This is not to say that they are complex for the sake of that quality alone. Rather, complex ideas cannot be expressed adequately in simplistic prose. The more complex a sentence, the more likely it is to contain an error, and the variety of errors that can be introduced are too many to enumerate. We can, however, provide illustrative sentences.

Parallelism, as you learned in a previous lesson, means using parallel (matching) grammatical forms for ideas that are parallel in meaning.

Manage lengthy, complex sentences by ensuring structural integrity and logical flow.

BASIC
INTERMEDIATE
ADVANCED

Example:

King John was adored by his subjects; he was generous, people were treated fairly by him, and he was courageous in battle. ✘

King John was adored by his subjects; he was generous, he treated people fairly, and he was courageous in battle. ✓

In the first sentence above, there is a failure of parallelism in the series of clauses following the semicolon. There are two active voice verbs and two passive voice verbs. The first occurrence of the passive voice is permissible since it appears before the semicolon and is not intended to parallel the three ideas that come after it. The second occurrence, however, is incorrect. Because being generous, treating people fairly, and being courageous in battle are all parallel ideas meant to explain *why* King John was adored by his subjects, they need to appear in parallel form, and in this case, that means in the active voice.

Complex sentences usually have both subordinate and independent clauses, and it is important to express the relationship between clauses clearly.

Example:

After carefully considering the presentations of both the developer and the community groups, the Board ruled when the interests of the community outweighed the interest of the property owner. ✗

After carefully considering the presentations of both the developer and the community groups, the Board ruled that the interests of the community outweighed the interest of the property owner. ✓

> In the original, the subordinating conjunction "when" is used to introduce what should be a noun clause, but "when" is used for adverbial clauses. "That" is needed to introduce the noun clause.

Complex sentences may include parenthetical expressions, and it is important that these be properly phrased.

Example:

At the time of his death, John Kennedy was widely acknowledged as, and continues to be, one of the greatest American presidents. ✗

> The problem here is that the parenthetical phrase is intended to incorporate the "acknowledged as" in order to complete the phrase but fails to do so. The error can be corrected in this way:

At the time of his death, John Kennedy was widely acknowledged as, and continues to be recognized as, one of the greatest American presidents. ✓

This sample of errors is by no means a list of all the things that go wrong with a complex sentence. Our best advice is to read such sentences for what they actually say, not for what they would like to say. That way, you'll be in a position to determine whether the writer has been successful.

EXERCISE 7

DIRECTIONS: In each of the following items, a word or phrase is underlined. Following each sentence or sentences are alternative suggestions for rewriting the underlined part. If you think the original is correct, choose NO CHANGE. Otherwise, choose the best alternative. Answers are on page 804.

81. During the 1907 season, Pop Warner created a new offense dubbed "the Carlisle formation," where a player could run, pass, or kick without revealing to the defense the offense's plan.

   A. NO CHANGE
   B. where a player would
   C. when a player would
   D. from which a player could

82. The usefulness of a transistor comes from its ability to use a small signal applied between one pair of its terminals to control a much larger signal at another pair of terminals, a property called gain that allows the transistor to act as an amplifier.

   F. NO CHANGE
   G. which is gain allowing
   H. and this is gain that
   J. while gain allows

83. When Scott Joplin was still a young child, his family left the farm on which his father, a former slave, worked as a laborer because they moved to the newly established town of Texarkana, which straddles the Texas-Arkansas border.

   A. NO CHANGE
   B. laborer, because
   C. laborer, and
   D. laborer, when

84. The formation of badlands is the result of deposition and erosion, the first the accumulation, over time, of layers of mineral material and the second the sedentary material subsequently erodes.

   F. NO CHANGE
   G. material and the second the subsequent erosion of the sedentary material
   H. material then the subsequent erosion of the sedentary material
   J. material, then the subsequently eroding sedentary material

85. The famous Las Vegas Strip has many of the largest hotels, casinos, and resort properties in the <u>world since fifteen</u> of the world's 25 largest hotels by room count, with a total of over 62,000 rooms, are located on the Strip.

    A. NO CHANGE
    B. world; fifteen
    C. world, since fifteen
    D. world for fifteen

86. Baseball <u>has and probably always will be</u> America's game with leagues for players of all ages ranging from t-ball for preschoolers to a senior circuit for retired professionals.

    F. NO CHANGE
    G. has been and probably always will be
    H. has and will probably always be
    J. was, probably and always,

87. NASCAR's history can be traced back to the moonshine runners of prohibition, who upgraded their vehicles in order to escape the pursuit of the <u>authorities who gathered</u> informally to race them to determine which was the fastest.

    A. NO CHANGE
    B. authorities which gathered
    C. authorities, and who gathered
    D. authorities gathering

88. In America, fox hunting is called fox chasing, as it is the practice not to pursue the fox once it has "gone to ground" (hidden in a hole); and some hunts may not catch a fox for many <u>seasons, despite chasing</u> several foxes in a single day of hunting.

    F. NO CHANGE
    G. seasons when they chase
    H. seasons, by chasing
    J. seasons when chasing

89. Aerobic bacteria require oxygen for continued growth and existence; anaerobic bacteria cannot tolerate gaseous oxygen and live deep in underwater sediments or other oxygen-free environments; and facultative <u>anaerobes, which prefer growing in the presence of oxygen, but</u> can continue to grow without it.

    A. NO CHANGE
    B. anaerobes prefer growing in the presence of oxygen but
    C. anaerobes preferring to grow in the presence of oxygen but
    D. anaerobes, prefer to grow in the presence of oxygen while they

90. With the development of music education in the public school system, high school and university marching bands became ubiquitous, and the importance of the trombone <u>continued, then</u> a typical band today includes two tenor trombones and perhaps a bass trombone.

    F. NO CHANGE
    G. continued; then
    H. continued, when
    J. continued, and

Conventions of Usage

Correct Pronoun Use

Reflexive pronouns end in "–self" and are self-referential: "myself," "yourself," "himself," "herself," "itself," "ourselves," "themselves."

Correctly use reflexive, relative, and possessive pronouns.

Examples:

I did not trust <u>myself</u> with the chocolate chip cookies.

<u>Erika</u> had to ask <u>herself</u> if it was worth all the effort.

The <u>directors</u> almost seemed to compete among <u>themselves</u> to see who could acquire the most lavish office decor.

Reflexive pronouns, of course, must agree with their antecedents, but this is usually not a problem because there are so few reflexive pronouns. The error that is perhaps most commonly made with this type of pronoun is the use of non-standard forms: "youself," "theyselves," and "theirselves." These are heard in conversation in various regions but are not considered acceptable in formal written English.

Relative pronouns link a relative clause to the rest of the sentence, and that function is described by the name "relative" pronouns. Relative pronouns include "that," "which," "who," "whom," "whoever," and "whomever."

The relative pronouns "that" and "which" generally refer to groups or things; "who" and "whom" refer to people.

Remember: Use "who" to refer to the subject of the clause or sentence. Use "whom" to refer to the object of a clause or sentence.

Examples:

After the waitress took my order, she turned to Benjamin, who ordered the fettuccine alfredo.

The person to whom the waitress should deliver the fettuccine alfredo is Benjamin.

Finally, be careful with commonly confused word pairs such as "it's" and "its," "you're" and "your," and "they're" and "their." "It's" is the contraction of "it is"; "its" is the third person singular possessive pronoun. "You're" is the contraction of "you are"; "your" is the second person possessive pronoun. "They're" is the contraction of "they are"; "their" is the third person plural possessive pronoun.

Examples:

My uncle was fond of saying that when <u>it's</u> time to build a railroad, people will build trains, meaning that a solution can be found to every problem.

My uncle was fond of saying that every dog has <u>its</u> day, meaning that everyone will, at some time or another, enjoy success.

<u>You're</u> not going to believe the news about Tina.

I just heard some really good news about <u>your</u> sister, Tina.

The lost hikers suffered no permanent harm, and <u>they're</u> very happy to be back home.

The lost hikers suffered no permanent harm and were glad to return to <u>their</u> homes.

DIRECTIONS: In each of the following items, a word or phrase is underlined. Following each sentence or sentences are alternative suggestions for rewriting the underlined part. If you think the original is correct, choose NO CHANGE. Otherwise, choose the best alternative. Answers are on page 804.

---

91. When giving a persuasive speech, <u>its important to organize the argument clearly and to back up your</u> position with authoritative evidence.

    A. NO CHANGE
    B. its important to organize the argument clearly and to back up you're
    C. it's important to organize the argument clearly and to back up your
    D. it's important to organize the argument clearly and to back up you're

92. The hostess invited her guests to make <u>theirselves</u> comfortable while she went to the kitchen to finish preparing the dinner.

    F. NO CHANGE
    G. themselves
    H. itself
    J. yourself

93. In football, the quarterback tells teammates what play they will run, sets the play in motion, and either hands the ball off to the running back, passes it to <u>one of the receivers, or runs it himself</u>.

A. NO CHANGE
B. one of the receivers, or runs it oneself
C. one of the receivers, or runs it themselves
D. receivers, and runs it themselves

94. The students at the Regional Fine Arts Festival waited anxiously to hear the judges' decision regarding the entry <u>what had won first prize and would</u> represent the region in the national competition.

F. NO CHANGE
G. that had won first prize and would
H. what had won first prize and that would
J. which had won first prize and what would

95. When I began taking diving lessons, I wondered how <u>I would ever convince me</u> to dive from a platform over 30 feet straight down into the water, much less do air-somersaults while dropping.

A. NO CHANGE
B. I would ever be convinced by myself
C. myself would ever be convinced
D. I would ever convince myself

96. Scholars are divided on the issue of whether <u>there was a real person to which Shakespeare wrote his sonnets</u>.

F. NO CHANGE
G. they're was a real person to which Shakespeare wrote his sonnets
H. there was a real person to whom Shakespeare wrote his sonnets
J. there was a real person to whom Shakespeare wrote his sonnets himself

97. Clinical studies are research programs designed to test specific medical products or procedures and are open <u>to whoever is willing to participate, as long as they meet</u> the specifications required by the nature of the particular study.

A. NO CHANGE
B. to whomever is willing to participate, as long as they meet
C. to whomever is willing to participate, as long as their meeting
D. to whoever is willing to participate, as long as they themselves meet

98. The United States provided the opportunity for millions of immigrants in the early twentieth century to make a life for themselves, but a reaction to World War I inspired a rise in <u>nativism, which opposes</u> the immigration and assimilation of specific ethnic or cultural groups.

    F. NO CHANGE
    G. nativism, who opposes
    H. nativism opposes
    J. nativists, which themselves oppose

99. There were two dwarf goats <u>who lived in the barn and grazed in the adjacent enclosure, which</u> also served as pasture for the donkey.

    A. NO CHANGE
    B. that lived in the barn and grazed in the adjacent enclosure, which
    C. that lived in the barn and grazed in the adjacent enclosure, what
    D. that lived in the barn and grazed in the adjacent enclosure; that

100. The rules of *Monopoly* state that <u>whomever is the first person to land on a particular property has the opportunity to buy the property, put houses on itself</u>, and collect rent from any other player who lands on the property.

    F. NO CHANGE
    G. whomever is the first person to land on a particular property has the opportunity to buy the property, put houses on it
    H. whomsoever is the first person to land on a particular property has the opportunity to buy the property, put houses on itself
    J. whoever is the first person to land on a particular property has the opportunity to buy the property, put houses on it

Ensure Agreement

Inverted Sentence Structure

You should pay careful attention to the agreement between subject and verb, but there are some sentence structures that create special problems. One is inverted sentence structure. In an inverted sentence, the verb precedes the subject.

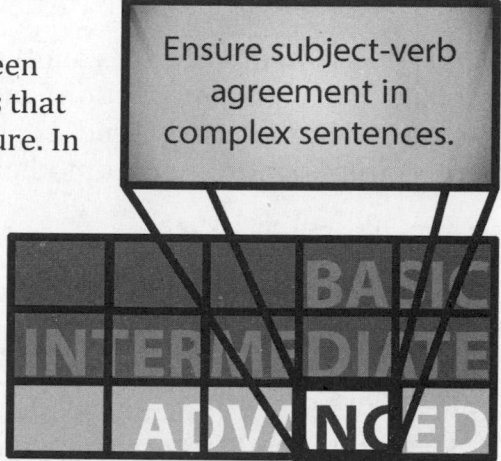

Ensure subject-verb agreement in complex sentences.

Examples:

Although the First Amendment to the Constitution does guarantee freedom of speech, the Supreme Court has long recognized that there <u>has</u> to be some *restrictions* on the exercise of this right. ✗

Jennifer must have been doubly pleased that day, for seated in the gallery to watch her receive the award <u>was</u> *her brother, her parents, and her husband.* ✗

In both of these sentences, the subjects and verbs do not agree. The relationships are obscured by the order in which the elements appear in the sentence—the verbs come before the subjects. These sentences should read:

Although the First Amendment to the Constitution does guarantee freedom of speech, the Supreme Court has long recognized that there <u>have</u> to be some *restrictions* on the exercise of this right. ✓

Jennifer must have been doubly pleased that day, for seated in the gallery to watch her receive the award <u>were</u> *her brother, her parents, and her husband.* ✓

Disjointed and Compound Subjects

As a matter of grammatical convention, subjects of the form "either . . . or" take the number of the element nearest the verb, and subjects of the form " . . . and . . ." are plural.

Examples:

Since the publishing company must meet the deadline for sending the book to print tomorrow, either the *editor or one of her assistants* <u>need</u> to stay at the office until the manuscript is complete. ✗

In this sentence, the subject has the form "either . . . or." When a subject consists of two or more parts joined by "or," the verb must agree with the element that follows "or." So, for the purpose of agreement, the subject of the sentence is "one." The correct construction is, "one . . . <u>needs</u>."

Jennifer, her parents, and her grandmother <u>intends</u> to have a celebratory dinner tonight, since, after months of test-taking, college applications, scholarship competitions, and much waiting, Jennifer has been granted a full scholarship. ✖

> This sentence contains another compound subject, but this time the elements are joined by the conjunction "and," and, by rule, a subject consisting of more than two elements joined by "and" is plural. So, the correct construction is, "Jennifer, her parents, and her grandmother <u>intend</u>."

Indefinite Pronouns

By grammatical convention, the following pronouns are considered singular and take singular verbs: "anyone," "each," "either," "everybody," "neither," "none," and "one."

Examples:

Each of the students <u>are</u> given the opportunity to submit a project for extra credit. ✖

Each of the students <u>is</u> given the opportunity to submit a project for extra credit. ✓

Everybody in the bleachers <u>were</u> given a rain check for one free admission to the grandstand. ✖

Everybody in the bleachers <u>was</u> given a rain check for one free admission to the grandstand. ✓

Subjects such as "all," "any," "half," "most," and "some" can take either singular or plural verbs depending on what they are referring to and the overall sense of the sentence.

Examples:

Because they had been packed haphazardly, *some* of the fine china dishes <u>were</u> broken when the movers mistook the open box for trash and threw it in the dumpster. ✓

Some of the water <u>was</u> spilled when I poured it into her glass. ✓

Intervening Grammatical Elements

Often grammatical elements such as phrases or even clauses that come between a subject and its verb can make it more difficult to determine what number of verb is required.

Examples:

In March 1941, faced with the task of sending a large number of troops abroad, the Navy commissioned an engineering team at Quonset Point, Rhode Island, to design light, portable, and inexpensive barracks; and by October, the *designs* for the Quonset, which means "long place" in the language of the Narragansett tribe, <u>was</u> finalized. ✖

In March 1941, faced with the task of sending a large number of troops abroad, the Navy commissioned an engineering team at Quonset Point, Rhode Island, to design light, portable, and inexpensive barracks; and by October, the *designs* for the

Quonset, which means "long place" in the language of the Narragansett tribe, <u>were</u> finalized. ✓

> The plural subject "designs" requires the plural "were." Notice that the relative clause that comes between the subject and the verb makes it difficult to make the connection. Additionally, the singular "tribe" seems to require the singular verb, even though "tribe" is not the subject.

Because they had been packed so carefully in layers of excelsior, *not one* of the fine china dishes <u>were</u> broken when the movers mistook the open box for trash and threw it in the dumpster. ✗

Because they had been packed so carefully in layers of excelsior, *not one* of the fine china dishes <u>was</u> broken when the movers mistook the open box for trash and threw it in the dumpster. ✓

> Again, intervening verbiage obscures the connection between subject and verb, and the proximity of the plural "dishes" makes it tempting to use a singular verb even though "dishes" is not the subject.

The chili *pepper*, which originated in the Americas, <u>have</u> been part of the human diet since at least 7,500 BCE. ✗

The chili *pepper*, which originated in the Americas, <u>has</u> been part of the human diet since at least 7,500 BCE. ✓

> The subject of this sentence is the singular "pepper," so the singular verb "has" is required. It's easy to overlook the failure of agreement in the original, however, because of the proximity of the plural "Americas."

EXERCISE 9

DIRECTIONS: In each of the following items, a word or phrase is underlined. Following each sentence or sentences are alternative suggestions for rewriting the underlined part. If you think the original is correct, choose NO CHANGE. Otherwise, choose the best alternative. Answers are on page 804.

101. <u>Principal Taylor explained that there is going to be some changes made in the school code</u> that will have an immediate effect on both teachers and students.

   A. NO CHANGE
   B. Principal Taylor explained that there are going to be some changes made in the school code
   C. Principal Taylor explained that there's going to be some changes made in the school code
   D. Principal Taylor explained that there's some changes that are going to be made in the school code

102. The number of people working out in gyms and health clubs <u>are</u> a good indication of the commitment of the younger generation to staying in good physical condition.

   F. NO CHANGE
   G. is
   H. to be
   J. being

103. Talking and texting are both forms of cell phone usage <u>that results in distracted driving and are leading causes</u> of motor vehicle crashes.

   A. NO CHANGE
   B. that result in distracted driving and are leading causes
   C. that results in distracted driving and is some leading causes
   D. which results in distracted driving and are leading causes

104. While it is true that many of the applicants to elite colleges <u>are turned down, there is</u> still thousands who receive acceptances.

   F. NO CHANGE
   G. is turned down, there is
   H. are turned down, they're
   J. are turned down, there are

105. According to legend, somewhere on the island <u>is buried</u> the remains of the notorious pirate along with a chestful of gold and jewels.

   A. NO CHANGE
   B. are buried
   C. buried
   D. was buried

106. The young soldier has been deployed overseas for nearly a year, and waiting for her when <u>she arrived home was</u> her entire family and most of the townspeople.

    F. NO CHANGE
    G. she was arriving home was
    H. she arrived home were
    J. upon arrival home was

107. Heart attack, cancer, and stroke, in that order, <u>is the leading cause</u> of death in the United States, with chronic lung disease and accidents in the fourth and fifth positions.

    A. NO CHANGE
    B. are the leading cause
    C. are the leading causes
    D. is the leading causes

108. The blue-gray stones that edge the flower box beside the curb <u>comes</u> from the shore of Devon, England, carried to Chestertown as ballast by trading ships that visited the once-bustling international port.

    F. NO CHANGE
    G. come
    H. is coming
    J. was coming

109. When the measure finally came up for a vote, neither of the council members <u>who had argued against expanding the economic empowerment zone were</u> present in the room.

    A. NO CHANGE
    B. who had argued against expanding the economic empowerment zone was
    C. which had argued against expanding the economic empowerment zone was
    D. that had argued against expanding the economic empowerment zone was

110. The restaurant's new management wants to reassure the dining public that neither the quality of the food <u>nor the prices is</u> going to change appreciably.

    F. NO CHANGE
    G. or the prices is
    H. or the prices are
    J. nor the prices are

Punctuation

In order to understand the use of the comma, it is necessary first to recognize elements that, while useful, are not essential to the meaning of a sentence.

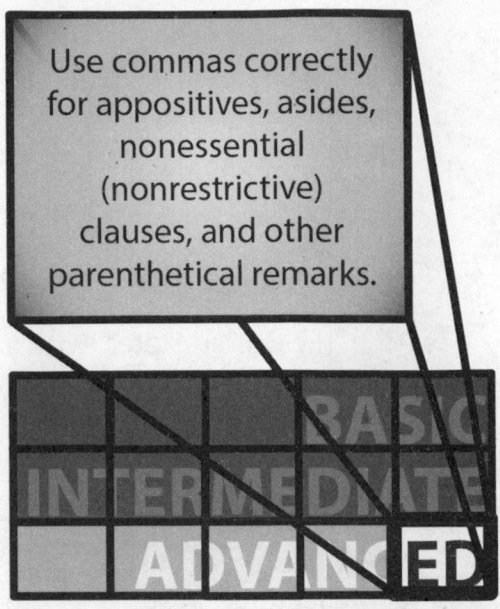

Use commas correctly for appositives, asides, nonessential (nonrestrictive) clauses, and other parenthetical remarks.

Examples:

At the 1936 Berlin Olympics, Jesse Owens won the 100-meter sprint, the long jump, and the 200-meter sprint. In the 200-meter sprint, he defeated Mack Robinson, the older brother of Jackie Robinson, in a time of 20.7 seconds.

The sentence is punctuated with several commas, and in other lessons we have covered the use of the comma to separate elements of a series. Here we are primarily interested in the two commas that set off the phrase "the older brother of Jackie Robinson." The phrase is an appositive, a noun construction used to identify, clarify, or further define a noun or noun phrase that comes before it in the sentence. The fact that Mack Robinson was the older brother of the baseball player Jackie Robinson is not essential to the sentence, but it is an interesting fact. So the fact set out in the appositive is interesting but not essential, and that is the reason for marking it with commas.

The lyrics to *A West Side Story* were, I believe, written by Stephen Sondheim and not, as is commonly thought, by Sondheim in collaboration with Leonard Bernstein.

Here we have two comments that are not essential to the meaning of the sentence: *I believe* and *as is commonly thought.* The second is perhaps more directly related to the central meaning than the first, but "importance" is not the test of whether commas are needed. If the aside interrupts the flow of the sentence and is not essential, then the commas are needed.

The question of whether an element is essential to the meaning of a sentence is most often a problem when deciding how to punctuate clauses. Compare the following:

The hotel requests that guests who use the towels that are provided in the pool area return towels to the pool attendant.

The hotel requests that guests who use the blue towels, which are provided in the pool area, return them to the pool attendant.

In the first sentence, the relative clause is essential to the meaning of the sentence because it identifies the towels that should be returned to the attendant: those provided in the pool area. In the second sentence, the towels identified as blue should be returned to the attendant, so the "which are provided in the pool area" is not essential (not required to identify the towels).

To explore the distinction further, consider the following pairs of sentences:

The professor, who was an authority on the Revolutionary War, was named Chair of the History Department. (Nonessential)

The professor who was an authority on the Revolutionary War was named Chair of the History Department. (Essential)

The vase, which is sitting on the coffee table, is an antique that is worth about $300. (Nonessential)

The vase that is sitting on the coffee table is an antique that is worth about $300. (Essential)

The supermarket, which remains open 24 hours a day, is located at the corner of Mulholland and Broad. (Nonessential)

The supermarket that remains open 24 hours a day is located at the corner of Mulholland and Broad. (Essential)

EXERCISE 10

DIRECTIONS: In each of the following sentences, add the necessary commas for each sentence. Answers are on page 804.

111. William Faulkner a great American author writes books that are both poetic and grotesque.

112. After the bubble burst many dot-com owners who were briefly worth millions on paper almost overnight found themselves looking for jobs.

113. Sergeant Rodriguez who served two tours of duty in Iraq was hard on new recruits because he wanted them to be well-prepared when they were finally deployed.

114. The naturally occurring grasslands of the southern Great Plains which includes large parts of South Dakota and Nebraska were replaced with cultivated fields.

115. Professional race car driver Dale Earnhardt, Sr. who won 76 races in his career was killed on the final lap of the 2001 Daytona 500 after making contact with another car and hitting the outside wall nose first.

116. Jack the Ripper is the best-known name given to an unidentified serial killer who was criminally active in the impoverished areas in and around the Whitechapel district of London in 1888.

117. During the Great Depression, the term "Okies" referred to very poor migrants from Oklahoma and surrounding states who moved to California in search of jobs after the ecological disaster called the "Dust Bowl."

118. Professional athletes because of the wear and tear on various joints are prone to develop arthritis in later life.

119. The moon which was not quite full cast eerie shadows on the lawn and the side of the house.

120. Jules Verne who is considered a major literary author in France and most of the rest of Europe is usually regarded by English readers as a writer of fiction and children's books.

121. The first electric chair was built for the state of New York by Harold P. Brown who was secretly paid by Edison to demonstrate that alternating current was more dangerous than direct current.

122. After placing his pregnant wife into Lifeboat #4, Colonel Astor stood on the starboard bridge wing smoking a cigarette with Jacques Futrelle an American writer of detective fiction; 30 minutes later the ship slipped into the icy waters of the North Atlantic.

123. *The Constitution* as *The Atlanta Constitution* originally was known was first published on June 16, 1868 and was so successful that by 1871 it had killed off the *Daily Intelligencer* the only Atlanta paper to survive the American Civil War.

124. At 11:30 a.m. local time on May 29, 1953, Edmund Hillary and Tenzing Norgay a Nepali Sherpa climber from Darjeeling reached the summit of Mount Everest the first climbers to do so.

125. The Hope Diamond also known as the Tavernier Blue is a large, 45.52-carat diamond with trace amounts of boron within its crystal structure that makes it appear blue to the naked eye.

126. A cummerbund is a broad, pleated waist sash often worn with tuxedos single-breasted dinner jackets first adopted by British military officers in colonial India as an alternative to a waistcoat.

127. Unlike other modes of diving which rely either on breath-hold or on air pumped from the surface scuba divers carry their own source of oxygen a system that allows greater freedom of movement.

128. Hypothermia a condition in which core body temperature drops below that required for normal metabolism and other bodily functions is the opposite of hyperthermia which is present in heat exhaustion and heat stroke.

129. The *Ride of the Valkyries* the popular title for the beginning of Act III of the opera of *Die Walküre* by Richard Wagner was used in *Apocalypse Now*, a 1979 war film.

130. Kate Chopin born Katherine O'Flaherty was an American author of short stories and novels who is now considered by some to have been a forerunner of feminist authors of the twentieth century.

Apostrophes

In English, we have two general methods for forming the possessives of nouns. One uses the apostrophe and the other uses "of."

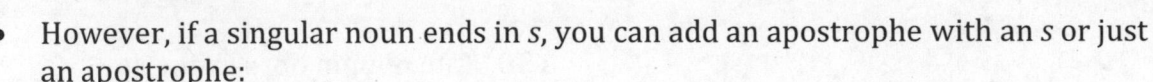

Correctly use apostrophes.

Examples:

The doctor's stethoscope was sitting on the nurse's desk.

The stethoscope of the doctor was sitting on the desk of the nurse.

You've heard the rules for forming the possessive with an apostrophe for years:

- For singular nouns, add an apostrophe and *s*:

  Maggie's dog

  the president's home

  pilot's hat

- However, if a singular noun ends in *s*, you can add an apostrophe with an *s* or just an apostrophe:

Chris's jacket	or	Chris' jacket
Dickens's second novel	or	Dickens' second novel
the actress's role	or	the actress' role

- For plural nouns ending in *s*, add an apostrophe:

  infants' cribs

  campers' tents

  radio stations' frequencies

- For plural nouns not ending in *s*, add an apostrophe and *s*:

  children's stories

  women's issues

  oxen's yokes

EXERCISE 11

DIRECTIONS: In each of the following items, a section of the sentence is underlined. Following each sentence or sentences are alternative suggestions for rewriting the underlined part. If you think the original is correct, choose NO CHANGE. Otherwise, choose the best alternative. Answers are on page 805.

131. <u>Matt's hat was hanging under a coat on the rack beside the barn's door.</u>

  A. NO CHANGE
  B. Matts' hat was hanging under a coat on the rack beside the barns' door.
  C. Matts's hat was hanging under a coat on the rack beside the door of the barn.
  D. Matts hat was hanging under a coat on the rack beside the barns's door.

132. We plant the oaks so that our <u>warriors' lives, sacrificed on this field of battle, will not go unremembered but will be commemorated each spring when the tree's</u> foliage is renewed.

  F. NO CHANGE
  G. warriors's lives, sacrificed on this field of battle, will not go unremembered but will be commemorated each spring when the tree's
  H. warriors's lives, sacrificed on this field of battle, will not go unremembered but will be commemorated each spring when the trees's
  J. warriors' lives, sacrificed on this field of battle, will not go unremembered but will be commemorated each spring when the trees'

133. Over the past 20 years, the <u>cities' populations have declined while the suburbs</u> have increased.

  A. NO CHANGE
  B. cities' populations have declined while the suburbs's
  C. cities' populations have declined while the suburbs'
  D. citys's populations have declined while the suburbs

134. The renovation of the <u>mens' locker room was finished just before the arrival of the new freshmen</u> class.

  F. NO CHANGE
  G. men's locker room was finished just before the arrival of the new freshmen's
  H. men's locker room was finished just before the arrival of the new freshmens'
  J. men's locker room was finished just before the arrival of the new freshmen

135. In the <u>childrens' story, the mices'</u>
home is described as cozy and tidy;
but in reality, mice live in excrement-
littered nests fabricated from foraged
debris.

A. NO CHANGE
B. childrens's story, the mice's
C. children's story, the mice's
D. children's story, the mouses's

Colons and Semicolons

In the Basic (p. 49) and Intermediate (p. 111) levels of this topic, we discussed techniques for combining clauses with commas and conjunctions to make more effective sentences. Semicolons can also be used for this purpose.

Examples:

Art Deco is an eclectic style that combines traditional craft motifs with Machine Age materials and imagery. It first appeared in France after World War I, flourished internationally in the 1930s and 1940s, and waned in the post-World War II era.

Art Deco is an eclectic style that combines traditional craft motifs with Machine Age materials and imagery; it first appeared in France after World War I, flourished internationally in the 1930s and 1940s, and waned in the post-World War II era.

In 1816, a succession of major volcanic eruptions caused a dramatic drop in global temperatures. The result was the "year without a summer."

In 1816, a succession of major volcanic eruptions caused a dramatic drop in global temperatures; the result was the "year without a summer."

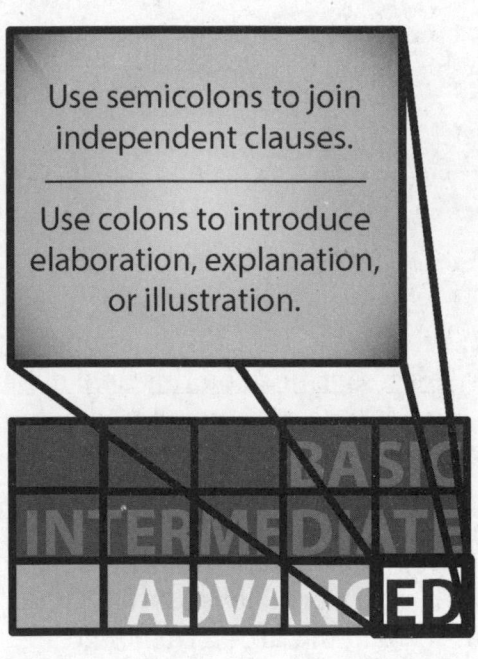

Use semicolons to join independent clauses.

Use colons to introduce elaboration, explanation, or illustration.

Colons are used to introduce an explanation or a series.

Examples:

The spacecraft *Challenger* disaster occurred on January 28, 1986, when the shuttle broke apart 73 seconds into its flight following the failure of an o-ring: a gasket in the shape of a torus designed to be seated in a groove and compressed during assembly between two or more parts, creating a seal at the interface.

Lenny really loves machinery and can service or repair almost any device with a small engine: lawnmowers, ATVs, chainsaws, weed whackers, and even motorcycles.

The most common error made in using the colon is to duplicate the function of the colon by including a phrase like "for example" or "such as":

The valved brass family includes all of the modern brass instruments such as: trumpet, French horn, euphonium, tuba, and variations on those instruments. ✗

The valved brass family includes all of the modern brass instruments: trumpet, French horn, euphonium, tuba, and variations on those instruments. ✓

EXERCISE 12

DIRECTIONS: In each of the following items, a word or phrase is underlined. Following each sentence or sentences are alternative suggestions for rewriting the underlined part. If you think the original is correct, choose NO CHANGE. Otherwise, choose the best alternative. Answers are on page 805.

136. In the eighteenth century, the British agriculturalist Charles Townshend started the British Agricultural Revolution by popularizing a four-field rotation: wheat, turnips, barley, and clover.

F. NO CHANGE
G. rotation such as: wheat
H. rotation using crops like: wheat
J. rotation with crops including: wheat

137. Ozone is a pale blue gas with a distinctively pungent smell; the name was given to the chemical substance by Christian Friedrich Schönbein, who called it *ozein*, the Greek verb meaning "to smell," from the peculiar odor in lightning storms.

A. NO CHANGE
B. smell, the name was given to
C. smell the name was given to
D. smell, naming

138. Aposematism is the exhibition by plants and animals of appearance and behavior that warns a predator of the inadvisability of taking a possible prey using a variety of <u>signals such as: conspicuous colors, sounds, and odors</u>.

   F. NO CHANGE
   G. signals: conspicuous colors, sounds, and odors
   H. conspicuous colors, sounds, and odors, as such signals
   J. signals like: conspicuous colors, sounds, and odors

139. Semiotics is the study of signs and sign <u>processes such as: indication</u>, designation, likeness, analogy, metaphor, symbolism, signification, and communication.

   A. NO CHANGE
   B. processes such as indication
   C. processes like: indication
   D. processes including: indication

140. Joel Chandler Harris acknowledged the debt to the storytellers from whom he learned the "Uncle Remus" <u>fables; indeed</u>, many of the stories that he recorded have direct equivalents in the African oral tradition, and it is thanks to Harris that their African-American form is preserved.

   F. NO CHANGE
   G. fables, indeed
   H. fables indeed
   J. fables: indeed

WRITING AN ESSAY | Planning an Essay

Understand the Assignment

Let the Prompt Be Your Topic

When presented with a prompt, always read it several times until you are completely familiar with the material. Sometimes it may be helpful to underline key words or phrases that are important.

The prompt is intended to be your topic and an inspiration for your writing. If you pay careful attention to the language of the prompt, it can actually help you to get started.

Consider this sample essay prompt:

> Human beings are often cruel, but they also have the capacity for kindness and compassion. In my opinion, an example that demonstrates this capacity is ––––.
>
> Complete the statement above with an example from current affairs, history, literature, or your own personal experience. Then write a well-organized essay explaining why you regard that event favorably.

This topic explicitly invites you to choose an example of kindness or compassion from history, current events, literature, or even personal experience. Thus, you could write about the end of a war (history), a mission of humanitarian aid (current events), the self-sacrifice of a fictional character (literature), or even about the day that your family helped a stranded motorist (personal experience). Remember that what you have to say is not as important as how you say it.

Develop a Point of View

Sometimes an essay prompt will invite you to present your opinion on an issue. When you encounter such prompts, you must decide whether you are in agreement or disagreement with the statement given.

Write Only on the Assigned Topic

While the types of prompts may differ among assignments or tests, the directions all agree on this point: you must write on the assigned topic. The assigned topic is often open-ended, which means that the essay graders are not looking for a particular opinion or answer, so you should have no problem coming up with something to write.

Organize Your Thoughts

Limit the Scope of Your Essay

The requirements of the writing assignment should determine the length and scope of your essay. Always remember to define the scope of an essay before beginning to write. This will improve your focus, and your essay will be more likely to accomplish only the assigned task, whether it is to defend a controversial position or to provide a definition. The more limited and specific your topic, the more successful your essay is likely to be since you will be better able to supply the specific details necessary to give depth and sophistication to your essay. You will also reduce the possibility of either straying onto tangential topics or under-developing a specific claim.

Develop a Thesis

A thesis statement provides the scope, purpose, and direction of an essay in one clear and focused statement. A thesis statement usually includes your claims or assertions and the reasoning and evidence you will use to support them. If possible, try to formulate the thesis of your composition in a single sentence during the pre-writing stage. When developing a thesis, keep in mind the following ideas:

IMPORTANT POINTS FOR DEVELOPING A THESIS
1. The thesis must not be too broad or too narrow.
2. The thesis must be clear to both you and the essay reader.
3. Everything in the essay must support your thesis.
4. Use specific details and examples rather than generalizations to support your thesis.

Identify Key Points

Identify the two or three (perhaps four) important points that you want to make. Then, decide on the order of presentation for those points.

Write an Outline

Once you gain a clear understanding of the assignment, its requirements, and what you want to write about, it's then important to organize the major points of your essay in a written outline. The purpose of an outline is to develop a logical structure to your arguments and to streamline your essay. An outline should include your thesis statement, the key points of your argument, and the concluding statement of your essay. A sample outline structure is presented below:

SAMPLE OUTLINE
I. Introduction: Thesis Statement

II. First Key Point
   A. Sub-Point 1
   B. Sub-Point 2

III. Second Key Point
   A. Sub-Point 1
   B. Sub-Point 2

IV. Third Key Point
   A. Sub-Point 1
   B. Sub-Point 2

V. Conclusion: Restatement of Thesis

Composition

Organize Ideas into Paragraphs

A good writer uses paragraphs effectively. Paragraphs are important because they provide the structure through which a writer conveys meaning. To illustrate this point with an analogy, imagine a grocery store in which items are not organized into sections. In this store, there is no fresh produce section, no canned goods section, no baked goods section, and no frozen foods section. Consequently, a single bin holds bunches of bananas, cans of beans, loaves of bread, and frozen turkeys. This lack of organization would make shopping very difficult. Likewise, essays without paragraphs (or with poorly organized paragraphs) are very difficult—if not impossible—to understand.

As you begin your essay, you will need to decide how many paragraphs you will write. Your essay should contain two to four important points that develop or illustrate your thesis. Each important point should be treated as its own paragraph.

Do not write simply to fill up space and make it seem like you have many ideas. This approach can result in repetition and wordiness, which is a sign of disorganization and unclear thinking. Write enough to demonstrate your writing ability and to prove your thesis. Five paragraphs (an introduction paragraph, three main body paragraphs, and a concluding paragraph) are usually sufficient.

Write the Essay

Many students become frustrated before they even begin to write. They sit and stare at the blank page and complain that they are "blocked." In other words, they can't think of anything to write. The secret to successfully beginning an essay is planning and pre-writing. Once you have completed the pre-writing stage (the most important part of writing), you begin writing. You may need to go back and revise some of your work, but doing the pre-writing (getting your ideas together before you begin your essay) is the easiest way to avoid writer's block. As you write your essay, follow this simple essay structure:

BASIC ESSAY STRUCTURE

I. Introduction: State the thesis of your essay.
    A. State your position clearly.
    B. State the elements that you will be using to support your position.

II. Body: Each paragraph in the body of your essay will be devoted to one of the supporting elements that were listed in the introduction. Elaborate on the elements by using examples.

III. Conclusion: Summarize your position and the reasons for your position.

The Introduction

During the pre-writing stage, you analyzed the topic. Now, use the introduction (the first paragraph) to write clear and concise sentences that describe the topic, your point of view on it, and what you plan to say to back up your position. In general, an introduction should let the reader know what direction your essay will take. However, don't spend too much time on an introduction. The remainder of the essay will be where you'll explain your ideas and give your examples in more detail.

When writing your introduction, keep these points in mind:

WRITING AN INTRODUCTION

1. Focus on the essay topic presented in the prompt and clearly state your point of view on this topic.

2. Use a tone that is sincere, straightforward, and clear. DO NOT be cute or funny, ironic or satiric, overly emotional or too dramatic.

3. DO NOT repeat the writing prompt word-for-word. Instead, paraphrase the prompt in your own words and then clearly state your point of view.

4. After stating your point of view, briefly state the evidence or arguments you will use to support your point of view.

Finally, an effective introduction often accomplishes one of the following tasks as well: it explains why readers should care about the topic at hand, or it grabs the reader's attention by describing briefly an incident in real life that is related to the topic.

The Body

The heart of the essay is the development which takes place in the body paragraphs. Here, the writer must attempt, in paragraph form, to support the main idea of the essay through illustrations, details, and examples. These body or developmental paragraphs must serve as a link in the chain of ideas and contribute directly to the essay's main idea or position.

Each paragraph should start with a transitional statement or phrase that describes the relationship of the paragraph to the previous paragraphs. The length of any one of these body paragraphs can vary, but each paragraph should only cover one main idea. You may do this through a style that is descriptive, narrative, or expository. You may take a factual or an anecdotal approach. Whatever approach you choose and whatever style you adopt, though, your writing must be coherent, logical, unified, and well-ordered.

When writing your essay, avoid the following common mistakes:

AVOID THESE COMMON ERRORS
1. DO NOT use sentences that include irrelevant material. In each body paragraph, only include sentences that relate specifically to the argument being made in that paragraph.
2. DO NOT use sentences that disrupt logical development. In each body paragraph, make sure each sentence logically follows from the sentence that comes before it.

Transitions

A good writer uses transitional words or phrases to connect thoughts, to provide for a logical sequence of ideas, and to link paragraphs. The following list includes some transitions and the logical relationships they indicate:

TRANSITIONAL WORDS AND PHRASES

Addition

again
also
and
besides
both...and
finally
first, second, third
furthermore
in addition
likewise
moreover
not only...but (also)
similarly

Alternation

either...or
neither...nor
nor
or
so that

Cause/Effect/Purpose

accordingly
as
as a consequence
as a result
because
consequently
for
for this purpose
hence
since
therefore
so

Conditions

as if (as though)
if
once...then
unless

Contrast

all the same
although
but
even though
however
instead
nevertheless
on the contrary
on the other hand
otherwise
still
though
yet

Space

here
in the middle
nearby
next to
opposite to
there
to the left/right
where
wherever

Support

for example
for instance
in fact
in general
such as

Summary

as shown above
in other words
in brief
in conclusion
in general
in short
in summary
to sum up

Time

after
as soon as
at the present time
before
during
eventually
finally
in (month, year)
later
meanwhile
since
then
until
when
whenever
while

The Conclusion

A successful writer knows when and how to end an essay. To conclude your essay effectively, you should have a strong and clear concluding paragraph. This concluding paragraph should make a reader feel that your essay has made its point; that your thesis has been explained; and that your point of view has been supported by specific examples, ideas, or arguments. A concluding paragraph can be as short as three to six sentences. The following are some guidelines for writing a successful concluding paragraph:

EFFECTIVE METHODS FOR CONCLUDING AN ESSAY
1. Restate your point of view on the essay topic.
2. Summarize the main arguments and evidence you used to support your point of view.
3. If time permits, conclude with a brief statement as to why your point of view is more defensible than a different point of view on the essay topic. What are the positive consequences of holding your point of view? What are the negative consequences of holding the opposite point of view?

The following is a quick overview of ineffective methods for writing a conclusion:

INEFFECTIVE METHODS FOR CONCLUDING AN ESSAY
1. DO NOT apologize for being unable to present all possible arguments in a limited amount of time.
2. DO NOT complain that the topic was uninteresting. DO NOT complain that the topic was too broad.
3. DO NOT introduce new material that you won't have time to develop. DO NOT introduce irrelevant material.

Principles of Good Writing

While writing, keep the three principles of good writing in mind: write grammatically, punctuate and spell correctly, and write concisely and clearly. If you follow these conventions, you will communicate your ideas clearly and effectively.

Write Grammatically

When writing an essay, the following principles of good grammar should be observed for an effective essay:

CORRECT GRAMMAR AND EFFECTIVE ESSAYS
1. Each sentence must have a conjugated (main) verb that agrees with its subject.
2. Each pronoun must have a referent (antecedent) with which it agrees.
3. Similar elements in a sentence must appear in parallel form.
4. Modifiers must agree with what they modify. They must also make sense.
5. Each sentence should use clear and concise language.

Punctuate and Spell Correctly

In addition to writing grammatically, concisely, and formally (without using slang or other informal language), you must punctuate and spell correctly. Since you are in charge of writing the essay, you can choose to avoid punctuation and spelling errors. If you are unsure about how to punctuate a particular construction or spell a particular word, choose an alternative.

Write Concisely and Clearly

Use simple and direct sentences. Avoid complex and convoluted sentences. In general, the most complicated sentence you should use is one with two independent clauses that are joined by a conjunction such as "and" or "but." Of course, you can also use sentences that include one dependent clause and one independent clause that are joined together by a conjunction such as "while" or "although." Again, you should try to express yourself simply and directly.

Also, avoid using any unnecessary or wordy phrases, such as those illustrated in the following chart:

AVOID THESE UNNECESSARY AND WORDY PHRASES	
Instead of:	*Say:*
In my opinion, I believe that	I believe that
In the event of an emergency	In an emergency
On the possibility that it may	Since it may
close to the point of	close to
have need for	need
with a view to	to
in view of the fact that	because
give consideration to	consider
mean to imply	imply
disappear from view	disappear
in this day and age	today
the issue in question	the issue

Finally, while neatness is not graded, it is almost certainly true that an illegible essay will not receive a good grade.

Revision and Scoring

Proofread Your Essay

Proofreading is an essential part of the writing process. The first draft of an essay will usually not be free of errors. This means that you will need to re-read the essay and correct any grammatical errors or logical inconsistencies. There are two categories of errors that generally appear in essays: structural errors and mechanics/usage errors.

Proofread for Structural Errors

When proofreading, first consider the structural elements of an essay. The three most important structural factors in an essay are unity, coherence, and support. Essays are judged by how well they meet these basic requirements. To improve your essay, ask yourself the following questions:

UNITY, COHERENCE, AND SUPPORT
1. Does the essay have a main thesis that is clearly stated in the introduction? What is it? What is the essay's point of view on the essay topic?
2. Does the introduction clearly state the arguments and evidence that will support the essay's point of view?
3. Does each body paragraph have a topic sentence? (A topic sentence is the first sentence of a paragraph, and it summarizes what will be argued or presented in that paragraph.)
4. Does each body paragraph make a different argument to support the essay's point of view?
5. Do the other sentences in each body paragraph all support the topic sentence? In other words, do the other sentences all further the argument or present evidence related to the main point made in the topic sentence?
6. Do the body paragraphs include specific details or examples to make the argument more vivid and interesting?
7. Does the essay use transitional words or phrases that allow the reader to move easily from one idea or paragraph to the next?
8. Does the essay have a conclusion that clearly re-states the essay's point of view on the essay topic?

Proofread for Mechanics/Usage Errors

After reviewing the structure of your essay, look for mechanics/usage errors. Although these are less important, mechanics/usage errors can prevent readers from focusing on the substance of an essay. The following is a list of common mechanics/usage errors:

COMMON MECHANICS/USAGE ERRORS
1. Omission of words—especially "the," "a," and "an"
2. Omission of final letters in words
3. Careless spelling errors
4. Incorrect use of capital letters
5. Faulty punctuation

Scoring Rubric

The rubric (scoring guide) below summarizes how your essay will likely be graded by the essay reader.

ESSAY SCORE QUALIFICATIONS	
Score	**Essay Qualities**
EXCELLENT	• demonstrates *clear and consistent competence*, though it may have occasional errors • effectively and insightfully addresses the writing task • is well-organized and fully developed • uses appropriate and innovative examples to support ideas • demonstrates a superior grasp of grammar and style, varies sentence structure, and uses a wide range of vocabulary
SUPERIOR	• demonstrates *reasonably consistent competence* with occasional errors or lapses in quality • effectively addresses the writing task • is generally well-organized and adequately developed • uses appropriate examples to support ideas • demonstrates a competent grasp of grammar and style, employs some syntactic variety, and uses appropriate vocabulary
GOOD	• demonstrates *adequate competence* with occasional errors and lapses in quality • addresses the writing task • is organized and somewhat developed • uses examples to support ideas • demonstrates an adequate but inconsistent grasp of grammar and style with minor errors in grammar and diction • displays minimal sentence variety

ESSAY SCORE QUALIFICATIONS	
Score	**Essay Qualities**
AVERAGE	• demonstrates *developing competence* • may contain one or more of the following weaknesses: inadequate organization or development; inappropriate or insufficient details to support ideas; and an accumulation of errors in grammar, diction, or sentence structure
BELOW AVERAGE	• demonstrates *some incompetence* • is flawed by one or more of the following weaknesses: poor organization; thin development; little or inappropriate detail to support ideas; and frequent errors in grammar, diction, and sentence structure
WEAK	• demonstrates *incompetence* • is seriously flawed by one or more of the following weaknesses: very poor organization, very thin development, and usage or syntactical errors so severe that meaning is somewhat obscured

EXERCISE 1

DIRECTIONS: You have 30 minutes to plan and write an essay. Read the prompt carefully and make sure you understand the instructions. A successful essay will have the following features: it will take a position on the issue presented in the writing prompt; it will maintain a consistent focus on the topic; it will use logical reasoning and provide supporting ideas; it will present ideas in an organized manner; and, finally, it will include clear and effective language in accordance with the conventions of standard written English. Sample essay responses and analyses begin on page 805.

Teachers evaluate the work of students by grading exams, homework, and other assignments, as well as class participation. The end-of-term report card with its letter or numerical grades is a time-honored tradition. Now, some teachers and administrators suggest that students be given the opportunity to grade teachers. They point out that students are in a unique position to assess the effectiveness of their teachers because they spend so much time with the teachers in the classroom. Some of those favoring this idea propose that students complete forms, ranking teachers according to relevant criteria, such as "Preparedness" and "Ability to Communicate." Other teachers and administrators oppose this idea and argue that students lack the experience and perspective to determine what makes an effective teacher. They also express concern that the evaluation forms could be used by students to retaliate against teachers for personal reasons. In your opinion, should students be given the opportunity to grade their teacher?

In your essay, take a position on this issue. You can write about either point of view presented here, or you can present a different point of view on this topic. Support your position with relevant reasons and/or examples from your own experience, observations, or reading.

ESSAY OUTLINE

Reading Skills Review

Course Concept Outline

	Main Idea and Voice (MID)	Explicit Details (SUP)	Development (REL)	Vocabulary (MOW)	Implied Ideas and Applications (GEN)
Basic	Identify the writer's topic and purpose for a particular passage. Identify the main idea or purpose of paragraphs in a particular passage.	Identify details in a passage such as names, dates, and events. Identify details at the sentence or paragraph level in a passage. Identify the purpose of a specific part of a passage.	Be alert to the sequence of events to determine when (or if) an event occurred in a passage. Identify the cause-effect relationships within a passage. Identify relationships between main characters in a passage. Identify cause-effect relationships in a single paragraph of a passage.	Use context clues to determine the meaning of unfamiliar words and phrases. Use contextual clues to determine alternative meanings and shades of meanings.	Draw conclusions about the people or events in straightforward narratives. Make generalizations and draw conclusions about people and ideas.
Intermediate	Infer the main idea or purpose of paragraphs in an uncomplicated literary passage. Understand the author's or narrator's approach (e.g., point of view, kinds of evidence used) in uncomplicated passages. Identify the main idea or purpose of paragraphs in uncomplicated passages. Infer the main idea or purpose of paragraphs in more complex passages. Summarize key events and ideas in more complex passages. Understand the author's or narrator's approach (e.g., point of view, kinds of evidence used) in more complex passages.	Locate important details in uncomplicated passages. Make simple inferences about the role of details in passages. Locate important details in more complex passages. Locate and interpret subtle details in uncomplicated passages. Discern details, which may appear in different parts of a passage, that support important points in more complex passages.	Order sequences of events in uncomplicated literary passages. Identify clear relationships between people, ideas, and so on in uncomplicated passages. Identify clear cause-effect relationships in uncomplicated passages. Understand relationships between people, ideas, and so on in uncomplicated passages. Identify clear relationships between characters, ideas, and so on in more complicated literary narratives. Order sequences of events in uncomplicated passages. Discern implied or subtly stated cause-effect relationships in uncomplicated passages. Identify clear cause-effect relationships in more complex passages.	Determine the meaning of figurative and nonfigurative words, phrases, and statements in uncomplicated passages using contextual clues. Determine, using context, the appropriate meaning of almost any word, phrase, or statement in uncomplicated passages. Determine, using context, the appropriate meaning of some figurative and nonfigurative words, phrases, and statements in more complex passages.	Draw generalizations and conclusions using details that support the main points of more challenging passages. Draw generalizations and conclusions about people, ideas, etc. in uncomplicated passages. Draw generalizations and conclusions about people, ideas, and so on in more complex passages. Draw subtle generalizations and conclusions about characters, ideas, and so on in uncomplicated literary narratives.
Advanced	Infer the main idea or purpose of more complex passages and paragraphs. Summarize events and ideas in almost any passage. Understand the author's or narrator's overall approach (e.g., point of view, kinds of evidence used) in almost any passage. Identify clear main ideas and purposes of challenging passages or paragraphs.	Locate and interpret subtle details in more complex passages. Use details that appear in different sections of complex informational passages to support specific points or arguments. Locate and interpret details in challenging passages. Understand the subtle or complex function of a part of a passage.	Order sequences of events in more complex passages. Understand the dynamics between people, ideas, etc. in more complex passages. Understand implied or subtly stated cause-effect relationships in more complex passages. Order sequences of events in challenging passages. Understand subtle relationships between people, ideas, etc. in almost any passage. Understand implied, subtle, or complex cause-effect relationships in almost any passage.	Determine the appropriate meaning of words, phrases, and statements from figurative or technical contexts. Determine the context-dependent meaning of words, phrases, or statements in almost any passage, even when the language is richly figurative and the vocabulary is difficult.	Draw generalizations and conclusions about people, ideas, etc. by using information from one or more sections of more complex passages. Draw complex or subtle generalizations or conclusions about people, ideas, etc. by combining information from different parts of the passage. Understand and generalize about parts of a complex literary narrative.

In this Reading Skills Review, you will focus on five important elements of reading comprehension:

- Main Idea and Voice
- Explicit Details
- Development
- Vocabulary
- Implied Ideas and Applications

The Reading Skills Review is divided into three levels (Basic, Intermediate, and Advanced). Each level features two lessons (with a total of six lessons across all three levels). Each lesson has a passage that walks through the five elements of reading comprehension. After you have reviewed these two passages, you will work through an exercise with additional passages. As you begin, keep in mind that you already possess all of these skills because you are already a reader. These lessons are designed to isolate and develop skills you already have.

BASIC | Lesson 1

Please read the following passage and refer to it as necessary throughout Lesson 1.

This passage is an excerpt from The Book of Animals, *a book by Arab writer and philosopher Al-Jahiz.*

In the fly there are two good qualities. One of these is the facility with which it may be prevented from causing annoyance and discomfort. For if any person wishes to make the flies quit his house and secure himself from being troubled by them without diminishing the amount of light in the house, he has first only to shut the door, and they will hurry forth
5 as fast as they can and try to outstrip each other in seeking the light and fleeing from the darkness. Then no sooner is the curtain let down and the door opened than the light will return and the people of the house will no longer be harassed by flies. If there be a slit in the door, or if, when it is shut, one of the two folding leaves does not quite close on the other, then that will serve them as a means of exit; and the flies often go out through the
10 gap between the bottom of the door and the lintel. Thus it is easy to get rid of them and escape from their annoyance. With the mosquito it is otherwise, for just as the fly has greater power for mischief in the light, so the mosquito is more tormenting and mischievous and bloodthirsty after dark; and it is not possible for people to let into their houses sufficient light to stop the activity of the mosquito, because for this purpose they
15 would have to admit the beams of the sun, and there are no mosquitoes except in summer

when the sun is unendurable. Hence, while it is easily possible to contrive a remedy against flies, this is difficult in the case of mosquitoes.

The second merit of the fly is that unless it ate the mosquito, which it pursues and seeks after on the walls and in the corners of rooms, people would be unable to stay in their

20 houses. I am informed by a trustworthy authority that Muhammad son of Jahm said one day to some of his acquaintances, "Do you know the lesson which we have learned with regard to the fly?" They said, "No." "The fact is," he replied, "that it eats mosquitoes and chases them and picks them up and destroys them. I will tell you how I learned this. Formerly, when I wanted to take the siesta, I used to give orders that the flies should be

25 cleared out and the curtain drawn and the door shut an hour before noon. On the disappearance of the flies, the mosquitoes would collect in the house and become exceedingly strong and powerful and bite me violently as soon as I began to rest. Now on a certain day I came in and found the room open and the curtain up. And when I lay down to sleep, there were no mosquitoes and I slept soundly, although I was very angry with the

30 slaves. Next day they cleared out the flies and shut the door as usual, and on my coming to take the siesta I saw a multitude of mosquitoes. Then on another day they forgot to shut the door, and when I perceived that it was open I rebuked them.

However, when I came for the siesta, I did not find a single mosquito and I said to myself, 'Methinks I have slept on the two days on which my precautions were neglected, and have

35 been hindered from sleeping whenever they were carefully observed. Why should not I try today the effect of leaving the door open? If I sleep three days with the door open and suffer no annoyance from the mosquitoes, I shall know that the right way is to have the flies and the mosquitoes together, because the flies destroy them, and that our remedy lies in keeping near us what we used to keep at a distance.' I made the experiment, and now the

40 end of the matter is that whether we desire to remove the flies or destroy the mosquitoes, we can do it with very little trouble."

Main Idea and Voice

Whether it's an advertisement, a news article, or even a shopping list, all writing happens for a reason. Every piece of writing has both a *focus* and a **purpose**. The *focus* of the piece is the topic, or what the writing is about. The **purpose** is the reason for the writing. Think of the focus as the "what" of a passage, and the purpose as the "why." Together, focus and purpose form the main idea of a passage.

Identify the writer's topic and purpose for a particular passage.

To identify the main idea of a passage, ask yourself:

- *What* is this passage about?

- *Why* is the writer telling me this?

Think of the main idea as a sentence you could write using the following template:

In this passage, the author describes _____ in order to _____. The first blank is the focus; the second blank is the purpose.

Now, let's apply this method to the sample passage above.

- *What* is this passage about? This passage is about methods of ridding the household of flies and mosquitoes.

- *Why* is the writer telling me this? To explain why flies are preferable pests to mosquitoes.

Using the example above, we could fill in that template to read:

In this passage, the author describes methods of ridding the household of flies and mosquitoes in order to suggest that flies are preferable pests to mosquitoes.

The clue to the main idea of this passage comes right at the beginning: Al-Jahiz states that the fly has two good qualities. He then uses the rest of the passage to explain what those qualities are: the ease with which they can be removed from the household, and their control of the mosquito population. He supports this claim by describing the differences between flies and mosquitoes.

Explicit Details

The line "The facts, ma'am, nothing but the facts" may make you think of old TV crime shows, when a grizzled detective questions a witness about the details of a crime. Those detectives wanted their witnesses to tell them some basic facts, including the **who**, **what**, **where**, and **when** of the event the detective was investigating. Similarly, when you read a passage, you should play the detective and note the explicit details, or supporting details, like the place, time, people involved, and location of events.

Identify details in a passage such as names, dates, and events.

Most explicit details are *facts*, or definite truths that can be backed up by specific words and passages in the reading. Think of each passage as a story with a beginning, middle, and end. The facts, or details, make up the **who**, **what**, **where**, and **when** of the story. You don't need to memorize these details as you read, but you should try to make a mental note of where you can find them if necessary to answer a question.

To find details, you must engage in careful reading, because facts can be forgotten or confused. If you've ever followed a recipe, you know how easy it is to confuse ingredients and measurements. You may have added two sticks of butter and one cup of milk to your cake batter when the recipe actually asked for one stick of butter and two cups of milk.

Your best bet in cooking, and in reading questions, is to double-check the passage first. Sometimes an Explicit Details question will provide many similar answers that may sound appealing because they change only one important detail from what is stated in the passage, or because they use almost identical language.

Now, let's look at a few details questions about the sample passage above:

1. The passage states that the mosquito is particularly annoying:

    A. during the day.
    B. after dark.
    C. in the winter.
    D. when flies are also present.

    This is a *when* question: When is the mosquito particularly annoying? (A) might sound right because daylight is discussed in the passage, but in relation to flies, not mosquitoes. (D) might also be enticing, since the interaction of flies and mosquitoes is also discussed in the passage. However, paragraph one states that the mosquitoes are especially bothersome after dark, (B).

2. The passage states that when offered an opening to the outdoors, flies in a darkened room will:

    F. escape from the room.
    G. retreat into the darkness.
    H. fly randomly about.
    J. search for prey.

    This is a *what* question: What do flies in a darkened room do when offered an opening to the outdoors? The first paragraph explains that a good way to remove flies is to darken the room but leave an opening to the outdoors. The flies are attracted by the light and fly out. Therefore, (F) is the correct answer. (G) is contradicted by the passage, and there is no evidence for (H) in the passage. (J) is a misreading of the details: flies will search for prey, but only in a room with the door open and curtains up, as we are told in the final two paragraphs.

In questions about explicit details, you sometimes might be asked to identify something that *isn't* a detail in the passage. Questions of this type will usually include words like NOT or EXCEPT. Thinking back to the recipe example, a question about that recipe might ask you "All of the following spices are included in the cake recipe EXCEPT?" or, "Which cake ingredient should NOT be included in the batter?" Correct answers for NOT or EXCEPT questions like these might be an ingredient that isn't included in the recipe anywhere, or the answer might be an ingredient that *is* included in the recipe, but for the frosting rather than the batter. Again, your best bet for these kinds of questions is to double-check the passage before making a decision.

3.   The passage states that all of the following are characteristics of the fly EXCEPT:

    A. they will fly towards a light source in a darkened room.
    B. they hunt mosquitoes.
    C. they carry diseases.
    D. they can easily be removed from the household.

    While it may be true that flies are known to carry diseases, the passage does not mention this detail, (C).

Development

In the previous section, we discussed how each passage tells a story. Besides the facts, or details in the story, we should also pay attention to how that story unfolds, or how it develops. In this lesson, you will learn to identify two different kinds of passage development: the sequence of events in a passage, and the cause-effect relationship between those events.

The development of a passage is a question of *when* something occurred. However, while in the previous section you learned to identify *when* an event took place in time, say, on "Tuesday at 3:00 p.m.," or in "October, 1996," Development questions will ask you to compare events in the passage as they relate to each other. This is a slightly different kind of *when* that will require you to keep the progress of the entire passage in mind as you read.

> Be alert to the sequence of events to determine when (or if) an event occurred in a passage.
>
> ---
>
> Identify the cause-effect relationships within a passage.

Sequence of Events Development

The **sequence of events** is the chronological order, or order in time, of the events described in a passage. To help you follow the sequence of events, many passages contain **signal words** that clarify the order in which events took place.

Think back to the recipe example we used in the previous lesson. The recipe might read:

"*Before* you begin mixing the batter, preheat the oven to 350°," "*First*, measure out $2\frac{1}{2}$

cups of flour," or "*While* the cake is baking, prepare the icing." In each sentence, a signal word alerts you to the sequence of events: you should preheat the oven before you begin, your first step while preparing the batter is to measure out flour, and you should make the icing at the same time that the cake is baking. Keep in mind that words that signal an event is taking place at the same time as another, like "during," "as," or "while" still place those events in time in relation to each other.

As this brief example suggests, there are many chronological signal words that you might encounter in a passage, including:

- Numerical signal words like "first," "second," or "third"

- Non-numerical chronological signal words like "then," "while," "later," "afterward," "before," "finally," "during"

Look back at the passage (p. 193) and circle all of the signal words you find.

You should have found a few numerical and non-numerical chronological signal words: in the first paragraph, "first" and "then"; and in the second paragraph, "next day" and "then." These words should help you answer questions like these:

4. Muhammad son of Jahm first had a mosquito-free nap after:

    F. his slaves accidentally left his door open and curtains up.
    G. his slaves closed his door and drew the curtains before his nap.
    H. he observed how easily flies could be removed from the room.
    J. his slaves cleared out the flies before his nap.

    This sequence-of-events question should be simple if you noted the signal words in the second paragraph, which tell you that Muhammad first had a mosquito-free nap "on a certain day" when his slaves left the door and window open, (F). This event occurs before the "next day," when they cleared out the flies (J) and closed his door and windows as usual (G).

As you can see from the above example, a sequence-of-events question doesn't always contain the word *when*. Development questions might also ask you what happened before, after, or during another event.

Development questions, like Explicit Details questions, might sometimes ask you about an event that didn't take place at all in the passage. For example, the question might ask when you should add brown sugar to your cake recipe, even though the recipe doesn't include brown sugar as an ingredient. Or in reference to the sample passage, a Development question might ask you when Muhammad son of Jahm became ill after having been bitten by mosquitoes, an event that does not take place in the passage at all. In these cases, read the answer choices carefully, and select one that indicates that the event does NOT take place in the passage.

Cause-Effect Development

The effect that one event has on another creates a **cause-effect relationship** between those events. Because you are developing your reading skills, for example, you will answer more reading test questions correctly. Your skill practice is a *cause*; its *effect* is an improvement in your test performance.

When you are determining cause and effect, you are identifying both the sequence of events and the relationship between those events. Whereas a chronological Development question might ask you when something occurred in relation to other events, a cause-effect relationship question will ask you why something occurred in relation to other events. To determine a cause-effect relationship, you should look for signal words that establish more than a simple timeline. For cause-effect questions you will look for words and phrases like "because," "since," "consequently," "as a result," and sentence constructions like "if...then." "Then" works as both a sequence-of-events signal word and a cause-effect signal word, depending on the context.

Look at the passage (p. 193) and circle all of the cause-effect signal words you find.

> The first paragraph contains "then," "if...then," and "because"; and the final paragraph contains a "because," all of which function as cause-effect signal words. These words should help you answer questions like this:

5.   According to the passage, the hot summer sun makes it impractical to:

A.   open doors and curtains.
B.   eliminate flies from the house.
C.   take a nap during the day.
D.   build a house with doors and windows.

> In the first paragraph, the signal word "because" indicates *why* curtains and doors can't be opened to let enough light in to dispel mosquitoes, because during the summer, when mosquitoes are common, "the sun is unendurable." The hot sun is the *cause*; the *effect* is that curtains must be drawn during the day to prevent sunlight from getting in. So, the correct answer is (A). (B) is a misreading of the details; (C) is incorrect because the passage shows that the narrator does take a "siesta," or nap, during the day. As for (D), it over exaggerates what the passage is saying. It may be impractical to open doors and curtains because of the hot summer sun, but that doesn't mean it is necessary to build a house with no doors or windows.

Vocabulary

As you read the sample passage, you probably encountered a few unfamiliar vocabulary words such as "outstrip," "contrived," and "rebuked." This will likely happen during test time, too, but there's no need to panic. While a good vocabulary is a great asset, you don't always need to know a dictionary definition to understand how a word is being used in the context of a passage. As a matter of fact, you've been learning the meaning of words from their context in a sentence or passage ever since you learned how to read; it's one of the major ways we learn new vocabulary and phrases. Most sentences contain clues you can use to determine the meaning of unfamiliar words.

> Use context clues to determine the meaning of unfamiliar words and phrases.
>
> BASIC
> INTERMEDIATE
> ADVANCED

Here's an example:

> My friend Jason, a guitarist, always plays *lugubrious*, mournful folk songs. Although he is an excellent musician, I wish he occasionally would play more upbeat tunes with happier lyrics.

6. In the context of the passage above, the word *lugubrious* most likely means:

    F. exciting.
    G. depressing.
    H. romantic.
    J. optimistic.

    You know from the passage that "lugubrious" probably has a similar meaning to "mournful," and that the writer would like Jason to play something happier instead. This suggests that "lugubrious" must mean the opposite of happy, so "depressing," (G), which is similar in meaning to "mournful," is the best choice here.

The question and explanation above illustrates two different ways you can determine the meaning of unfamiliar words. One is to look in the passage for synonyms for the unknown word. A **synonym** is a word that has the same meaning as another word. In the passage above, "lugubrious" and "mournful" must be synonyms, since they are separated with just a comma in the sentence. Furthermore, there is nothing to indicate in the sentence that the two words have dissimilar meanings, as would be the case if the passage read "lugubrious, *not* mournful folk songs," or "lugubrious, *rather than* mournful folk songs." The clues instead suggest that the two words must have almost the same meaning.

A second way of determining the meaning of unfamiliar words in a passage is through identification of **antonyms**, or words with opposite meaning to the unknown word.

Suppose you don't know the meaning of either "mournful" or "lugubrious." That's not a problem, as long as you pay attention to other clues in the passage. In the second sentence, the writer states that the tunes Jason plays are NOT happy or upbeat. "Lugubrious" must be the opposite, or antonym, of "upbeat" and "happy."

Let's try another example, using synonym and antonym clues:

> Following her long illness, Gina was *enervated*; she was exhausted all the time and couldn't find the energy she used to have to get through a long workday.

7. In the context of the sentence, the word *enervated* most likely means:

    A. healthy.
    B. excited.
    C. strengthened.
    D. weakened.

> The unknown word, "enervated," must be a synonym for "exhausted," since that is how Gina feels after her illness. Also, the unknown word must mean the opposite of feeling energetic, since we know that Gina doesn't have much energy now. The best answer, then, is (D), "weakened."

Now, try a few related to the sample passage (p. 193):

8. In the context of the passage, *secure* (line 3) means:

    F. restrain.
    G. expose.
    H. protect.
    J. amuse.

> The passage is talking about avoiding the annoyance caused by flies, so you are looking for a word that means "defend" or "avoid," since presumably the unknown word is something one can do to "himself" to avoid the assault of the flies. The unknown word, then, must be an antonym for "annoy" or "trouble," verbs used to describe the action of flies in the surrounding sentences. Of all of the answer choices, (H), "protect," is the best choice.

9. In the context of the passage, the word *rebuked* (line 32) most likely means:

    A. fired.
    B. departed.
    C. praised.
    D. scolded.

Muhammad son of Jahm states that the first day his slaves left the curtains up and door open, he was "very angry" with them. We can assume that since they repeat the mistake later, his reaction would be consistent with someone who is even angrier. This question is a bit tricky, however, because the passage doesn't provide a synonym or antonym for the unknown word. Instead, you must think of a word that would describe the action of someone whose servants had disobeyed his orders. Think of this as a synonym for "punish" or "yell at." Testing the choices in context will prove that only "scolded," (D), is a sensible replacement for "rebuked."

Implied Ideas and Applications

Sometimes an author doesn't directly state the purpose of the writing or what you, the reader, should take away from it. As a good reader, you should follow the clues left by the writer to draw conclusions about the information in the passage.

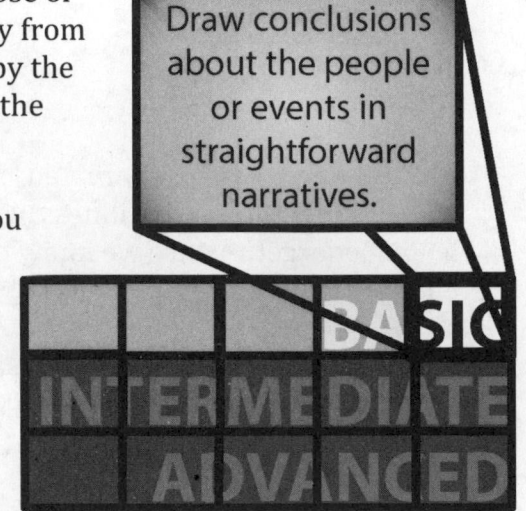

You already do this all the time, particularly when you read or view advertisements. Advertisements don't always state directly the value or purpose of a product, but we are still able to conclude from those advertisements that we should buy a certain product or service. Suppose, for example, that a soda company uses the slogan "Sunny Soda: It Puts the Pep in Your Step!" While the company doesn't ask you to buy Sunny Soda directly, the slogan *implies* that Sunny Soda will give you more energy. The company would like you to *conclude* from that slogan that you should buy some Sunny Soda because it will make you feel energetic.

The passages you are likely to encounter during tests probably won't be as straightforward as the Sunny Soda slogan, but they often work the same way. They might *imply*, or suggest without stating, something about people or events, or they might give you enough information to draw a **conclusion**, that is, a decision or judgment, about people or events. Both conclusions and implications are suggested by the passage rather than stated outright.

Implications and conclusions can be tricky to pick out of a passage, specifically because they require you to do your own detective work. You must gather the evidence and draw conclusions from it. The danger in this kind of detective work is that you might draw conclusions that aren't supported by the passage. Your conclusion about a passage should be directly supported by the passage, and not include any outside opinions or information. In other words, you must carefully consider whether an implied idea or conclusion is supported or not supported by the passage.

In the sample passage at the beginning of the lesson (p. 193), for example, Muhammad son of Jahm does not state the purpose of his experiment, nor does he state the results. Instead, you must look at the clues in the passage to determine these things.

10. The experiment mentioned in line 39 was designed to determine whether:

    F. mosquitoes were likely to bite the human residents of the house.
    G. flies in the house would be an effective control on mosquitoes.
    H. rooms in the house would be cooler with drapes drawn and doors closed.
    J. one sleeps more soundly during the day or at night.

    Muhammad son of Jahm is surprised to learn that he is not bothered by mosquitoes when flies are in the room, so he repeats the conditions under which flies were allowed to stay in the room while he napped. The implication is that the experiment will test whether or not the flies control the mosquito population, (G).

11. You can conclude from the passage that Muhammad son of Jahm's experiment:

    A. proved that mosquitoes do not like bright sunlight.
    B. failed to link the presence of flies with the control of mosquitoes.
    C. failed to prove that flies prefer darkness to sunlight.
    D. proved that flies will control the mosquito population.

    Muhammad son of Jahm doesn't state whether or not his experiment, in which he repeated the conditions under which he wasn't bitten for three consecutive days, proved or disproved his theory about flies. However, since in the last sentence he states that "I made the experiment, and now the end of the matter is that whether we desire to remove the flies or destroy the mosquitoes, we can do it with very little trouble," you can conclude that the results were as he predicted, (D), that the presence of flies meant fewer mosquitoes. Otherwise he would not be able to state so confidently that both pests are easy to deal with.

Lesson 2

Please read the following passage, and refer to it as necessary throughout Lesson 2.

*The passage below is from Gertrude Simmons Bonnin's short story, "The Soft-Hearted Sioux,"
published in* Harper's Monthly *in 1901.*

Beside the open fire I sat within our teepee. With my red blanket wrapped tightly about my
crossed legs, I was thinking of the coming season, my sixteenth winter. On either side of the
wigwam were my parents. My father was whistling a tune between his teeth while
polishing with his bare hand a red stone pipe he had recently carved. Almost in front of me,
5 beyond the center fire, my old grandmother sat near the entranceway. She turned her face
toward her right and addressed most of her words to my mother. Now and then she spoke
to me, but never did she allow her eyes to rest upon her daughter's husband, my father. It
was only upon rare occasions that my grandmother said anything to him. Thus his ears
were open and ready to catch the smallest wish she might express. Sometimes when my
10 grandmother had been saying things which pleased him, my father used to comment upon
them. At other times, when he could not approve of what was spoken, he used to work or
smoke silently.

On this night my old grandmother began her talk about me. Filling the bowl of her red
stone pipe with dry willow bark, she looked across at me. "My grandchild, you are tall and
15 are no longer a little boy." Narrowing her old eyes, she asked, "My grandchild, when are you
going to bring here a handsome young woman?" I stared into the fire rather than meet her
gaze. Waiting for my answer, she stooped forward and through the long stem drew a flame
into the red stone pipe. I smiled while my eyes were still fixed upon the bright fire, but I
said nothing in reply. Turning to my mother, she offered her the pipe. I glanced at my
20 grandmother. The loose buckskin sleeve fell off at her elbow and showed a wrist covered
with silver bracelets. Holding up the fingers of her left hand, she named off the desirable
young women of our village.

"Which one, my grandchild, which one?" she questioned. "Hoh!" I said, pulling at my blanket
in confusion. "Not yet!" Here my mother passed the pipe over the fire to my father. Then
25 she too began speaking of what I should do. "My son, always be active. Do not dislike a long
hunt. Learn to provide much buffalo meat and many buckskins before you bring home a
wife." Presently my father gave the pipe to my grandmother, and he took his turn in the
exhortation.

"Hoh, my son, I have been counting in my heart the bravest warriors of our people. There is
30 not one of them who won his title in his sixteenth winter. My son, it is a great thing for
some brave of sixteen winters to do." Not a word had I to give in answer. I knew well the

fame of my warrior father. He had earned the right of speaking such words, though he himself was a brave only at my age.

35 Refusing to smoke my grandmother's pipe because my heart was too much stirred and sorely troubled by their words and advice, I arose to go. Drawing my blanket over my shoulder, I said, as I stepped toward the entranceway: "I go to hobble my pony. It is now late in the night."

Main Idea and Voice

In Lesson 1, you learned that all writing has a *focus* and a *purpose*, which together form the main idea of the passage (p. 194). You learned how to question a passage to determine the main idea, asking "What is the passage about?" and "Why is the author telling me this?" You also learned that the main idea can be summed up using this template: "In this passage, the author describes _____ in order to _____.

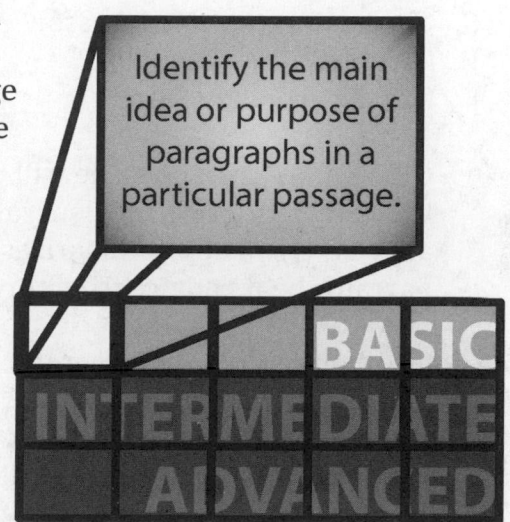

Identify the main idea or purpose of paragraphs in a particular passage.

In this lesson, we will take those skills and apply them to paragraphs rather than the entire passage. A good paragraph has one thing to say in relation to the overall passage, and one thing only. It has its own purpose, its own main idea that is closely connected to the main idea of the passage. For example, a paragraph might provide evidence for the main idea, it might give an example or a counter-example for the main idea, or it might give historical information you need to understand the main idea. These are just a few ways that paragraphs relate to a whole. As you read at the paragraph level, ask yourself, "Why is this paragraph here?"

A question about the main idea of a passage requires you to look at the big picture, that is, at the focus and purpose of the entire passage. A question about the main idea of a paragraph, however, requires you to break down the passage into its component parts, examining each paragraph to determine where it fits into the big picture.

Look at the passage at the beginning of this lesson. What do you think is the purpose of the second paragraph? To answer this question, you must first have a good idea of what the main idea of the passage is. Answer this question first:

1. The passage mainly describes:

    A. a family discussion about the young man's future.
    B. the family history of the father's passage to adulthood.
    C. the tension between the young man's father and his grandmother.
    D. an argument about the obligations of a boy to his family.

The passage describes an intimate family gathering around the fire. The grandmother initiates the discussion by asking the boy when he plans to marry. Then, the father and mother both offer their advice on his future plans. Therefore, the correct answer is (A).

You might also think about the main idea of a passage as something that would make a good title for it:

2.   Which of the following is the best title for this passage?

   F.   "My Sixteenth Winter"
   G.   "Father Teaches Me a Lesson"
   H.   "Grandmother's Opinion"
   J.   "Advice from My Family"

   Often, more than one title will be possible in questions like this, but only one will be the best. Title (F) is too general, whereas (G) and (H) are too specific. The correct answer, (J), neatly summarizes the action of the whole selection, in which the narrator hears advice from three members of his family.

Now, think about how each paragraph relates to the main idea of the passage, then answer this question:

3.   The second paragraph is mainly about:

   A.   the grandmother's opinion that the young man should marry soon.
   B.   the grandmother's suggestion that the young man should wait for marriage.
   C.   the father's suggestion that the young man should become a warrior soon.
   D.   the significance of the red stone pipe to the family.

   Since the main idea of the passage is that the young man is hearing advice about his marriage plans from his family, you can easily eliminate answer (D), since it is unrelated to that point. The pipe is clearly important in the family, but the paragraph is not about the pipe. Answer (C) is a misreading of the passage, since the father actually cautions his son against becoming a warrior too soon, and besides, that conversation doesn't take place in the second paragraph. For the remaining answers, you must read the details carefully. The grandmother clearly asks the young man when he will choose a wife, and proceeds to name off his choices. She obviously wants him to marry soon, so the correct answer is (A).

If you look carefully at the passage, you will see that the paragraphs are neatly organized, and each has a clear relationship to the main idea. The first paragraph introduces the family and the setting for the conversation. Then, the passage proceeds to give one paragraph to the opinions of each family member: after the grandmother, the mother gives her opinion, and then the father gives his. Finally, in the final paragraph, the speaker reacts to all of this family counsel. Each paragraph does one job and one job only.

Explicit Details

In Lesson 1, you learned to identify facts like *who*, *what*, *where*, and *when* that were clearly stated in the passage (p. 195). You took care to double-check your facts before selecting answers because many passages contain facts that can easily be confused (like recipe ingredients), and you also learned to look out for NOT or EXCEPT situations in which you are asked to exclude facts that aren't in the passage or that don't answer the specific question.

Identify details at the sentence or paragraph level in a passage.

Identify the purpose of a specific part of a passage.

BASIC

INTERMEDIATE

ADVANCED

Lesson 1 focused on details that could easily be located in a passage with careful reading. Identifying these details is not always so easy or concrete, however. In more challenging passages, you will be given many *wheres*, *whens*, *whos*, and even *whats*, and you must read the question and passage carefully to make sure you know exactly what details are called for. A passage about the signing of the Declaration of Independence might mention George Washington, Benjamin Franklin, and John Hancock, for example, but if a question asks you to identify the author of the Declaration, you would need to have read closely enough to select Thomas Jefferson.

In the passage at the beginning of the lesson (p. 204), for example, many *whats* are associated with the young man's grandmother:

4.   The passage mentions all of the following about the grandmother EXCEPT:

   F.   she is wearing silver jewelry.
   G.   she is smoking a stone pipe.
   H.   she has a blanket wrapped about her.
   J.   she is wearing buckskin clothing.

   (F), (G), and (J) are all mentioned in the description of the grandmother in paragraph two. (H) is a misreading of the passage. The passage states (in the second sentence) that the young man, not the grandmother, has a blanket, so (H) is the correct answer.

In other cases, you might be given only part of the information, or be asked to generalize from or to rephrase the given details. Instead of the year 1865 as the *when* of a passage, for example, you may have to infer from the clues in the passage that the events it describes took place at the end of the American Civil War. Similarly, a passage about the film director Orson Welles might not specifically mention his name at all, in which case the *who* of the passage might be something more vague, like "the film's director."

5.   It can be inferred from the passage that the narrator was "sorely troubled" in line 35 because:

A. he did not want to disappoint his family.
B. he was not ready to be married.
C. he believed pipe smoke was harmful.
D. he did not like to hunt.

After hearing the "words and advice" from his grandmother, mother, and father, it can be inferred that the narrator is worried about not living up to his family's expectations and disappointing them, (A).

Although complex passages contain many details, it's important that you remember that those details aren't there just to confuse you. Just as every paragraph has a job to do in relation to the main idea, every detail has a purpose as well.

As you consider unusual or seemingly unnecessary details, ask yourself, "What is this detail doing here?" or "Why is the writer giving me this detail?" You might be asked a question that tests your understanding of the purpose of explicit details in the passage.

6.   What is the significance of the red clay pipe?

F. The person holding the pipe will marry soon.
G. Unmarried people in the household cannot smoke the pipe.
H. A person who wishes to speak first passes the pipe.
J. The person holding the pipe is the only one who can speak.

This is a tricky Explicit Details question, since you must pay very careful attention to who is holding the pipe and who is speaking to arrive at the correct answer. (F) doesn't work, since every member of the family holds the lit pipe at some point, and the young man's parents are married; (G) doesn't work, since in the last paragraph the unmarried young man is offered the pipe (even though he refuses to smoke it). (J) might seem enticing, but if you read carefully, you will see that once the pipe is lit by the grandmother, the person who speaks is never holding the pipe while he or she speaks, but instead has already passed it to another family member. This leaves (H) as the correct answer.

Development

In Lesson 1, you learned two ways to understand the relationship of events in passages: the sequence of events in time, and cause-effect relationships between them (p. 197). You learned signal words that indicated those relationships as well. In this lesson, you will look at different kinds of relationships—those between people—and you will also apply the cause-effect skills you learned in Lesson 1 to complex paragraphs rather than to entire passages.

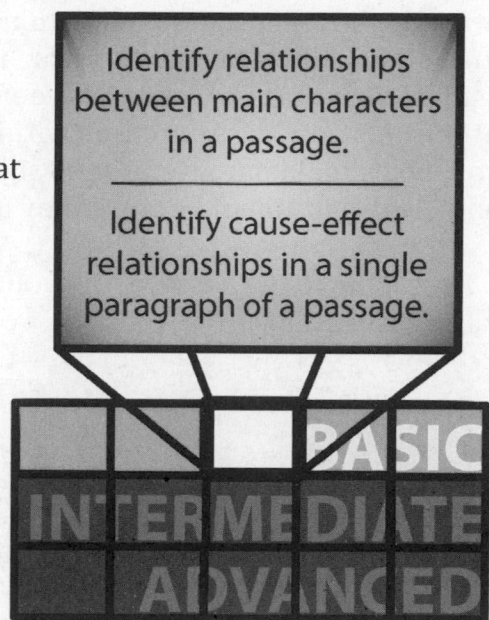

Identify relationships between main characters in a passage.

Identify cause-effect relationships in a single paragraph of a passage.

Relationships Between People

Passages often contain many basic relationships between people, like those between co-workers, family, or friends. Relationships between people, like relationships between events, are signaled by certain words.

Relationship signal words you might encounter in a passage include:

- Family relationship signal words like "daughter," "husband," "cousin," and "niece"

- Non-family relationship signal words like "friend," "boss," "coworker," and "teacher"

Look at the sample passage (p. 204), and circle all the relationship signal words you find.

> You should have noticed many family relationship words, like "father," "mother," "daughter's husband," "grandmother," and "grandchild." Noticing where these signal words are will help you answer questions like this:

7. According to the passage, the grandmother rarely speaks to:

    A. her daughter.
    B. her grandson.
    C. the young women.
    D. her son-in-law.

> The passage states that the grandmother rarely makes eye contact with "her daughter's husband," and in the following sentence it states that she speaks to him "on rare occasions." Therefore, (D) is the correct answer. Circling the family relationship signal words should have helped you locate the part of the passage you needed to answer this question quickly.

Cause-Effect Relationships in Paragraphs

In Lesson 1, you learned some of the signal words that indicate a cause and effect relationship in a passage (p. 199). In more complex passage, cause-effect relationships occur not just between paragraphs, but also within them. Just as cause-effect relationships are signaled by certain words between events in a passage, those same words signal relationships between sentences within paragraphs, as well. As you learned in the last lesson, you should pay attention to signal words like "because," "since," "therefore," "as a result," "so," and "then" because they usually signal a cause-effect relationship.

8.   According to the passage, the young man declines the offer of his grandmother's pipe because he is:

F.   angry.
G.   anxious.
H.   chilled.
J.   determined.

Notice the signal word "because" in the question stem; this suggests you are looking for a cause-effect relationship. The question asks you about a cause-effect relationship that takes place in a single paragraph of the passage: the last paragraph. The narrator's heart is "stirred," and he is also "troubled," and he decides to leave the conversation. The only answer choice that makes sense, then, is (G). There is nothing in his actions or thoughts to suggest anger, (F), or determination, (J), since he has not yet made a decision he might be determined to follow. While (H) might be a good explanation for why he draws his blanket over his shoulders, it doesn't explain why he refuses his grandmother's pipe.

Vocabulary

In Lesson 1, you learned to look for *synonyms* and *antonyms* to help you determine the meaning of an unknown word in a sentence (p. 200). While this is a good way to determine the meaning of an unfamiliar word or phrase, sometimes the sentence doesn't give you any clear synonyms or antonyms. Other times the unknown word or phrase is a phrase or saying that doesn't seem to make sense if you take it literally, even if you know what all of the words in it mean. In short, a word can have different meanings depending on who says it, where it is said, when it is said, and whether or not it is a common saying, or **idiom**. Even if the sentence doesn't include obvious synonyms or antonyms, you can still rely on contextual clues to determine the meaning of unknown words or idioms.

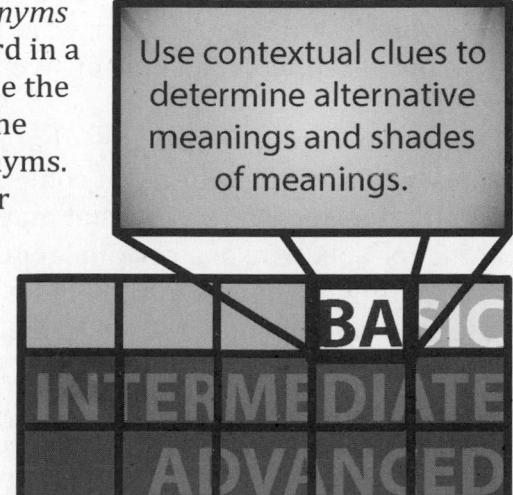

Here's an example:

> Old Joe had a *colorful* past, including the time he spent as a rodeo clown, a few years traveling with the circus as an elephant groomer, and even a month or two he spent traveling around the Midwest as a vacuum-cleaner salesman.

Now, you probably already know that "colorful" has more than one meaning. In this case, the word describes Joe's interesting and adventurous employment history. You probably didn't think that Joe's past was literally painted in many different colors. Even if you were unsure of the alternative meaning of "colorful," however, you could probably guess from the clues in the rest of the sentence that it means something like "lively," "varied," or "fascinating," all of which are synonyms for "colorful" in this context.

Now try this question about the sample passage (p. 204):

9. The word *hobble* in line 36 most likely means:

A. injure.
B. limp.
C. tie up.
D. ride.

You may be familiar with the verb "hobble" already, as meaning "to limp" or "to walk awkwardly," or even "to cause a limp." In the context of the passage, however, those meanings don't make sense. There is nothing to suggest that the narrator plans to do harm to the pony, (A), and (B) doesn't make grammatical sense if you try it as a replacement. (D) doesn't make sense because the unknown word here is something someone would do because, as the narrator states, "it is late in the night," an unlikely time to go for a ride. Even if you don't know that another meaning of "hobble" is "to tie up or tether an animal to prevent it from wandering," you should be able to arrive at (C) by eliminating the other answer choices, and because that is the only answer that makes sense in context.

You can use a similar technique—that is, looking for contextual clues in the rest of the sentence or passage—when you come across an *idiom* you don't recognize. An idiom is a common saying or expression that may not literally make sense, but that has a particular meaning for speakers of a certain language or of a certain culture. Right now, for example, you're "hitting the books," although it's unlikely that you're actually striking a book. The phrase is commonly understood to mean "studying."

Other common idioms in English include "letting the cat out of the bag," (accidentally exposing a secret) and "counting your chickens before they hatch" (acting on expected good news before it actually happens). You probably know or use many more that are even more common, like "that's just the tip of the iceberg." When you hear that idiom, you don't look around for a large block of ice. Instead, you know from context what it means.

Let's try a less common idiom:

These young reporters are *wet behind the ears*; they believe everything our politicians say, and are terrible at determining whether their story leads are credible.

10. In the context of the sentence, the phrase *wet behind the ears* probably means:

   F. inexperienced.
   G. ambitious.
   H. skillful.
   J. disobedient.

Even if you don't know what "wet behind the ears" means, you do know that the reporters are "young" and are making mistakes that those new to journalism might make, such as not questioning the words of elected officials, and not being able to determine good from bad information as they research new stories. This means they aren't very skillful yet, so (H) isn't correct. There's nothing to suggest that the young reporters are disobeying anyone, (J), and although they may be ambitious, the behavior described in the rest of the sentence doesn't describe ambitious behavior, (G). Instead, their behavior is naïve, youthful, and a result of inexperience, (F), which is the correct answer. "Wet behind the ears" is an idiom that comes from newborn babies, who after being cleaned off might still be wet behind the ears.

Implied Ideas and Applications

In Lesson 1, you learned that conclusions are often difficult to make (p. 202). Writers frequently *imply* their points of view and reasoning without stating them directly in the passage. It's up to you to draw *conclusions* that still remain grounded in the passage. In that lesson, we focused on drawing conclusions about people, places, events, and things. In this lesson, we will also draw conclusions about *ideas*.

Make generalizations and draw conclusions about people and ideas.

Conclusions are one way that you can take what the writer **implies** (suggests but doesn't state) and make a judgment or decision based on those suggestions. Another way to use the ideas and opinions implied by the author is to generalize about them. A **generalization** is a way of applying the information, ideas, and arguments in a passage more broadly. In other words, a generalization is a kind of conclusion you can draw about the ideas presented in the passage.

Unlike a conclusion, which is grounded in the passage, a generalization takes a conclusion and asks you to apply it more broadly, either by applying the information in it to a related situation (poor school lunches are a symptom of a larger food-quality problem), or by drawing a further conclusion about the information.

Now, look back at the sample passage (p. 204) and answer the following question:

11. All of the following can be inferred from the passage about Sioux culture EXCEPT:

    A. Sioux braves become warriors only after they are married.
    B. Sioux children do not take their family's opinions into account when making major life decisions.
    C. the opinions of Sioux elders are greatly respected.
    D. the opinions of female Sioux and male Sioux are equally valued.

    This is a thought-reversal question, since the EXCEPT suggests you are looking for a generalization about Sioux culture that is *not* likely, given the information in this passage. While none of these claims are stated clearly in the passage, you should be able to pick out the correct answer by thinking about the broader ideas suggested by the passage and generalizing from them. The narrator clearly respects the opinions of both of his parents and of his elderly grandmother, and both parents also show reverence for the grandmother, so (C) and (D) are incorrect. The words of the narrator's father suggest that a male Sioux becomes a warrior after marriage, so (A) is incorrect. Only (B) is contradicted by the passage, since the narrator's reactions to his family's advice suggest that he takes their opinions very seriously.

EXERCISE 1

DIRECTIONS: Each passage below is followed by one or more items based on its content. Answer the items on the basis of what is stated or implied in the corresponding passage. Answers are on page 810.

PASSAGE I

This passage is adapted from an informational article about flooding.

A flood is an overflow of water that covers lands that are normally not covered by water. A flood occurs, for example, when a stream or river overflows its banks. Small streams are subject to flash floods—that is, very rapid increases in water that may last only a few minutes. In larger streams, floods usually last from several hours to a few days, and a series
5 of storms might keep a river above flood stage for several weeks.

Floods can occur at any time, but weather patterns have a strong influence on when and where floods happen. Cyclones—similar in structure to tornadoes—bring moisture inland from the ocean, causing floods in the spring in the western United States. Thunderstorms are relatively small but intense storms that cause flash floods in smaller streams during the
10 summer in the Southwest. Frontal storms at the edge of large, moist air masses moving across the country cause floods in the northern and eastern parts of the United States during the winter.

The magnitude of a flood is described by a term called the *recurrence interval*, which is based upon long-term study of flow records for a stream. A five-year flood is one that
15 would occur, on the average, once every five years. A 100-year flood is expected to happen only once in a century. It is important to remember, however, that there is a one percent chance that a flood of that size could happen during any given year.

Of course, the frequency and magnitude of floods can be altered if changes are made in the drainage basin of a stream or river. Significantly, harvesting timber or changing land use
20 from farming to housing can cause the runoff to increase, resulting in an increase in the magnitude of flooding. On the other hand, dams can protect against flooding by storing storm runoff. Although the same volume of water must eventually move downstream, the peak flow can be reduced by temporarily storing water and then releasing it when water levels have fallen.

1. According to the passage, the flooding in the northern and eastern parts of the United States during the winter is mainly caused by:

   A. cyclones.
   B. tornados.
   C. frontal storms.
   D. thunderstorms.

2. The author's intention in writing the passage was to:

   F. explain some aspects of flooding.
   G. warn against the dangers of floods.
   H. persuade farmers to use more land.
   J. stop the harvesting of timber.

3. According to the author, flash floods are most likely to be caused by:

   A. large, moist air masses.
   B. cyclones passing over oceans.
   C. summer thunderstorms.
   D. heavy snow storms and blizzards.

4. According to the passage, the magnitude of a flood is measured by the:

   F. season in which it occurs.
   G. size of the storm that causes it.
   H. length of the drainage basin.
   J. recurrence interval.

5. According to passage, what is the maximum length of time that a river might remain above flood stage?

   A. A few minutes
   B. One or two hours
   C. A day or two
   D. Several weeks

6. You can conclude from the passage that increased runoff is one result of:

   F. five-year floods.
   G. deforestation.
   H. dam construction.
   J. cyclones.

7. According to the passage, a flood is defined as:

   A. a period of excessively heavy rain.
   B. a geographic feature of a waterway.
   C. any event happening only once a century.
   D. an overflow of water covering land not usually submerged.

8. The author states that dams help to control flooding by:

   F. temporarily delaying the flow of water.
   G. accelerating the flow of water downstream.
   H. diverting floodwater into other rivers.
   J. permanently storing quantities of run-off.

9. According to the passage, a 100-year flood is one that typically:

   A. happens every year for a century.
   B. takes place once in every hundred flood events.
   C. lasts approximately a century.
   D. occurs only once every century.

PASSAGE II

This passage is adapted from an article on the California Gold Rush.

In 1848, gold was discovered in California, and newspapers quickly spread the word. President James K. Polk confirmed the discovery in his 1848 State of the Union message to Congress. The president's words and the knowledge that taking the precious metal was completely unregulated in California were enough to trigger the greatest national mass
5 migration in US history and a global gold fever now called the California Gold Rush. People used their life savings, mortgaged their homes, and sold everything they had to travel to California in hopes of becoming wealthy. At the time gold was discovered, there were approximately 11,000 non-Native Americans living in California. Between the discovery and 1852, some 300,000 people, mostly young and male, traveled to California from all
10 quarters.

Regardless of where the hopeful travelers originated, the months-long trip was perilous. A journey across the continent meant rough conditions and possibly skirmishes with Native Americans and attacks by other travelers, both of which could result in injury and even death. Those coming by sea from Europe and the eastern United States had to travel around
15 stormy Cape Horn. The sea journey could be shortened by going overland through the jungles of the Isthmus of Panama, but it was a region rife with cholera and other diseases. From San Francisco, getting to the mining areas was difficult. There was little housing, disease was rampant, and food prices were astronomically high.

There were tales of people finding thousands of dollars of gold in only a few weeks, but
20 most miners just encountered hard times. To survive, some left mining or worked for wages in other men's operations. The problem for many was that they couldn't afford to return home, and any news of other people striking it rich would renew hope. Many people lost, but a few lucky ones won. By 1860, approximately $600 million in gold had been mined—more than $10 billion today.

10. In line 3, the word *precious* most nearly means:

    F. legal.
    G. common.
    H. beautiful.
    J. valuable.

11. According to the passage, how many people moved to California during the time between the discovery of gold and 1852?

    A. 11,000
    B. 300,000
    C. 600 million
    D. 10 billion

12. Which of the following is NOT mentioned in the passage as a way people obtained money for travelling to California?

   F. Selling personal belongings
   G. Mortgaging property
   H. Using life savings
   J. Robbing other travelers

13. The passage implies that travelers who crossed the Isthmus of Panama:

   A. generally came from the eastern US.
   B. arrived in California after the Gold Rush.
   C. did so to avoid the trip around Cape Horn.
   D. paid less than others for their trip.

14. In line 16, the word *rife* most nearly means:

   F. devoid.
   G. filled.
   H. immune.
   J. suspected.

15. The author mentions all of the following as difficulties facing travelers when they arrived in San Francisco EXCEPT:

   A. high food prices.
   B. a housing shortage.
   C. widespread disease.
   D. lack of work.

16. In line 11, the word *perilous* most nearly means:

   F. dangerous.
   G. lengthy.
   H. uneventful.
   J. expensive.

17. In line 12, *skirmishes* means:

   A. fights.
   B. trades.
   C. conversations.
   D. contests.

18. According to the selection, many people moved to California because:

   F. they hoped to become rich by mining gold.
   G. President Polk encouraged them to go.
   H. they wanted to open stores to sell goods to miners.
   J. they had no homes of their own.

19. What is the main focus of the selection?

   A. The conditions in San Francisco during the California Gold Rush
   B. The various modes of transportation available during the mid-1800s
   C. The demographic characteristics of the people who came to California
   D. The California migration triggered by the discovery of gold

20. The passage states that some people
mortgaged their homes in order to:

F.   get money to travel to California.
G.   ensure a place to return to.
H.   provide insurance against failure.
J.   purchase gold from California.

PASSAGE III

This passage is adapted from the book Old Indian Days *by Charles Eastman.*

It was now dark. The night was well-nigh intolerable for Antoine. The buffalo milled around him in countless numbers, regarding him with vicious glances. It was only by reason of their natural aversion to man that they gave him any space. The bellowing of the bulls grew louder, and there was a noticeable uneasiness on the part of the herd. This was a sign of
5   approaching storm.

On the western horizon, Antoine saw flashes of lightning. The cloud which had been a mere speck increased to large proportions. Suddenly the wind came, and lightning flashes became more frequent, showing the ungainly forms of the animals like strange monsters in the white light. The colossal herd was again in violent motion in a blind rush for shelter.
10   There seemed to be groaning in heaven and earth—millions of hoofs and throats roaring in unison. As a shipwrecked man clings to a piece of wood, so Antoine, although almost exhausted with fatigue, stuck to the saddle of his pony. As the mad rush continued, every flash of lightning displayed heaps of bison in death struggle under the hoofs of their companions.

15   The next morning, when Antoine awoke, he saw the herd had entered the strip of timber which lay on both sides of the river, and it was here that Antoine conceived his first distinct hope of saving himself. "Waw, waw, waw!" was the hoarse cry that came to his ears, perhaps from a human being in distress. Antoine strained his eyes and craned his neck to see who it could be. Through an opening in the branches ahead he saw a large grizzly bear
20   lying along an inclined limb and hugging it desperately to maintain his position. The bear was completely surrounded by the buffalo. He had taken his unaccustomed refuge after making a brave stand against several bulls, one of which lay dead nearby, while he himself was bleeding from several wounds. Antoine had been assiduously looking for a friendly tree, by means of which he hoped to effect his own escape from captivity by the army of
25   bison. His horse, by chance, made his way directly under the very box-elder that was supporting the bear and there was a convenient branch just within his reach.

He saw at a glance that the occupant of the tree would not interfere with him. The two were, in fact, companions in distress. Antoine tried to give a war-whoop as he sprang desperately from the pony's back and seized the cross-limb with both his hands. By the

30 middle of the afternoon the main body of the herd had passed, and Antoine's captivity had at last come to an end. He swung himself from his limb to the ground, and walked stiffly to the carcass of the nearest cow, which he dressed, and prepared himself a meal. But first he took a piece of liver on a long pole to the bear!

21. By "their natural aversion to man" (line 3), Eastman probably refers to the buffalo's:

A. fear of human beings.
B. awareness of the presence of a bear.
C. aggressive behavior when badly frightened.
D. primitive instinct to look for shelter.

22. The word *ungainly* (line 8) means:

F. graceful.
G. unpredictable.
H. awkward.
J. invisible.

23. The passage implies that the dead bull near the tree (line 22) was killed by:

A. Antoine.
B. other bulls.
C. the bear.
D. the storm.

24. By "unaccustomed refuge" (line 21), the author means that bears:

F. need shelter.
G. live in caves.
H. prefer the open range.
J. rarely climb trees.

25. Antoine walks "stiffly" (line 31) because he:

A. injured his leg in the jump.
B. was in the tree a long time.
C. was bitten by the bear.
D. doesn't want the buffalo to hear him.

26. The bear and Antoine are "companions in distress" (line 28) because they are:

F. constant companions.
G. mortal enemies.
H. mighty hunters.
J. both in danger.

27. The word *dressed* (line 32) is used to mean:

A. adorned.
B. clothed.
C. bound.
D. prepared.

28. The first sign that Antoine has that a storm is approaching is:

F. the restlessness of the herd.
G. flashes of lightning.
H. peals of thunder.
J. ominous storm clouds.

29. Which of the following best explains why Antoine brought the bear a piece of the cow's liver on a pole (lines 32–33)?

    A. He hoped to drive the bear away from the area.

    B. He wanted to share his food with a fellow survivor.

    C. He intended to antagonize the bear and then kill it.

    D. He wanted to learn whether the bear will eat while in the tree.

PASSAGE IV

This passage is from a lecture on adolescence and human development.

Early adolescence is the second most rapid time of growth and change in human development. Only infancy exceeds early adolescence in the rapidity of growth. Children from age 12 to 15 are considered to be in the stage of early adolescence.

Physically, young adolescents are experiencing a growth spurt and the onset of puberty.
5 They have special health and nutritional needs related to these physical changes. More important, however, are the emotional and social changes they experience. Young adolescents are looking for both a sense of uniqueness and a sense of belonging, both separation and commitment, and both future goals and personal past. On the one hand, for the first time in their lives they have awakened to a sense of personal destiny; on the other
10 hand, for the first time in their lives they see themselves as belonging to a particular generation.

Intellectually, young adolescents are exploring values and ideas in a new way. They are beginning to form abstractions, to generalize, and to think about thinking itself. This intellectual development enables them to shift away from an authoritarian and childlike
15 sense of right and wrong to a more open and complex approach to value formation. They also begin to struggle with conflicting concepts like individual rights and the overriding social good.

Because this is a critical time in human development, there is a tendency among many adolescents and adults to be apprehensive about the outcome of this tumultuous period. It
20 is important to remember, however, that the great majority of adolescents steer their way safely through the various dangers of a demanding period of life.

30. What is the most rapid time of growth and change in human development?

   F. Infancy
   G. Adolescence
   H. Early adulthood
   J. Middle age

31. What is the focus of the passage?

   A. The many changes in early adolescence.
   B. The emotional challenges of young adulthood.
   C. The differences between infancy and adolescence.
   D. The ethical development of children.

32. According to the passage, early adolescence is characterized by which of the following?

   I. Increasingly abstract thinking
   II. Reflection on moral values
   III. Rapid physical maturation

   F. I only
   G. II only
   H. II and III only
   J. I, II, and III

33. In the context of the passage, an *authoritarian* (line 14) sense of right and wrong most likely comes from:

   A. other children.
   B. an authority figure.
   C. TV shows and other media.
   D. an internal moral compass.

PASSAGE V

This passage describes the American folk art, fraktur.

Fraktur is a uniquely American folk art rooted in the Pennsylvania Dutch (Pennsylvania German) culture. In German, *fraktur* refers to a particular typeface used by printers. Derived from the Latin *fractura*, "breaking apart," fraktur suggests that the letters are broken apart and reassembled into designs. Fraktur as a genre of folk art refers to a text
5 (usually religious) that is decorated with symbolic designs.

Fraktur was primarily a private art dealing with the role of the individual in Pennsylvania Dutch society and its various rites of passage: birth and baptism; puberty and schooling; courtship and marriage; and death and funeral rites. Special fraktur documents were associated with each: the *Taufschein* or Birth-Baptismal Certificate, the *Vorschrift* for the
10 student, the *Trauschein* for marriage, and the *Denkmal* or Memorial. Of these, the *Taufschein* and the *Vorshrift* are the most numerous. Wedding and death certificates are rare because of the availability of alternative forms of memorialization, the wedding plate with its humorous inscription and the engraved tombstone.

In Pennsylvania during the early settlement era, fraktur art flowered, at least in part, to fill
15 an artistic vacuum that existed in the everyday world of the Pennsylvania Dutch farmer.

While fraktur was produced by folk artists, these were not studio artists producing public art for a wealthy clientele, but individuals who, in addition to their major occupation, produced private art for individuals. The great majority were either ministers in the Lutheran or Reformed Church or schoolmasters in parochial schools. Because of the close
20 association with religious life, fraktur was permitted as an art form in a culture that frowned upon public display in general. As art, fraktur both delights the eye and refreshes the spirit with its bright colors, ingenious combination of text and pictures, and symbols drawn from folk culture. For example, mermaids were often put on baptismal certificates to represent water spirits that, in Germanic mythology, were believed to deliver newborns to
25 midwives who then took them to their waiting mothers. Still, though art, fraktur was rarely displayed even in the home. Instead, it was usually kept in Bibles or other large books, pasted onto the inside lids of blanket chests, or rolled up in bureau drawers.

Fraktur is uniquely Pennsylvania Dutch, but manuscript art did develop in other American sectarian groups. The New England Puritans decorated family registers, the Shakers
30 produced "spirit drawings," and the Russian-German Mennonites created *Zierschriften* or ornamental writings.

34. What is the passage primarily about?

   F. German influences on American art
   G. Fraktur art of the Pennsylvania Dutch
   H. Symbolism in German mythology
   J. American manuscript folk art

35. By "private art" (line 6) the author means that fraktur:

   A. was created by individual artists.
   B. commemorated the lives of individuals.
   C. exhibited Germanic influences.
   D. was a form of manuscript art.

36. The wedding plate and the engraved tombstone correspond to the:

   F. *Taufschein* and *Vorschrift.*
   G. *Taufschein* and *Trauschein.*
   H. *Vorschrift* and *Denkmal.*
   J. *Trauschein* and *Denkmal.*

37. *Flowered* (line 14) most nearly means:

   A. exhibited bright colors.
   B. was publicly displayed.
   C. grew and spread vigorously.
   D. challenged conventional wisdom.

38. It can be inferred that the "artistic vacuum" (line 15) existed in part because:

    F. public displays of art were discouraged.
    G. few people had real artistic talent.
    H. fraktur art was primarily private art.
    J. artistic resources were in short supply.

39. A mermaid symbol would be most likely to appear on a:

    A. *Denkmal.*
    B. *Trauschein.*
    C. *Taufschein.*
    D. *Vorschrift.*

40. Which of the following is NOT a common characteristic of fraktur art?

    F. Humorous inscriptions
    G. Bright colors
    H. Text and pictures
    J. Folk symbols

41. The last sentence of the third paragraph serves further to demonstrate that fraktur:

    A. derived primarily from German roots.
    B. was largely a private art form.
    C. combined both text and pictures.
    D. is uniquely American.

42. It can be inferred that the Puritans, the Shakers, and the Mennonites:

    F. were sectarian groups.
    G. produced fraktur art.
    H. emigrated from Germany.
    J. were Lutheran or Reformed.

43. The author is considering adding the following sentence to the essay:

    In fact, in Europe and also in Pennyslvania, the earlier word for such pieces of art was Frakturschriften *or "Fraktur Writings."*

    If the author decided to add this sentence, it would most logically be placed after which of the following?

    A. The last sentence of the first paragraph
    B. The last sentence of the second paragraph
    C. The first sentence of the third paragraph
    D. The last sentence of the third paragraph

44. Which of the following topics would be a logical continuation for the passage?

    F. A discussion of the wedding plate and engraved tombstone
    G. A biographical sketch of a typical Pennsylvania Dutch family
    H. An analysis of the similarities between fraktur art and other manuscript art
    J. A listing of well-known Pennsylvania Dutch fraktur folk artists

PASSAGE VI

John James Audubon (1785-1851) was an ornithologist and naturalist whose descriptions and paintings of wild birds remain among the best ever made. In this essay on the wild turkey, his superb powers of observation are evident.

The great size and beauty of the wild turkey, its value as a delicate and highly prized article of food, and the circumstance of its being the origin of the domestic race now generally dispersed over both continents, render it one of the most interesting of the birds indigenous to the United States of America.

5 The unsettled parts of the States of Ohio, Kentucky, Illinois, and Indiana, an immense extent of country to the northwest of these districts, upon the Mississippi and Missouri, and the vast regions drained by these rivers from their confluence to Louisiana, including the wooded parts of Arkansas, Tennessee, and Alabama, are the most abundantly supplied with this magnificent bird. It is less plentiful in Georgia and the Carolinas, becomes still scarcer
10 in Virginia and Pennsylvania, and is now very rarely seen to the eastward of the last mentioned States. In the course of my rambles through Long Island, the State of New York, and the country around the Lakes, I did not meet with a single individual, although I was informed that some exist in those parts. Turkeys are still to be found along the whole line of the Allegheny Mountains, where they have become so wary as to be approached only with
15 extreme difficulty. While in the Great Pine Forest, in 1829, I found a single feather that had been dropped from the tail of a female, but saw no bird of the kind. Farther eastward, I do not think they are now to be found. I shall describe the manners of this bird as observed in the countries where it is most abundant, and having resided for many years in Kentucky and Louisiana, may be understood as referring chiefly to them.

20 The turkey is irregularly migratory, as well as irregularly gregarious. With reference to the first of these circumstances, I have to state, that whenever the mast of one portion of the country happens greatly to exceed that of another, the turkeys are insensibly led toward that spot, by gradually meeting in their haunts with more fruit the nearer they advance towards the place where it is most plentiful. In this manner flock follows after flock, until
25 one district is entirely deserted, while another, as it were, overflowed with them. But as these migrations are irregular, and extend over a vast expanse of country, it is necessary that I should describe the manner in which they take place.

About the beginning of October, when scarcely any of the seeds and fruits have yet fallen from the trees, these birds assemble in flocks, and gradually move towards the rich bottom
30 lands of the Ohio and Mississippi. The males, or, as they are more commonly called, the gobblers, associate in parties of from ten to a hundred, and search for food apart from the females; while the latter are seen either advancing singly, each with its brood of young, then about two-thirds grown, or in connection with other families, forming parties often amounting to seventy or eighty individuals, all intent on shunning the old cocks, which,
35 even when the young birds have attained this size, will fight with and often destroy them by repeated blows on the head. Old and young, however, all move in the same course, and

on foot, unless their progress be interrupted by a river, or the hunter's dog force them to take wing. When they come upon a river, they betake themselves to the highest eminences, and there often remain a whole day, or sometimes two, as if for the purpose of consultation.

40 During this time, the males are heard gobbling, calling, and making much ado, and are seen strutting about, as if to raise their courage to a pitch befitting the emergency. Even the females and young assume something of the same pompous demeanor, spread out their tails, and run round each other, purring loudly, and performing extravagant leaps. At length, when the weather appears settled, and all around is quiet, the whole party mounts
45 to the tops of the highest trees, whence, at a signal, consisting of a single cluck, given by a leader, the flock takes flight for the opposite shore.

45. In context, the word *indigenous* (line 4) most nearly means:

A. domesticated.
B. genuine.
C. confined.
D. native.

46. In the context of the passage, the word *unsettled* (line 5) most nearly means:

F. troubled.
G. uninhabited.
H. upset.
J. disorganized.

47. According to the passage, females with broods nearing maturity avoid older male birds because:

A. female turkeys raise exactly one brood per year.
B. the older males may injure or kill the younger ones.
C. additional birds will overtax the limited food supplies.
D. barriers between them are impossible to overcome.

48. The main purpose of the second paragraph is to:

F. define the range of the turkey.
G. compare the turkey to other birds.
H. describe turkey coloration.
J. explain one kind of turkey behavior.

49. The word *mast* (line 21) apparently refers to:

A. part of a sailing ship.
B. groups of turkeys.
C. feathers.
D. edible nuts and berries.

50. The third paragraph is primarily concerned with turkey:

F. hunting techniques.
G. mating behavior.
H. foraging habits.
J. migration patterns.

51. The passage is primarily based upon the author's:

    A. memoirs of childhood experiences.

    B. scientific experiments in the laboratory.

    C. reading of the diaries of others.

    D. direct observations of turkeys.

52. The word *eminences* (line 38) means:

    F. excellences.

    G. nobilities.

    H. prominences.

    J. heights.

PASSAGE VII

This passage was adapted from a book about ancient Greek culture.

Perhaps the best-known of the ancient Greek religious festivals are the panhellenic gatherings at Olympia, in honor of Zeus, where the Olympics originated in 776 BCE. These and other festivals in honor of Zeus were called "crown festivals" because the winning athletes were crowned with wreaths, such as the olive wreaths of Olympia. Yet in ancient
5 Greece there were at least 300 public, state-run religious festivals celebrated at more than 250 locations in honor of some 400 deities. Most of these were held in the cities, in contrast to the crown festivals, which were held in rural sanctuaries. In Athens, for example, four annual festivals honored Athena, the city's divine protectress, in addition to those for other gods. In all, some 120 days were devoted annually to festivals.

10 By far, the largest event of the Athenian religious calendar, rivaling the crown gatherings in prestige, was the Great Panathenaic festival. The development of the Panathenaic festival— the ritual embodiment of the cult of Athena—evolved from a purely local religious event into a civic and panhellenic one. This transformation, and that of the image of Athena from an aggressively martial goddess to a more humane figure of victory, parallels the great
15 political change that occurred in Athens from 560 BCE to 430 BCE, as it evolved from a tyranny to a democracy.

Athenian reverence for Athena originated in a myth that recounts a quarrel between Poseidon and Athena over possession of Attica. In a contest arranged by Zeus, Athena was judged the winner and made the patron goddess of Athens, to which she gave her name.
20 The origin of the Panathenaia, however, is shrouded in mystery. Perhaps it was founded by Erichthonius, a prehistoric king of Athens. According to legend, after having been reared by Athena on the Acropolis, he held games for his foster mother and competed in the chariot race, which he reputedly invented. The first archaeological evidence for the festival is a Panathenaic prize vase from 560 BCE depicting a horse race, so scholars infer that
25 equestrian events were part of the festival.

Much more is known about the Panathenaia after 566 BCE, when the festival was reorganized under the tyrant Peisistaros. At that time, the festival, in addition to its annual

celebration, was heightened every fourth year into the Great Panathenaia, which attracted
top athletes from all over the region to compete for valuable prizes—such as 140 vases of
30 olive oil for winning the chariot race—rather than for honorific wreaths.

From the mid-sixth century BCE until the end of antiquity, when the Christian emperors
suppressed the pagan religions, the high point of Athenian religious life was the Great
Panathenaia, held in July. Every four years, some 1,300 painted amphorae were
commissioned and filled with olive oil to be used as prizes. The accouterments of Athena—
35 helmet, spear, and shield—figured prominently in the iconic representations of the goddess
on these vases and served to identify the stylized figure and to associate the festival with
the goddess. So far as is known, none of the crown games commissioned any art for their
festivals. Yet, ironically, the images that are often associated with the modern Olympics are
taken from the Panathenaic vases.

53. What does the passage primarily
discuss?

   A. The origins of the modern
Olympic games.

   B. Minor religious festivals in
ancient Greece.

   C. Athletic contests centered in
ancient Athens.

   D. Use of military iconography on
Greek pottery.

54. Which of the following is NOT
mentioned as a characteristic of the
games at Olympia?

   F. The games were held in honor of
Zeus.

   G. Winners were crowned with
wreaths.

   H. The games originated in 776 BCE.

   J. The games were held in or near
cities.

55. Which of the following best summarizes the parallel development referred to in the second paragraph?

A.

Time	Athena	Festival	Government
Earlier	Symbol of Victory	Local, Religious	Tyranny
Later	Aggressive Warrior	Regional, Civic	Democracy

B.

Time	Athena	Festival	Government
Earlier	Symbol of Victory	Regional, Civic	Democracy
Later	Aggressive Warrior	Local, Religious	Tyranny

C.

Time	Athena	Festival	Government
Earlier	Aggressive Warrior	Local, Religious	Tyranny
Later	Symbol of Victory	Regional, Civic	Democracy

D.

Time	Athena	Festival	Government
Earlier	Aggressive Warrior	Local, Religious	Democracy
Later	Symbol of Victory	Regional, Civic	Tyranny

56. The author implies that the possibility that Erichthonius originated the Panathenaia is:

F. conclusively proved.
G. a theoretical possibility.
H. without any foundation.
J. a hoax perpetrated by Athenians.

57. The "equestrian events" mentioned in line 25 refer to activities involving:

A. weapons.
B. gods.
C. horses.
D. tyrants.

58. Which of the following was NOT true of the Great Panathenaia?

F. It was held every four years.
G. Contestants competed solely for honor.
H. It began at the time of Peisistaros.
J. It was held in July.

59. What word has most nearly the same meaning as *amphorae* (line 33)?

A. Vases
B. Wreaths
C. Representations
D. Panathenaia

60. *Iconic* (line 35) most nearly means:

    F. nonrealistic depiction.
    G. religious statue.
    H. painted amphorae.
    J. assorted weapons.

61. According to the passage, who is supposed to have created the chariot race?

    A. Poseidon
    B. Erichthonius
    C. Peisistaros
    D. Athena

62. According to the passage, the archaeological evidence for the Panathenaia dates from:

    F. 776 BCE
    G. 566 BCE
    H. 560 BCE
    J. 430 BCE

63. In which paragraph does the author mention objects traditionally associated with Athena?

    A. Paragraph two
    B. Paragraph three
    C. Paragraph four
    D. Paragraph five

PASSAGE VIII

This passage discusses early spirituality and shamanism.

Primitive humans believed that everything around them—trees, streams, and even rocks—contained spirits. Even the sophisticated Greeks believed in wood nymphs.

When humans first settled into primitive shelters, they became interested in the spirits of the sky and the earth and especially in how to prevent them from causing harm to
5 themselves. This concern gave rise to the shaman, a term that originated among the Mongol peoples of eastern Siberia and may be related to their word for ascetic, which means the practice of severe self-discipline. The shaman is a magician, medium, or healer who owes his powers to mystical communion with the spirit world. The shaman protects humans from destructive spirits.

10 Cave paintings, carved bones, and other artifacts indicate that shamanism was widespread 20,000 years ago. Surviving forms are seen even today among Siberians, Polynesians, Eskimos, and Native Americans. The close resemblance in many shaman rituals raises the question of whether practices arose spontaneously in several regions or whether they were spread by prehistoric migrations.

15 Occasionally, it was believed that shamans inherited their vocation, but more often it was thought that they were called by spirits. The calling, an event that could occur anytime between birth and manhood, would be signaled by some powerful sign such as lightning.

Novice shamans were subjected to severe trials, and their final ordination was marked by dramatic visions, trances, convulsions, or seizures.

20 The shaman dealt mostly with illnesses that were believed to arise from a disturbance of the spirit. A shaman might also practice herbal therapy, but most often that was left to a medicine man or other tribal member of lower standing. Through divination, or consultation with spirits, the shaman would make his diagnosis, usually a spirit loss. The shaman would travel through the underworld to locate the spirit and persuade it to return.

64. What is the main topic of the passage?

F. The origins of shamanism
G. The practice of herbal therapy
H. The training of shamans
J. Shamanism in modern cultures

65. According to the passage, the word *shaman* originated with what people?

A. Greeks
B. Mongols
C. Polynesians
D. Native Americans

66. Why does the passage mention cave paintings and carved bones?

F. To show how shamans were trained
G. To show how shamans diagnose spirit loss
H. To show that shamanism is an ancient practice
J. To show that shamanism was widespread

67. What can be inferred about the theory that shamanism was spread by prehistoric migrations?

A. The theory has been definitely proved.
B. Evidence for the theory is inconclusive.
C. Scholars don't take theory seriously.
D. The theory has been rejected.

INTERMEDIATE | Lesson 3

Please read the following passage, and refer to it as necessary as the lesson proceeds.

This passage is an excerpt from a speech by Elizabeth Cady Stanton at the 1848 Women's Rights Convention.

We have met here today to discuss our rights and wrongs, civil and political, and not, as some have supposed, to go into the detail of social life alone. We do not propose to petition the legislature to make our husbands just, generous, and courteous, to seat every man at the head of a cradle, and to clothe every woman in male attire. None of these points,

5 however important they may be considered by leading men, will be touched in this convention. As to their costume, these gentlemen need feel no fear of our imitating that, for we think it in violation of every principle of taste, beauty, and dignity; notwithstanding all the contempt cast upon our loose, flowing garments, we still admire the graceful folds and consider our costume far more artistic than theirs. Many of the nobler sex seem to agree

10 with us in this opinion, for the bishops, priests, judges, barristers, and lord mayors of the first nations on the globe, and the Pope of Rome, with his cardinals, too, all wear the loose flowing robes, thus tacitly acknowledging that the male attire is neither dignified nor imposing.

No, we shall not molest you in your philosophical experiments with stocks, pants,

15 high-heeled boots, and Russian belts. Yours be the glory to discover, by personal experience, how long the kneepan can resist the terrible strapping down which you impose, in how short time the well-developed muscles of the throat can be reduced to mere threads by the constant pressure of the stock, how high the heel of a boot must be to make a short man tall, and how tight the Russian belt may be drawn and yet have wind enough to sustain life.

20 But we are assembled to protest against a form of government existing without the consent of the governed—to declare our right to be as free as man is free, to be represented in the government which we are taxed to support, to have such disgraceful laws as give man the power to chastise and imprison his wife, to take the wages which she earns, the property which she inherits, and, in case of separation, the children of her love; laws which make her

25 the mere dependent on his bounty.

It is to protest against such unjust laws as these that we are assembled today, and to have them, if possible, forever erased from our statute books, deeming them a shame and a disgrace to a republic in the nineteenth century.

Main Idea and Voice

In the previous lesson, you learned that every paragraph has its own main idea (p. 205). You learned to look at the entire passage to determine what relationship the part (the paragraph) had to the whole (the passage). To determine that relationship, you had to make inferences from the information in the passage, since paragraphs don't always clearly state their purpose. The same goes for entire passages. In this lesson, you'll focus on inferring the main idea in passages where it is not clearly stated. You'll also take a closer look at the author of the passage and the tools he or she uses to achieve different purposes.

> Infer the main idea or purpose of paragraphs in an uncomplicated literary passage.
>
> ___
>
> Understand the author's or narrator's approach (e.g., point of view, kinds of evidence used) in uncomplicated passages.

Inferring the Main Idea

Main ideas aren't always easy to determine. A writer or speaker doesn't have to directly state either the topic or purpose of his or her writing, and this is particularly true in literature or fiction writing. Nevertheless, you can still infer the main idea from most passages. As you read, ask yourself: "What is the main idea?" and "Why is the author telling me (or his or her audience) this?" In the passage at the beginning of this lesson (p. 231), Stanton doesn't clearly state the purpose of her discussion of men's and women's garments, and the purpose of the passage isn't clear at all until the final paragraph.

1. The main point of the speech is to:

   A. demand the reform of laws discriminating against women.
   B. encourage women to reject all forms of authority.
   C. ask that men allow women to hold key governmental posts.
   D. invite leading men to sit down to discuss important issues.

   The speech is a protest against laws that discriminate against women. The laws make it so women have no say in government and no control over their own lives. The speech is demanding that the laws that allow women's husbands to imprison them, as well as take their wages, property, and even children, be changed, (A). Stanton is clear in this point when she suggests that "we are assembled to protest against a form of government existing without the consent of the governed."

Why, however, does Stanton include so much information about clothing in the passage? Even if Stanton didn't clearly state the purpose of her speech, you could probably infer a few things about the main idea from her discussion of clothing: that men's clothing is just as restrictive and impractical as men claim women's clothing to be, for example, or that men who claim that women's rights are a matter of complete role reversal as signified by dress are misunderstanding the arguments of suffragettes. Those inferences strongly suggest that the main idea of this passage is to fight for equal rights for women: Stanton's purpose (demanding equality) is expressed through her focus (gendered stereotypes of clothing.)

Considering the Author's Point of View

One method by which you can determine the main idea in more challenging passages is to consider the author's point of view. The author of an essay or nonfiction piece has chosen a subject and a stance on it for a reason. In literary passages, the author shares certain details about characters, places, and events for a reason, as well. When you consider the author's point of view, you are considering the underlying assumptions, beliefs, and intentions held by the author. In some cases, the author directly and clearly states these intentions and beliefs. In speeches and personal essays, for example, authors frequently explain why they have taken a particular stance on an issue by making reference to their personal history and beliefs. Most of the time, however, you must infer information about the author from the passage.

Questions you might ask (or be asked) about the author include:

- What does the author want me to believe?

- What side does the author take toward the topic of the passage?

- What is the author's background?

- Why does the author care about this issue?

- Did the place or time in which this passage was written influence the author?

- Who does the author perceive as the audience for this work?

- What are the author's biases? (i.e. likes, dislikes, prejudices, misconceptions)

- What is the author's reason for writing?

These questions can help you determine the main idea in challenging passages by giving you a better understanding of any unique perspectives from which the author is writing. As a result, you will have a better idea of the main idea of the passage.

2. In line 9, why does Stanton refer to the *nobler sex*?

    F. She believes that men are worthier than women.
    G. She is speaking about the upper classes.
    H. Her audience is made up entirely of women.
    J. She is using a cliché in a jesting tone.

    To answer this question you must think about who is speaking. A speaker at a women's rights convention wants her listeners to agree with her that current laws are unjust against women. She is speaking because she believes that these unjust laws need to be changed. Such a speaker is unlikely to seriously consider men the "nobler sex," (F). Instead, by considering the speaker and the speaker's purpose, you should understand that she uses the term ironically; that is, she doesn't consider men noble at all, (J). This idea is further emphasized by her discussion of the ridiculous impracticality of fashionable male clothing and accessories. Note that answers (G) and (H) are probably true and could be assumed by thinking about the author. However, neither answer explains why Stanton would use the term "nobler sex."

Tone

When you consider what point a writer is trying to make, one of the major considerations you must take into account is tone. **Tone** is the writer's attitude towards the subject, the material, or the audience. A speaker at a graduation ceremony might adopt a serious or inspirational tone; a frustrated parent might tell a teenager, "Don't you use that tone of voice with me!" to imply that the child's tone is inappropriate. Tone can make a huge difference in how we interpret a passage. In the Stanton passage, for example, it was important to recognize that the term "nobler sex" was being used for comedic effect in order to understand what it meant in context. Stanton's tone in the first half of the passage is fairly tongue-in-cheek, or humorous, even though her message is quite serious. You can tell from her tone that she doesn't really believe that men are the "nobler sex."

Tone is important because it helps you understand the direction from which an argument is given. It is also important because tone can be an excellent way to assess the quality of an argument; that is, whether or not a conclusion or implication is well-supported or compelling. It's hard to agree with someone who takes an unreasonably confrontational or overly emotional tone, for example.

You already use and understand a huge variety of tones in your speaking, but they are sometimes harder to pick out in writing, where vocal cues, gestures, and body language are largely absent. Nevertheless, you can pick out the tone of most passages. Think of the difference between these two sentences:

> The new reality show? I watched it, all right. I've never seen such a collection of mental giants. Honestly, I thought it was set at Harvard or something.

> The new reality show was surprisingly intelligent; I hope future shows feature such educated and poised participants.

Both sentences contain more or less the same information: there's a new reality show and the people in it are smart. Both are remarkably different in tone, however. The first is ironic and sarcastic in tone. You can tell by the use of hyperbole (the speaker has "never seen" such intelligence), paired with the false claims of honesty and the casual "or something," that the speaker isn't serious about the claims. While the speaker says the people in the new show are intelligent, the tone used implies just the opposite. The second sentence contains no hints that the speaker might be kidding. Instead, the speaker admits surprise and expresses optimism that the new show is a sign of good things to come in reality programming. The tone of the second sentence is serious and even optimistic.

Words you might use to describe tone include: "playful," "serious," "outraged," "indignant," "sarcastic," "alarmed," "ironic," "funny," "condescending," "skeptical," and "arrogant." An author's tone can also indicate his or her purpose in a passage.

Considering the Purposes of Writing

By this point, you have already learned to identify the purpose of a passage by using the template "In this passage, the author describes _____ in order to _____." Most answers to that final blank, where you would state the *purpose* of the passage, can be grouped into one of three categories:

- **Entertainment:** The writer's purpose in these passages is to entertain. Fiction writing entertains, as do many humorous or personal essays.

- **Education:** Many passages are simply trying to teach us about something: a historical event, how to do or make something, the life of a public figure or artist, a complicated medical procedure, or a scientific breakthrough. The purpose of this lesson, for example, is to teach you about different reading skills.

- **Persuasion:** Persuasive writing tries to convince readers to do something or believe something: to take a certain side of an argument, to take action, to change their behavior, to adopt the author's own viewpoint, to purchase a good or service, or take a trip to an exotic location.

Many passages will have two or even all three of these purposes. A vibrant description of life on a Caribbean Island, for example, might teach you about a culture with which you aren't familiar and persuade you to plan your next vacation there, while still providing an entertaining read. It's up to you to follow clues to determine what the major purpose of a passage is. Even if it contains elements of all three categories, you can probably determine which of the three is the main purpose. If that Caribbean Island description is published in a glossy travel magazine, for example, its purpose is probably persuasive. If it includes mostly bare facts and history, its purpose is more likely to educate. And, if the description is part of a novel or short story, and serves to set the scene for the action, its purpose is likely to entertain. Stanton's purpose in the passage above is to *persuade* her listeners to protest unjust laws that discriminate against women. If the speech was published in a newspaper with a general readership, its purpose might also be to educate readers on gender inequality. Note, however, that her purpose is *not* to persuade women that the laws are unjust—her audience at a women's rights convention probably already knows this and doesn't need education or persuasion on that point; instead, she is persuading her audience of like-minded women to protest.

The Means of Persuasion

To persuade readers, authors use three major tactics, which we can think of as the *means of persuasion*:

- **Authority:** Authors establish themselves as authority figures on an issue to establish credibility that will bolster their argument. Advertisements use this form of persuasion all the time—think of smiling doctors endorsing a vitamin supplement, or a famous athlete performing in a certain brand of athletic gear. The message is simple: if the authorities on this subject believe this, so should you.

- **Logic:** Appeals to logic rely on evidence, facts, and experiments. Articles in the sciences use this form of persuasion, but you can also see it at work elsewhere. Authors appealing to logic may break down the opposing viewpoint and point out its flaws, or they may make correlations between their own position and a similar one to suggest their viewpoint is warranted.

- **Emotion:** Authors frequently appeal to the emotions of their audience. For example, political speeches are filled with appeals to patriotism, pride, or even fear. Guilt is frequently used as a means to drive readers to action, as anyone who has ever read a plea to donate to a cause knows well. The emotions appealed to can range from the noble (honor, love, happiness, and goodwill) to the less noble (cruelty, hatred, anger, or revenge).

While in simple passages, like the advertisements mentioned above, you may find only one means of persuasion, in more challenging passages you might encounter two or three. Stanton relies a bit on all three: she appeals to authority by placing herself in the wronged group and referring to "we" throughout; she appeals to logic by giving evidence that male logic about what suffragettes actually want is flawed; and she appeals to emotion through her palpable anger at the injustice of "disgraceful" laws that "imprison" women.

Explicit Details

In the previous lesson, you began to ask questions about details, such as "why is this detail here?" (p. 207). In this lesson, we'll focus more specifically on these kinds of questions. Some details support the main point of the passage, while others support secondary ideas.

Look at the sample passage again (p. 231). Then answer these accompanying questions about details:

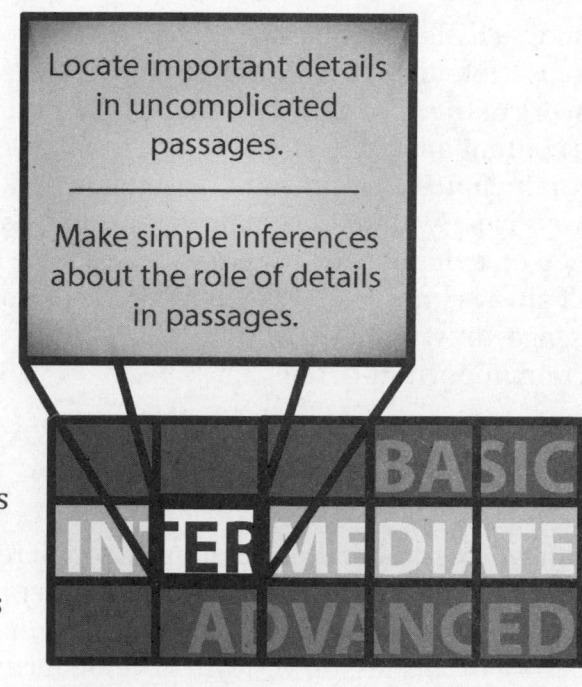

Locate important details in uncomplicated passages.

Make simple inferences about the role of details in passages.

3. The speaker's observation of the fact that the clergy, those in the legal profession, and high government officials wear formal robes shows that:

    A. women's attire is less dignified than men's attire.
    B. men's clothing is more practical than women's clothing.
    C. men, if given the opportunity, would prefer to wear robes.
    D. women find flowing robes and other garments too restrictive.

    This detail doesn't support the main idea of the passage: discriminatory laws are unjust. Rather, it supports a secondary idea: men who reduce women's rights to a matter of clothing don't really understand what suffragettes are fighting for. Moreover, those men are simply wrong about their understanding of gendered clothing. Stanton essentially says: "See, robes (that is, feminine clothing) are considered even by men to be better than pants because really important men wear robes." Therefore, (C) is the correct answer.

4. The speaker mentions "stocks, pants, high-heeled boots, and Russian belts" in order to suggest that:

    F. men's clothing is more practical than women's clothing.
    G. men's clothing is restrictive and uncomfortable.
    H. men's clothing is less restrictive than women's clothing.
    J. women would prefer to dress more like men.

    In lines 14–19, Stanton talks about how these articles of clothing, worn by men, choke and restrict, (G). This detail supports the same secondary point as the previous question: women are not fighting to dress like men. Stanton gives us a few practical reasons why: women's clothing is more aesthetically pleasing, robes and other loose garments are worn by many powerful men, anyway, and finally this point—that men's clothing is impractical and, in some cases, injurious.

In more challenging passages like this one, you might have to infer the significance of details. Note that Stanton never says that the "bishops, priests, judges, barristers, and lord mayors of the first nations on the globe, and the Pope of Rome" are important men; from the content and context of the passage, however, it is clear that these are all powerful men, so their choice to wear robes is significant. Remember that the main idea of a passage isn't always clearly stated; in some cases you must infer it from the text, or draw a conclusion based on evidence in the passage. The same thing goes for details: the purpose of a detail isn't always immediately evident. Instead, you may need to infer it from the rest of the passage, drawing on your understanding of the main idea to determine the significance of certain important details.

Development

You have learned in the previous lesson to recognize cause-effect relationships, family and other personal relationships, and the sequence of events in passages (p. 209). In this lesson you will develop further all three of those skills, learning to create a complete sequence of events in a passage, recognizing other types of relationships between people, places, things, and ideas, and learning to recognize cause-effect relationships in more challenging passages.

> Order sequences of events in uncomplicated literary passages.
>
> Identify clear relationships between people, ideas, and so on in uncomplicated passages.
>
> Identify clear cause-effect relationships in uncomplicated passages.
>
> BASIC
> INTERMEDIATE
> ADVANCED

Creating a Complete Sequence of Events

In Lesson 1 (p. 197) you learned to recognize numerical and non-numerical signal words like "first," "later," "finally," and "afterward" to determine when events in a passage took place. Even when those words aren't present, you can use them to create a complete sequence of events in a passage. This is especially helpful in passages that contain many dates, those that lack signal words, or those in which events aren't written down in the order in which they occurred.

The passage for this lesson above doesn't really contain a sequence of events, but many of the passages you've read up to this point do. Look back at the passage on the California Gold Rush (p. 216), for example. A complete sequence of events for that passage might look like this:

- First, gold was discovered in California in 1848.

- Next, the president confirmed the find.

- After the announcement, men from all over the country flocked to California to look for gold.

- During their travels, those men faced perilous and dangerous conditions.

- By 1852, however, 300,000 men had arrived in California.

- Finally, the rush ended, with over $600 million in gold discovered.

Notice that this sequence of events doesn't exactly match the order in which the same information is presented in the passage. Instead, it details all of the information in the passage in the order in which it occurred *in time*. This means that the number of men who traveled to California, 300,000, occurs later in the chronology than it does in the passage, since the men first had to travel before their numbers reached 300,000. As you read, try to take note of the complete sequence of events, creating your own list of events if necessary. As your reading passages get more complex, look out for events that aren't introduced in chronological order.

Complicated Relationships

Just as you sometimes have to pick up on subtle clues to help you determine the sequence of events, you may also have to read closely to determine more subtle relationships between people.

Think of the difference between these two descriptions:

> When Madison heard Jack call her name, she flinched and then took a deep breath, mentally bracing herself for the conversation she thought was about to happen.

> When Madison heard Jack call her name, she gasped with surprise and excitement, while mentally bracing herself for the conversation she thought was about to happen.

In the first sentence, the relationship between Madison and Jack isn't a positive one; Madison clearly doesn't want to have a conversation with Jack, but feels like she has to. In the second sentence, that relationship is much more positive. Madison is eager to have a conversation with Jack, as signaled by her gasp of excitement. She may have thought he was out of town, or they may be friends who have just made up after a fight. In either case, she is happy to see him. The sentences are nearly identical, but just a few words make the difference between a relationship of tension and one of joy. You must read between the lines, following verbal clues, described body language, and dialogue to determine how characters feel about each other, their surroundings, or a particular situation.

Furthermore, keep in mind that relationships don't just happen between people, but also between people and events, and between ideas, things, and places, as well. A person might belong to a club, for example, or a new product might be the result of a series of experiments. A pet cat belongs to someone; a film is produced by a studio. Locations might exist within or in relation to other locations (parts of a whole like the relationship of a state to a country) such as streets in a city. There are countless relationships between people, places, things, and ideas in your reading; these are just a few of the many kinds of relationships you'll be expected to recognize as you read.

Finally, take note of relationships between paragraphs in reading passages, as well. Now that you're familiar with strategies for determining the main idea of passages and paragraphs, you should be able to articulate how paragraphs relate to each other, and moreover, how the passage proceeds.

5.   Which of the following best describes the organization of the Stanton passage (p. 231)?

   A. The speaker describes a historical event, offers new evidence to support it, and
       then reiterates that the reigning interpretation of the event is correct.
   B. The speaker defines a popular term, explains why that definition is incorrect, and
       then proposes a new definition.
   C. The speaker states a claim, refutes a popular misconception about that claim, and
       then repeats the clarified claim.
   D. The speaker states a claim, provides several separate arguments to support it, and
       then offers evidence for a different claim.

   The answer to this question is signaled in the first sentence, when Stanton claims that "We have met here today to discuss our rights and wrongs, civil and political, and not, as some have supposed, to go into the detail of social life alone." The clue is "as some have supposed...." This signals that Stanton is going to tell us what others suppose, and why that is incorrect. She proceeds to tell us what she is *not* proposing, and through that tactic exposes many common misconceptions about the women's rights movement. Lines 2–4 refute some of the misconceptions about the women's rights movement, and Stanton then returns to her original claim, in lines 20–28, which now has more force. For questions like this, you can also arrive at the correct answer by eliminating some of the choices. (A) is obviously incorrect because Stanton is speaking about current events. (B) is incorrect because the speech is not concerned with defining terms, nor does Stanton propose a different definition for anything in the speech. (D) may look enticing, but note that Stanton only makes one major claim in the speech, and she makes it at the beginning and the end. Therefore, (C) is the correct answer.

More Challenging Cause-Effect Relationships

In Lesson 1 (p. 199) and Lesson 2 (p. 210), you looked at cause-effect relationships within sentences or paragraphs. In some cases, however, those relationships are spread out, so that, for example, the effect of a new school opening in a low-income neighborhood is described at the beginning of the passage, but the cause is not revealed until the end of the passage. For another example, you may read an essay in which a person's unusual hobby is described in great detail, but the motivation for that hobby is revealed somewhere in the middle of the passage. Words that signal cause-effect relationships are not generally used in these cases, and you must read across paragraphs to determine what caused a particular outcome, or what arose from a particular cause. An article about that new school opening might begin with the effects (new businesses in the neighborhood, a drop in vandalism, and a greater sense of community) before revealing the cause of this positive change (the opening of a new school).

Just remember: causes and effects are sometimes reversed in passages, or sometimes spread far apart, so that the effect of an event may be revealed several paragraphs after the cause.

Vocabulary

In the previous lesson, you learned to rely on contextual clues to help you determine the meaning of idioms (p. 211). Idioms are a kind of *figurative language*. Figurative language is any kind of language that doesn't make sense using literal definitions, but that nevertheless conveys meaning in context. If someone says "I'm so hungry I could eat a horse," for example, you don't believe that person is going to literally eat an entire horse. Instead, that person is using a common form of figurative language called **hyperbole**, or exaggeration.

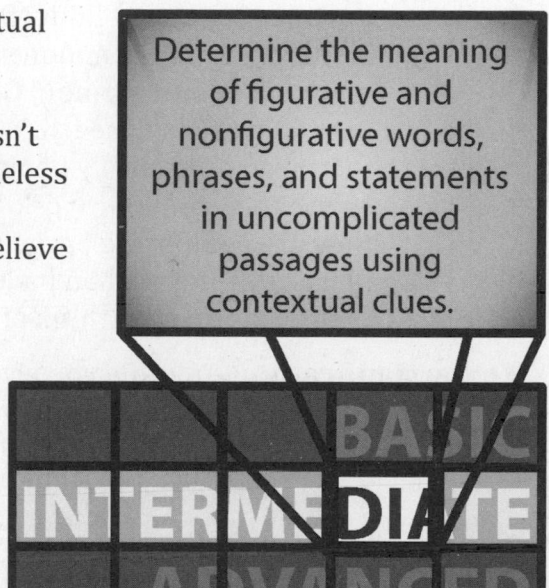

The Stanton passage (p. 231) uses a bit of hyperbole, as well, although Stanton attributes that exaggeration to men, who claim that the women's rights movement means that women want "to seat every man at the head of a cradle, and to clothe every woman in male attire." Stanton suggests that men who make those claims are exaggerating, since that is not what the women's rights movement is primarily about; although some changes in domestic responsibility and clothing norms went hand-in-hand with suffragism, early feminists were not advocating a full reversal of gender roles, as many men feared.

There are five major categories of figurative language, each of which you will encounter in your reading, particularly in more challenging passages. You probably are familiar with many of these categories already, even if you don't know their technical names. Don't worry too much about memorizing these vocabulary words, however. Instead, focus on becoming familiar with the kinds of figurative language you will encounter:

- **Idioms**: You already know this one. An idiom is a common saying or phrase that doesn't make literal sense, but still conveys a specific meaning in the specific cultural context.

- **Hyperbole**: Hyperbole is exaggerated language. Love songs make frequent use of it, with lyrics like "I'll love you until the rivers run dry." When you complain that "There's nothing to do in this town," you are likely using hyperbole as well.

- **Comparisons**: There are two major categories of comparisons, *simile* and *metaphor*.

    o Simile: A comparison between two unlike things using the words *like* or *as*. Examples: poet Robert Burns' famous line: "My love is like a red, red rose," or sayings like "I worked like a dog all day," or "I feel as big as a house."

    o Metaphor: A comparison between two unlike things without using the obvious signal words *like* or *as*. Metaphors can be trickier to spot, in part because they are so common. Sometimes you can spot them right away, as in the opening line of Emily Dickinson's poem, "Hope is the thing with feathers," or the common sayings, "You're the apple of my eye," or "He's my knight in shining armor." Other times they are less obvious because they are part of everyday speech. When someone has "fallen behind in their studies," they aren't physically behind anything. The comparison is between physical space and academic work. Similarly, if someone says "things are looking up," they are comparing optimism with physical space, as if good news is physically higher than bad news. Many metaphors like these are so common that we don't even think of them as comparisons between things.

- **Personification**: Anytime you give non-human things like animals, the weather, objects, or even ideas human characteristics, you are using personification. Examples: "That salsa had a bite to it," "The city never sleeps," "The wind whispered to the trees," "The announcement took me by surprise," "We were in a race against time."

- **Onomatopoeia**: These are words that mimic sounds, like "woof," "crack," "hoot," "bang," and "pow." Many of them are so common that you may not even realize that they are examples of onomatopoeia: "cackle," "jingle," "drip," "flutter," "babble," "giggle," "mumble," and "whisper," are all examples of onomatopoeia. Many of the words we use to describe animal sounds, speech, or sounds that occur in nature belong to this category of figurative language, which attempts to represent sounds or actions with words.

You can determine the meaning of figurative words or phrases, no matter how unfamiliar, by using the same techniques you learned in previous lessons. Look for synonyms and antonyms, or, if there are none, you can infer the meaning of these words or phrases from other contextual clues, like qualities or characteristics associated with the unknown word, re-statements of the unknown word or phrase, or actions that resulted from the unknown word or phrase.

Implied Ideas and Applications

In Lesson 1 (p. 202) and Lesson 2 (p. 213) you learned about conclusions and generalizations, both of which are ways to use information and ideas that are implied but not directly stated in a passage. In this lesson, you will use those same skills, in passages that are slightly more difficult.

In more challenging reading passages, you will be able to draw more than one conclusion or make more than one generalization from the evidence and details. In the Stanton passage (p. 231), for example, you could conclude that many nineteenth-century men misunderstood the cause of women's rights. You could also conclude, based on different evidence, that the women's rights movement was primarily concerned with legal rights, not social causes. You could also make more than one generalization about this passage, such as: those who oppose change frequently misrepresent the cause of those who demand it, or clothing is one of the major means by which cultures express gender differences.

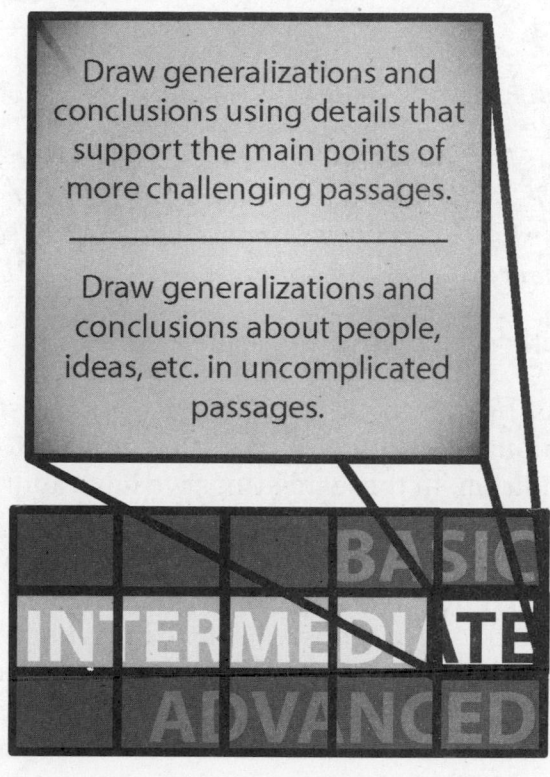

> Draw generalizations and conclusions using details that support the main points of more challenging passages.
>
> ———
>
> Draw generalizations and conclusions about people, ideas, etc. in uncomplicated passages.

You can probably think of more generalizations and conclusions about the information presented in that passage. Keep in mind, however, that *all of your inferences must remain grounded in the passage*, and you should therefore be able to point to details in the passage that support your conclusions. For example, if you concluded that the women's rights movement was primarily concerned with legal rights, not social causes, you could back up this conclusion by pointing out that Stanton tells the audience they have met to discuss more than just the details "of social life alone" (line 2) and that they are assembled to "protest against such unjust laws" (line 26).

Lesson 4

Please read the following passage, and refer to it as necessary as the lesson proceeds.

Henry Highland Garnet (1815-1882) was born a slave but escaped with his parents to New York. He became a missionary and a famous abolitionist, and later served as ambassador to Liberia. This excerpt is from Garnet's "Address to the Slaves of the United States of America," delivered at an 1843 abolitionists' convention in Buffalo, New York.

Brethren and Fellow Citizens:

Your brethren of the North, East, and West have been accustomed to meet together in National Conventions, to sympathize with each other, and to weep over your unhappy condition. In these meetings we have addressed all classes of the free, but we have never,
5 until this time, sent a word of consolation and advice to you. We have been contented in sitting still and mourning over your sorrows, earnestly hoping that before this day, your sacred liberties would have been restored. But, we have hoped in vain. Years have rolled on, and tens of thousands have been borne on streams of blood and tears, to the shores of eternity. While you have been oppressed, we have also been partakers with you; nor can
10 we be free while you are enslaved. We therefore write to you as being bound with you. Many of you are bound to us, not only by the ties of a common humanity, but we are connected by the more tender relations of parents, wives, husbands, children, brothers and sisters, and friends. As such, we most affectionately address you.

Slavery has fixed a deep gulf between you and us, and while it shuts out from you the relief
15 and consolation which your friends would willingly render, it afflicts and persecutes you with a fierceness which we might not expect to see in the fiends of hell. But still the Almighty Father of Mercies has left to us a glimmering ray of hope, which shines out like a lone star in a cloudy sky. Mankind are becoming wiser and better—the oppressor's power is fading, and you, every day, are becoming better informed and more numerous. Your
20 grievances, brethren, are many. We shall not attempt, in this short address, to present to the world all the dark catalogue of this nation's sins, which have been committed upon an innocent people. Nor is it indeed necessary; for you feel them from day to day, and all the civilized world look upon them with amazement.

Two hundred and twenty-seven years ago, the first of our injured race were brought to the
25 shores of America. They came not with glad spirits, to select their homes in the New World. They came not with their own consent to find an unmolested enjoyment of the blessings of this fruitful soil. The first dealings which they had with men calling themselves Christians exhibited to them the worst features of corrupt and sordid hearts; and convinced them that no cruelty is too great, no villainy and no robbery too abhorrent for even enlightened men
30 to perform, when influenced by avarice and lust. Neither did they come flying upon the wings of Liberty to a land of freedom. But they came with broken hearts, from their beloved

native land, and were doomed to unrequited toil and deep degradation. Nor did the evil of their bondage end at their emancipation by death. Succeeding generations inherited their chains, and millions have come from eternity into time and have returned again to the
35 world of spirits, cursed, and ruined by American Slavery.

The colonists threw the blame upon England. They said that the mother country entailed the evil upon them, and that they would rid themselves of it if they could. The world thought they were sincere, and the philanthropic pitied them. But time soon tested their sincerity. In a few years the colonists grew strong and severed themselves from the British
40 Government. Their independence was declared, and they took their station among the sovereign powers of the earth. The Declaration of Independence was a glorious document. Sages admired it, and the patriotic of every nation reverenced the God-like sentiments which it contained. When the power of Government returned to their hands, did they emancipate the slaves? No; they rather added new links to our chains. Were they ignorant
45 of the principles of Liberty? Certainly they were not. The sentiments of their revolutionary orators fell in burning eloquence upon their hearts, and with one voice they cried, Liberty or Death.

Brethren, arise, arise! Strike for your lives and liberties. Now is the day and the hour. Let every slave throughout the land do this, and the days of slavery are numbered. You cannot
50 be more oppressed than you have been—you cannot suffer greater cruelties than you have already. Rather die freemen than live to be slaves. Remember that you are four millions!

Where is the blood of your fathers? Has it all run out of your veins? Awake, awake; millions of voices are calling you! Your dead fathers speak to you from their graves. Heaven, as with a voice of thunder, calls on you to arise from the dust. Let your motto be resistance!
55 resistance! resistance! No oppressed people have ever secured their liberty without resistance. What kind of resistance you had better make, you must decide by the circumstances that surround you, and according to the suggestion of expediency. Brethren, adieu! Trust in the living God. Labor for the peace of the human race, and remember that you are four millions.

Main Idea and Voice

In the previous lesson, you began to think about the author (p. 232). This included analyzing the author's background, motivations, and biases, as well as the author's purpose (to educate, entertain, or persuade). You also learned to recognize different means of persuasion, or different strategies authors use to persuade their listeners or readers. In this lesson, you will learn to apply these skills to more challenging passages.

Together, all of these skills you've practiced so far should help you summarize a passage. A **summary** is a re-statement, in your own words, of the content of a passage. Summaries are an important tool to help you narrow down the main idea of a passage, and creating one will help you practice your comprehension of more challenging passages. Think of it this way: if you had to sum up the passage for a friend, what would you say it was about?

Once you have read a passage a few times, you should be able to rephrase its topic and purpose in just a few carefully chosen sentences. Challenge yourself to summarize the passage in three sentences, then two sentences, and, finally, in one sentence. As you write a summary, try not to look back at the passage for reference. If you need to look back at the passage, you may not understand it well enough yet to summarize it. Also, try to use as little of the language from the passage as possible. A summary should be *your version* of what the passage is about.

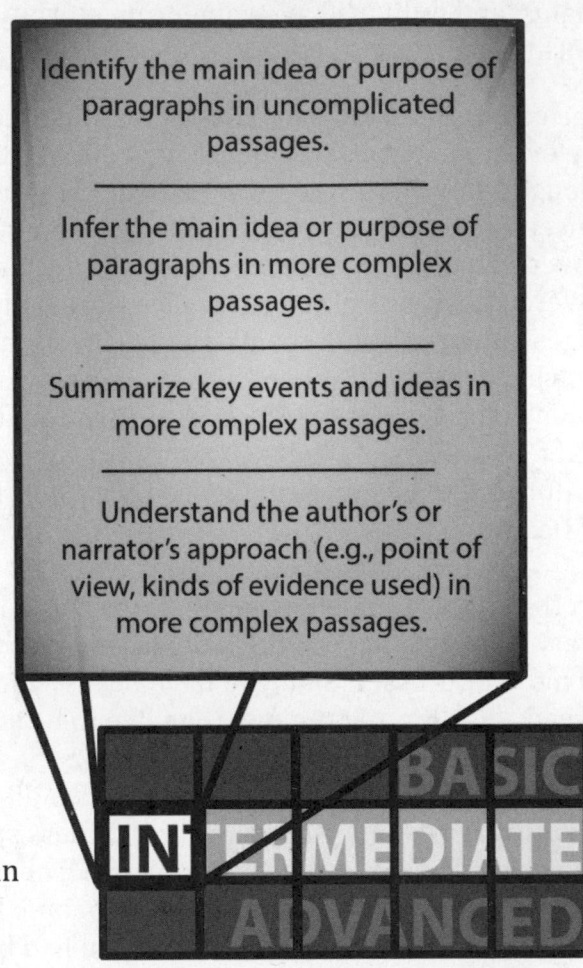

Identify the main idea or purpose of paragraphs in uncomplicated passages.

Infer the main idea or purpose of paragraphs in more complex passages.

Summarize key events and ideas in more complex passages.

Understand the author's or narrator's approach (e.g., point of view, kinds of evidence used) in more complex passages.

BASIC
INTERMEDIATE
ADVANCED

Like many main idea topics, the summary can be written following a template, although the template will vary a bit from passage to passage. Although there isn't a one-size-fits-all template for summary writing, you might start by filling in something like this:

> The purpose of this passage is to _____. To achieve this purpose, the author _____.

Or, you can try this even shorter template:

> In this passage, the author (does/explains/explores/argues something) in order to _____.

Now, let's put your new skills to work using the sample passage (p. 244). After you read the passage, write a summary of it. Then, answer the questions that follow about the author, purpose, and means of persuasion:

A two-sentence summary of this passage might look something like this:

> In this address, Garnet, a former slave, speaks to the enslaved as if they are in the crowd before him, detailing their miserable plight, the extent of their suffering, and the injustices they have endured since they were brought to America unwillingly from Africa. Garnet takes this approach in order to emphasize to his audience of abolitionists that slaves are their family and their brothers, thus suggesting that as long as slavery exists, neither slaves nor freemen are truly free.

This summary makes both the subject and purpose of the passage clear in as few words as possible, but never uses any language borrowed directly from the passage. Your summary of the passage might be shorter or longer, and this example shouldn't be taken as the only possible summary of the main idea of Garnet's speech.

Now, answer a few questions about the passage:

1. Garnet's main purpose in the first paragraph is to:

   A. argue that the institution of slavery can be ended by passive resistance.
   B. prove that, at the time, slavery was practiced in all parts of the United States.
   C. explore the connections between the members of the conference and those who are still enslaved.
   D. argue that slavery is contrary to both moral and divine law.

   > The speech uses a very clever rhetorical device. Though Garnet is literally speaking to the abolitionists who are attending the Buffalo conference, he speaks as though his audience were the people still enslaved, particularly in the South. You'll notice that he mentions "brethren of the North, East, and West" (line 2) in the third person, the implication being that the second person listeners are those still living in the South. Indeed, he calls attention to their absence by using the verb "write to" (line 10) rather than "speak to." He draws a distinction between those in attendance who actively oppose slavery as a political issue and those who are still actually enslaved (lines 9–10). And he notes that the two are joined not only by the issue of slavery but by affective bonds of friendship and family (lines 11–13). So, (C) is the correct answer.

2. The main purpose of the text of Garnet's speech is to:

   F. call for the conference attendees to invade the South.
   G. encourage Southern slaves to rebel against slaveholders.
   H. urge Southern slaves to demand to be emancipated by slaveholders.
   J. call for all persons of African descent to emigrate to Africa.

The main point of the speech is a call for rebellion against the institution of slavery, (G). In line 48, Garnet urges slaves to "Strike for your lives and liberties," and in line 54 tells them to "Let your motto be resistance!"

3. The main purpose of the third paragraph is to point out that:

   A. slavery was an institution that also existed in England and elsewhere.
   B. the Declaration of Independence was greatly admired by other nations.
   C. the American colonies adopted slavery because it existed in England.
   D. rhetoric of revolutionary liberty did not result in the emancipation of slaves.

This question nicely illustrates the difference between details and main purpose. It is true that the third paragraph mentions that slavery existed in England, (A) and (C), and that the Declaration of Independence was greatly admired, (B). But those are details used to make the main point that there was an inconsistency between the rhetoric of the American Revolution and the political practices that followed upon it, (D).

Explicit Details

In Lesson 2 (p. 207) you learned to locate simple details, like *who*, *what*, *when*, and *where*, in a passage, even when those details weren't always straightforward. In Lesson 3 (p. 237) you also began to think about *why* certain details were included in a passage, drawing inferences from the paragraph and the entire passage. In this lesson, you'll isolate those details again; only this time you'll focus not just on locating them and explaining their significance, but also on describing them.

If you've ever auditioned for a play, you probably read over the list of possible characters, which included a brief description of that character's personality. For example, *Edward: A mysterious, middle-aged millionaire who suspects his wife married him for his money alone. Sophia: Edward's much younger and naive wife, who came from a poor family and doesn't understand the social rules of her new class.* These directions give you some idea of how to approach those characters for your audition—how they would speak, what kind of body language they would use,

Locate important details in more complex passages.

———

Locate and interpret subtle details in uncomplicated passages.

———

Discern details, which may appear in different parts of a passage, that support important points in more complex passages.

BASIC
INTERMEDIATE
ADVANCED

and the kind of relationship they would have with each other. In short, the character sheet gives you a description of the *whos* in the play. Listing the characteristics of details in a passage requires you to do the opposite work: the passage gives you the "performance," and you must mentally create a description of the characters or the places described.

As you read, ask yourself these kinds of questions:

- **Who:** What kind of person is this character? What kind of person is the speaker? What adjectives would I use to describe this person? What kinds of adjectives would I use to describe this person's relationship with other people or characters?

- **Where:** What kind of place is this location? What adjectives would I use to describe it?

- **When:** What adjectives could I use to describe this time period? What adjectives would I use to describe this month/week/year?

- **What:** What kind of event is this? What adjectives could I use to describe it? How could I describe this object/idea? What are the qualities of this object/idea?

Also, remember that you must draw support from the passage for your descriptions.

For example, consider the passage for this lesson (p. 244). In the final paragraph, Garnet refers to "men calling themselves Christians." How would you describe those men? Garnet uses the term ironically, since he clearly doesn't consider the behavior of these men Christian at all. You might think of them as violent, hypocritical, uncharitable, cold, callous, and cruel. All of the descriptions are grounded in the passage. Likewise, you could describe *slavery* as it is presented in the passage as degrading, abusive, inhumane, cruel, and unjust. Again, all of these descriptions are grounded in the passage and can be supported by specific phrases and words within it.

As in the previous lesson, you should remember that important details might be scattered throughout the passage (p. 238). Your support for descriptions of details should and will also come from throughout the passage, and not just from the words and sentences immediately surrounding the detail. Think back to the police detective analogy from Lesson 1 (p. 195). To solve a mystery, a police detective will probably interview many witnesses, who will provide many details. The details necessary to solve the mystery, however, might come from any part of the witness's statements. The detective solves the mystery by picking up on the most important details. Likewise, you must draw from information throughout the passage to determine which details are most significant to the passage, and how to describe those details.

Development

In many ways, this lesson will build on the previous lesson, in which you focused on creating a sequence of events for passages, identified more complex relationships between people, places, things, ideas, and paragraphs, and paid attention to passages in which cause and effect are reversed or separated by several paragraphs (p. 238). In this lesson, you will learn about disruptions in the sequence of events, subtle clues for determining relationships, and methods for determining subtle cause-effect relationships in more challenging passages.

Flashbacks and Flash-Forwards

Events don't always take place in chronological order in a passage. Literary passages and non-fiction essays frequently employ *flashbacks* and *flash-forwards* in their writing. Authors use flashbacks to tell us something important that happened in the past that will help us understand the present:

> Shauna turned down the stranger's offer of a ride home. <u>Once, when she was younger</u>, she had accepted a ride home from work one night that she would never forget. That was the summer of 1973...

Understand relationships between people, ideas, and so on in uncomplicated passages.

Identify clear relationships between characters, ideas, and so on in more complicated literary narratives.

Order sequences of events in uncomplicated passages.

Discern implied or subtly stated cause-effect relationships in uncomplicated passages.

Identify clear cause-effect relationships in more complex passages.

BASIC
INTERMEDIATE
ADVANCED

Similarly, authors use flash-forwards to tell us how events in the present have an effect on the future.

> Shauna turned down the stranger's offer of a ride home. <u>Years later, she would recall</u> the incident when she saw that stranger again—this time on a movie screen. She would turn to her friend in the theatre and say...

Both flashbacks and flash-forwards are sudden and sometimes unexpected disruptions in the normal sequence of events in a passage, and both are usually temporary. The chronology is temporarily interrupted by a jump to the past or future, and then returns to the present of the passage. Frequently, they are marked by some kind of signal word or phrase, like the ones underlined above, that alert a reader that a shift in time is taking place. When you put together a sequence of events for a passage, don't forget to stay alert for these devices.

You should also keep in mind that writers don't mix up the chronological order of events just to confuse you. Instead, the writer might use complicated devices like flashbacks and flash-forwards to help you understand a character's motivations, to let you know the long term effect of a decision, or to emphasize a particularly important historical moment. Essays or news stories about historical events, for example, frequently include such devices. For example, an article about the civil rights movement might feature interviews with participants in marches and demonstrations as well as information on how those participants' lives were changed by that historic era. Such an essay would rely heavily on flashbacks and flash-forwards to illustrate the real human costs and payoffs of an important cultural moment.

Making Comparisons

As you learned in the previous lesson, relationships between people aren't always clearly stated; in many cases, you will have to pay attention to body language, adjectives, descriptions, and context to determine how characters feel about or interact with each other. The same thing is true with comparisons. Many of the characteristics of details can be determined by comparing them with other details in the passage. This is a tool authors use to help develop relationships between characters, ideas, objects, and places without directly stating those relationships. In many cases, these comparisons are made without any signal words. Here's an example:

> Jenna and Renee looked nothing alike. Jenna was short for her age, and she wore her brown hair cropped short and spiked up with gel. All of her clothes were black, and most of them were deliberately ripped or torn. Renee was tall and willowy. She was on the dance team, and she dressed like a ballerina: long, flowing skirts, gauzy blouses in pastel colors, and white ribbons she used to tie her long red hair into a ponytail. You can imagine my surprise, then, when Sean told me they were actually twin sisters.

The relationships in this passage are developed through comparison. Jenna and Renee are twin sisters, but their physical appearances are quite different. You can infer from those differences that the twins have very different personalities, as well. Notice that the passage doesn't contain any signal words alerting you that a comparison is being made. Instead, the proximity of the descriptions to each other, as well as the opening sentence, suggests a relationship of some sort between these two women that isn't confirmed until the final sentence. In more challenging passages, subtle comparisons can be made using information from anywhere in the passage.

Subtle Cause-Effect Relationships

Cause and effect might be reversed or separated by several paragraphs. In more challenging passages, those relationships might be difficult to spot. After all, a cause may have many effects, and an effect may have many causes. The author doesn't have to make that clear for you by using signal words or by keeping cause and effect close together.

One method of determining subtle cause-effect relationships is to locate a major event or action in the passage. Then, see if you can answer the following questions:

- Why did this event/action happen?

- What are the effects of this event/action?

Come up with as many answers as you can to these questions. Using the passage for this lesson (p. 244), for example, you might ask yourself: what was the result of Garnet's claim that "Two hundred and twenty-seven years ago, the first of our injured race were brought to the shores of America"? There are many answers to this question, and therefore many effects of the beginning of slavery in America: families were ripped apart, a gulf between slave and freemen was created, slaves suffered greatly, the children of slaves were also enslaved, millions of people have been oppressed, and freemen have become symbolically enslaved. These effects of slavery come from throughout the passage, but none of them come from outside of the passage. Remember that even the most subtle cause-effect relationships must be supported by the passage.

Vocabulary

In this lesson, you will apply the contextual vocabulary-building skills you have already learned to a more challenging passage. Remember that the context you need in order to understand unknown words, idioms, and other figurative language may not appear immediately around the unknown word or passage. Instead, you may need to rely on clues from throughout the passage. Some words or phrases have different meanings depending on the context. As we covered in the previous Vocabulary section (p. 241), figurative language is when something is described by comparing it to something else. These comparisons might not always be obvious, so it is important to use context clues to determine the meaning of figurative words, phrases, and statements.

Determine, using context, the appropriate meaning of almost any word, phrase, or statement in uncomplicated passages.

Determine, using context, the appropriate meaning of some figurative and nonfigurative words, phrases, and statements in more complex passages.

BASIC

INTERMEDIATE

ADVANCED

Answer the following questions, all of which come from the passage at the beginning of this lesson (p. 244):

4. What does Garnet mean by "dark catalogue" (line 21)?

    F. A record of enslaved Africans.
    G. A roster of the slaveholders.
    H. An inventory of nations opposed to slavery.
    J. A list of injustices done by slavery.

    Here, Garnet is using figurative language, since there is no actual catalog containing a complete list of "the nation's sins." (By the way, "the nation's sins" is an example of personification, since the "nation" is an idea, and it can't actually "sin" as a person can.) This Vocabulary question asks you to decipher a metaphor used by Garnet, in which he compares the wrongs done by Americans in the past to a list that might be written down or illustrated in a book. Return to the line cited and try out the choices in context. Only (J) fits.

5. In the passage, what "shines out like a lone star in a cloudy sky" (lines 17–18)?

    A. Enlightened attitudes of a few
    B. Hope of freedom from slavery
    C. Disapproval of the civilized world
    D. Knowledge of the evils of slavery

    This question asks you to identify what is being compared in a simile. The answer choices come from throughout the passage, and while several make sense, only one, (B), is specifically compared to "a lone star in a cloudy sky."

6. The word *eternity* in the first paragraph (line 9) most closely means:

    F. wisdom.
    G. death.
    H. time.
    J. soul.

    Garnet is saying that slavery has existed for years despite the hope that it would come to end. Tens of thousands of people have suffered under the system, their lives characterized by "blood and tears" until they finally die, still enslaved. The metaphor for life here is quite striking. Blood and tears are liquid in form and flow, like streams. These streams of suffering have carried the sorrowful throughout their lives, running their individual courses until they, inevitably, empty into *eternity* or death, (G).

Implied Ideas and Applications

Evaluating Generalizations and Conclusions

Good critical readers feel comfortable questioning what they read. In previous lessons, you've learned to question the evidence (details) used by writers to draw conclusions (p. 213), and you've learned to question the cause-effect relationships stated in a passage by using evidence to contradict what the writer states (p. 243). The same holds true with conclusions. Sometimes a writer comes to a different conclusion than you do about the details in the passage, or the author generalizes something about a situation or character that isn't supported by the details. Even in passages where the conclusion is implied rather than stated, you may find that you simply don't agree with the writer.

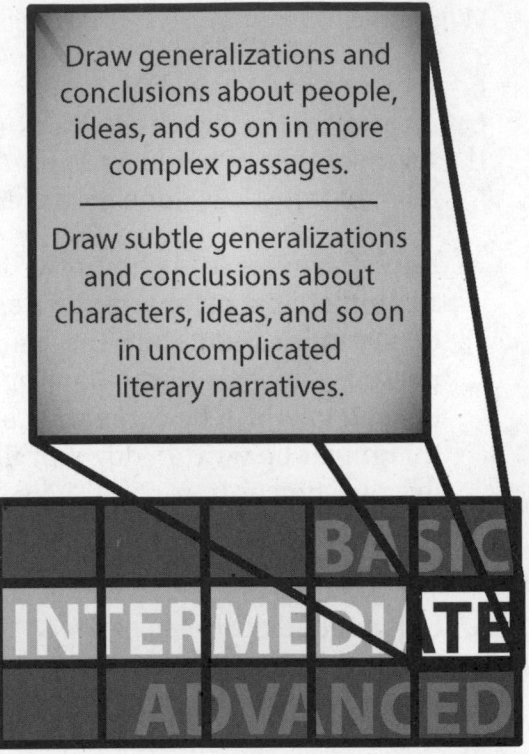

Draw generalizations and conclusions about people, ideas, and so on in more complex passages.

Draw subtle generalizations and conclusions about characters, ideas, and so on in uncomplicated literary narratives.

BASIC

INTERMEDIATE

ADVANCED

Take the following example:

> That cab driver drove us way out of the way last night. I'm sure he thought we wouldn't notice, but I know the fastest way to get to that restaurant. He was probably just trying to put more miles on the meter so we would have to pay more money. You just can't trust cab drivers; they'll do anything to make a few extra bucks.

In this passage, the speaker condemns *all* cab drivers based on an experience with one. Moreover, the author only gives one example of dishonest behavior to justify her conclusion, which is hardly enough evidence to generalize about an entire profession. Also, the evidence that is here could be explained by other details the author doesn't have or chose to omit. Perhaps the "fastest" way to get to the restaurant isn't the shortest in distance, so the cab driver was actually saving the author money. Maybe there was construction or an accident that forced the driver to take an alternate route. In any case, you might disagree with an author's generalizations or conclusions. You should be able to articulate *why* you disagree, though.

Logical Fallacies

There are many mistakes that an author may make that lead to faulty conclusions or generalizations. These errors are called **logical fallacies**, and you should be on the lookout for them when you read. If you've ever read the comments section of an article posted on the internet, particularly one about a contentious issue, you've probably encountered plenty of logical fallacies. Here are a few of the most common ones. As always, don't worry about memorizing their technical names; instead, just become familiar with what these faults in reasoning look like:

- **Slippery Slope:** Conclusions that suggest that if A happens, then after a series of tiny steps, Z will happen.

  o Example: If you fail this course, then your entire life will be ruined.

- **Hasty Generalization:** Drawing a large or sweeping conclusion based on limited or biased evidence.

  o Example: My parents won't let me go out tonight. They must hate me.

- **Ad Hominem Attack:** Attacking the opposing side using personal attacks on character, rather than reasoning or facts.

  o Example: My opponent's immigration reform plan will fail because he is ignorant and reckless.

- **False Cause:** This is a conclusion that is incorrectly attributed to a particular cause or attributed without evidence.

  o Example: The building collapsed after the owners fell behind on the rent. The owners must have caused the collapse.

- **False Dichotomy:** An argument that provides only two possible outcomes, choices, or sides, so that one side can look obviously better than the other. It's usually indicated by an either/or set of signal words.

  o Example: You're either with us, or you're against us.

There are many ways that an author can exhibit bad reasoning, but be sure to explain *why* their reasoning is faulty, even if you don't know exactly what the name for that fault is.

EXERCISE 1

DIRECTIONS: Each passage below is followed by one or more items based on its content. Answer the items on the basis of what is stated or implied in the corresponding passage. Answers are on page 810.

PASSAGE I

This passage explains the applications for geothermal energy.

Geothermal energy offers enormous potential for low-temperature applications. This new technology relies on the earth's natural thermal energy to heat or cool a house or multi-family dwelling directly without the need to convert steam or other high-temperature fluids into electricity using expensive equipment.

5 A geothermal system consists of a heat pump and exchanger plus a series of pipes, called a loop, installed below the surface of the ground or submerged in a pond or lake. Fluid circulating in the loop is warmed and carries heat to the home. The heat pump and exchanger use an electrically powered vapor compression cycle—the same principle employed in a refrigerator—to concentrate the energy and to transfer it. The concentrated
10 geothermal energy is released inside the home, and fans then distribute the heated air to various rooms through a system of ducts. In summer, the process is reversed: excess heat is drawn from the home, expelled to the loop, and absorbed by the earth.

Geothermal systems are more effective than conventional heat pumps that use the outdoor air as their heat source (on cold days) or heat sink (on warm days) because geothermal
15 systems draw heat from a source whose temperature is more constant than that of air. The temperature of the ground or groundwater a few feet beneath the earth's surface remains relatively stable—between 45°F and 70°F. In winter, it is much easier to capture heat from the soil at a moderate 50°F than from the atmosphere when the air temperature is below zero. Conversely, in summer, the relatively cool ground absorbs a home's waste heat more
20 readily than the warm outdoor air.

The use of geothermal energy through heat pump technology has almost no adverse environmental consequences and offers several advantages over conventional energy sources. Direct geothermal applications are usually no more disruptive of the surrounding environment than are normal water wells. Additionally, while such systems require
25 electricity to concentrate and distribute the energy collected, they actually reduce total energy consumption by one-fourth to two-thirds, depending on the technology used. For every 1,000 homes with geothermal heat pumps, an electric utility can avoid the installation of two to five megawatts of generating capacity. Unfortunately, only a modest part of the potential of this use for geothermal energy has been developed because the
30 service industry is small and the price of competing energy sources is low.

1. The author presents the new technology as:

    A. promising but underutilized.
    B. dependable but costly.
    C. inexpensive but unreliable.
    D. unproven but efficient.

2. The passage says that the low price of competing energy sources results in:

    F. a decrease in the cost for installing geothermal heating and cooling equipment.
    G. an economic incentive in favor of the continued use of conventional energy sources.
    H. an expanded reliance on direct geothermal technology for climate control of smaller structures.
    J. an increase in the number of new homes constructed using geothermal heating.

3. Which of the following would be the most logical continuation of the passage?

    A. A listing of geological features of the earth such as geysers and volcanoes that might be potential geothermal energy sources.
    B. A review of the history of the use of geothermal energy and associated technologies.
    C. A description of experimental techniques for converting geothermal energy into electricity.
    D. A discussion of some ways of expanding reliance on geothermal energy for direct, low-temperature applications.

4. The author refers to a refrigerator in line 9 in order to:

    F. demonstrate the feasibility of geothermal technology.
    G. provide the reader with a familiar example of heat pump technology.
    H. illustrate the distinction between direct and indirect geothermal technology.
    J. prove that geothermal energy can cool as well as heat.

5. In line 19, *waste* most nearly means:

    A. geothermal.
    B. exterior.
    C. reduced.
    D. unwanted.

6. Which of the following observations helps to illustrate why the new technology can be used for air conditioning as well as heating homes?

    F. A pool of still water freezes faster than a running stream.
    G. A drink of well water tastes cool on a hot summer day.
    H. Clothes on a line dry more quickly on a dry day than on a day with high humidity.
    J. It feels colder on a windy winter day than on a day with the same temperature and no wind.

PASSAGE II

This passage is adapted from a book about the future of technology.

The catchphrase "information age" is widely used but often with only casual effort to unpack its meaning. For many, this phrase means little more than the fact that computers and associated technologies are involved. Yet, it is clear that we are in the throes of the third great transformation of human communication.

5 Before any form of communication was possible, there must have been human thought. We all have an experience of an inner life in which we look into our minds or reflect upon our thoughts, but our inner thoughts are not, in and of themselves, accessible to others. To be sure, a scream, a sigh, or a grunt may signal pain, satisfaction, or disapproval; but raw experience is not thought. Instead, what was needed was a system of symbols to express
10 thoughts in ways that were susceptible to understanding by others, that is, a code. Speech sounds represent cognitions; and as language has developed, increasing richness and subtlety of expression have become possible.

With speech, the knowledge of individuals could not only be communicated, it could be accumulated, and so society began to acquire a common wisdom—stored usually in the
15 brains of elders. By memorizing the accumulated knowledge and passing it on to successive generations by word of mouth, the product of human minds achieved a durability beyond the life of a single human.

The second transformation occurred with the development of a code that made use of graphic symbols to record speech. The earliest known use of graphics is the cave drawings
20 of the Upper Paleolithic period, 30,000 to 10,000 BCE, but these drawings were not yet a primitive form of writing—only a way to represent important events in the same way as primitive music and dance. The first true use of graphic symbols to codify speech did not occur until around 3,500 BCE or about 500,000 years after humans evolved an oral tradition. The invention of the printing press, which made books, newspapers, magazines
25 and other printed matter available to everyone who could read, belongs to this second transformation.

We are now in the throes of a third transformation in communications, though when it began exactly is difficult to say. One might choose that evening of 1844 when Samuel Morse telegraphed the message "What has God wrought!" Or possibly the invention by Charles
30 Babbage of the "Analytic Engine," a mechanical device that prefigured the modern electronic computer. Or the ENIAC computer developed during World War II, the first digital electronic computer. In any case, it is estimated that it took about 150,000 years for human knowledge to first double, then 1,500 years for it to double again, and that it now doubles every 15 years or less.

7. What is the passage mainly about?

   A. The beginning of the information age.
   B. Transformations in communication.
   C. The evolution of human speech.
   D. The transmission of knowledge.

8. Which of the following most closely matches the sequence of events in the passage?

   F. Writing, thought, speech, electronic communication
   G. Speech, thought, writing, electronic communication
   H. Thought, speech, writing, electronic communication
   J. Screams, thought, writing, electronic communication

9. According to the passage, screams, sighs, and grunts are:

   A. basic thoughts.
   B. word concepts.
   C. raw experience.
   D. psychological states.

10. Which of the following best describes the connection between a word and a thought?

    F. The word represents the thought.
    G. The word creates the thought.
    H. The thought and word emerge together.
    J. The thought represents the word.

11. *Code* (line 10) most nearly means:

    A. system of symbols.
    B. accumulated knowledge.
    C. speech sounds.
    D. thought.

12. *Common* (line 14) most nearly means:

    F. ordinary.
    G. shared.
    H. ancient.
    J. insignificant.

13. In can be inferred that cave drawings occupy a middle ground between:

    A. thought and word.
    B. speech and writing.
    C. writing and printing.
    D. wisdom and computers.

14. According to the passage, true graphic symbols were first used approximately how many years ago?

    F. 150
    G. 5,500
    H. 10,000
    J. 500,000

15. Which of the following is implied in the last paragraph?

    A. Morse's telegraph and Babbage's Analytical Engine were forerunners of ENIAC.

    B. Babbage's Analytical Engine was a more advanced version of Morse's telegraph.

    C. ENIAC, like Babbage's Analytical Engine, was a mechanical computing device.

    D. Morse and Babbage developed ENIAC as a joint project.

16. The phrase *information age* (line 1) refers to:

    F. the world of pre-speech.

    G. the emergence of speech.

    H. the invention of graphic symbols.

    J. the third transformation.

17. What topic might the author logically take up next?

    A. How humans evolved the physical capacity for speech.

    B. Why thought must exist before speech is possible.

    C. Where the earliest graphics symbols appeared on earth.

    D. What the third transformation means for knowledge.

18. The primary purpose of the passage is to:

    F. explain the significance of a phrase.

    G. refute an accepted theory.

    H. predict the course of the future.

    J. propose a solution to a problem.

PASSAGE III

This passage explains how legislatures have changed and evolved.

Legislatures are increasingly becoming highly professionalized bodies. There have been profound changes in the organization of legislative life, shifts in the location of power, and alterations to the instruments by which power is exercised.

James S. Young's account of Washington DC from 1800 through 1828 describes a
5   community of sojourners, people temporarily in a place with little or no expectation of remaining long. Congressmen lived in boarding houses, and the boundaries between the makeshift social life of residents and their political duties were indistinct. Young's Washington was a city of cliques formed around regional and sectional affinities. For the modern legislator, social life has receded to the periphery. Legislators live in apartments
10   and have less to do with one another in groups outside of the formal interactions of the legislative body. Organized political units—conferences, caucuses, committees—have replaced the more personal clique arrangements of an earlier period. Additionally, membership is more likely to be a career in itself rather than a temporary status or a capstone to another career. Indeed, members describe themselves in terms of their status.
15   When asked to list their primary occupation, most describe themselves not as lawyers or business executives but as "legislators."

A second set of changes involves the internalization of control of the legislative body. In earlier periods, it was the Chief Executive who set the agenda for the body as whole. For example, the Chief Executive proposed the budget, and the legislature largely approved it.
20   Or the Chief Executive exercised control through a veto power that was regarded as nearly absolute. Now, legislatures are more likely to propose an agenda and to ignore that of the Chief Executive and to make it clear that a veto can be overridden when the issue is of sufficient importance to the membership. External control also used to reside in the hands of local party leaders who controlled nominations. Now, control over nominations is more
25   centralized and under the direction of legislative leaders.

Finally, there is the change in what counts as an instrument of power. Career legislators plan to be re-elected, so influencing a member's re-election chances becomes an important instrument of leadership. Leaders within the body itself now control the means to a successful campaign and distribute money and other assistance in exchange for loyalty.
30   Additionally, member items, budget allocations to specific districts over which members have considerable control, are an important tool of leadership. And there is growth of centers of policy activity where a legislator has created a special area of influence through expertise and the development of special relationships with influential groups.

19. What is the main point of the passage?

    A. The Chief Executive is now less important than the legislature.
    B. Legislative power is centered in the hands of a few.
    C. Democracy is at risk from recent political changes.
    D. Legislatures are now highly professional organizations.

20. Which of the following best describes the relationship amongst the second, third, and fourth paragraphs?

    F. Three independent arguments in support of a contention.
    G. One main argument followed by two minor arguments.
    H. A claim, a rebuttal, and an answer to the rebuttal.
    J. Three arguments presented in order of their importance.

21. Which of the following terms used by the author helps to define *sojourners* (line 5)?

    A. Community
    B. Temporarily
    C. Boundaries
    D. Indistinct

22. A *clique* (line 8) is a:

    F. governmental agency.
    G. legislative body.
    H. political party.
    J. social grouping.

23. Which of the following means most nearly the OPPOSITE of *periphery* (line 9)?

    A. Center
    B. Permanent
    C. Elected
    D. Later

24. Which of the following phrases could best be substituted for *capstone* (line 14)?

    F. Crowning achievement
    G. Acceptable alternative
    H. Political aspiration
    J. Second choice

25. Which of the following is NOT an example of external control (paragraph three)?

    A. Political influence of the Chief Executive.
    B. Veto power of the Chief Executive.
    C. Local party control over nominations.
    D. Centralized direction of nominations.

26. The controls mentioned in paragraph four would be LEAST effective if used on:

    F. a first term career legislator.
    G. a member facing stiff re-election opposition.
    H. a junior member who hopes for a prestigious party appointment.
    J. a member who has already announced retirement.

27. If the author wished to categorize the instruments of power mentioned in the last paragraph as either direct controls over party members or influence with others, which of the following tables would most accurately represent the author's understanding of those categories?

A.

Direct Control over Party Members	Influence over Others
Distribution of campaign money	Control of member items
Relations with influential groups	Policy expertise

B.

Direct Control over Party Members	Influence over Others
Distribution of campaign money	Policy expertise
Control of member items	Relations with influential groups

C.

Direct Control over Party Members	Influence over Others
Policy expertise	Control of member items
Distribution of campaign money	Relations with influential groups

D.

Direct Control over Party Members	Influence over Others
Policy expertise	Distribution of campaign money
Relations with influential groups	Control of member items

28. Where does the author mention how legislators view themselves?

F. Paragraph one
G. Paragraph two
H. Paragraph three
J. Paragraph four

29. Which of the following best describes the organization of the passage?

   A. The author states a thesis and then supports it with evidence.

   B. The author describes a popular position and then refutes it.

   C. The author explains the historical roots of a political problem.

   D. The author outlines the defects of a political institution.

30. Which of the following would be the most appropriate for the author to include in a fifth paragraph?

   F. Examples of the effects of professionalization on laws passed.

   G. An analysis of the declining power of the Chief Executive.

   H. More details on the social life of nineteenth century Washington DC.

   J. The names of prominent members of the legislature.

PASSAGE IV

This passage discusses alcohol abuse and alcoholism in a clinical context.

Alcohol abuse and dependence are serious problems affecting 10 percent of adult Americans, and the toll is high: 3 out of 100 deaths in the United States can be linked directly to alcohol. In addition to traffic crashes, injuries in the home and on the job, and serious long-term medical consequences, alcohol abuse has been implicated in aggression
5 and crime. The cost of alcohol abuse and alcohol dependence is estimated to be as high as $1 trillion annually.

Although patterns vary, it is possible to classify drinkers as social drinkers, alcohol abusers, and alcohol-dependent persons. While alcohol consumption is never entirely a risk-free activity, these categories represent a range from relatively benign to extremely problematic.

10 An evaluation of treatment for any alcohol-related disorder must be situated historically. For nearly two hundred years, the explanation of alcoholism as a disease competed with explanations in which character or moral defects were believed to lead to drinking behavior. It wasn't until the 1930s that serious consideration was given to the concept of alcoholism as a disease with psychological, biochemical, endocrinological, and neurological
15 implications. Even as late as the 1960s, some researchers still defined alcoholism broadly to include any drinking behavior that had harmful consequences.

Evidence accumulated, however, suggesting that alcohol abuse and alcohol dependence are distinguishable. "Alcohol abuse" refers either to transitory or long-term problems in accomplishing basic living activities in which alcohol is implicated, and "alcohol
20 dependence" describes a severe disability in which dependence brings about a reduction in the individual's ability to control the drinking behavior. This delineation was endorsed in 1987 by the Institute of Medicine which defined alcohol abuse as "repetitive patterns of heavy drinking associated with impairment of functioning and/or health" and discussed

alcoholism (dependency) as a separate phenomenon. Alcohol dependence is associated
25 with additional symptoms such as craving, tolerance, and physical dependence that bring
about changes in the importance of drinking in the individual's life and impaired ability to
exercise behavioral restraint.

The distinction has important clinical implications. For some nondependent alcohol
abusers, drinking patterns may be modified by exhortations or by societal sanctions. For
30 alcohol-dependent persons, exhortations and sanctions are insufficient, and the goal of
modified drinking inappropriate. The goal for these people is abstinence, and a range of
treatment options is available, including pharmacologic interventions, psychotherapy, and
counseling. But even alcohol-dependent persons do not constitute a homogeneous group.
They are not identical in personality, life experiences, family characteristics, or social status.
35 Knowledge of the differences among alcohol-dependent persons is important because
research shows that alcoholism treatment methods are differentially effective according to
patient characteristics.

31. What does the passage mainly discuss?

A. The history of alcoholism as a treatable disease.
B. The difference between alcohol abuse and alcohol dependence.
C. The injurious consequences associated with alcohol consumption.
D. The early view of alcohol abuse as a moral problem.

32. According to the second paragraph, which of the following represents the progression from least serious to most serious uses of alcohol?

F. Social drinking, alcohol abuse, alcohol dependence
G. Social drinking, alcohol dependence, alcohol abuse
H. Alcohol abuse, social drinking, alcohol dependence
J. Alcohol dependence, alcohol abuse, social drinking

33. It can be inferred that the author would consider the conclusions mentioned in the third paragraph as:

A. unfounded rejections of the traditional model.
B. scientific advances, but only partially correct.
C. conclusively proven and valid for current models.
D. irrelevant to the subject of discussion.

34. In paragraph three, the author contrasts which of the following?

F. Disease and moral defect
G. Psychological and biochemical implications
H. Alcoholism and harmful consequences
J. Disorder and alcoholism

35. In context, the word *benign* (line 9) means:

    A. addictive.
    B. immoral.
    C. illegal.
    D. harmless.

36. Which of the following is NOT mentioned as an implication of the early disease model of alcoholism?

    F. Social implications
    G. Psychological implications
    H. Endocrinological implications
    J. Neurological implications

37. Which of the following are used in the passage to distinguish alcohol dependence from alcohol abuse?

    I. Craving
    II. Tolerance
    III. Physical dependence

    A. I only
    B. II only
    C. III only
    D. I, II, and III

38. In context, *homogeneous* (line 33) means:

    F. may be modified.
    G. identical.
    H. important.
    J. research shows.

39. Where in the passage does the author cite an authority in support of the argument?

    A. Paragraph two
    B. Paragraph three
    C. Paragraph four
    D. Paragraph five

40. Where in the passage does the author outline different courses of treatment?

    F. Paragraph two
    G. Paragraph three
    H. Paragraph four
    J. Paragraph five

41. The mention of suicide as a consequence of alcohol-related depression would be an appropriate addition to which of the following sentences?

A. In addition to traffic crashes, injuries in the home and on the job, and serious long-term medical consequences, alcohol abuse has been implicated in aggression and crime.

B. It wasn't until the 1930s that serious consideration was given to the concept of alcoholism as a disease with psychological, biochemical, endocrinological, and neurological implications.

C. The goal for these persons is abstinence, and a range of treatment options is available, including pharmacologic interventions, psychotherapy, and counseling.

D. They exhibit differences in personality, life experiences, family characteristics and social status.

42. The passage is primarily concerned with:

F. drawing a distinction.
G. refuting a theory.
H. cataloguing sources.
J. criticizing behavior.

43. The most logical continuation of the passage would be:

A. further information about alcoholism as a moral problem.
B. an explanation of the physical effects of alcohol on the brain.
C. a brief historical summary of the attitudes toward alcohol.
D. a more detailed discussion of treatments for alcohol dependence.

PASSAGE V

This passage discusses early criminal law.

Early criminal law, which grew out of the blood feud, was almost totally lacking in the modern ethical notion of wrongdoing. Wherever a barbaric society was organized along the lines of blood kinship, revenge aimed not at atonement for the bodily harm inflicted but for the humiliation suffered by the family unit. So too, the primary goal of the early law was to
5 provide an alternative to the feud by substituting a system of monetary compensation, and there emerged a definite tariff or *wer* with amounts reflecting the affront to clan dignity. Thus, the Welsh King Howell the Good decreed that a scar on the face was worth eighty pence, while the permanent loss of a thumb (an injury that would disable the hand) brought only seventy-six pence.

10 In a parallel development, the institution of the *deodand* for cases involving a fatality required the surrender of the agent of death, whether that was a sword, a cart, a millwheel, or even an ox. It was not even required that the object have been under the direct control of the owner at the time, as in a case involving a sword hanging on a wall that fell killing a visitor. The fact that early law attributed responsibility to insensible objects is further

15 indication that the notion of ethical wrongdoing was a much later innovation.

44. What is the main topic of the selection?

   F. The significance of *wer* and *deodand*.
   G. The history of the death penalty.
   H. The origins of the blood feud.
   J. Modern notions of criminal liability.

45. The author cites the decree of King Howell the Good in order to:

   A. clarify the distinction between the *wer* and the *deodand*.
   B. prevent misunderstanding about forfeiture in cases resulting in fatalities.
   C. show that violence was common during the era of the blood feud.
   D. prove that the *wer* compensated the clan for loss of honor.

46. The author's argument would be most strengthened by an early case in which:

   F. the *wer* for a visible bruise was double that for a similar bruise concealed by clothing.
   G. the owner of an object had to forfeit it after using it to inflict injury.
   H. the *deodand* did not apply because the instrument of death had been misused.
   J. the payment for two persons of unequal rank was the same.

47. According to the selection, the primary purpose of the *wer* was to:

   A. deter people from injuring one another.
   B. provide alternative dispute resolution.
   C. punish wrongdoers for breaking the law.
   D. prevent clan members from suing one another.

48. In line 10, the word *parallel* most nearly means:

   F. violent.
   G. unending.
   H. similar.
   J. legal.

49. In line 14, the word *insensible* most nearly means:

A. inanimate.
B. dangerous.
C. unconscious.
D. useful.

50. The author mentions the sword in line 13 because:

F. people in violent societies frequently use arms.
G. it was not being used by anyone at the time of the death.
H. a sword is dangerous no matter who uses it.
J. a sword wound is usually worse than a farming injury.

51. In line 6, the word *affront* most nearly means:

A. advancement.
B. fatality.
C. insult.
D. atonement.

52. In line 6, the word *definite* most nearly means:

F. changeable.
G. expensive.
H. optional.
J. fixed.

53. The word *clan* in line 6 refers to what phrase used earlier in that paragraph?

A. Family unit
B. Blood feud
C. Ethical notion
D. Barbaric society

PASSAGE VI

This passage describes the impact of open government statutes in California.

Open government statutes in California have proved both beneficial and harmful. In the energy commission, for example, as in other government commissions, nearly all decisions must be made in a public session for which at least seven days' notice must be given. (Two notable exceptions to public participation in commission meetings are meetings that are
5   held to discuss pending litigation and meetings held to discuss staff personnel matters.) The determination of which decisions can be made by the executive director and which are strictly reserved for the commission becomes quite important in this context. If something is a matter for the commission, there must be a public hearing with attendant publicity and preparation of materials for distribution at the meeting. (A formal delegation of authority
10 authorizes the executive director to make purchases of goods and services, including consulting services, costing less than $5,000.)

Furthermore, no more than three of the commission's five commissioners may meet informally with one another or with the executive director or any member of his staff to discuss commission activities. Such behavior would be a violation of open government

15 statutes. Staff briefings must take place commissioner by commissioner or through a commissioner's advisers. More frequently, commissioners or their advisers contact the staff for information, but all such requests must be submitted in writing.

An example of the impact of open government on the operating procedures of a commission is the energy commission's budgetary process. The budget for the commission,
20 unlike that prepared in other state agencies, was prepared in a public session by the five commissioners. The session was not simply a "review and comment" session, since the commissioners had not previously discussed the budget. Every item proposed for the budget could be commented on by anyone who attended the hearings. The budget was then forwarded to the governor's office prior to submission to the legislature as part of the
25 executive budget. In a recent case involving development of regulations to ban the use of gas pilot lights in new equipment sold in the state, much of the actual development of the regulations was performed by an advisory committee of both environmental and industrial representatives in public workshops.

Perhaps open government's effect has been greatest in the promulgation of rules and
30 regulations. Complaints have arisen from the news media and several legislators about the slowness of the energy commission in setting regulations. In fact, the commission may be unable to meet the original legislatively mandated deadlines for several sets of regulations, including standards for newly constructed nonresidential buildings. If, however, a commission attempts to handle more matters without input from state agencies and
35 interested groups in open meetings, it will be criticized for circumventing the open government intentions of the legislation. Thus, if present practices continue, the commission will continue to be criticized for moving too slowly; but if it attempts to move more quickly, the commissioners open themselves up to charges of attempting to circumvent the letter and spirit of the open government law.

54. The author is primarily concerned with discussing the:

F. disadvantages of California's open government legislation.

G. effect of an open government statute on California's energy commission.

H. methods by which California energy commissioners obtain information.

J. energy policies adopted by the California Energy Commission under the open government statute.

55. The passage implies the open government statute is intended to accomplish all of the following EXCEPT:

  A. to minimize the likelihood of secret political deals.
  B. to allow an opportunity for the public to influence government decisions.
  C. to ensure that government officials are held accountable for their policies.
  D. to guarantee that a government agency can respond quickly to a problem.

56. The passage most strongly supports which of the following conclusions about a decision that is within the authority of the executive director of an agency?

  F. It would be made more quickly than a decision reserved for a commission.
  G. It would be made with the assistance of the agency's commissioners.
  H. It would be a highly publicized event attended by members of the media.
  J. It would deal with a matter of greater importance than those handled by the commission.

57. In the final paragraph, the author discusses:

  A. an analogy.
  B. a theory.
  C. a contradiction.
  D. a dilemma.

58. The author makes all of the following points about the rules governing the commission EXCEPT:

  F. public sessions can be held only on seven days' notice.
  G. at a public session, anyone wishing to be heard may comment.
  H. meetings to discuss personnel matters do not require a public hearing.
  J. a meeting of commissioners cannot be held without a quorum of three commissioners.

59. It can be inferred from the passage that the executive director is authorized to make certain purchases costing less than $5,000 in order to:

  A. avoid the necessity of holding public hearings on routine matters.
  B. take the commission's budget outside the scope of public review.
  C. allow commissioners to make their own decisions on matters of staffing.
  D. protect the executive director from being sued as an individual.

60. Which of the following statements about a "review and comment" session can be inferred from the selection?

F. A "review and comment" session is held to provide members of the legislature with an opportunity to ask commissioners to justify their budget requests.
G. A "review and comment" session is likely to be much lengthier and more detailed than public sessions required by the open government statute.
H. A "review and comment" session is held to invite those in attendance to remark on decisions that already have been made.
J. At a "review and comment" session, the public is given an opportunity to ask specific questions of government officials.

61. The author's primary concern is to:

A. criticize a government agency.
B. analyze the functioning of a government agency.
C. propose changes in government regulations.
D. respond to criticisms.

62. The author's treatment of the subject matter of the selection can best be described as:

F. unemotional and objective.
G. detached and indifferent.
H. enthusiastic and supportive.
J. mistrustful and skeptical.

PASSAGE VII

This passage describes the history of the American apprenticeship system.

At the beginning of the nineteenth century, skilled workers enjoyed the benefits of a well-organized apprenticeship system. Skilled workers were differentiated from unskilled workers by their knowledge of a specific skill which provided the opportunity for better earnings and for advancement. The unskilled fared poorly, with laborers, weavers, and mill
5 workers, who constituted perhaps forty percent of the urban working class, receiving about a dollar per day. Skilled workers—variously known as craftsman, artisans, or mechanics—were paid nearly double that. The tools they owned and their proficiency in using them gave skilled workers marketable assets. Working independently or with others in small shops directed by master craftsmen who supervised the production of goods for a custom
10 market, young apprentices could realistically anticipate becoming journeymen and even masters someday.

The technological and economic changes of the nineteenth century had a marked impact on the American apprenticeship system. Improvements in turnpikes or toll roads were

followed by "canal fever" accompanied by the appearance of steamboats. In the 1830s and
15 1840s, railroads were built. The resulting sharp reduction in transportation costs enabled
sellers to compete successfully in distant markets, opening up great profit-making
opportunities to efficient large-scale manufacturers. Limited custom order and local trade
gave way to a massive national market, inevitably affecting the conditions of the workers
who produced for this market.

20 Merchants increasingly assumed control not only over the sale of goods but over their
production. Their possession of substantial capital and easy access to credit enabled them
to contract for massive orders all over the country. The size of their operations enabled
them to cut prices below those fixed by masters and journeymen.

On the surface little seemed to have changed. In the typical shop, the master was still the
25 chief, and the apprentices and journeymen he presided over still owned their tools. Their
style of work in many cases differed little from what it had been in the eighteenth century.
But now the merchant capitalist supplied the raw materials and owned and marketed the
finished product made in the shop. The masters became small contractors employed by the
merchant capitalist and, in turn, employed one to a dozen apprentices and journeymen.
30 Since the profits of masters came solely out of wages and work, they sought to lessen
dependence on skill and to increase speed of output. To increase profits, masters demanded
greater productivity from skilled workers and resorted to cheaper labor—prisoners,
women, children, and the unskilled. Under the increasing economic pressure, the
apprentice system eventually broke down.

63. What is the passage primarily concerned with?

   A. The fairness of compensation paid to laborers.
   B. The decline and collapse of the apprentice system.
   C. The history of different modes of transportation.
   D. The living conditions of unskilled laborers.

64. Which of the following was NOT a skilled worker?

   F. Mechanic
   G. Artisan
   H. Craftsman
   J. Weaver

65. Which of the following did NOT separate the skilled worker from the unskilled worker?

   A. Geographical location of the workplace.
   B. Ownership of the tools of the trade.
   C. Ability to use tools to make goods.
   D. Prospect of advancement within the trade.

66. *Proficiency* (line 7) most nearly means:

   F. effort.
   G. skill.
   H. direction.
   J. independence.

67. The possibility of filling orders for a national market was due to:

   A. changed conditions for all workers.
   B. new machinery for producing goods.
   C. advances in modes of transportation.
   D. decreased demand for local goods.

68. Which of the following did NOT contribute to the rise of the merchants?

   F. Easy access to credit.
   G. Cheaper transportation.
   H. Shortage of skilled labor.
   J. Control over substantial capital.

69. According to the passage, substantial capital and easy access to credit were of greatest importance to:

   A. unskilled workers.
   B. merchants.
   C. masters.
   D. journeymen.

70. Masters who were under contract to merchants replaced skilled workers in order to:

   F. reduce the cost of labor.
   G. lower the cost of materials.
   H. raise the price of finished goods.
   J. obtain local orders.

71. According to the passage, the most important change in the structure of the workplace was:

   A. the hierarchy of workers.
   B. style of working.
   C. ownership of tools.
   D. financial arrangement.

72. What can be inferred about a typical shop at the beginning of the nineteenth century?

   F. Masters owned all of the tools.
   G. Masters supplied raw materials and sold finished goods.
   H. Unskilled workers competed against skilled workers.
   J. Finished goods had to be shipped long distances.

73. The *apprentice system* (line 2) refers to the:

   A. organization of workers according to skill and experience.
   B. practice of paying skilled workers more than unskilled ones.
   C. classification of industry by goods produced.
   D. division of markets into local, custom, and national.

74. The passage is primarily concerned with:

  F. analyzing an economic development.
  G. arguing for social reform.
  H. encouraging the use of skilled labor.
  J. describing manufacturing processes.

75. The author is considering adding the following sentence to the essay:

While the dollar of 1800 was worth at least seven or eight times as much as that of today, the wages of unskilled labor were too low to maintain a decent living.

If the author decided to add this sentence, it would most logically be placed at which of the following?

  A. After "day" and before "Skilled" in line 6
  B. After "system" and before "Improvements" in line 13
  C. After "changed" and before "In" in line 24
  D. After "output" and before "To" in line 31

PASSAGE VIII

This passage is adapted from a laboratory report on electromechanical batteries.

Electromechanical batteries, or EMBs, can power an electric car as well as electrochemical batteries. An EMB is a modular device that contains a flywheel integrated with a generator motor. The EMB is "charged" by spinning its rotor to maximum speed with the motor in "motor mode." It is "discharged" by slowing the rotor to draw out the kinetically stored
5 energy in "generator mode."

Compared to stationary EMB applications such as wind turbines, vehicular applications pose two special problems. First, gyroscopic forces create problems when a vehicle turns. The effects can be minimized by orienting the axis of rotation vertically, and by operating the EMB modules in pairs—one spinning clockwise and the other counterclockwise—so
10 that the net gyroscopic effect on the car is nearly zero.

The other problem associated with EMBs for vehicles is failure containment. The amount of kinetic energy stored is determined by the mass of the flywheel and its speed of rotation: the heavier the wheel and the faster it spins, the greater the energy stored. So it might seem that metal flywheels would be the automatic choice for EMBs. The problem is that any
15 spinning rotor has an upper speed limit determined by the tensile strength of the material from which it is made, and when that limit is exceeded, the result is catastrophic failure. In other words, the flywheel tears apart.

As it turns out, a low-density wheel can be spun up to a higher speed where it stores the same amount of kinetic energy as a heavier wheel spinning more slowly. Lightweight
20 graphite fiber, for example, is ten times more effective per unit mass for kinetic energy storage than steel. Plus, tests show that a well-designed rotor made of graphite fibers that fails turns into an amorphous mass of broken fibers. This failure is far more benign than that of metal flywheels, which typically break into shrapnel-like pieces that are difficult to contain.

76. The author is primarily concerned with:

F. discussing solutions to problems with the usage of EMBs to power cars.
G. reporting on new technology that makes EMB-powered cars competitive with gasoline-powered vehicles.
H. proving that EMBs can operate more efficiently than conventional batteries.
J. designing field tests to determine whether or not mobile EMBs can be used effectively.

77. The author mentions wind turbines in line 6 because they:

A. produce electricity.
B. store energy.
C. use wind power.
D. are stationary.

78. In line 8, the word *orienting* most nearly means:

F. reducing.
G. spinning.
H. aligning.
J. discharging.

79. It can be inferred that a low-density flywheel with stored kinetic energy equal to that of a high-density flywheel is:

A. discharging energy as it spins.
B. spinning in the opposite direction.
C. rotating at a higher speed.
D. made of graphite fibers.

80. In line 22, the word *amorphous* most nearly means:

F. shapeless.
G. weightless.
H. motionless.
J. worthless.

81. It can be inferred that when a flywheel is slowing down it is:

A. gaining weight.
B. spinning clockwise.
C. moving horizontally.
D. losing energy.

82. In line 22, the phrase *more benign* means:

F. less dangerous.
G. more reliable.
H. more stable.
J. less expensive.

83. The author regards the new EMB technology as:

A. overrated.
B. unattainable.
C. promising.
D. impractical.

84. The author states that the gyroscopic effect of EMB modules operating in pairs can be minimized if they are:

F. constructed of high-density metal.
G. rotated in opposite directions.
H. operating in their "motor" mode.
J. spinning at high speeds.

85. Which of the following best describes the logical development of the selection?

A. It mentions some technological challenges and describes some possible solutions.
B. It identifies some technological problems and dismisses attempts to solve them.
C. It outlines technological demands of an engineering application and minimizes their significance.
D. It presents a history of a technological question but offers no answers.

PASSAGE IX

This passage is adapted from an article about Asian elephants.

From the first appearance of a fairly small tapir-like mammal in what is now Egypt 45 million years ago, elephants evolved from a number of species which at one time inhabited nearly every continent. By the end of the Pleistocene glaciation about 10,000 years ago, however, only two species survived—the Asian elephant (*Elephas maximus*) and the African
5 elephant (*Loxodonta africana*). The position of the Asian elephant is somewhat paradoxical. Because it is the elephant species usually seen in zoos and circuses, it may be more familiar to the average American citizen. Yet, its status is generally less well known by the media and the general public than that of its larger cousin in Africa. With all of the publicity about the decline of the African elephant, they are still more than ten times more numerous than
10 the Asian species, which now numbers only 35,000 to 45,000 animals.

The story of the dramatic decline of the African elephant, primarily from large-scale poaching, is well known. The dramatic decline of Asian elephant numbers due to the

ever-increasing population of the Asian continent is relatively undocumented. The Asian elephant must share its habitat with some of the largest and poorest human populations in
15 the world. The combination of pressures on the environment brought on by these conditions has resulted in the conversion of forest cover to agriculture and villages, fragmenting elephant habitat and populations. There are only about ten populations with over 1,000 elephants, with half of these located in India. The majority of remaining populations is small, with less than 100 elephants each and some with lone bulls. The
20 dynamics of human population growth have inevitably led to increasing conflicts between humans and elephants, and people's tolerance for elephants has dropped. Where people once revered the elephant and tolerated the occasional crop raiding and destruction, now they are striking back, unfortunately often with lethal results.

Asian elephants have not traditionally been threatened by poaching for the ivory trade,
25 perhaps because females are tuskless and only 60 percent of the males carry tusks. However, recent trends indicate that poaching for ivory is on the upswing, especially in southern India. The proportion of sub-adult and adult elephants with tusks in various populations over the last 20 years has dropped dramatically, in some areas by as much as 75 percent. In one outstanding example, out of 1,000 elephants in the Periyar Tiger Reserve
30 only five adult males are left, and only two of those have tusks. This preferential decrease in the number of elephants with tusks strongly suggests increased poaching pressure for ivory.

This marked sexual disparity will result in changes in population structures, not only among adults but among sub-adults and juveniles. A drastic reduction in fertility has
35 already been seen which will affect the long term demographic structure of this population. Even if poaching is brought under control, it may take years for normal birth rates and juvenile survival to be restored.

The Asian elephant is listed as "endangered," and most of the thirteen Asian elephant range countries, including India, reinforce these international listings with domestic laws of their
40 own. However, some illegal ivory obtained from poaching continues to move from country to country. Many Asian countries have the strong desire to reduce the levels of poaching and stop all illegal trade, but they need assistance if they are to improve their ability to enforce these laws. In addition, while national legislation has afforded the elephant with maximum protection on paper, local conditions often serve to make this safety net more
45 illusory than real. Forests in many areas can be owned by local District Councils or private individuals and subject to uncontrolled slash and burn, shifting cultivation, leading to disappearance of prime elephant habitats. Erratic economic and political situations as well as lack of emphasis on wildlife-related crimes have made it difficult for some countries to effectively enforce laws and to efficiently manage their elephant populations and other
50 natural resources. For these reasons, the Asian elephant is in trouble—and it will take more than legal paperwork to ensure its survival.

86. The main purpose of the passage is to:

    F. contrast the problems facing the Asian elephant with those facing the African elephant.

    G. explain the reasons for the decline in the population of elephants on the Asian continent.

    H. describe how humans can benefit from their interaction with animals in the wild.

    J. list the various protections enacted by the governments of countries in Asia that have elephant populations.

87. In line 5, the word *paradoxical* most nearly means:

    A. dangerous.

    B. enviable.

    C. contradictory.

    D. insignificant.

88. The passage states that the two species of elephant that exist today, *Elephas maximus* and *Loxodonta africana*, were the only two elephant species surviving:

    F. 45 million years ago.

    G. 35,000 to 45,000 years ago.

    H. 10,000 years ago.

    J. 1,000 years ago.

89. According to information provided in the passage, African elephants are:

    A. larger and more numerous than Asian elephants.

    B. larger but less numerous than Asian elephants.

    C. smaller and more numerous than Asian elephants.

    D. smaller and less numerous than Asian elephants.

90. In line 17, the word *fragmenting* most nearly means:

    F. breaking up.

    G. adding to.

    H. bringing together.

    J. opening onto.

91. In the second paragraph, the author implies that elephants:

    A. are unable to live in proximity to humans.

    B. require forest cover for their habitat.

    C. prefer to live in groups smaller than 100.

    D. feed primarily upon crops planted for human use.

92. The author states that Asian elephants have traditionally not been targeted by ivory poachers because:

F. the herds of Asian elephants are smaller than the herds of African elephants.
G. the African elephants are, on average, larger than Asian elephants.
H. only the female Asian elephants have tusks that are sources of ivory.
J. Asian elephant females as well as many males do not have ivory tusks.

93. The author regards the conclusion that elephants in the Periyar Tiger Reserve have been killed by ivory poachers as:

A. unlikely but not impossible.
B. misguided but not surprising.
C. rash but plausible.
D. likely but not proven.

94. According to the passage, the primary threat to the populations of Asian elephants has been:

F. elephant hunters.
G. competition with humans.
H. predation by the Periyar Tiger.
J. competition with African elephants.

95. According to the passage, modern elephants evolved from an animal that first appeared in:

A. Egypt.
B. India.
C. Periyar.
D. Asia.

ADVANCED | Lesson 5

Please read the following passage and refer to it as necessary as the lesson proceeds.

This passage discusses the effect of microwave radiation on organisms.

Behavior is one of two general responses available to endothermic (warm-blooded) species
for the regulation of body temperature, the other being innate (reflexive) mechanisms of
heat production and heat loss. Human beings rely primarily on the first to provide a
hospitable thermal microclimate for themselves, in which the transfer of heat between the
5 body and the environment is accomplished with minimal involvement of innate
mechanisms of heat production and loss. Thermoregulatory behavior anticipates hyperthermia, and the organism adjusts its behavior to avoid becoming hyperthermic: it removes
layers of clothing, it goes for a cool swim, etc. Organisms can also respond to changes in the
temperature of the body core, as is the case during exercise; but such responses result from
10 the direct stimulation of thermoreceptors distributed widely within the central nervous
system, and the ability of these mechanisms to help the organism adjust to gross changes in
its environment is limited.

Until recently it was assumed that organisms respond to microwave radiation in the same
way that they respond to temperature changes caused by other forms of radiation. After all,
15 the argument runs, microwaves are radiation and they heat body tissues. This theory
ignores the fact that the stimulus to a behavioral response is normally a temperature
change that occurs at the surface of the organism. The thermoreceptors that prompt
behavioral changes are located within the first millimeter of the skin's surface, but the
energy of a microwave field may be selectively deposited in deep tissues, effectively
20 bypassing these thermoreceptors, particularly if the field is at near-resonant frequencies.
The resulting temperature profile may well be a kind of reverse thermal gradient in which
the deep tissues are warmed more than those of the surface. Since the heat is not conducted
outward to the surface to stimulate the appropriate receptors, the organism does not
"appreciate" this stimulation in the same way that it "appreciates" heating and cooling of
25 the skin. In theory, the internal organs of a human being or an animal could be quite
literally cooked well-done before the animal even realizes that the balance of its
thermomicroclimate has been disturbed.

Until a few years ago, microwave irradiations at equivalent plane-wave power densities of
about 100 mW/cm^2 were considered unequivocally to produce "thermal" effects;
30 irradiations within the range of 10 to 100 mW/cm^2 might or might not produce "thermal"
effects, while effects observed at power densities below 10 mW/cm^2 were assumed to be
"nonthermal" in nature. Experiments have shown this to be an oversimplification, and a
recent report suggests that fields as weak as 1 mW/cm^2 can be thermogenic. When the heat
generated in the tissues by an imposed radio frequency (plus the heat generated by
35 metabolism) exceeds the heat-loss capabilities of the organism, the thermoregulatory

system has been compromised. Yet surprisingly, not long ago, an increase in the internal body temperature was regarded merely as "evidence" of a thermal effect.

Main Idea and Voice

In Lesson 4, you learned to pay attention to the purpose and subject of a passage and to consider the author's point of view, purpose, and means of persuasion (p. 246). The following questions about the sample passage for Lesson 5 build on those skills.

First, some questions ask you to identify the main idea or the author's purpose in writing individual paragraphs or complete passages. You may also need to summarize the events in a passage.

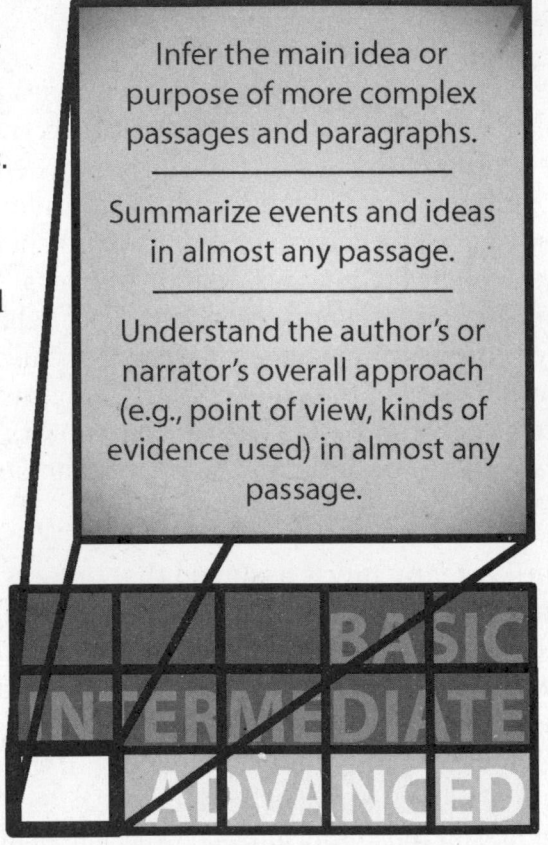

Infer the main idea or purpose of more complex passages and paragraphs.

Summarize events and ideas in almost any passage.

Understand the author's or narrator's overall approach (e.g., point of view, kinds of evidence used) in almost any passage.

1. The author is primarily concerned with:

    A. showing that behavior is a more effective way of controlling body temperature than are innate mechanisms.
    B. criticizing researchers who will not discard their theories about the effects of microwave radiation on organisms.
    C. demonstrating that effects of microwave radiation are different from those of other forms of radiation.
    D. analyzing the mechanism by which an organism maintains its bodily temperature in a changing thermal environment.

    The author is concerned with demonstrating that earlier theories were incorrect, (C). (A) is wrong because, while it describes a point made in the passage (in the last sentence in the first paragraph), this is not the overall or main point of the passage. (B) is wrong because the focus of the passage is the scientific evidence of the effects of microwaves, not a judgment about the people who once advanced those now out-of-date theories. As for (D), while the author does analyze the mechanisms for maintaining body temperature in a changing thermal environment, the behavior is one test of the effect of microwaves on the body. Thus, it is a supporting detail rather than the main idea.

Second, some questions may require you to determine the author's strategy or approach. To answer these questions it is important to note the author's point of view, the tone of the passage, and what kinds of evidence the author uses.

2. The author's strategy in lines 25–27 is to:

    F. introduce a hypothetical example to dramatize a point.
    G. propose an experiment to test a scientific hypothesis.
    H. cite a case study to illustrate a general contention.
    J. produce a counterexample to disprove an opponent's theory

In the lines indicated, the author states that it is possible that an organism could be cooked by microwave radiation (because the radiation penetrates into the core) before it even realizes its temperature is rising. The verb tense here, "could," clearly indicates that the author is introducing a hypothetical possibility, (F). Given the shocking nature of the example, we should conclude that the author has introduced it to dramatize a point.

3. The author's discussion can best be described as:

    A. analytical.
    B. alarmed.
    C. speculative.
    D. noncommittal.

The author gives facts and analyzes or discusses a problem; therefore, the tone could be called analytical, (A). The author is clearly interested in microwaves and notes their potential danger, but the overall tone of the passage is not "alarmed," (B). As for (C), the scientific evidence presented shows that the author is not merely speculating, (C). And as for (D), the author does commit to a definite position on microwaves, (D).

Explicit Details

In Lesson 4 you learned to locate and describe details, to infer their significance in a passage, and to look for evidence supporting your conclusions about them from the entire passage (p. 248). In this lesson, you'll learn to apply those skills to a more challenging technical passage like the sample passage, where details may be unfamiliar or difficult to describe.

The biggest challenge in technical passages is the sheer number of unfamiliar details. In the passage above, for example, many of the important details may also be unfamiliar processes or technical terms. Take the following sentence from the final paragraph:

> Until a few years ago, microwave irradiations at equivalent plane-wave power densities of about 100 mW/cm² were considered unequivocally to produce "thermal" effects; irradiations within the range of 10 to 100 mW/cm² might or might not produce "thermal" effects; while effects observed at power densities below 10 mW/cm² were assumed to be "nonthermal" in nature.

Locate and interpret subtle details in more complex passages.

Use details that appear in different sections of complex informational passages to support specific points or arguments.

When you encounter passages like this, don't panic! All of the information you need to answer any questions about details, whether you understand the processes described or not, is located in the passage. Rephrase the passage using words you understand and taking out the most confusing information.

> Until recently, scientists thought that microwave irradiations of a higher density produced thermal effects, those with a slightly lower density may or may not produce thermal effects, and those below a certain threshold were thought to be nonthermal in nature.

Underneath the technical jargon, this passage is simply giving readers some basic parameters by which scientists have traditionally defined the levels of internal heat generated by microwave irradiation. Why does the author include this detail? The "until recently" signals that something about these parameters has recently been proven incorrect or inadequate. The author is giving us this information so we understand later in the passage what it is that he or she finds incorrect, or, rather, an "oversimplification" of thermal processes.

In other cases, you may not need to rephrase a difficult passage to understand the details being described or how they are being used. Even if you don't know what a detail means, you can use grammatical and syntactical clues in the passage to answer questions about it.

Simply filter out the unknown language and focus on locating the detail in the passage. Read the surrounding sentences or that paragraph again carefully before selecting your answer, and you might find that the question isn't so difficult, after all. Try the following question about the sample passage (p. 281):

4. According to the passage, innate mechanisms for heat production:

    A. are not governed by thermoreceptors inside the body of the organism.
    B. are not affected by microwave radiation.
    C. trigger the type of response needed to counteract gross changes in environmental temperatures.
    D. are a less effective means of compensating for gross changes in temperature than are behavioral strategies.

    The correct answer is (D). Where does the author mention innate mechanisms for heat production? Even if you don't know what that means, you can still locate those words in the first paragraph, so start there to find the answer. In the final sentence of the first paragraph, the author states that the second type of mechanism for regulating temperature is less effective for adjusting to gross changes in temperature than is the first type, (D). Even without a full understanding of the processes described, you simply needed to track down the detail mentioned in the passage to answer this question. (A) is wrong because, while the author establishes that there are two general responses available to warm-blooded animals for regulating body temperature (behavioral and innate mechanisms), the author goes on to state that humans rely primarily on the first type of response, but the organism also responds to changes in temperature in the core of the body (the second type of response) and these changes *are* triggered by thermoreceptors distributed throughout the central nervous system. (B) is wrong because the author does not provide any information about the effect of microwave radiation on internal thermoreceptors. (C) is wrong because the problem cited by the author is not that internal thermoreceptors do not respond to changes in the temperature of the core of the body, but that they do not trigger the type of response needed to counteract gross changes in environmental temperatures.

Remember that all details are included for a reason, and you can answer plenty of questions about those details, including their role in a passage, without fully understanding the complete vocabulary or implications of a detail.

Development

You learned in Lesson 4 to recognize various relationships in passages, such as cause and effect relationships, interpersonal relationships, and relationships between paragraphs (p. 250). In this lesson, you will practice applying those same skills to a complex technical passage in which cause and effect may have to be inferred, relationships are subtle or implied, and paragraphs have more subtle relationships.

Answer the following Development questions about the sample passage (p. 281):

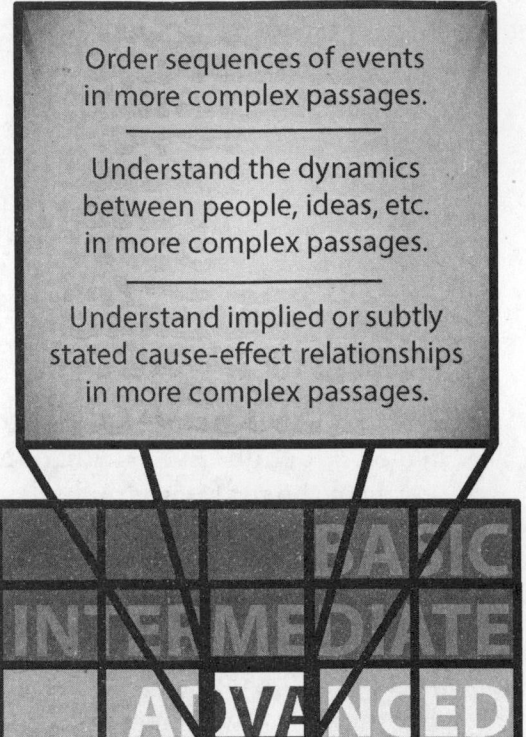

Order sequences of events in more complex passages.

Understand the dynamics between people, ideas, etc. in more complex passages.

Understand implied or subtly stated cause-effect relationships in more complex passages.

5. The third paragraph is related in which way to the second paragraph?

A. The third paragraph offers a counterargument to the idea presented in the second paragraph.
B. The second and third paragraphs provide different evidence that common assumptions about the same topic are incorrect.
C. The second paragraph introduces a term that is defined in the third paragraph.
D. The third paragraph provides further evidence for the argument made in the second paragraph.

(B) is the correct answer. This question requires you to explore the relationship between the paragraphs in a complex passage. Notice that both paragraphs begin with the same basic structure: "until recently, *x* was believed about microwave irradiation." Each paragraph debunks a common assumption about microwave irradiation, but these paragraphs are not about the *same* assumption, so (D) is incorrect. Paragraph 2 is about the assumption of how organisms respond to microwave radiation, and paragraph 3 debunks assumptions about what levels of microwave radiation produce thermal effects.

6. Which one of the following would be the most logical topic for the author to discuss following the final paragraph of the passage?

    F. A discussion of the strategies used by various species to control hyperthermia.

    G. A suggestion for new research to be done on the effects of microwaves on animals and human beings.

    H. A proposal that the use of microwave radiation be prohibited because it is dangerous.

    J. A survey of the literature on the effects of microwave radiation on human beings.

The correct answer is (G). Since the last paragraph deals with a recent report suggesting that previous assumptions about microwaves were incorrect, the author would probably go on to talk about the need for more research, (G). (F) is wrong because a discussion of the strategies used by various species to control hyperthermia would not follow logically from the author's remarks that microwave radiation has not been correctly understood. The discussion of such strategies early in the passage is only intended to set the stage for the main point of the passage. (H) is wrong because it overstates the case: there is no evidence to suggest that microwave radiation is so dangerous that it should be prohibited, only that it should be understood and regulated. Finally, (J) is wrong because clearly the author is concerned with new information about microwave radiation. He or she has already suggested that what we now believe is erroneous, so a survey of current literature and theories would not be helpful.

Vocabulary

If you encounter an unfamiliar word in a technical passage, ask yourself the following questions:

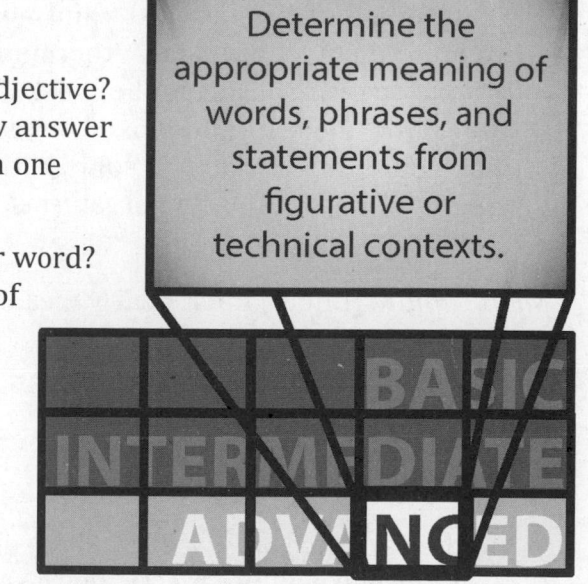

Determine the appropriate meaning of words, phrases, and statements from figurative or technical contexts.

- What part of speech is the word? Noun? Adjective? Adverb? This may help you eliminate a few answer choices, if the choices represent more than one part of speech.

- Does this word sound like another familiar word? If it's a compound word (a word made up of two separate words, like "doghouse") do you recognize the meaning of any part of it?

- Does the word contain any prefixes at the beginning or suffixes at the end? These common syllables may help you determine the part of speech of an unknown word, or at least the nature of the word (i.e. whether it's a positive or negative term.)

- ○ A **prefix** is a series of letters that precede the root of a word, but that don't make sense on their own like *ex-* (ex-husband), *non-* (non-refundable), *re-* (recreate), or *un-* (unoriginal). Prefixes alter the quality of the word that follows, so being aware of what a prefix seems to do to other familiar words may help you eliminate an answer choice or two.

- ○ A **suffix** also alters the quality of the word it modifies, only through letters that come at the end of a word. Think *–ly* (sleepily), *-ing* (frequenting), or *–itis* (appendicitis). A suffix often changes the part of speech of a word, so that may help you eliminate answer choices as well.

- What do I know about this word from context? Make a list of any context clues.

Now, try a few questions about the technical terms in the sample passage (p. 281):

7. The word *thermoreceptor* (line 10) most likely means:

   A. cold sensor.
   B. pain sensor.
   C. heat transmitter.
   D. heat sensor.

   (D) is the correct answer. *Thermoreceptor* can be broken into parts: the prefix "thermo-" and the word "receptor." Even if you don't know that a receptor is an organ that senses and responds to a stimulus, the word sounds like words that you probably do know, like "receiver" or "reception," all of which suggest the sensing or receiving of information, rather than the transmission of information. With this clue you can eliminate (C). Next, think about the prefix "thermo-." Words that may come to mind include "thermal," "thermometer," and "thermos," all of which refer to the retention or measurement of heat. Even though you might still conclude that "thermo-" means "cold" based on that evidence (after all, a thermometer measures heat, but it also measures cold), in the context of the passage, which discusses the effects of heat stimuli on organisms, the answer that makes the most sense is (D).

8. *Microclimate* (line 4) most nearly means:

   F. very small environment.
   G. large weather system.
   H. heat source.
   J. extremely hot.

   In the sentence, *microclimate* is clearly a noun because it acts as a direct object. You can therefore eliminate (J), which suggests the word is an adjective. While "climate" might refer to either environment or weather, the prefix "micro-" suggests something small, not large, so (F) is the best answer. You could also create a list of characteristics of a *microclimate*: it's something that requires "minimal involvement" and that can be created by removing layers of clothing or going for a swim. (F) is the only answer choice that could have all of those characteristics.

Implied Ideas and Applications

In Lesson 4, you learned to identify logical fallacies in arguments to determine whether or not you agree with the writer (p. 254). More technical passages may not include the typical elements of an argument, such as a clearly stated premise and conclusion. Nevertheless, the questions that accompany these passages may require you to identify flaws in the author's logic. In more challenging passages, you will need to rely on clues from the passage to determine the implied conclusions and generalizations.

Draw generalizations and conclusions about people, ideas, etc. by using information from one or more sections of more complex passages.

Now, answer the following questions about the sample passage (p. 281):

9.   Which of the following best represents the flaw in logic the author identifies in the second paragraph?

   A.   If *a* happens, then *b* will inevitably happen, as well.
   B.   Because *a* is a kind of *c*, and *b* is a kind of *c*, both *a* and *b* will affect *d* in exactly the same way.
   C.   Whenever *a* happens, *b* happens, so *a* must cause *b*.
   D.   *a* is a kind of *c*, and *b* is a kind of *c*, so *a* = *b*.

   (B) is the correct answer. To answer this question, you must first determine exactly what the author thinks is wrong with previous theories about microwave radiation: what kind of logical fallacy does the author identify? In the second paragraph the author states that previous theories have treated microwave radiation and other forms of radiation in the same way with regards to how organisms sense and react to the changes in body temperature they create. The flaw in this logic, according to the writer, is that microwave radiation heats from the inside-out, not the outside-in. The organism will therefore not sense temperature changes from microwave radiation the same way it will sense changes from external thermal stimuli. Microwave radiation and other forms of radiation are not the same kind of radiation, so they will not have the same effect on warm-blooded organisms.

The flaw here is one of hasty generalization: previous assumptions have incorrectly generalized from one scenario (exposure to other forms of radiation) how an organism will react to another scenario (exposure to microwave radiation), but those generalizations are based on incorrect or faulty evidence. So, you are looking for another situation in which a false comparison of two unlike things results in an assumption that both things will have the same effect on a third thing. While (D) almost fits this scenario, it leaves out that important "third thing" element. (A) represents the slippery slope fallacy and (C) the false cause fallacy, neither of which correctly represents the logical flaw identified in this passage.

10. The author implies that the proponents of the theory that microwave radiation acts on organisms in the same way as other forms of radiation based their conclusions primarily on:

F. laboratory research.
G. unfounded assumption.
H. control group surveys.
J. outdated research.

The correct answer is (G). This is another way of coming at the same logical flaw discussed in the previous question. (H) is neither mentioned nor implied in the passage, so it can be eliminated. (F) seems appealing, but note that in the last paragraph laboratory research is cited to debunk rather than support previous assumptions, thereby implying that proponents of the theory are not using laboratory tests. (J) is also appealing, but the author doesn't imply that previous research is outdated, but instead suggests that it is simply incorrect or hasn't been undertaken at all. (G) works nicely because it captures the language of the second paragraph and because it adequately describes the fallacy (one based on hasty generalizations, or assumptions without evidence).

Lesson 6

In a test environment, you will encounter a variety of passages about multiple topics written in a range of difficulty levels. While all of the skills you've encountered in these lessons have built upon one another, don't forget that questions and passages might come from all different levels. Some passages will seem easy, now that you've encountered more difficult works. Others are designed to challenge your reading and interpretation skills. In other words, you may get a mix of questions for a single passage that draws from the simplest skills you've learned over the past five lessons (such as identifying the topic of a passage) to the most complicated (such as identifying the relationship of paragraphs to each other).

Furthermore, as you may have noticed as the difficulty of lessons progressed, some questions will no longer fit neatly into each content area. Some questions might require you to understand both the purpose (Main Idea) and the organization (Development) of the passage, or both a difficult term (Vocabulary) and why it is included (Explicit Details). While the questions below are still organized based on which category the stem most obviously suggests, be aware that you may have to draw from two or more skills to arrive at the correct answer.

In this final lesson, you'll review all of the previous lessons for each content area. You will encounter a range of questions that will challenge you to recall all of the skills we've discussed over the past five lessons and apply them to a complex and challenging passage. Good luck!

Please read the following passage and refer to it as necessary as the lesson proceeds.

This passage discusses the English alphabet and how it relates to spelling.

In an alphabet that is accurately constructed and used, there is one, and only one, symbol for each significant speech sound, and only one speech sound is represented by any given symbol. Under these conditions, spelling is determined solely by pronunciation. Such a phonetically correct and simple orthography requires no special considerations apart from
5 the alphabet to be used.

Spelling of this precision does not exist, though in certain languages there is a fairly close approximation to it. In customary spelling, each of the above-stated principles is violated. There is an alphabetic inadequacy, or the lack of symbols to represent certain important speech sounds; redundancy, or the use of two or more symbols or combinations of symbols
10 to represent the same sound; and repetition, or the use of the same symbol or combination of symbols to represent two or more sounds. Moreover, since every language varies from age to age and from locality to locality, the phonetic character that every alphabet originally possessed could be maintained only by continuous adaptation to these alterations of uttered words.

15 The natural tendency toward phonetic corruption was intensified by the establishment of a standard, relatively unchanging orthography, due principally to the introduction of the printing press. The practical need for uniformity of spelling caused certain spellings, then customary, to be accepted as correct. Thus, not only were existing faults of spelling institutionalized, but the imperfect tendency to respond to phonetic change was almost
20 wholly suppressed. Pronunciation has continued to change, often radically, but spelling has lagged behind.

Another important source of confusion in English spelling, closely associated with this process of fixation, is the influence of the revival of learning that brought words of classic origin into special prominence. The idea developed that, regardless of their pronunciation,
25 such words should be made to conform as exactly as possible to the Latin and Greek terms from which they were ultimately derived. This etymological theory, which offered a wide opportunity for pedants, gained strength both from the weakness of the contemporary feeling for phonetic accuracy and from the printer's practical difficulty in making a selection among existing forms in his quest for uniformity. A result was the introduction of
30 many forms that were erroneous from both the phonetic and the true philological points of view; for, apart from the indefensibility of this use of spelling as a means of rendering derivation obvious to the eye, the method was dangerous in the hands of men whose knowledge of the history of the language was necessarily inadequate. A familiar example is the present English *debt* (from the Early Modern English and Middle English *det, dette,* from
35 Old French *dette),* in which the *b* was etymologically inserted both in French (though later abandoned) and in English to make the spelling suggest more directly the original Latin *debita,* though the *b* has never been pronounced. On the other hand, this process actually corrupted pronunciation in some cases. For example, the *l* in *fault* (Middle English and Old French *faute),* which was inserted in the same way to suggest the Latin *fallere,* has actually

40 come to be pronounced, though the correct pronunciation (which survived as late as the time of Alexander Pope) makes the word rhyme with *ought, thought,* and *taught.*

The result of this history, as embodied in English orthography, is apparent. First, while all of the other principal European alphabets have retained with comparatively small variations the Roman values of the letters, the English alphabet has to a very large extent abandoned

45 them. This is especially true of the long vowels. Second, the letters of the English alphabet are used with a great diversity of sound values. Thus, of the vowels, accented and unaccented, *a* has nine, as in *name, bare, man, father, water, want, ask, village, data.* Third, the various English speech sounds are written with an even greater variety of symbols. The ways in which this occurs are too numerous to be given and illustrated in full, but the

50 orthographic situation will be understood from the following examples: *i (it),* accented or unaccented, is represented by *i, y, e, o, u, ie, ee, ui, ai, hi, ive, eo, ia, ei, ey, ea, eig, ehea, ewi, ois, uy, oi, igh, ay, ieu,* as in the following words: *fit, hymn, pretty, women, busy, sieve, breeches, build, Saint John* (sin'jun), *exhibit , fivepence* (tip' ens), *Theobald* (tib'ald), *carriage, forfeit, donkey, guinea, sovereign, James's forehead, housewife* (hus'if), *chamois, plaguy, Jervois*

55 (jer'vis), *Denbigh, Rothesay (roth'si), Beaulieu* (bew'li).

The confusion of English spelling, however, while great, is not so complete as might be expected from its above-stated theoretical defects; it exhibits a certain amount of system, and it is also possible to demonstrate a very considerable phonetic element in it. Its chief practical defects are the ambiguities in the use of letters such as *c* and *k (cat, kill)*, *c* and *s*

60 *(cinder, seat),* and *f* and *ph (fool, philosopher),* and the employment of silent letters, that is, letters that, if omitted, would leave the symbol a simpler and, generally, more common one for the same sound, as in *guard, add, feign,* and *though.*

Main Idea and Voice

Back in Lesson 1, you began thinking about the Main Idea by articulating the *focus* (what) and *purpose* (why) of the passage (p. 194). Sometimes the Main Idea is stated directly in the passage. Other times, as you learned in Lesson 3, you have to infer the Main Idea (p. 232). Then, in Lesson 2, you applied the same idea to paragraphs (p. 205). Each paragraph does just one thing, and it relates to the Main Idea of a passage in a particular way. You may have to infer the purpose or topic of each paragraph, as well.

> Identify clear main ideas and purposes of challenging passages or paragraphs.

In Lesson 3, you began to think more about the author's point of view as a tool to determine the Main Idea: his or her background, time period, reason for writing, stance on the issue, and biases, as well as the side the author takes on an issue, his or her perceived audience, and why the author cares about it (p. 232). You also considered the purposes of the passage: to entertain, educate/inform, or persuade, and the means of persuasion: appeals to logic, authority, and emotion. Then, in Lesson 5, you turned your attention to the audience. You considered the tone, degree of specialization, definition of complex ideas and terms, context, and purpose of the passage to identify its implied audience (p. 282).

To determine the Main Idea of the passage, especially complex passages, you will need to draw from several different skill areas: the purpose, tone, means of persuasion, and the author's point of view. For especially difficult passages, as you learned in Lesson 4, it might be helpful to write a one, two, or three sentence summary, written in your own words, to test your comprehension (p. 246).

Now, answer a few Main Idea questions about the sample passage at the beginning of this lesson (p. 292):

1. It can be inferred that the author believes:

   A. that dictionaries should be updated frequently, allowing standardized usage to reflect the use of slang.
   B. that dictionaries should be updated frequently, allowing new words, such as scientific terms, to be incorporated into standard usage.
   C. that the dictionary should be entirely rewritten and the spelling standardized.
   D. that since the advent of the printing press, the development of English orthography has been virtually nonexistent.

   (D) is the correct answer. This question asks you to consider the author's point of view as well as to identify ideas implied by the passage. The author is explaining why the English language is less than perfect phonetically. He places much of the blame upon the invention of the printing press, which has created uniformity of spelling but only by arresting orthographic development.

2. What is the main subject of paragraph 4?

   F. The orthographic history of the word *debt*
   G. The influence of the Classical revival on English spelling
   H. How the invention of the printing press standardized English spelling
   J. The need for English spelling to more accurately reflect its pronunciation

   The correct answer is (G). This question requires attention to specific details as well as a bit of inference, since the author never specifically mentions the classical revival of the nineteenth century. However, the first few sentences of the paragraph state as much by telling us that the "revival of learning that brought words of classic origin into special prominence" led to some corruption in English spelling. The author then goes on to detail that corruption, citing specific examples of classical origins of modern corrupted spellings. (F) is mentioned in the paragraph, but is too specific to be its main concern. (H) is mentioned in paragraph 3, not 4, and (J), besides not being a concern of the paragraph in question, is a misreading of the purpose of the passage in general, which is not to persuade but to inform.

3. It may be inferred from the passage that the author would accept which of the following statements?

I. The use of *ch* to represent the speech sound in *chocolate* is an indication of the inadequacy of the English alphabet.
II. Ideally, the spelling of a language ought to reflect the current pronunciation of the language.
III. Part of the difficulty students have in recognizing rhyme in Shakespeare's work stems from the fact that the pronunciation embodied in Shakespeare's spelling has largely disappeared.

A. I
B. I and II
C. II and III
D. I, II, and III

(C) is the correct answer. This question asks you to make an inference based on the author's point of view, so it is both a Main Idea and an Implied Ideas question. Since statement (I) may not be inferred from the passage, you can eliminate (A) and (B) and (D). The author speaks of groups of letters being used to represent sounds. The alphabet would be inadequate only if it were necessary to use the same combination of letters to represent different sounds. Statement (II) is inferable. The author is critical of the fact that the English language does not reflect pronunciation because this interferes with the objective of spelling. Statement (III) may also be inferred. If spelling has not changed, but pronunciation has, this may account for some of the difficulty of reading older written English. The author even mentions another poet, Alexander Pope, as an example of a poet whose sense of rhyme was different from ours today because of changes in pronunciation.

Explicit Details

You began your study of details with the basics, identifying the *who*, *what*, *where*, and *when* of straightforward passages through careful reading. Details, you recall, are like the ingredients in a recipe: you must pay careful attention to avoid making a mistake. More challenging passages will contain many details or might require you to generalize or infer the details from the information presented, as you learned in Lesson 2 (p. 207). In that lesson, you also began to question *why* details were included, since every detail in the passage is there for a reason.

Locate and interpret details in challenging passages.

Understand the subtle or complex function of a part of a passage.

Determining why a detail is included in a passage often means making inferences about that detail, a skill you developed in Lesson 3 (p. 237). You may have to infer the significance of a detail from anywhere in the passage or the passage as a whole and not just from the paragraph or sentence in which it appears. You practiced this skill further in Lesson 4, where you began to describe details and draw conclusions about them in order to understand their importance to the passage (p. 248). Ask yourself questions of the details, like "What kind of person is this character?", "What kind of place is this?", "How could I describe this time period?", or "What qualities does this event or this idea have?"

Finally, in Lesson 5 you learned a strategy for unpacking the significance of details in complex technical passages, which frequently contain many unfamiliar or abstract details (p. 284). Rephrasing technical passages is a good way to clarify the relationship of details to each other and their significance in the passage. Don't forget, however, to always ground all of your conclusions and descriptions using the information in the passage.

Now, answer a few Explicit Details questions about the sample passage (p. 292):

4. Which of the following is NOT an indictment of the spelling of the English language mentioned in the passage?

   F. Many letters or groups of letters are used to represent the same sound in the spoken language.
   G. There are too few characters in the English alphabet to adequately represent every sound that occurs in the spoken language.
   H. A single letter in the alphabet may be used to represent a myriad of speech sounds that occur in the spoken language.
   J. The spelling of the English language does not accurately reflect the changing pronunciation of words.

(G) is the correct answer. This Explicit Details question contains a thought-reverser: you are looking for the one detail in the choices that is *not* included in the passage. (F) is an indictment made by the author in the fifth paragraph. His or her long list of symbols used to represent the *i* sound of *fit* is offered in proof of this indictment. (H) is the contention evidenced by the discussion of the letter *a* in paragraph 4, and (J) is one of the major points made in the passage, and is detailed in paragraphs 4 and 5.

5.   The author of the passage views the function of spelling as:

A. a way of standardizing the pronunciation of a language.
B. a way of representing words by combinations of alphabetic symbols.
C. a way of standardizing the structure of a language.
D. a way of ensuring the purity of a language by keeping it free from slang and colloquial expressions.

The correct answer is (B). This Explicit Details question is disguised as a Main Idea question, since it asks about the author's point of view on something. However, the author states his or her view on spelling quite clearly in the first paragraph, which indicates that spelling is the representation of the spoken word, so this question is really a matter of recalling the location of a detail. This question also requires some development skills, since you must understand the relationship between spelling and language as it is described in the first paragraph. (A) is incorrect because the causal relationship described is reversed. According to the passage, pronunciation should determine spelling. (C) confuses the meaning of *standardization* as the author uses it. The term is meant not in the sense of maintaining a high standard or preserving the language from impurity or slang, but instead as uniformity of spelling. For the same reason, (D) is incorrect.

6.   Why does the author tell us that the letter *a* has nine different sounds?

F. Because the letter *a* is common in Greek and Latin words.
G. Because it is an example of a sound that can be represented by a variety of symbols.
H. Because it is an example of the diversity of sounds values attributed to English letters.
J. Because the letter *a* is commonly employed as a silent letter in English words.

(H) is the correct answer. This question asks you about the significance of a detail to the passage. All of the answer choices use the language and content of the passage, but only (H) correctly identifies the purpose of the *a* example in the passage, which is to demonstrate that one result of standardized spelling in English is that letters now represent a variety of sounds.

Development

You may have noticed as lessons progressed that Development sections often contained the most content of the five content areas. This is because the development, or how a passage progresses, depends on several kinds of relationships: from simple cause-effect or chronological progressions to complex relationships between paragraphs. The larger heading of "development" embodies some of the most challenging reading comprehension skills. Nevertheless, you can still think about this category as primarily focused on relationships between events, people, places, things, ideas, and structural elements like sentences and paragraphs.

In Lesson 1, you learned to look out for signal words like *first, second, third, then, while, later, afterward, before, finally*, or *during* in order to determine a basic sequence of events in simple passages (p. 197). Simple questions about the sequence of events will ask you *when* an event in the passage occurred, but those questions may not always include the word *when* in them. Likewise, questions about cause and effect, another common relationship in passages, may not always contain the words *why* or *as a result*, but they will nevertheless be interested in which events caused or were the effect of other events in the passage. In simple passages, cause and effect relationships are signaled by words and phrases like *because, since, consequently, as a result*, and sentence constructions like *if...then*. In Lesson 2, you focused on these relationships as they occurred at the paragraph level rather than the entire passage (p. 209), and in Lesson 3 you learned that the sequence of events may not unfold in chronological order in a passage, and that in more challenging passages, cause-effect relationships may be reversed as well (p. 238).

You also began, starting in Lesson 2, to identify a different set of relationships: family and non-family relationships between people in passages (p. 209). Relationships between people are sometimes subtle or difficult to determine, and you have to infer those relationships from the passage, as you learned in Lesson 3 (p. 238). In that lesson, you also paid closer attention to other relationships in passages: between ideas, things, and places. Even paragraphs have relationships, and many questions will ask you how paragraphs relate to each other, or what might happen in the next paragraph after the end of the passage. In Lesson 4, you were also introduced to the concept of comparisons, a tool used by authors to develop relationships without stating them directly (p. 250).

As your lessons progressed, you encountered more complex relationships. In more challenging passages, as you learned in Lesson 4, cause-effect relationships might be difficult to identify, and you may have to ask, "Why did this event/action happen?" and "What are the effects of this event/action?" to make those relationships clearer (p. 252). Likewise, more challenging passages might use flash-forwards or flashbacks to disrupt the sequence of events, and you should be prepared to identify why the authors employ these devices. Finally, in Lesson 5, you brought all of these skills to bear on complex technical passages, which may contain subtle cause and effect, personal, and chronological relationships requiring a nuanced understanding of how the argument proceeds (p. 286).

Now, answer a few Development questions about the sample passage (p. 292):

7. The revived interest in classical origin of words resulted in all of the following EXCEPT:

    A. suppression of the ability of orthography to respond to phonetic change.
    B. the introduction of erroneous forms containing unpronounced letters.
    C. a sense that spelling of words should reflect as closely as possible their Latin and Greek origins.
    D. corrupted pronunciation of some words.

    The correct answer is (A). This cause-effect question focuses on the relationships developed in paragraph 4, but it also requires attention to supporting details as well. (B), (C), and (D) are all mentioned as effects of the Classic revival in the fourth paragraph, but the effect mentioned in (A) is the result of a different development discussed in the previous paragraph: the introduction of the printing press.

8. When did Alexander Pope write poetry (lines 40–41)?

    F. Before the establishment of a standard, unchanging English orthography.
    G. Before the intrusive *l* in *fault* influenced the pronunciation of the word.
    H. At a time when English letters still had only one pronunciation.
    J. Before the insertion of the intrusive *l* into the word *fault*.

    (G) is the correct answer. Even though there aren't many sequence-of-events signal words in this passage, you can still put together a basic sequence of events in the passage. (H) can be eliminated easily because the author tells us that a perfect system does not exist. (F) can be eliminated simply because there isn't enough evidence in the passage to support or deny it. While the printing press and classical revival did establish a relatively stable orthography, the Pope example suggests that some changes were still being made after the invention of the printing press. So, although development is slow, changes do still happen. (J) is a misunderstanding of the point of the Pope example, which is evidence not of a poet who wrote before the spelling of the word had changed, but one who wrote before its pronunciation had changed to reflect the changed spelling, (G).

9. Which of the following best describes the relationship between paragraphs 2, 3, and 4?

    A. Introduction of an argument, one reason why it is accurate, then a counterexample to reinforce the writer's stance

    B. Three paragraphs describing different historical events in support of a larger argument

    C. Introduction of a historical process, one large significant event impacting that process, then discussion of another significant event impacting that process

    D. Introduction of a historical process, one large application of that process, then a detailed discussion of that application

The correct answer is (C). The second paragraph introduces the process by which a language's orthography and pronunciation become disconnected. Over time, the author tells us, the spoken word of a language changes, but changes to spelling adapt more slowly. In paragraph 3, we are given a significant event, the invention of the printing press, that exacerbated the "natural tendency" described in paragraph 2. Paragraph 4 gives us "another" event that impacted the disconnection process: the classical revival. (D) is an appealing choice, but the printing press is not an "application" of the process of disconnect, but a source of that disconnection. Furthermore, paragraph 4 is not subordinate to paragraph 3, as (D) suggests, but instead offers a second and equally important illustration of a process. (A) and (B) are incorrect because of the purpose of the passage: the author isn't trying to persuade but to inform, so there is no particular argument here in need of support. Besides, paragraph 2 does not describe a historical event, but a historical process, so (B) is incorrect.

Vocabulary

No matter how unfamiliar a word or phrase might be, you have learned strategies to determine its meaning in the context of even the most complex passages. In Lesson 1, you focused on determining the meaning of unknown words by looking for *synonyms* (words with the same meaning) or *antonyms* (words with the opposite meaning) in the passage (p. 200). Sometimes, as you learned in Lesson 2, you may know one meaning of the unknown word, but it has other meanings or shades of meaning with which you may be unfamiliar (p. 211). In these cases, the more common meaning might be an answer choice, but it won't make sense in context.

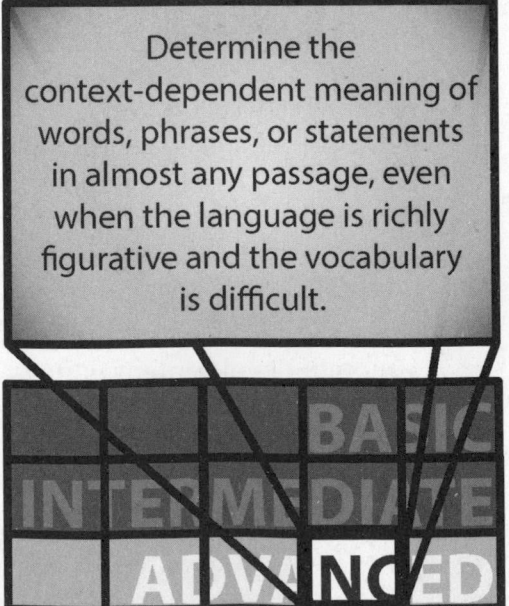

Determine the context-dependent meaning of words, phrases, or statements in almost any passage, even when the language is richly figurative and the vocabulary is difficult.

Unknown words and phrases may also be examples of *figurative language*, or language that doesn't make literal sense, but nevertheless conveys meaning. One common type of figurative language is the *idiom*, a common saying that conveys a particular meaning in a particular cultural or historical context. Other types of figurative language to which you were introduced in Lesson 3 (p. 241) include: *hyperbole* (exaggeration), *simile* (comparison using "like" or "as"), *metaphor* (comparison without using "like" or "as"), *personification* (attributing human characteristics to animals or other non-human objects or phenomena), and *onomatopoeia* (words that attempt to mimic the sounds they describe). Like unknown words or those with several meanings, figurative language can be identified and defined through close attention to contextual clues. As you learned in Lesson 4, those clues may come from anywhere in the passage, and not just from the sentence or paragraph in which the unknown word appears (p. 252).

Even when you encounter technical terms or what seem to be nonsense words, you can still employ strategies that may help you determine their meaning. In Lesson 5, you learned to define unknown words by making a list of their characteristics, identifying their part of speech, defining them by association with similar-sounding words, paying attention to what their *prefixes* and *suffixes* mean, and breaking compound words into their component parts (p. 287).

Now, answer a few Vocabulary questions about the sample passage (p. 292):

10. *Practical defects* (line 59) could most accurately be restated as:

    F. realistic mistakes.
    G. functional flaws.
    H. effective errors.
    J. realistic assets.

> (G) is the correct answer. This vocabulary question hinges on the many shades of the meaning of *practical.* One common meaning is "realistic," (F), but that doesn't make sense in this context, since the paragraph isn't about mistakes that are more or less likely to succeed because of their practicality, which is how *practical* in a realistic sense is meant. So, both (F) and (J) (which is doubly incorrect because it inaccurately identifies "asset" as a synonym for "defects") can be eliminated. Then, think more about words that are similar to *practical*: "practice" and "practitioner" come to mind. Both suggest something hands-on, something actually done rather than discussed as an abstract idea. In the context of the passage, this meaning makes sense, since it's about defects in the actual usage of English letters. This meaning is underscored by the words "use" and "employment" in the following sentences. *Practical* in this sense is therefore most like "functional," (G). (H) contains another shade of meaning for *practical*, in the sense of being suitable for a certain task. That meaning doesn't make sense in this context, though.

11. An *etymological theory* (line 26) is one concerned with:

A. the source of words.
B. the sound of words.
C. the spelling of words.
D. the history of the alphabet.

The correct answer is (A). Breaking down this word into the parts you understand isn't particularly effective in this case, unless you already know what an *etymom* (word) is. "-ological" is somewhat helpful, since it suggests the study of something (like "psychological," or "sociological"), but it doesn't really eliminate any of the answer choices. So, focus instead on how to describe the unknown word: the pronoun "this" that comes just before it suggests that the unknown phrase is a rewording of what came just before it, which is "the idea that … words should be made to conform as exactly as possible to the Latin and Greek terms from which they were ultimately derived." This clearly suggests (A), that an *etymological theory* is one that concerns the origins of words.

12. *Phonetic* and *orthographic* refer to what qualities or words, respectively?

F. Spelling and sound
G. Sound and origin
H. Sound and spelling
J. Spelling and origin

(H) is the correct answer. Both words are used several times in the passage. Besides the similarity to "phone" and "phonics," you should be able to tell that *phonetic* refers to sound in the passage, particularly in paragraph 3, in which we learn that spelling didn't respond to "phonetic change," which is associated with "pronunciation," after the introduction of the printing press. You can therefore eliminate (F) and (J), since neither associates sound with *phonetics*. The clue to the meaning of *orthography* is in paragraph 5, in which the "orthographic situation" of English is illustrated with a single sound in English, "i (it)," that can be spelled in 25 different ways. This is a strong clue that *orthography* refers to spelling, an idea supported by its use in the first paragraph, which describes a "correct and simple orthography" as one in which "spelling is determined by pronunciation." As far as origin goes, (G) and (J), you should already know from the previous question (item 11) that the word for that would be "etymological."

Implied Ideas and Applications

In Lesson 1, you learned about *implications*, which are a kind of information that is strongly suggested by the passage, but that isn't actually directly stated in the passage (p. 202). Writers frequently *imply* what they would like you to take away from the passage, or what you should *conclude* from it. When you are asked to apply the ideas in the passage, whether stated or implied, to another situation or idea, you are *generalizing*, as you learned in Lesson 2 (p. 213). When a question asks you which scenario is most like the one described in the passage, or how the information in the passage might work when applied to a different situation, you are being asked to *generalize* from the passage. Nevertheless, you should always be sure to ground all generalizations, conclusions, and inferences in information from the passage to avoid misrepresenting its content.

> Draw complex or subtle generalizations or conclusions about people, ideas, etc. by combining information from different parts of the passage.
>
> ───────────
>
> Understand and generalize about parts of a complex literary narrative.

BASIC INTERMEDIATE ADVANCED

In Lesson 4, you were introduced to several common logical fallacies, including: *slippery slope*, *over-generalization*, *ad-hominem attack*, *false cause*, and *false dichotomy* (p. 254). Even if you don't remember all of these terms, you may be required to identify information that the author has missed, overlooked, or deliberately left out of his or her argument. You also may be asked to identify a flaw similar to the one the author makes, or one similar to the one the author accuses others of making, as you learned in Lesson 5 (p. 289). Now, answer a few questions about the Implied Ideas and Applications of the sample passage (p. 292).

13. Which of the following would be an example of the alteration of spelling to indicate the etymology of a word?

   A. The addition of the letter *s* to the word *iland* to indicate its relationship to the Latin *insula*.

   B. The elimination of the silent *b* from *debt* because the letter is no longer pronounced as it was in the Latin *debitatis*.

   C. The use of the prefix *psych-*, from the Greek *psyche*, to indicate a function of the mind.

   D. The joining of two words such as *house* and *boat* to represent a concept that joins some of the essential characteristics of the things described by each of the words.

(A) is the correct answer. This Application question, in which you must generalize using the information in the passage, is also a vocabulary question testing your understanding of the word "etymology." The author points out that some spellings have been changed, not to reflect their pronunciation, but to reflect the origin (or "etymology") of the word despite the fact that the pronunciation will not be altered. The *s* is silent in the word *island*. (B) is wrong because it is not representative of the process discussed—changes of spelling to reflect origin (not pronunciation). (C) and (D) are examples of words whose spelling indicates their origins, but they are not instances of words whose spelling has been altered in order to reflect their origins.

14. Which of the following, if true, would undermine the author's point about the spelling of "i (it)" in paragraph 5?

    F. The author includes many spellings of the "i" sound that aren't consistent with its sound in the word "it."
    G. The Norman Conquest of 1066 resulted in the mixture of English and French phonetics and orthography.
    H. The Great Vowel Shift, which took place from the fourteenth through the eighteenth centuries, resulted in a markedly different pronunciation of many English words.
    J. The sound for "e (led)" has 19 different spellings in English orthography.

    The correct answer is (F). The key to this question lies in staying focused on the question. (G) and (H) both describe historical influences on the evolution of the English language. Both facts actually could support the author's Main Idea, which is that the language has changed far faster than spelling, resulting in the spelling of many English words not reflecting their pronunciation. Furthermore, neither has much effect on the author's point about "i (it)," since those events are likely responsible for some of the disconnect in the pronunciation and spelling of that sound. (J) is actually another example of the author's point, so it certainly wouldn't undermine his observations about "i (it)." (F), however, would undermine the point at least a bit, since, if true, it would appear that the author has committed a fallacy of including false evidence for dramatic effect.

15. Which of the following would be an example of a redundancy in the spelling of a language as described by the author?

    A. The use of *qu* to represent the sounds in the words *liquor* and *quick.*
    B. The use of *e* to represent the sound in *jest* and the use of *ee* to represent the sound in *seem.*
    C. The presence of *gh* in *caught.*
    D. The use of *ow* and *ou* to represent the sounds in *bowl* and *soul.*

The correct answer is (D). According to the second paragraph of the passage, a redundancy is the use of more than one symbol to represent a single sound, and the question asks you to apply this term to another scenario. (A) shows the use of one symbol to communicate two sounds. This would be an example of repetition. (B) is merely an example of two different letters or groups of letters being used to represent two different sounds. (C) is an example of a silent letter, discussed elsewhere in the passage.

EXERCISE 1

DIRECTIONS: Each passage below is followed by one or more items based on its content. Answer the items on the basis of what is stated or implied in the corresponding passage. Answers are on page 811.

PASSAGE I

This passage discusses advances in computer technology.

Can computers reason? Reasoning requires the individual to take a given set of facts and draw correct conclusions. Unfortunately, errors frequently occur, and we are not talking about simple carelessness as occurs when two numbers are incorrectly added, nor do we mean errors resulting from simple forgetfulness. Rather, we have in mind errors of a logical
5 nature—those resulting from faulty reasoning. Now, or at least soon, computers will be capable of error-free logical reasoning in a variety of areas. The key to avoiding errors is to use a computer program that relies on the last two decades' research in the field of automated theorem proving. AURA (Automated Reasoning Assistant) is the program that best exemplifies this use of the computer.

10 AURA solves a problem by drawing conclusions from a given set of facts about the problem. The program does not learn, nor is it self-analytical, but it reaches logical conclusions flawlessly. It uses various types of reasoning and, more importantly, has access to very powerful and sophisticated logical strategies.

AURA seldom relies on brute force to find solutions. Instead it solves almost all problems by
15 using sophisticated techniques to find a contradiction. One generally starts with a set of assumptions and adds a statement that the goal is unreachable. For example, if the problem is to test a safety system that automatically shuts down a nuclear reactor when instruments indicate a problem, AURA is told that the system will not shut the reactor down under those circumstances. If AURA finds a contradiction between the statement and the system's
20 design assumptions, then this aspect of the reactor's design has been proved satisfactory. This strategy, known as the set of support strategy, lets AURA concentrate on the problem at hand and avoid the many fruitless steps required to explore the entire theory underlying the problem. Almost never does the program proceed by carrying out an exhaustive search.

The chief use for AURA at this time is for electronic circuit design validation, but a number
25 of other uses will arise. For example, there already exist "expert systems" that include a
component for reasoning. An expert system is a special-purpose program designed to
automate reasoning in a specific area such as medical diagnosis. These expert programs,
unlike human experts, do not die. Such systems continue to improve and have an indefinite
life span. Moreover, they can be replicated for pennies. A human who can expertly predict
30 where to drill for oil is in great demand. A program that can predict equally well would be
invaluable and could be duplicated any number of times.

Will the computer replace the human being? Certainly not. It seems likely that computer
programs will reproduce—that is, design more clever computer programs and more
efficient, more useful components. Reasoning programs will also analyze their own
35 progress, learn from their attempts to solve a problem, and redirect their attack on a
problem. Such programs will assist, rather than replace, humans. Their impact will be felt in
design, manufacturing, law, medicine, and other areas. Reasoning assistants will enable
human minds to turn to deeper and far more complex ideas. These ideas will be partially
formulated and then checked for reasoning flaws by a reasoning program. Many errors will
40 be avoided.

1. Which of the following titles best
describes the content of the passage?

A. Scientific Applications of
Computers
B. Theories of Artificial Intelligence
C. Some Suggested Applications for
AURA
D. Using Computers to Assist Human
Reasoning

2. According to the passage, all of the
following are advantages of expert
programs EXCEPT:

F. they have an indefinite life span.
G. they cost little to reproduce.
H. many copies can be made
available.
J. they are self-analytical.

3. If the design of an electronic circuit
were tested by AURA, and the
conclusion that under certain
circumstances a switching device
would remain open generated a
contradiction, this would lead to the
conclusion that:

A. the circuit was properly designed.
B. the switch would remain closed
under the circumstances.
C. the switch would remain open
under the circumstances.
D. an error in human reasoning
invalidated the design

4. The author's attitude toward the
developments he describes can best
be described as:

F. enthusiastic.
G. reluctant.
H. cautious.
J. skeptical.

5. The author is primarily concerned with:

    A. discussing recent developments.
    B. correcting a misconception.
    C. proposing a theory.
    D. refuting an objection.

PASSAGE II

This passage is an excerpt from a critical literary essay on George Orwell's Nineteen Eighty-Four.

When we are speaking casually, we call *Nineteen Eighty-Four* a novel, but in a more exacting context we call it a political fable. This is not refuted by the fact that the book is preoccupied with an individual, Winston Smith, who suffers from a varicose ulcer, or by the fact that it takes account of other individuals, including Julia, Mr. Charrington, Mrs. Parsons, Syme, and
5 O'Brien.

The figures claim our attention, but they exist mainly in their relation to the political system that determines them. It would indeed be possible to think of them as figures in a novel, though in that case they would have to be imagined in a far more diverse set of relations. They would no longer inhabit or sustain a fable, because a fable is a narrative relieved of
10 much contingent detail so that it may stand forth in an unusual degree of clarity and simplicity. A fable is a structure of types, each of them deliberately simplified lest a sense of difference and heterogeneity reduce the force of the typical. Let us say, then, that *Nineteen Eighty-Four* is a political fable, projected into a near future and incorporating historical references mainly to document a canceled past.

15 Since a fable is predicated upon a typology, it must be written from a certain distance. The author cannot afford the sense of familiarity that is induced by detail and differentiation. A fable, in this respect, asks to be compared to a caricature, not to a photograph. It follows that in a political fable there is bound to be some tension between a political sense, which deals in the multiplicity of social and personal life, and a sense of fable, which is committed
20 to simplicity of form and feature. If the political sense were to prevail, the narrative would be drawn away from fable into the novel, at some cost to its simplicity. If the sense of fable were to prevail, the fabulist would station himself at such a distance from any imaginary conditions in the case that his narrative would appear unmediated, free, or bereft of conditions. The risk in that procedure would be considerable: a reader might feel that the
25 fabulist has lost interest in the variety of human life and has fallen back upon an unconditioned sense of its types, that he has become less interested in lives than in a particular idea of life. The risk is greater still if the fabulist projects his narrative into the future: the reader cannot question by appealing to the conditions of life he already knows.

He is asked to believe that the future is another country and that "they just do things
30 differently there."

In a powerful fable, the reader's feeling is likely to be mostly fear: he is afraid that the
fabulist's vision of any life that is likely to arise may be accurate and will be verified in the
event. The fabulist's feeling may be more various. Such a fable as *Nineteen Eighty-Four*
might arise from disgust, despair, or world-weariness, induced by evidence that nothing,
35 despite one's best efforts, has changed, and that it is too late now to hope for the change
one wants.

6. In drawing an analogy between a fable and a caricature (lines 16–17), the author would most likely regard which one of the following pairs of ideas as also analogous?

   F. The subject of a caricature and the topic of a fable.

   G. The subject of a caricature and the main character in *Nineteen Eighty-Four.*

   H. The subject of a fable and the artist who draws the caricature.

   J. The artist who draws the caricature and a novelist.

7. The author uses the contrast between a caricature and a photograph to emphasize the point that a political fable:

   A. is a more accurate rendering of social life than is a novel.

   B. is more likely to cause a reaction of fear in the reader than is a novel.

   C. is less likely to be understood by the reader than is a novel.

   D. lacks much of the contingent detail that characterizes a novel.

8. Which one of the following best explains why the author mentions that Winston Smith suffers from a varicose ulcer?

   F. To demonstrate that a political fable must emphasize type over detail.

   G. To show that Winston Smith has some characteristics that distinguish him as an individual.

   H. To argue that Winston Smith is no more important than any other character in *Nineteen Eighty-Four.*

   J. To illustrate one of the features of the political situation described in *Nineteen Eighty-Four.*

9. The "tension" that the author mentions in line 18 refers to the:

 A. necessity of striking a balance between the need to describe a political situation in simple terms and the need to make the description realistic.
 B. reaction that the reader feels because he or she is drawn to the characters of the fable as individuals but repulsed by the political situation.
 C. delicate task faced by a literary critic who must interpret the text of a work while attempting to accurately describe the intentions of the author.
 D. danger that too realistic a description of a key character will make the reader feel that the fable is actually a description of his or her own situation.

10. The author's attitude toward *Nineteen Eighty-Four* can best be described as:

 F. condescending.
 G. laudatory.
 H. disparaging.
 J. scholarly.

11. The author uses the phrase "another country" (line 29) to describe a political fable in which:

 A. political events described in a fable occur in a place other than the country of national origin of the author.
 B. a lack of detail makes it difficult for a reader to see the connection between his own situation and the one described in the book.
 C. too many minor characters create the impression of complete disorganization, leading the reader to believe he is in a foreign country.
 D. the author has allowed his personal political convictions to infect his description of the political situation.

12. The author's primary concern is to:

 F. define and clarify a concept.
 G. point out a logical inconsistency.
 H. trace the connection between a cause and an effect.
 J. illustrate a general statement with examples.

PASSAGE III

This passage discusses techniques used for insect and pest management.

Traditional strategies for controlling insect-pests tend to rely on the use of nonselective insecticides that cause extensive ecological disruption. The alternative sterile insect technique, in which members of the target species are irradiated to cause sterility, has enjoyed some modest success. When released into an infested area, the sterile insects mate
5 with normal insects but produce no offspring. Unfortunately, the irradiation weakens the insects, making it less likely that they will mate; and, in any event, sterile insects do not search selectively for non-sterile mates. A third, newly developed strategy is based on parasite release.

Pest hosts and their associated parasites have evolved biological and behavioral
10 characteristics that virtually ensure that the relative numbers of hosts and parasites in the ecosystem they inhabit remain within relatively narrow limits—even though coexisting populations may fluctuate up to 100-fold during a single season. The close numerical relationships are entirely consistent with nature's balancing mechanisms, which permit closely associated organisms to live together in harmony. Thus, in natural populations, the
15 ratios of parasites to hosts are not high enough to result in dependable control. However, it is possible to mass-rear parasites so that they can be released at strategic times and in numbers that result in parasite-to-host ratios sufficient to control host populations.

Biosteres tryoni, for example, has a strong affinity for medfly larvae. Let us assume that a new medfly infestation is discovered. It is likely to have originated from a single female and,
20 even in an area with a good surveillance program, to be in the third reproductive cycle. The rate of population increase is tenfold per generation; so at the time the infestation comes to light, about 1,000 males and 1,000 females are emerging and will produce a total of approximately 80,000 larvae. Reproduction will be concentrated in an area of about one square mile, but scattered reproduction will occur anywhere within a 25-square mile area.
25 At first glance, the odds of controlling the infestation by parasite release seem low, but with new techniques for mass-producing parasites, it is possible to release one million males and one million females into the infested area. This would mean an average of 62 females per acre, and the average female parasitizes about 30 host larvae during its lifetime.

Additionally, the parasites actively search for host habitats by using the kairomone signals
30 emanating from infested fruit. Even assuming that only ten percent of the released females are successful and, further, that they parasitize an average of only ten larvae, they could still parasitize one million larvae. Only 80,000 larvae are available, however; so the actual ratio would be 12.5:1. A ratio as low as 5:1 results in 99 percent parasitism.

This method of pest eradication presents no health or environmental problems and is
35 actually cheaper. The cost of mass-rearing and distributing *B. tryoni* is about $2,000 per
million. So, even if six million parasites of both sexes are released during a period
corresponding to three medfly reproductive cycles, the total cost of the treatment would be
$12,000—compared to $25,000 for a single insecticide spray application to the same 25-
square mile area.

13. The author implies that the sterile
insect release strategy is not
completely effective because:

A. some sterile insects mate with
other sterile insects.
B. weakened sterile insects refuse to
mate with healthy insects.
C. the cost of producing a sufficient
number of sterile insects is
prohibitive.
D. sterile insects are incapable of
producing offspring.

14. According to the passage, *Biosteres
tryoni* is effective in controlling
medfly infestations because:

F. female *B. tryoni* feed on adult
medflies.
G. male and female *B. tryoni*
parasitize medfly larvae.
H. female *B. tryoni* parasitize medfly
larvae.
J. male *B. tryoni* prevent male
medflies from mating.

15. It can be inferred that if *B. tryoni*
were not attracted by kairomone
signals from medfly-infested fruit,
that the parasite release strategy
would be:

A. less effective because some *B.
tryoni* would remain in areas not
infested.
B. less effective because none of the
B. tryoni would parasitize medfly
larvae.
C. equally as effective because *B.
tryoni* do not damage fruit crops.
D. more effective because some *B.
tryoni* would fail to reproduce.

16. In the development of the passage,
the author:

F. explains a scientific theory and
then offers evidence to refute it.
G. cites statistics to compare the
relative effectiveness of different
strategies.
H. speculates on the probable course
of scientific developments.
J. states a general principle and
then provides an example of its
application.

17. Which one of the following statements about medfly reproduction can be inferred from the passage?

A. Only about 25 percent of larvae reach adulthood.
B. The medfly is capable of reproducing asexually.
C. A typical generation contains ten times as many females as males.
D. A new generation of medfly is produced once a year.

18. It can be inferred that an insecticide application for the hypothetical infestation would treat a 25-square mile area because:

F. the cost for a single spray application to the area is $25,000.
G. *B. tryoni* would tend to concentrate themselves in infested areas.
H. medfly reproduction might occur anywhere within that region.
J. the spray would repel medflies from fruit not already infested.

19. The author is primarily concerned with:

A. criticizing the use of nonselective insecticides.
B. defending the use of parasite release programs.
C. explaining the workings of a new pest-control method.
D. refuting the suggestion that parasite release is costly

PASSAGE IV

This passage explains the complexity of the Japanese language.

What we expect of translation is a reasonable facsimile of something that might have been said in our language, but there is involved in this notion a debate between critics as to what constitutes a reasonable facsimile. Most of us at heart belong to the "soft-line" party: a given translation may not be exactly "living language," but the facsimile is generally reasonable.
5 The "hard-line" party aims only for the good translation. The majority of readers never notice the difference, as they read passively, often missing stylistic integrity so long as the story holds them. Additionally, a literature like Japanese may even be treated to an "exoticism handicap."

Whether or not one agrees with Roy A. Miller's postulation of an attitude of mysticism by
10 the Japanese toward their own language, it is true that the Japanese have special feelings toward the possibilities of their language and its relation to life and art, and these feelings

have an effect on what Japanese writers write about and how they write. Many of the special language relationships are not immediately available to the non-Japanese (which is only to say that the Japanese language, like every other, has some unique features). For
15 example, in my own work on Dazai Osamu, I have found how close to the sense of the rhythms of spoken Japanese his writing is, and how hard that is to duplicate in English. Juda's cackling hysterically, "Heh, heh, heh" (in *Kakekomi uttae*), or the coy poutings of a schoolgirl (in *Joseito*) have what Masao Miyoshi has called, in *Accomplices of Silence*, an "embarrassing" quality. It is, however, the embarrassment of recognition that the reader of
20 Japanese feels. The moments simply do not work in English.

Even the orthography, or the rules of spelling, of written Japanese is a resource not open to us. Tanizaki Jun'ichiro, who elsewhere laments the poverty of "indigenous" Japanese vocabulary, writes in *Bunsho tokuhon* of the contribution to literary effect—to "meaning," if you will—made simply by the way a Japanese author chooses to "spell" a word. In Shiga
25 Naoya's *Kinosaki nite*, for example, the onomatopoeic "bu-n" with which a honeybee takes flight has a different feeling for having been written in *hiragana* instead of *katakana*. I read, and I am convinced. Arishima Takeo uses onomatopoeic words in his children's story *Hitofusa no budo*, and the effect is not one of baby talk, but of gentleness and intimacy that automatically pulls the reader into the world of childhood fears, tragedies, and
30 consolations, memories of which lie close under the surface of every adult psyche.

This, of course, is hard to reproduce in translation, although translators labor hard to do so. George Steiner speaks of an "intentional strangeness," a "creative dislocation," that sometimes is invoked in the attempt. He cites Chateaubriand's 1836 translation of Milton's *Paradise Lost*, for which Chateaubriand "created" a Latinate French to approximate Milton's
35 special English as an example of just such a successful act of creation. He also laments what he calls "the 'moon in pond like blossom weary' school of instant exotica," with which we are perhaps all too familiar.

20. The author is primarily concerned with:

   F. criticizing translators who do not faithfully reproduce the style of works written in another language.

   G. discussing some of the problems of translating Japanese literature into English.

   H. arguing that no translation can do justice to a work written in another language.

   J. demonstrating that Japanese literature is particularly difficult to translate into English.

21. It can be inferred that *Accomplices of Silence* is:

   A. an English translation of Japanese poetry.

   B. a critical commentary on the work of Osamu.

   C. a prior publication by the author on Japanese literature.

   D. a text on Japanese orthography.

22. The author cites Shiga Naoya's *Kinosaki nite* in order to:

   F. illustrate the effect that Japanese orthography has on meaning.
   G. demonstrate the poverty of indigenous Japanese vocabulary.
   H. prove that it is difficult to translate Japanese into English.
   J. acquaint the reader with an important work of Japanese literature.

23. With which one of the following statements would the author most likely agree?

   A. The Japanese language is the language best suited to poetry.
   B. English is one of the most difficult languages into which to translate any work written in Japanese.
   C. It is impossible for a person not fluent in Japanese to understand the inner meaning of Japanese literature.
   D. Every language has its own peculiar potentialities which present challenges to a translator.

24. It can be inferred that the Japanese word *bu-n* (line 25) is most like which one of the following English words?

   F. Bee
   G. Honey
   H. Buzz
   J. Flower

25. The author uses all of the following EXCEPT:

   A. examples to prove a point.
   B. citation of authority.
   C. analogy.
   D. personal knowledge.

26. It can be inferred that the "exoticism handicap" (line 8) mentioned by the author is:

   F. the tendency of some translators of Japanese to render Japanese literature in a needlessly awkward style.
   G. the attempt of Japanese writers to create for their readers a world characterized by mysticism.
   H. the lack of literal, word-for-word translational equivalents for Japanese and English vocabulary.
   J. the expectation of many English readers that Japanese literature can only be understood by someone who speaks Japanese.

PASSAGE V

Social Studies: This passage addresses the debates that surround healthcare.

Since World War II, considerable advances have been made in the area of healthcare services. These include better access to healthcare (particularly for the poor and minorities), improvements in workplace safety, and increased numbers of physicians and other healthcare personnel. All have played a part in the recent improvement in life
5   expectancy. But there is mounting criticism of the large remaining gaps in access to healthcare, the unbridled cost inflation, the further fragmentation of service, the excessive indulgence in wasteful high-technology "gadgeteering," and the breakdown in doctor-patient relationships. In recent years, proposed solutions and new programs—small and large—have proliferated at a feverish pace, and disappointments have multiplied at almost
10 the same rate. This has led to an increased pessimism—"everything has been tried and nothing works"—that sometimes borders on cynicism or even nihilism.

It is true that the automatic "pass through" of rapidly spiraling costs to government and insurance carriers, which was set in a publicized environment of "the richest nation in the world," produced for a time a sense of unlimited resources and allowed a mood to develop
15 whereby every practitioner and institution could "do his own thing" without undue concern for the "Medical Commons." The practice of full-cost reimbursement encouraged capital investment, and now the industry is overcapitalized. Many cities have hundreds of excess hospital beds; hospitals have a superabundance of high-technology equipment; and structural ostentation and luxury are the order of the day. In any given day, one-fourth of all
20 community beds are vacant; expensive equipment is underused or, worse, used unnecessarily. Capital investment brings rapidly rising operating costs.

Yet, in part, this pessimism derives from expecting too much from healthcare. It must be realized that care is, for most people, a painful experience, often accompanied by fear and unwelcome results. Although there is vast room for improvement, healthcare will always
25 retain some unpleasantness and frustration. Moreover, the capacities of medical science are limited. Humpty Dumpty cannot always be put back together again. Too many physicians are reluctant to admit their limitations to patients and too many patients and families are unwilling to accept such realities. Nor is it true that everything has been tried and nothing works, as shown by the prepaid group practice plans of the Kaiser Foundation and at Puget
30 Sound. In the main, however, such undertakings have been drowned by a veritable flood of public and private moneys that have supported and encouraged the continuation of conventional practices and subsidized their shortcomings on a massive, almost unrestricted scale. Except for the most idealistic and dedicated, there have been no incentives to seek change or to practice self-restraint or frugality. In this atmosphere, it is not fair to condemn
35 as failures all attempted experiments; it may be more accurate to say many have never had a fair trial.

27. The author implies that the Kaiser Foundation and Puget Sound plans (lines 29–30) differed from other plans by:

    A. encouraging capital investment.
    B. requiring physicians to treat the poor.
    C. providing incentives for cost control.
    D. employing only dedicated and idealistic doctors.

28. The author mentions all of the following as consequences of full-cost reimbursement EXCEPT:

    F. rising operating costs.
    G. underused hospital facilities.
    H. overcapitalization.
    J. lack of service for minorities.

29. The tone of the passage can best be described as:

    A. light-hearted and amused.
    B. objective but concerned.
    C. detached and unconcerned.
    D. cautious but sincere.

30. According to the author, the "pessimism" mentioned in line 22 is partly attributable to the fact that:

    F. there has been little real improvement in healthcare services.
    G. expectations about healthcare services are sometimes unrealistic.
    H. large segments of the population find it impossible to get access to healthcare services.
    J. advances in technology have made healthcare services unaffordable.

31. The author cites the prepaid plans (lines 29–30) as:

    A. counterexamples to the claim that nothing has worked.
    B. examples of healthcare plans that were overfunded.
    C. evidence that healthcare services are fragmented.
    D. proof of the theory that no plan has been successful.

32. It can be inferred that the sentence "Humpty Dumpty cannot always be put back together again" means that:

    F. the cost of healthcare services will not decline.
    G. medical science cannot cure every illness.
    H. medical care is not really essential to good health.
    J. illness is often unpleasant and even painful.

33. With which one of the following descriptions of the system for the delivery of healthcare services would the author most likely agree?

    A. It is biased in favor of doctors and against patients.
    B. It is highly fragmented and completely ineffective.
    C. It has not embraced new technology rapidly enough.
    D. It is generally effective but can be improved.

34. Which one of the following best describes the logical structure of the passage?

    F. The third paragraph is intended as a refutation of the first and second paragraphs.
    G. The second and third paragraphs are intended as a refutation of the first paragraph.
    H. The second and third paragraphs explain and put into perspective the points made in the first paragraph.
    J. The first paragraph describes a problem, and the second and third paragraphs present two horns of a dilemma.

35. The author's primary concern is to:

    A. criticize physicians and healthcare administrators for investing in technologically advanced equipment.
    B. examine some problems affecting the delivery of healthcare services and assess their severity.
    C. defend the medical community from charges that healthcare has not improved since World War II.
    D. analyze the reasons for the healthcare industry's inability to provide quality care to all segments of the population.

PASSAGE VI

This passage deals with the issues involved in policymaking.

Because some resources must be allocated at the national level, we have created policies that reflect the aggregated attributes of our society. The federal budget determines the proportion of federal resources to be invested in social welfare programs and how these resources are distributed among competing programs. This budget is arrived at through a
5 reiterative, aggregative political process which mediates the claims of groups interested in health, education, welfare, and so on, thus socializing the continuing conflict generated by their separate aspirations. The test of whether a policy is "good" under this system is whether it can marshal sufficient legitimacy and consent to provide a basis for cohesion and action. Technical criteria may play a role in the process, but the ultimate criteria are
10 political and social.

Whether a policy that is "good" in the aggregate sense is also "good" for a particular person, however, is a different matter. If everyone had identical attributes, these criteria of goodness would produce identical outcomes. With any degree of complexity or change, however, these criteria will always produce different outcomes. Any policy negotiated to
15 attain an aggregate correctness will be wrong for every individual to whom the policy applies. The less a person conforms to the aggregate, the more wrong it will be.

When a policy is not working, we normally assume that the policy is right in form but wrong in content. It has failed because insufficient intelligence has informed its construction or insufficient energy its implementation. We proceed to replace the old policy
20 with a new one of the same form. This buys time, since some time must elapse before the new policy can fully display the same set of symptoms of failure as the old. We thus continue to invest our time, energy, and other resources as if every new discovery of a nonworking policy is a surprise, and a surprise that can be corrected with some reorganized model. But if policies based on complex, aggregated information are always
25 wrong with respect to the preferences of every person to whom they apply, we should concentrate on limiting such policies to minima or "floors." Rather than trying for better policies, we should try for fewer policies or more limited aggregated ones. Such limitations could be designed to produce policies as spare and minimal as possible, for the resources not consumed in their operation would then be usable in non-aggregative, person-specific
30 ways—that is, in a disaggregated fashion. This will require more than just strengthened "local" capacity; it will require the development of new procedures, institutions, roles, and expectations.

36. Which one of the following best states the central theme of the passage?

    F. Policies designed to meet the needs of a large group of people are inherently imperfect and should be scaled down.

    G. Policies created by the democratic process are less effective than policies designed by a single, concentrated body of authority.

    H. The effectiveness of a social policy depends more upon the manner in which the policy is administered than upon its initial design.

    J. Since policies created on the federal level are inherently ineffective, all federal social welfare programs should be discontinued.

37. According to the passage, the test of whether a policy is successful in the aggregate sense is whether or not it:

    A. applies to a large number of people.

    B. satisfies the needs of the people to whom it applies.

    C. appeals to a sufficiently large number of people.

    D. can be revised periodically in response to changing conditions.

38. Which one of the following would the author probably agree is NOT an example of a policy based on a process of aggregation?

    F. A school dietician prepares menus based on a survey of the taste preferences of students.

    G. A state requires licensed drivers to take an eye examination only once every ten years because most people's eyes do not change radically in a shorter period of time.

    H. The trainer for a baseball team prescribes exercises for injured team members according to the nature of the injury and the physical makeup of the player.

    J. The senate passed a law lowering the legal driving limit to 0.08, based on studies that determined impairment as a function of blood-alcohol levels.

39. In line 11, the author places the word "good" in quotation marks in order to:

    A. emphasize that the word is ambiguous when applied to public policies.

    B. stress that no two people will agree on what is "good" and what is not.

    C. minimize the need to describe public policies in value terms.

    D. point out that the word can be applied to individuals but not to groups.

40. Which one of the following words, when substituted for the word *aggregate* (line 15), would LEAST change the meaning of the sentence?

F.   Extreme
G.   Group
H.   Average
J.   Quantity

41. The author regards the use of aggregative policies as:

A.   enlightened but prohibitively expensive.
B.   undesirable but sometimes necessary.
C.   wasteful and open to corruption.
D.   essential and praiseworthy.

42. Which one of the following, if true, would most weaken the author's argument?

F.   Many aggregative social welfare policies enacted during the 1930s are still in effect even though they have been modified several times.
G.   A study by the General Services Administration of the federal government concluded that waste and mismanagement in government programs has declined in recent years.
H.   Many government programs can be made more efficient by applying sophisticated computer models and other advanced technology to the problems they are designed to solve.
J.   The resources that would be freed by limiting aggregative policies exist only as tax revenues, which cannot be distributed except through aggregative policies.

43. According to the passage, a policy based on aggregation will be wrong for every person to whom it applies because:

A.   no individual fits precisely the group profile.
B.   technical criteria aren't given sufficient emphasis.
C.   individuals who have no need for a program may still fit its eligibility criteria.
D.   some administrators may not apply policies uniformly to all.

PASSAGE VII

This passage explains the idea of a system of taxation called a single tax.

A single tax is a tax levied upon a single item or a single type of transaction that is intended to meet all or at least the principal revenue needs of a nation or other political jurisdiction. The concept of a single tax on the rent of land was introduced into general economic discussion about the middle of the eighteenth century by the Physiocrats and was
5   popularized in the late nineteenth century by Henry George, particularly in his book *Progress and Poverty* and in his New York mayoral campaign of 1886. George advocated the abolition of all taxes on industry and its products and the appropriation by taxation of the annual rental value of all the various forms of natural opportunities embraced under the general term "land."

10 The single tax proposed by Henry George was defended by its supporters as consonant with the theory of natural rights. A human being, they asserted, has an absolute inalienable right to life, equality of opportunity, and the pursuit of property. By virtue of these general rights, a person may claim access to land, which is necessary for the maintenance of life. But land, most of which is privately held, differs in fertility and value. Thus, those who hold
15 poorer land or no land at all are denied their natural rights of life, equality of opportunity, and pursuit of property. These natural rights, argued the supporters of the single tax, give everyone a joint claim to the difference between the value of the worst and the best lands. This differential value, called economic rent, belongs to the community as a whole.

Against this position, it was argued that the theory of natural rights also holds that a person
20 is entitled to the fruits of his or her labor and that the taking of property created by individual effort is confiscatory. Supporters of the single tax argued, however, that any scheme of private ownership was inherently unjust. Because of the scarcity of land and the differences in productivity among various parcels of land, some people are necessarily denied their right of equality of opportunity. Consequently, a single tax on land would not
25 confiscate that which belongs rightly to the landowner but would merely reclaim from the landowner that which by natural right belonged to the entire community.

A second general argument for the single tax on land rested upon the economic theory of distribution. With increases in population, people are forced to bring into cultivation poorer and poorer lands. But as this is done, economic rent—the difference between the
30 productivity of the best and the worst lands under cultivation—increases. As a result, wages decrease because wages in general are fixed by the income that can be earned by occupiers and tillers of freely held land. The share of capital in the product of industry, George maintained, follows the same course as wages (capital being in all essential respects simply labor impressed or congealed into matter). Thus, wages and interest rates rise and
35 fall together, varying inversely with rent.

Not only does rent increase with the increase in population, according to supporters of the single tax on land, every invention involves a further demand upon the soil for raw produce, thus increasing rent. Everything that lowers interest rates depresses wages and elevates

rent; every increment of capital, being a demand for land, and every additional laborer has
40 the same effect. Under private ownership of land, increases in population, science that
stimulates invention, frugality that multiplies capital—in short, material progress itself—
are synonymous with poverty.

Finally, advocates of the single tax on land argued that it would be more expeditious than
other methods of taxation. First, it would eliminate a large army of tax collectors. Second, it
45 would enormously increase the production of wealth by removing the taxes upon capital,
production, and consumption which, they theorized, repressed or discouraged industry,
and by forcing into use lands held idle for speculative purposes.

44. The author of the selection is primarily concerned with:

    F. persuading the reader that a single tax on land is economically efficient.

    G. encouraging legislators to adopt a single tax on land in lieu of other taxes.

    H. describing some nineteenth century arguments in favor of a single tax on land.

    J. discussing the relationship between tax rates and other economic factors such as interest rates.

45. According to the passage, Henry George regarded which of the following as the primary determinant of the wage level?

    A. Amount of income produced by owners of freely held land

    B. Number of employers in a geographical region

    C. Rate of taxation by the government of wages and salaries

    D. Level of rents paid by renters for the use of land owned by others

46. It can be inferred from the passage that Henry George entitled his work *Progress and Poverty* because he thought that under the existing tax structure:

    F. progress would inevitably lead to greater poverty.

    G. poverty would inevitably lead to more progress.

    H. progress would inevitably lead to a reduction in poverty.

    J. higher interest rates would inevitably lead to lower wages.

47. It can be inferred that an opponent of the single tax on land would regard the economic value created by the efforts of a landowner to improve that land as a:

    A. property right.

    B. loss of capital.

    C. legitimately taxable transaction.

    D. cause of unemployment.

48. If a government makes previously unoccupied fertile lands available to the general population, then economic rent, as that term was used by the supporters of a single tax on land, should:

    F. increase.
    G. decrease.
    H. remain unchanged.
    J. become zero.

49. According to the supporters of a single tax on land, an increase in wages should be accompanied by:

    A. a decrease in interest rates.
    B. an increase in rent.
    C. an increase in interest rates.
    D. an increase in population.

50. According to the selection, supporters of a single tax on land claimed that the single tax would do all of the following EXCEPT:

    F. reduce government bureaucracy.
    G. discourage land speculation.
    H. increase production of wealth.
    J. burden poor laborers.

PASSAGE VIII

This passage provides information on antipsychotic drugs called neuroleptics.

In the 1950s, the development of antipsychotic drugs called neuroleptics radically changed the clinical outlook for patients in mental institutions who had previously been considered hopelessly psychotic. Daily medication controlled delusions and made psychotherapy possible. Many, who otherwise might never have left institutions, returned to society. Now,
5 physicians have learned that there is a price to be paid for these benefits. Approximately 10 to 15 percent of patients who undergo long-term treatment with antipsychotic drugs develop a cluster of symptoms called tardive dyskinesia, the most common symptoms of which are involuntary repetitive movement of the tongue, mouth, and face, and sometimes the limbs and trunk.

10 Neuroleptic drugs interfere with the action of dopamine, an important neurotransmitter in the brain, by binding to the dopamine receptors of nerve cells. Dopamine is a prime suspect in the pathophysiology of schizophrenia. Large doses of drugs such as amphetamines, which stimulate secretion of dopamine, produce a psychosis resembling schizophrenia. Reducing the activity of this neurotransmitter alleviates the delusions that cause 25 percent
15 of psychotic behavior. Although the inhibition of dopamine activity can control psychotic behavior, researchers now believe that the central nervous system of some patients adapts to long-term therapy by increasing the number of specific dopamine binding sites. The net result is dopamine hypersensitivity, which is correlated with the subsequent appearance of tardive dyskinesia.

20 The risk of developing tardive dyskinesia is not so great that doctors have considered abandoning the use of antipsychotic drugs. Patients generally are bothered only slightly by the physical side effects, though the abnormal movements are troubling and may hinder social adjustment. Additionally, early diagnosis and prompt discontinuation of the neuroleptics might result in a decrease in the incidence of the movement disorders.
25 Unfortunately, without neuroleptic drugs, psychotic behavior returns. So, researchers have tried to achieve a satisfactory balance between the two effects, lowering dosages to a level that minimizes movement disorders yet controls psychosis. In a five-year study of twenty-seven psychiatric patients treated with neuroleptics representing all classes of antipsychotic drugs, researchers attempted to decrease drug doses to their lowest effective
30 levels. Patient responses suggested that low to moderate doses of antipsychotic drugs could control psychoses just as well as high doses, and tardive dyskinesia symptoms stabilized and gradually diminished or completely disappeared.

The fact that psychoses can be controlled at the same time that tardive dyskinesia symptoms are reduced suggests that a drug more specifically affecting the mechanism of
35 psychoses might not cause movement disorders. Sulpiride, a drug not available in the United States but widely used in Europe, where it was developed, may be one such alternative. The drug selectively blocks D–2 dopamine receptors, perhaps especially those in the limbic area of the brain, which is involved in emotion and behavior. It does not adversely affect the adenylate cyclase-linked D–1 dopamine receptors. Sulpiride has proven
40 effective in the short term, but whether it suppresses tardive dyskinesia over a long period of treatment is not yet known.

51. Which one of the following titles best describes the content of the passage?

    A. The Therapeutic Value of Antipsychotic Drugs

    B. The Tradeoff in the Use of Neuroleptic Drugs

    C. The Connection between Psychotherapy and Neuroleptic Drugs

    D. Recent Developments in the Treatment of Mental Illness

52. It can be inferred that neuroleptic drugs control psychosis by:

    F. suppressing the production of dopamine in the brain.

    G. blocking the nerve impulses transmitted to the muscles.

    H. preventing the absorption of dopamine by brain cells.

    J. creating a hypersensitivity to dopamine.

53. According to the passage, neuroleptic drugs are:

   A. generally effective but have unwanted side effects.
   B. gradually replacing psychotherapy.
   C. experimental and still not widely accepted.
   D. reserved for the most serious cases of psychosis.

54. It can be inferred that the primary danger of tardive dyskinesia is the:

   F. psychological effect on the patient.
   G. long-term therapeutic use of drugs.
   H. addiction of a patient to dopamine.
   J. physical injuries caused by violent muscle spasms.

55. If a patient showed symptoms of tardive dyskinesia, a doctor would probably:

   A. discontinue the use of all antipsychotic drugs.
   B. increase the dosage of dopamine.
   C. confine the patient to an institution.
   D. reduce the dosage of any neuroleptic drug.

56. The author cites the effects of large doses of drugs such as amphetamines in order to:

   F. demonstrate that dopamine may be the cause of some psychotic behavior.
   G. prove that neuroleptic drugs produce symptoms of tardive dyskinesia.
   H. give an example of a neuroleptic drug that does not necessarily cause tardive dyskinesia.
   J. show that smaller dosages of neuroleptic drugs can effectively control psychotic behavior.

57. According to the passage, which of the following statements about D-2 dopamine receptors are true?

   I. They are located only in the limbic area of the brain.
   II. Their functioning is affected by the drug sulpiride.
   III. They are responsible for initiating motor movements.

   A. I only
   B. II only
   C. I and II only
   D. II and III only

58. The tone of the final paragraph of the passage can best be described as:

   F. cautiously optimistic.
   G. bitterly disappointed.
   H. unconcerned.
   J. alarmed.

Math Skills Review

Course Concept Outline

ii. Compound Interest
d) Mixture Problems
7. Exercise 6 (Items #138–152, pp. 582–584)
8. Solve Linear Inequalities (p. 584)
9. Absolute Value in Algebraic Expressions, Equations, and Inequalities (p. 585)
10. Solving Quadratic Equations (p. 587)
11. Solving Systems of Equations (p. 588)
   a) Substitution
   b) Linear Combination (Elimination)
12. Exercise 7 (Items #153–172, pp. 592–593)

E. Graphical Representations (p. 594)

1. Find the Distance Between Two Points (p. 594)
2. Find Equations of Lines or Points (p. 596)
   a) Parallel Lines
   b) Horizontal and Vertical Parallel Lines
   c) Perpendicular Lines
3. Inequalities on the Number Line (p. 597)
   a) Linear Inequalities
   b) Quadratic Inequalities
3. Parabolas, Circles, and Graphs (p. 601)
   a) Identifying Graphs of Quadratic Functions
   b) Domain and Range of Graphed Functions
   c) Identifying Characteristics of Circles
4. Use Coordinate Graphs and Solve Complex Geometry Problems (p. 605)
   a) Graphing Geometric Figures
   b) Interpreting Information from Graphs
   c) Transformation Effects on Graphs
      i. Vertical Translations
      ii. Horizontal Translations
5. Exercise 8 (Items #173–207, pp. 608–616)

F. Plane Figures (p. 617)

1. Triangles (p. 617)
   a) Pythagorean Theorem
   b) Special Properties of 45°-45°-90° Triangles
   c) Special Properties of 30°-60°-90° Triangles
   d) Similar Triangles
2. Exercise 9 (Items #208–227, pp. 620–623)
3. Circle Properties and Formulas (p. 624)
4. Solve Multi-Step Geometric Problems (p. 627)
5. Exercise 10 (Items #228–242, pp. 629–634)

G. Measurement (p. 635)

1. Area, Perimeter, and Volume (p. 635)
2. Scale Factors (p. 642)
3. Composite Figures (p. 643)
4. Exercise 11 (Items #243–274, pp. 649–654)

H. Functions (p. 655)

1. Composite Functions (p. 655)
2. Trigonometry (p. 657)
3. Unit Circle Trigonometry (p. 659)
4. Identify Trigonometric Graphs (p. 661)
5. Exercise 12 (Items #275–288, pp. 664–665)

	Basic Manipulations (BOA)	Statistics and Data Presentations (PSD)	Number Concepts (NUM)	Algebraic Expressions, Equations, and Inequalities (XEI)
Basic	Perform simple one-operation calculations, such as addition, subtraction, multiplication, and division, using whole numbers and decimals. Perform simple conversions such as inches to feet or minutes to hours. Solve simple one-step and two-step arithmetic problems involving whole numbers, fractions, decimals, and percents.	Determine the average of a list of positive whole numbers. Determine the average of a list of numbers. Determine the average of a data set given the number of values and the sum of the values. Use the relationship between an event probability and the probability of its complement. Read tables and graphs. Solve one-step and multi-step calculations using information from tables and graphs.	Identify equivalent fractions, fractions in lowest terms, one-digit factors, and place value of digits.	Show familiarity with basic algebraic expressions. Evaluate simple expressions using whole numbers. Combine like terms. Solve simple equations involving whole numbers, integers, or decimals.
Intermediate	Solve multi-step arithmetic problems involving percents, proportions, rates, computing with a given average, and unit conversions.	Determine the missing data value given the average and all the values but one. Determine the average given the frequency counts of all data values. Determine the probability of events and common situations. Show familiarity with simple counting techniques and use Venn diagrams. Manipulate and translate data in tables and graphs.	Show familiarity with primes, greatest common factor, least common multiple, and working with numerical factors. Show familiarity with basic number concepts, such as rounding, ordering decimals and fractions, absolute value, and identification of patterns. Work with simple exponents, such as squares and square roots, cubes and cube roots, and positive exponents. Work with scientific notation. Determine when expressions are undefined. Show familiarity with complex numbers.	Evaluate simple expressions using integers. Add and subtract simple expressions. Multiply two binomials. Add, subtract, and multiply polynomials. Solve simple first-degree equations. Execute simple word-to-symbol translations. Use first-degree equations to solve real-world problems. Create single-variable expressions, equations, or inequalities for common pre-algebra situations such as rate, distance, and proportion. Identify simple quadratic equation solutions. Factor simple quadratic expressions such as the difference of squares and perfect square trinomials. Solve simple first-degree inequalities not requiring reversal of the inequality sign.
Advanced	Solve complex word problems involving percentages, proportions, ratios, rates, or averages.	Calculate and utilize weighted averages. Understand the differences between mean, median, and mode. Calculate the probability when the event or sample space is not explicitly given. Calculate joint and contingent probabilities. Use counting techniques. Understand, use, analyze, and draw conclusions from information in tables, graphs, and figures.	Apply number properties such as prime factorization, factors/multiples, odd/even numbers, and positive/negative numbers. Draw conclusions based on number concepts, algebraic properties, and relationships between numbers and expressions. Apply exponent rules. Show familiarity with logarithms and geometric sequences. Multiply two complex numbers. Apply properties of complex numbers.	Manipulate algebraic expressions and equations. Create expressions, equations, and inequalities for common algebra situations. Create expressions requiring planning and/or manipulation to model real-world situations. Create equations and inequalities requiring planning, manipulation, and/or solving. Solve linear inequalities requiring reversal of the inequality sign. Solve linear equations and simple inequalities involving absolute value. Solve quadratic equations. Solve simultaneous equations.

Graphical Representations (GRE)	Plane Figures (PPF)	Measurement (MEA)	Functions (FUN)
Locate numbers on a number line and in the first quadrant of the coordinate plane.	Show familiarity with angles associated with parallel lines.	Calculate or estimate line segment lengths given other lengths. Determine the perimeter of a polygon given all side lengths. Determine the area of a rectangle given whole number dimensions.	
Locate points in the coordinate plane. Demonstrate understanding of length on the number line. Determine the midpoint of a line segment. Identify graphical representations of inequalities on the number line. Show familiarity with slope and determine slope from linear equations or coordinate points. Identify graphs of linear equations.	Show familiarity with basic angle properties and special angle sums such as 90°, 180°, and 360°. Determine angle measures using properties of parallel lines. Determine an unknown angle measure using several angle properties. Use isosceles triangle properties. Identify Pythagorean triples.	Determine the perimeter and area of triangles in one-step and multi-step problems. Determine the perimeter and area of rectangles and squares in one-step and multi-step problems. Determine the circumference and area of circles in one-step and multi-step problems. Use geometric formulas when all the required information is given. Determine the perimeter of composite figures.	Evaluate quadratic and polynomial functions using integer values. Express basic trigonometric relationships for an angle in a right triangle.
Use the distance formula. Determine line equations or point coordinates using properties of parallel and perpendicular lines. Identify number line graphs of solution sets to linear and simple quadratic inequalities. Identify special characteristics of parabolas and circles, such as the center and radius of a circle. Identify characteristics of graphs based on a set of conditions or an equation, such as $y = ax^2 + c$. Comprehend, analyze, and apply information in coordinate graphs. Solve problems involving multiple algebraic and/or geometric concepts.	Use the Pythagorean theorem. Apply properties of special triangles such as 30°-60°-90°, 45°-45°-90°, similar, and congruent. Use relationships between arcs, angles, and distances in circles. Solve multi-step geometric problems.	Compute a measure using relationships between perimeter, area, and volume of geometric figures. Use scale factors to calculate the magnitude of a size change in geometric figures. Determine the area of composite geometric figures when planning or visualization is required.	Evaluate composite functions using integer values. Create an expression for the composite of two simple functions. Apply basic trigonometric ratios. Use trigonometric concepts and identities. Show familiarity of unit circle trigonometry. Identify graphs of basic trigonometric functions.

BASIC | Basic Manipulations

Simple Calculations

Properties of Whole Numbers

Properties of All Whole Numbers

Whole numbers are the positive integers, plus the number zero: $\{0, 1, 2, 3, 4,...\}$.

> Perform simple one-operation calculations, such as addition, subtraction, multiplication, and division, using whole numbers and decimals.
>
> ———————
>
> Perform simple conversions such as inches to feet or minutes to hours.

sum (total):   The result of adding numbers together. The **sum**, or total, of 2 and 3 is 5: $2+3=5$.

difference: The result of subtracting one number from another. The **difference** between 5 and 2 is 3: $5-2=3$.

product: The result of multiplying numbers together. The **product** of 2 and 3 is 6: $2 \cdot 3 = 6$.

quotient: The result of dividing one number by another. The **quotient** when 6 is divided by 2 is 3: $6 \div 2 = 3$.

remainder: In division, if the quotient is not itself a whole number, the result can be written as a whole number quotient plus a whole number remainder. For example, $7 \div 3 = 2$, plus a **remainder** of 1.

Properties of the Integers 0 and 1

The integers 0 and 1 have special properties that differ from other integers. First, the integer 0 is neither positive nor negative. If n is any number, then $n \pm 0 = n$ and $n \cdot 0 = 0$. Also, division by 0 is not defined. Therefore, it is never allowable to divide anything by 0. The integer 1 multiplied by any number n is equal to the original number; that is, $1 \cdot n = n$. Also, for any number $n \neq 0, n \cdot \dfrac{1}{n} = 1$. Note that the number 1 can be expressed in many ways; for example, $\dfrac{n}{n} = 1$ for any number $n \neq 0$. Finally, multiplying or dividing an expression by 1, in any form, does not change the value of that expression.

Examples:

$$4 + 0 = 4 \qquad\qquad 3 \cdot 0 = 0 \qquad\qquad 2 \cdot \frac{1}{2} = 1$$

$$4 - 0 = 4 \qquad\qquad 1 \cdot 5 = 5 \qquad\qquad \frac{4}{4} = 1$$

Working with Decimals

Adding and Subtracting Decimals

Decimals can be manipulated in very much the same way as whole numbers. You can add and subtract decimals.

Examples:

$$0.2 + 0.3 + 0.1 = 0.6$$

$$0.7 - 0.2 = 0.5$$

Adding zeros to the end of a decimal number does not change the value of that number. If the decimals do not have the same number of decimal places, add zeros to the right of those that do not until every number has the same number of decimal places. Then, line up the decimal points and combine the decimals as indicated. Follow the same process for subtracting decimals.

Examples:

1. $0.75 - 0.1125 \Rightarrow$
$$\begin{array}{r} 0.7500 \\ -0.1125 \\ \hline 0.6375 \end{array}$$

2. $0.125 + 0.6 + 0.115 \Rightarrow$
$$\begin{array}{r} 0.125 \\ 0.600 \\ +0.115 \\ \hline 0.840 \end{array}$$

3. $0.999 - 0.000001 \Rightarrow$
$$\begin{array}{r} 0.999000 \\ -0.000001 \\ \hline 0.998999 \end{array}$$

4. $2.14 + 0.125 + 0.0005 \Rightarrow$
$$\begin{array}{r} 2.1400 \\ 0.1250 \\ +0.0005 \\ \hline 2.2655 \end{array}$$

5. $0.8 - 0.1111 \Rightarrow$
$$\begin{array}{r} 0.8000 \\ -0.1111 \\ \hline 0.6889 \end{array}$$

6. $0.11 + 0.9 + 0.033 \Rightarrow$
$$\begin{array}{r} 0.110 \\ 0.900 \\ +0.033 \\ \hline 1.043 \end{array}$$

Multiplying Decimals

As with fractions, there is no need to find a common denominator or line up the decimal points when multiplying decimals: the multiplication process generates its own common denominator. Simply multiply as with whole numbers and then adjust the decimal point. To find the correct position for the decimal point first, count the total number of decimal places in the numbers that are being multiplied. Then, in the final product, place the decimal point that many places to the left, counting from the right side of the last digit.

Examples:

$0.25 \cdot 0.2 = ?$

Ignore the decimals and multiply: $25 \cdot 2 = 50$. Now, adjust the decimal point. Since 0.25 has two decimal places, and 0.2 has one decimal place, count three places to the left, starting at the right side of the zero in 50; the final product is $0.050 = 0.05$.

$0.1 \cdot 0.2 \cdot 0.3 = 0.006$ ($1 \cdot 2 \cdot 3 = 6$, and there are three decimal places in the multiplication.)

$0.02 \cdot 0.008 = 0.00016$ ($2 \cdot 8 = 16$, and there are five decimal places in the multiplication.)

$2 \cdot 0.5 = 1$ ($2 \cdot 5 = 10$, and there is one decimal place in the multiplication.)

$2.5 \cdot 2.5 = 6.25$ ($25 \cdot 25 = 625$, and there are two decimal places in the multiplication.)

$0.10 \cdot 0.10 \cdot 0.10 = 0.001$ ($10 \cdot 10 \cdot 10 = 1,000$, and there are six decimal places in the multiplication.)

To simplify the process of multiplying decimals, drop any final zeros before multiplying. Thus, in the case of the last example, $0.10 \cdot 0.10 \cdot 0.10 = 0.1 \cdot 0.1 \cdot 0.1 = 0.001$ since there are three decimal places in the multiplication.

Dividing Decimals

Like multiplication, division generates a common denominator by a suitable adjustment of zeros. However, there are two situations in which division of decimals is a little tricky. Let's review them one at a time.

First, when the divisor (the number doing the dividing) is a whole number, place the decimal point in the quotient (result of division) immediately above the decimal point in the dividend (the number being divided). Then, keep dividing until there is no remainder, adding zeros as needed to the right of the dividend. This is the procedure whenever the divisor is a whole number—even if the dividend is also a whole number.

Examples:

$$0.25 \div 5 \Rightarrow 5\overline{)0.25} \quad \begin{array}{r} 0.05 \\ \end{array}$$

$$\begin{array}{r} -25 \\ \hline 0 \end{array}$$

$$2.5 \div 2 \Rightarrow 2\overline{)2.50} \quad \begin{array}{r} 1.25 \\ \end{array}$$

$$\begin{array}{r} -2 \\ \hline 05 \end{array}$$

$$\begin{array}{r} -4 \\ \hline 10 \end{array}$$

$$\begin{array}{r} -10 \\ \hline 0 \end{array}$$

$$1.75 \div 25 \Rightarrow 25\overline{)1.75} \quad \begin{array}{r} 0.07 \\ \end{array}$$

$$\begin{array}{r} -1\,75 \\ \hline 0 \end{array}$$

$$1.44 \div 12 \Rightarrow 12\overline{)1.44} \quad \begin{array}{r} 0.12 \\ \end{array}$$

$$\begin{array}{r} -12 \\ \hline 24 \end{array}$$

$$\begin{array}{r} -24 \\ \hline 0 \end{array}$$

$$0.1 \div 250 \Rightarrow 250\overline{)0.1000} \quad \begin{array}{r} 0.0004 \\ \end{array}$$

$$\begin{array}{r} -1000 \\ \hline 0 \end{array}$$

$$9 \div 2 \Rightarrow 2\overline{)9.0} \quad \begin{array}{r} 4.5 \\ \end{array}$$

$$\begin{array}{r} -8 \\ \hline 10 \end{array}$$

$$\begin{array}{r} -10 \\ \hline 0 \end{array}$$

The second tricky situation occurs when the divisor is a decimal. In these cases, "clear" the fractional part of the decimal by moving the decimal point to the right. For example, if dividing by 0.1, change 0.1 to 1; if dividing by 2.11, convert that to 211 by moving the decimal point two places to the right. However, you must also move the decimal point of the dividend by the same number of places to ensure that their relative values are not changed. Notice that in the following examples both decimal points are moved the same number of places to the right.

Examples:

$$5 \div 2.5 \Rightarrow 2.5\overline{)5.0} \quad \begin{array}{r} 2. \\ \end{array}$$

$$\begin{array}{r} -5\,0 \\ \hline 0 \end{array}$$

$$10 \div 1.25 \Rightarrow 1.25\overline{)10.00} \quad \begin{array}{r} 8. \\ \end{array}$$

$$\begin{array}{r} -10\,00 \\ \hline 0 \end{array}$$

$$50 \div 0.05 \Rightarrow 0.05\overline{)50.00} \quad \begin{array}{r} 1000. \\ \end{array}$$

$$\begin{array}{r} -50\,00 \\ \hline 0 \end{array}$$

There are two final things to say about dividing decimals. First, as mentioned previously, you can use division of decimals to convert fractions to decimals. For example, to convert $\frac{9}{2}$ to a decimal number, simply divide 9 by 2.

Examples:

$$\frac{9}{2} = 2\overline{)9} \Rightarrow 2\overline{)9.0}^{\,4.5}$$
$$\underline{-\,8}$$
$$1\,0$$
$$\underline{-\,1\,0}$$
$$0$$

$$\frac{3}{4} = 4\overline{)3} \Rightarrow 4\overline{)3.00}^{\,0.75}$$
$$\underline{-\,2\,8}$$
$$2\,0$$
$$\underline{-2\,0}$$
$$0$$

Second, some fractions do not have exact decimal equivalents. Try converting $\frac{1}{3}$ to a decimal using the division route. You will be at it forever, because you get an endless succession of "3"s. Try converting $\frac{1}{9}$ to a decimal using the division method. Again, you will get an endless succession, this time of repeating "1"s. By convention, repeating decimals are indicated using an overbar: $0.1\overline{1}$.

Simple Conversions

Some word problems require you to perform a unit conversion. For example, you might need to convert inches into feet. Always read carefully to see what units are required for the answer.

Example:

A four-piece entertainment center has a height of 81 inches. How tall, in feet, is the entertainment center?

A. 0.20   C. 6.75   E. 12.00
B. 6.00   D. 8.10

There are 12 inches in 1 foot. To find the height of the entertainment center in feet, convert 81 inches to feet:

$$81 \text{ inches} \cdot \frac{1 \text{ foot}}{12 \text{ inches}} = \frac{81}{12} \text{ feet} = 6.75 \text{ feet}$$

If a problem requires conversion between common units such as inches and feet or minutes and hours, you should already be familiar with the units required. Sometimes you may be given a problem that involves conversion of units with which you are not familiar. In that case, either the problem itself will provide you with the needed information or you will have to look up the conversion in a chart.

Example:

The Honey-Badger Scout Patrol went on a 15-mile hike in the Lolo National Forest in west central Montana. Approximately what distance did the Scout Patrol hike in kilometers? (1 kilometer ≈ 0.62 miles)

A. 6.2   C. 10.0   E. 62.0
B. 9.3   D. 24.2

Convert miles to kilometers using the equivalence given:

$$15 \text{ miles} \cdot \frac{1 \text{ kilometer}}{0.62 \text{ miles}} \approx 24.2 \text{ kilometers}$$

If you look again at the two items we just covered, you will notice that converting units involves multiplying and dividing. A common mistake is to invert the conversion. For example, suppose that you tried to convert 15 miles to kilometers as follows:

$$15 \cdot \frac{0.62}{1} = 9.3$$

This result is wrong. Fortunately, there is an easy way to make sure that you are doing the conversion correctly: include the units. In the wrong conversion just shown:

$$15 \text{ miles} \cdot \frac{0.62 \text{ miles}}{1 \text{ kilometer}} = \frac{9.3 \text{ miles} \cdot \text{miles}}{\text{kilometers}}$$

But $\frac{\text{miles} \cdot \text{miles}}{\text{kilometers}}$ is not a real unit. The **correct** solution is:

$$15 \text{ \cancel{miles}} \cdot \frac{1 \text{ kilometer}}{0.62 \text{ \cancel{miles}}} \approx 24.2 \text{ kilometers}$$

In the correct solution, the "miles" unit in the numerator and the "miles" unit in the denominator cancel each other out. You can always be sure that you've done the conversion correctly if you include the units in your calculations.

EXERCISE 1

DIRECTIONS: Choose the correct answer to each of the following items. Answers are on page 812.

1. What is the sum of 5, 7, and 8?

    A. 12   C. 20   E. 28
    B. 15   D. 25

2. What is the difference between 8 and 3?

    F. 24   H. 8   K. 3
    G. 11   J. 5

3. What is the product of 2 and 8?

    A. 4   C. 10   E. 24
    B. 6   D. 16

4. What is the remainder when 12 is divided by 7?

    F. 1   H. 3   K. 5
    G. 2   J. 4

5. What is the remainder when 50 is divided by 2?

    A. 0   C. 3   E. 50
    B. 1   D. 25

6. What is the product of 6 and $\dfrac{1}{6}$?

    F. 0   H. 1   K. 36
    G. $\dfrac{1}{6}$ J. 6

7. The sum of 7 and 0 is:

    A. –7   C. $\dfrac{1}{7}$ E. 14
    B. 0   D. 7

8. $0.1 + 0.1 = ?$

    F. 0.002   H. 0.2   K. 20
    G. 0.02   J. 2

9. $0.528 + 0.116 + 0.227 = ?$

    A. 0.871   C. 0.243   E. 0.0012
    B. 0.583   D. 0.112

10. $1.23 + 0.00001 = ?$

    F. 1.24   J. 1.2300001
    G. 1.2301   K. 1.230000001
    H. 1.23001

11. $0.01 + 0.001 + 0.0001 + 0.00001 = ?$

    A. 1   D. 0.01111
    B. 0.1111   E. 0.001111
    C. 0.1

12. $0.27 + 0.36 + 2.1117 + 3.77777 + 1.42 = ?$

    F. 5.44   J. 12.223479
    G. 7.93947   K. 14.002785
    H. 8.11143

13. $0.7 - 0.3 = ?$

   A. 0.004   C. 0.04   E. 0.4
   B. 0.021   D. 0.21

14. $1.35 - 0.35 = ?$

   F. 1   H. 0.1   K. 0.00001
   G. 0.35   J. 0.0035

15. $1 - 0.00001 = ?$

   A. 0.9   C. 0.999   E. 0.99999
   B. 0.99   D. 0.9999

16. $0.1 \cdot 0.1 \cdot 0.1 = ?$

   F. 0.3   H. 0.01   K. 0.0001
   G. 0.1   J. 0.001

17. $0.11 \cdot 0.33 = ?$

   A. 0.363   D. 0.000363
   B. 0.0363   E. 0.0000363
   C. 0.00363

18. $5 \cdot 0.25 = ?$

   F. 1.25   J. 0.00125
   G. 0.125   K. 0.000125
   H. 0.0125

19. $100 \cdot 0.00052 = ?$

   A. 0.0052   C. 5.2   E. 520
   B. 0.052   D. 52

20. $1.000 \cdot 1.000 \cdot 1.000 \cdot 1.000 = ?$

   F. 1   H. 0.01   K. 0.0001
   G. 0.1   J. 0.001

21. $0.2 \div 5 = ?$

   A. 0.4   C. 0.004   E. 0.00004
   B. 0.04   D. 0.0004

22. $25.1 \div 2.51 = ?$

   F. 100   H. 0.1   K. 0.001
   G. 10   J. 0.01

23. $2 \div 2.5 = ?$

   A. 8   C. 0.8   E. 0.008
   B. 5   D. 0.5

24. $111 \div 0.111 = ?$

   F. 1   H. 11   K. 1,000
   G. 10   J. 110

25. $0.12345 \div 0.012345 = ?$

   A. 100   C. 1   E. 0.01
   B. 10   D. 0.1

26. On the day of a footrace, it began to rain. Because of the rain, officials delayed the race 17 minutes. By how many seconds was the race delayed?

   F. 510   J. 2,040
   G. 1,020   K. 3,400
   H. 1,700

27. The maximum takeoff weight for a particular cargo airplane is 910,000 pounds. What is the maximum takeoff weight of the cargo airplane in tons? (1 ton = 2,000 pounds)

   A. 0.002   D. 400
   B. 45   E. 455
   C. 200

28. As part of servicing an off-road truck, a mechanic has drained all of the oil from the engine. The service manual states that 5 quarts of oil should then be added. If the service garage measures oil in pints, how many pints of oil should the mechanic add? (1 quart = 2 pints)

F. 2.5   H. 7   K. 11
G. 3   J. 10

29. A hot air balloon is hovering over an expanse of open farmland at an altitude of 6,500 feet. What is the altitude of the balloon in meters? (1 foot ≈ 0.30 meters)

A. 1,500   D. 6,500
B. 1,950   E. 9,000
C. 2,025

30. The driving distance from Chicago to Phoenix is approximately 1,800 miles. Approximately how many kilometers is the driving distance from Chicago to Phoenix? (1 kilometer ≈ 0.62 miles)

F. 180   J. 2,903
G. 1,116   K. 3,600
H. 2,000

One-Step and Two-Step Arithmetic Story Problems

Story problems are mathematical manipulations presented in everyday contexts. Story problems are more difficult than a basic manipulation because the situation presented may seem distracting or confusing. In order to correctly answer a story problem, identify each piece of information, determine how the information fits together, and then solve the problem.

> Solve simple one-step and two-step arithmetic problems involving whole numbers, fractions, decimals, and percents.

One-Step Whole Number Story Problems

Some story problems involve whole numbers.

Example:

You work at a department store. Brand X shirts are on sale for $12 each. A customer purchases 3 Brand X shirts. How much should you charge for the shirts, before tax?

F. $12   H. $24   K. $48
G. $15   J. $36

Translate the story problem: $\dfrac{\$12}{\text{shirt}} \cdot 3 \text{ shirts} = \$36$.

One-Step Fraction and Decimal Story Problems

Similarly, story problems may include fractions or decimals.

Examples:

Your recipe for a soufflé calls for $1\frac{1}{3}$ cups of milk for every 5 eggs. If you plan to use 10 eggs, how many cups of milk will you need?

F. $1\frac{1}{3}$ H. $2\frac{1}{3}$ K. 4

G. 2   J. $2\frac{2}{3}$

The number of eggs doubles, so double the amount of milk: $1\frac{1}{3} \cdot 2 = 2\frac{2}{3}$.

Or, more formally: $\dfrac{1\frac{1}{3} \text{ cups of milk}}{5 \text{ eggs}} \cdot 10 \text{ eggs} = 2\frac{2}{3} \text{ cups of milk}$.

Gasoline costs $4.10 a gallon. When Tom refueled his car, he bought 9.4 gallons of gasoline. What was the total cost of the gasoline?

F. $4.10   H. $13.50   K. $38.54

G. $8.20   J. $36.00

Translate the story problem: $\dfrac{\$4.10}{1 \text{ gallon}} \cdot 9.4 \text{ gallons} = \$38.54$.

One-Step Percent Story Problems

There are three basic variations of the one-step percent problem:

- What is x percent of some quantity?

- What percent is this of that?

- This is x percent of what?

Notice that in each of the three forms, there is the phrase "of that" (or "of what") and the phrase "is this" (or "this is"). When you set up a fraction for the percent, always place the "is this" value over the "of that" value. This allows us to write the "is-over-of" equation for percents: $\dfrac{\text{is}}{\text{of}} = \dfrac{\%}{100}$.

Examples:

If Paula had 50 marbles and gave 20% of them to her friend Paul, how many marbles did Paula give to Paul?

Simplify the item stem: "x is 20% of 50." Thus, $\dfrac{\text{is}}{\text{of}} = \dfrac{\%}{100} \Rightarrow \dfrac{x}{50} = \dfrac{20}{100} \Rightarrow$

$x = \dfrac{20 \cdot 50}{100} = \dfrac{20}{2} = 10$.

John received a paycheck for $200. Of that amount, he paid Ed $25. What percentage of the paycheck did John give Ed?

Simplify the item stem: "$25 is x% of $200." Thus, $\dfrac{\text{is}}{\text{of}} = \dfrac{\%}{100} \Rightarrow \dfrac{\$25}{\$200} = \dfrac{x}{100} \Rightarrow$

$x = \dfrac{25 \cdot 100}{200} = \dfrac{25}{2} = 12.5\%$.

Seven students attended a field trip. If these seven students were $6\frac{1}{4}$% of all the 9th graders, find the total number of 9th graders.

Simplify the item stem: "7 is 6.25% of x." Thus, $\dfrac{\text{is}}{\text{of}} = \dfrac{\%}{100} \Rightarrow \dfrac{7}{x} = \dfrac{6.25}{100} \Rightarrow$

$x = \dfrac{7 \cdot 100}{6.25} = 7 \cdot 16 = 112$.

Two-Step Story Problems

Some story problems require more than one step in order to reach the solution.

Examples:

You need 5 pounds of nails for an upcoming project, and you are comparing the price of two brands of stainless steel nails of equal length. Brand X nails come in 5 pound packages for $24, and Brand Y nails come in 2.5 pound packages for $15. How much do you save by buying Brand X (disregarding sales tax)?

Find the cost of Brand X and Brand Y for 5 pounds of nails:

$$\text{Brand } X: \; 5 \text{ pounds} \cdot \frac{\$24}{5 \text{ pounds}} = \$24$$

$$\text{Brand } Y: \; 5 \text{ pounds} \cdot \frac{\$15}{2.5 \text{ pounds}} = \$30$$

Now, subtract the price of Brand X from the price of Brand Y to determine your savings: $30 – $24 = $6.

Mr. Saunders works at Brown's Department Store, where he is paid $80 per week in salary plus a 4% commission on all his sales. How much does he earn in a week in which he sells $4,032 worth of merchandise?

Find 4% of $4,032: $4,032 \cdot 0.04 = \$161.28$.

Add this amount to $80: $161.28 + \$80 = \$241.28$.

EXERCISE 2

DIRECTIONS: Choose the correct answer to each of the following items. Answers are on page 812.

31. Subtracting 1 from which digit in the number 12,345 will decrease the value of the number by 1,000?

    A. 1   C. 3   E. 5
    B. 2   D. 4

32. Adding 1 to each digit of the number 222,222 will increase the value of the number by how much?

    F. 333,333   H. 100,000   K. 1
    G. 111,111   J. 10

33. What is the sum of the product of 2 and 3 and the product of 3 and 4?

    A. 6   C. 18   E. 72
    B. 12   D. 35

34. One brass rod measures $3\frac{5}{16}$ inches long and another brass rod measures $2\frac{3}{4}$ inches long. What is the total length, in inches, of the two rods combined?

    F. $6\frac{9}{16}$ H. $5\frac{1}{2}$ K. $5\frac{1}{32}$
    G. $6\frac{1}{16}$ J. $5\frac{1}{16}$

35. Which of the following equals the number of half-pound packages of tea that can be taken out of a box that holds $10\frac{1}{2}$ pounds of tea?

    A. 5   C. 11   E. 21
    B. $10\frac{1}{2}$ D. 20

36. If each bag of tokens weighs $5\frac{3}{4}$ pounds, how many pounds do 3 bags weigh?

    F. $7\frac{1}{4}$ H. $16\frac{1}{2}$ K. $17\frac{1}{2}$
    G. $15\frac{3}{4}$ J. $17\frac{1}{4}$

37. For three months, Pete saved part of his monthly allowance. He saved $4.56 the first month, $3.82 the second month, and $5.06 the third month. How much did Pete save altogether?

    A. $12.04   C. $13.04   E. $14.44
    B. $12.44   D. $13.44

38. If the outer radius of a metal pipe is 2.84 inches and the inner radius is 1.94 inches, what is the thickness, in inches, of the metal?

    F. 0.85   H. 1.00   K. 1.25
    G. 0.90   J. 1.18

39. 80 is what percentage of 20?

    A. 4%   C. 40%   E. 400%
    B. 8%   D. 200%

40. What percentage of 10 is 1?

    F. 0.1%   H. 10%   K. 1,000%
    G. 1%   J. 100%

41. What number is 250% of 12?

    A. 3   C. 24   E. 36
    B. 15   D. 30

42. The Wildcats won 10 out of 12 games. To the nearest whole percent, what percentage of their games did the Wildcats win?

    F. 3   H. 38   K. 94
    G. 8   J. 83

43. If 75% of 240 cars in a certain parking lot are sedans, how many of the cars in the parking lot are sedans?

    A. 18   C. 60   E. 210
    B. 24   D. 180

44. If the price of an item increases from $5.00 to $8.00, the old price is what percentage of the new price?

    F. 20%   H. 62.5%   K. 160%
    G. 60%   J. 92.5%

45. If the price of a share of stock drops from $200 to $160, the old price is what percentage of the new price?

    A. 20%   C. 50%   E. 125%
    B. 25%   D. 80%

46. During one week, a man traveled $3\frac{1}{2}$, $1\frac{1}{4}$, $1\frac{1}{6}$, and $2\frac{3}{8}$ miles. The next week, he traveled $\frac{1}{4}$, $\frac{3}{8}$, $\frac{9}{16}$, $3\frac{1}{16}$, $2\frac{5}{8}$, and $3\frac{3}{16}$ miles. How many more miles did he travel the second week than the first week?

    F. $1\frac{37}{48}$ H. $1\frac{1}{2}$ K. $\frac{47}{48}$
    G. $1\frac{3}{4}$ J. 1

47. A certain type of board is sold only in lengths of multiples of 2 feet. The shortest board sold is 4 feet and the longest is 12 feet. A builder needs a large quantity of this type of board in $3\frac{1}{2}$-foot lengths. To minimize waste, which of the following board lengths should be ordered (ignore the width of the cut)?

    A. 4-foot   C. 8-foot   E. 12-foot
    B. 6-foot   D. 10-foot

48. The population of a town was 54,000 in the last census. Since then it has increased by two-thirds. Which of the following equals its present population?

    F. 18,000   H. 72,000   K. 108,000
    G. 36,000   J. 90,000

49. A car is run until the gas tank is $\frac{1}{8}$ full. The tank is then filled to capacity by putting in 14 gallons. What is the gas tank's capacity, in gallons?

A. 8   C. 16   E. 28
B. 14   D. 20

50. Pete earns $20.56 on Monday, $32.90 on Tuesday, and $20.78 on Wednesday. He spends half of all that he earned during the 3 days. How much does he have left?

F. $36.42   H. $37.12   K. $38.42
G. $36.72   J. $37.72

51. What is the total cost of $3\frac{1}{2}$ pounds of meat at $1.70 per pound and 20 lemons at $2.70 per dozen?

A. $4.40   C. $10.45   E. $12.15
B. $6.20   D. $11.35

52. A reel of cable weighs 1,279 pounds. If the empty reel weighs 285 pounds and the cable weighs 7.1 pounds per foot, how many feet of cable are on the reel?

F. 140   H. 160   K. 180
G. 150   J. 170

53. How much will 345 fasteners at $4.20 per hundred cost if the fasteners can be purchased individually at the same price?

A. $13.29   C. $14.29   E. $14.99
B. $13.99   D. $14.49

54. A certain radio costs a merchant $72. At what price must he sell it if he is to make a profit of 20% of the selling price?

F. $86.40   H. $90   K. $448
G. $88   J. $444

55. A baseball team has won 40 games out of 60 played. It has 32 more games to play. How many of these games must the team win to make a record 75% win rate for the season?

A. 28   C. 30   E. 34
B. 29   D. 32

Probability, Statistics, and Data Analysis

Mean

Calculating a Mean (Average)

To calculate an ***average (arithmetic mean)***, add the quantities contributing to the average and then divide that sum by the number of quantities involved. For example, the average of 3, 7, and 8 is $\frac{3+7+8}{3} = \frac{18}{3} = 6$. The term "average" is often used instead of "mean" or "arithmetic mean." The generalized formula for an average is given by the following equation:

Average (Arithmetic Mean) =

$$\overline{x} = \frac{x_1 + x_2 + x_3 + \dots + x_n}{n}.$$

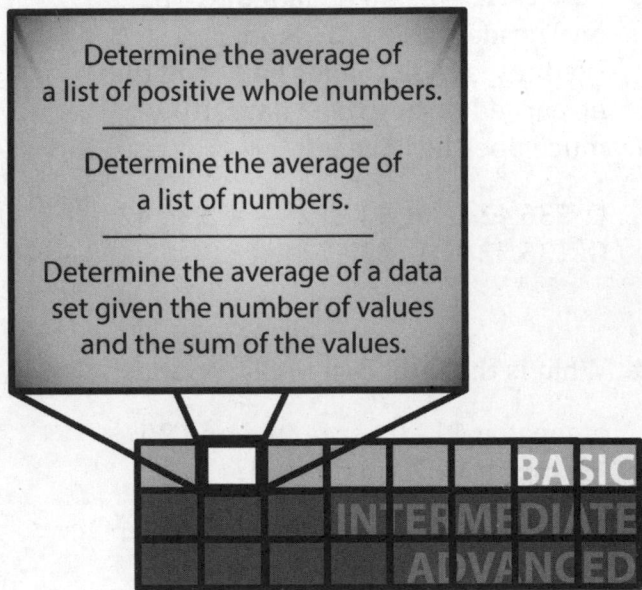

Determine the average of a list of positive whole numbers.

Determine the average of a list of numbers.

Determine the average of a data set given the number of values and the sum of the values.

BASIC
INTERMEDIATE
ADVANCED

Example:

A student's final grade is the average of her scores on five exams. If she receives scores of 78, 83, 82, 88, and 94, what is her final grade?

To find the average, add the five grades and divide that sum by 5:

$$\frac{78 + 83 + 82 + 88 + 94}{5} = \frac{425}{5} = 85.$$

A list of numbers to be averaged can include fractions, decimals, or negative numbers.

Examples:

Beth is trying to determine the optimal amount of sugar to use in her raspberry iced tea recipe. Four different recipes instruct her to use $\frac{1}{4}$ cup, $\frac{2}{3}$ cup, $\frac{3}{4}$ cup, or $\frac{1}{3}$ cup of sugar to make 1 large pitcher of tea. Beth averages the four amounts of sugar to determine how much sugar to use. How much sugar does Beth use?

Simplify by working with decimal equivalents: Average = $\dfrac{0.25+0.\overline{66}+0.75+0.\overline{33}}{4}=$

$\dfrac{2}{4}=\dfrac{1}{2}$ cup.

Stephen is on the cross country team. In the last five meets, he ran the 5K race in 15.75 minutes, 15.5 minutes, 16.25 minutes, 14.75 minutes, and 15.0 minutes, respectively. What is his average race time for the last five races?

$$\text{Average} = \frac{15.75+15.5+16.25+14.75+15.0}{5}=\frac{77.25}{5}=15.45\text{ minutes}$$

During the winter, an 8th grade class collected the coldest temperatures recorded in their state each day for seven days. The temperatures were –2°F, –2°F, –1°F, 5°F, 6°F, 1°F, and 0°F. What was the average temperature, in degrees Fahrenheit, for the seven days?

$$\text{Average} = \frac{(-2)+(-2)+(-1)+5+6+1+0}{7}=\frac{7}{7}=1°F$$

Calculating a Mean Given the Number of Values and Sum of the Values

For some average problems, you might not have a nice, neat list of numbers to work with. You may be given just the number of values (*n*) and the sum of all the values and asked to find the average. But don't panic. These types of problems are actually saving you a step—you don't have to add a bunch of numbers together since they're already added for you! You will simply need to divide the sum by *n*.

Example:

A group of 6 numbers totals $18\dfrac{3}{4}$. What is the average value of this group of numbers?

$$\text{Average} = \frac{18.75}{6}=3.125=3\frac{1}{8}$$

The Fundamentals of Probability

One of the fundamental principles of probability can be summed up in the statement, "The likelihood of outcome A + the likelihood of not-outcome A = 100%," or $A + (-A) = 100\%$.

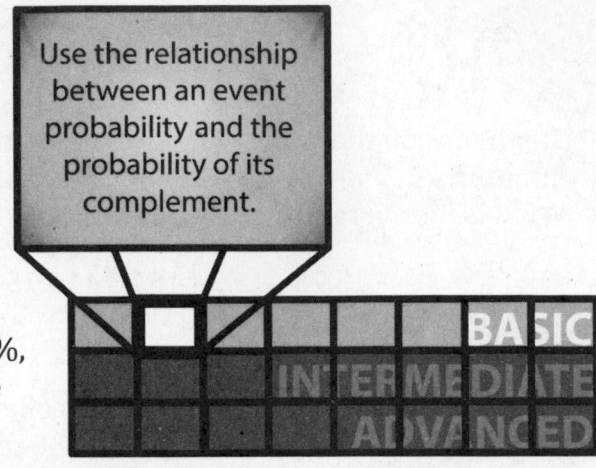

Use the relationship between an event probability and the probability of its complement.

For example, a jar contains some green marbles and some blue marbles. You choose one of the marbles completely at random. If the probability that you'll pick a green marble is 20%, then the probability that the marble will NOT be green is 100% − 20% = 80%. And, in this case, since there are only two kinds of marbles in the jar, green and blue, the probability of picking a blue marble is 80%.

Examples:

In a particular school assembly of 120 students, there are 40 first-graders. If one student is chosen at random to assist with a demonstration on stage, what is the probability that a first-grader will be chosen?

A. 40   C. 1   E. $\dfrac{1}{3}$

B. $\dfrac{4}{3}$ D. $\dfrac{2}{3}$

Since 40 of the 120 students are first-graders, the probability of picking a first-grader is $\dfrac{40}{120} = \dfrac{1}{3}$.

In a particular school assembly of 120 students, there are 40 first-graders. If one student is chosen at random to assist with a demonstration on stage, what is the probability that the student chosen will NOT be a first-grader?

F. 80   H. 1   K. $\dfrac{1}{3}$

G. $\dfrac{4}{3}$ J. $\dfrac{2}{3}$

We know from the previous problem that the probability that a first-grader will be chosen is $\dfrac{1}{3}$. So, the probability that a first-grader will NOT be chosen is $1 - \dfrac{1}{3} = \dfrac{2}{3}$.

Data Interpretation: Tables and Graphs

The procedure for solving a problem using information from a table or a chart is the same procedure for solving a word problem:

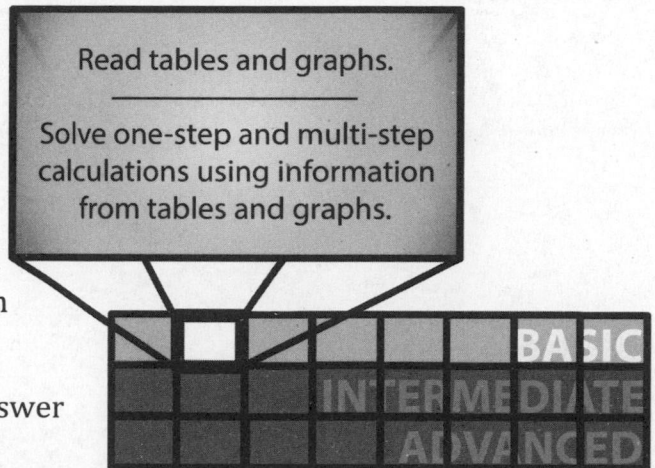

Read tables and graphs.

Solve one-step and multi-step calculations using information from tables and graphs.

1. Read carefully. Then isolate the question asked.

2. Determine how the information given will answer the question.

3. Do the computations necessary to answer the question.

Example:

The tables below show the number, type, and cost of candy bars bought during one week at two local drugstores.

NUMBER OF CANDY BARS BOUGHT						
	Type A		Type B		Type C	
	Large	Giant	Large	Giant	Large	Giant
Drugstore P	60	20	69	21	43	17
Drugstore Q	44	18	59	25	38	13

COST PER CANDY BAR	Large	Giant
Type A	$0.45	$0.69
Type B	$0.45	$0.79
Type C	$0.55	$0.99

What is the total cost of all Type B candy bars bought at these two drugstores during the week?

1. The question is: What is the **total cost** of all **Type B** candy bars bought at these **two drugstores** during the week? (The key terms in this question are in bold.)

2. From the table on the left you can see that Type B candy bars were sold in *both* drugstores and in *two different sizes*: Large and Giant. From the table on the right you can find the cost of Large and Giant Type B candy bars. The product of the number of Type B candy bars of a particular size and its corresponding cost will produce the cost, in dollars, for that many candy bars of that size. Adding the products will result in the total cost.

3. Find the total cost of all Type B bars bought at the two drugstores:
    $69(0.45) + 21(0.79) + 59(0.45) + 25(0.79) = \$93.94$.

This procedure can also be applied to graphs.

Example:

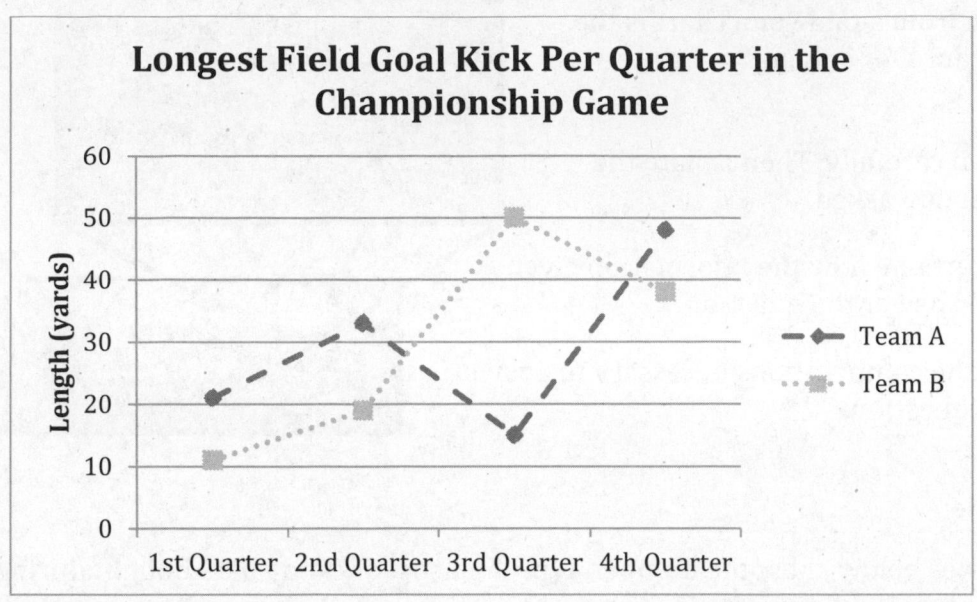

What was the approximate average length of the longest kick per quarter in the championship game made by Team A?

A. 10 yards   D. 48 yards
B. 21 yards   E. 117 yards
C. 29 yards

1. The question is: What is the **approximate average length** of the longest kicks in the championship game made by **Team A**? (The key terms in this question are in bold.)

2. The graph provides four values for each team, so to find the average, total the four values and divide by the number of values (4).

3. Average $= \dfrac{21+33+15+48}{4} = \dfrac{117}{4} = 29.25 \approx 29$ yards.

EXERCISE 3

DIRECTIONS: Choose the correct answer to each of the following items. Answers are on page 812.

56. What is the average of 5, 11, 12, and 8?

   F. 6   H. 9   K. 12
   G. 8   J. 10

57. Find the mean of the following 6 numbers: −3, 2, 6, 5, 2, and 0.

   A. 1   C. 5   E. 8
   B. 2   D. 6

58. What is the average of $\dfrac{1}{4}$, $\dfrac{3}{4}$, $\dfrac{5}{8}$, $\dfrac{1}{2}$, and $\dfrac{3}{8}$?

   F. $\dfrac{3}{32}$ H. $\dfrac{1}{2}$ K. $\dfrac{27}{32}$
   G. $\dfrac{5}{16}$ J. $\dfrac{5}{8}$

59. What is the average of $0.78, $0.45, $0.36, $0.98, $0.55, and $0.54?

   A. $0.49   C. $0.56   E. $0.61
   B. $0.54   D. $0.60

60. What is the average of 0.03, 0.11, 0.08, and 0.5?

   F. 0.18   H. 0.28   K. 1.0
   G. 0.25   J. 0.50

61. Mr. Whipple bought five different items costing $4.51, $6.25, $3.32, $4.48, and $2.19. What is the average cost of the five items?

   A. $3.40   C. $3.90   E. $4.15
   B. $3.80   D. $4.00

62. Nadia received scores of 8.5, 9.3, 8.2, and 9.0 in four different gymnastics events. What is the average of her scores?

   F. 8.5   H. 8.9   K. 9.1
   G. 8.75   J. 9

63. Five people have ages of 44, 33, 45, 44, and 29 years. What is the average of their ages in years?

   A. 36   C. 40   E. 43
   B. 39   D. 41

64. In a chemical test for Substance X, a sample is divided into five equal parts. If the purity of the five parts is 84%, 89%, 87%, 90%, and 80%, what is the average purity of the sample (expressed as a percentage)?

   F. 83   H. 86   K. 88
   G. 84   J. 87

65. The grades received on a test by four students were 55, 75, 80, and 65. What is the average of these grades?

A. 55   C. 70   E. 80
B. 68.75   D. 72.25

66. A group of eight numbers totals $41\frac{1}{2}$.

What is the average value of this group of numbers?

F. 332   H. 8.415   K. $5\frac{3}{16}$

G. $41\frac{1}{16}$ J. $5\frac{1}{2}$

67. A group of ten numbers totals –4. What is the average value of this group of numbers?

A. –4   C. –0.04   E. 4
B. –0.4   D. 0.4

68. After an intense rainfall that lasted for four days, a particular county's rainfall total was 9.2 inches. What was the average daily rainfall during this storm?

F. 2.0 inches   J. 4.0 inches
G. 2.2 inches   K. 36.8 inches
H. 2.3 inches

69. Joshua spent a total of $16\frac{2}{3}$ hours fixing eight computers for his customers. What was the average amount of time Joshua spent working on each computer?

A. $2\frac{1}{12}$ hours   D. $4\frac{2}{3}$ hours

B. $2\frac{1}{4}$ hours   E. $21\frac{1}{3}$ hours

C. $2\frac{2}{3}$ hours

70. In a certain government office, if 360 staff hours are needed to process 120 building permit applications, on average how long (in hours) does it take to process one application?

F. 3   H. 12   K. 36
G. 6   J. 24

71. Dominic is one of a group of students being considered to read the morning announcements over the intercom system at school. One student will be chosen at random. If the probability that Dominic will be chosen is $\frac{1}{4}$, what is the probability that Dominic will NOT be chosen?

A. 0   C. $\frac{1}{2}$ E. 1

B. $\frac{1}{4}$ D. $\frac{3}{4}$

72. A game is played by spinning an unbiased spinner which, when it finally stops, points to a color. The result of a spin of the spinner is purely random. On any given spin, if the probability that the spinner will point to the color red is $\frac{1}{10}$, what is the probability that the spinner will NOT point to the color red?

F. $\frac{1}{11}$ H. $\frac{1}{9}$ K. $\frac{11}{10}$

G. $\frac{1}{10}$ J. $\frac{9}{10}$

73. A machine dispenses bouncy balls, 1 ball for 25 cents, at random. If the machine currently has 12 blue and 48 green bouncy balls, what is the probability that the next bouncy ball will NOT be green?

A. 0.25   C. 0.75   E. 4.00
B. 0.5   D. 1.00

74. Rita and Sam are playing a card game, and Rita must choose a card at random from a pile of 5 cards. If the probability that Rita will choose a card that is NOT red is $\frac{2}{5}$, what is the probability that Rita will choose a card that is red?

F. $\frac{2}{5}$ H. $\frac{3}{5}$ K. 1

G. $\frac{5}{10}$ J. $\frac{2}{3}$

75. Sandra has a packet of flower seeds. A seed will produce flowers of one color, either red, yellow, or orange. If Sandra picks a seed at random, the probability that it is one that will produce an orange flower is $\frac{1}{2}$. What is the probability that the seed will NOT produce an orange flower?

A. $\frac{1}{3}$ C. $\frac{2}{3}$ E. 1

B. $\frac{1}{2}$ D. $\frac{3}{4}$

76. The table below shows the daily change in the weather temperatures for a certain city last week. What was the net change (total change), in degrees Celsius, in the weather temperature for the week?

Day	Daily Change in Temperature (°C)
Sunday	+5.5
Monday	+1.7
Tuesday	−3.9
Wednesday	−3.3
Thursday	−0.5
Friday	+0.8
Saturday	−0.2

F. −5.7   H. 0.1   K. 5.7
G. −0.1   J. 5.3

Questions 77–78 refer to the following graph.

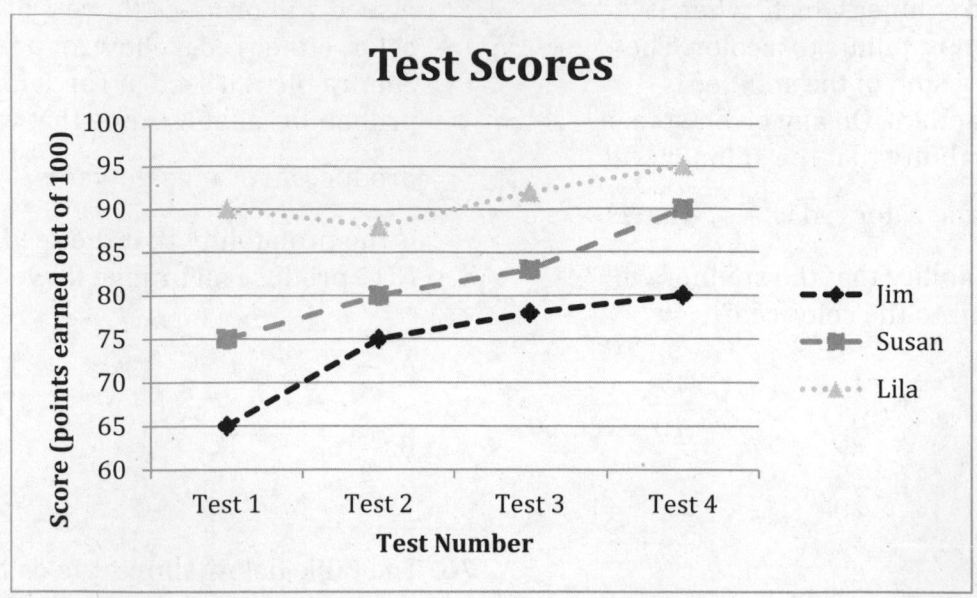

77. Approximately how many more points did Lila earn on the fourth test than Susan?

A. 5   C. 80   E. 95

B. 10   D. 90

78. What is the average score of the three students for Test 1?

F. 75   H. 80   K. 90

G. $76\frac{2}{3}$ J. $82\frac{1}{2}$

Questions 79–80 refer to the following graph.

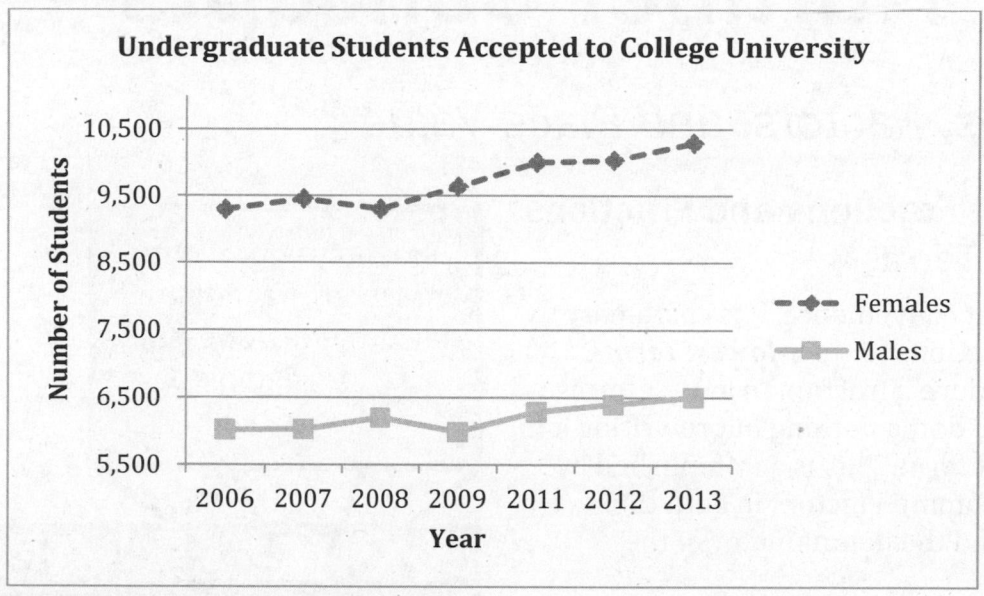

79. Approximately how many male undergraduate students were accepted to College University in 2008?

A. 5,800   C. 6,200   E. 9,300
B. 6,000   D. 6,500

80. Between what years did the number of male students accepted increase while the number of female students accepted decreased?

F. 2006–2007   J. 2009–2010
G. 2007–2008   K. 2010–2011
H. 2008–2009

Number Concepts

Fractions, Factors, and Place Value

Equivalent Fractions and Fractions in Lowest Terms

For reasons of convenience, it is customary to reduce all fractions to their **lowest terms**. When you reduce a fraction to lowest terms, you really are doing nothing but rewriting it in an equivalent form. This is accomplished by eliminating common factors in both the numerator and the denominator of the fraction.

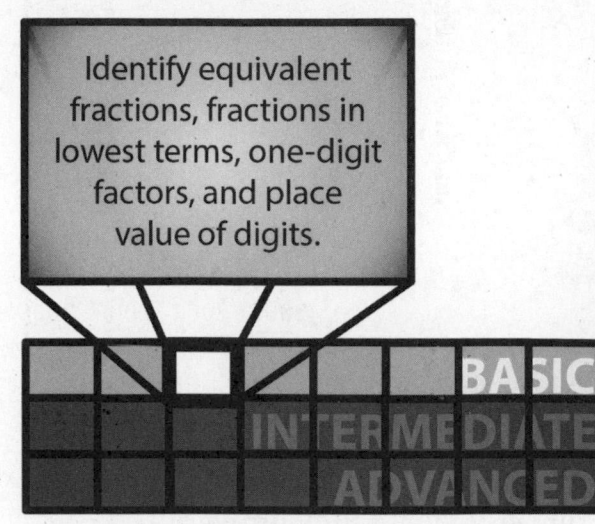

Identify equivalent fractions, fractions in lowest terms, one-digit factors, and place value of digits.

BASIC
INTERMEDIATE
ADVANCED

Example:

$$\frac{8}{16} = \frac{1(8)}{2(8)} = \frac{1}{2}$$

There are various ways of describing what goes on when you reduce a fraction. You might think of it as factoring out a greatest common factor, such as 8 in this example, and then dividing 8 into 8 (canceling). It is also possible to think of the process as dividing both the numerator and the denominator by the same number: $\frac{8}{16} = \frac{8 \div 8}{16 \div 8} = \frac{1}{2}$.

It does not matter how you describe the process, so long as you know how to reduce a fraction to its lowest terms. A fraction is expressed in lowest terms when there is no number (other than 1) that can be evenly divided into both the numerator and the denominator. For example, the fraction $\frac{8}{15}$ is in lowest terms, since there is no number (other than 1) that evenly goes into 8 and 15. On the other hand, the fraction $\frac{8}{12}$ is not in lowest terms, since both 8 and 12 can be evenly divided by 4. Reducing $\frac{8}{12}$ by a greatest common factor of 4 gives $\frac{2}{3}$, which is in lowest terms since nothing (other than 1) evenly divides into both 2 and 3.

Examples:

$$\frac{12}{36} = \frac{1 \cdot 12}{3 \cdot 12} = \frac{1}{3} \qquad \frac{42}{48} = \frac{7 \cdot 6}{8 \cdot 6} = \frac{7}{8} \qquad \frac{50}{125} = \frac{2 \cdot 25}{5 \cdot 25} = \frac{2}{5}$$

If a fraction is particularly large, you may need to reduce it in steps. The process is largely a matter of trial and error, but there are a couple of divisibility rules that can guide you. Remember that if both the numerator and the denominator are even numbers, you can reduce the fraction by a factor of 2. Also, if both the numerator and the denominator end in either 0 or 5, they are both divisible by 5.

Examples:

$$\frac{32}{64} = \frac{16(2)}{32(2)} = \frac{8(2)}{16(2)} = \frac{4(2)}{8(2)} = \frac{2(2)}{4(2)} = \frac{1(2)}{2(2)} = \frac{1}{2}.$$

$$\frac{55}{100} = \frac{11(5)}{20(5)} = \frac{11}{20}$$

Factors and Multiples

Numbers that evenly divide another number are called the *factors* of that number. If a number is evenly divisible by another number, it is considered a *multiple* of that number. 1, 2, 3, 4, 6, and 12 are all factors of 12: 12 is a multiple of 2, a multiple of 3, and so on.

Example:

A unit of soldiers includes 144 members. The commander wants the soldiers to assemble in a formation that has an equal number of rows and columns. How many soldiers should be in each row?

A. 9   C. 11   E. 15
B. 10   D. 12

Since $(12)(12) = 144$, a formation of 12 by 12 will have an equal number of rows and columns.

There is a time-saving rule for finding the factors of a number:

Divide the number, N, by 1, 2, 3, ..., n. All numbers that divide N evenly are factors; those that do not divide N evenly are not factors. And check numbers only up to the point at which $n^2 \geq N$. For example, for the number 36, once you have identified that 1 (and 36), 2 (and 18), 3 (and 12), 4 (and 9), and 6 (and 6) are factors, recognize that $6^2 \geq 36$, so you have identified all the factors.

Example:

Write down all the unique factors of 45.

$1 \cdot 45 = 45$
$2 \ldots$ not a factor
$3 \cdot 15 = 45$
$4 \ldots$ not a factor
$5 \cdot 9 = 45$
$6 \ldots$ not a factor
$7 \ldots$ not a factor

Since $7^2 > 45$, we can stop. The factors of 45 are 1 and 45, 3 and 15, and 5 and 9.

Place Value

Counting numbers and their place values are organized from right to left in units, groups of ten (tens), groups of ten tens (hundreds), and groups of ten ten-tens (thousands), and so on:

1 HUNDRED THOUSANDS
2 TEN THOUSANDS
3, THOUSANDS
4 HUNDREDS
5 TENS
6 UNITS

We use a digit's position to determine whether that digit counts units, or groups of ten, or groups of ten tens, and so on. So the number 36 means "three groups of ten plus six additional units," and 44 means "four groups of ten plus four additional units."

Example:

In the number 45,176, which digit is the hundreds digit?

A. 1   C. 5   E. 7
B. 4   D. 6

The third place from the right is the hundreds place: 1. The number is shorthand for 4 groups of 10,000 plus 5 groups of 1,000 plus 1 group of 100 plus 7 groups of ten plus 6 units.

A decimal is nothing more than a special way of writing fractions using a denominator of ten, one hundred, one thousand, and so on. The place value positions are listed from left to right (starting after the decimal point), as tenths, hundredths, thousandths, and so on.

$$0 \ . \ 1 \ 2 \ 3 \ 4 \ 5$$

TENTHS

HUNDREDTHS

THOUSANDTHS

TEN THOUSANDTHS

HUNDRED THOUSANDTHS

Example:

In the decimal 0.34562, which digit occupies the thousandths place?

F. 2   H. 4   K. 6
G. 3   J. 5

The third digit from the left (starting after the decimal point) is the thousandths place: 5.

EXERCISE 4

DIRECTIONS: Choose the correct answer to each of the following items. Answers are on page 812.

81. Which of the following is NOT equal to $\dfrac{3}{8}$?

    A. $\dfrac{6}{16}$ C. $\dfrac{31}{81}$ E. $\dfrac{120}{320}$

    B. $\dfrac{15}{40}$ D. $\dfrac{33}{88}$

82. Which of the following is NOT equal to $\dfrac{5}{6}$?

    F. $\dfrac{25}{30}$ H. $\dfrac{50}{60}$ K. $\dfrac{100}{120}$

    G. $\dfrac{45}{50}$ J. $\dfrac{55}{66}$

83. What is $\dfrac{3}{12}$ expressed in lowest terms?

A. $\dfrac{1}{6}$ C. $\dfrac{1}{3}$ E. $\dfrac{3}{4}$

B. $\dfrac{1}{4}$ D. $\dfrac{1}{2}$

84. What is $\dfrac{125}{625}$ expressed in lowest terms?

F. $\dfrac{1}{10}$ H. $\dfrac{2}{5}$ K. $\dfrac{4}{5}$

G. $\dfrac{1}{5}$ J. $\dfrac{7}{10}$

85. What is $\dfrac{121}{132}$ expressed in lowest terms?

A. $\dfrac{1}{11}$ C. $\dfrac{9}{10}$ E. $\dfrac{11}{12}$

B. $\dfrac{1}{10}$ D. $\dfrac{10}{11}$

86. What is $\dfrac{8}{30}$ expressed in lowest terms?

F. $\dfrac{2}{15}$ H. $\dfrac{1}{5}$ K. $\dfrac{2}{3}$

G. $\dfrac{3}{15}$ J. $\dfrac{4}{15}$

87. What is $\dfrac{15}{64}$ expressed in lowest terms?

A. $\dfrac{15}{64}$ C. $\dfrac{5}{8}$ E. $\dfrac{64}{15}$

B. $\dfrac{3}{8}$ D. $\dfrac{15}{8}$

88. What is $\dfrac{9}{57}$ expressed in lowest terms?

F. $\dfrac{1}{57}$ H. $\dfrac{3}{19}$ K. $\dfrac{9}{19}$

G. $\dfrac{1}{9}$ J. $\dfrac{3}{11}$

89. Which of the following is (are) equivalent to $\dfrac{1}{3}$?

I. $\dfrac{40}{120}$

II. $\dfrac{75}{100}$

III. $\dfrac{120}{360}$

A. I only   D. II and III only
B. III only   E. I, II, and III
C. I and III only

90. Which of the following is equivalent to $\dfrac{9}{9}$?

F. 0   H. 9   K. 81
G. 1   J. 18

91. Which of the following is a factor of 64?

    A. 6   C. 16   E. 37
    B. 10   D. 34

92. Which of the following is NOT a factor of 72?

    F. 2   H. 18   K. 38
    G. 8   J. 24

93. Which of the following is NOT a factor of 88?

    A. 4   C. 11   E. 88
    B. 8   D. 24

94. Which of the following is a complete list of all the factors of 56?

    F. {1, 56}
    G. {1, 2, 28, 56}
    H. {1, 2, 4, 14, 28, 56}
    J. {1, 2, 4, 7, 8, 14, 28, 56}
    K. {1, 2, 4, 7, 8, 14, 27, 28, 56}

95. Which of the following is a factor of 256, 120, and 200?

    A. 3   C. 10   E. 20
    B. 8   D. 16

96. In the number 1,327,589, which digit signifies the number of thousands?

    F. 1   H. 3   K. 7
    G. 2   J. 5

97. In the number, 1,327,589, decreasing which digit by 1 decreases the value of the number by 10,000?

    A. 1   C. 3   E. 7
    B. 2   D. 5

98. In the number 5,014,789, increasing which digit by 5 increases the value of the number by 5,000?

    F. 0   H. 4   K. 9
    G. 1   J. 5

99. In the decimal 0.14576, which digit occupies the hundredths place?

    A. 1   C. 5   E. 7
    B. 4   D. 6

100. In the decimal 0.145783, which digit occupies the ten thousandths place?

    F. 1   H. 5   K. 8
    G. 4   J. 7

Algebraic Expressions, Equations, and Inequalities

Elements of Algebra

Algebra is the branch of mathematics that uses letter symbols to represent numbers. The letter symbols are, in essence, placeholders. They function somewhat like "someone" or "somewhere" in that they do not represent a definite value. For example, in the sentence "Someone took the book and put it somewhere," neither the identity of the person in question nor the new location of the book is known. We can rewrite this sentence in algebraic terms: "x put the book in y place." The identity of x is unknown, and the new location of the book is unknown. It is for this reason that letter symbols in algebra are often referred to as "unknowns."

Algebra, like English, is a language, and for making certain statements, algebra is much better than English. For example, the English statement "There is a number such that, when you add 3 to it, the result is 8" can be rendered more easily in algebraic notation: $x + 3 = 8$. In fact, learning the rules of algebra is like learning the grammar of any language. Keeping this analogy between algebra and English in mind, let's begin by studying the components of the algebraic language.

> Show familiarity with basic algebraic expressions.
>
> Evaluate simple expressions using whole numbers.
>
> Combine like terms.
>
> Solve simple equations involving whole numbers, integers, or decimals.
>
> BASIC
> INTERMEDIATE
> ADVANCED

The basic unit of the English language is the word. The basic unit of algebra is the **term**. In English, a word consists of one or more letters. In algebra, a term consists of one or more letters or numbers. For example, x, $2z$, xy, N, 2, $\sqrt{7}$, and π are all algebraic terms. A term can be a product, quotient, or single symbol.

In English, a word may have a root, a prefix, a suffix, an ending, and so on. In algebra, a term may have a coefficient, an exponent, a sign, etc. Of course, algebraic terms also include a variable, sometimes referred to as the base.

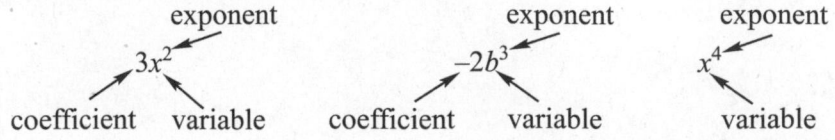

Just as with numbers, when the sign of an algebraic term is positive, the "+" is not written (e.g., $3x$ is equivalent to $+3x$). Additionally, when the coefficient is 1, the "1" is not written (e.g., x rather than $1x$).

The elements in an algebraic term are all joined by the operation of multiplication. The coefficient and its sign are multiplied by the variable(s). For example: $-3x = (-3)(x)$; $5a = (+5)(a)$; and $\frac{1}{2}N = (+\frac{1}{2})(N)$.

The exponent, as you have already learned, also indicates multiplication. Thus, x^2 means x times x; a^3 means a times a times a; and N^5 means N times N times N times N times N. Be careful not to confuse the coefficient with the exponent: $3x$ means "+3 times x," while x^3 means "x times x times x." Of course, many terms have both a coefficient and an exponent. For example, $3x^2$ means "+3 times x times x," and $-5a^3$ means "−5 times a times a times a."

Evaluating Algebraic Expressions

In English, words are organized into phrases. In algebra, terms are grouped together in **expressions**. An expression is a collection of algebraic terms that are joined by addition, subtraction, or both.

Examples:

$x + y$

$-2x + 3y + z$

Evaluate an expression by plugging given numbers into the expression in the place of the indicated variable(s).

Examples:

What is the value of $3x^2$ if $x = 5$?

Plug in the given value to solve the expression: $3x^2 = 3(5)^2 = 3(25) = 75$.

What is the value of xy if $x = 2$ and $y = 7$?

Plug in the given values to solve the expression: $xy = (2)(7) = 14$.

Combining Like Terms

In algebra, only **_like terms_** may be combined. Like terms are terms with the same variables having the same exponent values. Coefficients do not factor into whether or not terms are similar.

Examples:

$3x^2$, $40x^2$, $-2x^2$, and $\sqrt{2}x^2$ are like terms.

$3x$ and $3x^2$ are NOT like terms.

xy, $5xy$, $-23xy$, and πxy are like terms.

xy and x^2y are NOT like terms.

$10xyz$, $-xyz$, and xyz are like terms.

xy, yz, and xz are NOT like terms.

To combine like terms, do the indicated operation(s).

Examples:

$3x^2 + 40x^2 = 43x^2$

$xy - 5xy + 23xy = 19xy$

Algebraic Equations

Basic Principle of Equations

The fundamental rule for working with any equation is: whatever you do to one side of an equation, you must do exactly the same thing to the other side of the equation. This rule implies that you can add, subtract, multiply, and divide both sides of the equality by any value without changing the statement of equality. The only exception is that you cannot divide by zero. The following example illustrates the validity of this principle using an equation containing only real numbers.

Example:

$5 = 5$

> This is obviously a true statement. You can add any value to both sides of the equation, say 10, and the statement will remain true. Add 10: $5 + 10 = 5 + 10 \Rightarrow$ $15 = 15$. You can also subtract the same value from both sides, e.g., 7: $15 - 7 = 15 - 7 \Rightarrow 8 = 8$. You can multiply both sides by the same value, e.g., -2: $8 \cdot -2 = 8 \cdot -2 \Rightarrow -16 = -16$. Finally, you can divide both sides by the same value (except zero); e.g., -4: $-16 \div -4 = -16 \div -4 \Rightarrow 4 = 4$.

This principle for manipulating equations applies to algebraic equations with variables, as the following example illustrates.

Example:

$5 + x = 5 + x$

Add x: $5 + x + x = 5 + x + x \Rightarrow 5 + 2x = 5 + 2x$. Whatever x is, since it appears on both sides of the equation, both sides of the equation must still be equal. Now, subtract a value, e.g., y: $5 + 2x - y = 5 + 2x - y$. Again, since y appears on both sides of the equation, the statement that the two expressions are equal remains true. Multiply by 9: $9(5 + 2x - y) = 9(5 + 2x - y) \Rightarrow 45 + 18x - 9y = 45 + 18x - 9y$. Just as with addition and subtraction, both sides are multiplied by 9 and the equation remains true. Finally, divide by 3: $\dfrac{45 + 18x - 9y}{3} = \dfrac{45 + 18x - 9y}{3} \Rightarrow 15 + 6x - 3y = 15 + 6x - 3y$. Both sides are divided by 3 and the equation remains true.

Do NOT multiply both sides of an equation by zero if the equation contains a variable. You may lose special characteristics of the variable. For example, the equation $2x = 8$ is true only if $x = 4$. However, the equation $0(2x) = 0(8)$ is true for any value of x.

Solving Algebraic Equations

To solve an algebraic equation, manipulate the equation until the variable is isolated.

Example:

If $3x = 15$, $x = ?$

Isolate the variable: $3x = 15 \Rightarrow \dfrac{3x}{3} = \dfrac{15}{3} \Rightarrow x = 5$.

EXERCISE 5

DIRECTIONS: Choose the correct answer to each of the following items. Answers are on page 812.

101. What is the coefficient in the algebraic expression $\dfrac{3}{4}y^2$?

A. $\dfrac{3}{4}$ C. 3   E. y

B. 2   D. 4

102. If x is a positive integer, which of the following is equivalent to x^1?

F. x^0 H. 1   K. x^x

G. 0   J. x

103. $x + 2x + 3x = ?$

   A. $6x^6$ C. $6x$ E. $x - 6$

   B. x^6 D. $x + 6$

104. $a^3 - 12a^3 + 15a^3 + 2a^3 = ?$

   F. $6a^3$ H. $6a$ K. a

   G. $2a^2$ J. $3a$

105. $-7nx + 2nx + 2n + 7x = ?$

   A. 0 D. $9nx + 9xn$

   B. $-5nx + 2n + 7x$ E. $4nx$

   C. $18nx$

106. $2x^2 + 2x^2 + 2x^2 = ?$

   F. $6x^6$ H. $6x^2$ K. 6

   G. $2x^6$ J. $6x$

107. If $3x = 12$, then $x = ?$

   A. 2 C. 4 E. 10

   B. 3 D. 6

108. If $7x - 5x = 12 - 8$, then $x = ?$

   F. 0 H. 2 K. 4

   G. 1 J. 3

109. If $a - 8 = 10 - 2a$, then $a = ?$

   A. -2 C. 2 E. 6

   B. 0 D. 4

110. If $12x + 3 - 4x - 3 = 8$, then $x = ?$

   F. -5 H. 0 K. 5

   G. -1 J. 1

111. If $a + 2b - 3 + 3a = 2a + b + 3 + b$, then $a = ?$

   A. -1 C. 2 E. 6

   B. 0 D. 3

112. If $-4 - x = 12 + x$, then $x = ?$

   F. -8 H. 2 K. 8

   G. -4 J. 4

113. If $\dfrac{2x}{3} + \dfrac{x}{4} + 4 = \dfrac{x}{6} + 10$, then $x = ?$

   A. $\dfrac{11}{12}$ C. 5 E. 20

   B. $\dfrac{3}{2}$ D. 8

114. If $\dfrac{1}{p} + \dfrac{2}{p} + \dfrac{3}{p} = 1$, then $p = ?$

   F. $\dfrac{1}{6}$ H. 1 K. 6

   G. $\dfrac{3}{4}$ J. 2

115. If $\dfrac{5 - x}{5} = 1$, then $x = ?$

   A. -5 C. 0 E. 5

   B. -1 D. 1

Graphical Representations

The Number Line

Several devices that you use almost every day are, in essence, number lines. For example, a thermometer:

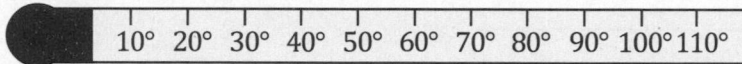

Just as you can locate or indicate a position or point on a thermometer, you can locate or indicate a point on the number line.

> Locate numbers on a number line and points in the first quadrant of the coordinate plane.

Example:

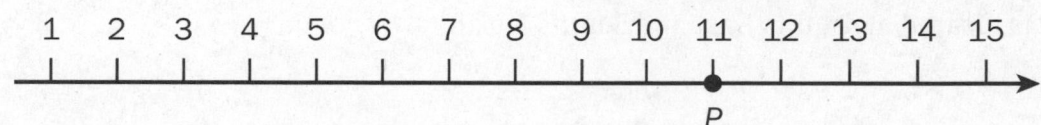

Point *P* is located at the number 11.

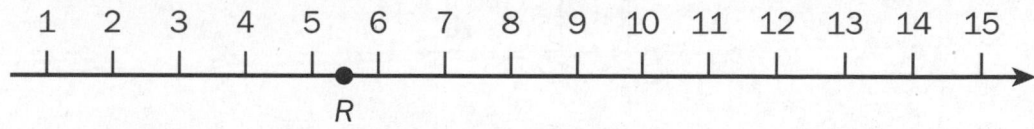

Point *R* is located between the number 5 and the number 6.

Technically speaking, the number line has a point that represents every real number, including whole numbers, fractions, square roots, and so on:

$$\frac{1}{4} \quad \frac{1}{2} \quad \frac{3}{4} \quad 1 \quad \frac{5}{4} \quad \frac{3}{2} \quad \frac{7}{4} \quad 2 \quad \frac{9}{4} \quad \frac{5}{2} \quad \frac{11}{4} \quad 3 \quad \frac{13}{4} \quad \frac{7}{2} \quad \frac{15}{4}$$

The procedure for reading a number line is always the same: the position or location of a point indicates the number with which it is associated.

The Coordinate Plane

The easiest way to understand the coordinate axis system is as an analog to the points of the compass. If we take a plot of land, we can divide it into quadrants:

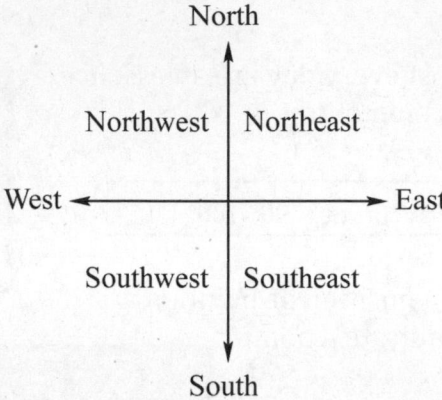

Now, if we add measuring units along each of the directional axes, we can actually describe any location on this piece of land by two numbers.

Example:

Point P is located at 4 units East and 5 units North.

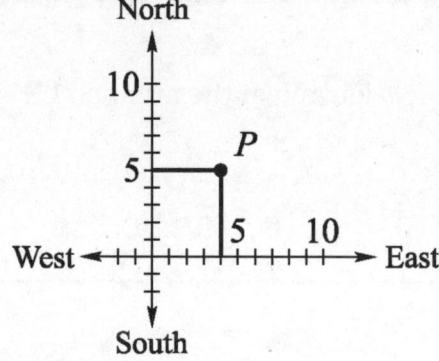

An **ordered pair** of coordinates has the general form (x, y). The first element refers to the **x-coordinate**: the distance left or right of the **origin**, or intersection of the axes. The second element gives the **y-coordinate**: the distance up or down from the origin.

Example:

Plot $(3,2)$.

Move to the positive 3 value on the x-axis, 3 units to the right. Then, from there move up two units on the y-axis, as illustrated by the graph on the left. The graph on the right demonstrates an alternative method: the point $(3,2)$ is located at the intersection of a line drawn through the *x*-value 3 parallel to the *y*-axis and a line drawn through the *y*-value 2 parallel to the *x*-axis.

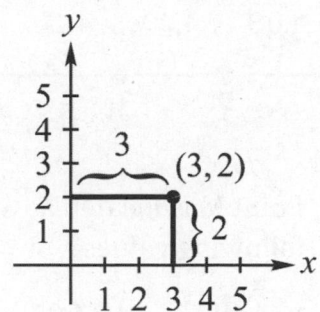

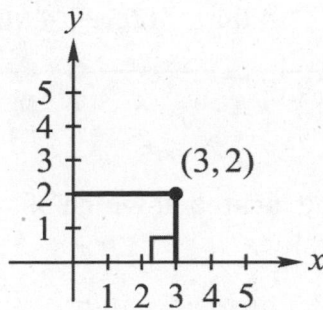

EXERCISE 6

DIRECTIONS: Choose the correct answer to each of the following items. Answers are on page 812.

Questions 116–120 refer to the following figure.

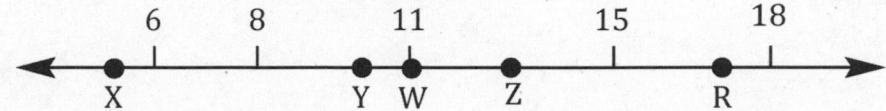

116. Which of the points shown on the number line is located at 11?

    F. X   H. W   K. R
    G. Y   J. Z

117. Point Y is located between which two numbers?

    A. 6 and 8   D. 15 and 18
    B. 8 and 11   E. 18 and 20
    C. 11 and 15

118. Point R could be located at which of the following values?

    F. 7   H. 15   K. 18
    G. 10   J. 17

119. Which of the points shown on the number line is less than 6?

    A. X   C. W   E. R
    B. Y   D. Z

120. Point Z is greater than which of the following pairs of points?

    F. W and Y   J. W and Z
    G. X and R   K. X and Z
    H. W and R

Questions 121–125 refer to the following figure.

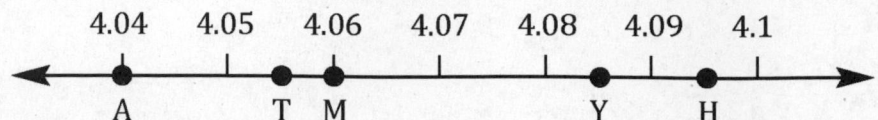

121. Point T could be located at which of the following values?

A. 4.045   C. 4.055   E. 4.5
B. 4.05   D. 4.15

124. Point M is located at which of the following values?

F. 4.04   H. 4.055   K. 4.065
G. 4.05   J. 4.06

122. Point Y is located between which of the following values?

F. 4.05 and 4.06
G. 4.06 and4.07
H. 4.07 and 4.08
J.   4.08 and 4.09
K. 4.09 and 4.1

125. Which of the following points is located at 4.04?

A. H   C. M   E. A
B. Y   D. T

123. Point H could be located at which of the following values?

A. 4.085   C. 4.15   E. 4.96
B. 4.096   D. 4.5

Questions 126–130 refer to the following figure.

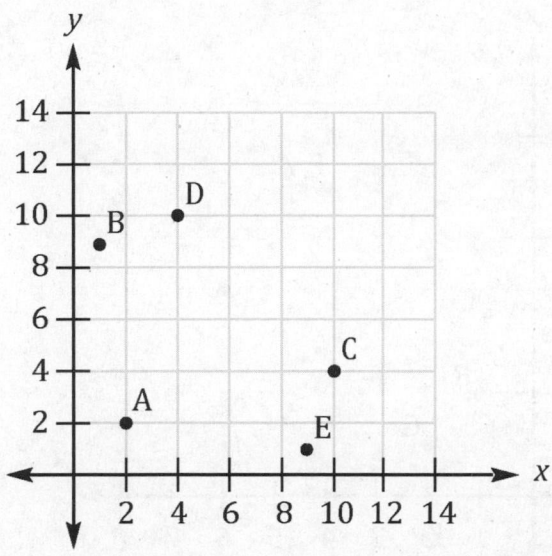

126. Which of the points shown is located at (2,2) on the coordinate grid?

F. A H. C K. E
G. B J. D

127. Which of the points shown is located at (4,10) on the coordinate grid?

A. A C. C E. E
B. B D. D

128. Which of the points shown is located at (9,1) on the coordinate grid?

F. A H. C K. E
G. B J. D

129. Which of the points shown is located at (1,9) on the coordinate grid?

A. A C. C E. E
B. B D. D

130. Which of the points shown is located at (10,4) on the coordinate grid?

F. A H. C K. E
G. B J. D

Questions 131–135 refer to the following figure.

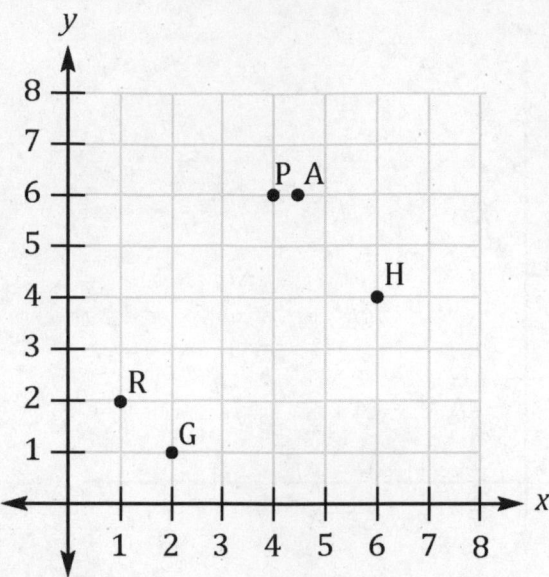

131. Which of the points shown is located at (1,2) on the coordinate grid?

A. G   C. A   E. H
B. R   D. P

132. Which of the points shown is located at (6,4) on the coordinate grid?

F. G   H. A   K. H
G. R   J. P

133. Which of the points shown is located at (4.5,6) on the coordinate grid?

A. G   C. A   E. H
B. R   D. P

134. Which of the points shown is located at (2,1) on the coordinate grid?

F. G   H. A   K. H
G. R   J. P

135. Which of the points shown is located at (4,6) on the coordinate grid?

A. G   C. A   E. H
B. R   D. P

Plane Figures

Parallel Lines

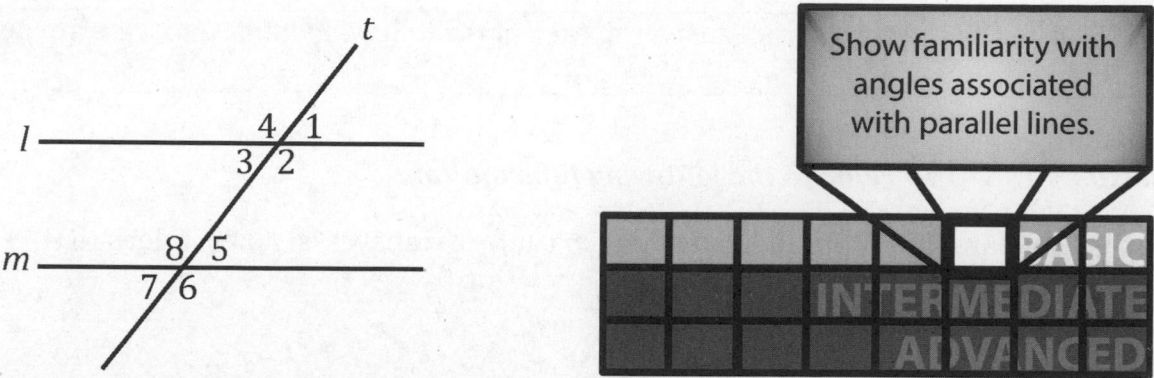

In the figure above, line *l* and line *m* are parallel lines. The line cutting across the parallel lines, line *t*, is called a ***transversal***. The angles are labeled according to their positions. The transversal forms two sets of quadrants, one with line *l* and one with line *m*. Angles 1 and 5 are located in the same position relative to the intersection of line *t* with respect to line *l* or line *m*. Such angles are called ***corresponding angles***. Similarly, angles 2 and 6, angles 3 and 7, and angles 4 and 8 are also corresponding angles. They are called corresponding angles because the relative position of one in the figure is the same as that of the other—so they correspond to each other.

Angles 2 and 8 and angles 3 and 5 are on opposite sides of the transversal and between (on the interior of) the parallel lines. We call these pairs of angles ***alternate interior*** angles.

Angles 1 and 7 and angles 4 and 6 are on opposite sides of the transversal and above and below (exterior to) the parallel lines. We call these pairs of angles ***alternate exterior*** angles.

In summary:

$$\angle 1 = \angle 3 = \angle 5 = \angle 7$$
$$\angle 2 = \angle 4 = \angle 6 = \angle 8$$

Each pair of corresponding angles, alternate interior angles, and alternate exterior angles are equal in measure to each other, which leads to the following:

$$\angle 1 + \angle 2 = 180°$$
$$\angle 3 + \angle 8 = 180°$$
$$\angle 4 + \angle 7 = 180°$$
$$\angle 5 + \angle 6 = 180°$$

There is a special case of this theorem when the transversal crosses the parallel lines at 90°. When parallel lines are cut by a transversal on a right angle, all angles are equal, and any two angles equal 180°.

EXERCISE 7

DIRECTIONS: Choose the correct answer to each of the following items. Answers are on page 813.

Questions 136 –140 refer to the following information.

The figure below shows parallel lines *l* and *m* cut by a transversal *t*. Line *t* does NOT intersect *l* and *m* at 90°.

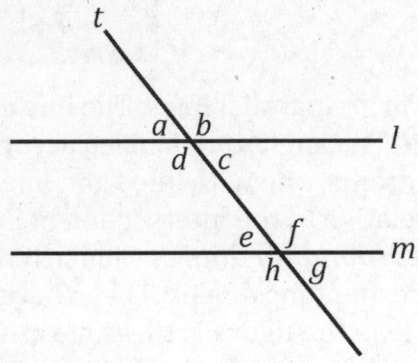

136. Which of the following angle pairs add up to 180 degrees?

   I.   ∠*b* and ∠*c*
   II. ∠*b* and ∠*g*
   III. ∠*d* and ∠*e*

  F. I only   J. I and III only
  G. I and II only K. I, II, and III
  H. II and III only

137. Which pair of angles are corresponding angles?

  A. ∠*a* and ∠*d*   D. ∠*b* and ∠*f*
  B. ∠*a* and ∠*h*   E. ∠*b* and ∠*g*
  C. ∠*b* and ∠*d*

138. Which of the following angles is equal to ∠*g*?

  F. ∠*a*   H. ∠*d*   K. ∠*h*
  G. ∠*b*   J. ∠*f*

139. Which of the following pairs of angles are alternate interior angles?

   I.   ∠*a* and ∠*g*
   II. ∠*c* and ∠*e*
   III. ∠*d* and ∠*f*

  A. I only   D. II and III only
  B. II only   E. I, II, and III
  C. I and III only

140. Which of the following pairs of angles are alternate exterior angles?

   I. $\angle a$ and $\angle g$
   II. $\angle b$ and $\angle h$
   III. $\angle a$ and $\angle h$

   F. I only
   G. II only
   H. I and II only
   J. II and III only
   K. I, II, and III

141. Which of the following is (are) necessarily true in the figure below?

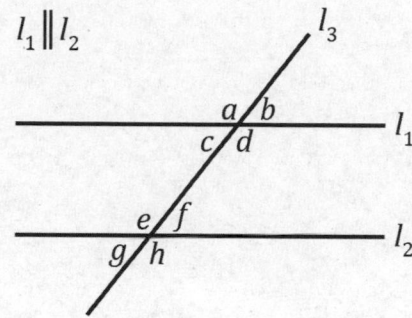

   I. $\angle b = \angle c$
   II. $\angle d = \angle c$
   III. $\angle g = \angle e$

   A. I only
   B. III only
   C. I and III only
   D. II and III only
   E. I, II, and III

Questions 142–143 refer to the following information.

The figure below shows parallel lines r and s cut by a transversal t:

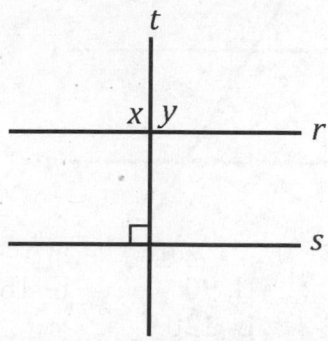

142. What is the degree measure of $\angle y$?

   F. 30°
   G. 60°
   H. 90°
   J. 120°
   K. 180°

143. What is the total degree measure of $\angle x$ and $\angle y$ when added together?

   A. 45°
   B. 60°
   C. 90°
   D. 120°
   E. 180°

144. In the figure below, if parallel lines *l* and *m* are cut by transversal *t*, then *x* = ?

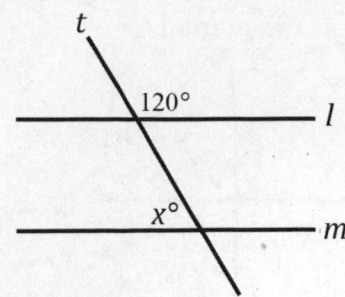

F. 45 H. 90 K. 180
G. 60 J. 120

145. In the figure below, if parallel lines *l* and *m* are cut by transversal *t*, then *x* = ?

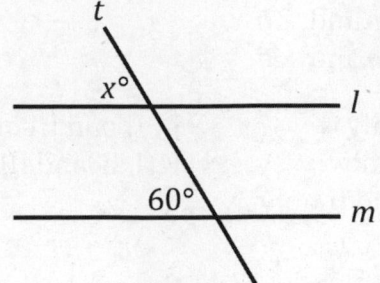

A. 30 C. 90 E. 180
B. 60 D. 120

Measurement

Line Segment Lengths

All linear measurement presupposes that there is some agreed upon unit of measure. Without a unit of measure, you can't even talk about distance. You can't say how long a stick is, how far the next town is, or how tall your friend is. Without units, the best that you can do is to say whether two lengths are equal or unequal and, if they are not equal, which one is longer and which one is shorter. But you can't say *how much* longer or *how much* shorter.

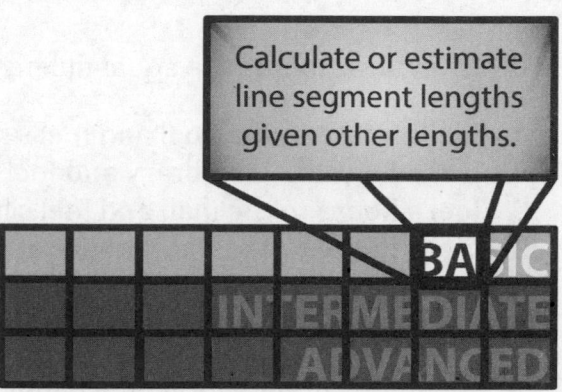

Calculate or estimate line segment lengths given other lengths.

Examples:

The figure below shows line segments connecting Joel's house to various places in a town.

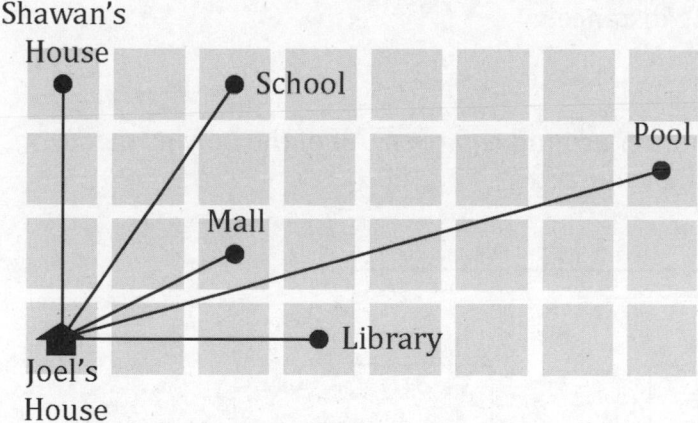

Which of the segments is the longest?

A. Joel's house to Shawan's House
B. Joel's house to the pool
C. Joel's house to the mall
D. Joel's house to the library
E. Joel's house to the school

Which of the segments is the shortest?

F. Joel's house to the school
G. Joel's house to the library
H. Joel's house to Shawan's house
J. Joel's house to the pool
K. Joel's house to the mall

Which two segments are equal in length?

A. Joel's house to the pool and Joel's house to the school
B. Joel's house to the library and Joel's house to the pool
C. Joel's house to the mall and Joel's house to the library
D. Joel's house to Shawan's house and Joel's house to the library
E. Joel's house to the school and Joel's house to the mall

You can actually answer all three questions based upon the appearance of the line segments in the figure: which looks longest, which looks shortest, and which two look equal. The longest segment is Joel's house to the pool, the shortest is Joel's house to the mall, and Joel's house to Shawan's house and Joel's house to the library are equal in length.

In other instances you may be given values and units for various distances and asked to calculate the total distance or a missing distance.

Example:

The figure below represents the border around a garden. All of the border pieces intersect at right angles. What is the value of x?

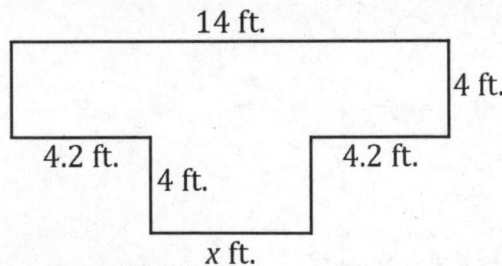

A. 4.6   C. 6.4   E. 22.4
B. 5.6   D. 8.4

Since all angles are right angles, set up an equation and solve for the missing length:

$$x + 4.2 + 4.2 = 14$$
$$x + 8.4 = 14$$
$$x = 5.6$$

Polygons

The perimeter of a figure is the sum of the lengths of the sides of the figure:

Perimeter = $side_1$ + $side_2$ + $side_3$ . . . $side_n$

where "side" is the length of the side and n is the number of sides of the figure. Actually, that is a lot of mathematical talk for a very simple idea, which is illustrated by the following examples.

> Determine the perimeter of a polygon given all side lengths.

> BASIC
> INTERMEDIATE
> ADVANCED

Example:

What is the perimeter of the triangle shown below?

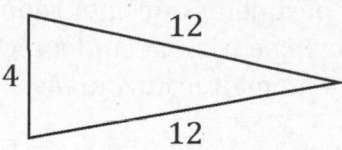

A. 4   C. 16   E. 28
B. 12   D. 24

The perimeter is the sum of the three sides: 4 + 12 + 12 = 28.

What is the perimeter of the rectangle shown below?

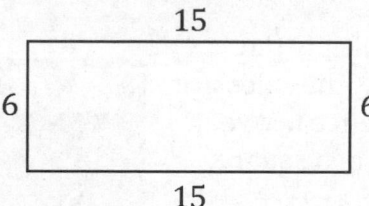

F. 6   H. 21   K. 90
G. 15   J. 42

The perimeter is the sum of the four sides: 6 + 15 + 6 + 15 = 42.

What is the perimeter of the octagon shown below, given that all of the octagon's sides are equal?

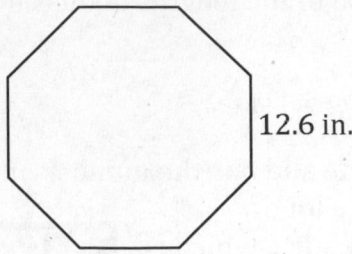

12.6 in.

A. 8 in.   C. 75.6 in.   E. 158.76 in.
B. 12.6 in.   D. 100.8 in.

The perimeter is the sum of the eight sides, which are equal, so $12.6 \cdot 8 = 100.8$ in.

The figure in the example above is a regular polygon, or enclosed figure with equal sides and equal angles. But the notion of perimeter does not require that the sides be equal, as seen in the first two examples featuring a triangle and a rectangle. The perimeter is simply the sum of the lengths of the sides—no matter how many sides or what their lengths.

Area

Remember, a **rectangle** is any four-sided figure that has four right angles. Since the opposite sides of a rectangle are congruent, it is customary to speak of the two dimensions of a rectangle: width and length. A **square** is a rectangle with four congruent sides.

Determine the area of a rectangle given whole number dimensions.

BASIC
INTERMEDIATE
ADVANCED

To find the **area** of a rectangle, multiply the width times the length. In a square, the sides are all congruent, so there is no difference between length and width. To find the area of a square, just square the length of one side.

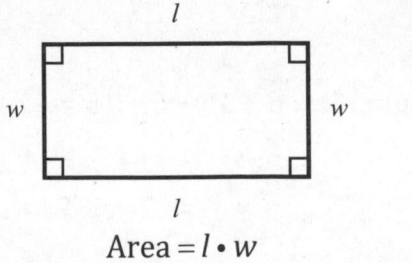

l
w w
l
Area $= l \cdot w$

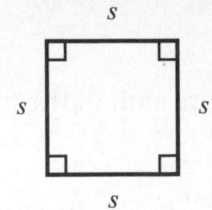

s
s s
s
Area $= s \cdot s = s^2$

EXERCISE 8

DIRECTIONS: Choose the correct answer to each of the following items. Answers are on page 813.

Questions 146–150 refer to the following diagram.

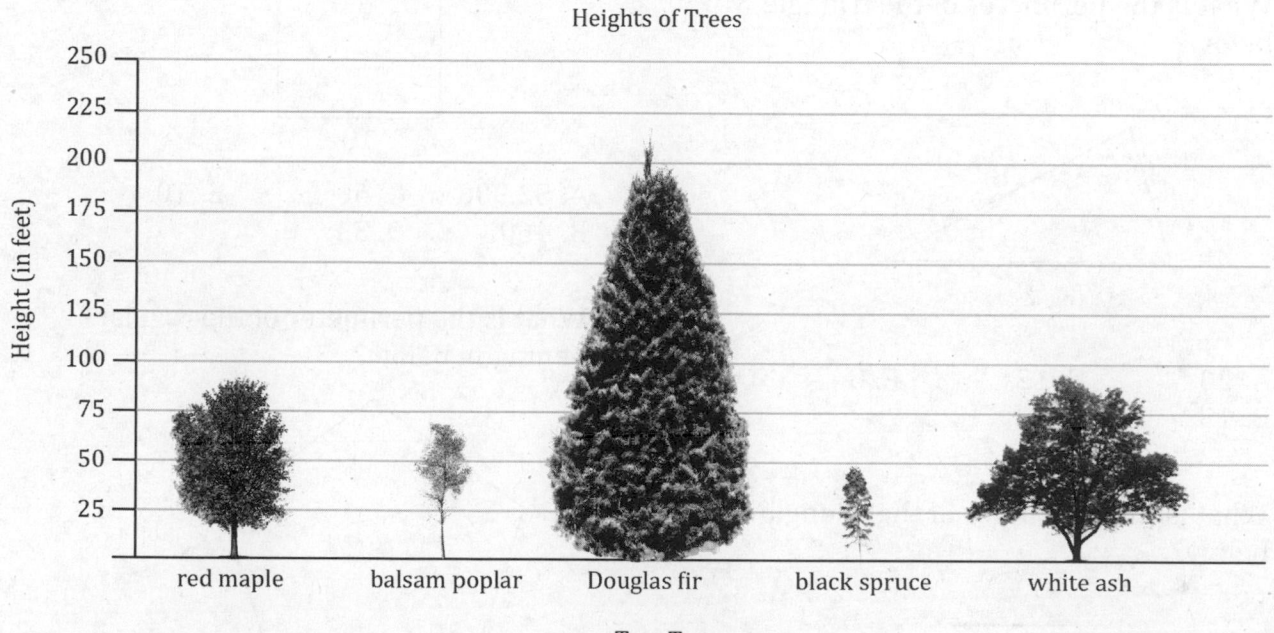

146. What is the tallest tree shown in the diagram?

    F. red maple   J. black spruce
    G. balsam poplar   K. white ash
    H. Douglas fir

147. What is the shortest tree shown in the diagram?

    A. red maple   D. black spruce
    B. balsam poplar   E. white ash
    C. Douglas fir

148. What is the approximate height of the balsam poplar shown in the diagram?

    F. 35 feet   K. 90 feet
    G. 70 feet   J. 215 feet
    H. 80 feet

149. What is the approximate height of the black spruce shown in the diagram?

    A. 50 feet   D. 90 feet
    B. 70 feet   E. 215 feet
    C. 80 feet

150. Approximately how much taller is the Douglas fir tree than the red maple tree?

F. 180 feet   K. 50 feet
G. 145 feet   J. 15 feet
H. 125 feet

151. What is the perimeter of the triangle below?

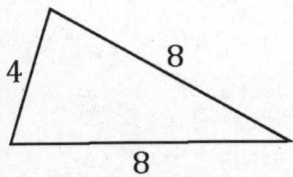

A. 20   C. 12   E. 8
B. 18   D. 10

152. What is the perimeter of the triangle below?

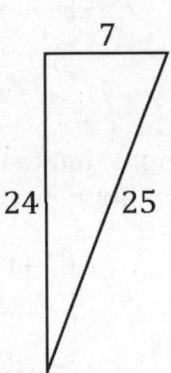

F. 4200   H. 199   K. 56
G. 607   J. 193

153. What is the perimeter of the rectangle below?

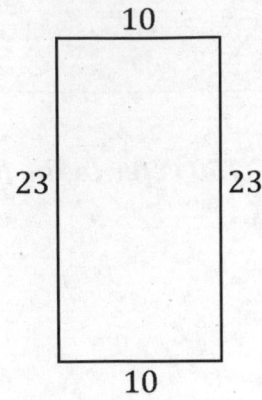

A. 52,900   C. 66   E. 10
B. 460   D. 33

154. What is the perimeter of the regular pentagon below?

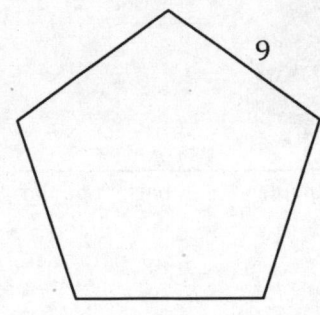

F. 9   H. 36   K. 81
G. 27   J. 45

155. What is the perimeter of the figure below?

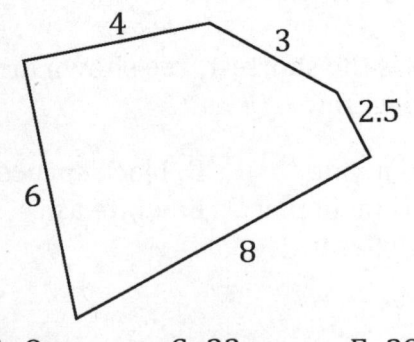

A. 8   C. 23   E. 28.5
B. 19.5   D. 23.5

156. What is the area of the figure below?

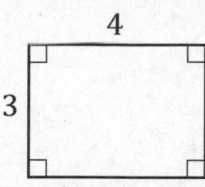

F. 6 H. 12 K. 24
G. 8 J. 14

157. In the figure below, $\overline{AB} = 5$. What is the area of square *ABCD*?

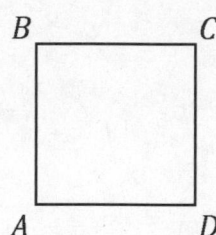

A. 5 C. 20 E. 40
B. 10 D. 25

158. What is the area of the rectangle below?

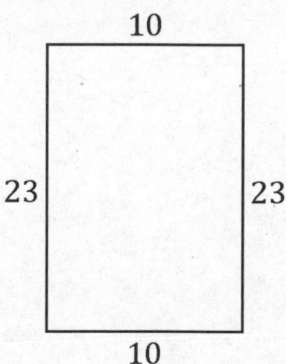

F. 66 H. 230 K. 529
G. 100 J. 460

159. The figure below shows a rectangular area where a whiteboard will be hung. If the entire area is to be covered with the whiteboard material, how many square feet of material are needed? (Ignore any waste.)

16 ft.

3.5 ft.

A. 12.5 square feet
B. 19.5 square feet
C. 28 square feet
D. 39 square feet
E. 56 square feet

160. A school flag is made from a rectangular piece of fabric 4 feet by 7.6 feet. How many square feet of material is the flag?

F. 11.6 square feet
G. 23.2 square feet
H. 30.4 square feet
J. 60.8 square feet
K. 73.76 square feet

INTERMEDIATE | Basic Manipulations

Throughout your lifetime you will regularly encounter everyday situations that require multi-step arithmetic manipulations. This section presents a few of those scenarios, including percents, proportions, rates, averages, unit conversions, and planning.

Multi-Step Percent Problems

Common multi-step percent problem scenarios include taxes, discounts, and profits.

Solve multi-step arithmetic problems involving percents, proportions, rates, computing with a given average, and unit conversions.

Taxes

Taxes are calculated as a percent of money spent or money earned.

Examples:

Dane County collects a 7% sales tax on automobiles. If the price of a used car is $5,832 before taxes, what will it cost when the sales tax is added in?

> Find 7% of $5,832 to determine the amount of tax: ($5,832)(0.07) = $408.24. Then add that amount to $5,832: $5,832 + $408.24 = $6,240.24. This can be done in one step by finding 107% of $5,832: ($5,832)(1.07) = $6,240.24.

If a salesperson earns a commission on yearly sales at the rate of 10% for the first $10,000 of sales, 15% for the next $10,000, 20% for the next $10,000, and 25% for all earnings over $30,000, how much income tax must be paid on a yearly income of $36,500?

> Find the commission earned at each percentage rate and add them:

$$
\begin{array}{rcl}
10\% \text{ of first } \$10,000 &=& \$1,000 \\
15\% \text{ of next } \$10,000 &=& \$1,500 \\
20\% \text{ of next } \$10,000 &=& \$2,000 \\
+\ \ 25\% \text{ of next } \$6,500 &=& \$1,625 \\
\hline
\text{Total Commission} &=& \$6,125
\end{array}
$$

Discounts

A discount is expressed as a percent of the original price that will be deducted from that price to determine the sale price.

Examples:

Bill's Hardware offers a 20% discount on all appliances during a sale week. How much must Russell pay for a washing machine priced at $280?

$20\% \cdot \$280 = 0.2 \cdot \$280 = \$56$ discount $\Rightarrow \$280 - \$56 = \$224$ sale price. Alternatively, the following shortcut simplifies the solution: if there is a 20% discount, Russell will pay 80% of the marked price: $80\% \cdot \$280 = 0.8 \cdot \$280 = \$224$ sale price.

A store offers a television set marked at $340 less consecutive discounts of 10% and 5%. Another store offers the same set marked at $340 less a single discount of 15%. How much does the buyer save buying at the lower price?

Store 1
Initial 10% discount: $340(0.1) = $34, and $340 – $34 = $306
Second 5% discount: $306(0.05) = $15.30, and $306 – $15.30 = $290.70

Store 2
single 15% discount: $340(0.15) = $51, and $340 – $51 = $289

Thus, the second store will have a lower sale price, and the buyer saves $290.70 – $289.00 = $1.70 buying at the better price.

Profit

Gross profit is equal to revenues minus expenses, that is, the selling price minus the cost.

Example:

A used car lot paid $5,000 for a trade-in car. At what price should the salesperson sell the used car in order to make a gross profit of 60% of the cost of the car?

The cost of the car is $5,000, so the gross profit is 60% of $5,000, or 0.6(5,000) = $3,000. Since the gross profit is equal to the selling price minus cost, the selling price of the car must be gross profit plus cost, or $3,000 + $5,000 = $8,000.

Multi-Step Proportion Problems

A ***proportion*** is the mathematical equivalent of a verbal analogy. For example, $2:3::8:12$ is equivalent to "two is to three as eight is to twelve." The main difference between an analogy and a proportion is the precision. A verbal analogy depends upon words that do not have unique and precise meanings, while mathematical proportions are made up of numbers, which are exact.

In a mathematical proportion, the first and last terms are called the "extremes" of the proportion because they are on the extreme outside, and the two middle terms are called the "means" ("mean" can mean "middle"). In a mathematical proportion, the product of the extremes is always equal to the product of the means. For example, in the proportion $2:3::8:12$, $2\cdot12=3\cdot8$.

Direct Proportions

The use of proportions can be a powerful problem-solving tool. ***Direct proportions*** equate ratios of two quantities having a direct relationship. The more there is of one quantity, the more there is of the other quantity, and vice versa.

> **Example:**
>
> If the cost of a dozen donuts is $3.60, what is the cost of 4 donuts? Assume there is no discount for buying in bulk.
>
> Relate the quantities using a direct proportion: $\dfrac{\text{Total Cost } X}{\text{Total Cost } Y} = \dfrac{\text{Number } X}{\text{Number } Y} \Rightarrow$
>
> $$\frac{\$3.60}{x} = \frac{12 \text{ donuts}}{4 \text{ donuts}} \Rightarrow x = \frac{4 \text{ donuts} \cdot \$3.60}{12 \text{ donuts}} = \frac{\$3.60}{3} = \$1.20.$$

Note that in the previous example, we set up the proportion by grouping "like terms": the "cost of the donuts" is on one side of the proportion and the number of donuts is on the other side. It is equally correct to set up the proportion as $\dfrac{\text{Total Cost } X}{\text{Number } X} = \dfrac{\text{Total Cost } Y}{\text{Number } Y}$.

However, setting up direct proportions by grouping like terms is the first step in solving inverse proportions, as we'll see in the next subsection, so it is generally a good idea to group like terms to avoid confusion. The following examples illustrate additional typical situations involving direct proportions.

The LONGER the travel time, the GREATER the distance traveled (and vice versa), assuming a CONSTANT speed.

Example:

If a plane moving at a constant speed flies 3,000 miles in 6 hours, how far will the plane fly in 8 hours?

Use a direct proportion: $\dfrac{3,000 \text{ mi}}{x} = \dfrac{6 \text{ hr}}{8 \text{ hr}} \Rightarrow (x)(6 \text{ hr}) = (3,000 \text{ mi})(8 \text{ hr}) \Rightarrow$

$x = \dfrac{8 \cancel{\text{ hr}} \cdot 3,000 \text{ mi}}{6 \cancel{\text{ hr}}} = 4,000 \text{ mi}.$

The LONGER the time of operation, the GREATER the output (and vice versa).

Example:

If an uninterrupted stamping machine operating at a constant rate postmarks 320 envelopes in 5 minutes, how long will it take the machine to postmark 480 envelopes?

Use a direct proportion: $\dfrac{320 \text{ envelopes}}{480 \text{ envelopes}} = \dfrac{5 \text{ min}}{x} \Rightarrow (320 \text{ envelopes})(x) =$

$(480 \text{ envelopes})(5 \text{ min}) \Rightarrow x = \dfrac{480 \cancel{\text{ envelopes}} \cdot 5 \text{ min}}{320 \cancel{\text{ envelopes}}} = 7.5 \text{ min}.$

The GREATER the number of items, the GREATER the weight (and vice versa).

Example:

If 20 jars of preserves weigh 25 pounds, how much do 15 jars of preserves weigh?

Use a direct proportion: $\dfrac{20 \text{ jars}}{15 \text{ jars}} = \dfrac{25 \text{ lbs}}{x} \Rightarrow (20 \text{ jars})(x) = (15 \text{ jars})(25 \text{ lbs}) \Rightarrow$

$x = \dfrac{15 \cancel{\text{ jars}} \cdot 25 \text{ lbs}}{20 \cancel{\text{ jars}}} = 18.75 \text{ lbs}.$

Inverse Proportions

In some situations, quantities are related **inversely**; that is, an increase in one results in a decrease in the other, and vice versa. For example, the more workers doing a job, the less time it takes to finish the job. In this case, quantities are related inversely to each other. To solve problems involving inverse relationships, use the following procedure to set up an inverse proportion.

Step 1: Set up an ordinary proportion—make sure to group like terms (with like units).

Step 2: Invert one side of the proportion.

Step 3: Solve for the unknown quantity.

Example:

Assuming a constant rate of 125 kilometers per hour, a train makes the trip from Tokyo to Kyoto in 4 hours. How long will the trip take if the train travels at a constant rate of 200 kilometers per hour?

The greater the rate of travel, the shorter the duration of the trip, so use an inverse proportion. First, set up a direct proportion, grouping like terms:
$\dfrac{125 \text{ kph}}{200 \text{ kph}} = \dfrac{4 \text{ hours}}{x}$. Now, invert one side of the equation and solve for the

unknown quantity: $\dfrac{125 \text{ kph}}{200 \text{ kph}} = \dfrac{x}{4 \text{ hrs}} \Rightarrow \left(200 \text{ kph}\right)\left(x\right) = \left(125 \text{ kph}\right)\left(4 \text{ hrs}\right) \Rightarrow$

$\left(200 \text{ kph}\right)\left(x\right) = 500 \text{ kph} \cdot \text{hrs} \Rightarrow x = \dfrac{500 \ \cancel{\text{kph}} \cdot \text{hrs}}{200 \ \cancel{\text{kph}}} = 2.5 \text{ hrs}.$

Multi-Step Rate Problems

Another type of problem which uses proportions is a **rate** problem. Note that the following words are frequently used in rate problems: *for, in, per, to, each*. For example: $100 *for* 5 hours of work, 3 widgets produced *in* 5 minutes, 55 miles *per* hour, 13 floors *to* a building, 7 cards *each*.

Example:

During a 4-hour party, 5 adults consumed appetizers costing $120. For the same appetizer costs per person per hour, what would be the cost of appetizers consumed by 4 adults during a 3-hour party?

The ratio in question is appetizer costs per person per hour, so equate two ratios

and solve for the missing value: $\dfrac{\$120}{5 \text{ adults}/4 \text{ hours}} = \dfrac{x}{4 \text{ adults}/3 \text{ hours}} \Rightarrow$

$\dfrac{\$120 \cdot 4 \text{ hours}}{5 \text{ adults}} = \dfrac{x \cdot 3 \text{ hours}}{4 \text{ adults}} \Rightarrow x = \dfrac{\$120 \cdot 16 \ \cancel{\text{adults} \cdot \text{hours}}}{15 \ \cancel{\text{adults} \cdot \text{hours}}} = \$128.$

Computing with a Given Average

Some average problems involve computation of an average rate. These problems may require you to use the formula $\text{Rate} = \dfrac{\text{Distance}}{\text{Time}}$.

Examples:

Ivan left Austin to drive to Boxville at 6:15 p.m. and arrived at 11:45 p.m. If he averaged 50 miles per hour while driving and stopped one hour for dinner, how many miles is Boxville from Austin?

A. 200   C. 250   E. 300
B. 225   D. 275

> In this case, average is really just a rate: 50 miles in 1 hour. From 6:15 p.m. to 11:45 p.m. equals a total elapsed time of 5.5 hours. However, one hour was used for dinner. Therefore, Ivan drove at 50 miles per hour for 4.5 hours, covering
>
> $\dfrac{50 \text{ miles}}{\text{hour}} \cdot 4.5 \text{ hours} = 225 \text{ miles, (B)}.$

A log kept by military guards recorded that an average of 26 vehicles per hour passed through a checkpoint over a three-day period. At this rate, how many vehicles would pass through the checkpoint in a 24-hour period?

F. 52   H. 78   K. 1,872
G. 72   J. 624

> The average given is just a rate:
>
> $\dfrac{26 \text{ vehicles}}{\text{hour}} \cdot 24 \text{ hours} = 624 \text{ vehicles, (J)}.$

As a biology project, a student calculated a density of 12.3 earthworms per square foot in the top soil of a large and uniform grassy area. Based upon this finding, how many earthworms should the student expect to find in 20 square feet of the grassy area?

A. 110.7   C. 246   E. 3,321
B. 180   D. 842

> Again, the average given is just a rate:
>
> $\dfrac{12.3 \text{ earthworms}}{\text{square foot}} \cdot 20 \text{ square feet} = 246 \text{ earthworms, (C)}.$

Multi-Step Unit Conversions

Some multi-step arithmetic questions may involve different units of measure. For any problem requiring conversion from one unit of measure to another, other than for units of time, the relationship between those units will be given.

Example:

A car travels at a constant rate of 37 miles per hour. If 1 kilometer is equal to 0.62 miles, approximately how many kilometers does the car travel in 20 minutes?

$$\text{Rate} \cdot \text{Time} = \text{Distance} \Rightarrow \left(\frac{37 \text{ mi}}{\text{hr}} \cdot \frac{1 \text{ km}}{0.62 \text{ mi}} \right) \cdot \left(20 \text{ min} \cdot \frac{1 \text{ hr}}{60 \text{ min}} \right) =$$

$$\frac{37 \text{ km}}{0.62 \text{ hr}} \cdot \frac{20 \text{ hr}}{60} \approx \frac{60 \text{ km}}{3} = 20 \text{ km}$$

EXERCISE 1

DIRECTIONS: Choose the correct answer to each of the following items. Answers are on page 813.

1. If a textbook costs $30 plus 8.5% sales tax, what is the total cost of one textbook?

   A. $3.55   C. $23.55   E. $33.55
   B. $12.55   D. $32.55

2. A suit is sold for $68 while priced at $80. What is the rate of discount?

   F. 15%   H. $17\frac{11}{17}$%   K. 24%

   G. 17%   J. 20%

3. A stereo was discounted by 20% and sold at the discount price of $256. Which of the following equals the price of the stereo before the discount?

   A. less than $300
   B. between $300 and $308
   C. between $308 and $316
   D. between $316 and $324
   E. more than $324

4. The regular price of a bedding set is $118.80. Which of the following equals the price of the bedding set after a sale price reduction of 20%?

   F. $158.60   J. $95.04
   G. $148.50   K. $29.70
   H. $138.84

5. Two dozen ping pong balls and four badminton shuttlecocks are to be purchased for a playground. The ping pong balls are priced at $0.35 each and the shuttlecocks at $2.75 each. The playground receives a discount of 30% from these prices. Which of the following equals the total cost of this equipment?

A. $7.29   C. $13.58   E. $19.40
B. $11.43   D. $18.60

6. If 240 widgets cost $36, what is the cost of 180 widgets?

F. $8   H. $24   K. $32
G. $16   J. $27

7. Orville claims that 3 bags of his popcorn will yield 28 ounces when popped. If this is the case, how many ounces will 5 bags of his popcorn yield when popped?

A. 23   C. $54\frac{1}{2}$ E. $64\frac{2}{3}$

B. $46\frac{2}{3}$ D. 64

8. In a poll of 1,000 people, 420 said they would vote for Mason. Based on this poll, how many people would be expected to vote for Mason if 60,000,000 people actually vote?

F. 25,200,000   J. 26,200,000
G. 25,500,000   K. 26,500,000
H. 26,000,000

9. A snapshot measures $2\frac{1}{2}$ inches by $1\frac{7}{8}$ inches. If it is enlarged so that the longer dimension is 4 inches, what is the length, in inches, of the enlarged shorter dimension?

A. $2\frac{1}{2}$ C. $3\frac{3}{8}$ E. 5
B. 3   D. 4

10. It costs $3.10 per square foot to lay tile flooring. How much will it cost to lay 180 square feet of flooring?

F. $162   H. $558   K. $1,800
G. $186   J. $620

11. If Joey earns $352 in 16 days, how much will he earn in 117 days?

A. $3,050   C. $2,285   E. $1,170
B. $2,574   D. $2,080

12. Assuming that on a blueprint $\frac{1}{8}$ inch equals 12 inches of actual length, what is the actual length, in inches, of a steel bar represented on the blueprint by a line $3\frac{3}{4}$ inches long?

F. $3\frac{3}{4}$ H. 36   K. 450
G. 30   J. 360

13. If p pencils cost d dollars, how many pencils can be bought for c cents?

A. $\dfrac{100pc}{d}$ C. $\dfrac{pd}{c}$ E. $\dfrac{cd}{p}$

B. $\dfrac{pc}{100d}$ D. $\dfrac{pc}{d}$

14. If a truck travels 275 miles on 25 gallons of fuel, then what is the average fuel consumption for the entire trip expressed in miles per gallon?

F. 25   H. 15   K. 7
G. 18   J. 11

15. A gear 50 inches in diameter turns a smaller gear 30 inches in diameter. If the larger gear makes 15 revolutions, how many revolutions does the smaller gear make in that same time?

A. 9   C. 20   E. 30
B. 12   D. 25

16. If Maria bicycles at an average speed of 15 miles per hour, her trip from the park to her house takes 3 hours. How long, in hours, will the trip take if she bicycles at an average rate of 20 miles per hour?

F. 2   H. 2.5   K. 2.8
G. 2.25   J. 2.75

17. If El kayaks at an average speed of 6 miles per hour, the trip across the lake takes 2 hours. How long, in hours, will the trip take if El's average speed is 5 miles per hour?

A. 1   C. 1.6   E. 2.4
B. 1.2   D. 1.8

18. If 4 workers take an hour to pave a road, how long should it take 12 workers to pave the same road?

F. $\dfrac{1}{4}$ hour   H. $\dfrac{1}{2}$ hour   K. 3 hours

G. $\dfrac{1}{3}$ hour   J. 1 hour

19. If the trip from Soldier Field to Wrigley Field takes two hours walking at a constant rate of four miles per hour, how long (in hours) will the same trip take walking at a constant rate of five miles per hour?

A. 2.5   C. 1.6   E. 1.25
B. 1.75   D. 1.5

20. A swimming pool is filled by either of two pipes. Pipe A supplies water at the rate of 200 gallons per hour and takes eight hours to fill the pool. If Pipe B can fill the pool in five hours, what is the rate (in gallons per hour) at which Pipe B supplies water?

F. 125   H. 360   K. 575
G. 320   J. 480

$19. \dfrac{x}{2} = \dfrac{4mph}{5mph}$ $5x = 8$

21. If Bruce can eat $2\frac{1}{2}$ bananas per day, how many bananas can Bruce eat in 4 weeks?

   A. 70   C. 80   E. 90
   B. 75   D. 85

22. If a kilogram of a certain cheese costs $9.60, what is the cost of 450 grams of the cheese? (1 kilogram = 1,000 grams)

   F. $2.78   H. $3.88   K. $5.12
   G. $3.14   J. $4.32

23. If 48 liters of a certain liquid weigh 50 kilograms, then how much, in grams, will 72 liters of the liquid weigh? (1 kilogram = 1,000 grams)

   A. 25   C. 75,000   E. 120,000
   B. 75   D. 90,000

24. Nikki is making party favors and needs ribbon to tie the favor bags. If she can cut exactly 8 strips out of 2 yards of ribbon, how many strips can she cut from 15 feet of ribbon? (3 feet = 1 yard)

   F. 6   H. 15   K. 25
   G. 10   J. 20

25. Sandi traveled 6800 miles from Dubai to New York in 14 hours. Using the same rate, how long would it take to travel 2720 km from New York to Denver? (1 km = 0.62 miles) Round your answer to the nearest tenth.

   A. 3 hours   D. 5.6 hours
   B. 3.5 hours   E. 6 hours
   C. 4 hours

robability, Statistics, and Data Analysis

Averages

An average is the sum of a set of values divided by the total number of values, such as the average high temperature over a period of 5 days or the average cost of four books. However, the unknown value in an average problem is not always the average of a set of values.

Determining Missing Elements in Averages

Some items provide the average of a group of numbers and some—but not all—of the quantities involved. You are then asked to find the **missing element(s)**. For example, if the average of 3, x, and 8 is 6, what is the

Determine the missing data value given the average and all the values but one.

───────────

Determine the average given the frequency counts of all data values.

value of x? Since the average of the three numbers is 6, the sum (or total) of the three numbers is $3 \cdot 6 = 18$. The two given numbers are equal to $3 + 8 = 11$, so the third number

must be 18 − 11 = 7. Check the solution by averaging 3, 8, and 7: $\dfrac{3+8+7}{3} = \dfrac{18}{3} = 6$.

Examples:

For a certain five-day period, the average high temperature (in degrees Fahrenheit) for Chicago was 30°. If the high temperatures recorded for the first four of those days were 26°, 32°, 24°, and 35°, what was the high temperature recorded on the fifth day?

The sum of the five numbers is $5 \cdot 30 = 150$. The sum for the first four days is: $26 + 32 + 24 + 35 = 117$. Thus, the fifth day must have had a high temperature of $150 - 117 = 33$. Note that this is the same as setting up an equation for the average

and solving for the missing element: $\dfrac{26 + 32 + 24 + 35 + x}{5} = 30 \Rightarrow$

$x = (30 \cdot 5) - (26 + 32 + 24 + 35) = 150 - 117 = 33$.

The average of Jose's scores on four tests is 90. If three of those scores are 89, 92, and 94, what is his fourth score?

The sum of all four scores must be $4 \cdot 90 = 360$. The sum of the three known scores is $89 + 92 + 94 = 275$. Thus, the remaining score must be $360 - 275 = 85$. Note that this is the same as setting up an equation for the average and solving for the missing element: $\dfrac{89 + 92 + 94 + x}{4} = 90 \Rightarrow x = (90 \cdot 4) - (89 + 92 + 94) =$ $360 - 275 = 85$.

The average of a group of eight numbers is 9. If one of these numbers is removed from the group, the average of the remaining numbers is 7. What is the value of the number removed?

The sum of the original numbers is $8 \cdot 9 = 72$. The sum of the remaining numbers is $7 \cdot 7 = 49$, so the value of the number that was removed must be $72 - 49 = 23$.

Determining Missing Elements in Averages Using Frequency Counts

Another variation on average problems asks about more than one missing element.

Example:

In a group of children, three of the children are ages 7, 8, and 10, and the other two are the same age. If the average of the ages of all five children is 7, what is the age of the other two children?

The total sum of the five ages must be $5 \cdot 7 = 35$. The sum of the known ages is $7 + 8 + 10 = 25$, so the ages of the two other children must equal 10. Since there are two of them of the same age, each one must be 5 years old.

Single-Event Probability

Probability is concerned with experiments that have a finite number of outcomes. Probabilities occur in games, sports, weather reports, etc. The probability that some particular outcome or set of outcomes (called an **event**) will occur is expressed as a ratio. The numerator of a probability ratio is the number of ways that the event of interest can occur. The denominator is the total number of outcomes that are possible. This **probability ratio** is true for

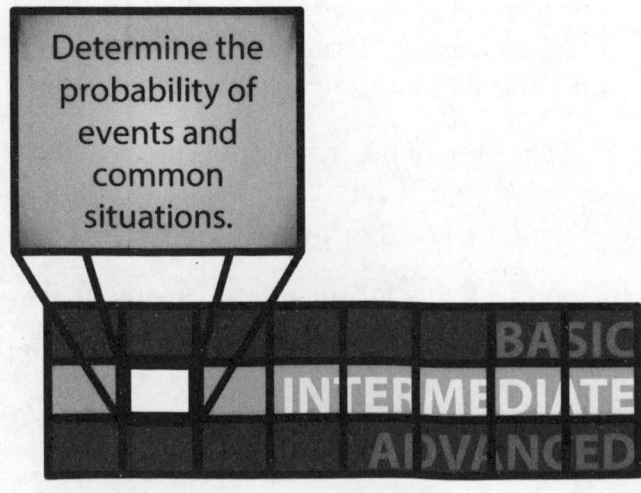

experiments in which all of the individual outcomes are equally likely:

$$\text{Probability of event} = \frac{\text{number of ways that event can happen}}{\text{total number of outcomes possible}}$$

Example:

If a six-sided die is tossed, what is the probability that you will get a number greater than 4?

There are a total of six ways a die can land: 1, 2, 3, 4, 5, or 6. Each of these six events is equally likely. There are two possible outcomes that are greater than 4: 5 or 6.

Therefore, the probability of the die landing with a number greater than 4 is $\frac{2}{6} = \frac{1}{3}$.

Counting Methods

The Multiplication Principle for Counting

The ***multiplication principle for counting*** states that if one object is to be chosen from a set of m objects and a second object is to be chosen from a different set of n objects, the total number of ways of choosing both objects simultaneously is mn. In other words, if an operation takes two steps and the first step can be performed in m ways, and if, for each of

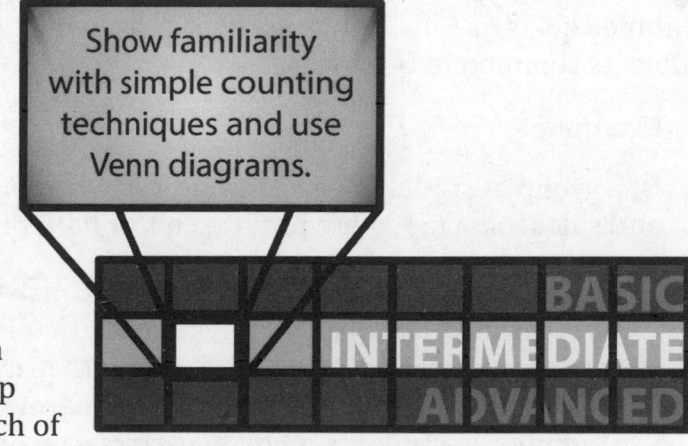

Show familiarity with simple counting techniques and use Venn diagrams.

BASIC
INTERMEDIATE
ADVANCED

those ways, the second step can be performed in n ways, the total number of ways of performing the operation is mn. Note that the two sets are separate and independent of each other.

Examples:

A litter of boxer puppies contains 4 with brindle coloring and 5 with fawn coloring. In how many ways can a pair of one brindle puppy and one fawn puppy be chosen from this litter of puppies?

There are 4 choices for a brindle puppy and 5 choices for a fawn puppy. By the multiplication principle for counting, the total number of possible pairs is:
$4 \cdot 5 = 20$.

From a garden with 6 flower varieties, a bouquet of 3 different types of flowers is to be picked. How many different possible bouquets are there?

Extend the multiplication principle for counting to a three-step process: there are 6 choices of flower varieties for the first pick of the bouquet, for the second flower there are 5 choices (because one flower type has been eliminated). Furthermore, for each of these pairs, there are 4 remaining flower choices for the third pick (because two flower types have been eliminated, having been picked as the first and second flowers in the bouquet). Therefore, the total number of possible bouquets is: $6 \cdot 5 \cdot 4 = 120$.

The Addition Principle for Counting

The **addition principle for counting** is the first of several useful methods for counting objects and sets of objects without actually listing the elements to be counted. According to the theorem, if set A contains m objects and set B contains n objects (and there are no objects common to the two sets) then the total number of objects in the two sets combined is $m+n$. However, if there are k objects common to the two sets, then the total in the combined set is $m + n - k$. In other words, you must take into account the double-counting of objects common to both sets.

Example:

Of a group of students at a campus cafe, 9 ate pizza and 5 had salad. If 3 had both pizza and salad, how many ate pizza, salad, or both pizza and salad?

The question describes two sets: one consisting of students that ate pizza (set P: $m = 9$), and one consisting of students that had salad (set S: $n = 5$). Since the question states that 3 students ate both pizza and salad, the number of students common to the two sets is 3 ($k = 3$). Therefore, the total in the combined set (number of students who ate pizza, salad, or both) is: $m + n - k = 9 + 5 - 3 = 11$.

This kind of situation involving sets that overlap is most easily handled by displaying the given information in a **Venn diagram**.

Example:

Two circles are drawn on a floor. 20 people are standing in circle A. 15 people are standing in circle B. 9 people are standing in both circles. Find the total number of people standing in the two circles.

One set has 20 people ($m = 20$). The other set has 15 people ($n = 15$). Nine people are in both sets ($k = 9$). The total number of people, then, is the sum of people in each group minus the people who are counted twice (because they are in two groups): Total = $m + n - k = 20 + 15 - 9 = 26$ people.

Alternatively, the item can be illustrated with a Venn diagram:

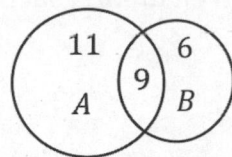

From the diagram, it can be seen that there are a total of 11 + 9 + 6 or 26 people.

Data Presentations

Data presentations such as the table below provide a quick reference for data interpretation and analysis. However, sometimes one form of data is more helpful than another form of data in making a point or analyzing a problem.

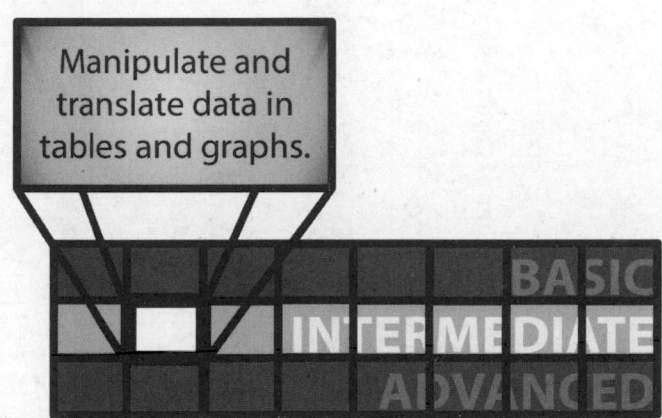

Manipulate and translate data in tables and graphs.

Example:

Sports Trading Cards Albert Collected
(Over Five Months)

	January	February	March	April	May
Baseball	52	34	38	46	40
Football	12	10	16	23	25
Hockey	8	10	15	19	17
Cricket	5	4	7	6	2
Rugby	3	1	4	2	1

The table above is helpful in answering questions such as:

How many baseball cards did Albert collect in March? 38

How many rugby cards did Albert collect in May? 1

The table is helpful as far as it goes. But there are more efficient ways to determine the total number of cards Albert purchased in a given month, such as by using a cumulative bar graph.

Example:

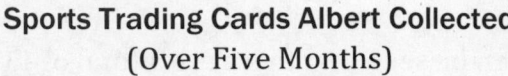

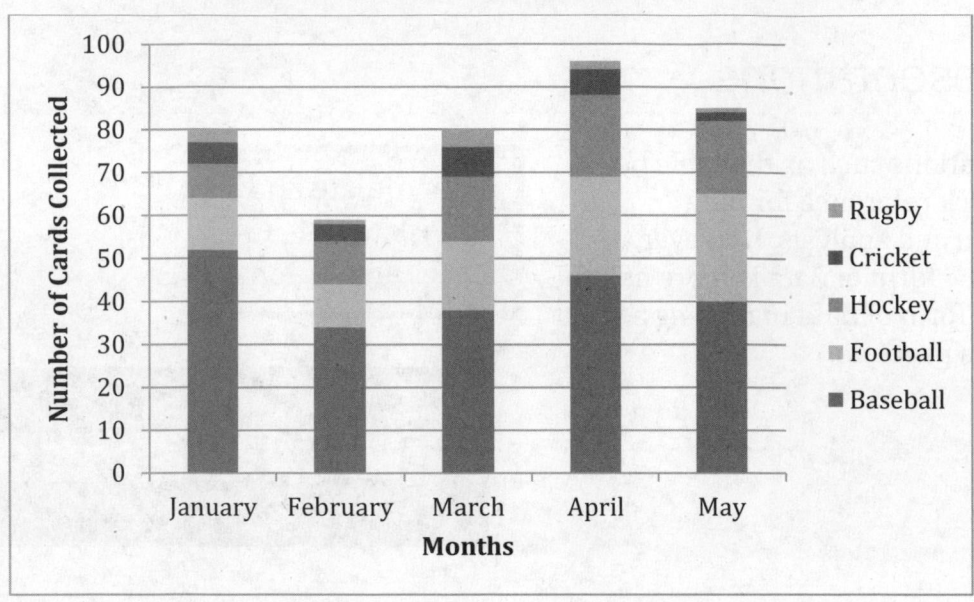

Approximately how many cards did Albert collect in April?

Using the table, you could determine the total: 46 + 23 + 19 + 6 + 2 = 96. But it is much faster to look at the cumulative bar graph and see that the total for April is approximately 95 cards.

Similarly, line graphs present helpful information about the rise and fall of data within a particular series.

Example:

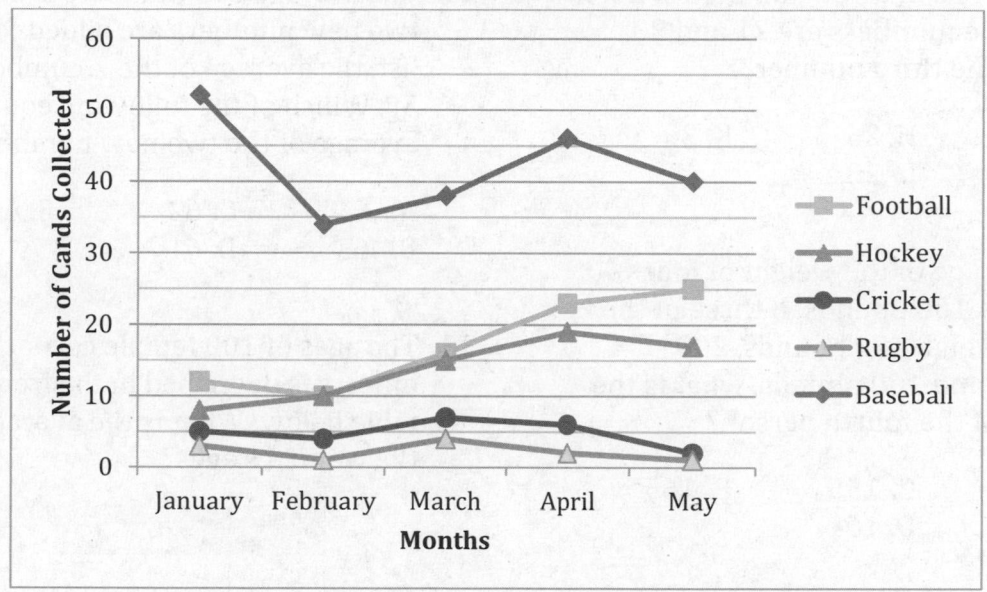

Sports Trading Cards Albert Collected
(Over Five Months)

This type of chart is particularly good for answering questions such as:

For which type of trading card did the number of cards collected increase from April to May?

> The line takes an upward turn for football cards.

Fewer cards were collected in February than in January for how many types of trading cards?

> Four: football, cricket, rugby, and baseball

EXERCISE 2

DIRECTIONS: Choose the correct answer to each of the following items. Answers are on page 813.

26. The average of three numbers is 24. If two of the numbers are 21 and 23, what is the third number?

    F. 20   H. 26   K. 30
    G. 24   J. 28

27. The average of the weight of four people is 166 pounds. If three of the people weigh 150 pounds, 200 pounds, and 180 pounds, what is the weight of the fourth person?

    A. 134   C. 155   E. 165
    B. 140   D. 161

28. Robert made the following deposits into a savings account:

Amount	Frequency
$15	4 times
x	2 times
$25	4 times

    If the average of all 10 deposits is $20, what was the amount, x, of the deposits he made 2 times?

    F. $18.50   H. $21.50   K. $22.50
    G. $20.00   J. $22.00

29. The average of 5 numbers is 56. If two new numbers are added to the list, the average of the 7 numbers is 58. Which of the following equals the average of the two new numbers?

    A. 64   C. 62   E. 60
    B. 63   D. 61

30. The ages of 100 female corporate officers is described in the frequency table below. What is the average of the women's ages?

Ages	Frequency
25	12
35	26
45	28
55	34

    F. 16   H. 43.4   K. 45
    G. 43   J. 44.3

31. The probability that an event will happen can be shown by the fraction
$$\frac{\text{winning events}}{\text{total events}} \text{ or } \frac{\text{favorable events}}{\text{total events}}.$$
From the 8-digit number 12,344,362, Helen selects a digit at random. What is the probability that she selected 4?

    A. $\dfrac{1}{8}$ C. $\dfrac{1}{4}$ E. $\dfrac{4}{1}$

    B. $\dfrac{1}{5}$ D. $\dfrac{1}{2}$

32. One of the letters in the alphabet is selected at random. What is the probability that the letter selected is a letter found in the word "MATHEMATICS"?

F. $\dfrac{1}{26}$ H. $\dfrac{5}{13}$ K. $\dfrac{6}{13}$

G. $\dfrac{4}{13}$ J. $\dfrac{11}{26}$

33. Larry has 4 red ties, 2 pink ties, and 4 blue ties. What is the probability that he chooses a pink tie?

A. 20%   C. 60%   E. 80%
B. 40%   D. 75%

34. Jim's fishbowl contains 5 tetras, 3 goldfish, and x platies. He removes one fish from the fishbowl at random. If the probability of removing a goldfish from the bowl is 1 out of 3, how many fish does Jim have?

F. 1   H. 5   K. 9
G. 3   J. 8

35. Lisa has 2 red dresses, 3 green dresses and x blue dresses hanging in her closet. If Lisa chooses one dress at random, the probability that Lisa will choose a red dress is 25%. How many blue dresses does Lisa have?

A. 1   C. 3   E. 5
B. 2   D. 4

36. Robert is making an eclectic playlist. He has narrowed it down to 5 pop songs, 4 country songs, 3 rap songs, 2 folk songs, and 1 heavy metal song. If he wants his playlist to consist of 1 song from each type of music, how many combinations of songs are possible?

F. 5   H. 30   K. 240
G. 15   J. 120

37. Susan decides to spend 30 minutes a week doing an aerobic exercise and 30 minutes a week doing a strength exercise. If there are 6 types of aerobic exercises and 3 types of strength exercises available for Susan to do, how many different combinations of exercises are possible to accomplish this task?

A. 2   C. 11   E. 36
B. 9   D. 18

38. Anna is putting a new outfit on her Barbie doll. She has 2 hats, 6 shirts, 4 pairs of pants, and 2 pairs of shoes to choose from. If an outfit consists of 1 hat, 1 shirt, 1 pair of pants, and 1 pair of shoes, how many different outfits can Anna create?

F. 4   H. 30   K. 100
G. 14   J. 96

39. Sally collects stuffed animals. She has 8 teddy bears, 6 kittens, 6 bunnies, and 4 puppies. She decides to trade 1 of her teddy bears, 1 of her bunnies and 1 of her puppies with her friend Lyle. How many different combinations of these animals can she trade with Lyle?

A. 18   C. 192   E. 1152
B. 27   D. 288

40. Jeremy wants to buy a new bike. He goes to the bike store and finds 3 models that he can afford. Each of the three models comes in 4 colors and 2 types of seats. How many different choices does he have if each choice consists of 1 model, 1 color, and 1 type of bike seat?

F. 3   H. 9   K. 24
G. 6   J. 18

41. The table below shows the number of students in three sports at East High School. 8 students are in both basketball and tennis, 5 students are in both basketball and volleyball, and 3 students are in both volleyball and tennis. No student is in all three sports. What is the total number of students that participate only in basketball or tennis?

Sport	Number of Students
Basketball	35
Volleyball	15
Tennis	40

A. 22   C. 50   E. 75
B. 29   D. 51

42. At Jamie's bank, 20 bankers manage personal loans and 15 bankers manage business loans. Of those, 3 bankers manage both. If the bank only offers these two types of loans, how many bankers does it employ?

F. 12   H. 32   K. 38
G. 17   J. 35

43. A geometry teacher has a box of 50 shapes in her classroom. If 25 are regular polygons (figures with sides of equal length), 18 are rectangles, and 7 are squares, how many shapes in the box are not regular polygons, rectangles or squares?

A. 7   C. 14   E. 25
B. 11   D. 18

44. The Pizza Pie surveyed 30 of their customers to find out which pizza toppings they liked better, veggie or meat. 14 people liked veggie, and 13 liked meat. Of those, 4 liked both. How many people surveyed did not like either type of pizza topping?

F. 4   H. 10   K. 27
G. 7   J. 23

45. In a class of 80 students, 48 are enrolled in math, 49 are enrolled in English, and 33 are enrolled in both. How many students are not enrolled in either math or English?

A. 16   C. 32   E. 47
B. 31   D. 33

Questions 46–50 refer to the following information.

Five classrooms are collecting box tops for their school. The table below shows the number of box tops collected each week, over a period of five weeks.

NUMBER OF BOX TOPS						
Teacher	Week 1	Week 2	Week 3	Week 4	Week 5	*Total*
Mrs. Abbott	23	32	51	64	82	*252*
Miss Baker	21	30	42	58	75	*226*
Mr. Clemens	31	37	59	56	90	*273*
Mrs. Davis	28	40	54	74	89	*285*
Mr. Eaton	32	26	48	60	80	*246*

Questions 46–48 refer to the following graph.

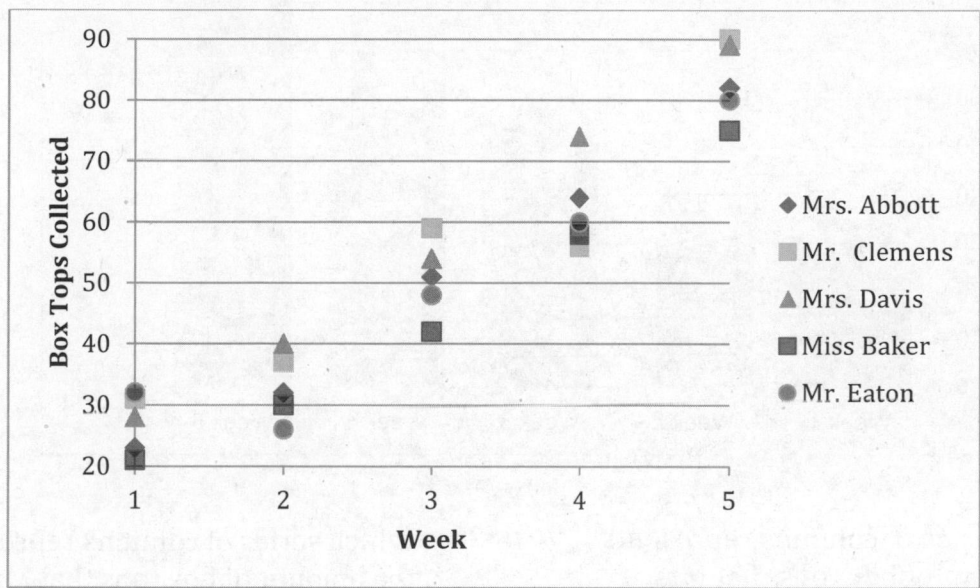

46. During Week 2, how many more box tops did Mr. Clemens' class collect than Miss Abbott's class?

F. 2   H. 5   K. 10
G. 4   J. 7

47. Over the course of five weeks, which class collected the greatest amount of box tops?

A. Mrs. Abbott's class
B. Miss Baker's class
C. Mr. Clemens' class
D. Mrs. Davis' class
E. Mr. Eaton's class

48. Which class collected fewer box tops in Week 4 than in Week 3?

    F. Mrs. Abbott's class
    G. Miss Baker's class
    H. Mr. Clemens' class
    J. Mrs. Davis' class
    K. Mr. Eaton's class

Questions 49–50 refer to the following graph.

Box Tops Collected

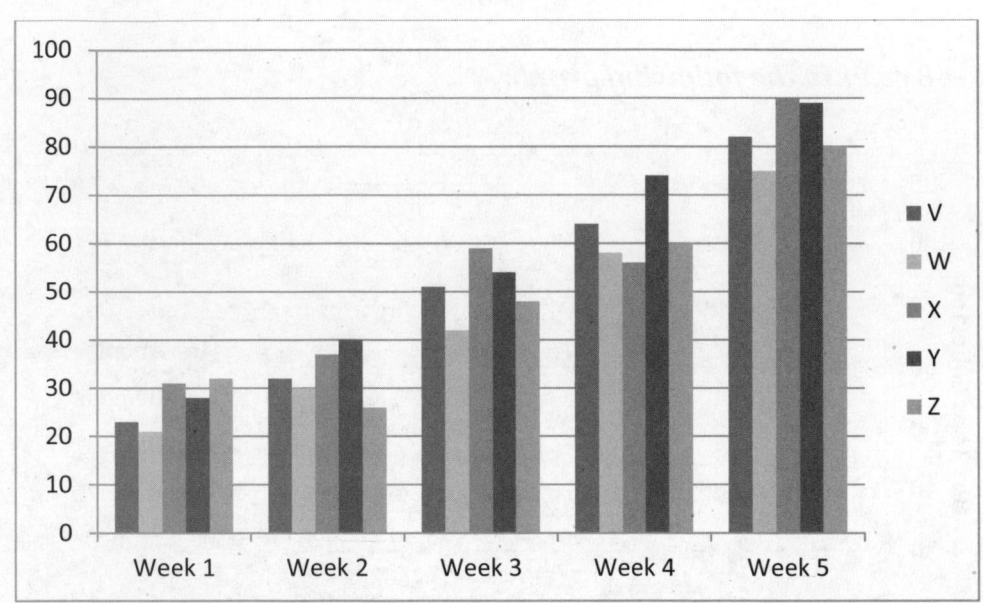

49. Which series of columns represents the amount of box tops that Mrs. Davis' class collected over the course of five weeks?

    A. V   C. X   E. Z
    B. W   D. Y

50. Which series of columns represents the amount of box tops that Mrs. Baker's class collected over the course of five weeks?

    F. V   H. X   K. Z
    G. W   J. Y

Number Concepts

Primes, Factors, and Multiples

A **prime number** is a whole number (other than 1) that is only evenly divisible by 1 and by itself. For example, 13 is a prime number because it is evenly divisible by 1 and 13 but not by any other whole number. <u>Note:</u> 1 is NOT considered a prime number. The following are examples of prime numbers: 2, 3, 5, 7, 11, 13, 17, 19, and 23.

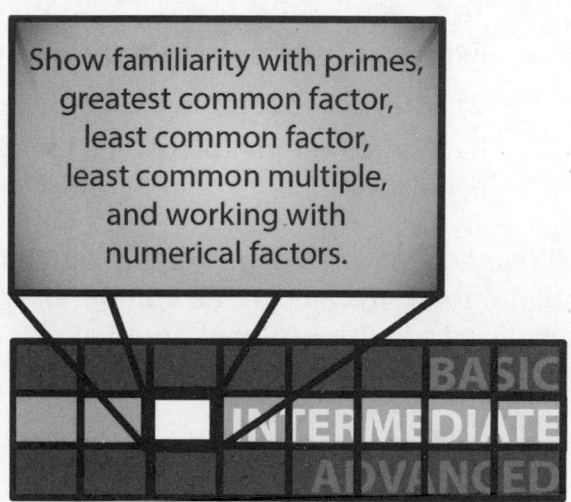

Example:

Which of the following is equal to the ratio of the number of prime numbers between 0 and 20 with one digit to the number of prime numbers between 0 and 20 with two digits?

A. $\dfrac{1}{2}$ C. 1   E. 2

B. $\dfrac{3}{4}$ D. $\dfrac{4}{3}$

List the number of primes between 0 and 20: 2, 3, 5, 7, 11, 13, 17, and 19. Thus, four have one digit and four have two digits. The ratio is $\dfrac{1}{1} = 1$, (C).

The **greatest common factor** of two numbers is the largest factor shared by both numbers. Recall that numbers that evenly divide another number are factors of that number.

Examples:

What is the greatest common factor of 12 and 16?

Factors of 12 are 1, 2, 3, 4, 6, and 12, and factors of 16 are 1, 2, 4, 8, and 16, so the greatest common factor of 12 and 16 is 4.

If a is the greatest common factor of 12 and 18 and b is the greatest common factor of 24 and 15, what is the value of ab?

F. 3   H. 12   K. 24
G. 9   J. 18

The greatest common factor of 12 and 18 is 6 and the greatest common factor of 24 and 15 is 3. Therefore, the value of *ab* is (6)(3) = 18, (J).

Let $D = 120$. How many positive factors, including 1 and 120, does D have?

A. Three   C. Six   E. Sixteen
B. Five   D. Eight

Express 120 as a product of prime factors with exponents: $120 = 2(2)(2)(3)(5) = 2^3(3)(5)$. To find the total number of positive factors, add 1 to the exponent of each base and multiply the results together: $(3+1)(1+1)(1+1) = (4)(2)(2) = 16$ positive factors, (E).

The ***least common multiple*** of two numbers is the smallest number that is a multiple of both numbers. Recall that if a number is evenly divisible by another number, it is considered a multiple of that number.

Examples:

What is the least common multiple of 96, 120, and 252?

F. 210   H. 1,440   K. 10,080
G. 420   J. 2,016

Express each of the three numbers as a product of primes with exponents:

$$96 = (2)(2)(2)(2)(2)(3) = \left(2^5\right)(3)$$

$$120 = (2)(2)(2)(3)(5) = \left(2^3\right)(3)(5)$$

$$252 = (2)(2)(3)(3)(7) = \left(2^2\right)\left(3^2\right)(7)$$

Now, to find the least common multiple, choose for each base the one with the highest exponent and multiply them together: $\left(2^5\right)\left(3^2\right)(5)(7) = 10,080$, (K).

If x is the least common multiple of the set {4, 5, 9, 12} and y is the greatest common factor of the set {60, 120, 42, 36}, what is the value of $\dfrac{x}{y}$?

A. 6   C. 60   E. 180
B. 30   D. 100

Write the values in the first set as products of prime factors with exponents. Multiple together the highest exponential value of each base to find the least common multiple:

$$4 = 2^2$$
$$5 = 5$$
$$9 = 3^2$$
$$12 = \left(2^2\right)(3)$$

So, the least common multiple is $\left(2^2\right)(5)\left(3^2\right) = 180$. And write the values in the second set as prime factors:

$$60 = (2)(2)(3)(5)$$
$$120 = (2)(2)(2)(3)(5)$$
$$42 = (2)(3)(7)$$
$$36 = (2)(2)(3)(3)$$

So, the greatest common factor is $(2)(3) = 6$. Thus, the value of $\dfrac{x}{y}$ is $\dfrac{180}{6} = 30$, (B).

Items testing your ability to work with factors are often presented as word problems. The strategy is the same: determine whether the greatest common factor or least common multiple is required and use the quickest method to find it.

Examples:

The clerk at a bakery must divide 72 cupcakes and 64 muffins into "Day Old" bags to be sold at a discount. Each bag will contain both cupcakes and muffins. If the clerk wants to create the greatest possible number of identical bags so that no items are left over, how many cupcakes and muffins will be in each bag?

F. 18 cupcakes and 16 muffins
G. 16 cupcakes and 18 muffins
H. 12 cupcakes and 9 muffins
J. 9 cupcakes and 8 muffins
K. 8 cupcakes and 9 muffins

This question asks for the greatest common factor of 72 and 64:

$$72 = \left(2^3\right)\left(3^2\right)$$

$$64 = 2^6$$

So, the greatest common factor—the number of pastry bags—is $2^3 = 8$. Therefore, there are $\dfrac{72}{8} = 9$ cupcakes and $\dfrac{64}{8} = 8$ muffins in each bag, (J).

Hot dogs come in packages of 8 and buns come in packages of 6. Assuming one hot dog per bun, what is the smallest number of packages that must be purchased to avoid any leftover dogs or buns?

A. 2 packages of hotdogs and 4 packages of buns
B. 3 packages of hotdogs and 3 packages of buns
C. 3 packages of hotdogs and 4 packages of buns
D. 4 packages of hotdogs and 3 packages of buns
E. 6 packages of hotdogs and 8 packages of buns

This problem asks for the least common multiple of 6 and 8. Test multiples of 6 until you find one that is also a multiple of 8: 6, 12, 18, 24. Or, you can write each as a product of primes with exponents and multiply the largest exponential of each base: 6 = (2)(3) and $8 = 2^3$, so the least common multiple is $(2^3)(3) = 24$. So, 24 hotdog/bun combinations is the minimum number that doesn't leave any leftovers: 3 packages of hotdogs and 4 packages of buns, (C).

If x is divisible by 3 and y is an even number, then $x^3 y^2$ must be divisible by which of the following?

F. 5   H. 54   K.   216
G. 8   J. 108

Any number divisible by 3 can be written as $3a$ and any even number can be written as $2b$, where a and b are integers. So: $x^3 y^2 = (3a)^3 (2b)^2 = 27a^3 (4b^2) = 108a^3 b^2$. Therefore, $x^3 y^2$ must be divisible by 108, (J).

Rounding

The number system is designed to support representation of exact numerical values, such as 123,587.4327. However, not all situations require such specificity. Sometimes it is easier to work with "rounded" numbers.

To round a number, determine the digit you would like to round to, such as the hundreds digit. This digit is in the **rounding position**. The number immediately to its right is the **check digit.** If the check digit is greater than 4, increase the digit in the rounding position by one. If the check digit is less than or equal to 4,

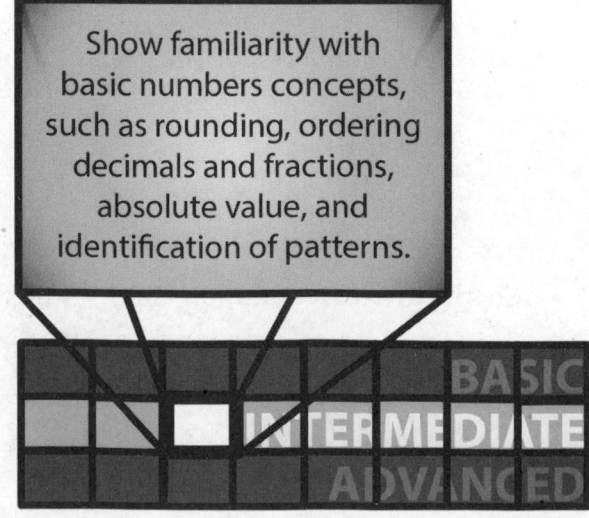

Show familiarity with basic numbers concepts, such as rounding, ordering decimals and fractions, absolute value, and identification of patterns.

BASIC
INTERMEDIATE
ADVANCED

do not change the digit in the rounding position. Use zeroes to represent the check digit and all digits to its right.

The presentation of these items requires knowledge of the names of the digit places, so it's worth reviewing again. First, some of the digit places to the left of the decimal:

1 HUNDRED THOUSANDS
2 TEN THOUSANDS
3, THOUSANDS
4 HUNDREDS
5 TENS
6 . UNITS
0

And the digit places to the right of the decimal:

0 . 1 TENTHS
2 HUNDREDTHS
3 THOUSANDTHS
4 TEN THOUSANDTHS
5 HUNDRED THOUSANDTHS

Examples:

What is the value of 1,736.0194, rounded to the nearest hundred?

A. 1,800.000
B. 1,736.020
C. 1,736.019
D. 1,700.000
E. 1,600.000

The digit in the tens place is less than 5, so the digit in the hundreds place remains the same and the digits to the right are replaced with zeroes. Therefore, the value of 1,736.0194 rounded to the hundreds place is 1,700.000, (D).

What is the value of 2,340.2679 rounded to the nearest thousandth?

F. 2,000.000
G. 2,300.000
H. 2,400.000
J. 2,340.268
K. 2,340.270

The digit in the ten thousandth place (9) is greater than 5, so the digit in the thousandth place (7) increases by 1 and the digit to the right is dropped. Therefore, 2,340.2679 rounded to the nearest thousandth is 2, 340.268, (J).

What is the value of 4,358 + 1,423 – 3,256 rounded to the nearest thousand?

A. 1,000   C. 3,000   E. 5,000
B. 2,000   D. 4,000

Do the indicated operations: 4,358 + 1,423 – 3,256 = 2,525. Since the digit in the hundreds place (5) is equal to 5, the digit in the thousands place (2) increases by 1. Therefore, the value of 2,525 rounded to the nearest thousand is 3,000, (C).

Ordering Decimals and Fractions

The only trick to ordering decimals is to remember that more decimal places does NOT necessarily translate to a larger value. To order decimals, compare two at a time. Look at the first whole number (the value to the left of the decimal point)—if that number is different, follow the rules for ordering whole numbers. If the number is the same, then look to the digits to the right of the decimal point. Then, compare one place at a time, beginning with the tenths place until the digits are different. Comparison of those digits puts the values in order.

Example:

Which one of the following correctly lists the values in order from largest to smallest?

F. 1.13467, 1.13, 0.1346, 0.135, 0.13467
G. 1.13467, 1.13, 0.135, 0.13467, 0.1346
H. 1.13467, 1.13, 0.13467, 0.135, 0.1346
J   1.13467, 1.13, 0.13467, 0.1346, 0.135
K. 0.1346, 0.13467, 0.135, 1.13, 1.13467

Of the listed values, two have a 1 in the ones place, and the rest have 0. Therefore, compare 1.13467 and 1.13 to determine the larger: the two values are the same up to the thousandths place—so, the one with digits to right is the larger, 1.13467, and 1.13 the next larger. Next, of the three decimal values, they are the same until the thousandths place: 0.135 is the next largest. And of the remaining two 0.13467 is larger than 0.1346. So, the correct order, from largest to smallest, is: 1.13467, 1.13, 0.135, 0.13467, 0.1346, (G).

When comparing fractions, don't waste valuable time converting each to a decimal. In fact, this method can easily backfire by the introduction of errors due to calculator entry mistakes. Instead, memorize these important "benchmark" fraction values and compare fractions using these benchmarks.

MEMORIZE THESE DECIMAL FRACTION EQUIVALENTS		
$\frac{1}{2} = 0.50$	$\frac{1}{5} = 0.20$	$\frac{1}{8} = 0.125$
$\frac{1}{3} = 0.3\overline{3}$	$\frac{1}{6} = 0.1\overline{6}$	$\frac{1}{9} = 0.1\overline{1}$
$\frac{1}{4} = 0.25$	$\frac{1}{7} = 0.\overline{142857}$	$\frac{1}{10} = 0.10$

Any fraction can be written in terms of the above listed equivalents. For example, consider $\frac{5}{8}$ and $\frac{4}{9}$: $\frac{1}{8}$ is 0.125, so $\frac{5}{8}$ is $5 \cdot 0.125$, or 0.625; $\frac{1}{9}$ is approximately 0.111, so $\frac{4}{9}$ is approximately $4 \cdot 0.111$, or 0.444.

Example:

The following table gives five monthly precipitation totals for Seattle. List the months according to precipitation from most to least.

MONTH	PRECIPITATION
January	$37\frac{1}{2}$ inches
February	$37\frac{2}{5}$ inches
March	$39\frac{3}{4}$ inches
April	$39\frac{3}{5}$ inches
May	38 inches

A. March, April, May, January, February
B. May, March, April, January, February
C. February, January, May, April, March
D. March, April, January, February, May
E. March, May, January, February, April

The correct answer is (A). You only need to compare two sets of numbers: January with February and March with April. January, at $37\frac{5}{10}$ inches is greater than February, at $37\frac{4}{10}$ inches. And March, at $39\frac{7.5}{10}$ inches is greater than April, at $39\frac{6}{10}$ inches. Therefore, the order, from most precipitation to least, is: March, April, May, January, February.

Absolute Value

A number's ***absolute value*** is its distance on the number line from the origin, without regard to direction: $|x| = |-x|$. The absolute value of a number is its value without any sign and so its value is always zero or more: $|x| \geq 0$. Therefore, $|x| = x$ if $x \geq 0$ and $|x| = -x$ if $x < 0$.

Examples:

$|4| = 4$

$|-10| = 10$

$|5| - |3| = 5 - 3 = 2$

$|-2| + |-3| = 2 + 3 = 5$

$|1| + |-2| + |3| + |-4| + |5| + |-6| + |7| + |-8| + |9| + |-10| + |11| + |-12| = ?$

F. –12   H. 6   K. 78
G. –6   J. 12

Perform the indicated operations, dropping the negative sign for any absolute value: $|1| + |-2| + |3| + |-4| + |5| + |-6| + |7| + |-8| + |9| + |-10| + |11| + |-12| =$
$1 + 2 + 3 + 4 + 5 + 6 + 7 + 8 + 9 + 10 + 11 + 12 = 78$, (K).

This idea of value, without regard to direction, helps to clarify negative number operations. However, items that test the concept of absolute value without giving actual values can be confusing. Simply make it real by substituting actual values and testing the answer choices.

Example:

If m is positive and n is negative, $|m| + |n| = ?$

A. $m + n$ D. 1
B. $m - n$ E. 0
C. $n - m$

This item is easier if you pick a positive value for m and a negative value for n, say 3 and –2, respectively. Thus: $|m| + |n| = |3| + |-2| = 3 + 2 = 5$. So, you know the answer isn't (D) or (E). Plug $m = 3$ and $n = -2$ into the remaining answer choices. The correct choice will return the value 5:

A. $m + n = 3 + -2 = 1$ ✗

B. $m - n = 3 - -2 = 5$ ✓

C. $n - m = -2 - 3 = -5$ ✗

Pattern Identification

A sequence is a set of numbers that follow a pattern. Each number in the sequence is a term. We'll come back to sequences again in Advanced, Number Concepts, with geometric sequences. For now, we'll stick with arithmetic sequences: sequences in which each term is found by adding or subtracting the same value from one term to the next. When consecutive terms are found by adding the same value from one term to the next, the value is called the "common sum"; when the value is subtracted from one term to the next, the value is called the "common difference." Thus, if the difference is positive, the sequence increases, and if the difference is negative, the sequence decreases.

Example:

What is the next term in the arithmetic sequence 3, 11, 19, ... ?

F. −5 H. 8 K. 35
G. 0 J. 27

> In any arithmetic sequence, the same number (called the common sum) is always added to get from one term to the next. To get from the first term, 3, to the second, 11, the value 8 is added. To get from the 11 to 19, the value 8 is added. Thus, 8 is the common sum. Therefore, the fourth term in the sequence is 19 + 8 = 27, (J).

To find the nth term of any arithmetic sequence, use the formula $a_n = a_1 + d(n-1)$, where d represents the common sum or difference between terms.

Examples:

Find the 5th term of the arithmetic sequence $a_n = 4 - 6(n-1)$

A. −20 C. 5 E. 24
B. −10 D. 20

> The fifth term corresponds to $n = 5$: $a_5 = 4 - 6(5-1) = 4 - 6(4) = -20$, (A).

Which one of the following expressions correctly models the arithmetic sequence 6, 10, 14, ...?

F. $6 - 4(n - 1)$ J. $4 + 6(n - 1)$
G. $6 + 4(n + 1)$ K. $4 - 6(n - 1)$
H. $6 + 4(n - 1)$

> Find the difference between the terms: +4. And $a_1 = 6$. Therefore, the correct expression for modeling the sequence is $6 + 4(n - 1)$, (H).

Which one of the following statements is true about the arithmetic sequence shown below?

$$-24, -12, 0, 12, \ldots$$

A. Every term in the sequence is divisible by 24.
B. The ratio between consecutive terms is 2:1
C. The fifth term is 36.
D. The common sum is −12.
E. The sum of the first five terms is 0.

The sum of the first five terms is 0, (E). The ratio between the first two terms is 2:1, but this isn't true for the remainder of the terms (terms are related by constant ratios in geometric sequences, not arithmetic sequences). The fifth term is 24. The common sum is +12.

EXERCISE 3

DIRECTIONS: Choose the correct answer to each of the following items. Answers are on page 813.

51. How many prime numbers are there between 50 and 60?

A. 0   C. 2   E. 4
B. 1   D. 3

52. Which of the following numbers is (are) prime?

I.   12,345
II. 999,999,999
III. 1,000,000,002

F. I only
G. III only
H. I and II only
J. I, II, and III
K. Neither I, II, nor III

53. What is the greatest common factor of both 6 and 9?

A. 1   C. 6   E. 12
B. 3   D. 9

54. What is the greatest common factor of 18, 24, and 36?

F. 6   H. 12   K. 18
G. 9   J. 15

55. What is the least common multiple of both 5 and 2?

A. 7   C. 20   E. 40
B. 10   D. 30

56. $25 + 50 + 100 = ?$

    F. $5(1+2+3)$ J. $25(1 + 2 + 4)$
    G. $5(1+2+4)$ K. $25(1+5+10)$
    H. $25(1+2+3)$

57. $1,234(96) - 1,234(48) = ?$

    A. $1,234(48)$
    B. $1,234(96)$
    C. $1,234(48+96)$
    D. $(1,234 \cdot 1,234)$
    E. $2 \cdot 1,234$

58. A certain tree flowers every 7 years and a certain insect hatches every 6 years. If the tree flowered and the insect hatched in 1980, what is the next year in which the flowering of the tree and the hatching of the insects coincide?

    F. 1993   H. 2008   K. 2024
    G. 1994   J. 2022

59. Charles is ordering office supplies. He wants to order an equal number of pens and pencils but pens come in boxes of 24 and pencils come in boxes of 15. To have the same number of each, and to order as few as possible, how many boxes of pens does Charles order?

    A. 3   C. 8   E. 24
    B. 5   D. 15

60. There are 56 boys and 48 girls attending a day camp. The campers are to be split into teams with only boys or only girls on each team. If the number of campers on each team is equal and all the campers are on a team, what is the greatest number of campers possible on a team?

    F. 4   H. 12   K. 84
    G. 8   J. 48

61. In a warehouse, televisions in boxes 36 inches tall are stacked next to stereos in boxes 24 inches tall. What is the minimum height at which the two stacks are equal?

    A. 24 inches   D. 144 inches
    B. 36 inches   E. 824 inches
    C. 72 inches

62. Eggs come in cartons of 12 and English muffins come in packages of 10. What is the least number of packages of each that can be bought to make egg muffin sandwiches with no eggs or muffins leftover?

    F. 3 egg cartons, 4 muffin packages
    G. 6 egg cartons, 5 muffin packages
    H. 4 egg cartons, 6 muffin packages
    J. 5 egg cartons, 3 muffin packages
    K. 5 egg cartons, 6 muffin packages

63. As the quality control officers at a factory, Jill checks every 9th widget and Joe checks every 15th widget. If they begin a shift by both checking the same widget, which widget off the assembly line is the next widget that both Jill and Joe check?

    A. 16th   C. 28th   E. 91st
    B. 19th   D. 46th

64. If a and b are positive integers such that the least common multiple of a^3b^2 and a^2b^3 is 1,000, what is the greatest common factor?

F. 10   H. 100   K. 1,000
G. 25   J. 200

65. At the airport, shuttle vans leave the terminal every 20 minutes and the tram leaves every 25 minutes. If a van and the tram leave the terminal at the same time, after how many minutes will that van and the tram again leave the terminal at the same time?

A. 45 minutes   D. 90 minutes
B. 60 minutes   E. 100 minutes
C. 75 minutes

66. A store display is decorated with three strings of lights. One string blinks every 8 seconds, the second blinks every 10 seconds, and the third blinks every 12 seconds. If the three strings blink simultaneously when the display is turned on, over the next 11 minutes, how many times do the three strings blink at the same time?

F. 5   H. 8   K. 18
G. 6   J. 10

67. Which one of the following expressions is equivalent to $ab^2 + a^2bc - a^3d$?

A. $a^2(b^2 + bc - ad)$

B. $a(b^2 + abc - ad)$

C. $a(b^2 + a[bc - ad])$

D. $a(b^2 + a^2[bc - d])$

E. $a(b^2 - a[bc + ad])$

68. If x and y are positive integers, the greatest common factor and least common multiple of x^2y and x^3y^2 are:

F. x^2y and x^3y^2, respectively.

G. x^3y^2 and x^2y, respectively.

H. x^2y^2 and x^2y^2, respectively.

J. xy and x^2y, respectively.

K. xy^2 and x^3y^2, respectively.

69. What is the value of 372 + 533 + 147, rounded to the nearest hundred?

A. 800   C. 1,000   E. 1,200
B. 900   D. 1,100

70. What is the sum of 187.312, 16.162, and 6.621 rounded off to the nearest hundredth?

F. 200.00   H. 210.09   K. 210.90
G. 210.01   J. 210.10

71. Eli works at the local sandwich shop and makes $7.80 per hour. In one week he works 23 hours. How much did Eli make in that week rounded to the nearest dollar?

A. $31   C. $179   E. $184
B. $161   D. $180

72. Put the following numbers in descending order; 2.573, 2.057, 2.57, 2.5, 2.0612.

F. 2.0612, 2.057, 2.5, 2.57, 2.573
G. 2.5, 2.57, 2.573, 2.0612, 2.057
H. 2.057, 2.0612, 2.573, 2.57, 2.5
J. 2.573, 2.57, 2.5, 2.0612, 2.057
K. 2.573, 2.57, 2.5, 2.057, 2.0612

73. Which one of the following fractions is the smallest?

A. $\dfrac{3}{8}$ C. $\dfrac{1}{4}$ E. $\dfrac{2}{5}$

B. $\dfrac{5}{16}$ D. $\dfrac{6}{11}$

74. The heights of five children are listed in the table below. What is the correct order of the children from shortest to tallest?

CHILD	HEIGHT
Carlos	$73\dfrac{1}{5}$ inches
Raena	$72\dfrac{1}{4}$ inches
Zed	$72\dfrac{5}{8}$ inches
Henry	$73\dfrac{2}{3}$ inches
Azaree	$72\dfrac{2}{5}$ inches

F. Henry, Carlos, Zed, Azaree, Raena
G. Raena, Zed, Azaree, Carlos, Henry
H. Azaree, Raena, Zed, Carlos, Henry
J. Raena, Azaree, Zed, Henry, Carlos
K. Raena, Azaree, Zed, Carlos, Henry

75. $|6| + |6| = ?$

A. –12   C. 1   E. 36
B. 0   D. 12

76. $|-8| + |8| = ?$

F. –16   H. 16   K. 64
G. 0   J. 24

77. For all real numbers x such that $x \neq 0$, which of the following expressions are equal?

   I. $|-x|$
  II. $-|x|$
 III. $-|-x|$

A. I and II only
B. I and III only
C. II and III only
D. I, II, and III
E. Neither I, II, nor III

78. If $|6 - x| = 18$, then $x = ?$

F. $\{-12, -24\}$ J. $\{3, 4\}$
G. $\{-12, 24\}$ K. $\{12, -24\}$
H. $\{-3, 4\}$

79. Consider the following sequence of numbers:

$$34, \underline{\quad}, \underline{\quad}, 52$$

What two numbers should be placed in the blanks so that the difference between consecutive terms in the sequence is the same?

A. 43, 52   D. 43, 46
B. 40, 43   E. 46, 50
C. 40, 46

80. Which one of the following expressions correctly models the arithmetic sequence 16, 13, 10, 7, ...?

F. $-3n - 19$ J. $n - 3$
G. $3n - 19$ K. $n + 19$
H. $19 - 3n$

Exponents, Squares, Cubes, and Roots

We've already worked with powers and exponents when we learned to write numbers as products of prime factors. A *power* of a number indicates repeated multiplication.

The notation system for designating the power of a number is a superscript following the number. The number being multiplied is the *base*, and the superscript is the *exponent*. The exponent indicates the operation of repeated multiplication.

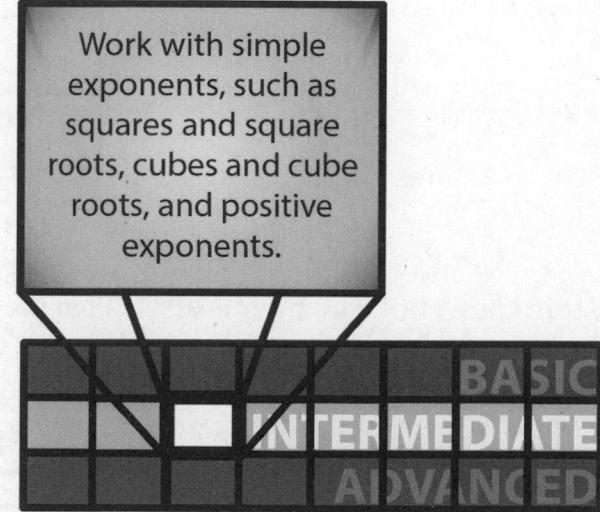

Work with simple exponents, such as squares and square roots, cubes and cube roots, and positive exponents.

Examples:

The third power of 2 is written as 2^3: base

$\rightarrow 2^3 \leftarrow$ exponent $= (2)(2)(2)$.

The fifth power of 3 is written as 3^5: base $\rightarrow 3^5 \leftarrow$ exponent $= (3)(3)(3)(3)(3)$.

The seventh power of x is written as x^7: base $\rightarrow x^7 \leftarrow$ exponent $= (x)(x)(x)(x)(x)(x)(x)$

A base without an exponent is unchanged and represents the *first power* of the number. Since $x^1 = x$, the exponent 1 is not explicitly noted.

Examples:

$2^1 = 2$

$1{,}000^1 = 1{,}000$

$n^1 = n$

The second power of a number is also called the *square* of the number. This refers to a square with sides equal in length to the number; the square of the number is equal to the area of the aforementioned square.

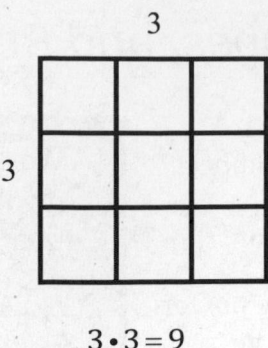

$$3 \cdot 3 = 9$$

The third power of a number is also called the *cube* of that number, which refers to a cube with sides equal in length to the number. The cube of a number is equal to the volume of that cube.

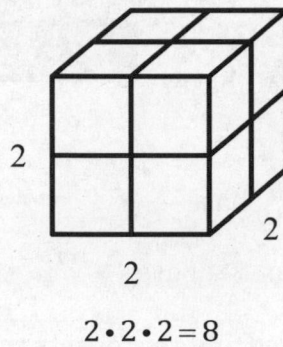

$$2 \cdot 2 \cdot 2 = 8$$

Beyond the square and the cube, powers are referred to by their numerical names, e.g., fourth power, fifth power, sixth power, and so on.

Properties of Integer Exponents

We can expand our understanding of exponents easily beyond squares and cubes by applying the generalized rules for operations involving exponents. We'll return to applying properties of integer exponents in Advanced, Number Concepts.

PROPERTIES OF POSITIVE INTEGER EXPONENTS	

1. $(x^m)(x^n) = x^{(m+n)}$

2. $(x^m)^n = x^{mn}$

3. $(xy)^m = (x^m)(y^m)$

4. $\left(\dfrac{x}{y}\right)^m = \dfrac{x^m}{y^m}$

5. $x^0 = 1$, when $x \neq 0$

Example:

If x and y are real numbers, which one of the following is equivalent to $x^4 x^3 - \left(x^4\right)^3$?

A. x^{19} D. $x^7 - x^{12}$

B. x^5 E. $x^{12} - x^7$

C. $x^{12} + x^7$

Apply the first and second properties of integer exponents: $x^4 x^3 = x^{4+3} = x^7$ and $\left(x^4\right)^3 = x^{4(3)} = x^{12}$. Plug this value into the given equation: $x^4 x^3 - \left(x^4\right)^3 = x^7 - x^{12}$, (D).

Square Roots and Cube Roots

A *square root* of a number x is a solution to the equation $\sqrt{x} = b$, in which $x = b^2$. When you perform the multiplication indicated by an exponent, you are in effect answering the question, "What do I get when I multiply this number by itself so many times?" Now ask the opposite question, "What number, when multiplied by itself so many times, will give me a certain value?" For example, when you raise 2 to the third power, you find out that $2^3 = 8$. Now, ask the question in the other direction. What number, when raised to the third power, is equal to 8?

This reverse process is called "finding the root of a number." Why roots? Look at the following diagram; the picture resembles plant roots. Finding the prime factorization of a number is essentially finding the base numbers that the number of interest grew from. In the example below, since $2^6 = 64$, the sixth root of 64 is 2.

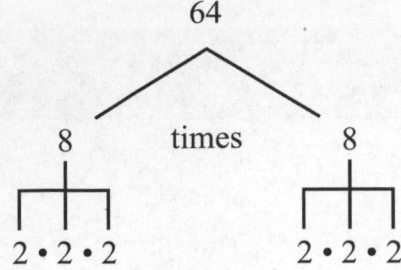

Of course, we rarely deal with sixth roots. Mostly, we deal with two roots: $8 \cdot 8 = 64$, so the second or **square root** of 64 is 8; and occasionally with numbers having three roots: $(4)(4)(4) = 64$, so the third or **cube root** of 64 is 4.

The operation of taking a square root of a number is signaled by the *radical* sign, $\sqrt{}$. *Radical* comes from the Latin word "radix," which means "root."

MEMORIZE THESE IMPORTANT SQUARE ROOTS	✓

$$\sqrt{1} = 1 \qquad \sqrt{16} = 4 \qquad \sqrt{49} = 7 \qquad \sqrt{100} = 10$$
$$\sqrt{4} = 2 \qquad \sqrt{25} = 5 \qquad \sqrt{64} = 8 \qquad \sqrt{121} = 11$$
$$\sqrt{9} = 3 \qquad \sqrt{36} = 6 \qquad \sqrt{81} = 9 \qquad \sqrt{144} = 12$$

The symbol $\sqrt{}$ always denotes a positive number. Later, when we get to the topic of quadratic equations in algebra, we will run across a "$\pm$" sign preceding the radical; this signifies both the positive and negative values of the root.

If a radical sign is preceded by a superscript number, then the number, or *index*, indicates a root other than the square root. In the notation $\sqrt[n]{a}$, n is the root or index, $\sqrt{}$ is the radical, and a is the radicand.

Example:

$\sqrt[3]{8} = ?$

F. 4   H. $2\sqrt{2}$ K. 1

G. $\dfrac{8}{3}$ J. 2

Factor out any perfect cubes from 8: $\sqrt[3]{8} = \sqrt[3]{(2)(2)(2)} = 2$, (J).

IMPORTANT PROPERTIES OF SQUARES AND SQUARE ROOTS

1. Squaring a negative number yields a positive result.

2. The square root of a number x is written as $\sqrt{x}$. A square root is always a positive number.

3. A number is a perfect square when the square root of that number is a whole number.

If a number is a perfect square (e.g., 4, 9, 16, etc.), then extracting its square root is easy. Simply use the values given in the examples of square roots above. Not every number, however, has an exact square root. In such cases, you can do one of two things. First, you may be able to find in the number a factor that does have an exact square root and extract that factor from under the radical sign.

Example:

$\sqrt{468} = ?$

A. $\sqrt{13}$ C. $6\sqrt{13}$ E. 78

B. $5\sqrt{13}$ D. 22

Factor out all the perfect squares from 468: $\sqrt{468} = \sqrt{4(117)} = \sqrt{4(9)(13)} = (2)(3)\sqrt{13} = 6\sqrt{13}$, (C).

Knowledge of the approximate values for common square roots may save you time. For example, it is useful to know that $\sqrt{2}$ is approximately 1.4 and that $\sqrt{3}$ is approximately 1.7. Other values can be approximated by using ranges; e.g., $\sqrt{7}$ must be between 2 and 3 ($\sqrt{4} < \sqrt{7} < \sqrt{9}$). Since 7 is closer to 9 than to 4, a good approximation of $\sqrt{7}$ is between 2.6 and 2.7.

Properties of Rational Exponents

As with the expansion of properties of square and cubes to integer exponents, we can expand our coverage of square roots and cube roots to generalized properties of radicals. Radicals can be rewritten using **rational (fractional) exponents**. This simplifies the process of working with radicals, since all of the rules for exponents apply to fractional exponents and thus to radicals. The relationship between a rational exponent and the radical representing a given root is: $\sqrt[n]{x^m} = x^{\frac{m}{n}}$, where m and n are integers, and $n \neq 0$.

Examples:

$$\sqrt{x} = x^{\frac{1}{2}} \qquad\qquad \sqrt{4} = 4^{\frac{1}{2}} = 2$$

$$\sqrt[3]{x} = x^{\frac{1}{3}} \qquad\qquad \sqrt[3]{8} = 8^{\frac{1}{3}} = 2$$

When you multiply a square root by itself, the result is the radicand: $\left(\sqrt{x}\right)\left(\sqrt{x}\right) = x$. This can be explained using the product rule for exponents as illustrated in the following example.

Example:

$$\left(\sqrt{2}\right)\left(\sqrt{2}\right) = ?$$

F. $\sqrt{2}$ H. 2   K.   4

G. $2\frac{1}{4}$ J. $2\sqrt{2}$

When multiplying similar bases, add the exponents: $\left(\sqrt{2}\right)\left(\sqrt{2}\right) = 2^{\frac{1}{2}} \cdot 2^{\frac{1}{2}} = 2^1 = 2$, (H).

OPERATIONS INVOLVING RADICALS (RATIONAL EXPONENTS)

1. Product Rule: $\sqrt{x} \cdot \sqrt{x} = x^{\frac{1}{2}}x^{\frac{1}{2}} = x^1 = x$

2. Quotient Rule: $\dfrac{\sqrt[m]{x}}{\sqrt[n]{x}} = \dfrac{x^{\frac{1}{m}}}{x^{\frac{1}{n}}} = x^{\left(\frac{1}{m}-\frac{1}{n}\right)}$

3. Power Rule: $\left(\sqrt[m]{x}\right)^n = \left(x^{\frac{1}{m}}\right)^n = x^{\frac{n}{m}}$

4. Product Power Rule: $\sqrt[m]{x^n y^p} = \left(x^n y^p\right)^{\frac{1}{m}} = x^{\frac{n}{m}} y^{\frac{p}{m}} = \sqrt[m]{x^n} \cdot \sqrt[m]{y^p}$

5. Quotient Power Rule: $\sqrt[m]{\dfrac{x^n}{y^p}} = \left(\dfrac{x^n}{y^p}\right)^{\frac{1}{m}} = \dfrac{x^{\frac{n}{m}}}{y^{\frac{p}{m}}} = \dfrac{\sqrt[m]{x^n}}{\sqrt[m]{y^p}}$

The power rules for working with exponents are the ones you are most likely to use when working with radicals. The following example illustrates how the product power rule applies to radicals.

Example:

$\sqrt{125} = ?$

A. 5   C. $5\sqrt{5}$ E. 25

B. $3\sqrt{5}$ D. $10\sqrt{5}$

Apply the product power rule: $\sqrt{125} = 125^{\frac{1}{2}} = (25 \cdot 5)^{\frac{1}{2}} = 25^{\frac{1}{2}} \cdot 5^{\frac{1}{2}} = \left(\sqrt{25}\right)\left(\sqrt{5}\right) = 5\sqrt{5}$, (C).

Notice that this is just the process of extracting a square root by finding a factor that is a perfect square, but what makes this process work is the product power rule of exponents. The quotient power rule is used in the following example.

Example:

$$\sqrt{\frac{4}{9}} = ?$$

F. $\sqrt{\dfrac{2}{3}}$ H. $\dfrac{2}{3}$ K. $\dfrac{4}{3}$

G. $\dfrac{\sqrt{2}}{3}$ J. $\dfrac{4}{9}$

Apply the quotient power rule: $\sqrt{\dfrac{4}{9}} = \left(\dfrac{4}{9}\right)^{\frac{1}{2}} = \dfrac{4^{\frac{1}{2}}}{9^{\frac{1}{2}}} = \dfrac{\sqrt{4}}{\sqrt{9}} = \dfrac{2}{3}$, (H).

Importantly, since radicals are fractional exponents and obey the rules for exponents, you cannot simply add radicals. $\sqrt{4} + \sqrt{9}$ is not equal to $\sqrt{13}$, and you can prove this by taking the square root of 4, which is 2, and the square root of 9, which is 3. $2+3$ is 5, which does not equal $\sqrt{13}$.

IMPORTANT RULES FOR WORKING WITH RADICAL SIGNS

$\sqrt{a}$ means the "square root of a." $\sqrt[3]{a}$ means the "cube root of a."

$\sqrt{a}\sqrt{b} = \sqrt{ab}$

$\sqrt[n]{a^n} = a$

$\sqrt[n]{\sqrt[m]{a}} = \sqrt[nm]{a}$

Example:

$$\left(\sqrt{8m^2}\right)\left(\sqrt{2n^4}\right) = ?$$

A. $2mn^2$ C. $4m^2n$ E. $16\sqrt{mn}$
B. $4mn^2$ D. $16mn^2$

Apply the rules for working with radicals: $\left(\sqrt{8m^2}\right)\left(\sqrt{2n^4}\right) =$

$\left(\sqrt{8}\right)\left(\sqrt{m^2}\right)\left(\sqrt{2}\right)\left(\sqrt{n^4}\right) = \left(\sqrt{16}\right)\left(m^2\right)^{1/2}\left(n^4\right)^{1/2} = 4mn^2$, (B).

Scientific Notation

In English, we often use abbreviations or acronyms for objects or ideas with long or difficult names. For example, "Incorporated" is often abbreviated "Inc." Similarly, when working with large numbers we can use scientific notation to more quickly and easily express that number. For instance, the distance from the planet Neptune to the sun is 2,798,000,000 miles, which is more easily expressed using scientific notation.

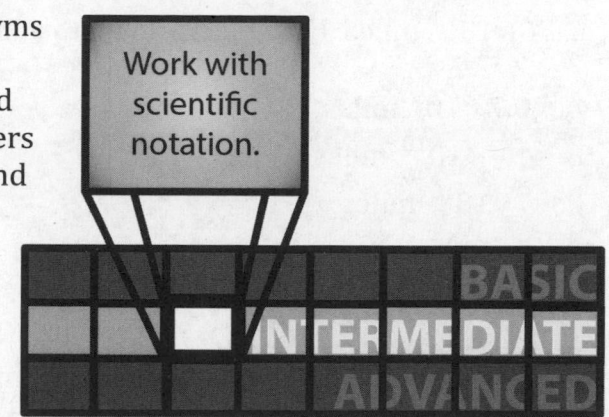

To express a number in scientific notation, use the form $a \times 10^n$, where $1 \le a < 10$ and n is an integer.

To convert a number to scientific notation, move the decimal point until the number is in the correct format. Each time you move the decimal point one unit to the left, increase the exponent value of the base 10 by 1. Each time you move the decimal point one unit to the right, decrease the exponent value of the base 10 by 1.

For example, 468,000,000,000 written in scientific notation would be 4.68×10^{11} because the decimal point was moved 11 places to the left. Likewise, 0.0000000575 written in scientific notation would be 5.75×10^{-8} because the decimal point was moved 8 places to the right.

Examples:

Which one of the following is equal to 364,000,000?

F. 3.64×10^{-8}

G. 3.64×10^{-7}

H. 3.64×10^{7}

J. 3.64×10^{8}

K. 3.64×10^{9}

Writing the number as 3.64 means moving the decimal point 8 units to the left. Therefore, $364{,}000{,}000 = 3.64 \times 10^{8}$, (J).

The distance from our solar system to the closest star, Proxima Centauri, is 2.49×10^{13} miles. The distance from our solar system to the next closest star, Alpha Centauri, is 2.56×10^{13} miles. How much closer to our solar system is the closer star?

A. 0.7×10^9 miles
B. 1.4×10^{10} miles
C. 7×10^{10} miles
D. 7×10^{11} miles
E. 14×10^{11} miles

Find the difference between the distances: $2.56 \times 10^{13} - 2.49 \times 10^{13} = (2.56 - 2.49) \times 10^{13} = 0.07 \times 10^{13}$ miles. Writing the number in scientific notation means moving the decimal point two places to the right. This decreases the exponent on the base 10 by 2: $0.07 \times 10^{13} = 7 \times 10^{11}$ miles, (D).

Undefined Expressions

An expression is undefined when a particular value causes it to violate math rules. This occurs for two scenarios: 1) having a zero in the denominator (bottom) of a fraction or 2) having a negative number in a square root (or any even root). For example, both $\dfrac{4-x}{0}$ and $\sqrt{-2}$ are undefined expressions.

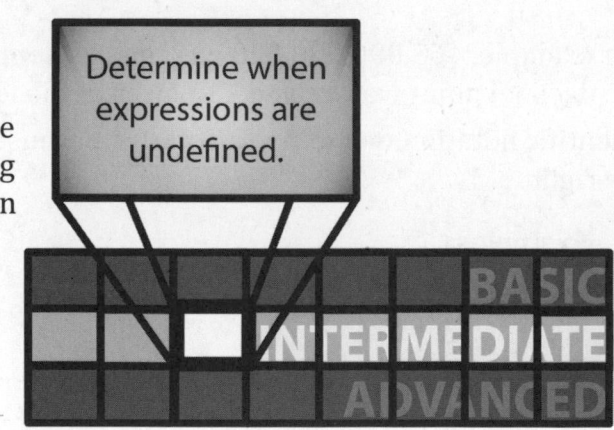

Example:

For what value(s) of x is $\dfrac{(x-3)^2}{x^2}$ undefined?

A. 0 only
B. 0 and 3 only
C −3 only
D. 0 and −3 only
E. −3, 0, and 3 only

There are only two things that can make $\dfrac{(x-3)^2}{x^2}$ undefined: a denominator equal to zero or a negative in a square root. Since the expression doesn't involve a square root, only the value of x that makes the denominator equal to zero makes the expression undefined. This occurs for $x = 0$, (A).

Complex Numbers

The *imaginary unit* is defined as i, where $i^2 = -1$; that is, i is the square root of -1:

$$i = \sqrt{-1}$$

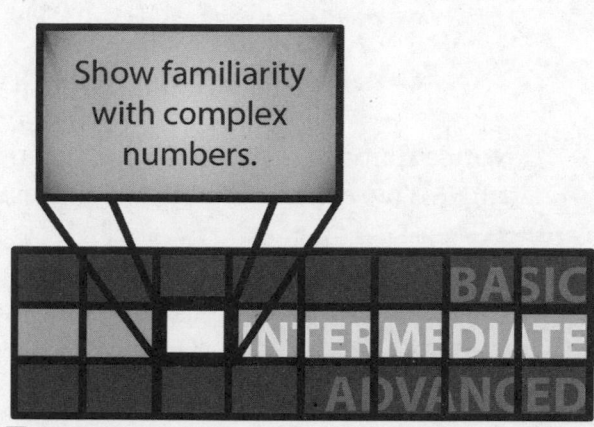

Note that i is not a real number—it cannot be placed on a number line. The square root of any negative number can be written as an imaginary number, i, times the square root of the same positive number:

$$\sqrt{-x} = \sqrt{-1}\sqrt{x} = i\sqrt{x} \text{ for } x > 0$$

Examples:

Which one of the following is equivalent to $\sqrt{-4} + \sqrt{-9}$?

F. $3 + 5i$ H. $5i$ K. -5
G. $5 + 3i$ J. $i\sqrt{13}$

Simplify the expression: $\sqrt{-4} + \sqrt{-9} = \sqrt{-1}\sqrt{4} + \sqrt{-1}\sqrt{9} = 2i + 3i = 5i$, (H).

What is the value of $(\sqrt{-9})(\sqrt{-9})$?

A. -9 C. $3i$ E. 9
B. -3 D. 3

Since $\sqrt{-9} = (\sqrt{-1})(\sqrt{9}) = i\sqrt{9} = 3i$, $(\sqrt{-9})(\sqrt{-9}) = (3i)(3i) = 9i^2 = 9(-1) = -9$, (A). Notice that $(\sqrt{-9})(\sqrt{-9})$ is NOT equal to $\sqrt{(-9)(-9)} = \sqrt{81} = 9$, since the square root of -9 is an imaginary number; it is not a real number.

If x is a positive integer, which one of the following could be the value of i^{2x} ?

F. i H. 1 K. 4
G. 0 J. 2

Test the first several possible values for x:

$$x = 1: i^{2x} = i^2 = \sqrt{-1}\sqrt{-1} = -1$$

$$x = 2: i^{2x} = i^4 = \left(i^2\right)\left(i^2\right) = (-1)(-1) = 1$$

$$x = 3: i^{2x} = i^6 = (-1)(-1)(-1) = -1$$

$$x = 4: i^{2x} = i^8 = (-1)(-1)(-1)(-1) = 1$$

Notice that as i is raised to consecutive positive integers, the value flips between -1 and 1. Therefore, of the listed values, only (H) is possible.

Which one of the following is an imaginary number?

A. $-\sqrt{2}$ C. $\dfrac{2}{-\sqrt{3}}$ E. $-\sqrt[3]{2}$

B. $-\dfrac{\sqrt{2}}{2}$ D. $\sqrt{-3}$

Taking the square root of a negative number yields an imaginary number. Therefore, (D) is the only imaginary number: $\sqrt{-3} = \sqrt{-1}\sqrt{3} = i\sqrt{3}$.

A complex number is any real number multiplied by or added to i. Thus, any complex number can be written as $a + bi$, where a is the real part and bi is the imaginary part. Two complex numbers are equal only if both parts, real and imaginary, are equal.

All the same rules of arithmetic apply to complex numbers as for real numbers, simply combine real parts with real parts and imaginary parts with imaginary parts.

Examples:

$(14i - 3) - (5 + 9i) = ?$

F. $-8 + 5i$ J. $126i + 15$
G. $-141 + 43i$ K. $70i + 27i$
H. $-8 + 23i$

Perform the indicated operations, combining like terms (real with real and imaginary with imaginary): $(14i - 3) - (5 + 9i) = 14i - 3 - 5 - 9i = -8 + 5i$, (F).

Notice that the final expression contains both a real part, -8, and an imaginary part, $5i$.

If $3(6x - i) = 36 + yi$, which of the following are values for $\{x, y\}$?

A. $\{-2, -1\}$ C. $\{2, -3\}$ E. $\{3, 2\}$
B. $\{-2, 1\}$ D. $\{2, 3\}$

Perform the indicated operations:

$$3(6x - i) = 36 + yi$$

$$18x - 3i = 36 + yi$$

Set the real parts as equal and the imaginary parts as equal and solve both for the unknown:

$$18x = 36$$

$$x = 2$$

And:

$$-3i = yi$$

$$y = -3$$

To multiply together two imaginary numbers, apply the FOIL method for multiplying two binomials: First, Outer, Inner, Last. Refer to page 445 for an in-depth review of the FOIL method.

Example:

$(2 + 4i)(3 - 5i) = ?$

F. -16 J. $14 - 2i$
G. $6 - 20i$ K. $-14 + 12i$
H. $26 + 2i$

Multiply the two complex numbers, treating them as binomial expressions: apply the FOIL method. Combine the products of the first terms, outer terms, inner terms, and last terms: $(2 + 4i)(3 - 5i) = (2)(3) + (2)(-5i) + (4i)(3) + (4i)(-5i) =$
$6 - 10i + 12i - 20i^2 = 6 + 2i - 20i^2$.

And since $i^2 = -1$: $6 + 2i - 20i^2 = 6 + 2i - 20(-1) = 26 + 2i$, (H).

To divide with complex numbers, multiply the numerator and denominator by the conjugate of the denominator. For a complex number $a + bi$, the complex conjugate is $a - bi$.

Example:

Which one of the following expressions is equivalent to $\dfrac{4+3i}{5-2i}$?

A. $\dfrac{1}{7}$ D. $\dfrac{20+17i}{29}$

B. $\dfrac{14+23i}{29}$ E. $29+23i$

C. $14+23i$

To get rid of the complex number in the denominator, multiply the numerator and the denominator by the complex conjugate of the denominator, using the FOIL method: $\dfrac{4+3i}{5-2i}=\dfrac{4+3i}{5-2i}\left(\dfrac{5+2i}{5+2i}\right)=\dfrac{(4+3i)(5+2i)}{(5-2i)(5+2i)}=\dfrac{20+8i+15i+6i^2}{25+10i-10i-4i^2}=$

$\dfrac{20+23i+6(-1)}{25-4(-1)}=\dfrac{14+23i}{29}$, (B).

EXERCISE 4

DIRECTIONS: Choose the correct answer to each of the following items. Answers are on page 814.

81. What is the third power of 3?

A. 1 C. 9 E. 27
B. 3 D. 15

82. What is the first power of 1,000,000?

F. 0 J. 10

G. $\dfrac{1}{1,000,000}$ K. 1,000,000

H. 1

83. $\sqrt{36}=?$

I.   6
II. -6
III. $3\sqrt{3}$

A. I only D. II and III only
B. I and II only E. I, II, and III
C. I and III only

84. $\sqrt{52}=?$

F. $\sqrt{5}+\sqrt{2}$ H. $2\sqrt{13}$ K. 13^2
G. 7 J. $13\sqrt{4}$

85. $\dfrac{\sqrt{81}}{\sqrt{27}} = ?$

   A. $\sqrt{3}$ C. $3\sqrt{3}$ E. $9\sqrt{3}$
   B. 3 D. 9

86. $2\sqrt{2}$ is approximately equal to which of the following?

   F. 2.8 H. 4 K. 12
   G. 3.4 J. 7

87. $\sqrt{2}\left(2\sqrt{3}\right) = ?$

   A. $-2\sqrt{6}$ C. 2 E. $2\sqrt{6}$
   B. $-\sqrt{6}$ D. $\sqrt{6}$

88. $\sqrt{3^2 + 5^2} = ?$

   F. 6 H. 7 K. 8
   G. $\sqrt{34}$ J. $\sqrt{51}$

89. $\dfrac{15\sqrt{96}}{5\sqrt{2}} = ?$

   A. $7\sqrt{3}$ C. $11\sqrt{3}$ E. $40\sqrt{3}$
   B. $7\sqrt{12}$ D. $12\sqrt{3}$

90. Which of the following radicals is a perfect square?

   F. $\sqrt{420}$ J. $\sqrt{500}$
   G. $\sqrt{480}$ K. $\sqrt{525}$
   H. $\sqrt{484}$

91. Which of the following statements are equivalent?

   I. $\dfrac{1}{x} < \dfrac{1}{2}$
   II. $-2 < x < 2$
   III. $x^2 < 4$

   A. I and II only
   B. II and III only
   C. I and III only
   D. I, II, and III
   E. None of the statements are equivalent

92. If a is a real number such that $a^2 = 16$, then $a^3 - \sqrt{a} = ?$

   F. 4 H. 24 K. 64
   G. 16 J. 62

93. For all real numbers $x, y,$ and z, $\sqrt[3]{x} = y^2$ and $y^3 = z^2$. Which one of the following equations expresses x in terms of z?

   A. $x = z^{\frac{3}{4}}$ C. $x = \sqrt[3]{z}$ E. $x = z^4$
   B. $x = \dfrac{z^4}{4}$ D. $x = z^2$

94. If $x^3 = 64$ and $y^3 = 125$, what is the value of $y - x$?

   F. -1 H. 1 K. 3
   G. 0 J. 2

95. Which one of the following expressions is equal to $\left(4x^2y\right)\left(6xy^3\right)\left(3x\sqrt{y}\right)$?

A. $13x^2y^3$

B. $13x^4y^{1/2}$

C. $24x^{3/2}y^{9/2}$

D. $72x^4y^{9/2}$

E. $72x^4y^2$

96. If n is an integer and 1.2345×10^n is greater than 1,000,000, what is the least possible value of n?

F. 2 H. 4 K. 6

G. 3 J. 5

97. Which one of the following is equal to 80,000 + 40,000?

A. 0.12×10^{-6}

B. 1.2×10^{-5}

C. 1.2×10^5

D. 12×10^4

E. 120×10^3

98. 0.01 x 45 = ?

F. 0.45×10^1

G. 0.45×10^2

H. 4.5×10^{-2}

J. 4.5×10^{-1}

K. 4.5×10^1

99. The moon travels at approximately 1 kilometer per second in orbit around the earth. Approximately how far does the moon travel in 28 days?

A. 8.64×10^3

B. 10.1×10^3

C. 4.03×10^4

D. 2.64×10^5

E. 2.42×10^6

100. Using turbidity measurements, the number of bacteria in a pond sample was estimated to be 5×10^7 per milliliter. Following installation of a filtration pump in the pond, the number of bacteria was found to have decreased to 1/1,000th that of the unfiltered level. What was the estimated bacteria count following filtration?

F. 5×10^4 per milliliter

G. 5×10^5 per milliliter

H. 5×10^7 per milliliter

J. 5×10^9 per milliliter

K. 5×10^{10} per milliliter

101. If 1×10^5 is increased by 200% and then decreased by 75%, the final value is:

A. 1.25×10^7

B. 5×10^5

C. 1.5×10^5

D. 5×10^4

E. 1.5×10^4

102. For what value(s) of x is the expression $\dfrac{\sqrt{4-x}}{x-2}$ undefined?

F. $x = 2$ only

G. $x = 2$ and $x = 4$ only

H. $x = 2$ and $x < 4$ only

J. $x = 2$ and $x > 4$ only

K. $x = 2$ and $x \geq 4$ only

103. If $\dfrac{x^2 + 2x}{x + 2} = x$, what does x equal?

    A. −2
    B. 2
    C. any value except −2
    D. any value except 2
    E. any value

104. $i^3 = ?$

    F. $3i$ H. −1   K. 1
    G. i J. $-i$

105. $i^8 = ?$

    A. $8i$ C. −1   E. 1
    B. i D. $-i$

106. $(2 + 3i) + (-7 - i) - (i^2) = ?$

    F. $-6 + 2i$ J. $5 - 2i$
    G. $10 + 4i$ K. $-5 + 2i$
    H. $-4 + 2i$

107. $5i(11 - 2i) = ?$

    A. $65i$ D. $-10 + 55i$
    B. $10 + 55i$ E. $10i - 55$
    C. $45i$

108. $-4i(8 - 3i) = ?$

    F. $-12 - 32i$ J. $32i + 12$
    G. $-32i + 12$ K. $-44i$
    H. $12 - 23i$

109. $(5 + 3i)(8 - 9i) = ?$

    A. 67   D. $13 - 21i$
    B. $67 - 6i$ E. $67 - 21i$
    C. $13 - 6i$

110. Which one of the following expressions is equivalent to $\dfrac{36 + 7i}{3i}$?

    F. $\dfrac{7 - 36i}{3}$ J. $7 + 21i$

    G. $\dfrac{21 + 108i}{9}$ K. $33 + 4i$

    H. $7 - 12i$

Algebraic Expressions, Equations, and Inequalities

Algebraic Expressions

Algebraic expressions are classified according to the number of **terms** the expression contains.

Examples of terms:

x^2 $\qquad\qquad$ yz

$3x$ $\qquad\qquad$ 4

A **polynomial** is an algebraic expression with one or more terms. A **monomial** is a polynomial with exactly one term. A **binomial** is a polynomial with exactly two terms. A **trinomial** is a polynomial with exactly three terms.

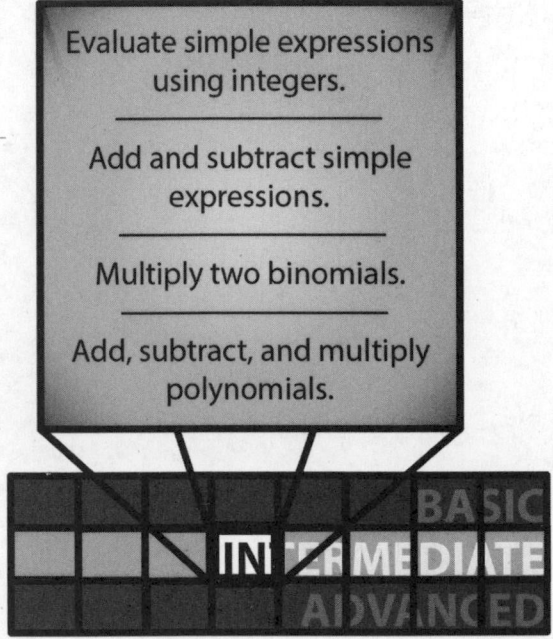

Evaluate simple expressions using integers.

Add and subtract simple expressions.

Multiply two binomials.

Add, subtract, and multiply polynomials.

Examples:

Monomial: x^2, $4ab$, xy^2

Binomial: $x + 6$, $x^2 - xy$, $3x^2 - 2y^2$

Trinomial: $x^2 + 4x - 2$, $x + y - 3$, $x^2 + y^{20} - z^{12}$

The highest power of the variable term in any polynomial expression determines the degree of the polynomial. A **first degree** (or **linear**) **polynomial** only includes variable(s) raised to the first power. A **second degree** (or **quadratic**) **polynomial** includes a variable that is squared, and none of the variables are raised to a higher power than 2.

Examples:

$x + 3$ (linear binomial)

$3x^2 - 8x - 3$ (quadratic trinomial)

MATH | INTERMEDIATE • 443

Evaluating Simple Algebraic Expressions

The process of assuming a value for a variable, substituting that value for the variable in an expression, and performing the indicated operations is called **evaluating** an expression.

Examples:

If $x = 5$, what is the value of $\dfrac{3x+1}{2}$?

A. 4   C. 6   E. 8
B. 5   D. 7

$$\frac{3x+1}{2} = \frac{3(5)+1}{2} = \frac{16}{2} = 8$$

If $x = -2$, what is the value of $x + 5x - 3x - \dfrac{x}{2}$?

F. −17   H. $-\dfrac{1}{2}$ K. 5

G. −5   J. $\dfrac{5}{2}$

$$x + 5x - 3x - \frac{x}{2} = (-2) + 5(-2) - 3(-2) - \frac{(-2)}{2} = (-2) - 10 + 6 + 1 = -5$$

Adding and Subtracting Algebraic Terms

To simplify an algebraic expression, group like terms and add/subtract the numerical coefficients of each group. Variables and exponents of combined similar terms remain unchanged.

Examples:

$x^2 + 2x^2 + 3x^2 = ?$

All three terms are similar: x^2 with a coefficient. Combine the terms by adding the coefficients: $1 + 2 + 3 = 6$. Thus, the result is $6x^2$.

$y + 2x + 3y - x = ?$

With two different types of terms, group the similar terms together: $(2x - x) + (y + 3y)$. Add the coefficients for each type of term. For the x terms, the combined coefficient is $2 - 1 = 1$; for the y terms, $1 + 3 = 4$. The result is $x + 4y$.

Notice that when all similar terms are combined, it is not possible to carry the addition or subtraction any further.

Multiplying Algebraic Expressions

The fundamental rule for multiplying two expressions is that every term of one expression must be multiplied by every term of the other expression.

First, let's look at the case in which a polynomial is to be multiplied by a single term. One way of solving the item is to first add and then multiply. Alternatively, we can use the **distributive property** to multiply every term inside the parentheses by the term outside the parentheses, and then we can add the terms: $x(y+z) = xy + xz$. The result is the same regardless of the method used. The following example illustrates these two methods using real numbers.

Example:

$2(3+4+5) = 2(12) = 24$

The distributive property returns the same result:
$2(3+4+5) = (2 \cdot 3) + (2 \cdot 4) + (2 \cdot 5) = 6 + 8 + 10 = 24$.

The following examples apply the distributive property to algebraic expressions.

Examples:

$x(y + z) = xy + xz$

$a(b + c + d) = ab + ac + ad$

To multiply two polynomials, either add the polynomials and then multiply the result or use distributive property to multiply and then add the result.

Example:

$(2+3)(1+3+4) = (5)(8) = 40$

The distributive property returns the same result:

$(2+3)(1+3+4) = (2 \cdot 1) + (2 \cdot 3) + (2 \cdot 4) + (3 \cdot 1) + (3 \cdot 3) + (3 \cdot 4) =$
$2 + 6 + 8 + 3 + 9 + 12 = 40$

Multiplying Binomials

Use the distributive property when multiplying binomials. The **_FOIL method_** can be used to simplify the process. To multiply two binomials using the FOIL method, follow these steps for combining the binomial terms: (1) multiply the _first_ terms, (2) multiply the _outer_ terms, (3) multiply the _inner_ terms, (4) multiply the _last_ terms, and (5) combine like terms. The FOIL method is simply a mnemonic shortcut derived from the distributive property. The following diagram illustrates application of the FOIL method.

MULTIPLYING TWO BINOMIALS

(FOIL: First, Outer, Inner, Last)

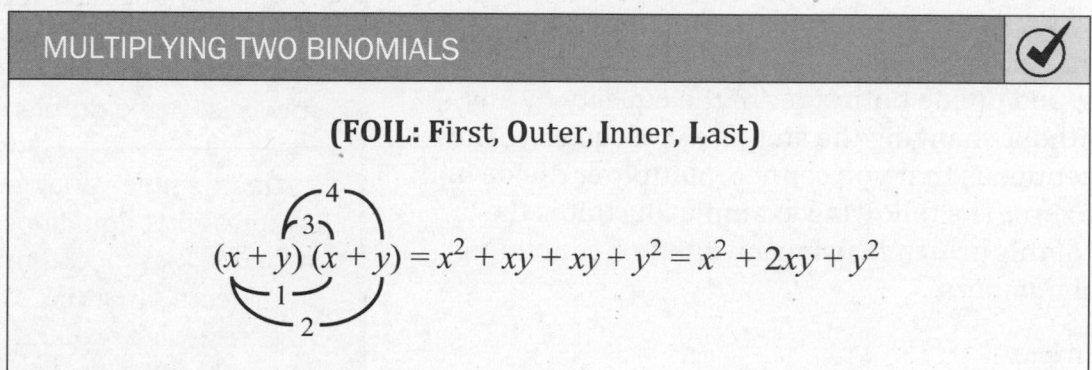

$$(x+y)(x+y) = x^2 + xy + xy + y^2 = x^2 + 2xy + y^2$$

Examples:

$(x+y)(x-y) = ?$

First: $(x)(x) = x^2$.
Outer: $(x)(-y) = -xy$.
Inner: $(y)(x) = xy$.
Last: $(y)(-y) = -y^2$.

Add: $x^2 - xy + xy - y^2 = x^2 - y^2$.

$(x-y)(x-y) = ?$

First: $(x)(x) = x^2$.
Outer: $(x)(-y) = -xy$.
Inner: $(-y)(x) = -xy$.
Last: $(y)(-y) = -y^2$.

Add: $x^2 - xy - xy + y^2 = x^2 - 2xy + y^2$.

First-Degree Equations and Story Problems

Solving First-Degree Equations

An ***algebraic equation*** is a statement that sets two algebraic expressions equal to each other. The fundamental rule for working with any equation states that whatever you do to one side of an equation, you must do exactly the same thing to the other side of the equation. This rule implies that you can add, subtract, multiply, and divide both sides of the equality by any value without changing the statement of equality. The only exception is that you cannot multiply or divide both sides by zero. The following example illustrates the validity of this principle using an equation containing only real numbers.

Solve simple first-degree equations.

Execute simple word-to-symbol translations.

Use first-degree equations to solve real-world problems.

Create single-variable expressions, equations, or inequalities for common pre-algebra situations such as rate, distance, and proportion.

Example:

$$8 = 8$$

Add 12 to both sides. $8 + 12 = 8 + 12$

$$20 = 20$$

Divide both sides by 2. $\dfrac{20}{2} = \dfrac{20}{2}$

$$10 = 10$$

Multiply both sides by 4. $10 \cdot 4 = 10 \cdot 4$

$$40 = 40$$

Subtract 32 from both sides. $40 - 32 = 40 - 32$

$$8 = 8$$

Do NOT, however, multiply both sides of an equation by zero if the equation contains a variable. You may lose special characteristics of the variable. For example, the equation $2x = 8$ is true only if $x = 4$. However, the equation $0(2x) = 0(8)$ is true for any value of x. Therefore, do NOT multiply by 0.

This fundamental rule of equations is the key to solving linear equations. To solve for an unknown variable, manipulate both sides of the equation in the same way to isolate the variable on one side. Be sure to reduce the other side of the equation by combining like terms.

Examples:

If $-3x + 15 = x + 3$, then what is the value of x?

A. –6   C. 2   E. 6
B. –3   D. 3

To isolate x, manipulate the equation to isolate x. Subtract x from both sides:

$$-3x + 15 - x = x + 3 - x$$
$$-4x + 15 = 3$$

Next, subtract 15 from both sides:

$$-4x + 15 - 15 = 3 - 15$$
$$-4x = -12$$

Lastly, divide both sides by –4.

$$\frac{-4x}{-4} = \frac{-12}{-4} \Rightarrow x = 3$$

If $x + 5 = 10$, then $x = ?$

F. 0   H. 2   K. 20
G. 1   J. 5

To solve for x, subtract 5 from both sides:

$$x + 5 - 5 = 10 - 5$$
$$x = 5$$

$$\frac{2x + 5}{3} = 9$$

To isolate x, multiply both sides by 3 and simplify:

$$(3)\left(\frac{2x + 5}{3}\right) = (3)(9)$$
$$2x + 5 = 27$$

Subtract 5 from both sides and divide by 2:

$$2x + 5 - 5 = 27 - 5$$

$$2x = 22$$

$$\frac{2x}{2} = \frac{22}{2}$$

$$x = 11$$

Some math problems require you to translate words or phrases into algebraic equations before you solve to find the value of an unknown variable.

Examples:

English	_Algebra_
Ed is three years older than Paul	$E = P + 3$
Paul is twice as old as Mary	$P = 2M$
Ned has \$2 more than Ed	$N = E + 2$
Bill has three times as much money as does Ted	$B = 3T$

Solving Story Problems

Using the skill of translating provided information into an algebraic expression or equation, you can solve story problems such as motion and variation problems.

The fundamental relationship in all **_motion problems_** is $\text{distance} = \text{rate} \cdot \text{time}$. The problems at the level of this examination usually derive their equation from a relationship concerning distance. Most problems fall into one of three types: motion in opposite directions, motion in the same direction, and round trips.

Motion in Opposite Directions

When two objects moving at the same speed start at the same time and move in opposite directions, or when two objects start at points at a given distance apart and move toward each other with the same speed until they meet, then the distance the second travels will equal one-half the total distance covered. Either way, the total distance $= d_1 + d_2$:

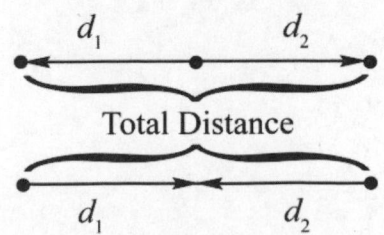

Motion in the Same Direction

This type of item is sometimes called the "catch-up" problem. Two objects leave the same place in the same direction at different times and at different rates, but one "catches up" to the other. In such a case, the two distances must be equal.

Round Trip

In this type of problem, the rate going is usually different from the rate returning. The times are also different. But if we go somewhere and then return to the starting point, the distance must be the same.

To solve any motion problem, it is helpful to organize the data in a box with columns for rate, time, and distance. A separate row should be used for each moving object. Remember that if the rate is given in *miles per hour*, the time must be in *hours* and the distance in *miles.*

Examples*:*

Two cars leave a restaurant at 1 p.m., with one car traveling east at 60 miles per hour and the other west at 40 miles per hour along a straight highway. At what time will they be 350 miles apart?

Create a table summarizing the provided information:

	Rate ×	Time	= Distance
Eastbound	60	x	$60x$
Westbound	40	x	$40x$

Notice that the time is unknown, since we must determine the number of hours traveled. However, since the cars start at the same time and stop when they are 350 miles apart, their times are the same: $60x + 40x = 350 \Rightarrow 100x = 350 \Rightarrow x = 3.5$. Therefore, in 3.5 hours, it will be 4:30 p.m.

Gloria leaves home for school, riding her bicycle at a rate of 12 miles per hour. Twenty minutes after she leaves, her mother sees Gloria's English paper on her bed and leaves to bring it to her. If her mother drives at 36 miles per hour, how far must she drive before she reaches Gloria?

Since the rate is in miles per hour and the distance is in miles, the time must be in hours. Create a table summarizing the provided information:

	Rate	× Time	= Distance
Gloria	12	x	$12x$
Mother	36	$x - \dfrac{1}{3}$	$36\left(x - \dfrac{1}{3}\right)$

The 20 minutes has been converted to $\dfrac{1}{3}$ of an hour. In this problem, the times are not equal, but the distances are: $12x = 36\left(x - \dfrac{1}{3}\right) \Rightarrow 12x = 36x - 12 \Rightarrow 12 = 24x \Rightarrow$

$x = \dfrac{1}{2}$. Thus, if Gloria rode for $\dfrac{1}{2}$ hour at 12 miles per hour, the distance covered was 6 miles. So, Gloria's mother must drive 6 miles before she reaches Gloria.

Nisha leaves home at 11 a.m. and rides to Andrea's house to return her bicycle. She travels at 12 miles per hour and arrives at 11:30 a.m. She turns right around and walks home. How fast does she walk if she returns home at 1 p.m.?

Create a table summarizing the provided information:

	Rate	× Time	= Distance
Going	12	$\dfrac{1}{2}$	6
Return	x	$1\dfrac{1}{2}$	$\dfrac{3x}{2}$

The distances are equal: $6 = \dfrac{3x}{2} \Rightarrow 12 = 3x \Rightarrow x = 4$ miles per hour.

Variation Problems

Variation in mathematics refers to the interrelationship of variables such that a change of value for one variable produces a corresponding change in another. There are three basic types of variation: direct, inverse, and joint.

First, variation problems may involve direct variation. The expression "x varies directly with y" can be described by either of the following equations:

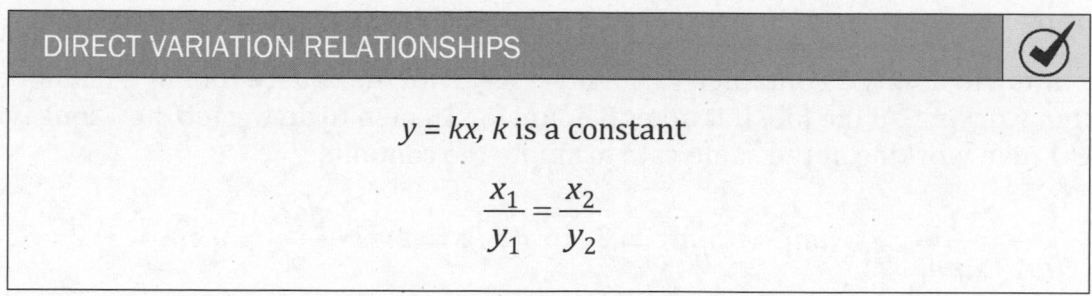

DIRECT VARIATION RELATIONSHIPS

$$y = kx, \ k \text{ is a constant}$$

$$\frac{x_1}{y_1} = \frac{x_2}{y_2}$$

Two quantities are said to vary directly if they change in the same direction. As one increases, the other increases and their ratio is equal to the positive constant.

For example, the amount you must pay for milk varies directly with the number of quarts of milk you buy. The amount of sugar needed in a recipe varies directly with the amount of butter used. The number of inches between two cities on a map varies directly with the number of miles between these cities.

Example:

If x varies directly as y^2, and $x = 12$ when $y = 2$, what is the value of x when $y = 3$?

Notice that the variation involves the square of y. Therefore,

$$\frac{x_1}{\left(y_1\right)^2} = \frac{x_2}{\left(y_2\right)^2} \Rightarrow \frac{12}{2^2} = \frac{x}{3^2} \Rightarrow \frac{12}{4} = \frac{x}{9} \Rightarrow x = 27 \ .$$

Second, variation problems may involve inverse variation. The expression "x varies inversely as y" can be described by either of the following equations:

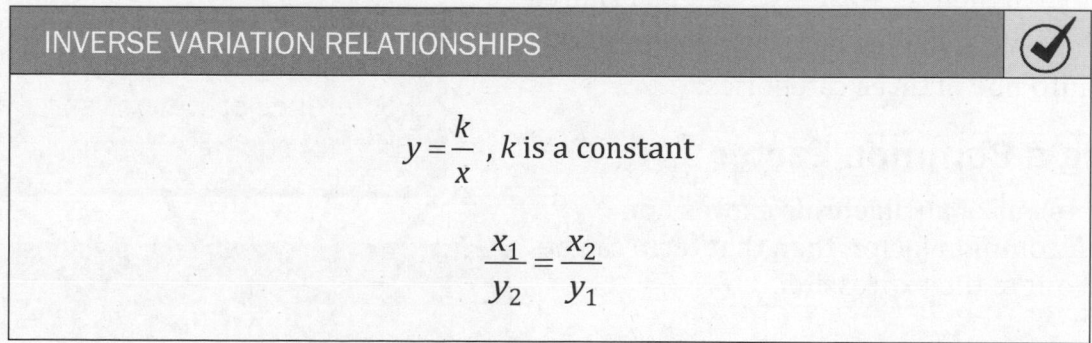

INVERSE VARIATION RELATIONSHIPS

$$y = \frac{k}{x} \ , \ k \text{ is a constant}$$

$$\frac{x_1}{y_2} = \frac{x_2}{y_1}$$

Two quantities vary inversely if they change in opposite directions. As one quantity increases, the other quantity decreases.

For example, the number of people hired to paint a house varies inversely with the number of days the job will take. A doctor's stock of flu vaccine varies inversely with the number of patients she injects. The number of days a given supply of cat food lasts varies inversely with the number of cats being fed.

Example:

The time t to empty a container varies inversely with the square root of the number of men m working on the job. If it takes 3 hours for 16 men to do the job, how long will it take 4 men working at the same rate to empty the container?

$$\frac{t_1}{\sqrt{m_2}} = \frac{t_2}{\sqrt{m_1}} \Rightarrow t_1\sqrt{m_1} = t_2\sqrt{m_2} \Rightarrow 3\sqrt{16} = t\sqrt{4} \Rightarrow t = 3 \cdot \frac{\sqrt{16}}{\sqrt{4}} = 3\left(\sqrt{4}\right) = 3 \cdot 2 = 6.$$

Finally, variation problems may involve joint variation. The expression "x varies jointly as y and z" can be described by any of the following equations:

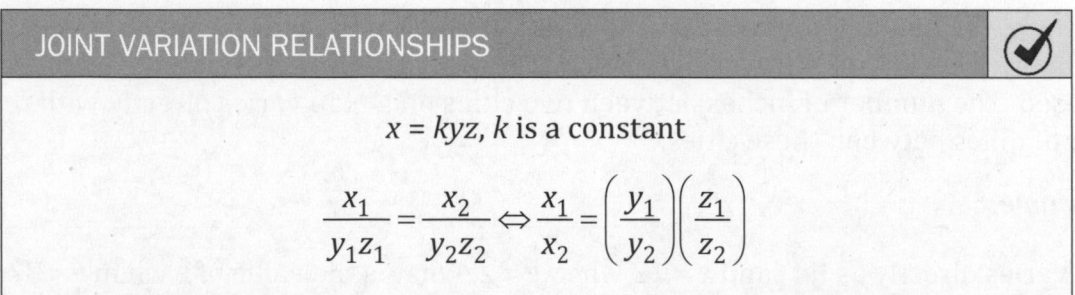

JOINT VARIATION RELATIONSHIPS

$$x = kyz, k \text{ is a constant}$$

$$\frac{x_1}{y_1 z_1} = \frac{x_2}{y_2 z_2} \Leftrightarrow \frac{x_1}{x_2} = \left(\frac{y_1}{y_2}\right)\left(\frac{z_1}{z_2}\right)$$

Quadratic Equations and Expressions

The term **factoring** may intimidate you, but factoring is nothing more than reverse multiplication. For example, if $(x + y)(x + y) = x^2 + 2xy + y^2$, then $x^2 + 2xy + y^2$ can be factored into $(x + y)(x + y)$. Most factoring you need to do will fall into one of three categories.

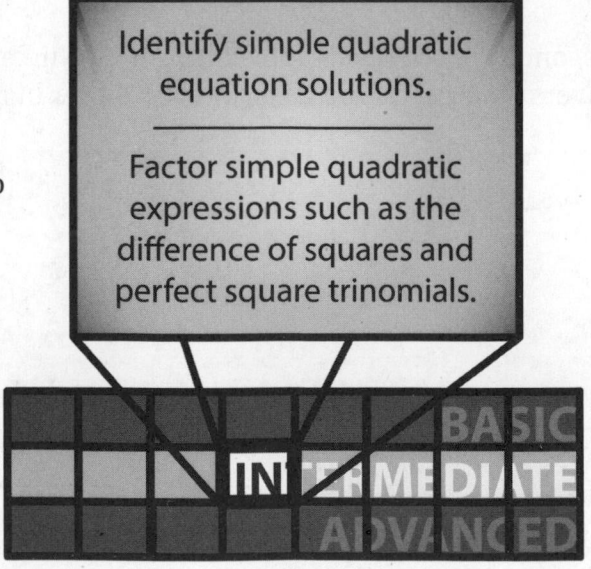

Identify simple quadratic equation solutions.

Factor simple quadratic expressions such as the difference of squares and perfect square trinomials.

BASIC
INTERMEDIATE
ADVANCED

Finding a Common Factor

If all the terms of an algebraic expression contain a common factor, then that term can be factored out of the expression.

Examples:

$$ab + ac + ad = a(b + c + d)$$

$$abx + aby + abz = ab(x + y + z)$$

$$x^2 + x^3 + x^4 = x^2\left(1 + x + x^2\right)$$

$$3a + 6a^2 + 9a^3 = 3a\left(1 + 2a + 3a^2\right)$$

Reversing a Known Polynomial Multiplication Process

Three situations arise with such frequency that you should memorize the results to simplify the calculation.

THREE COMMON MULTIPLICATIONS INVOLVING POLYNOMIALS
1. $(x + y)^2 = (x + y)(x + y) = x^2 + 2xy + y^2$
2. $(x - y)^2 = (x - y)(x - y) = x^2 - 2xy + y^2$
3. $.(x + y)(x - y) = x^2 - y^2.$

The three patterns can also be reversed.

THREE COMMON POLYNOMIAL MULTIPLICATION REVERSALS
1. Perfect square trinomial: $x^2 + 2xy + y^2 = (x + y)(x + y)$
2. Perfect square trinomial: $x^2 - 2xy + y^2 = (x - y)(x - y)$
3. Difference of two squares: $x^2 - y^2 = (x + y)(x - y)$

Reversing an Unknown Polynomial Multiplication Process

Occasionally, you may find it necessary to factor an expression that does not fall into one of the three categories presented above. The expression will most likely have the form $ax^2 + bx + c$; e.g., $x^2 + x - 6$. To factor such expressions, set up a blank diagram: ( )( ). Then, fill in the diagram by answering the following series of questions.

Step 1: What factors will produce the first term, ax^2?

Step 2: What possible factors will produce the last term, c?

Step 3: Which of the possible factors from step 2, when added together, will produce the middle term, bx?

Examples:

Factor $x^2 + 3x + 2$.

What factors will produce the first term, ax^2, where $a = 1$? x times x yields x^2, so the factors, in part, are $(x\ \ )(x\ \ )$. What possible factors will produce the last term? The possibilities are {2,1} and {–2,–1}. Which of the two sets of factors just mentioned, when added together, will produce a result of $+3x$? The answer is {2,1}: $2 + 1 = 3$, as the FOIL method confirms: $(x + 2)(x + 1) = x^2 + x + 2x + 2 = x^2 + 3x + 2$.

Factor $x^2 + 4x - 12$.

What factors will generate x^2? $(x\ \ )(x\ \ )$. What factors will generate –12? {1,–12}, {12,–1}, {2,–6}, {6,–2}, {3,–4}, and {4,–3}. Which factors, when added together, will produce the middle term of $+4x$? The answer is {6,–2}: $6 + (–2) = 4$. Thus, the factors are $(x + 6)$ and $(x - 2)$, as the FOIL method confirms: $(x + 6)(x - 2) = x^2 - 2x + 6x - 12 = x^2 + 4x - 12$.

Algebraic Inequalities

An **inequality** is very much like an equation except, as the name implies, it is a statement that two quantities are not equal. Four different symbols are used to make statements of inequality:

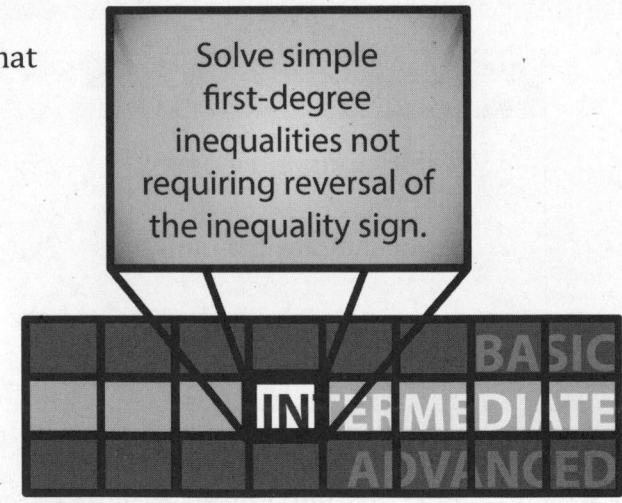

Solve simple first-degree inequalities not requiring reversal of the inequality sign.

- $>$ greater than
- $<$ less than
- $\geq$ greater than or equal to
- $\leq$ less than or equal to

Examples:

$5 > 1$ ....5 is greater than 1.

$2 > -2$ ......2 is greater than –2.

$x > 0$ ....x is greater than zero.

$x > y$ ....x is greater than y.

$8 < 9$ ....8 is less than 9.

$-4 < -1$ ...–4 is less than –1.

$x < 0$ ....x is less than zero.

$y < x$ ....y is less than x.

$x \geq 0$ ....x is greater than or equal to zero. (x could be zero or any number larger than zero.)

$x \geq y$ ....x is greater than or equal to y. (Either x is greater than y, or x and y are equal.)

$x \leq 0$ ....x is less than or equal to zero. (x could be zero or any number less than zero.)

$x \leq y$ ....x is less than or equal to y. (Either x is less than y, or x and y are equal.)

The fundamental rule for working with inequalities is similar to that for working with equalities: Treat each side of the inequality exactly the same. You can add or subtract the same value to each side of an inequality without changing the value of the inequality, and you can multiply or divide each side of an inequality by any *positive* value without changing the value of the inequality. If you multiply or divide each side of an inequality by any *negative* value, the direction of the inequality changes.

Example:

$$5 > 2$$

Add 25 to both sides. $5 + 25 > 2 + 25$

$$30 > 27$$

Subtract 6 from both sides. $30 - 6 > 27 - 6$

$$24 > 21$$

Multiply both sides by 2. $24 \cdot 2 > 21 \cdot 2$

$$48 > 42$$

Divide both sides by 6. $48 \div 6 > 42 \div 6$

$$8 > 7$$

Multiply both sides by -2. $8(-2) < 7(-2)$

$$-16 < -14$$

Divide both sides by -1. $-16 \div -1 > -14 \div -1$

$$16 > 14$$

EXERCISE 5

DIRECTIONS: Choose the correct answer to each of the following items. Answers are on page 814.

111. If $x = 7$, what is the value of $\dfrac{x}{21} + \dfrac{4}{3}$?

A. $\dfrac{1}{3}$ C. 1   E. 2

B. $\dfrac{2}{3}$ D. $\dfrac{5}{3}$

112. If $x = -3$, what is the value of $\dfrac{2x - 10}{4}$?

F. −4   H. −1   K. 4
G. −2   J. 1

113. If $a = 4$ and $b = 5$, what is the value of $3a + 4b$?

A. −8   C. 31   E. 79
B. 9   D. 32

114. If $x = 5$ and $y = 6$, what is the value of $\dfrac{2xy}{6}$?

F. 2   H. 10   K. 15
G. 5   J. 12

115. If $x = 4$, $y = 2$ and $z = -3$, what is the value of $4x - (y + z)$?

A. 1   C. 11   E. 17
B. 7   D. 15

116. $x^2 + 2xy - 3x + 4xy - 6y + 2y^2 + 3x - 2xy + 6y = ?$

F. $x^2 - 2xy + y^2$

G. $x^2 + y^2 + 3x + 2y$

H. $x^2 + 2y^2 + 4xy + 6x + 6y$

J. $x^2 + 2y + 4xy + 6x$

K. $x^2 + 2y^2 + 4xy$

117. $3(a + b + c + d) = ?$

A. $3abcd$
B. $3a + b + c + d$
C. $3a + 3b + 3c + 3d$
D. $3ab + 3bc + 3cd$
E. $12a + 12b + 12c + 12d$

118. $3a^2(ab + ac + bc) = ?$

F. $3a^3b^2c$
G. $3a^3 + 3b^3 + 3c$
H. $3a^2b + 3a^2c + 3a^2bc$
J. $3a^3b + 3a^3c + 3a^2bc$
K. $3a^5b + 3a^5c$

119. $(a+b)^2 = ?$

    A. $a^2 + b^2$
    B. $a^2 - b^2$
    C. $a^2 + 2ab - b^2$
    D. $a^2 - 2ab + b^2$
    E. $a^2 + 2ab + b^2$

120. $(a+b)(a-b) = ?$

    F. $a^2 - b^2$
    G. $a^2 + b^2$
    H. $a^2 + 2ab + b^2$
    J. $a^2 - 2ab + b^2$
    K. $a^2 + 2ab - b^2$

121. $(2-x)^2 = ?$

    A. $4 - x^2$
    B. $x^2 + 4$
    C. $x^2 + 4x + 4$
    D. $x^2 - 4x + 4$
    E. $x^2 - 4x - 4$

122. $(x-y)(x+2) = ?$

    F. $x^2 + 2xy + 2y$
    G. $x^2 + 2xy + x + y$
    H. $x^2 + 2xy + x - 2y$
    J. $x^2 - xy + 2x - 2y$
    K. $x^2 + 2x + 2y - 2$

123. $(w+x)(y-z) = ?$

    A. $wxy - z$
    B. $wy + xy - yz$
    C. $wy - wz + xy + xz$
    D. $wy + wz + xy - xz$
    E. $wy - wz + xy - xz$

124. $(2+x)(3+x+y) = ?$

    F. $x^2 + 6xy + 6$
    G. $x^2 + 6xy + 3x + 2y + 6$
    H. $x^2 + 2xy + 6x + 6y + 6$
    J. $x^2 + xy + 5x + 2y + 6$
    K. $x^2 + 3xy + 2x + y + 6$

125. $(x-y)^3 = ?$

    A. $x^3 - 3x^2 y + 3xy^2 - y^3$
    B. $x^3 + 3x^3 y + 3xy^3 + y^3$
    C. $x^3 + 3x^2 y - 3xy^2 - y^3$
    D. $x^3 + 6x^2 y^2 + y^3$
    E. $x^2 + 6x^2 y^2 - y^3$

126. If $5 - x = 2$, then $x = ?$

    F. 0   H. 5   K. 9
    G. 3   J. 7

127. If $20 = 3x + 5$, then $x = ?$

    A. 20   C. 7   E. 3
    B. 15   D. 5

128. If $7 = 5x + 2$, then $x = ?$

    F. −1   H. 1   K. 3
    G. 0   J. 2

129. If $\dfrac{x}{30} - 2 = 5$, then what is the value of x?

A. 90   C. 210   E. 300
B. 150   D. 240

130. If $-x + 10 = x + 4$, then what is the value of x?

F. –7   H. 0   K. 7
G. –3   J. 3

131. Which of the following shows the correct expression for *four more than x*?

A. $4 + x$ C. $x > 4$ E. $4 - x$
B. $4 > x$ D. $x - 4$

132. Which of the following is the correct expression for *7 less than y*?

F. $y + 7$ H. $y - 7$ K. $\dfrac{7}{y}$

G. $7 - y$ J. $\dfrac{y}{7}$

133. Which of the following is the correct expression for *twice the sum of x and 3*?

A. $2x + 3$ D. $x + 6$
B. $2(x + 3)$ E. $2(x - 3)$
C. $2x + 6$

134. Which of the following shows the correct equation for *twice a certain number is 10*?

F. $2 + x = 10$ J. $2(2 + x) = 10$
G. $2x = 10$ K. $2 - x = 10$
H. $(2)(10) = x$

135. A 4-person relay team ran a race in 52 seconds. Which of the following equations represents the average time per person, x?

A. $\dfrac{52}{4} = x$ D. $52x = 4$

B. $52 - 4 = x$ E. $\dfrac{4}{52} = x$

C. $52 - x = 4$

136. Two boats leave the dock at the same time. One boat is traveling north at 30 miles per hour and the other boat is traveling south at 50 miles per hour. After how many hours will they be 200 miles apart?

F. 1 hour   H. 2 hours   K. 3 hours
G. 1.5 hours   J. 2.5 hours

137. If the number n of newspapers sold per week varies with the price p in dollars according to the equation $n = 40 - 3p$, what would be the total weekly revenue from the sale of newspapers costing $1 each?

A. $30   C. $35   E. $40
B. $33   D. $37

138. The variable m varies directly as the square of t. If m is 7 when $t = 1$, what is the value of m when $t = 2$?

F. 28   H. 7   K. 2

G. 14   J. $3\dfrac{1}{2}$

139. Mr. Carlson receives a salary of $500 a month and a commission of 5% on all sales. What must be the amount of his sales in July so that his total monthly income is $2,400?

A. $48,000   D. $3,800
B. $38,000   E. $2,000
C. $7,600

140. A taxi charges a $1.10 fee for any new passenger plus $1.40 for each mile driven. How far would a passenger ride for $9.50?

F. 4 miles   H. 6 miles   K. 8 miles
G. 5 miles   J. 7 miles

141. $2x^2 + 4x^3 + 8x^4 = ?$

A. $2x^2\left(1 + 2x + 4x^2\right)$

B. $2x^2\left(1 + 2x + 4x^3\right)$

C. $2x^2\left(x + 2x + 4x^2\right)$

D. $2x^2\left(x + 2x^2 + 4x^3\right)$

E. $2x^2\left(x^2 + 2x^3 + 4x^4\right)$

142. $144^2 - 121^2 = ?$

F. 23
G. $(144 + 121)(144 - 121)$
H. $(144 + 121)(144 + 121)$
J. 23^2
K. $(144 + 121)^2$

143. $x^2 + 3x + 2 = ?$

A. $(x+1)(x-2)$ D. $(x-2)(x-1)$
B. $(x+2)(x+1)$ E. $(x+3)(x-1)$
C. $(x+2)(x-1)$

144. $x^2 + x - 20 = ?$

F. $(x+5)(x-4)$ J. $(x+10)(x-2)$
G. $(x+4)(x-5)$ K. $(x+20)(x-1)$
H. $(x+2)(x-10)$

145. $x^2 + 8x + 16 = ?$

A. $(x+2)(x+8)$ D. $(x+4)(x-4)$
B. $(x+2)(x-8)$ E. $(x+4)(x+4)$
C. $(x-4)(x-4)$

146. $a^2 - 3a + 2 = ?$

F. $(a-2)(a-1)$ J. $(a-3)(a+1)$
G. $(a-2)(a+1)$ K. $(a+3)(a+1)$
H. $(a+1)(a-2)$

147. $4x^2 + 12x + 9 = ?$

A. $(x+9)(x+1)$ D. $(2x+4)(x+3)$
B. $(x+3)(4x+3)$ E. $(4x+3)(x+9)$
C. $(2x+3)(2x+3)$

148. $2x^2 + 5x - 3 = ?$

    F. $(x-1)(x+3)$ J. $(3x+1)(x+3)$
    G. $(2x-1)(x+3)$ K. $(3x-1)(2x+3)$
    H. $(2x+1)(x-3)$

149. If $15x^2 + bx - 28 = (5x-4)(3x+7)$, then $b = ?$

    A. 7   C. 23   E. 33
    B. 14   D. 28

150. $x^2 - 9y^4 = ?$

    F. $\left(x+3y^2\right)\left(x-3y^2\right)$

    G. $\left(x-3y^2\right)\left(x-3y^2\right)$

    H. $\left(x+3y^2\right)\left(x+3y^2\right)$

    J. $\left(2x+3y^2\right)\left(2x+3y^2\right)$

    K. $\left(2x-3y^2\right)\left(2x-3y^2\right)$

151. For what values of x is $3 + 4x < 28$?

    A. $x < 4$ C. $x < 6.25$ E. $x \geq 0$
    B. $x > 4$ D. $x > 6.25$

152. If x is an integer and $5 \leq x \leq 7$, then which of the following values is (are) possible for x?

    I.   5
    II. 6
    III. 7

    F. II only   J. II and III only
    G. I and II only   K. I, II, and III
    H. I and III only

153. If x and y are integers, $5 > x \geq 2$, and $6 < y \leq 9$, then which of the following is the *minimum* value of xy?

    A. 14   C. 20   E. 54
    B. 18   D. 45

154. For what values of x is $\dfrac{x}{2} - 12 \leq 11$?

    F. $x \leq 10$ H. $x \leq 32$ K. $x \leq 46$
    G. $x \leq 23$ J. $x \leq 33$

155. For what values of x is $2x + 7 > x - 10$?

    A. $x > -17$ C. $x > -3$ E. $x > 12$
    B. $x > -12$ D. $x > 3$

Graphical Representations

The Coordinate Plane

An easy way of understanding the coordinate system is to imagine a map of a piece of land.

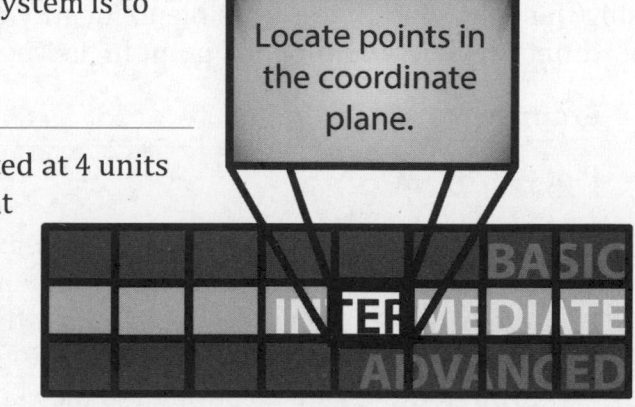

Locate points in the coordinate plane.

Example:

Relative to the Origin (0,0), Point *P* is located at 4 units East and 5 units North; Point *Q* is located at 4 units West and 5 units North; Point *R* is located at 4 units West and 2 units South; and Point *T* is located at 3 units East and 4 units South.

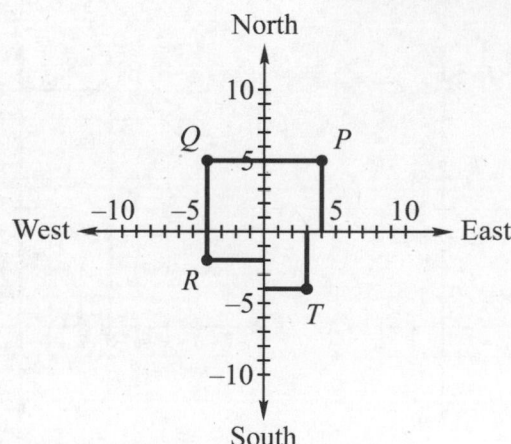

The coordinate system used in coordinate geometry differs from a land map because *x*- and *y*-axes are divided into negative and positive regions.

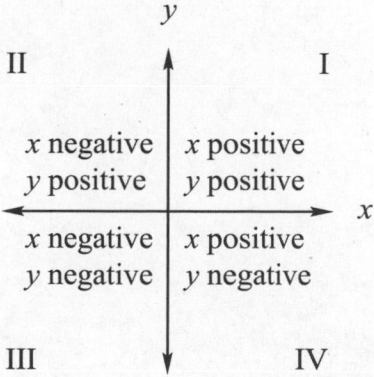

It is easy to see that ***Quadrant I*** corresponds to our Northeast quarter, in which the measurements on both the x- and y-axes are positive. ***Quadrant II*** corresponds to our Northwest quarter, in which the measurements on the x-axis are negative and the measurements on the y-axis are positive. ***Quadrant III*** corresponds to our Southwest quarter, in which both the x-axis measurements and the y-axis measurements are negative. Finally, ***Quadrant IV*** corresponds to our Southeast quarter, in which the x-values are positive while the y-values are negative.

Using this information it is possible to identify the ordered pairs for any point in the coordinate system and plot any point in the coordinate system.

Example:

Plot (–3, 8).

Move to the negative 3 value on the x-axis. Then, from there move up eight units on the y-axis, as illustrated by the graph on the left. The graph on the right demonstrates an alternative method: the point (–3,8) is located at the intersection of a line drawn through the x-value –3 parallel to the y-axis and a line drawn through the y-value 8 parallel to the x-axis.

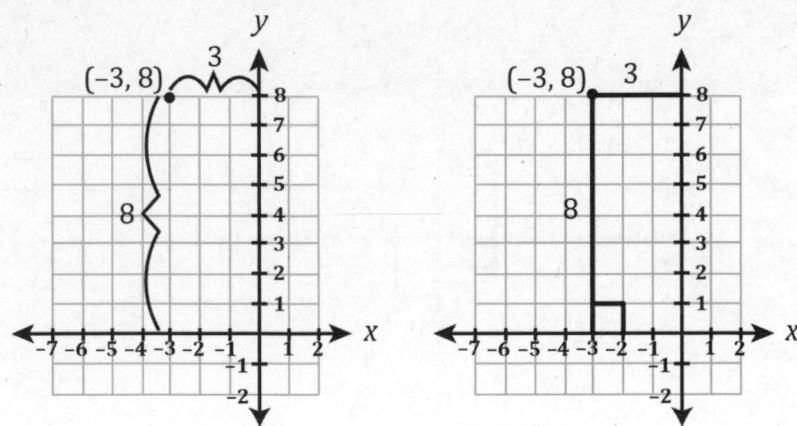

Number Lines and Line Segments

Length on the Number Line

Implicit in the concept of the number line is the notion of distance. As you move from one point to another, you move a certain distance:

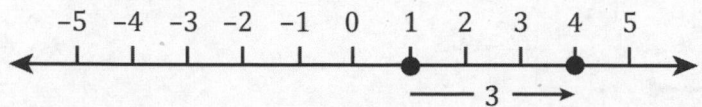

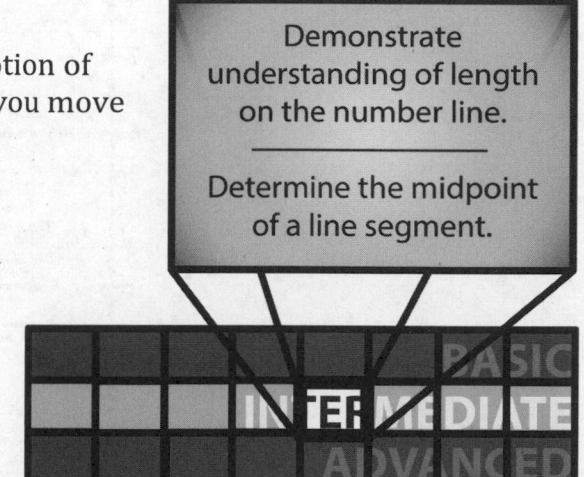

Demonstrate understanding of length on the number line.

Determine the midpoint of a line segment.

The distance separating the point with coordinate 4 from the point with coordinate 1 is: $4 - 1 = 3$.

The negative values are handled in similar fashion. The distance between -4 and 2 is $2 - (-4) = 6$:

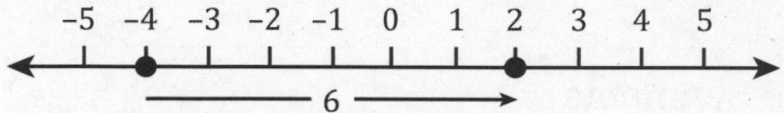

Note that the distance between points on the number line is the same regardless of the direction, because distance is always positive:

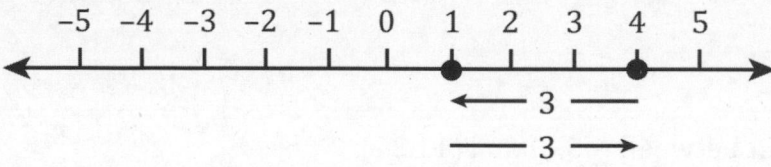

Line segments may also appear in the coordinate plane:

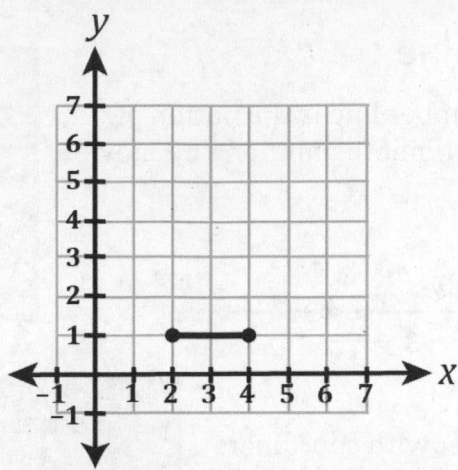

The length of lines parallel to either the *x*-axis or the *y*-axis in the coordinate plane can be measured in the same way as length is measured on a number line. The distance of line segments in the coordinate plane that are not parallel to one of the axes can also be measured, but this requires a formula that will be introduced in the Advanced level of this review.

Midpoint of Line Segments

For a line segment between two points, (x_1, y_1) and (x_2, y_2), the

midpoint $= \left(\dfrac{x_1 + x_2}{2}, \dfrac{y_1 + y_2}{2} \right)$. The *x*-coordinate of the midpoint is the average of the two

x-axis endpoints and the *y*-coordinate of the midpoint is the average of the two *y*-axis endpoints.

Examples:

Find the midpoint between (–5,8) and (11,34).

The midpoint is $\left(\dfrac{x_1 + x_2}{2}, \dfrac{y_1 + y_2}{2} \right) = \left(\dfrac{-5 + 11}{2}, \dfrac{8 + 34}{2} \right) = \left(\dfrac{6}{2}, \dfrac{42}{2} \right) = (3, 21)$.

One endpoint of a circle diameter is located at (13,1). If the center of the circle is (15,10), find the other endpoint.

The midpoint of the diameter is (15,10), so solve for x_2 and y_2:

$15 = \dfrac{x_1 + x_2}{2} \Rightarrow 15 = \dfrac{13 + x_2}{2} \Rightarrow x_2 = (15 \bullet 2) - 13 = 17$ and $10 = \dfrac{y_1 + y_2}{2} \Rightarrow$

$10 = \dfrac{1 + y_2}{2} \Rightarrow y_2 = (10 \bullet 2) - 1 = 19$. Thus, $(x_2, y_2) = (17, 19)$.

Linear Inequalities and their Graphs

A linear inequality is similar to a linear equation, except an inequality symbol is used instead of an equals sign to represent a relationship in which one side of the equation is more than, less than, or equal to the other side of the equation. For example, the linear inequality $x \leq -5$, read as "x is less than or equal to −5," means that x can be negative 5 or any value that is smaller than negative 5, for example, −5.5, −7, −100, etc. On the other hand, the linear inequality $x > 2$, read as "x is greater than 2," means that x can be values bigger than 2, but not including the value 2, for example, 2.01, 3, 50, etc. Linear inequalities are often represented by a graph. This can be seen in the examples below. Note that "greater than" and "less than" inequalities are represented by a closed dot, while "greater than or equal to" and "less than or equal to" inequalities are represented by an open dot.

Identify graphical representations of inequalities on the number line.

Examples:

Write the equation of the linear inequality that is graphed below:

$x > -2$: read as "x is greater than −2." The circle is open and the arrow points right, so the solutions of x include values greater than, but not including, −2. Possible solutions for x include: −1.99, −1, 0.6, 2.3, 4, 500, etc. There are infinitely many solutions.

Write the equation of the linear inequality that is graphed below:

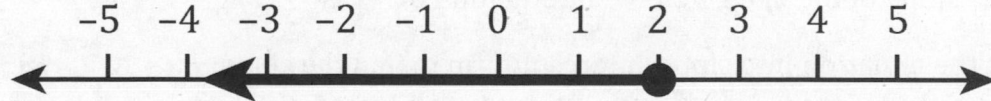

$x \leq 2$: read as "x is less than or equal to 2." The circle is closed and the arrow points left, so the solutions of x include values less than and including 2. Possible solutions for x include: 2, 1.8, −2.7, −8, −100....etc. There are an infinite number of solutions.

Write the equation of the linear inequality that is graphed below:

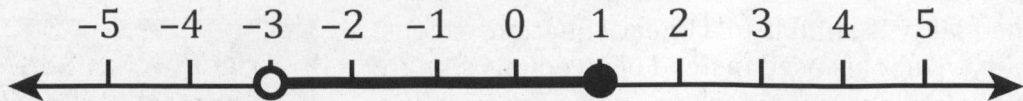

$-3 < x \leq 1$: read as "x is greater than -3 and less than or equal to 1." The circle is open at negative 3 and closed at 1 with the segment in between the values. Possible solutions for x include: -2.8, -1.1, 0, 0.25, 0.999, and 1.

Slope-Intercept Form

If x and y are related by a linear equation, then y is a **linear function**. Except for a vertical line, every linear equation is a linear function that can be represented in **slope-intercept form**: $y = mx + b$, where m is the slope of the line and b is the y-intercept. The y-intercept is the y-coordinate of the point where the line intersects the y-axis, or where $x = 0$. The **slope**, m, of a line describes the steepness of the line. It is defined as the change in y-values divided by the change in x-values, or rise over run:

$$\text{slope} = m = \frac{y_2 - y_1}{x_2 - x_1} = \frac{\text{rise}}{\text{run}}.$$

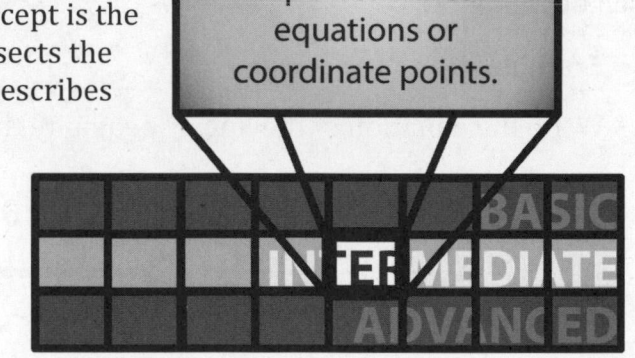

Show familiarity with slope and determine slope from linear equations or coordinate points.

Examples:

Find the slope of the line containing $(3,2)$ and $(8,22)$.

$$m = \frac{y_2 - y_1}{x_2 - x_1} = \frac{22 - 2}{8 - 3} = \frac{20}{5} = 4.$$

Find the slope of the line given by the equation $6x + 12y = 13$.

Put the equation into slope-intercept form to find the slope: $6x + 12y = 13 \Rightarrow$

$12y = -6x + 13 \Rightarrow y = \frac{-6x + 13}{12} \Rightarrow y = -\frac{x}{2} + \frac{13}{12}$. Therefore, the slope is $-\frac{1}{2}$.

The points $(-5,12)$, $(0,7)$, and $(10,-3)$ lie on a line. What is the y-intercept of this line?

The y-intercept is what y equals when $x = 0$. The x-coordinate of the second point is 0. Therefore, this point's y-coordinate, 7, is the y-intercept of the line.

Matching Graphs and Their Equations

The coordinate axis system provides a framework for plotting equations. Simply plot several pairs of points for the given equation.

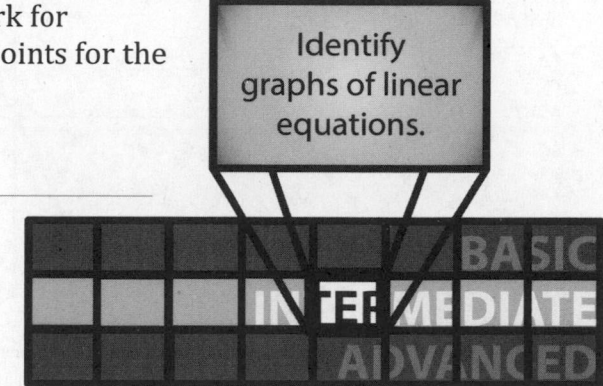

Identify graphs of linear equations.

Examples:

Plot the equation $y = x$.

This equation has infinitely many solutions, including:

x	1	2	3	5	0	−3	−5
y	1	2	3	5	0	−3	−5

Plot these pairs of x and y on the axis system. Draw a line through them to produce a plot of the original equation. The complete picture of the equation $y = x$ is a straight line including all the real numbers such that x is equal to y.

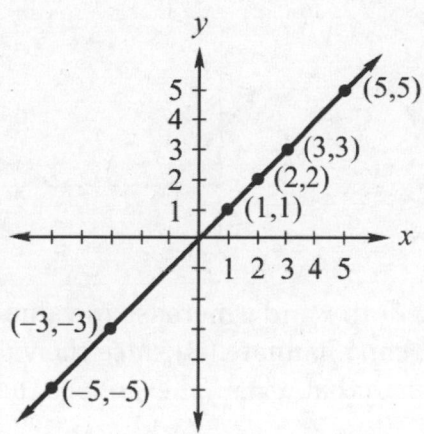

Plot the equation $y = 2x$.

This equation has infinitely many solutions, including:

x	−4	−2	−1	0	1	2	4
y	−8	−4	−2	0	2	4	8

After entering the points on the graph, complete the picture. It is a straight line, but it rises more rapidly than does $y = x$.

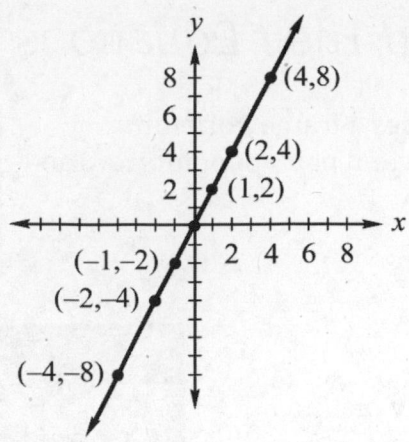

You may be asked simply to identify graphs of linear functions. The graph of a linear function is a straight line.

Examples:

The line of best fit for $y = f(x)$ for the ordered pairs $(-4,-12)$, $(1,3)$, $(2,6)$, $(3,9)$, and $(4,12)$ is best represented by which of the following graphs?

A. 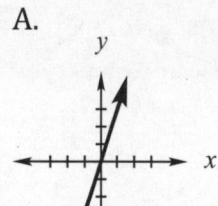   B. 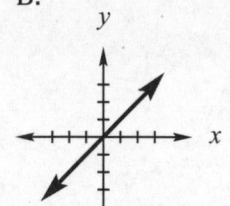   C. 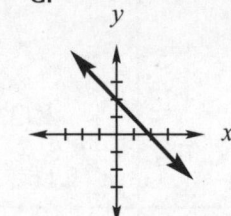   D. 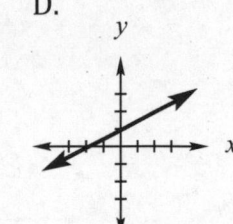   E.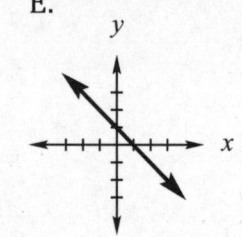

The correct answer is (A). Both x and y increase in value for each ordered pair, so eliminate (C) and (E). You can eliminate (B) since the values of x and y in the given ordered pairs clearly indicate that $x \neq y$. The slope is the change in y over the change in x. The slope for (A) is $\frac{3}{1} = 3$. The slope for (D) is $\frac{1}{2}$. Choose two of the given points and determine the slope of the line: $\frac{6-3}{2-1} = \frac{3}{1} = 3$.

EXERCISE 6

DIRECTIONS: Choose the correct answer to each of the following items. Answers are on page 814.

Questions 156–157 refer to the following diagram.

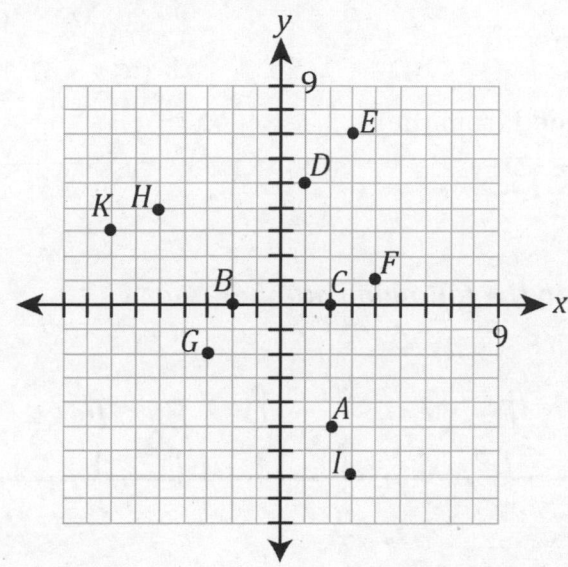

156. Which of the following points has coordinates (–7,3)?

F. *I*   H. *H*   K. *G*
G. *E*   J. *K*

157. Which of the following points have the same *y*-coordinate?

A. *A* and *D*   C. *F* and *J*   E. *B* and *C*
B. *H* and *J*   D. *G* and *I*

158. Points $(x, -4)$ and $(-1, y)$ (not shown in the figure below) are in Quadrants III and II, respectively. If $x \neq 0$ and $y \neq 0$, in which quadrant is point (x,y)?

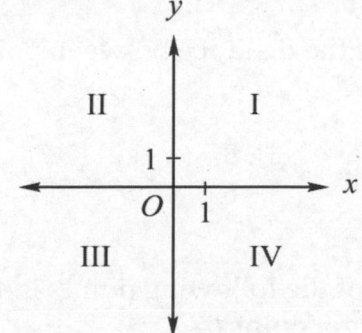

F. I
G. II
H. III
J. IV
K. Cannot be determined from the given information

159. On a coordinate plane, point B is located 7 units to the left of point A. The x-coordinate of point A is x, and the y-coordinate of point A is y. What is the x-coordinate of point B?

A. $x - 7$

B. $x + 7$

C. $y + 7$

D. $y - 7$

E. Cannot be determined from the given information

160. Point R is represented on the coordinate plane by (x,y). The vertical coordinate of point S is three times the vertical coordinate of point R and the two points have the same horizontal coordinate. The ordered pair that represents point S is:

F. $(3x, y)$ H. $(x, y-3)$ K. $(x, 3y)$

G. $(x, y+3)$ J. $(3x, 3y)$

Questions 161–165 refer to the following number line.

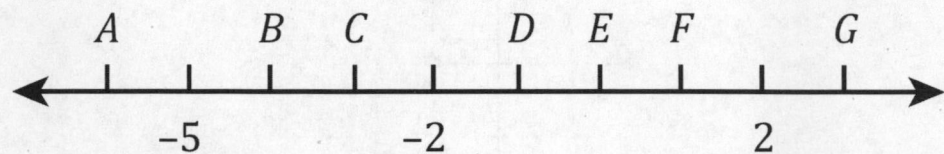

161. What is the coordinate of point C?

A. –6   C. –3   E. 3

B. –4   D. 0

162. What is the distance between points A and D?

F. –6   H. 5   K. 7

G. –1   J. 6

163. Which of the following points is 4 units from point D?

A. F D. B

B. G E. A

C. C

164. Which of the following segments have the same length?

F. $\overline{GC}$ and $\overline{AC}$

G. $\overline{BD}$ and $\overline{DG}$

H. $\overline{GF}$ and $\overline{AC}$

J. $\overline{AC}$ and $\overline{BD}$

K. $\overline{DE}$ and $\overline{CD}$

165. Which set(s) of points is (are) 5 units apart?

A. F and C

B. B and E

C. B and D

D. B and D; E and G

E. A and D; F and B

166. What is the midpoint between (−2,15) and (8,17)?

F. (6,16)   H. (5,16)   K. (6,32)
G. (3,16)   J. (5,32)

167. What is the midpoint between (−2,−3) and (−6,−11)?

A. (−4,−7)   D. (4,7)
B. (2,4)   E. (−2,−4)
C. (−7,−4)

168. Segment *AB* has the coordinates *A*(−12,14) and *B*(6,21). What is the location of the midpoint, *M*, of $\overline{AB}$?

F. *M* (3,−3.5)   J. *M* (−3,3.5)
G. *M* (−4,17.5)   K. *M* (−6,35)
H. *M* (−3,17.5)

169. The midpoint, *M*, of Segment *JG* has the coordinates *M*(4,5). If the endpoint *G* has the coordinates *G*(8,11), what are the coordinates of endpoint *J*?

A. *J* (6,8)   D. *J* (0,−1)
B. *J* (4,−1)   E. *J* (2,3)
C. *J* (16,21)

170. One endpoint of a circle's diameter is located at (−22,7). If the center of the circle is(−11,1), find the other endpoint.

F. (−44,1)   J. (−44,9)
G. (−11,9)   K. (−22,−5)
H. (0,−5)

171. Which of the following inequalities is represented by the graph below?

A. $x > -6$ C. $x < -6$ E. $x \geq -6.1$
B. $x < -7$ D. $x \leq -6$

172. Which of the following inequalities is represented by the graph below?

3   4   5   6   7   8   9   10 11 12 13

F. $x \geq 6$ H. $6 \leq x < 9$
G. $9 \leq x \leq 6$ J. $6 \leq x \leq 9$
K. $x \leq 9$

173. Which of the following is the graph of $x > 1$?

A.   −5 −4 −3 −2 −1 0 1 2 3 4 5

B.   −5 −4 −3 −2 −1 0 1 2 3 4 5

C.   −5 −4 −3 −2 −1 0 1 2 3 4 5

D.   −5 −4 −3 −2 −1 0 1 2 3 4 5

E.   −5 −4 −3 −2 −1 0 1 2 3 4 5

174. Which of the following points is a solution to the inequality graphed below?

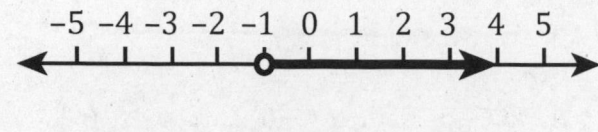

F. –2   H. –1.5   K. –0.9
G. –1.9   J. –1

175. Which of the following is the graph of $-3 < x \leq 2$?

A.
$\quad$ –5 –4 –3 –2 –1 0 1 2 3 4 5

B.
$\quad$ –5 –4 –3 –2 –1 0 1 2 3 4 5

C.
$\quad$ –5 –4 –3 –2 –1 0 1 2 3 4 5

D.
$\quad$ –5 –4 –3 –2 –1 0 1 2 3 4 5

E.
$\quad$ –5 –4 –3 –2 –1 0 1 2 3 4 5

176. What is the slope of a line that passes through $(0, -5)$ and $(8, 27)$?

F. 4   H. $\dfrac{8}{32}$ K. –4

G. 2   J. $-\dfrac{8}{32}$

177. The slope of a line that passes through points $(3, 7)$ and $(12, y)$ is $\dfrac{1}{3}$. What is the value of y?

A. 2   C. $6\dfrac{2}{3}$ E. 10

B. 4   D. $7\dfrac{1}{3}$

178. What is the slope of the line $y = 5x + 7$?

F. 7   H. 2   K. $\dfrac{1}{5}$

G. 5   J. $\dfrac{7}{5}$

179. A line passes through points $(3, 8)$ and $(w, 2k)$. If $w \neq -3$ or 3 and $k \neq 4$, what is the slope of the line?

A. $\dfrac{8 - 2k}{3 + w}$ C. $\dfrac{2k - 8}{w - 3}$ E. $\dfrac{3}{8}$

B. $\dfrac{2k + 8}{w + 3}$ D. $\dfrac{w - 3}{2k - 8}$

180. The graph of the following ordered pairs for (x, y) is approximately a straight line of the form $y = mx + b$: $(1, 18), (2, 23), (3, 27), (4, 32), (5, 38)$. Which of the following best approximates the value of b?

F. 13   H. 20   K. 25
G. 18   J. 23

181. A line passes through the points $\left(1, -\dfrac{7}{2}\right)$ and $(2, -4)$. What is the value of b?

A. –5   C. 0   E. 5

B. –3   D. 3

182. Given the linear function graphed below, which of the following statements is true?

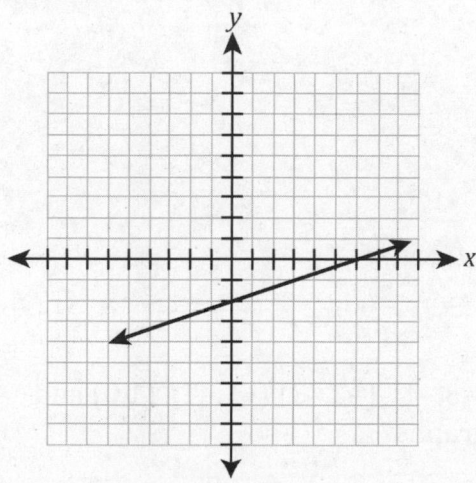

F. The x-intercept is 7, the y-intercept is –2 and the slope is $m = \dfrac{7}{2}$.

G. The x-intercept is 7, and the slope is $m = -\dfrac{2}{7}$.

H. The y-intercept is –2 and the slope is $m = -\dfrac{7}{2}$.

J. The x-intercept is 7, the y-intercept is –2 and the slope is $m = \dfrac{2}{7}$.

K. The y-intercept is 7 and the slope is $m = \dfrac{2}{7}$.

183. The following are all points on the graph of the line $y = \dfrac{2}{5}x - 3$ EXCEPT:

A. $(-10, -7)$ D. $(1, -2)$

B. $(-5, -5)$ E. $(10, 1)$

C. $(0, -3)$

184. Which of the following graphs below is the graph of the function $y = 2x - 1$?

F.
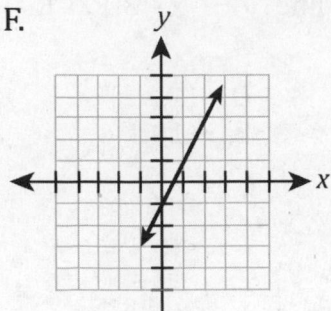

H.
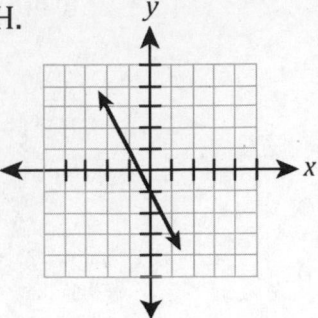

K.
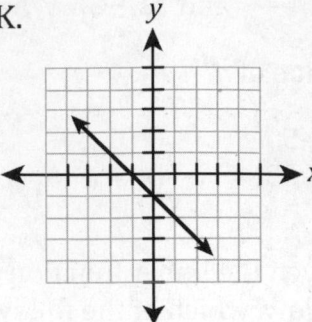

G.
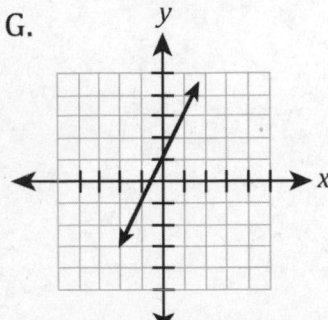

J.
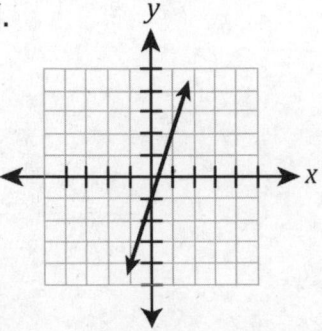

185. The line of best fit for $y = f(x)$ for the ordered pairs (–3,–4), (–2,–3) (–1,–2), (1,0) and (5,4) is best represented by which of the following graphs?

A.
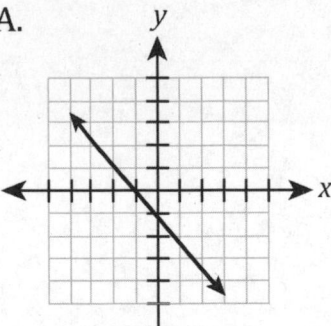

C.
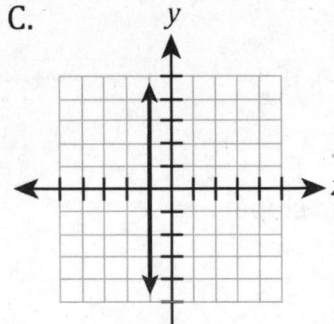

E.
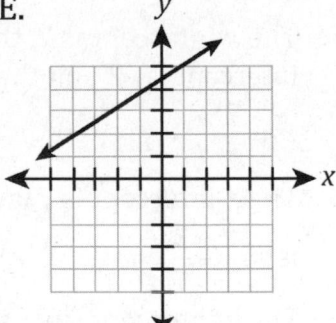

B.
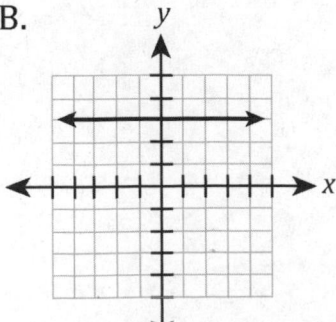

D.
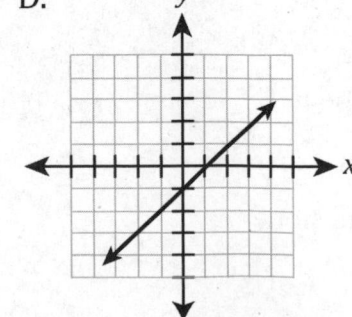

Plane Figures

Using Angle Properties

When two lines intersect, they form an **angle**, and their point of intersection is called the **vertex** of that angle.

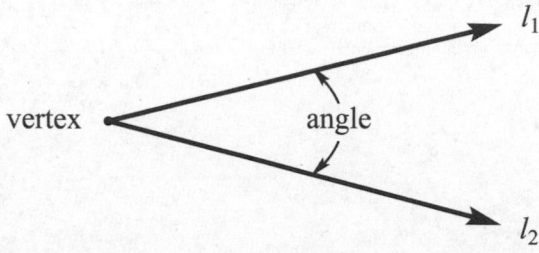

The size of an angle is measured in **degrees**. Degrees are defined in reference to a circle. A circle is divided into 360 equal parts, or degrees.

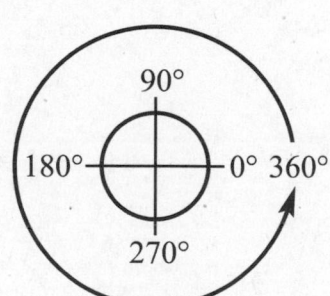

Show familiarity with basic angle properties and special angle sums such as 90°, 180°, and 360°.

Determine angle measures using properties of parallel lines.

Determine an unknown angle measure using several angle properties.

A 90° angle is also called a **right angle**. A right angle is often indicated in the following way:

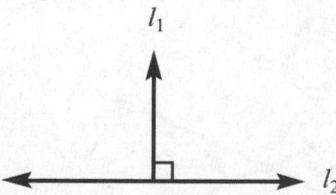

Two right angles form a straight line:

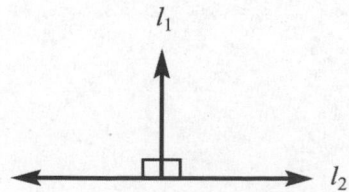

Since two right angles form a straight line, the degree measure of the angle of a straight line is $90° + 90° = 180°$:

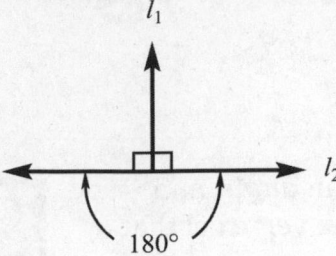

An angle that is less than 90° is called an **acute angle**. In the figure below, $\angle PQR$ is an acute angle:

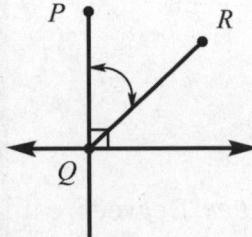

An angle that is greater than 90° but less than 180° is called an **obtuse angle**. In the figure below, $\angle PQR$ is an obtuse angle:

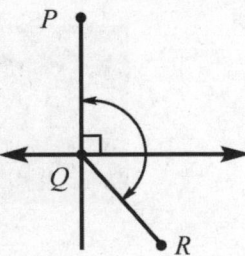

When two lines intersect, the opposite (or vertical) angles created by their intersection are **congruent**, or their measures are equal:

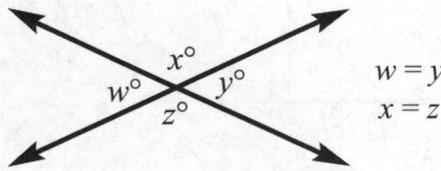

Two lines in the same plane that do not intersect regardless of how far they are extended are **parallel** to each other. In the following figure, the symbol ‖ indicates that l_1 and l_2 are parallel.

$$l_1 \parallel l_2$$

When parallel lines are intersected by a third line, called a **transversal**, the following angle relationships are created:

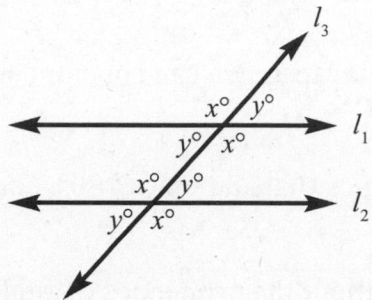

All angles labeled x are equal.

All angles labeled y are equal.

Any x plus any y totals 180. (x and y are **supplementary** angles.)

Thus, if you know the value of one angle, you can determine the value of any other angle.

Example:

$$l_1 \parallel l_2$$

If $b = 60$, then $e = ?$

b is a little angle and e is a big angle, so $b + e = 180$. Therefore, $b = 120$.

Two lines in the same plane that are **_perpendicular_** to the same line are parallel to each other:

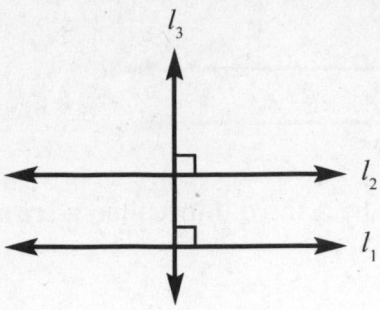

Since l_1 and l_2 are both perpendicular to l_3, we can conclude that l_1 and l_2 are parallel to each other.

Supplementary angles are two angles that add up to 180°. **_Complementary angles_** are two angles that add up to 90°.

You can use all of this information about the properties of angles and lines to determine unknown angle measures, whether the figures presented include parallel lines, perpendicular lines, or special angle degrees, such as 90°, 180°, and 360°.

Example:

In the figure below, x = ?

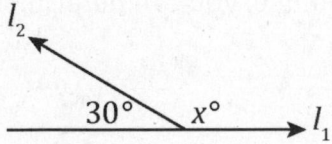

A straight line is a 180° angle. Therefore, the sum of all angles forming a straight line is 180°: $x° + 30° = 180°$, so $x = 150$.

EXERCISE 7

DIRECTIONS: Choose the correct answer to each of the following items. Answers are on page 814.

186. If $e = 120$, then $g = ?$

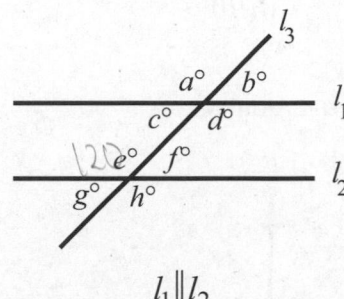

$$l_1 \| l_2$$

F. 60   H. 120   K. 180
G. 90   J. 150

187. In the diagram below, line a is parallel to line b. Which of the following is (are) true in the diagram below?

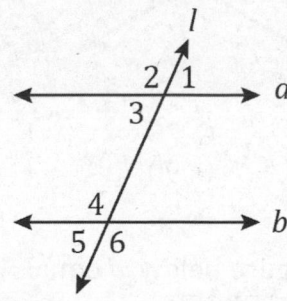

I. $\angle 1 \cong \angle 5$
II. $\angle 2 \cong \angle 6$
III. $\angle 3 + \angle 4 = 180°$

A. I only   D. II only
B. I and III only   E. I, II, and III
C. III only

188. In the diagram below, line l is parallel to line m. What is the number of degrees in $\angle ABC$?

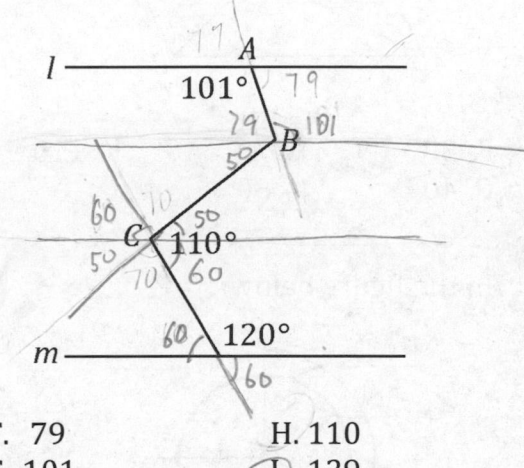

F. 79   H. 110
G. 101   J. 129
H. 105

189. In the diagram below, the line containing points A, B, and C is parallel to the line containing points D, E, and F. If $\angle ABE = (7x + 12)°$ and $\angle DEB = (2x + 42)°$, what is the number of degrees in $\angle CBE$?

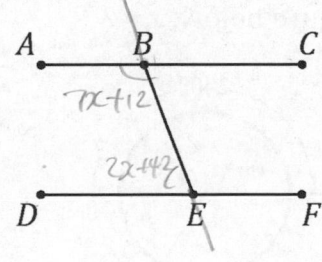

A. 70   C. 35
B. 54   D. 30
C. 42

190. In the diagram below, *ABCD* is a parallelogram with $\overline{AD} \parallel \overline{BC}$ and $\overline{AB} \parallel \overline{DC}$. The diagonals intersect at *E*. If $\angle DAC = 30°$ and $\angle DEA = 70°$, what is the degree measure of $\angle CBD$?

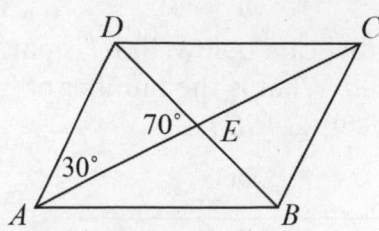

F. 30   H. 70   K. 110
G. 40   J. 80

191. In the figure below, *x* = ?

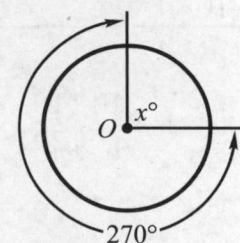

O is the center of the circle.

A. 30   C. 90   E. 270
B. 60   D. 120

192. In the figure below, *x* = ?

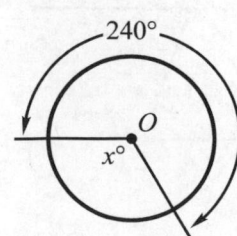

F. 60   H. 120   K. 180
G. 90   J. 150

193. In the figure below, *x* = ?

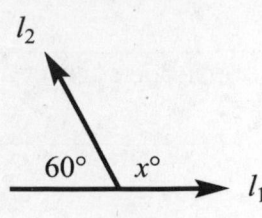

A. 15   C. 45   E. 120
B. 30   D. 90

194. In the figure below, *x* = ?

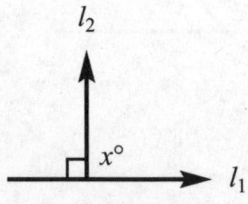

F. 15   H. 45   K. 90
G. 30   J. 60

195. In the figure below, *x* = ?

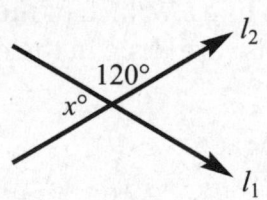

A. 45   C. 75   E. 120
B. 60   D. 90

196. In the figure below, *a* equals all of the following EXCEPT

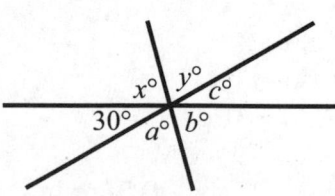

F. *y*   J. $150 - b$
G. $150 - x$ K. $180 - x - y$
H. $180 - b - c$

197. In the figure below, x = ?

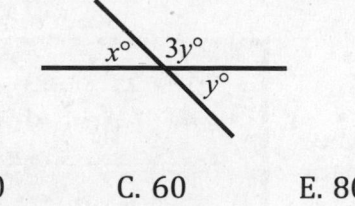

A. 30   C. 60   E. 80
B. 45   D. 65

198. In the figure below, $\overline{OM} \parallel \overline{PJ}$, and $\overline{FG}$ and $\overline{EG}$ divide $\angle CGO$ into 3 congruent angles. What is the degree measure of $\angle EGC$?

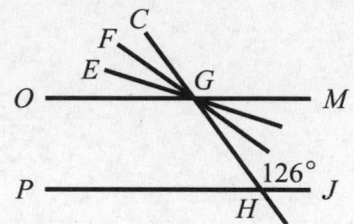

F. 18°   H. 42°   K. 63°
G. 36°   J. 54°

199. In the figure below, x = ?

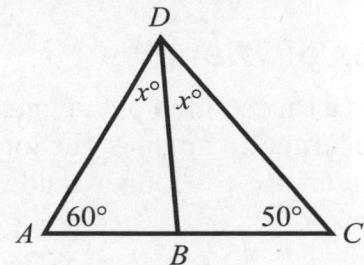

A. 30   C. 35   E. 70
B. 32   D. 40

200. In the figure below, x = ?

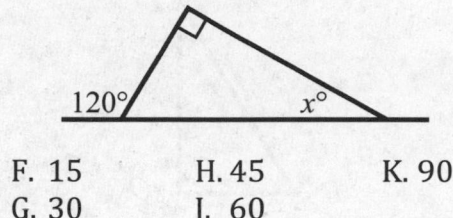

F. 15   H. 45   K. 90
G. 30   J. 60

Triangles

Properties of Triangles

A **triangle** is a three-sided plane figure. Within a given triangle, the larger an angle is, the longer the side opposite the angle is; conversely, the longer a side is, the larger the opposite angle is.

Use isosceles
triangle properties.
_____

Identify
Pythagorean triples.

Examples:

In the following figure, since $\overline{PR} > \overline{QR} > \overline{PQ}$,
$\angle Q > \angle P > \angle R$.

In the following figure, since $\angle P > \angle Q > \angle R$, $\overline{QR} > \overline{PR} > \overline{PQ}$.

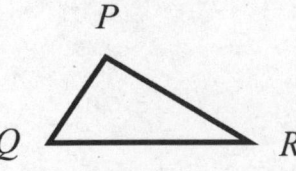

Within a given triangle, if two sides are equal, then the angles opposite the two sides are equal, and vice versa:

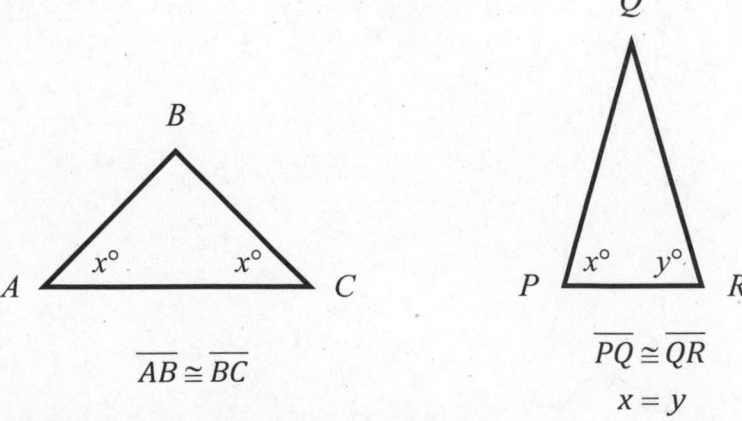

$$\overline{AB} \cong \overline{BC}$$

$$\overline{PQ} \cong \overline{QR}$$
$$x = y$$

A triangle with exactly two equal sides is called an **isosceles triangle**.

A triangle with exactly three equal sides is called an ***equilateral triangle***.

Example:

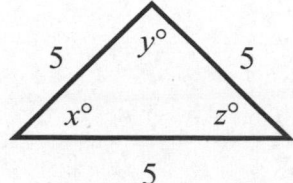

An equilateral triangle has three equal sides and therefore three equal angles: $x = y = z$. Since the three interior angles of any triangle add up to 180°, each angle must be 60°.

A triangle with a right angle is called a ***right triangle***. The longest side of the right triangle, which is opposite the 90° angle, is called the ***hypotenuse***.

Pythagorean Theorem and Pythagorean Triples

The sides of every right triangle fit a special relationship called the ***Pythagorean theorem***: the square of the hypotenuse is equal to the sum of the squares of the other two sides. This is easier to understand when it is summarized in a formula.

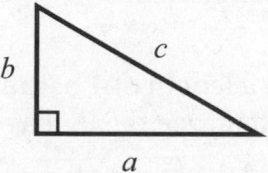

Pythagorean theorem: $c^2 = a^2 + b^2$

In any right triangle in which the lengths of any two sides are known, you can use the Pythagorean theorem to find the length of the missing side. One shortcut to the Pythagorean theorem is to recognize common groups of side lengths, also known as ***Pythagorean triples***.

Since $3^2 + 4^2 = 5^2$, the (3, 4, 5) right triangle is an example of a Pythagorean triple. And since $5^2 + 12^2 = 13^2$, the (5, 12, 13) right triangle is a second example of a Pythagorean triple.

This means that if a triangle has legs of lengths 3 and 4, the hypotenuse must be 5. You can memorize the triple to save time.

Or, if a triangle has one leg of length 5 and a hypotenuse of length 13, then, without plugging numbers into the Pythagorean theorem, you know that the second leg must have a length of 12.

You can also identify multiples of common Pythagorean triples, such as the 3, 4, 5 triple, to find more Pythagorean triples:

(3, 4, 5) multiplied by 2: (6, 8, 10)

(3, 4, 5) multiplied by 3: (9, 12, 15)

(3, 4, 5) multiplied by $\frac{1}{3}$: $\left(1, 1\frac{1}{3}, 1\frac{2}{3}\right)$

These groups of triples are sometimes called ***Pythagorean families***.

Remember: when using a Pythagorean triple to solve a problem, correctly identify which value is the hypotenuse.

Examples:

In the figure below, what is the length of $\overline{AB}$?

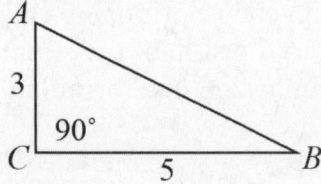

The missing side does not have a length of 4 because the missing side is the hypotenuse. To solve this problem, use the Pythagorean theorem:

$$3^2 + 5^2 = \left(\overline{AB}\right)^2 \Rightarrow 9 + 25 = \left(\overline{AB}\right)^2 \Rightarrow \sqrt{34} = \overline{AB}$$

In the figure below, what is the value of x?

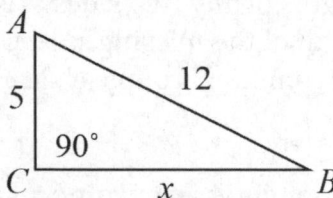

The missing side does not have a length of 13 because the missing side is a leg. The longest side is the hypotenuse, so to solve this problem, use the Pythagorean theorem: $5^2 + x^2 = 12^2 \Rightarrow 25 + x^2 = 144 \Rightarrow x = \sqrt{119}$.

You can also use Pythagorean triples to find the area of a right triangle when one of the side lengths is missing.

Find the area of the triangle in the figure below.

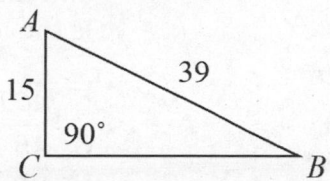

This right triangle is a member of the (5, 12, 13) family; each value has been multiplied by 3. So the missing length is 3(12), or 36. To find the area,

$$A = \frac{bh}{2} = \frac{15(36)}{2} = \frac{540}{2} = 270.$$

EXERCISE 8

DIRECTIONS: Choose the correct answer to each of the following items. Answers are on page 814.

201. In the figure below, if $\overline{AE} \parallel \overline{BD}$ and $\overline{BD} \cong \overline{DC}$, then $\angle BDC$ = ?

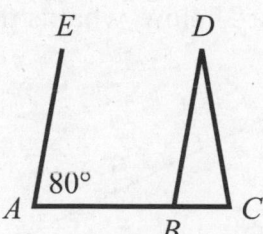

A. 10°   C. 18°   E. 24°
B. 15°   D. 20°

202. In the figure below, x = ?

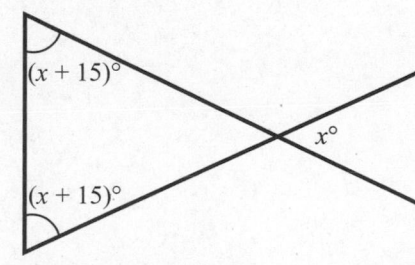

F. 20   H. 50   K. 90
G. 35   J. 65

203. Which of the following is (are) true of the figure below?

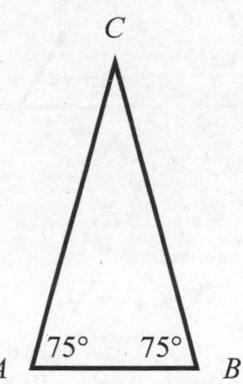

I. $\overline{AB} \cong \overline{BC}$
II. $\overline{BC} \cong \overline{AC}$
III. $\overline{AC} \cong \overline{AB}$

A. I only   D. I and III only
B. II only   E. I, II, and III
C. I and II only

204. Which of the following is (are) true of the figure below?

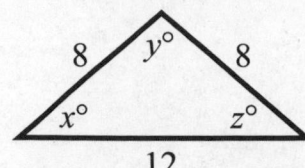

   I. $x = y$
   II. $y = z$
   III. $z = x$

F. I only
G. II only
H. III only
J. I and II only
K. I, II, and III

205. Which of the following is (are) true of the figure below?

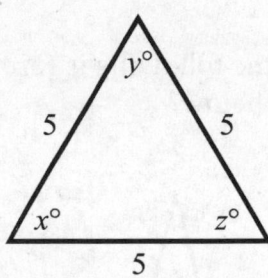

   I. $x = y$
   II. $y = z$
   III. $z = x$

A. I only
B. I and II only
C. I and III only
D. II and III only
E. I, II, and III

206. In $\triangle ABC$, the measure of $\angle A$ is 40° and the measure of $\angle B$ is 70°. What is the longest side of $\triangle ABC$?

F. $\overline{AC}$
G. $\overline{AB}$
H. $\overline{BC}$
J. $\overline{AC} \cong \overline{AB}$ (there is no longest side)
K. $\overline{AC} \cong \overline{BC}$ (there is no longest side)

207. In the figure below, what is the value of x?

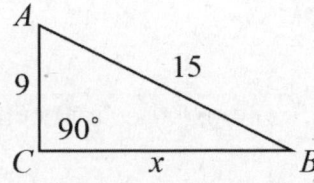

A. 9
B. 12
C. 13
D. 14
E. 15

208. In the figure below, what is the value of c?

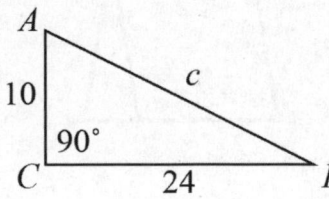

F. 10
G. 17
H. 24
J. 26
K. 34

209. In the figure below, what is the value of k?

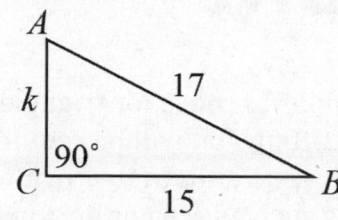

A. 4

B. 8

C. 12

D. 32

E. 64

210. In the figure below, what is the length of $\overline{AB}$?

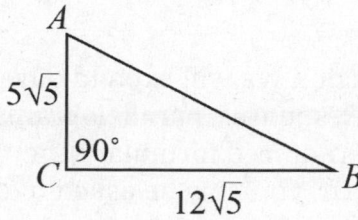

F. $\sqrt{5}$

G. $5\sqrt{13}$

H. 13

J. $13\sqrt{5}$

K. 65

Measurement

In this section we will expand our review of geometric formulas to those for triangles, rectangles, squares, parallelograms, trapezoids, and circles. Often, you will be required to know the required formula, either in a direct, no-frills, application situation or in a word problem. Or, you may be asked to calculate geometric values such as area or perimeter using a provided formula, which combines what you already know about geometry and algebra. Typically, direct-application situations require no more than one or two steps, while word problems involving geometric measures require multi-step solutions.

Recall that the perimeter of a figure is the sum of the lengths of its sides, and the area of a figure is the measure of square units contained within the figure's perimeter. Now, let's look at both of these measurements in more depth for each of the basic geometric shapes.

Perimeter and Area of Triangles

To find the perimeter of a **triangle**, add the lengths of the three sides together. The **altitude** of a triangle, or **height**, is a line drawn from a vertex perpendicular to the opposite side. To find the **area** of a triangle, multiply one-half by the height and the base. Note that the base can be the length of any side, while the height is the length of a perpendicular line originating from the base to one of the triangle's vertices.

Determine the perimeter and area of triangles in one-step and multi-step problems.

BASIC

INTERMEDIATE

ADVANCED

PERIMETER AND AREA OF TRIANGLES

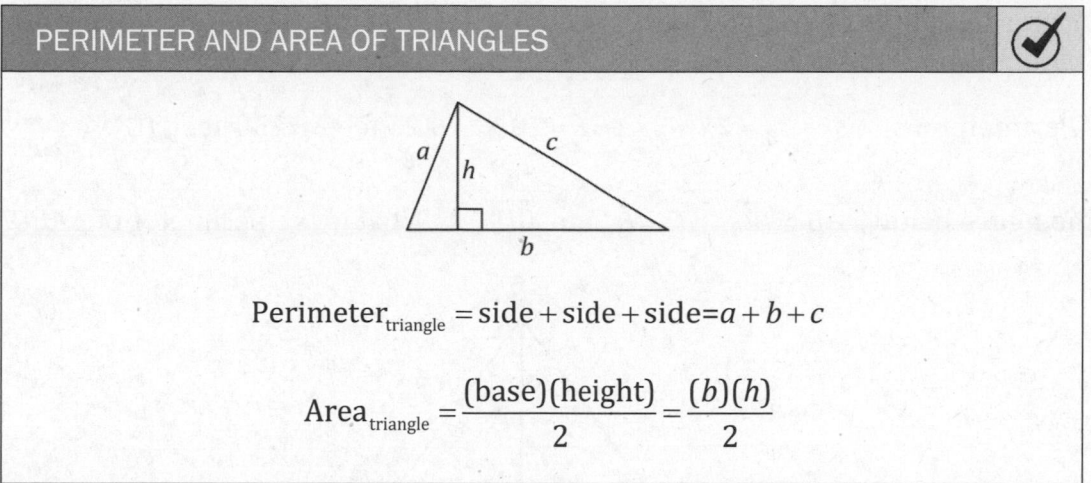

$$\text{Perimeter}_{\text{triangle}} = \text{side} + \text{side} + \text{side} = a + b + c$$

$$\text{Area}_{\text{triangle}} = \frac{(\text{base})(\text{height})}{2} = \frac{(b)(h)}{2}$$

Examples:

In the following figure, what is the area of the triangle?

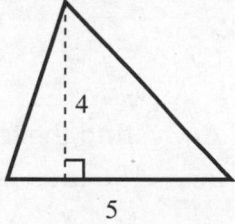

A. 8   C. 12   E. 20
B. 10   D. 15

The altitude is 4 and the base is 5. Apply the area formula for a triangle:

$$\text{Area}_{\text{triangle}} = \frac{(b)(h)}{2} = \frac{(4)(5)}{2} = 10, \text{(B)}.$$

A parking lot shaped like the triangle in the figure below is completely fenced during a street fair. If x equals 25 feet, what is the total length, in feet, of the fence?

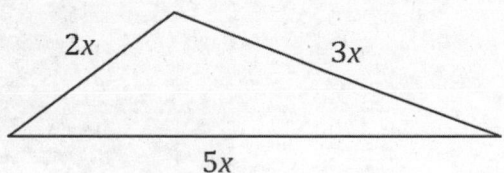

F. 100   H. 500   K. 2,500
G. 250   J. 1,250

Regardless of the presentation, the solution is the same: the perimeter of a triangle is the sum of the three sides.

$$\text{Perimeter} = s_1 + s_2 + s_3 = 2x + 3x + 5x = 10x = 10(25 \text{ feet}) = 250 \text{ feet, (G)}.$$

In the figure below, $\overline{AB} \cong \overline{BC}$, $\overline{AC} = 6$, and $\overline{BD} = 4$. What is the perimeter of $\triangle ABC$?

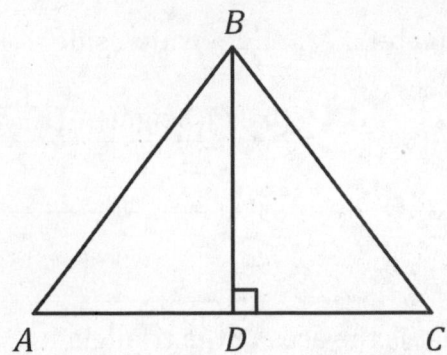

A. 10 C. 16   E. $16\sqrt{2}$
B. 12 D. 20

To determine the perimeter of $\triangle ABC$, find the lengths of the three sides using the given information. Since $\overline{AB} \cong \overline{BC}$, $\triangle ABC$ is an isosceles triangle and

$\overline{DC} = \dfrac{\overline{AC}}{2} = \dfrac{6}{2} = 3$. This means that $\triangle BCD$ is a 3-4-5 triangle, so $\overline{BC} = 5$ and $\overline{AB} = 5$.

Therefore, the perimeter of $\triangle ABC$ is 5 + 5 + 6 = 16, (C).

Perimeter and Area of Rectangles

The *area* of a rectangle is the width times the length. In a square, there is no difference between length and width. To find the *perimeter* of either a rectangle or a square, simply add the lengths of the four sides.

Determine the perimeter and area of rectangles and squares in one-step and multi-step problems.

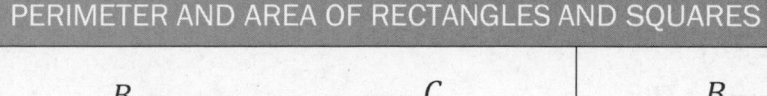

PERIMETER AND AREA OF RECTANGLES AND SQUARES

$$\overline{AB} \cong \overline{CD}; \ \overline{BC} \cong \overline{AD}$$

$$\angle A = \angle B = \angle C = \angle D = 90°$$

$$\text{Perimeter}_{\text{rectangle}} = 2(\text{width}) + 2(\text{length})$$
$$= 2w + 2l$$
$$= 2(w + l)$$

$$\text{Area}_{\text{rectangle}} = (w)(l)$$

$$\overline{AB} \cong \overline{CD} \cong \overline{BC} \cong \overline{AD}$$

$$\angle A = \angle B = \angle C = \angle D = 90°$$

$$\text{Perimeter}_{\text{square}} = 4(\text{side}) = 4s$$

$$\text{Area}_{\text{square}} = (s)(s) = s^2$$

Examples:

What is the perimeter of the figure below?

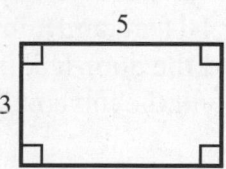

F. 8   H. 14   K. 16
G. 12   J. 15

The unlabeled sides are equal to the lengths of the opposite parallel sides, so the total perimeter is 2(3) + 2(5) = 6 + 10 = 16, (K).

If the perimeter of a rectangle is 68 yards and the width is 48 feet, what is the length?

A. 10 yards   C. 20 feet   E. 54 feet
B. 18 feet   D. 46 feet

Begin by converting the given perimeter to feet: $68 \ \text{yards} \cdot \dfrac{3 \ \text{feet}}{1 \ \text{yard}} = 204 \ \text{feet}$.

Now, use the perimeter formula to solve for the missing dimension:

$$\text{Perimeter} = 2l + 2w$$
$$204 = 2l + 2(48)$$
$$2l = 204 - 96 = 108$$
$$l = \frac{108}{2} = 54 \text{ feet}$$

If the diagonal of a square is $5\sqrt{2}$, what is the area of the square?

F. 5	H. 25	K. 35
G. 20	J. 30	

The diagonal of a square is the hypotenuse of the two isosceles triangles created inside the square by the presence of the diagonal. The two sides of the square are the same length, s, and the length of the hypotenuse is given as $5\sqrt{2}$. Use the Pythagorean theorem to find the length of the sides:

$$s^2 + s^2 = \left(5\sqrt{2}\right)^2 \Rightarrow 2s^2 = 50 \Rightarrow s = \sqrt{25} = 5$$

Now, solve for the area of the square:

$$\text{Area} = s^2 = 5^2 = 25$$

A painter is hired to paint a room that has two walls that measure 8 feet by 12 feet, a third wall that measures 8 feet by 10 feet, and a fourth wall that measures 8 feet by 4 feet. The room has no window, and the door will be painted, too. If the painter charges $1.50 per square foot, how much will the job cost?

A. $213	C. $304	E. $456
B. $180	D. $327	

Determine the square footage for each of the four walls and sum them:

$$
\begin{aligned}
&\text{Wall 1: } (8)(12) = 96\\
&\text{Wall 2: } (8)(12) = 96\\
&\text{Wall 3: } (8)(10) = 80\\
+\ &\underline{\text{Wall 4: } (8)(4)\ \ = 32}\\
&\qquad\qquad\quad 304 \text{ square feet}
\end{aligned}
$$

And since the painter charges $1.50 per square foot, the total cost is:

$$304 \text{ sq. ft.} \cdot \frac{\$1.50}{\text{sq. ft.}} = \$456$$

In the figure below, rectangle $ABCD$ has an area of 15. What is the length of the diagonal $\overline{AC}$?

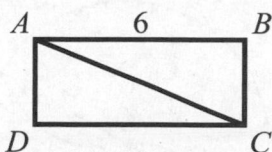

F. 4   H. 6.5   K. 7.5
G. 5   J. 7

The correct answer is (C). First, find the length of the second leg in $\triangle ABC$ from the area of the rectangle:

$$\text{Area} = 15 \Rightarrow \left(\overline{AB}\right)\left(\overline{BC}\right) = 15 \Rightarrow 6\left(\overline{BC}\right) = 15 \Rightarrow \overline{BC} = \frac{15}{6} = \frac{5}{2}$$

Now, find the length of diagonal $\overline{AC}$ by applying the Pythagorean theorem to $\triangle ABC$:

$$\left(\overline{AC}\right)^2 = 6^2 + \left(\frac{5}{2}\right)^2 \Rightarrow \left(\overline{AC}\right)^2 = 36 + \frac{25}{4} \Rightarrow \left(\overline{AC}\right)^2 = \frac{169}{4} \Rightarrow \overline{AC} = \sqrt{\frac{169}{4}} = \frac{13}{2} = 6.5.$$

Circumference and Area of Circles

The perimeter of a circle is known as the circle's circumference. To find the circumference of a circle, multiply two by pi, designated as π, and the radius ($C = 2\pi r$), or multiply π and the diameter ($C = \pi d$). Note that π is approximately 3.14. To find the area of a circle, multiply π and the squared value of the radius ($A = \pi r^2$).

Determine the circumference and area of circles in one-step and multi-step problems.

CIRCUMFERENCE AND AREA OF CIRCLES

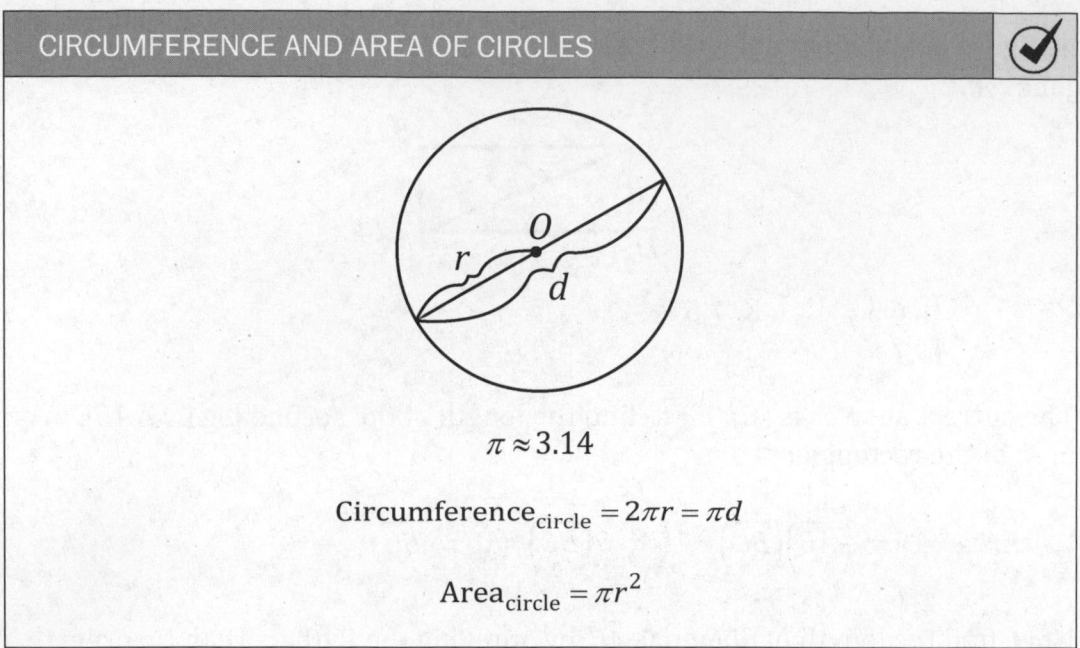

$$\pi \approx 3.14$$

$$\text{Circumference}_{\text{circle}} = 2\pi r = \pi d$$

$$\text{Area}_{\text{circle}} = \pi r^2$$

Examples:

What is the circumference of a circle with a radius of $\dfrac{5}{2}$?

A. $\dfrac{2\pi}{5}$ C. π E. 5π

B. $\dfrac{5\pi}{4}$ D. 2π

Use the formula for the circumference of a circle in terms of its radius:

$$\text{Circumference} = 2\pi r = 2\pi\left(\frac{5}{2}\right) = 5\pi$$

Polly has a round hot tub with a diameter of 6 feet and a depth of 5 feet. She wants to purchase a circular tarp large enough to cover the top of the hot tub with no more than an additional 6 inches overlap on the sides. Of the following available round tarp sizes, which one should she buy?

F. 24 square feet   J. 40 square feet
G. 28 square feet   K. 44 square feet
H. 36 square feet

Note that the depth of the tub is irrelevant. The minimum required area is the area of a circle of diameter 6 feet and the maximum required area is the area of a circle of diameter 7 feet (6 feet plus 0.5 feet on each side):

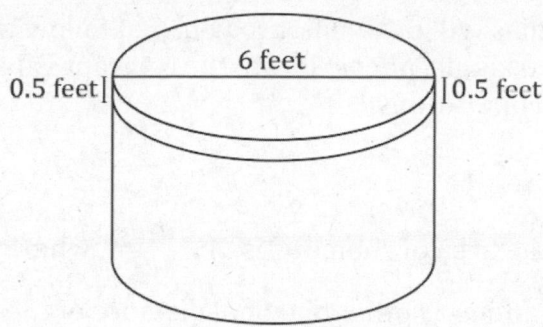

$$\text{Minimum Area } = \pi r^2 = \pi\left(\frac{d}{2}\right)^2 = \pi\left(\frac{6}{2} \text{ feet}\right)^2 = 9\pi \text{ square feet} \approx 28.3 \text{ square feet}$$

$$\text{Maximum Area } = \pi r^2 = \pi\left(\frac{d}{2}\right)^2 = \pi(\frac{7}{2} \text{ feet})^2 = \frac{49}{4}\pi \text{ square feet} \approx$$

38.5 square feet

The only tarp that falls within these measurements is (H), 36 square feet.

Use Geometric Formulas

Often, items will provide the necessary geometric formula and all the necessary information to solve for the required measurement. These formulas may be familiar, such as the area of a triangle, or more obscure, such as the area of a rhombus. Regardless of the formula given, the strategy is the same: plug in the given information into the formula and solve for the unknown measurement.

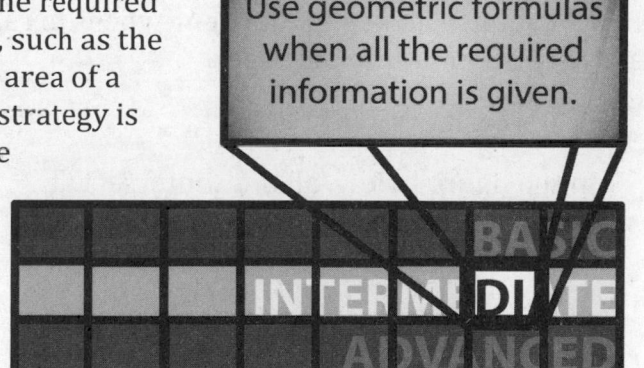

Use geometric formulas when all the required information is given.

Example:

The formula for calculating the area of a triangle is $A = \frac{1}{2}bh$, where b is the base and h is the height. If a triangle has a base of 10 and a height of 8, what is the area of the triangle?

A. 2   C. 18   E. 80
B. 9   D. 40

The best approach to the problem is just to substitute the values given into the formula and perform the indicated operations: $\text{Area} = \frac{(b)(h)}{2} = \frac{(8)(10)}{2} = 40$, (D).

Again, not all geometry formulas will be familiar to you. Just follow the same procedure we used for finding the area of a triangle, above: locate the relevant values, plug them into the formula, and do the indicated operations.

Example:

The formula for finding the area of rhombus is $A = \dfrac{d_1 d_2}{2}$, where d_1 is one diagonal distance of the rhombus and d_2 is other diagonal distance of the rhombus. If a rhombus has diagonals of lengths 4 and 6, what is the area of the rhombus?

F. 3   H. 6   K. 12
G. 4   J. 7

Just substitute the values given into the formula and do the required operations:

$$\text{Area} = \frac{d_1 d_2}{2} = \frac{(4)(6)}{2} = \frac{24}{2} = 12, \text{ (K)}.$$

Perimeter and Area of Composite Figures

Problems asking you to find the perimeter of composite shapes with unknown side lengths require you to first determine the unknown lengths from the given information and then calculate the perimeter. The key to this item-type is to recognize that given lengths serve multiple purposes.

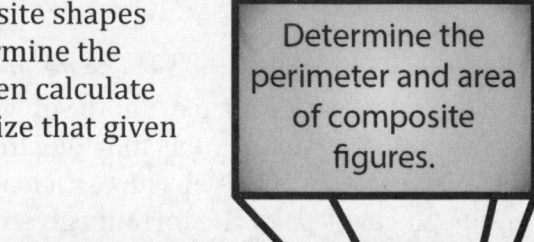

Determine the perimeter and area of composite figures.

Examples:

In the figure below, all lines intersect at right angles. What is the perimeter of the figure?

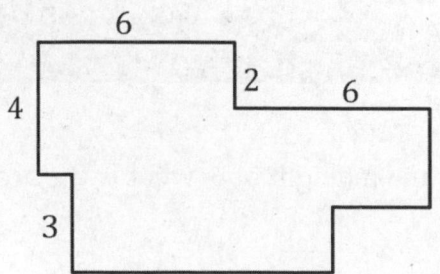

A. 21   C. 42   E. Cannot be determined from the given information
B. 38   D. 84

The correct answer is (B). While the figure does not give the lengths of all the sides, this information is not necessary. The trick is to recognize that the lengths of the sides on the left of the figure must equal those of the sides on the right, and the lengths of the sides on the top of the figure must equal those on the bottom. Therefore, the total perimeter is equal to 2(4 + 3) + 2(6 + 6) = 2(7) + 2(12) = 14 + 24 = 38.

In the figure below, *ABCD* is a square and *CDE* is a right triangle. If $\overline{BC} = 12$ inches and $\overline{DE} = 16$ inches, what is the perimeter of the combined figure *ABCED*?

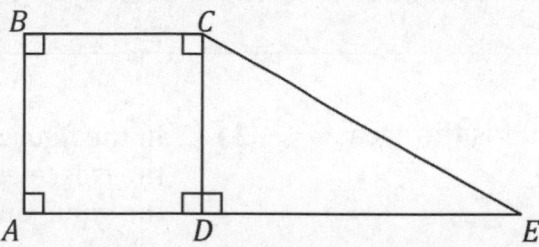

F. 48
G. 50

H. 72
J. 77

K. 153

Since the square and the triangle share a side, and the sides of a square are equal, the height of the triangle is 12 inches. Since the legs of the triangle are multiples of 3 and 4 (12 = (3)(4) and 16 = (4)(4)), the triangle is a Pythagorean triple: the hypotenuse is equal to (5)(4) = 20. (The length of the hypotenuse can also be found by directly applying the Pythagorean theorem.) The total perimeter of the composite figure is 12 + 12 + 12 + 16 + 20 = 72 inches, (H).

In the figure below, *BCDE* is a square with an area of 4. What is the perimeter of △*ABE* ?

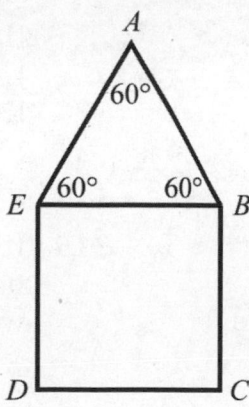

A. 3
B. 4

C. 6
D. 8

E. 12

The correct answer is (C). The only information given in the item is the area of the square. Notice that one side of the square is also a side of the triangle. Since the square's area is 4, the side of the square is 2 ($area_{square} = s^2 = 4 \Rightarrow s = \sqrt{4} = 2$).

Furthermore, $\triangle ABE$ has three 60° angles, so it is an equilateral triangle and the three sides are of equal length. Thus, the triangle's perimeter is $3s = 3(2) = 6$.

EXERCISE 9

DIRECTIONS: Choose the correct answer to each of the following items. Answers are on page 814.

211. In the figure below, what is the area of the triangle?

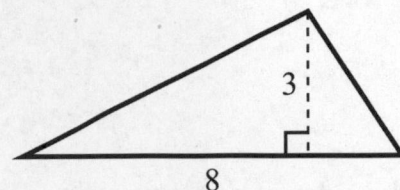

A. 3   C. 12   E. 24
B. 6   D. 18

212. In the figure below, what is the area of the triangle?

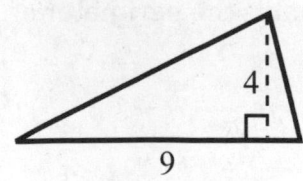

F. 6   H. 15   K. 24
G. 12   J. 18

213. What is the area of a right triangle with legs of lengths 4 and 5?

A. 6   C. 12   E. 24
B. 10   D. 20

214. In the figure below, the perimeter of the isosceles triangle is 24. What is the value of x?

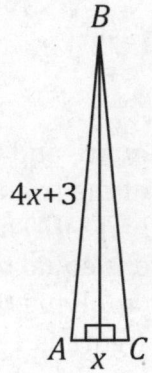

F. 2

G. $\dfrac{9}{4}$

H. 3

J. 4

K. Cannot be determined from the given information.

215. If the length of a rectangle is 12 inches and the width is 4 inches, what is the perimeter?

A. 16 inches   D. 36 inches
B. 24 inches   E. 48 inches
C. 32 inches

216. A swimming pool measuring 22 feet long by 16 feet wide is completely surrounded by a fence. How long is the fence?

F. 38 feet   J. 76 feet
G. 52 feet   K. 352 feet
H. 67 feet

217. In the figure below, what is the area, in square meters, of the rectangle?

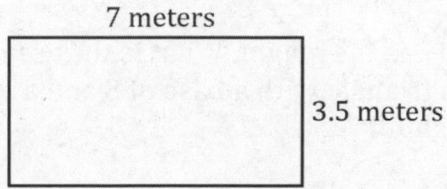

7 meters

3.5 meters

A. 21.0   C. 30.0   E. 49.0
B. 24.5   D. 35.5

218. The length of a rectangle is equal to twice its width. If the width of the rectangle is 5 centimeters, what is the area of the rectangle?

F. 25 cm²   H. 75 cm²   K. 200 cm²
G. 50 cm²   J. 150 cm²

219. If each of the following rectangles has an area of 6, which one has a width of $\frac{2}{3}$? (Note: Figures not drawn to scale.)

A. $\frac{2}{3}$ width

D. 6   width

B. $\frac{3}{2}$ width

E. 9   width

C. 3   width

220. If the area of the rectangle shown below is equal to 1, then $l =$?

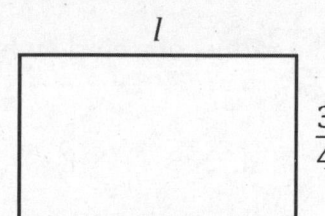

l

$\frac{3}{4}$

F. $\frac{4}{9}$ H. $\frac{4}{3}$ K. $\frac{9}{4}$
G. 1   J. 2

221. If the radius of a circle is 5, what is the circumference?

A. 5π C. 15π E. 24π
B. 10π D. 20π

222. If the radius of a circle is 3, what is the area?

    F. π H. 6π K. 12π
    G. 3π J. 9π

223. If the diameter of a circle is 8, what is the area?

    A. 16π C. 10π E. 4π
    B. 12π D. 8π

224. What is the radius of a circle with an area of 49?

    F. 7   H. $\dfrac{7}{\sqrt{\pi}}$ K. π^2

    G. 7π J. $\dfrac{7}{\pi}$

225. A circle has an area of $36\pi^3$. What is the radius of the circle?

    A. 6   C. $6\pi^2$ E. $6\pi^4$
    B. 6π D. $6\pi^3$

226. What is the radius of a circle whose area is 12π?

    F. 40π H. $2\sqrt{3}$ K. 3
    G. 1   J. 2

227. A circle has an area of $\dfrac{49\pi}{4}$. What is the diameter of the circle?

    A. 49   C. $\pi\sqrt{7}$ E. $\dfrac{7\sqrt{\pi}}{2}$

    B. 7π D. 7

228. At the county fair, the minimum area requirements for a circular holding pen is 24π square meters. What is the minimum radius, in meters, of such a holding pen?

    F. $\sqrt{6}$ H. 4   K. $4\sqrt{6}$
    G. 2   J. $2\sqrt{6}$

229. The formula for finding the area of a triangle is $A = \dfrac{bh}{2}$, where b is the base and h is the height. What is the area of a triangle with a base of 8 and a height of 7?

    A. 14   C. 30   E. 106
    B. 28   D. 56

230. The formula for finding the area of a rectangle is $A = wl$, where w is the width of the rectangle and l is the length. If a rectangle has a width of 7 and a length of 12, what is the area of the rectangle?

    F. 5   H. 38   K. 84
    G. 19   J. 42

231. The formula for finding the area of a parallelogram is $A = bh$, where b is the base, and h is the height. What is the area of a parallelogram with a base of 8 and a height of 6?

    A. 12   C. 24   E. 48
    B. 14   D. 28

232. What is the volume of a cube with an edge of length 3? ($V = e^3$, where e is the length of the edge)

    F. 3   H. 9   K. 27
    G. 6   J. 18

233. A rectangular solid has a width of 2, a length of 3, and a height of 2.5. What is the volume of the rectangular solid? ($V = wlh$, where w is the width, l is the length, and h is the height.)

    A. 4.5   C. 7.5   E. 15
    B. 6   D. 12

234. The formula for finding the area of a trapezoid is $A = \left(\dfrac{b_1 + b_2}{2}\right)(h)$, where b_1 and b_2 are the bases of the trapezoid and h the height. If a trapezoid has bases of 4 and 5 and a height of 3, what is the area of the trapezoid?

    F. 6   H. 13.5   K. 60
    G. 12   J. 30

235. The formula for finding the volume of a right circular cylinder with a radius r and height h is $V = \pi r^2 h$. What is the volume of a cylinder with a height of 10 and a radius of 4?

    A. 14π C. 160π E. $4{,}000\pi$
    B. 40π D. 400π

236. The formula for the volume of a sphere with radius r is $\dfrac{4\pi r^3}{3}$. If the radius of a soccer ball is 4 inches, what is the approximate volume of the ball in cubic inches?

    F. 120   H. 268   K. 768
    G. 180   J. 350

237. What is the perimeter of the figure below?

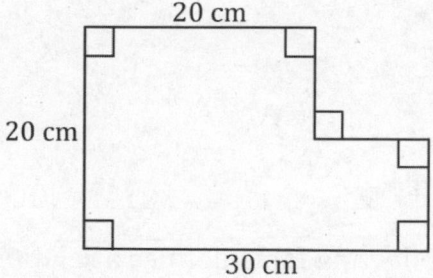

    A.   70 cm
    B.   75 cm
    C.   100 cm
    D.   600 cm
    E.   Cannot be determined from the given information

Functions

Evaluate Quadratic and Polynomial Functions

Function notation is used to rewrite a mathematical equation that represents a relationship between two variables. The relationship can be represented through a list of ordered pairs (x,y), an equation, or a graph.

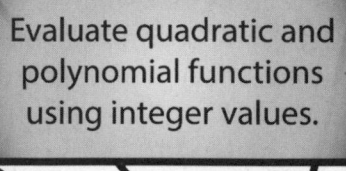
Evaluate quadratic and polynomial functions using integer values.

Example:

The following table defines a relationship through ordered pairs:

Weekday Meals	
Day of the Week	Meal
Monday	Turkey Meatloaf
Tuesday	Grilled Cheese and Pickles
Wednesday	Roasted Lemon Pepper Cod
Thursday	Stuffed Pork Chops
Friday	BBQ Chicken

The table defines the relationship between elements of the two groups "day of the week" (domain) and "meal" (range). According to the table, there are exactly five ordered pairs (day of the week, meal), where each pair represents the information in a single row of the table.

Our world is filled with relationships. Listing ordered pairs is one way of representing some of these relationships.

Examples:

A group of five friends purchased tickets for a Chicago White Sox game at US Cellular Field. Rohan's seat is in section 124, row 5, seat 1, Omar's seat is in section 124, row 5, seat 2, James' seat is in section 124, row 5 seat 3, Jack's seat is in section 124, row 5, seat 4, and Andrew's seat is in section 124, row 5, seat 5. Thus, the relationship between attendee (domain) and seat (range) represents five ordered pairs.

On a singing reality show, each one of seven singers in the contest is assigned a text message number. A viewer can vote for his favorite singer by texting the word "VOTE" to that singer's assigned number during the show. Thus, the relationship between singer (domain) and text message number (range) represents seven ordered pairs.

Mathematical Relationships

Unlike the examples above, mathematical relationships can be summarized by mathematical equations.

Example:

$$y = x^2 - 6$$

This equation describes the relationship between the elements in the set of x (domain) and the elements in the set of y (range). Thus, possible solutions include ordered pairs such as (–1,–5), (0,–6), and (2,–2).

Function Notation

Function notation uses the symbol $f(x)$ to represent the value returned by the function upon the input, that is, the element in the second set of values that is matched up with the element in the first set of values.

Examples:

$$f(x) = x^3 - 4$$

In this mathematical relationship, $f(x)$, read as "f of x," represents the matching element for any x selected from the first set of values.

What is the value of $f(2)$?

$$f(2) = (2)^3 - 4 = 4$$

In other words, the value 2 in the first set of values is matched to 4 from the second set of values.

What is the value of $f(-3)$?

$$f(-3) = (-3)^3 - 4 = -31$$

What is the value of $f(0)$?

$$f(0) = (0)^3 - 4 = -4$$

Mathematical relationships can also be represented graphically. We can draw a graph of $f(x) = x^3 - 4$ to show all the relationships of the function:

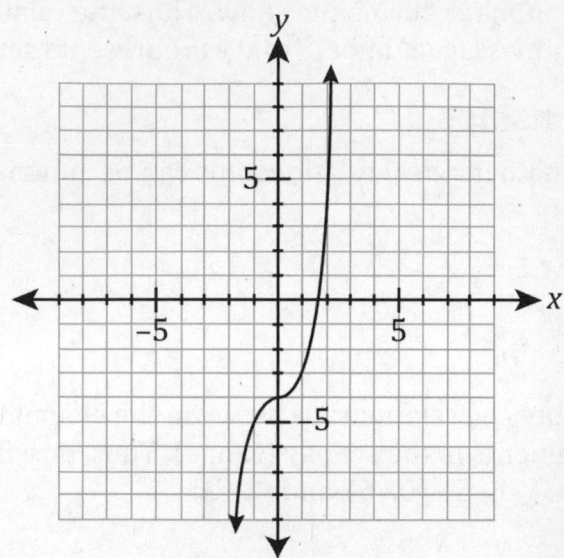

To summarize, a function is a set of ordered pairs (x,y) such that for each value of x, there is exactly one value of y. For every input, x, there is exactly one output, y. We say that "y is a function of x," which is written using a letter to designate the function: $y = f(x)$ or $y = g(x)$, which, for example, might stand for $y = f(x) = 3x - 2$ or $y = g(x) = 5x + 1$. The set of possible values for x is called the **domain** of the function. The set of corresponding values for y is called the **range** of the function.

Evaluating Quadratic Functions

Examples:

If $f(x) = -x^2 + 5$, what is $f(-2)$?

A. –9   C. –1   E. 9
B. –3   D. 1

The correct answer is (D):

$$f(-2) = -(-2)^2 + 5 = -(4) + 5 = 1$$

If $f(x) = -x^2 + x + 3$, what is $f(-2)$?

F. –5   H. 5   K. 24
G. –3   J. 9

The correct answer is (G):

$$f(-2) = -(-2)^2 + (-2) + 3 = -4 - 2 + 3 = -3$$

If $f(x) = 2x - 7$ and $g(x) = x^2 - 3$, what is the value of $f(g(-1))$?

A. –15   C. –17   E. 78
B. –11   D. 18

The correct answer is (B):

$$g(-1) = (-1)^2 - 3 = 1 - 3 = -2$$

$$f(-2) = 2(-2) - 7 = -11$$

$$f(g(-1)) = -11$$

Evaluating Polynomial Functions

Examples:

If $f(x) = 2x^2 - x - x^0$, then $f(4) = ?$

F. 59   H. 27   K. 11
G. 28   J. 12

The correct answer is (H):

$$f(x) = 2x^2 - x - x^0$$
$$f(4) = 2(4)^2 - (4) - (4)^0$$
$$= 2(16) - 4 - 1$$
$$= 27$$

If $f(x) = 3x^3 + x^2 - x$, then $f(-2) = ?$

A. –24   C. 20   E. 26
B. –18   D. 24

The correct answer is (B):

$$f(x) = 3(-2)^3 + (-2)^2 - (-2) = 3(-8) + 4 + 2 = -24 + 4 + 2 = -18$$

If $f(x) = -x^5 - x^3 + x$, then $f\left(\dfrac{1}{2}\right) = ?$

F. $-\dfrac{1}{38}$ H. $\dfrac{13}{32}$ K. 38

G. $\dfrac{11}{32}$ J. 32

The correct answer is (G):

$$f\left(\frac{1}{2}\right)=-\left(\frac{1}{2}\right)^{5}-\left(\frac{1}{2}\right)^{3}+\frac{1}{2}=-\left(\frac{1}{32}\right)-\left(\frac{1}{8}\right)+\frac{1}{2}=-\frac{1}{32}-\frac{4}{32}+\frac{16}{32}=\frac{11}{32}$$

Trigonometry

For every right triangle, lengths of sides and measures of angles can be found using the sine, cosine, and tangent functions. These functions are the functions used in right triangle trigonometry.

Express basic trigonometric relationships for an angle in a right triangle.

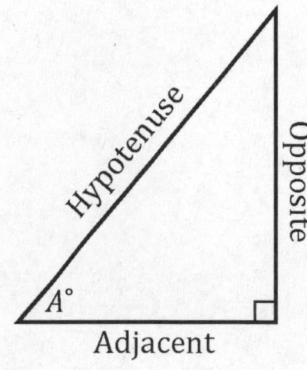

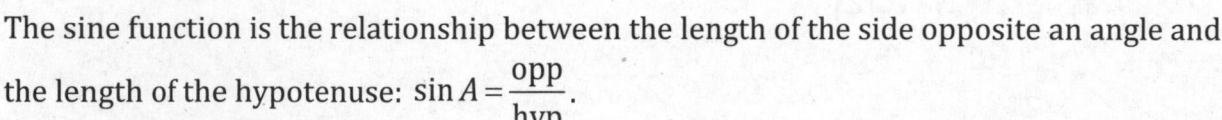

The sine function is the relationship between the length of the side opposite an angle and the length of the hypotenuse: $\sin A=\dfrac{\text{opp}}{\text{hyp}}$.

The cosine function is the relationship between the length of the side adjacent an angle and the length of the hypotenuse: $\cos A=\dfrac{\text{adj}}{\text{hyp}}$.

The tangent function is the relationship between the length of the side opposite an angle and the length of the side adjacent to the same angle: $\tan A=\dfrac{\text{opp}}{\text{adj}}$.

To find the length of a side or an angle measure, determine which side is adjacent to an angle and which side is opposite that angle. Then plug those values into the correct trigonometric function.

Examples:

In the figure below, *a* = ?

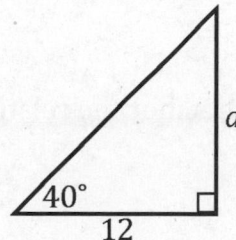

Label the sides in relation to the 40° angle; label side *a* "opp" (opposite) because it is opposite the 40° angle, label 12 "adj" (adjacent) because it is adjacent to the 40° angle.

Next, set up an equation using the tangent function, since the tangent function uses the opposite and adjacent sides, and solve for the unknown.

$$\tan 40° = \frac{a}{12} \Rightarrow a = 12 \tan 40°$$

In the figure below, *b* = ?

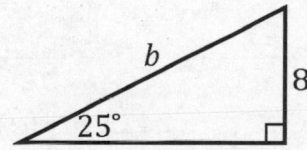

The two labeled sides are the side opposite the given angle and the hypotenuse, so use the sine function.

$$\sin 25° = \frac{8}{b} \Rightarrow b \sin 25° = 8 \Rightarrow b = \frac{8}{\sin 25°}$$

In the figure below, *c* = ?

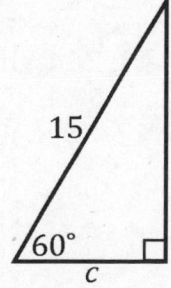

The two labeled sides are the side adjacent the given angle and the hypotenuse, so use the cosine function.

$$\cos 60° = \frac{c}{15} \Rightarrow c = 15 \cos 60°$$

The acronym SOH-CAH-TOA helps to remember the relationships for the sine, cosine, and tangent functions.

$$\text{Sin} = \frac{\text{Opp}}{\text{Hyp}}; \text{SOH}$$

$$\text{Cos} = \frac{\text{Adj}}{\text{Hyp}}; \text{CAH}$$

$$\text{Tan} = \frac{\text{Opp}}{\text{Adj}}; \text{TOA}$$

EXERCISE 10

DIRECTIONS: Choose the correct answer to each of the following items. Answers are on page 815.

238. If $f(x) = 2x - 4$, then $f(-3) = ?$

F. –10   H. 2   K. 12
G. –7   J. 10

239. If $f(x) = 0.25x - 11$, then $f(8) = ?$

A. –13   C. –7   E. 3
B. –9   D. –3

240. If $f(x) = 3(-5x - 1)$, then $f(-2) = ?$

F. –33   H. 14   K. 33
G. 12   J. 27

241. If $f(x) = 2x^2 + 5$, then $f(-3) = ?$

A. –13   C. 23   E. 75
B. 17   D. 41

242. If $f(x) = (-x)^3 - 7$, then $f(-4) = ?$

F. –71   H. 9   K. 71
G. –19   J. 57

243. If $f(x) = 5x^3 - 8x + 6$, then $f(-2) = ?$

A. –19   C. –2   E. 62
B. –18   D. 20

244. If $f(x) = x^3 + 2x^2 - x$, then $f(5) = ?$

F. 17   H. 55   K. 220
G. 30   J. 170

245. If $f(x) = -3x^4 + 2x^3 - x^0 + 6$, then $f(-3) = ?$

A. -292 C. -184 E. 91
B. -288 D. -91

246. If $f(x) = \left(\dfrac{12 - x^3}{\frac{1}{16}} \right)$, then $f(-2) = ?$

F. $\dfrac{5}{4}$ H. 128 K. 320
G. 64 J. 256

247. If $f(x) = \dfrac{x|3x|}{4}$, then $f(-5) = ?$

A. $-\dfrac{75}{4}$ C. 10 E. 75

B. $\dfrac{5}{2}$ D. $\dfrac{75}{4}$

248. In the figure below, $a = ?$

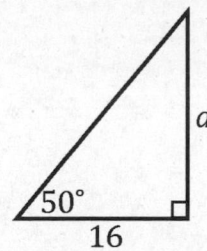

F. $16 \sin 50°$ J. $16 \tan 40°$
G. $16 \cos 50°$ K. $16 \cos 40°$
H. $16 \tan 50°$

249. In the figure below, $b = ?$

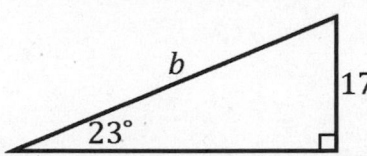

A. $\dfrac{17}{\sin 23°}$ D. $17 \cos 23°$

B. $\dfrac{17}{\cos 23°}$ E. $17 \tan 23°$

C. $17 \sin 23°$

250. In the figure below, $c = ?$

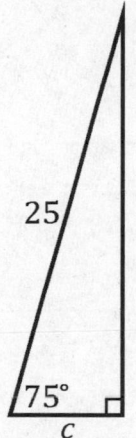

F. $25 \sin 75°$ J. $25 \tan 15°$
G. $25 \cos 75°$ K. $25 \cos 15°$
H. $25 \tan 75°$

ADVANCED | Basic Manipulations

Manipulation problems at the advanced level require the use of the same arithmetic skills that are covered in the basic and intermediate levels: percentages, ratios, proportions, averages, etc. But advanced level items are more complex. Typically, they require two, three, or even four steps, and the values involved can include fractions and decimals as well as integers.

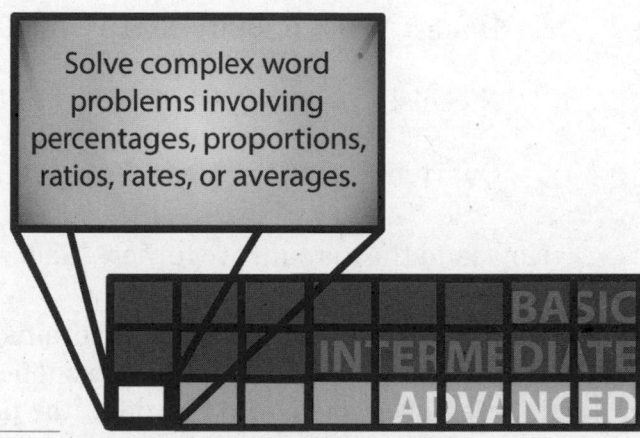

Solve complex word problems involving percentages, proportions, ratios, rates, or averages.

Examples:

SCHEDULE FOR COMPLETING PROJECT X					
	Mon.	Tue.	Wed.	Thu.	Fri.
Percentage of work to be completed each day	8%	17%	25%	33%	17%

By the end of which day is $\frac{3}{4}$ of the work scheduled to be completed?

A. Monday
B. Tuesday
C. Wednesday
D. Thursday
E. Friday

First, $\frac{3}{4}$ is equal to 75%. Next, find the day on which 75% of the work will have been completed:

Mon.: 8%

Tue.: 8% + 17% = 25%

Wed.: 25% + 25% = 50%

Thu.: 50% + 33% = 83%

And 83% > 75%, so the correct answer is (D).

A bag contains 800 coins. Of these, 10% are dimes, 30% are nickels, and the rest are quarters. What is the total face value of all the coins in the bag?

F. $32.00

G. $48.00

H. $80.00

J. $140.00

K. $480.00

Calculate the amount for each coin type:

Dimes: $(10\% \text{ of } 800) \cdot \$0.10 = \$8.00$

Nickels: $(30\% \text{ of } 800) \cdot \$0.05 = \$12.00$

Quarters: $(100\% - [10\% + 30\%] \text{ of } 800) \cdot \$0.25 = \$120.00$

Now, add the amounts together: $\$8.00 + \$12.00 + \$120.00 = \$140.00$, (J).

A wading pool is equipped with two drains, Drain A and Drain B. When the pool is filled to capacity and both drains are opened, the pool empties in 20 minutes. When Drain A is closed and Drain B is open, the pool empties in 30 minutes. If Drain B is closed and Drain A is open, how many minutes will it take to empty the pool?

A. 20 minutes

B. 30 minutes

C. 50 minutes

D. 60 minutes

E. 120 minutes

This item involves rates. Drain B works at the rate of 1 pool full of water every 30 minutes: $\dfrac{1}{30}$. Drain A and Drain B work at the combined rate of 1 pool full of water every 20 minutes: $\dfrac{1}{20}$. Therefore:

$$\text{Rate}_A + \text{Rate}_B = \text{Rate}_{A+B}$$

$$\text{Rate}_A + \frac{1}{30} = \frac{1}{20}$$

$$\text{Rate}_A = \frac{1}{20} - \frac{1}{30} = \frac{3(1)}{3(20)} - \frac{2(1)}{2(30)} = \frac{1}{60}$$

So Drain A working alone takes 60 minutes to empty the pool, (D).

Emily works in a food manufacturing facility where she operates a machine to mix corn flour and wheat flour in quantities to yield 1,000 pounds of mixture that is 15 percent corn flour by weight. If the required amount of corn flour is added and then a mechanical malfunction prevents 250 pounds of the wheat flour from being added, what percent, by weight, of the resulting mixture is corn flour?

F. 5%   H. 25%   K. 60%

G. 20%   J. $33\frac{1}{3}\%$

The mixture should contain 150 pounds of corn flour and 850 pounds of wheat flour; but because of the malfunction, it contains 150 pounds of corn flour and 600 pounds of wheat flour. So, the concentration of corn flour is $\dfrac{150}{(150+600)} = 20\%$, (G).

The town of Merryville collects a sales tax of m percent on all purchases, and Newtown collects a sales tax of n percent on all purchases. If the sales tax collected on a $300 purchase by Merryville is $3.00 more than the sales tax collected by Newton, what is the difference between the tax rate of Merryville and the tax rate of Newtown?

A. 0.5 cents per dollar
B. 1 cent per dollar
C. 1.5 cents per dollar
D. 3 cents per dollar
E. 60 cents per dollar

The sale tax in each town on a $300 item is $\dfrac{m}{100}(300) = 3m$ and $\dfrac{n}{100}(300) = 3n$, respectively. Since the difference is $3, $3m - 3n = 3$, so $m - n = 1$. Therefore, the difference between tax rate m and tax rate n is 1%. And a difference of 1% in terms of cents per dollar is 1 cent per dollar, (B).

It takes Maxine 15 minutes less to drive from Hooverton to Grantville at an average speed of 60 miles per hour than at an average speed of 50 miles per hour. What is the distance, in miles, that Maxine drives from Hooverton to Grantville?

F. 12.5 miles   J. 50 miles
G. 23 miles   K. 75 miles
H. 25 miles

Since the distance traveled is the same regardless of speed (or rate), set up an equation for $r_1 t_1 = r_2 t_2$:

$$\left(\frac{50 \text{ miles}}{\text{hour}}\right)(t \text{ hours}) = \left(\frac{60 \text{ miles}}{\text{hour}}\right)(t - 0.25)\text{hour}$$

$$50t = 60t - 15$$

$$10t = 15$$

$$t = 1.5 \text{ hours}$$

So, traveling 1.5 hours at 50 miles per hour, Maxine travels

$$1.5 \text{ hours} \cdot \frac{50 \text{ miles}}{\text{hour}} = 75 \text{ miles}, \text{ (K)}.$$

One year, 1% of the athletes playing a professional sport used and tested positive for a banned substance. However, 20% of the athletes who used the banned substance did not test positive. What percentage of the athletes playing the sport used the banned substance?

A. 0.20%   C. 1.21%   E. 21.00%
B. 0.21%   D. 1.25%

If t is the number of athletes in the population, and b is the number who took the banned substance, then $0.01t$ took the substance and tested positive while $0.2b$ took the substance and did not test positive. Thus, $0.8b$ took the substance and tested positive, and $0.8b = 0.01t$. Therefore, $\dfrac{b}{t} = \dfrac{0.01}{0.8} = 0.0125 = 1.25\%$, (D).

A building owner rents part of the ground floor to a jewelry store for $720 per month. The store's owner wants to rent an additional 30 square feet at the same rate per square foot. If the rent for the additional space will be $45 per month, what is the number of square feet occupied by the jewelry store <u>before</u> the new space is added?

F. 450   H. 510   K. 600
G. 480   J. 540

Find the monthly rent per square foot: $\dfrac{\$45}{30 \text{ sq. ft.}} = \$1.50/\text{sq. ft.}$ Using that figure,

find the number of square feet in the original configuration: $\dfrac{\$720}{\$1.50/\text{sq. ft.}} =$

480 sq. ft., (G).

One-third of a 72,000 square foot building project was originally set aside for "public use" with the rest designated as "retail use." If the originally planned square footage is reduced by 25% but the number of square feet designated for "public use" remains unchanged, what will be the ratio of the number of square feet designated for "public use" to the number of square feet now designated for "retail use?"

A. $\dfrac{1}{4}$ C. $\dfrac{1}{2}$ E. $\dfrac{4}{5}$

B. $\dfrac{1}{3}$ D. $\dfrac{3}{5}$

Originally, $\dfrac{1}{3}$ of 72,000 or 24,000 square feet was designated as "public use."

Reducing the overall project by 25% leaves $(0.75)(72,000) = 54,000$ square feet. "Public use" is still 24,000 square feet, so "retail use" is now: $54,000 - 24,000 = 30,000$ square feet. And the ratio of "public use" to "retail use" is $\dfrac{24,000}{30,000} = \dfrac{4}{5}$, (E).

On Monday, the price of a share of stock of MegaPix, Inc. dropped by 10%. On Tuesday, the price of a share rose by 10%. What was the net change in the price of the stock?

F. A decrease of 99%
G. A decrease of 1%
H. No net change
J.   An increase of 1%
K. An increase of 99%

Let P be the original price of the stock. A 10% drop would reduce the price to $0.9P$. Then, an increase of 10% would add $0.1(0.9P) = 0.09P$ to the new price: $0.9P + 0.09P = 0.99P$. Therefore, the final price is 99% of the original price, which indicates a decrease of 1%, (G).

In the figure below, *PQRS* is a rectangle, and *T* is a point on $\overline{PQ}$. What is the ratio of the area of the shaded portion of the figure to the area of the unshaded portion of the figure?

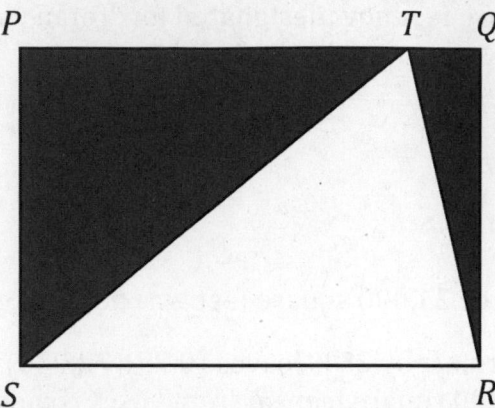

A. $\dfrac{1}{4}$ C. $\dfrac{1}{2}$ E. Cannot be determined from the given information

B. $\dfrac{1}{3}$ D. 1

The base of the triangle that defines the unshaded portion is the length of the rectangle, and the altitude of the triangle is equal to the width of the rectangle.

Therefore, $\dfrac{\text{Area}_{\text{shaded}}}{\text{Area}_{\text{unshaded}}} = \dfrac{\text{Area}_{\text{rectangle}} - \text{Area}_{\text{triangle}}}{\text{Area}_{\text{triangle}}} = \dfrac{bh - \dfrac{1}{2}bh}{\dfrac{1}{2}bh} = \dfrac{\dfrac{1}{2}bh}{\dfrac{1}{2}bh} = 1$, (D).

EXERCISE 1

DIRECTIONS: Choose the correct answer to each of the following items. Answers are on page 815.

1. A car owner insures her car for 80% of the car's fair market value. The premium for the policy is $348, calculated as 2.5% of the amount for which the car is insured. What is the fair market value of the car?

   A. $19,000　　D. $17,400
   B. $18,400　　E. $13,920
   C. $18,000

2. In a school in which 40% of the enrolled students are boys, 80% of the boys are present on a certain day. If 1,152 boys are present, which of the following equals the total school enrollment?

   F. 1,440　　J. 5,400
   G. 2,880　　K. 5,760
   H. 3,600

3. A salesperson at Quality Paper Company earns commissions based on total sales for the period. For the first $2,000 in sales, no commissions are paid; for the portion of total sales over $2,000 up to (and including) $6,000, a commission of 5% is paid; for the portion of total sales in excess of $6,000, a commission of 8% is paid. What is the commission paid during a period in which sales of a salesperson is $8,000?

   A. $40　　C. $200　　E. $640
   B. $160　　D. $360

4. Mr. Bridges can wash his car in 15 minutes, while his son Dave takes twice as long to do the same job. If they work together, how many minutes will the job take them?

   F. 5　　　　H. 10　　　　K. 30
   G. $7\frac{1}{2}$　　J. $22\frac{1}{2}$

5. A travel agency routinely sells cruises at a discount of 40 percent off the price advertised by the cruise line. If the travel agency offers an additional 25 percent off its already discounted price, what is the travel agency's price for a cruise priced by the cruise line at $3,200?

   A. $2,720　　D. $1,290
   B. $2,080　　E. $1,120
   C. $1,440

6. Molly is deciding which of two job offers to accept. Company X will pay $5,400 a month plus a commission equal to 4 percent of the salesperson's total sales for the month in excess of $60,000. Company Y will pay a commission equal to 6 percent of total sales for the month. For what level of sales would the compensation offered by the two companies be equal?

   F. $78,000　　J. $258,000
   G. $150,000　　K. $545,000
   H. $210,000

7. The ratio of acceptances to rejections sent out by a college is 7 to 36. If an additional 39 rejections are sent out, the ratio of acceptances to rejections will be 7 to 39. How many rejections have been sent out already?

   A. 28   C. 283   E. 1404
   B. 169   D. 468

8. From 1950 to 1960, production of a particular agricultural commodity decreased by 20 percent while the price per bushel of the commodity increased by 20 percent. If total sales of the commodity in 1960 were $6 billion (and the number sold equals the number produced), sales of the commodity, in dollars, in 1950 were approximately:

   F. $2.4 billion.   J. $6.25 billion.
   G. $5.76 billion.   K. $6.4 billion.
   H. $6.0 billion.

9. For the afternoon showing of a film, a theater sold 100 tickets, each of which was either a $7.50 ticket for a child or a $10.00 ticket for an adult. If the theater collected a total of $812.50 for the tickets, how many adult tickets were sold?

   A. 20   C. 40   E. 75
   B. 25   D. 60

10. A $1 million grant is to be divided among four charities, J, K, L, and M. If L and M will each be awarded $125,000 more than K and $325,000 less than J, how much of the grant will be awarded to M?

    F. $75,000   J. $200,000
    G. $125,000   K. $375,000
    H. $175,000

11. In the figure below, $\triangle ABC \sim \triangle DEF$. What is the length of $\overline{AC}$.

    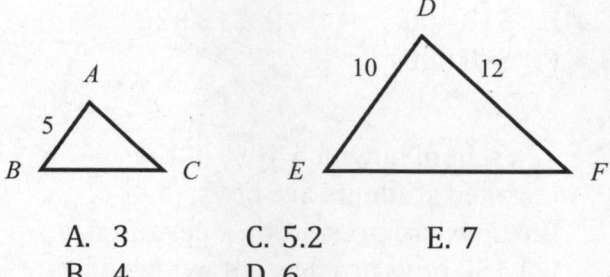

    A. 3   C. 5.2   E. 7
    B. 4   D. 6

12. In the figure below, a circle is inscribed in a square with an area of 324. What is the approximate ratio of the area of the circle to the area of the square?

    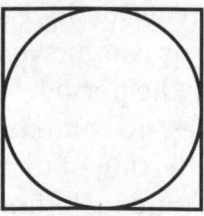

    F. 0.180   H. 0.324   K. 0.785
    G. 0.306   J. 0.330

13. In the figure below, a rectangle, a portion of which is shaded is shown in the coordinate plane. If a point inside the rectangle is selected at random, what is the probability that the point also lies in the shaded region?

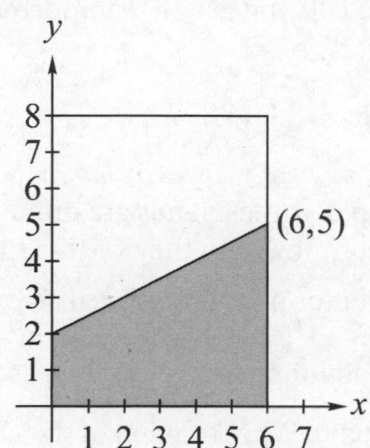

A. $\dfrac{1}{4}$ C. $\dfrac{3}{8}$ E. $\dfrac{1}{2}$

B. $\dfrac{1}{3}$ D. $\dfrac{7}{16}$

14. In calculating the cost of producing the school's yearbook, the editor knows that the fixed set-up cost will be $6,000 and the cost of printing will be $2 per copy. If the yearbook sells for $10 per copy, how many copies must be sold in order to exactly cover the cost of producing and printing the yearbook?

F. 300   H. 750   K. 1,250
G. 600   J. 1,000

15. In a certain community, the property tax is equal to the tax rate applied to the assessed value of the property. If the assessed value of a property is increased by 25 percent while the tax rate is decreased by 25 percent, what is the net effect on the taxes on the property?

A. An increase of 18.75 percent
B. An increase of 6.25 percent
C. No net change
D. A decrease of 6.25 percent
E. A decrease of 18.75 percent

16. Working independently, Machine X can fill an order in 15 hours. Working independently, Machine Y can fill the same order in 10 hours. If Machine X works independently for 12 hours to fill an order and then Machine Y works independently to complete the order, how many hours does it take Machine Y to complete the order?

F. 2   H. $\dfrac{4}{5}$ K. $\dfrac{1}{5}$

G. 1   J. $\dfrac{3}{4}$

17. In the figure below, O is the center of the circle. What is the ratio of the area of the shaded portion of the figure to the area of the unshaded portion of the figure?

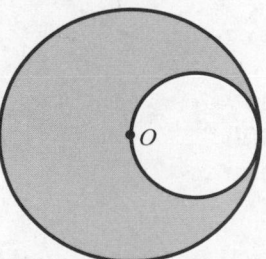

A. 4 : 1   C. 3 : 1   E. 2 : 1
B. π : 1   D. 5 : 2

18. At the close of trading on Tuesday, the price per share of a certain stock was 20 percent less than the price per share at the close of trading on Monday. On Wednesday, the price per share at closing was 25 percent less than that on Tuesday. If on Thursday, the price per share at closing was equal to the closing price on Monday, what was the percent increase in the price per share of the stock from closing Wednesday to closing Thursday?

F. 45%

G. $66\frac{2}{3}$%

H. 75%

J. 145%

K. $166\frac{2}{3}$%

19. The figure below shows the various categories of expenses for Day School. If Capital Improvements totaled approximately $285,000, which of the following is the best approximation of the amount allocated to Student Aid?

BUDGET FOR DAY SCHOOL

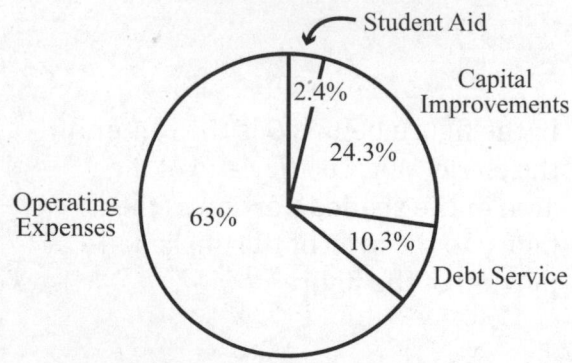

A. $28,000

B. $122,000

C. $300,000

D. $1,220,000

E. $2,800,000

20. Jan works at a clothing store where 60 percent of all the articles are imported and 20 percent of all the articles are priced at $100 or more. If 40 percent of the articles priced at $100 or more are imported, what percent of the articles are priced <u>under</u> $100 and are NOT imported?

F. 28%   H. 8%   K. 2%

G. 12%   J. 4.8%

21. A group of three friends ate dinner at a restaurant. When they settled the check, Peter paid $\frac{4}{5}$ as much as John paid, and John paid $\frac{1}{3}$ as much as Ralph paid. What fraction of the check did John pay?

A. $\frac{24}{5}$

B. $\frac{4}{5}$

C. $\frac{15}{24}$

D. $\frac{1}{3}$

E. $\frac{5}{24}$

22. The pie charts below show the percentage of all employees of a company who earn the amounts shown. What percentage of all employees earn more than $15,000 but not more than $25,000?

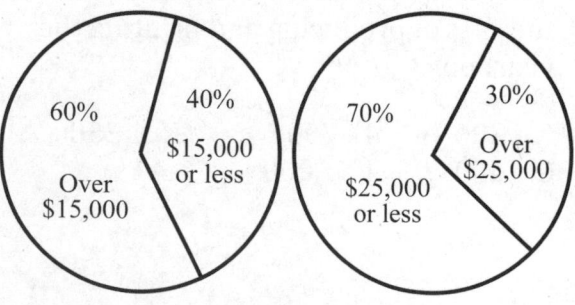

F. 10%

G. 12%

H. 28%

J. 30%

K. 42%

23. According to the data provided in the table below, what was the percent decrease in the number of people who enrolled for the seminar from Week 3 to Week 4?

ENROLLMENTS FOR A ONE-WEEK SEMINAR	
Week Number	Number of Enrollees
1	10
2	25
3	20
4	15
5	30

A. 5   C. 20   E. 50
B. 15   D. 25

24. In one classroom, exactly $\frac{1}{2}$ of the seats are occupied. In another classroom with double the seating capacity of the first, exactly $\frac{3}{4}$ of the seats are occupied. If the students from both rooms are transferred into a third, empty classroom that has a seating capacity exactly equal to the first two combined, what fraction of the seats in the third classroom is occupied?

F. $\frac{1}{4}$ H. $\frac{3}{8}$ K. $\frac{3}{4}$

G. $\frac{1}{3}$ J. $\frac{2}{3}$

25. A certain dairy packing plant has two machines, P and Q, that process milk at constant rates of 30 gallons per minute and 45 gallons per minute, respectively. A day's run of milk can be processed by Machine P operating alone in 6 hours, by Machine Q operating alone in 4 hours, or by both machines operating simultaneously in 2.4 hours. If a day's run of milk is processed using Machine Q alone for half the time and both machines together for half the time, how many hours does it take to complete the run?

A. 1.5   C. 3.75   E. 5.0
B. 3.0   D. 4.2

Probability, Statistics, and Data Analysis

Weighted Averages

In the average problems that appear in the Basic and Intermediate sections of this book, each element in the average is given equal weight. Sometimes, however, averages are created that give greater weight to one component than to another.

Calculate and utilize weighted averages.

BASIC
INTERMEDIATE
ADVANCED

Examples:

Cody bought 4 books that cost $6.00 each and 2 books that cost $3.00 each. What is the average cost of the 6 books?

A. $1.50   C. $5.00   E. $9.00
B. $3.00   D. $7.50

The average cost of the 6 books is not just the average of $6.00 and $3.00, which is $4.50. Cody bought more of the higher priced books, so the average must reflect that fact. Conceptually, you could treat each book as a separate expense:

$$\text{Average} = \frac{\$6 + \$6 + \$6 + \$6 + \$3 + \$3}{6} = \frac{\$30}{6} = \$5, \text{ (C)}.$$

Mathematically, it is simpler to "weight" the two different costs:

$$\text{Average} = \frac{\$6(4) + \$3(2)}{6} = \frac{\$30}{6} = \$5.$$

In your American History course, you will have five quizzes, one mid-term, and a final. Your teacher will give twice as much weight to the final exam as to the mid-term and will weight the mid-term and the average of the five quizzes equally. If your scores on the five quizzes are 80, 90, 87, 83, and 85, your mid-term score is 90, and your final exam score is 95, what will be your final grade in the course?

F. 85   H. 88.75   K. 93.5

G. 87.5   J. 91.25

When you set up the equation for the final grade in the course, make sure that the mid-term is weighted equally with the *average* of the quizzes. The average of the quizzes is:

$$\frac{80+90+87+83+85}{5}=85$$

And the weighted average of the three scores is:

$$\text{Final Grade} = \frac{\text{quiz avg.}+\text{mid term}+(2\cdot\text{final})}{4} \Rightarrow \frac{85+90+(2\cdot95)}{4}=91.25$$

(You divide by four because you essentially have that many scores: one quizzes average, one mid-term, but <u>two</u> finals.)

A commercial cookie company produces only two kinds of cookies, chocolate chip and oatmeal raisin cookies. Each kind of cookie is packaged separately. One day, $\frac{1}{120}$ of the packages containing chocolate chip cookies failed to seal properly and were rejected by quality control. On the same day, $\frac{1}{180}$ of the packages containing oatmeal raisin cookies failed to seal properly and were rejected by quality control. If the company produced twice as many packages of chocolate chip cookies as oatmeal raisin that day, what proportion of all the packages produced were rejected?

A. $\frac{1}{420}$ C. $\frac{1}{210}$ E. $\frac{1}{135}$

B. $\frac{1}{300}$ D. $\frac{1}{145}$

Create an equation that weights the rejection rate for chocolate chip cookie packages twice as heavily as that for oatmeal raisin:

$$\text{Average}=\frac{2\left(\frac{1}{120}\right)+\frac{1}{180}}{3}=\frac{\frac{1}{45}}{3}=\frac{1}{135}$$

Mean, Median, and Mode

You already understand that **mean** is another term for **average**.

The **median** is the numerical value separating the higher half from the lower half of a data sample, a population, or a probability distribution. The median of a finite list of numbers can be found by arranging all the values from lowest value to highest value and picking the middle one. For example, the median of {5, 7, 9} is 7. If the set contains an even number of values, the median is the mean of the two middle values.

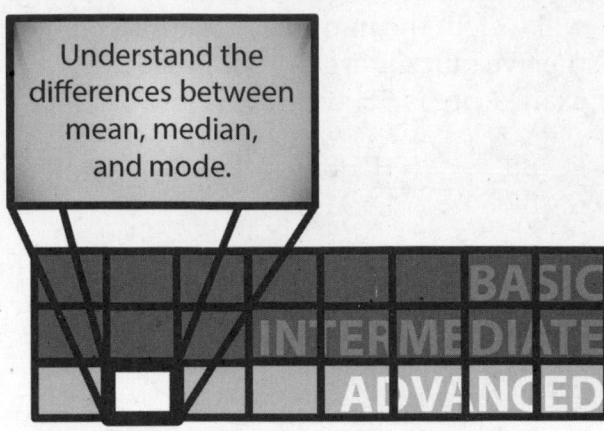

Understand the differences between mean, median, and mode.

BASIC
INTERMEDIATE
ADVANCED

Examples:

What is the median of {1, 1, 2, 3, 4, 5, 6, 7, 7, 7, 8, 8, 9}?

F. 4   H. 5.5   K. 6.5
G. 5   J. 6

The set contains an odd number of data values, 13, so the median is the middle value: 6, (J).

What is the median of {7, 9, 10, 16}?

A. 9   C. 10   E. 13
B. 9.5   D. 11.5

The set contains an even number of data values, so the median is the average of the two middle values: $\dfrac{9+10}{2} = 9.5$, (B).

What is the median of the set of values {–6, 0, 1, –3, 7}?

F. –3   H. 0   K. 4
G. –0.5   J. 1

Arrange the values in ascending order: –6, –3, 0, 1, 7. The middle value is 0, (H).

The **mode** is the value that appears most frequently in a data set. Depending on the values in a particular set, some data sets have multiple modes, while others have no modes. For example, the set {2, 4, 5, 5, 5, 6, 6, 19, 2} has a mode of 5. The set {–3, 5, 6, –3, –2, 7, 5, –3, 6, 5, 5, –3} is bimodal (has 2 modes) because –3 and 5 each occur four times. And the group of numbers $\{-8, 5, 4, -2, 7, 12\}$ does not have a mode because all values appear exactly one time.

Examples:

What is the mode for the set of numbers: $\{8, -1, -12, 2, 0, 7, 0\}$?

A. −2   C. 0   E. 2
B. −1   D. 1

The mode is 0, (C), since it appears twice in the set, while the other values appear only once.

What is (are) the mode(s) for the set of numbers $\{-7, 2, 8, 2, 3, -1, 1, 0, 3, 2, 3\}$?

F. 0   H. 2   K. 2 and 3
G. 0.5   J. 3

Both 2 and 3 appear three times, so the set is bimodal, (K).

Probability

Probability is the ratio between the number of defined outcomes and the collection of all possible outcomes of some action. For example, a single roll of one die (cube with one to six pips on each face) can produce one of six outcomes: 1, 2, 3, 4, 5, or 6. The collection of possible results is called the "sample space." Then, we can define an outcome that will be considered an "event." You might think of an event as being a successful attempt. For example, suppose that we wish to roll "3," then "3" (the face with the three pips facing upward) is the "event," the "sample space" is the six possible outcomes, and

the probability of the event occurring is $\frac{1}{6}$.

> Calculate the probability when the event or sample space is not explicitly given.
>
> ———
>
> Calculate joint and contingent probabilities.
>
> BASIC
> INTERMEDIATE
> ADVANCED

Things become more interesting when we use two dice rolled simultaneously, as you would in playing a board game such as Monopoly. Suppose, for example, that your token is on the space "Illinois Avenue," so that a 6 will land you on "GO DIRECTLY TO JAIL." (In which case, you do not pass GO, and you do not collect $200; and don't worry if you're not familiar with the Monopoly board, we've given you all the information you need.) What is the probability that you are going to roll a 6?

First, we'll need to define the sample space, or all possible outcomes:

Die A	1	1	1	1	1	1	2	2	2	2	2	2	3	3	3	3	3	3
Die B	1	2	3	4	5	6	1	2	3	4	5	6	1	2	3	4	5	6
Total	2	3	4	5	6	7	3	4	5	6	7	8	4	5	6	7	8	9

Die A	4	4	4	4	4	4	5	5	5	5	5	5	6	6	6	6	6	6
Die B	1	2	3	4	5	6	1	2	3	4	5	6	1	2	3	4	5	6
Total	5	6	7	8	9	10	6	7	8	9	10	11	7	8	9	10	11	12

As the table shows, the sample space includes 36 possible outcomes $(6 \cdot 6) = 36$, of which, five outcomes (1, 5; 2, 4; 3, 3; 4, 2; 5, 1) qualify as the event. So the probability of going to jail is $\dfrac{\text{event}}{\text{sample space}} = \dfrac{5}{36}$.

Let's say that in the example above you rolled a 6 and landed in jail. Now, you've just been released from jail and want your token to land on Pennsylvania Railroad or Free Parking on the next roll. What is the probability? You'll need a 5 or 10. How many outcomes will satisfy this definition of event? As the table shows, there are four possible outcomes that are 5 (1, 4; 2, 3; 3, 2; 4, 1) and three that total 10 (6, 4; 5, 5; 4, 6). So, the probability of rolling a 5 or a 10 is $\dfrac{4+3}{36} = \dfrac{7}{36}$.

Now, let's suppose that you manage to roll a 10 and land on Free Parking. You'd like to land next on Ventnor Avenue and need a 7. What is the probability you'll roll a 7? As the table shows, there are six outcomes that qualify (1, 6; 2, 5; 3, 4; 4, 3; 5, 2; 6, 1). So, the probability is $\dfrac{6}{36} = \dfrac{1}{6}$.

What makes these last two examples a bit more interesting than the first is that the outcome that qualifies as a successful event is not explicitly given. It was necessary to figure out which totals would be considered successful, e.g., 5 or 10.

Of course, nothing mathematical turns on the specifics of the Monopoly game board. A problem could as easily be presented without these details, as in the following example.

Example:

If two standard dice are rolled simultaneously, what is the probability that the total rolled value will be greater than 9?

A. $\dfrac{11}{12}$ C. $\dfrac{1}{4}$ E. $\dfrac{1}{12}$

B. $\dfrac{3}{4}$ D. $\dfrac{1}{6}$

There are six outcomes that produce a rolled value greater than 9 (4, 6; 5, 5; 6, 4; 6, 6; 6, 5; 5, 6). Therefore, the probability is $\dfrac{6}{36} = \dfrac{1}{6}$, (D).

Probability for Joint Events

Situations in which there are multiple events but the outcome of one event does not affect the outcome of another event are termed ***independent events***. For example, you are in New York City and ask Amy, who is standing next to you to pick a number between 1 and 6, inclusive, while, at the same time, your colleague in Los Angeles asks Fred to do the same thing. The choice by Amy does not influence the choice by Fred and vice versa.

In the table used to calculate the probabilities of the outcomes of a throw of two dice, we treated the sum as a single event. This was a simplifying assumption. In fact, the roll of each of the dice is, as you might suspect, a separate event, even when they occur simultaneously. The important aspect of the throw of two dice is that the two dice are independent of one another. Thus, the outcomes of the throw of two dice are multiple independent events.

Conceptually, the throw of the two dice is no different than throwing one die, waiting for it to come to rest, and then throwing the other die or throwing one die twice.

Use the ***Product Rule*** to solve the probability of joint events: Probability(A and B) = Probability(A) • Probability(B).

Examples:

Maureen is playing a board game with rules that require her to roll a single die twice and then move her board token a number of spaces equal to the total of the two rolls. What is the probability for a single turn that Maureen will roll two 3s?

F. $\dfrac{1}{36}$ H. $\dfrac{1}{12}$ K. $\dfrac{1}{3}$

G. $\dfrac{1}{13}$ J. $\dfrac{1}{6}$

Use the Product Rule: Probability(A) = $\dfrac{1}{6}$ and Probability(B) = $\dfrac{1}{6}$, so $\dfrac{1}{6} \cdot \dfrac{1}{6} = \dfrac{1}{36}$, (F).

Maureen is playing a board game with rules that require her to roll a single die twice and then move her board token a number of spaces equal to the total of the two rolls. What is the probability in a single turn that the total of the pips on the two rolls will be 7?

A. $\dfrac{1}{36}$ C. $\dfrac{1}{12}$ E. $\dfrac{1}{3}$

B. $\dfrac{1}{13}$ D. $\dfrac{1}{6}$

We know from prior analysis that 1, 2, 3, 4, 5, and 6 coupled with 6, 5, 4, 3, 2, and 1 total 7. The probability of rolling any of the six numbers on the first roll is 1. Then, for any one of the numbers thrown on the first roll, the probability of rolling the complement on the second roll is $\dfrac{1}{6}$. Using the Product Rule, the probability of

rolling a 7 is the two probabilities multiplied together: $1\left(\dfrac{1}{6}\right) = \dfrac{1}{6}$, (D).

What is the probability that the product of one element chosen at random from the set {1, 2, 3} and one element chosen from the set {4, 5, 6} will be odd?

F. $\dfrac{1}{9}$ H. $\dfrac{1}{3}$ K. $\dfrac{7}{9}$

G. $\dfrac{2}{9}$ J. $\dfrac{1}{2}$

There are nine possible products:

	4	5	6
1	4	5	6
2	8	10	12
3	12	15	18

And two of those, 5 and 15, are odd, so the probability is $\dfrac{2}{9}$, (G).

Probability for Contingent Events

A contingent event is one in which the outcome of the first event affects the probability of the outcome of the second event. For example, if a jar contains five red marbles and five black marbles, the probability of drawing two red marbles from the jar on the first two draws depends upon the first draw (without replacing the first marble drawn). The

probability of drawing a red marble on the first draw is $\dfrac{5}{10} = \dfrac{1}{2}$; and if a red marble is drawn, then the probability of drawing a second red marble is $\dfrac{5-1}{10-1}=\dfrac{4}{9}$. Therefore, the

probability of two red marbles on the first two draws is $\dfrac{1}{2} \cdot \dfrac{4}{9}=\dfrac{4}{18}=\dfrac{2}{9}$.

Example:

If a jar contains three red marbles and seven black marbles, what is the probability that two red marbles will be drawn from the jar on the first two random draws (without replacing the first marble drawn)?

A. $\dfrac{1}{21}$ C. $\dfrac{1}{15}$ E. $\dfrac{3}{10}$

B. $\dfrac{1}{20}$ D. $\dfrac{2}{25}$

Since three out of the ten marbles are red, the probability that the first marble

drawn is red is $\dfrac{3}{10}$. After drawing one red marble, this leaves two red marbles in

the jar out of nine. Therefore, the probability that the second marble drawn will

also be red is $\dfrac{2}{9}$. And the probability that both marbles drawn will be red is

$\dfrac{3}{10} \cdot \dfrac{2}{9}=\dfrac{6}{90}=\dfrac{1}{15}$, (C).

Counting Techniques

Permutations

If a set of n objects is to be ordered from 1st to nth , then there are n choices for the first object, $n-1$ choices for the second object, $n-2$ choices for the third object, and so on, until there is only one choice for the nth object. Therefore, the number of ways of ordering the n objects, also called **n factorial**, is as follows:

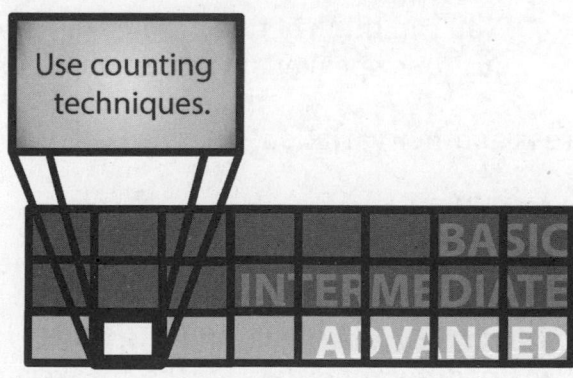

$n! = n(n-1)(n-2)\ldots(3)(2)(1)$

For example, four different colored beads can be arranged on a string in 4! or $4 \cdot 3 \cdot 2 \cdot 1 = 24$ different sequences. Each different sequence is a permutation.

Example:

Five speakers, Alice, Brad, Clara, Debbie, and Elaine, will address the student body. Each speaker will speak only once. If the speakers draw lots to determine the order in which they will speak, how many different orders for the speakers are possible?

F. 5 H. 30 K. 120
G. 6 J. 60

It is possible to conceptualize the number of different orders in the following way. Any one of the five could speak first. And for any selection for first speaker, there would be four speakers left to select from second. So, for the first two positions, there are $5 \cdot 4 = 20$ different pairs. Then, for each of those pairs, there are three speakers left for the third position, making $5 \cdot 4 \cdot 3 = 60$ triads. And then two left for fourth: $5 \cdot 4 \cdot 3 \cdot 2 = 120$. And one more to fill in the final position: $5 \cdot 4 \cdot 3 \cdot 2 \cdot 1 = 120$. That is, $5! = 120$, (K).

If the order is in any way restricted, then it will be necessary to modify the procedure, as in the following example.

Example:

Five speakers, Alice, Brad, Clara, Debbie, and Elaine, will address the student body. Each speaker will speak only once. If the speakers draw lots to determine the order in which they will speak, and if Brad will speak immediately after Alice, how many different orders for the speakers are possible?

A. 4 C. 24 E. 60
B. 6 D. 48

You can think of this problem as involving only four speakers, that is, treat A-B as just one speaker since that suborder is fixed: $4! = 4 \cdot 3 \cdot 2 \cdot 1 = 24$, (C).

Here is another variation:

Example:

Five speakers, Alice, Brad, Clara, Debbie, and Elaine, will address the student body. Each speaker will speak only once. If the speakers draw lots to determine the order in which they will speak, and if Brad will speak immediately before <u>or</u> after Alice, how many different orders for the speakers are possible?

F. 4 H. 24 K. 60
G. 6 J. 48

We can begin just as we did for the problem just above: $4! = 4 \cdot 3 \cdot 2 \cdot 1 = 24$. But in this case, the order of our pair of speakers will be <u>either</u> Alice-Brad <u>or</u> Brad-Alice. So there are $2 \cdot 24 = 48$ different orders, (J).

If you are asked to find the number of ways to arrange a smaller group that is being drawn from a larger group, you can use the following ***permutation formula***:

$$P = \frac{n!}{(n-k)!}$$

where n is the number of elements in the larger set and k is the number of elements being arranged.

Example:

Five candidates are running for office. The candidates who come in first, second, and third place will be elected president, vice-president, and treasurer, respectively. How many outcomes for president, vice-president, and treasurer are there?

A. 12	C. 30	E. 120
B. 24	D. 60	

Using the permutation formula: $P = \dfrac{n!}{(n-k)!} = \dfrac{5!}{(5-3)!} = \dfrac{5!}{2!} = \dfrac{5 \cdot 4 \cdot 3 \cdot 2 \cdot 1}{2 \cdot 1} = $

$5 \cdot 4 \cdot 3 = 60$. Notice that the formula is the same as applying the following logic: Any of the five candidates could come in first place, leaving four candidates who could come in second place, leaving three candidates who could come in third place, for a total of $5 \cdot 4 \cdot 3 = 60$ possible outcomes for president, vice-president, and treasurer, (D).

Combinations

A ***combination*** problem is similar to the problem type just discussed (a subset created from a larger set) with the difference that the order or arrangement of the smaller group that is being drawn from the larger group does NOT matter. Rather than the permutation formula, use the following ***combination formula***:

$$C = \frac{n!}{k!(n-k)!}$$

where n is the number of elements in the larger set and k is the number of elements being arranged. Note that in the previous example (five candidates running for office) order *did* matter. For every subgroup of 3 candidates there were 6 unique combinations, 3!, and each combination was counted. When order does not matter, each subgroup of 3 is treated as a single success so the duplicates need to be removed by dividing by $k!$.

Example:

How many different ways are there to choose four socks from a drawer containing nine socks?

Since the order or arrangement of the four socks being drawn from the drawer containing nine socks does not matter, use the combination formula:

$$C = \frac{9!}{4!(9-4)!} = \frac{9!}{4! \cdot 5!} = \frac{9 \cdot 8 \cdot 7 \cdot \cancel{6} \cdot \cancel{5}!}{4 \cdot \cancel{3} \cdot \cancel{2} \cdot 1 \cdot \cancel{5}!} = \frac{9 \cdot 8 \cdot 7}{4} = 126.$$

Data Analysis

Already in this book, you have been shown examples of the most common types of charts and graphs and shown how to read them. At this advanced level, the "pictures" are really not all that different. To be sure, a few may be noticeably more complex, but most of the skill required at this level is understanding subtleties. We'll focus our attention on three different variations on the general skill of "analyzing and drawing conclusions" from charts and graphs. So that the discussion can be specific, we'll use the following pair of pie charts.

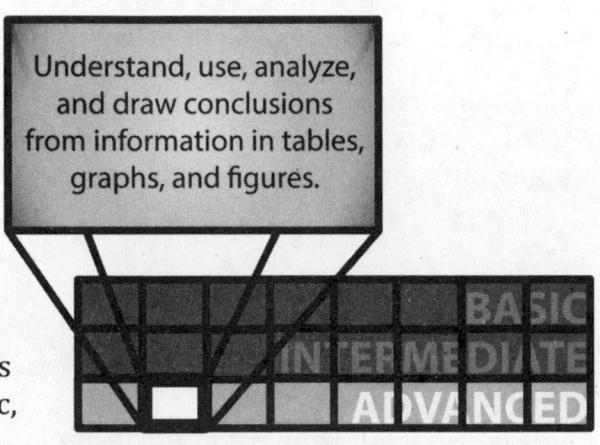

Understand, use, analyze, and draw conclusions from information in tables, graphs, and figures.

BASIC
INTERMEDIATE
ADVANCED

DISTRIBUTION OF PRIVATE SECTOR WORKFORCE

WASHINGTON COUNTY

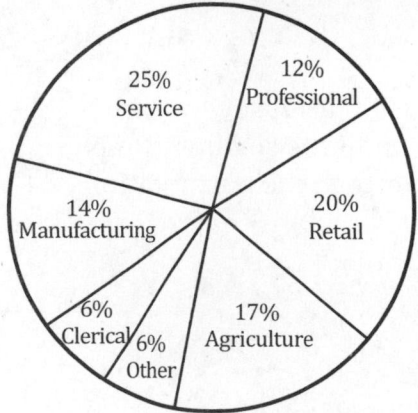

25% Service
12% Professional
14% Manufacturing
20% Retail
6% Clerical
6% Other
17% Agriculture

Approximate Total = 120,000

WARREN COUNTY

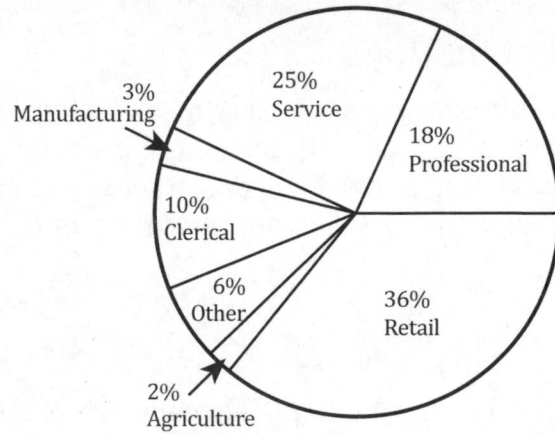

3% Manufacturing
25% Service
18% Professional
10% Clerical
6% Other
36% Retail
2% Agriculture

Approximate Total = 160,000

Performing Calculations Using Charts or Graphs

Advanced level questions sometimes ask you to pull together data from two or more charts.

Example:

Warren County has how many more people in the Clerical category than Washington County?

F. 8,800   J. 4,500
G. 7,000   K. 3,200
H. 5,600

This item requires you to pull data about clerical employment from both charts:
Warren Clerical – Washington Clerical $= 10\% \cdot 160,000 - 6\% \cdot 120,000 = 8,800$, (F).

Finding Shortcuts

Above we performed the needed calculation, but the numbers were easy to work with and didn't require a lot of time. Sometimes an advanced problem will seem to require a longer calculation but actually conceal the possibility of a shortcut.

Example:

For Warren County, how many employment categories include more than 24,000 people?

A. One   C. Three   E. Five
B. Two   D. Four

At first glance, it would seem that you are required to multiply the percentage for each sector for Warren County by the total of 160,000, but there is an easier approach. Find the percentage that, when multiplied by the total, will return the value 24,000:

$x\%$ of 160,000 = 24,000

$$x = \frac{24,000}{160,000} = 15\%$$

There are 3, (C), sectors that exceed 15%: Service, Professional, and Retail.

Read Carefully

You may not think that careful reading is an element of math, but it is. Of course, you have to read any question stem carefully lest you answer correctly the *wrong* question. You also have to understand the chart or graph and not draw unwarranted inferences.

Examples:

How many more people are employed in the Service sector in Warren County than in Washington County?

A. 0
B. 2,500
C. 5,000
D. 10,000
E. 25,000

> Make sure you do not confuse percentages with absolute numbers. In this case, the sizes of the Service sectors in the two counties are equal: 25%. But Warren County has a greater population. So, the answer is: $25\%(160,000) - 25\%(120,000) =$
>
> $25\%(160,000 - 120,000) = 25\%(40,000) = 10,000$, (D).

How many more people are employed as professional lawyers in Warren County than in Washington County?

F.   1.5
G.   6
H. 2,400
J. 14,400
K. Cannot be determined from the given information

> The charts tell you the percentage of employment in the Professional sector in the two counties, but they say nothing about the distribution of jobs within the category (i.e., they say nothing about lawyers), so (K) is correct.

EXERCISE 2

DIRECTIONS: Choose the correct answer to each of the following items. Answers are on page 815.

26. Sue bought 10 items at an average price of $3.60. The cost of eight of the items totaled $30. If the other two items were the same price, what was the price she paid for each?

F. $15.00   J. $3.00
G. $7.50   K. $1.50
H. $6.00

27. In a certain group, twelve of the children are age 10, and eight are age 15. What is the average of the ages of all the children in the group?

A. 9.6   C. 11   E. 12
B. 10.6   D. 11.5

28. The average of the weights of six people sitting in a boat is 145 pounds. After a seventh person gets into the boat, the average of the weights of all seven people in the boat is 147 pounds. What is the weight, in pounds, of the seventh person?

F. 160   H. 155   K. 147
G. 159   J. 149

29. What is the average grade for a student who received 90 in English, 84 in algebra, 75 in French, and 76 in music, if the subjects have the following weights: English 4, algebra 3, French 3, and music 1?

A. 81   C. 82   E. 83
B. $81\frac{1}{2}$ D. $82\frac{1}{2}$

30. The Paradise Dairy has two breeds of dairy cows: Holsteins and Jerseys. On Wednesday, the Holsteins produced milk with an average fat content of 3.5% by weight, and the Jerseys produced milk with an average fat content of 5% by weight. If the average fat content by weight of the day's production was 3.8%, what percentage of the day's production did the Holsteins contribute?

F. 16   H. 25   K. 80
G. 20   J. 60

Questions 31–33 refer to the following information.

During the 14 games of a season, a basketball player scored the following points per game: 42, 35, 29, 42, 33, 37, 26, 38, 42, 47, 51, 33, 30, and 40.

31. What is the median number of points scored by the player in the 14 games?

   A. 35.4   C. 36   E. 38
   B. 35.7   D. 37.5

32. What is the mode of the values in the list of points scored?

   F. 35.4   H. 38   K. 44
   G. 37.5   J. 42

33. What was the average (arithmetic mean) number of points scored by the player in the 14 games?

   A. 30   C. 37.5   E. 44
   B. 35   D. 42

34. What is the median for the following data set:
{2, −3, 8, 4, 9, −16, 12, 8, 4, 2}.

   F. 2   H. 3.5   K. 4.2
   G. 3   J. 4

35. A set of seven numbers contains the numbers 1, 4, 5, and 6. The other three numbers are represented by $2x + 8$, $x − 4$, and $7x − 4$. If the mode of these seven numbers is a negative even integer, then what is a possible value for x?

   A. 0   C. 2   E. 5
   B. 1   D. 4

36. A set of numbers $S = \{−5, −5, −3, −3, −2, −2, 0, 0, 0, 0, 4, 4, 6, 6\}$. If a zero is removed from the set S the resulting set is S'. Which of the following properties of S and S' are the same?

   I. Mean
  II. Mode
 III. Median

   F. I only   J. II and III only
   G. I and II only   K. I, II, and III
   H. I and III only

37. If S is a set of 15 different integers, which of the following operations CANNOT affect the value of the median?

   A. Doubling every number in the set
   B. Adding 15 to every number in the set
   C. Increasing the smallest number in the set
   D. Decreasing the smallest number in the set
   E. Decreasing the largest number in the set

Questions 38–39 refer to the following information.

A census shows that on a certain neighborhood block the number of children in each family is 3, 4, 4, 0, 1, 2, 0, 2, and 2.

38. What is the median number of children of the families on the block?

F. 1   H. 3   K. 5
G. 2   J. 4

39. What is the mode of the number of children per family?

A. 0   C. 2   E. 4
B. 1   D. 3

40. *A* is a set containing five different numbers. *B* is a set containing four different numbers, all of which are members of *A*. Which of the following statements CANNOT be true?

F. The mean of *A* is equal to the mean of *B*.
G. The median of *A* is equal to the median of *B*.
H. The range of *A* is equal to the range of *B*.
J. The mean of *A* is greater than the mean of *B*.
K. The range of *A* is less than the range of *B*.

41. If the variables *A*, *B*, and *C* take on only the values 1, 2, 3, 4, or 5 with frequencies indicated by the shaded regions of the figure below, for which of the frequency distributions is the mean equal to the median?

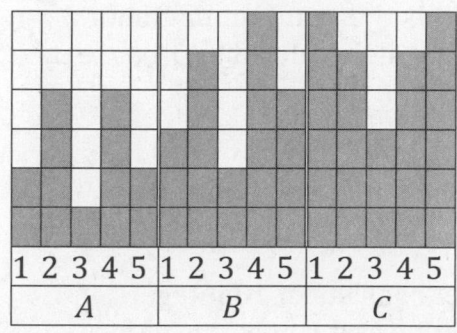

A. *A* only   D. *A* and *C* only
B. *B* only   E. *A*, *B*, and *C*
C. *C* only

42. Victoria had 10 pairs of shoes. When her family moved to a new apartment, 7 individual shoes were lost. What is the greatest number of pairs of shoes she can now have?

F. 4   H. 6   K. 8
G. 5   J. 7

43. How many different three-digit <u>even</u> integers can be made using the three digits 6, 7, and 8?

A. 2   C. 4   E. 12
B. 3   D. 6

44. How many two-element subsets of {*a*, *b*, *c*, *d*, *e*} do not contain *a* or *e*?

F. Two   H. Five   K. Nine
G. Three   J. Six

45. As a quality control procedure, a chemical lab includes in each sample to be tested a randomly chosen blank consisting of a single known chemical or a combination of two known chemicals. If protocol requires the lab to have available 12 different blanks, what is the minimum number of chemicals required to prepare the blanks?

A. 5   C. 12   E. 24
B. 6   D. 18

46. A set consists of 10 integers, p positive and n negative. If the probability that a number chosen at random from the set is positive is $\frac{1}{5}$, how many of the numbers are negative?

F. Two   H. Five   K. Eight
G. Four   J. Six

47. The probability that a coin will land heads up on any given toss is $\frac{1}{2}$. If the coin is tossed three times, what is the probability that at least one of the tosses will land heads up?

A. $\frac{1}{8}$ C. $\frac{1}{2}$ E. $\frac{7}{8}$

B. $\frac{1}{3}$ D. $\frac{3}{4}$

48. Two urns each contain 10 marbles. In one of the urns, there are 5 red marbles and 5 green marbles. In the other urn, there are 5 red marbles and 5 blue marbles. If one marble is selected at random from each of the urns, what is the probability that both will be red?

F. $\frac{1}{10}$ H. $\frac{1}{4}$ K. $\frac{1}{2}$

G. $\frac{1}{8}$ J. $\frac{1}{3}$

49. An urn contains 5 red marbles and 5 green marbles. If two marbles are drawn from the urn, what is the probability that both will be red?

A. $\frac{1}{10}$ C. $\frac{1}{3}$ E. $\frac{9}{10}$

B. $\frac{2}{9}$ D. $\frac{1}{2}$

50. If 5 books, each by a different author, are randomly stacked one on top of the other, what is the probability that the books will be stacked, from bottom to top, in alphabetical order according to author?

F. $\frac{1}{120}$ H. $\frac{1}{24}$ K. $\frac{1}{6}$

G. $\frac{1}{60}$ J. $\frac{1}{12}$

51. The stronger the relationship between two variables, the more closely the points on a scatter plot will approach some linear or curvilinear pattern. Which of the scatter plots below represents the strongest relationship between the two variables?

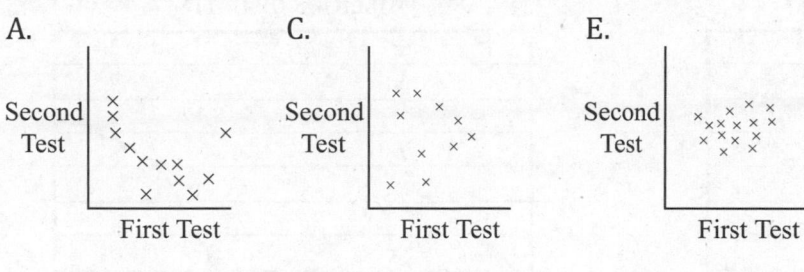

A.

Second Test

First Test

C.

Second Test

First Test

E.

Second Test

First Test

B.

Second Test

First Test

D.

Second Test

First Test

52. The table below represents the number of voters in five counties that voted in a general election and the percent change in the number of voters from the previously held primary election. Which county had the greatest net increase in voters between the primary and the general elections?

County	Number of Voters in General Election (in millions)	Percent Change from Primary Election
M	5.67	−23%
N	2.34	+14%
O	1.25	−2%
P	4.56	+4%
Q	6.23	+8%

F. County M   J. County P
G. County N   K. County Q
H. County O

Questions 53–55 refer to the following graphs.

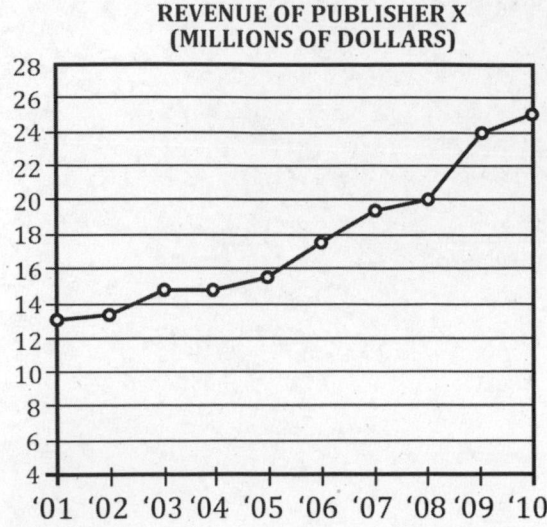

REVENUE OF PUBLISHER X
(MILLIONS OF DOLLARS)

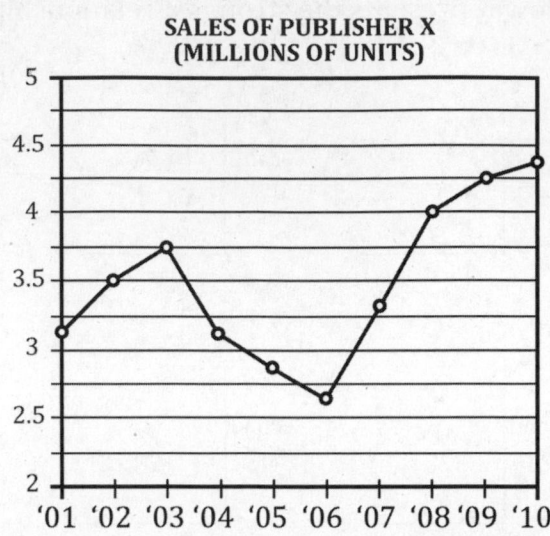

SALES OF PUBLISHER X
(MILLIONS OF UNITS)

53. In 2002, Publisher X sold 700,000 units from its fiction line. The fiction line accounted for what percentage of the total number of units sold?

A. 5%   C. 15%   E. 25%
B. 10%   D. 20%

54. How many years after 2001 show both an increase in unit sales and an increase in revenues?

F. Two   H. Four   K. Six
G. Three   J. Five

55. What was the approximate difference between the average revenue per unit generated in 2008 and in 2002?

A. $1.15   D. $3.25
B. $1.70   E. $4.10
C. $2.50

Number Concepts

Apply Number Properties

Advanced Level number properties and concepts problems require the application of basic properties such as factors/multiples, prime factorization, even/odd numbers, and positive/negative numbers. Let's review each of these properties with a few examples.

Apply number properties such as prime factorization, factors/multiples, odd/even numbers, and positive/negative numbers.

Consider the simple equation $2 \cdot 5 = 10$:

> 2 and 5 are *factors* of 10.
>
> 10 is a *multiple* of 2 and 5.
>
> 10 is *divisible* by 2 and 5.

Stated more formally, this translates to: If an integer *m* is divided by a second integer *n*, and the result is a third integer with no remainder, then *m* is a multiple of *n*, *n* is a factor of *m*, and *m* is divisible by *n*.

Recall the following important points about factors:

IMPORTANT POINTS ABOUT FACTORS ✓

1. An integer is a factor of itself, except 0, which has no factors and is not a factor of any integer.

2. 1 is a factor of all integers except 0.

3. An integer's largest factor (other than itself) will not be greater than one half the value of the integer.

The following divisibility rules are shortcuts for finding factors and can be especially helpful when factoring large integers or solving advanced application problems.

> ### FACTORIZATION SHORTCUTS
>
> 1. Divisible by 2: Integers ending in 0, 2, 4, 6, or 8
>
> 2. Divisible by 3: Integers whose digits sum to a multiple of 3
>
> 3. Divisible by 4: Integers whose last two digits represent a multiple of 4
>
> 4. Divisible by 5: Integers ending in 5 or 0
>
> 5. Divisible by 6: Integers divisible by both 2 and 3
>
> 6. Divisible by 8: Integers whose last three digits represent a multiple of 8
>
> 7. Divisible by 9: Integers whose digits sum to a multiple of 9

Examples:

Which of the following is a complete list of the positive factors of 3,477 that are less than 10?

F. {3}　　　H. {3, 8}　　　K. There are no positive factors less than 10.
G. {2, 4}　　J. {3, 9}

Use the shortcut methods for finding the factors. Since 3,477 doesn't end in 0, 5, or an even number, 2 5, and 6 are not factors. The number formed by the last two digits, 77, is not divisible by 4, so 4 isn't a factor, and the number formed by the last three digits, 477, is not divisible by 8, so 8 isn't a factor. However, the digits sum to 21, which is a multiple of 3 but not 9, so 3 is a factor, while 9 is not. Therefore, (F) is correct.

If $A = 2^2(3)(7) = 84$, how many positive factors does A have?

A. 12　　　C. 36　　　E. 84
B. 24　　　D. 42

The given equation represents the prime factorization of 84, so 2, 3, and 7 are factors. Identify additional unique combinations of these three factors: 6, 14, 21, and 42. Next, remember to include the square of 2, as well as related unique factors: 4, 12, and 28. Lastly, include 1 and 84. Thus, the total number of factors is 12, (A).

A **prime number** is a positive integer having only two positive factors, 1 and itself. Zero and 1 are not considered prime numbers. Prime factorization is the process of finding all the prime factors that multiply together to get a certain number. The best method is to begin by starting from the smallest prime number, which is 2.

Example:

If x is the sum of all unique prime factors of 54 and y is the sum of all unique prime factors of 76, what is the value of $y - x$?

F. 5   H. 16   K. 21

G. 11   J. 19

First, find the prime factors of 54 by dividing by 2, the smallest prime number:

$54 \div 2 = 27$

Now, check the next smallest prime number, 3, by dividing 27 by 3:

$27 \div 3 = 9$

And 9 divides by 3 three times. So, the prime factorization of 54 is:

$54 = (2)(27) = (2)(3)(9) = (2)(3)(3)(3)$

And the unique prime factors of 54 are {2, 3}. Similarly, find the prime factors of 76:

$76 = (2)(38) = (2)(2)(19)$

So, the unique prime factors of 76 are {2, 19}. Thus, the sum of the prime factors of 54, x, is $2 + 3 = 5$, and the sum of the prime factors of 76, y, is $2 + 19 = 21$. Therefore, $y - x = 21 - 5 = 16$, (H).

Recall the following important principles that govern the behavior of odd and even integers.

PRINCIPLES OF ODD AND EVEN INTEGERS	

1. EVEN ± EVEN = EVEN   5. EVEN • EVEN = EVEN

2. EVEN ± ODD = ODD   6. EVEN • ODD = EVEN

3. ODD ± EVEN = ODD   7. ODD • EVEN = EVEN

4. ODD ± ODD = EVEN   8. ODD • ODD = ODD

Note that due to the commutative property (see p. 546), the second and third principles above are identical, and the six and seventh principles are identical.

Remember that the rules for multiplication do NOT apply to division. For example, if you divide the even number 4 by the even number 8, the result is $\frac{1}{2}$. Odd and even are characteristics of whole numbers and negative integers, but not fractions. A fraction is neither odd nor even.

Example:

If n is a positive even integer, and if $n \div 4$ results in a quotient with a remainder of 2, which of the following expressions is NOT evenly divisible by 4?

A. $2n$ D. $n + 2$
B. $n - 2$ E. $3n + 2$
C. $n + 1$

Test the positive even integers (2, 4, 6, 8, etc.) as the value of n to determine which values result in a quotient with a remainder of 2:

$$n = 2: \frac{2}{4} = \frac{1}{2} \; \times$$

$$n = 4: \frac{4}{4} = 1 \; \times$$

$$n = 6: \frac{6}{4} = 1, \text{plus a remainder of 2} \; \checkmark$$

$$n = 8: \frac{8}{4} = 2 \; \times$$

$$n = 10: \frac{10}{4} = 2, \text{plus a remainder of 2} \; \checkmark$$

$$n = 12: \frac{12}{4} = 3 \; \times$$

$$n = 14: \frac{14}{4} = 3, \text{plus a remainder of 2} \; \checkmark$$

Thus, the values of n that if divided by 4 result in a quotient with a remainder of 2 are those in the sequence {6, 10, 14, ...}, in which each subsequent number increases by 4. Substitute a test value for n into the answer choices to determine which one is not divisible by 4, say $n = 10$:

$$\text{A. } 2n = 2(10) = 20: \frac{20}{4} = 5$$

$$\text{B. } n - 2 = 10 - 2 = 8: \frac{8}{4} = 2$$

$$\text{C. } n + 1 = \frac{11}{4} = 2, \text{plus a remainder of 3}$$

D. $n + 2 = 10 + 2 = 12$: $\dfrac{12}{4} = 3$

E. $3n + 2 = 3(10) + 2 = 32$: $\dfrac{32}{4} = 8$

Therefore, (C) is the only expression that is not evenly divisible by 4.

Problems can also focus on the properties of positive and negative numbers. Recall the following principles for working with negative numbers.

> ### PRINCIPLES FOR WORKING WITH NEGATIVE NUMBERS
>
> 1. Subtraction of a negative number is equivalent to addition of a positive number.
>
> 2. Addition of a negative number is equivalent to subtraction of a positive number.
>
> 3. Multiplication or division involving an odd number of negative numbers always results in a negative number.
>
> 4. Multiplication or division involving an even number of negative numbers always results in a positive number.

Examples:

If n is any positive number, which of the following must be positive?

   I. $-n - (-n)$

   II. $-n \cdot -n$

   III. $n \div (-n \cdot -n)$

A. I only   D. I and III only
B. II only   E. II and III only
C. III only

(I) is incorrect because $-n + n = 0$ (e.g., $-1 + 1 = 0$), and 0 is neither positive nor negative. (II) is correct because the product of an even number of negative numbers must result in a positive number. Finally, (III) is correct because a positive number divided by another positive number must result in a positive number. Therefore, (E) is correct.

If x and y are negative integers and $\dfrac{x-y}{2}=1$, what is the least possible value of xy?

F. 0   H. 2   K. 6
G. 1   J. 3

According to the principles of working with negative integers, multiplying two negative integers together results in a positive value, so the least possible value of xy results for negative integer values of x and y closest to 0. Since $\dfrac{x-y}{2}=1$, $x = y + 2$. In order for this to be true for negative integer values for x and y, y must be at least –3, in which case $x = -1$. Therefore, the least possible value of xy is $(-1)(-3) = 3$, (J).

Draw Conclusions

Other problems at this level require you to make conclusions based on basic number concepts and algebraic properties. The basic rules for combining and simplifying mathematical expressions apply not just to numbers but also to variables. Recall the following fundamental properties governing combining numbers and other terms.

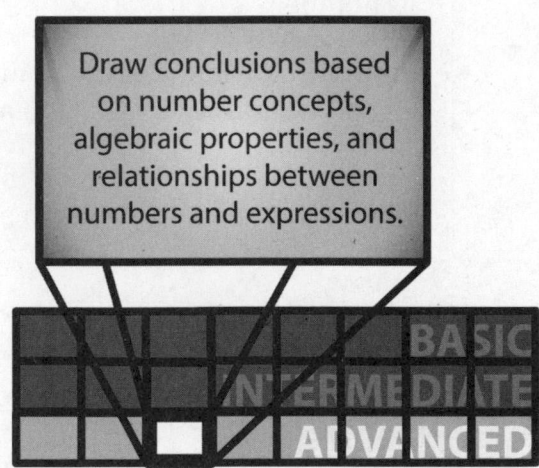

Draw conclusions based on number concepts, algebraic properties, and relationships between numbers and expressions.

BASIC ALGEBRAIC PROPERTIES	

Associative Properties:	$a + (b + c) = (a + b) + c$ $a(bc) = (ab)c$
Commutative Properties:	$a + b = b + a$ $ab = ba$
Distributive Properties:	$a(b + c) = ab + ac$ $a - (b + c) = a - b - c$ $\dfrac{a+b}{c} = \dfrac{a}{c} + \dfrac{b}{c}$

And note that these properties apply to addition and multiplication only.

Examples:

The expression $a[b - c(d + f)]$ is equivalent to:

A. $ab - cd + f.$
B. $ab - cd - cf.$
C. $ab - acd + acf.$
D. $ab - acd - acf.$
E. $ab - acd - cf.$

This item requires application of the distributive property: both the a and the c must be distributed across the contents of the associated parentheses. First, distribute the $-c$:

$$a[b - c(d + f)] = a(b - cd - cf)$$

Next, distribute the a:

$$a(b - cd - cf) = ab - acd - acf$$

Let $x = 2a - 3b + c$. What happens to the value of x if the value of a decreases by 1, the value of b increases by 2, and the value of c remains constant?

F. It increases by 8.
G. It increases by 4.
H. It remains unchanged.
J. It decreases by 5.
K. It decreases by 8.

Let x', a', b', and c' equal the new values of x, a, b, and c: $a' = a - 1$, $b' = b + 2$, and $c' = c$. So:

$$x' = 2a' - 3b' + c' = 2(a-1) - 3(b+2) + c = 2a - 2 - 3b - 6 + c = 2a - 3b + c - 8 = x - 8$$

Therefore, the value of x decreases by 8, (K).

Often, problems requiring application of number properties involve consecutive integers or consecutive odd/even numbers. Consecutive integers are one number apart: x, $x+1$, $x+2$, etc. Consecutive even or odd integers are two numbers apart: x, $x+2$, $x+4$, etc.

Examples:

If a and b are consecutive integers such that $a > b > 0$, then $a^2 - b^2 = ?$

A. b C. $b + 1$ E. $2b + 2$
B. $2b$ D. $2b + 1$

Since a and b are consecutive integers and $a > b$, $a = b + 1$. Substitute $b + 1$ for a in the expression and simplify:

$$a^2 - b^2 = (b+1)^2 - b^2 = (b+1)(b+1) - b^2 = b^2 + 2b + 1 - b^2 = 2b + 1$$

Three consecutive odd integers have a sum of 33. What is the largest of these integers?

F.   9   H. 11   K. 13
G. 10   J. 12

Represent the integers as x, $x+2$, and $x+4$. Write an equation indicating the sum is 33: $x+x+2+x+4=3x+6=33 \Rightarrow 3x=27 \Rightarrow x=9$. Thus, the integers are 9, 11, and 13, and the largest integer is 13, (K).

Five consecutive even numbers add up to 560. If the third number is x, what is the value of the largest number?

A. 59   C. 112   E. 116
B. 106   D. 114

If the third value is x, the remaining values are $x - 4$, $x - 2$, $x + 2$, and $x + 4$. Set the sum of the five numbers equal to 560 and solve for x:

$$(x - 4) + (x - 2) + (x) + (x + 2) + (x + 4) = 560$$
$$5x = 560$$
$$x = 112$$

Since the largest number is equal to $x + 4$, its value is $112 + 4 = 116$, (E).

Finally, arithmetic application problems at this level may require you to make conclusions based on relationships between numbers and expressions. Consider the following examples.

Examples:

If x and y are integers such that $x > 2$, $y > 3$, and m is the average of x and y, then $\dfrac{m+x+y}{3}$ is equal to which of the following?

F. 0
G. 1
H. $m + x + y$
J.   The average of x and y
K.   The absolute value of the difference between x and y

Since m is the average of x and y, $m = \dfrac{x+y}{2} = \dfrac{x}{2} + \dfrac{y}{2}$. Therefore:

$$\frac{m+x+y}{3} = \frac{\dfrac{x}{2}+\dfrac{y}{2}+x+y}{3} = \frac{\dfrac{3x}{2}+\dfrac{3y}{2}}{3} = \frac{x}{2}+\frac{y}{2} = \frac{x+y}{2}$$

And $\dfrac{x+y}{2}$ is equal to the average of x and y, (J).

If $\sqrt{m} + \sqrt{n} = \sqrt{m+n}$, then which of the following must be true?

A. $mn = 1$
B. $\sqrt{m} = \sqrt{n}$
C. $m = 0$ and $n = 0$
D. $m = 0$ or $n = 0$
E. $m = 1$ or $n = 1$

Square both sides of the equation to eliminate the radical signs and simplify:

$$\left(\sqrt{m} + \sqrt{n}\right)^2 = \left(\sqrt{m+n}\right)^2$$
$$\left(\sqrt{m} + \sqrt{n}\right)\left(\sqrt{m} + \sqrt{n}\right) = \left(\sqrt{m+n}\right)\left(\sqrt{m+n}\right)$$
$$m + 2\sqrt{mn} + n = m + n$$
$$2\sqrt{mn} = 0$$

Thus, either m or n must be 0, (D). Note that both could be 0, but this is not necessarily true.

EXERCISE 3

DIRECTIONS: Choose the correct answer to each of the following items. Answers are on page 815.

56. Which of the following integers has the same number of unique factors as 25?

F. 3   H. 6   K. 10
G. 5   J. 9

57. How many unique factors does the number 36 have?

A. Two   D Eight
B. Six   E. Nine
C. Seven

58. What is the sum of the unique prime factors of 156?

F. 3   H. 15   K. 78
G. 5   J. 18

59. What is the greatest common factor of $8x^3y^4z^6$, $12x^5y^3z^7$, and $24x^4yz^5$?

A. $2x^{12}y^8z^{18}$ D. $4x^3y^3z^6$
B. $4yz^5$ E. $24x^3yz^5$
C. $4x^3yz^5$

60. If *m* is the greatest prime factor of 42 and *n* is the greatest prime factor of 35, what is *m* − *n*?

F. 0   H. 2   K. 7
G. 1   J. 5

61. If *x* equals the number of unique odd prime factors in 180, *y* equals the number of two-digit prime numbers less than 30, and *z* equals the number of even prime numbers, what is the value of *y* − *xz*?

A. −2   C. 2   E. 6
B. 0   D. 4

62. If *a* equals the number of primes divisible by 13, *b* equals the number of even primes, *c* equals the number of unique prime factors in 136, and *d* equals the greatest common factor of 36 and 90, what is the value of *d* − (*a* + *b* + *c*)?

F. 4   H. 14   K. 18
G. 5   J. 16

63. If *m* and *n* are positive integers that have remainders of 1 and 5, respectively, when divided by 7, which of the following could NOT be the value of *m* + *n*?

A. 20   C. 55   E. 76
B. 34   D. 68

64. The positive integer *m* is a multiple of 6 and also a multiple of 8. What is the minimum possible value for 2*m*?

F. 4   H. 24   K. 96
G. 12   J. 48

65. If *m* and *n* are positive integers such that the greatest common factor of m^2n and mn^3 is 24 and $m^2n < mn^3$, then which of the following is a possible value for *m*?

A. 2   C. 4   E. 12
B. 3   D. 6

66. Let the symbol =*n*= be defined as the number of different pairs of positive integers the product of which is *n*. For example, =12= is 3 because (1)(12) = 12, (2)(6) = 12, and (3)(4) = 12. What is the value of =24=?

F. 3   H. 5   K. 7
G. 4   J. 6

67. Consider the following four-digit number with a missing digit represented by *x*:

$$5{,}6\,x\,4$$

If the four-digit number is a multiple of 3 and the sum of the four digits equals a multiple of 4, what is the value of *x*?

A. 1
B. 3
C. 6
D. 9
E. Cannot be determined from the given information

68. For any positive integer n, which of the following MUST be odd?

   I. $3(n+1)$

  II. $3n+2n$

 III. $2n-1$

F. I only
G. II only
H. III only
J. I and II only
K. I, II, and III

69. For any negative number n, which of the following MUST be negative?

   I. $n \cdot -n$

  II. $-n \cdot -n$

 III. $-n+n$

A. I only
B. II only
C. III only
D. II and III only
E. I, II, and III

70. Claude is standing in a line for movie tickets. He is eighth in line from the front and seventh in line from the back. How many people are standing in line?

F. 14   H. 16   K. 18
G. 15   J. 17

71. The least integer of a set of consecutive integers is –15. If the sum of these integers is 51, how many integers are in the set?

A. 15   C. 30   E. 34
B. 16   D. 31

72. If the sum of three consecutive odd integers, x, y, and z, is 21, what is the value of x?

F. 5   H. 7   K. 11
G. 6   J. 9

73. If the sum of three consecutive even integers, a, b, and c, is 24, what is the value of c?

A. 2   C. 6   E. 10
B. 4   D. 8

74. The sum of four consecutive even integers—a, b, c, and d—is 20. What is the median of the set $\{a, b, c, d, 20\}$?

F. 4   H. 8   K. 32
G. 6   J. 16

75. If x, y, and z are three consecutive odd integers such that $x < y < z$ and $3x = 2z + 3$, what is the value of z?

A. 9   C. 13   E. 17
B. 11   D. 15

76. If 15 is the fifth number in a series of five consecutive odd integers, what is the third integer in the series?

F. 5   H. 9   K. 13
G. 7   J. 11

77. If x, y, and z are consecutive negative odd integers such that $x < y < z$, which of the following must be a positive even integer?

A. $x + y + z$ D. $yz - x$
B. $(xyz)^2$ E. $x^2 + y^2 + z^2$
C. $(z - x - y)^2$

78. Three unique numbers are chosen, one from each of the sets A, B, and C:

$A = \{3, 9, 12\}$
$B = \{4, 6, 12\}$
$C = \{8, 10, 12\}$

What is the greatest possible sum of the three numbers?

F. 21   H. 31   K. 36
G. 26   J. 33

79. If M and N are two unique positive integers such that the units digit of N is equal to the tens digit of M and the tens digit of N is equal to the units digit of M, which of the following CANNOT be the sum of M and N?

A. 33   C. 121   E. 252
B. 88   D. 220

80. If n is an integer and $n = \dfrac{(2)(3)(5)(7)(11)(13)}{55k}$, which of the following could be the value of k?

F. 20   H. 30   K. 53
G. 22   J. 39

81. If x and y are unique two-digit integers that have the same digits but in reverse order, which of the following must be an integer?

A. $\dfrac{x+y}{10}$ D. $\dfrac{x-y}{9}$

B. $\dfrac{x+y}{9}$ E. $\dfrac{x-y}{10}$

C. $\dfrac{x-y}{2}$

Exponents

Complex expressions may require the application of two or more operations involving exponents. No matter how complex an item gets, it can be solved by a series of simple steps following the eight rules for working with exponents explained below. Remember to follow the rules for order of operations. Also, be careful when negative signs are involved.

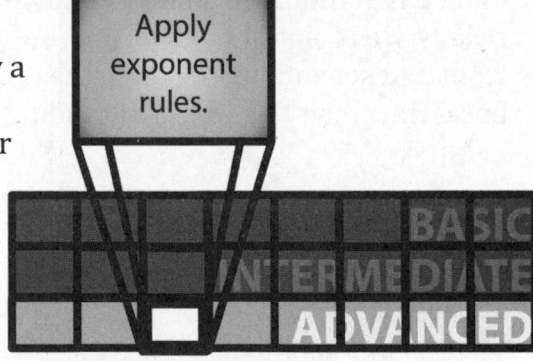

Apply exponent rules.

BASIC
INTERMEDIATE
ADVANCED

These rules for working with exponents provide simple shortcuts, as verified by explicitly executing all indicated operations. When you begin to manipulate algebraic expressions, not only will these same shortcuts apply, but they will become indispensable.

1. $x^1 = x$

2. $x^0 = 1$, if $x \neq 0$

3. $x^{-n} = \dfrac{1}{x^n}$

4. Product Rule: $x^m \cdot x^n = x^{m+n}$

5. Quotient Rule: $\dfrac{x^m}{x^n} = x^{m-n}$

6. Power Rule: $\left(x^m\right)^n = x^{m \cdot n}$

7. Product Power Rule: $\left(x^m \cdot y^p\right)^n = x^{mn} \cdot y^{pn}$

8. Quotient Power Rule: $\left(\dfrac{x^m}{y^p}\right)^n = \dfrac{x^{mn}}{y^{pn}}$

Examples:

If $9^x = 3$, then $9^{4x} = ?$

F. $\sqrt{3}$ H. $9(\sqrt[3]{3})$ K. 81
G. 12   J. 27

Rewrite the second expression in terms of the first by applying the rules of exponents: $9^{4x} = (9^x)^4$. And since $9^x = 3$, $(9^x)^4 = 3^4 = 81$, (K).

If $\left(\dfrac{1}{16}\right)^{n-1} = 2\sqrt{2}$, then $n = ?$

A. $-\dfrac{3}{2}$ C. 0   E. $\dfrac{5}{8}$

B. $-\dfrac{5}{8}$ D. 1

Rewrite the equation with equal bases:

$$(2^{-4})^{n-1} = (2)^1 (2)^{1/2}$$

$$2^{-4(n-1)} = 2^{1+1/2}$$

$$2^{-4n+4} = 2^{3/2}$$

Now that the bases are the same, drop them and solve the equation for n:

$$-4n + 4 = \frac{3}{2}$$

$$4n = \frac{5}{2}$$

$$n = \frac{5}{8}$$

If a, b, and c are positive numbers such that $(4^{16})(5^{16})(6^{16}) = (2^{4a})(3^{b^2})(10^{32c})$, what is the value of $a - b - c$?

F. −2   H. 2   K. 4

G. 1   J. $\dfrac{7}{2}$

Apply the product power rule of exponents to the left side of the equation and manipulate the expression until the bases match those on the right side of the equation:

$$(4^{16})(5^{16})(6^{16}) = 2^{16} \cdot 2^{16} \cdot 5^{16} \cdot 2^{16} \cdot 3^{16} = 2^{16} \cdot 2^{16} \cdot 3^{16} \cdot 10^{16} = 2^{32} \cdot 3^{16} \cdot 10^{16}$$

Now, set the exponents on the left side equal to the exponents on the right side for the corresponding identical base and solve each equation for the unknown variable. Remember that a, b, and c must be positive numbers:

$32 = 4a$
$a = 8$

$16 = b^2$
$b = 4$

$16 = 32c$
$c = \dfrac{1}{2}$

Therefore, $a - b - c = 8 - 4 - \dfrac{1}{2} = 3\dfrac{1}{2} = \dfrac{7}{2}$, (J).

Logarithms and Geometric Sequences

Now, let's expand our coverage of exponents to logarithms. Recall that $3^2 = 9$ is read as "3 raised to the second power equals 9." However, note that this can also be read as "2 is the exponent to which 3 must be raised to equal 9." This exponent is also called the logarithm. Thus, the statement "$3^2 = 9$" is equivalent to the statement "$\log_3 9 = 2$," or "the base 3 logarithm of 9 is 2." In other words, a logarithm is an exponent in reverse.

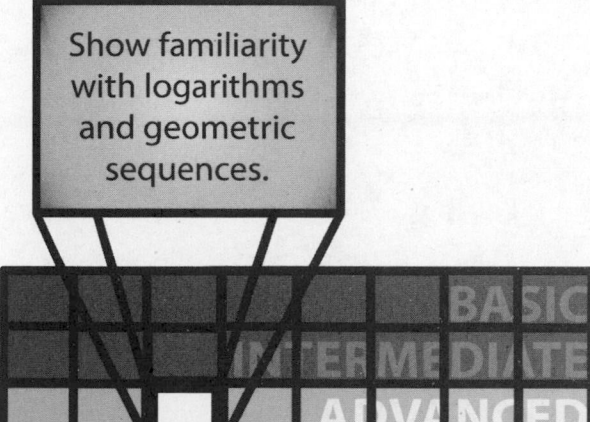

Show familiarity with logarithms and geometric sequences.

The following logarithm rules follow directly from the laws of exponents. Note that base 10 logarithms are sometimes written without the base indicated: $\log_{10} x = \log x$.

BASIC LOGARITHM RULES

For any positive base $b \neq 1$ and positive numbers $x, y,$ and n:

1. $\log_b b = 1$

2. $\log_b 1 = 0$

3. If $x = b^y$, then $\log_b x = y$

4. $\log_b(xy) = \log_b x + \log_b y$

5. $\log_b\left(\dfrac{x}{y}\right) = \log_b x - \log_b y$

6. $\log_b x^n = n\log_b x$

7. $\log_b x = \dfrac{\log_{10} x}{\log_{10} b}$ (change of base 10 formula)

Using the definition of a logarithm as laid out in the first rule above allows you to solve problems such as the following example.

Example:

What is the value of $\log_9 27$?

A. 1   C. $\sqrt{3}$ E $3\sqrt{3}$

B. $\dfrac{3}{2}$ D. 3

Let $\log_9 27 = x$, so $9^x = 27$. And since $9 = 3^2$ and $27 = 3^3$:

$$9^x = 27$$
$$(3^2)^x = 3^3$$
$$3^{2x} = 3^3$$

Since the bases are the same, set the exponents as equal and solve for x:

$$2x = 3$$
$$x = \frac{3}{2}$$

Items that involve exponential growth test knowledge of exponential growth sequences, also called *geometric sequences*. In a geometric sequence, the ratio, r, of any term to its preceding term is constant; that is, it's a sequence of numbers in which a certain number is multiplied by each preceding term to arrive at the next.

If the terms of a geometric sequence are designated by a_1, a_2, a_3, ..., a_n, then $a_n = a_1 r^{n-1}$.

Example:

What is the next term after $\dfrac{1}{2}$ in the geometric sequence $\{2, -1, \dfrac{1}{2}, ...\}$?

F. $-\dfrac{1}{4}$ H. 0   K. $\dfrac{1}{4}$

G. $-\dfrac{1}{2}$ J. $\dfrac{1}{2}$

The ratio between each term and the preceding term is $-\dfrac{1}{2}$. Thus, the next term is

$$\left(\frac{1}{2}\right)\left(-\frac{1}{2}\right) = -\frac{1}{4}, \text{ (F).}$$

What is the eighth term in the geometric sequence {4, 12, 36, ...}?

A. 324   D. 8,748
B. 2,187   E. 26,244
C. 4,374

The ratio between each term and the preceding term is 3. Use the equation for a geometric sequence to find the eighth term:

$$a_n = a_1 r^{n-1} \Rightarrow a_8 = 4(3)^{8-1} = 4(3)^7 = 4(2,187) = 8,748$$

Sequences that involve exponential growth have real-life applications, such as determining population growth over a specific period.

Example:

On June 1, 1990, the population of Grouenphast was 50,250. If the population is increasing at an annual rate of 8.4%, what is the approximate population of Grouenphast on June 1, 2010?

F. 31,524   J. 252,186
G. 94,570   K. 273,370
H. 126,093

An annual increase of 8.4% means that each year the population will be 108.4% of the previous year's population. Thus, the ratio between terms, r, is 1.084. The population on June 1, 1990 is the starting term: $a_1 = 50,250$. Since June 1, 2010 is 20 years later, the population at that time is the 21st term in the sequence: $n = 21$. So, the population on June 1, 2010 is: $a_n = a_1 r^{n-1} \Rightarrow a_{21} = 50,250(1.084)^{20} \approx$ 252,186, (J).

The previous example involving growth over time suggests an alternate form of the geometric sequence equation called the ***exponential growth equation***: $a_t = a_0 r^{\frac{t}{T}}$. In this equation, a_t is the amount after time, a_0 is the initial amount ($t = 0$), r is the growth rate per T, t is the total period of growth, and T is the time per cycle of growth. Note that this equation also applies to exponential decay, where the initial amount is larger than the amount after time t.

Complex Numbers

To multiply complex numbers, simply apply the same method as for multiplying two binomials: First, Outer, Inner, and Last, also known as the "FOIL" method (see Intermediate, p. 445 for an in-depth review of the FOIL method).

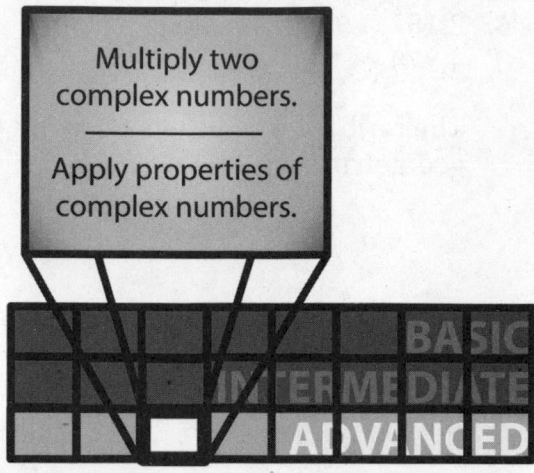

Multiply two complex numbers.
_____
Apply properties of complex numbers.

Example:

If $x = 2 - 3i$ and $y = 4 + 2i$, what is the value of xy?

A. $-2 - 8i$ D. $14 + 8i$
B. $-2 + 8i$ E. $14 - 8i$
C. $14 - 14i$

Multiply the two complex numbers as you would two binomials: multiply the first terms, then the outer terms, the inner terms, and finally the last terms:

$$xy = (2 - 3i)(4 + 2i) = (2)(4) + (2)(2i) + (-3i)(4) + (-3i)(2i) = 8 + 4i - 12i - 6i^2 =$$
$$8 - 8i - 6(-1) = 14 - 8i$$

To divide two complex numbers, multiply the numerator and denominator by the conjugate of the denominator. Recall that the conjugate of $x + y$ is $x - y$; therefore, the conjugate of a complex number $a + bi$ is $a - bi$.

Example:

Which of the following expressions is equal to $\dfrac{3+2i}{4-i}$?

F. $\dfrac{11}{17}i$ J. $\dfrac{10+11i}{17}$

G. $\dfrac{3}{4} - 2i$ K. $\dfrac{14+5i}{15}$

H. $\dfrac{10-11i}{15}$

Multiply both the numerator and the denominator by the conjugate of $4 - i$ and carry out the indicated operations:

$$\frac{3+2i}{4-i} = \frac{(3+2i)(4+i)}{(4-i)(4+i)} = \frac{12+3i+8i+2i^2}{16+4i-4i-i^2} = \frac{12+11i+2(-1)}{16-(-1)} = \frac{10+11i}{17}$$

An important property of the imaginary number, i, comes from raising i to consecutive integer powers, which creates a sequence that repeats with every interval of 4:

$$i^1 = i$$
$$i^2 = -1$$
$$i^3 = (i)(i)(i) = i(i^2) = i(-1) = -i$$
$$i^4 = (i)(i)(i)(i) = (i^2)(i^2) = (-1)(-1) = 1$$
$$i^5 = (i)(i^4) = (i)(1) = i$$
$$i^6 = (i)(i^5) = (i)(i) = -1$$
$$i^7 = (i)(i^6) = (i)(-1) = -i$$
$$i^8 = (i)(i^7) = (i)(-i) = -i^2 = -(-1) = 1$$

Thus, we have the following powerful shortcut for working with powers of i:

SHORTCUT FOR POWERS OF i	
For any positive integer $n > 3$: If n is a multiple of 4, $i^n = 1$. If n is not a multiple of 4, $i^n = i^r$, where r is the remainder when n is divided by 4.	

Example:

If $i^2 = -1$, what is the value of $i^{34} - (-i)^{30}$?

A. $-2i$ C. -2 E. $2i$
B. I D. 0

Applying our shortcut for powers of i, $i^{34} = i^2$ since the remainder of 34 divided by 4 is 2. And $(-i)^{30} = (-1)^{30}(i)^{30} = (1)(i^{30}) = i^2$ since the remainder of 30 divided by 4 is 2. Thus, $i^{34} - (-i)^{30} = i^2 - i^2 = 0$, (D).

EXERCISE 4

DIRECTIONS: Choose the correct answer to each of the following items. Answers are on page 815.

82. $\left(x^2\right)^3 = ?$

   F. x^5 H. $2x^5$ K. 6^x
   G. x^6 J. $2x^6$

83. $\dfrac{x^6 y^3 z^9}{x^4 y^3 z^8} = ?$

   A. x^2yz C. xyz E. x^2z
   B. x^2yz^2 D. x^2y

84. $\sqrt[12]{x^6} = ?$

   F. x^6 H. x^2 K. x^{-2}
   G. x^{-6} J. $x^{\frac{1}{2}}$

85. If $9a^3\sqrt{b} = a^5b^2$, what is a in terms of b?

   A. $3b^{-3}$ D. $9b^{3/4}$
   B. $3b^{-3/4}$ E. $(9b^{1/4})^{3/5}$
   C. $9b^{-3/2}$

86. The expression $\sqrt[k]{6^{2km}}$ must be a positive integer if which of the following is true?

   F. k is a positive integer.
   G. k is a multiple of 3.
   H. k is less than zero.
   J. m is a non-negative common fraction.
   K. m is a non-negative integer.

87. If $1 > x > 0$, which of the following must be true?

   A. $x^2 > x > \sqrt{x}$
   B. $x^2 > \sqrt{x} > x$
   C. $\sqrt{x} > x > x^2$
   D. $\sqrt{x} > x^2 > x$
   E. $x > \sqrt{x} > x^2$

88. For what value of x is $18^x = (3^6)(6^6)$?

   F. 2   H. 6   K. 18
   G. 3   J. 12

89. If $(3^a)(3^b) = 3^8$, what is the average (arithmetic mean) of a and b?

   A. 2   C. 4   E. 12
   B. 3   D. 8

90. If $3^x = 729$, what is the value of x?

   F. 2   H. 6   K. 13
   G. 3   J. 9

91. If $\left[(5^a)(5^b)\right]^c = \dfrac{5^d}{5^e}$, which of the following expressions is equal to e?

   A. $d - ac - b$ D. $\dfrac{d}{ca} + \dfrac{d}{cb}$
   B. $d - c(a + b)$ E. $c - d(a + b)$
   C. $\dfrac{d}{c(a+b)}$

92. If n is a positive integer, which of the following <u>CANNOT</u> be the units digit of n^2?

    F. 1   H. 4   K. 6
    G. 2   J. 5

93. If $4^{x-2} = 2^{1/2}$, then $x = ?$

    A. -2 C. 1   E. $\dfrac{9}{2}$

    B. $-\dfrac{1}{2}$ D. $\dfrac{9}{4}$

94. If $4^{2x+5} = 64$, what is the value of x?

    F. $-\dfrac{1}{2}$ H. 1   K. 4

    G. -1 J. 2

95. Which of the following is equivalent to $\sqrt[3]{64x^{12}y^6}\sqrt{9x^4y^2}$?

    A. $2\sqrt{x^9y^3}\sqrt{3x^2}$ D. $12x^8y^2$

    B. $12\sqrt[3]{x^6y^3}$ E. $12x^8y^4$

    C. $12x^6y^3$

96. If $3^m = 4^n$, which of the following represents the ratio of m to n?

    F. $\dfrac{\log 3x}{\log 4x}$ J. $\dfrac{\log 4}{\log 3}$

    G. $\log\dfrac{3}{4}$ K. $\log 4 - \log 3$

    H. $\dfrac{\log 3}{\log 4}$

97. Which of the following expressions is equal to $\log_n m$?

    A. m^n D. $\log_{10} n - \log_{10} m$

    B. $-\log_m n$ E. $\dfrac{\log_m n}{\log_{10} m}$

    C. $\dfrac{1}{\log_m n}$

98. If $a = 16$, $b = 2$, and $c = 4$, $\log_c\left(\dfrac{a^2}{b^4}\right) = ?$

    F. -4 H. $\dfrac{1}{2}$ K. 4

    G. -2 J. 2

99. If $\log_m 4 = x$ and $\log_m 3 = y$, what is $\log_m 36$ in terms of x and y?

    A. $2x - y$ C. $x + 2y$ E. $3xy$

    B. $x^2 + 2y$ D. $2(x + y)$

100. Which of the following expressions is equal to

$$\log x + 2\log_y y + \frac{1}{2}\log\frac{x}{y} - \frac{2}{3}\log z \ ?$$

F. $2 + \log\dfrac{\sqrt{x^3}}{\left(\sqrt{y}\right)\left(\sqrt[3]{z^2}\right)}$

G. $2 + \log\dfrac{\sqrt[3]{z^2}}{\left(\sqrt{x^3}\right)\left(\sqrt{y}\right)}$

H. $2 + \log\sqrt[3]{z^2}\sqrt{x^3}\sqrt{y}$

J. $\dfrac{1}{2} + \log\dfrac{\sqrt{y}}{\left(\sqrt{x^3}\right)\left(\sqrt[3]{z^2}\right)}$

K. $\dfrac{1}{2} + \log\dfrac{\left(\sqrt{x^3}\right)\left(\sqrt[3]{z^2}\right)}{\sqrt{y}}$

101. If m is a positive number such that $\log_m\left(\dfrac{1}{32}\right) = -5$, what is the value of m?

A. $\dfrac{1}{4}$ C. 2 E. 37

B. $\dfrac{1}{2}$ D. 4

102. If $8^{1/3} = \dfrac{1}{2}$, which of the following is true?

F. $-\log_8\dfrac{1}{2} = 3$

G. $-\log_8\dfrac{1}{3} = \dfrac{1}{2}$

H. $\log_2\left(-\dfrac{1}{3}\right) = 8$

J. $\log_8\dfrac{1}{2} = -\dfrac{1}{3}$

K. $\log_8\dfrac{1}{2} = \dfrac{1}{3}$

103. A geometric sequence is a sequence of numbers formed by continually multiplying by the same number; e.g., {81, 27, 9, 3, ...} is a geometric sequence formed by continually multiplying by $\dfrac{1}{3}$. What is the next term in the geometric sequence of {2, 8, 32, 128, ...}?

A. 132 D. 512
B. 256 E. 1,024
C. 384

104. The number of rabbits in a certain population doubles every 3 months. Currently, there are 5 rabbits in the population. How many rabbits will there be 3 years from now?

F. 64
G. 4,096
H. 9,064
J. 20,480
K. 20,840

105. Barb is writing a report on Fort Ann City, where she lives. She has learned that the population of the city doubled every 10 years from 1990 to 2010. If the population in 1990 was x people and continues to grow at the same rate, what will be the population of the city, in terms of x, in 2040?

A. $5x$

B. $10x$

C. $2x^5$

D. $\left(2^5\right)(x)$

E. $\left(2^5\right)^x$

106. Hannah took out a simple interest loan of $1,000. The interest rate on the loan is 5%. If no payments are made, how much money, in dollars, will she owe at the end of 7 years?

F. $(1.5)^7$
G. $(1.05)^7$
H. $7(1.05)$
J. $1{,}000 + (0.05)^7$
K. $1{,}000 + 7(0.05)$

107. The number of bacteria in a certain culture doubles every 15 minutes. If the number was initially 10^3, what was the number in the population 1 hour later?

A. $2^{(15/60)}(10^3)$
B. $2^{(60/15)}(10^3)$
C. $2^3(10)^{(60/15)}$
D. $(10^3)2^{(15/60)}$
E. $(10^3)2^{(60/15)}$

108. During a two-year period of political instability in a country, the price of a "market basket" of essential goods doubled every six months from its base price of 1 wint, the unit of currency of the country. Which of the lines on the graph below best represents the rise in the price of the market basket?

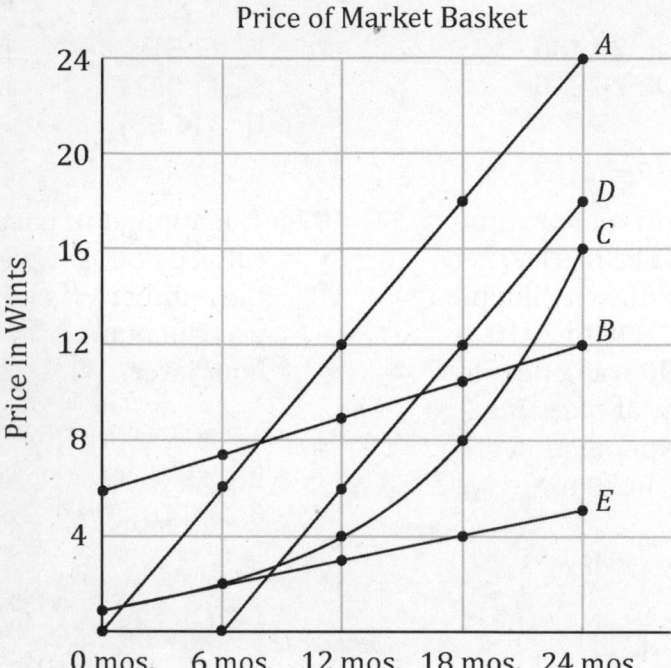

Price of Market Basket

F. A   H. C   K. E
G. B   J. D

109. Which of the following is a pure imaginary number?

A. $3 + 1$ C. $-1 + i^2$ E. $\sqrt{(-1)^2}$
B. i^2 D. $3\sqrt{-1}$

110. What is the value of i^{83}?

F. -1 H. -1 K. 1
G. 1 J. 0

111. If $x = 3 + 2i$ and $y = 4 - 3i$, which of the following is equal to $x + y$?

A. $i - 7$ C. $7 - 1$ E. 6
B. $7i + 7$ D. $i + 7$

112. If $m = 1 - 3i$ and $n = \dfrac{1}{2} + i$, which of the following is equal to $m^2 n$?

F. $-10 - 5i$ J. $2 - 11i$
G. $-10 + 5i$ K. $10 + 5i$
H. $2 + 5i$

Algebraic Expressions, Equations, and Inequalities

Algebraic Expressions

Use the arithmetic ***rules of exponents*** to multiply or divide algebraic terms. Remember that $x^0 = 1$ when $x \neq 0$, and $x^1 = x$. You'll recognize these rules from the summary of operations involving exponents in the previous section.

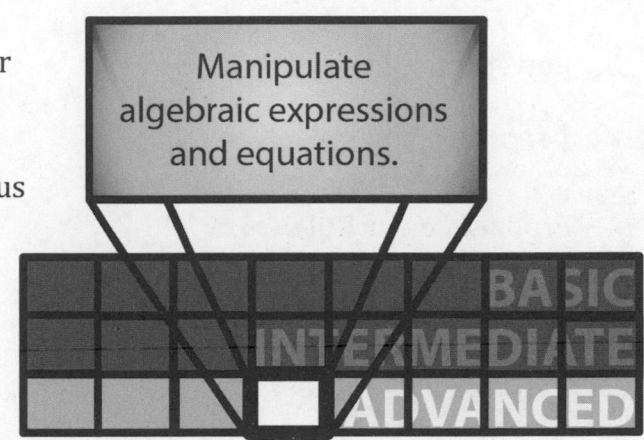

Manipulate algebraic expressions and equations.

BASIC
INTERMEDIATE
ADVANCED

RULES OF EXPONENTS

1. **Product Rule:** $x^m \bullet x^n = x^{m+n}$ and $ax^m \bullet bx^n = abx^{m+n}$

2. **Quotient Rule:** $\dfrac{x^m}{x^n} = x^{m-n}$

3. **Power Rule:** $\left(x^m\right)^n = x^{mn}$

4. **Product Power Rule:** $\left(x^m \bullet y^p\right)^n = x^{mn} \bullet y^{pn}$

5. **Quotient Power Rule:** $\left(\dfrac{x^m}{y^p}\right)^n = \dfrac{x^{mn}}{y^{pn}}$

6. **Negative Exponents:** $x^{-n} = \dfrac{1}{x^n}$

Examples:

1. Product Rule:

$$\left(3x^2\right)(xy) = (3 \cdot 1)\left(x^2 \cdot xy\right) = 3 \cdot x^{2+1} \cdot y = 3x^3 y$$

$$(2xyz)(3xy)(4yz) = (2 \cdot 3 \cdot 4)(xyz \cdot xy \cdot yz) = 24 \cdot x^{1+1} \cdot y^{1+1+1} \cdot z^{1+1} = 24x^2 y^3 z^2$$

2. Quotient Rule:

$$\frac{2x^4 y^3}{x^2 y^2 z} = \frac{2}{1} \cdot \frac{x^4 y^3}{x^2 y^2 z} = 2 \cdot \frac{x^{4-2} y^{3-2}}{z} = \frac{2x^2 y}{z}$$

3. Power Rule:

$$\left(4x^2\right)^3 = 4^3 x^{(2)(3)} = 64x^6$$

4. Product Power Rule:

$$\left(3x^2 y^3\right)^2 = 3^2 x^{(2)(2)} y^{(3)(2)} = 9x^4 y^6$$

5. Quotient Power Rule:

$$\left(\frac{x^2}{y^3}\right)^2 = \frac{x^{(2)(2)}}{y^{(3)(2)}} = \frac{x^4}{y^6}$$

$$\left(\frac{4a^3}{b^{-3}}\right)^2 = \frac{4^2 a^{(3)(2)}}{b^{(-3)(2)}} = \frac{16a^6}{b^{-6}} = 16a^6 b^6$$

Rational Expressions

A ***rational expression*** is a fraction containing algebraic terms.

Examples:

$$\frac{x^2}{xy - y^2}$$

$$\frac{3 + \dfrac{1}{x}}{9 - \dfrac{1}{x^2}}$$

Adding and Subtracting Rational Expressions

Adding and subtracting rational expressions, like adding and subtracting numerical fractions, require common denominators. If the denominators are the same, simply add/subtract the numerators: $\dfrac{a}{x} \pm \dfrac{b}{x} = \dfrac{a \pm b}{x}$.

Examples:

$$\frac{2x}{y} - \frac{x}{y} = \frac{2x - x}{y} = \frac{x}{y}$$

$$\frac{a^2 + x}{c^3 d} + \frac{x}{c^3 d} = \frac{a^2 + 2x}{c^3 d}$$

To add or subtract rational expressions with unlike denominators, you must first find a common denominator. Usually, this can be accomplished by using the same method as with numerical fractions: $\dfrac{a}{x} \pm \dfrac{b}{y} = \dfrac{ay}{xy} \pm \dfrac{bx}{xy} = \dfrac{ay \pm bx}{xy}$.

Example:

$$\frac{2x}{y} + \frac{3y}{x} = \frac{2x}{y} \searrow + \nearrow \frac{3y}{x} = \frac{2x^2 + 3y^2}{xy}$$

Multiplying and Dividing Rational Expressions

To multiply rational expressions, follow the rule for multiplying numeric fractions. Multiply terms in the numerators to create a new numerator, and multiply terms in the denominator to create a new denominator: $\dfrac{a}{c} \cdot \dfrac{b}{d} = \dfrac{ab}{cd}$.

Examples:

$$\frac{2}{x} \cdot \frac{3}{y} = \frac{6}{xy}$$

$$\frac{x^2 y^3}{z} \cdot \frac{x^3 y^2}{wz} = \frac{x^5 y^5}{wz^2}$$

To divide rational expressions, follow the rule for dividing numeric fractions. Invert the divisor, or second fraction, and multiply: $\dfrac{a}{c} \div \dfrac{b}{d} = \dfrac{a}{c} \cdot \dfrac{d}{b} = \dfrac{ad}{cb}$.

Examples:

$$\frac{2}{y} \div \frac{3}{x} = \frac{2}{y} \cdot \frac{x}{3} = \frac{2x}{3y}$$

$$\frac{2x^2}{y} \div \frac{y}{x} = \frac{2x^2}{y} \cdot \frac{x}{y} = \frac{2x^3}{y^2}$$

Radical Expressions

Radicals in algebraic expressions are manipulated in the same way as numeric radicals using the rules of exponents.

Example:

$$\frac{3\sqrt{x}+\sqrt{x^3}}{x}=?$$

Apply the rules of exponents: $\dfrac{3\sqrt{x}+\sqrt{x^3}}{x}=\dfrac{3\sqrt{x}}{x}+\dfrac{\sqrt{x^3}}{x}=\dfrac{3x^{\frac{1}{2}}}{x}+\dfrac{x^{\frac{3}{2}}}{x}=$

$$3x^{\left(\frac{1}{2}-1\right)}+x^{\left(\frac{3}{2}-1\right)}=3x^{-\frac{1}{2}}+x^{\frac{1}{2}}=\frac{3}{\sqrt{x}}+\sqrt{x}.$$

When simplifying expressions containing roots and radicals that are inverse operations of one another, it is important to note that the sign of the variable impacts the sign of the result. Consider $\sqrt{x^2}$: if $x \geq 0$, then $\sqrt{x^2}=x$; if $x<0$, then $\sqrt{x^2}=-x$.

Examples:

$$\sqrt{2^2}=2 \qquad\qquad\qquad \sqrt{(-2)^2}=-(-2)=2$$

Algebraic Equations

Solving Equations by Factoring

Factoring is an alternative shortcut method for solving some equations. Before factoring, rewrite the equation with all of the terms on one side of the equation and zero on the other side. If the nonzero side of the equation can be factored into a product of expressions, then use the following property to yield simpler equations that can be solved: if $xy = 0$, then $x = 0$ or $y = 0$. This is called the **zero-product property**. The solutions of the simpler equations will be solutions, or **roots**, of the factored equation.

Examples:

If $\dfrac{4x^3+8x^2-x-2}{x+4}=0$ and $x \neq -4$, what is the set of all possible values for x?

Factor the numerator of the fraction (for a review on factoring algebraic expressions, see page 452):

$$\frac{\left(4x^2 - 1\right)(x + 2)}{x + 4} = 0$$

Applying the zero-product property, either $4x^2 - 1 = 0$ or $x + 2 = 0$. In each instance, solve for x:

$$4x^2 - 1 = 0 \qquad\qquad x + 2 = 0$$
$$x^2 = \frac{1}{4} \qquad \text{or} \qquad x = -2$$
$$x = \pm\frac{1}{2}$$

Therefore, the set of all possible values for x is $\left\{-2, -\dfrac{1}{2}, \dfrac{1}{2}\right\}$

If $x^3 + 2x^2 + x = 3(x + 1)^2$, what is the set of all possible values for x?

Move all the terms to one side of the equality and simplify by factoring like terms:

$$x^3 + 2x^2 + x - 3(x + 1)^2 = 0$$
$$x\left(x^2 + 2x + 1\right) - 3(x + 1)^2 = 0$$
$$x(x + 1)^2 - 3(x + 1)^2 = 0$$
$$(x - 3)(x + 1)^2 = 0$$
$$x - 3 = 0 \text{ or } x + 1 = 0$$

Therefore, the set of all possible values for x is $\{-1, 3\}$.

Rational Equations

A rational equation is one in which one or more terms is a fractional one. When manipulating rational equations, follow the same rules as discussed with rational expressions. Rational equations may involve ***extraneous solutions***, which are NOT true when plugged into the original equation. Extraneous solutions to rational equations are possible when the equation includes a variable in the denominator. Thus, always test solutions that involve variables in the denominator.

Examples:

If $\dfrac{x}{x+6} = \dfrac{y^3 - 1}{(y+1)\left(y^2 - y + 1\right) + 4}$, then $x = ?$

Perform the indicated operations using an expanded version of the FOIL method:

$$\frac{x}{x+6} = \frac{y^3 - 1}{y^3 - y^2 + y + y^2 - y + 1 + 4} = \frac{y^3 - 1}{y^3 + 5} = \frac{y^3 - 1}{y^3 - 1 + 6} = \frac{y^3 - 1}{\left(y^3 - 1\right) + 6}.$$

Therefore, $x = y^3 - 1$.

If $\dfrac{5}{2x-2} = \dfrac{15}{x^2 - 1}$, then $x = ?$

Cross-multiply and evaluate:

$$\frac{5}{2x-2} = \frac{15}{x^2 - 1}$$

$$5\left(x^2 - 1\right) = 15\left(2x - 2\right)$$

$$5x^2 - 5 = 30x - 30$$

$$5x^2 - 30x + 25 = 0$$

Now, factor:

$$(5x - 5)(x - 5) = 0$$

Therefore, $x = 1$ or $x = 5$. Since the equation involves a variable in the denominator, test whether $2x - 2 = 0$ or $x^2 - 1 = 0$ for $x = 1$ or $x = 5$:

$$2(1) - 2 = 0 \text{ and } 1^2 - 1 = 0 \text{, so } x \neq 1$$
$$2(5) - 2 = 8 \text{ and } 5^2 - 1 = 24 \text{, so } x = 5$$

Radical Equations

Expressions in equations may include radicals. The same principles for working with radicals in expressions apply to equations. Test solutions to radical equations when finding the solution involves squaring both sides of the equation.

Example:

If $\sqrt{x-3}+5=x$, what is the value of x?

Solve for x:

$$\sqrt{x-3}+5=x$$
$$\sqrt{x-3}=x-5$$
$$\left(\sqrt{x-3}\right)^2=(x-5)^2$$
$$\left(\sqrt{x-3}\right)\left(\sqrt{x-3}\right)=(x-5)(x-5)$$
$$x-3=x^2-10x+25$$
$$0=x^2-11x+28$$
$$0=(x-7)(x-4)$$
$$x=7 \text{ or } 4$$

Since the solution involved squaring both sides, check both solutions:

$x=7$: $\sqrt{(7)-3}+5=7$ This statement is true, so $x=7$.

$x=4$: $\sqrt{(4)-3}+5=4$ This statement is NOT true, so $x\neq4$.

Exponents in Algebraic Equations and Inequalities

Rational Exponents

Rational equations and inequalities can include terms with rational exponents. The same rules for working with exponents apply to equations as they apply to expressions when manipulating these terms.

Example:

Find the value of $x^{-2/3}$ when $x=27$.

Substitute 27 for x in the given expression:
$$x^{-2/3}=(27)^{-2/3}=\frac{1}{27^{2/3}}=\frac{1}{\left(\sqrt[3]{27}\right)^2}=\frac{1}{3^2}=\frac{1}{9}.$$

Algebraic Exponents

When solving equations that involve algebraic exponential terms, try to find a common base to use throughout the problem. For a review of working with exponents in algebraic expressions, see page 552.

Example:

If $4^{x+2} = 8^{3x-6}$, what is the value of x?

Since $4 = 2^2$ and $8 = 2^3$:

$$\left(2^2\right)^{x+2} = \left(2^3\right)^{3x-6}$$

$$2^{2x+4} = 2^{9x-18}$$

Now, the bases are equal, so drop them and solve for x:

$$2x + 4 = 9x - 18$$

$$22 = 7x$$

$$x = \frac{22}{7}$$

EXERCISE 5

DIRECTIONS: Choose the correct answer to each of the following items. Answers are on page 815.

113. $\left(xy^2\right)\left(x^2 z\right)\left(y^2 z\right) = ?$

    A. $8xyz$

    B. $x^2 y^4 z$

    C. $x^3 y^4 z^2$

    D. $x^3 y^3 z^2$

    E. $x^3 y^3 z^3$

114. $\dfrac{a^3 b^4 c^5}{abc} = ?$

    F. $a^2 b^3 c^4$

    G. $a^3 b^4 c^5$

    H. $a^4 b^5 c^6$

    J. $(abc)^{12}$

    K. $(abc)^{60}$

115. $\left(\dfrac{a^2}{b^3}\right)^3 = ?$

    A. $\dfrac{a^5}{b}$

    B. $\dfrac{a^6}{b^9}$

    C. $\dfrac{a^5}{b}$

    D. $a^6 b$

    E. $a^6 b^9$

116. $\left(\dfrac{c^4 d^2}{c^2 d}\right)^3 = ?$

    F. $c^5 d^3$

    G. $c^5 d^5$

    H. $c^6 d^3$

    J. $c^6 d^4$

    K. $c^6 d^6$

117. $\left(\dfrac{abc^2}{abc^3}\right)\left(\dfrac{a^2b^2c}{ab}\right) = ?$

A. $\dfrac{ab}{c}$ C. ab E. abc

B. $\dfrac{bc}{a}$ D. c

118. $\dfrac{ab}{x} + \dfrac{bc}{x} + \dfrac{cd}{x} = ?$

F. $\dfrac{abcd}{x}$ J. $\dfrac{ab+bc+cd}{3x}$

G. $\dfrac{a+b+c+d}{x}$ K. $\dfrac{ab+bc+cd}{x^3}$

H. $\dfrac{ab+bc+cd}{x}$

119. $\dfrac{a}{b} - \dfrac{b}{a} = ?$

A. $\dfrac{ab}{a-b}$ D. $\dfrac{ab-ba}{ab}$

B. $\dfrac{a-b}{b-a}$ E. $\dfrac{a^2-b^2}{ab}$

C. $\dfrac{a-b}{ab}$

120. $\dfrac{x}{a} + \dfrac{y}{b} + \dfrac{z}{c} = ?$

F. $\dfrac{xyz}{abc}$

G. $\dfrac{x+y+z}{a+b+c}$

H. $\dfrac{xbc+yac+zab}{abc}$

J. $\dfrac{xbc+yac+zab}{a+b+c}$

K. $\dfrac{xa+yb+zc}{abc}$

121. $\dfrac{8x^{-4}}{2x} = ?$

A. $\dfrac{4}{x^4}$ C. $\dfrac{3}{x^5}$ E. $\dfrac{8}{x^5}$

B. $\dfrac{2}{x^5}$ D. $\dfrac{4}{x^5}$

122. $\dfrac{6x^{-5}y^2}{3^{-1}x^{-4}y} = ?$

F. $\dfrac{2y}{x}$ H. $\dfrac{16y^5}{x^4}$ K. $\dfrac{18y^2}{x^3}$

G. $\dfrac{18y}{x}$ J. $\dfrac{16y^4}{x^5}$

123. $\left(2x + \sqrt{3}\right)^2 = ?$

A. $3x^2 + 3x\sqrt{3} + 3$
B. $3x^2 - 4x\sqrt{3} - 3$
C. $4x^2 - 4x\sqrt{3} - 3$
D. $-4x^2 + 4x\sqrt{3} + 3$
E. $4x^2 + 4x\sqrt{3} + 3$

124. $\left(\dfrac{x^2 y^3 x^5}{2^{-1}}\right)^2 = ?$

F. $\dfrac{1}{4}x^{14}y^6$　　J. $4x^{14}y^6$

G. $\dfrac{1}{4}x^{49}y^9$　　K. $4x^{49}y^9$

H. $4x^{12}y^{66}$

125. $1 - \dfrac{x}{y} = ?$

A. $\dfrac{x-y}{x}$　　D. $\dfrac{1-x}{1-y}$

B. $\dfrac{y-x}{y}$　　E. $\dfrac{y-x}{xy}$

C. $\dfrac{x-y}{y}$

126. $\dfrac{1 + \dfrac{1}{x}}{\dfrac{y}{x}} = ?$

F. $\dfrac{x+1}{y}$　　H. $\dfrac{x^2+1}{xy}$

G. $\dfrac{x+1}{x}$　　J. $\dfrac{y+1}{y}$

H. $\dfrac{y(x+1)}{x^2}$

127. $\dfrac{\dfrac{1}{x} + \dfrac{1}{y}}{3} = ?$

A. $\dfrac{3x+3y}{xy}$　　D. $\dfrac{x+y}{3xy}$

B. $\dfrac{x+y}{3}$　　E. $\dfrac{3xy}{x}$

C. $\dfrac{xy}{3}$

128. If $x \geq 0$, then $\sqrt{\dfrac{x^2}{9} + \dfrac{x^2}{16}} = ?$

F. $\dfrac{x}{5}$　　H. $\dfrac{7x}{12}$　　K. $\dfrac{25x^2}{144}$

G. $\dfrac{5x}{12}$　　J. $\dfrac{5x^2}{12}$

129. $\sqrt{a^2 + b^2} = ?$

A. $a+b$
B. $a-b$
C. $\sqrt{a^2} + \sqrt{b^2}$
D. $(a+b)(a-b)$
E. None of these

130. If factored as completely as possible,
$16x^4 - 81y^{16} = ?$

F. $(4x^2 + 9y^4)(4x^2 - 9y^4)$

G. $(4x^2 + 9y^8)(4x^2 - 9y^8)$

H. $(16x^2 + 81y^8)(x - y^2)(x - y^2)$

J. $(4x^2 + 9y^8)(2x + 3y^4)(2x - 3y^4)$

K $16x^4 - 81y^{16}$

131. If $\dfrac{0.2 + x}{3} = \dfrac{\frac{5}{6}}{4}$, then $x = ?$

A. $-\dfrac{40}{17}$ C. 0   E. $\dfrac{40}{17}$

B. $-\dfrac{17}{40}$ D. $\dfrac{17}{40}$

132. If $3^{8x+4} = 27^{2x+12}$, then $x = ?$

F. $\dfrac{1}{16}$ H. $\dfrac{4}{3}$ K. 16

G. $\dfrac{3}{4}$ J. 5

133. If x is a real number such that $x \neq 0$, y is a real number, $x^5 = 8y$, and $x^4 = y$, then $x = ?$

A. 8   C. $8y$ E. $8y^2$

B. $7y$ D. $7y^2$

134. If $2\sqrt{x+3} + 5 = 21$, then $x = ?$

F. 1   H. 61   K. 253
G. 5   J. 64

135. If x represents a real number, how many different values of x satisfy the equation $x^{128} = 16^{32}$?

A. Zero
B. One
C. Two
D. More than two, but not infinite
E. Infinite

136. If $\dfrac{5}{x+1} + 2 = 5$, then $x = ?$

F. $-\dfrac{2}{7}$ H. $\dfrac{7}{2}$ K. 10

G. $\dfrac{2}{3}$ J. 7

137. If $x = k + \dfrac{1}{2} = \dfrac{k+3}{2}$, then $x = ?$

A. $\dfrac{1}{3}$ C. 1   E. $\dfrac{5}{2}$

B. $\dfrac{1}{2}$ D. 2

Solving Algebraic Formulas

An ***algebraic formula*** is an equation that typically involves a relationship between literal quantities. Problems that involve formulas often ask you to solve for a particular unknown (variable) using substitution. Algebraic formulas can take many different forms, including functions, scientific equations, geometric formulas, and story problems. Regardless of the format, the concept is the same: replace the variables with the values that are given and solve for the unknown variable.

Create expressions, equations, and inequalities for common algebra situations.

Create expressions requiring planning and/or manipulation to model real-world situations.

Create equations and inequalities requiring planning, manipulation, and/or solving.

Example:

The volume of a sphere is $\dfrac{4\pi r^3}{3}$, where r is the radius of the sphere. Find the radius of a sphere with a volume of 288π.

Set the volume of the sphere equal to 288π and solve for r:

$$288\pi = \frac{4\pi r^3}{3}$$
$$864\pi = 4\pi r^3$$
$$216 = r^3$$
$$6 = r$$

Algebraic formulas that represent real life situations often involve variables with units of measure, such as inches or gallons. You must ensure that all variables have similar units on both sides of the equation in order for the equality to remain true. To maintain consistency, it may be necessary to convert units using equivalent expressions (e.g., $\dfrac{12 \text{ inches}}{1 \text{ foot}}$, $\dfrac{3 \text{ feet}}{1 \text{ yard}}$, $\dfrac{60 \text{ minutes}}{1 \text{ hour}}$). Thus, when dealing with quantities given in units of any type, it helps to explicitly write out the units in the expressions.

Example:

If string costs k cents per foot at the hardware store, how much will w feet and j inches of the string cost, in dollars?

Explicitly write out the units in the expression and cancel like units in the numerator and denominator:

$$\text{Cost of string (dollars)} = \frac{k \text{ cents}}{1 \text{ ft. of string}} \cdot \text{length of string (ft.)} \cdot \frac{1 \text{ dollar}}{100 \text{ cents}}$$

$$= \frac{k \text{ cents}}{1 \text{ ft.}} \cdot \left[w \text{ ft.} + \left(j \text{ in.} \cdot \frac{1 \text{ ft.}}{12 \text{ in.}} \right) \right] \cdot \frac{1 \text{ dollar}}{100 \text{ cents}}$$

$$= \frac{k \text{ cents}}{1 \text{ ft.}} \cdot \left[w \text{ ft.} + \left(j \text{ in.} \cdot \frac{1 \text{ ft.}}{12 \text{ in.}} \right) \right] \cdot \frac{1 \text{ dollar}}{100 \text{ cents}}$$

$$= \frac{k \text{ cents}}{1 \text{ ft.}} \cdot \left(w + \frac{j}{12} \right) (\text{ft.}) \cdot \frac{1 \text{ dollar}}{100 \text{ cents}}$$

$$= k \text{ cents} \cdot \left(w + \frac{j}{12} \right) \cdot \frac{1 \text{ dollar}}{100 \text{ cents}}$$

$$= \frac{k}{100} \left(w + \frac{j}{12} \right) \text{ dollar}$$

Therefore, the cost of the string, in dollars, is $\frac{k}{100}\left(w + \frac{j}{12} \right)$.

Story problems may test arithmetic, algebra, or geometry in the context of a "story." You should have everything you need to solve these problems. However, remember that if a math story item stumps you, you have the answer at hand. Simply work backwards from the answer choices—the right answer has to be one of the choices. Since quantitative (i.e., numerical value) choices are arranged in size order, starting with the middle answer choice will result in the fewest calculations.

In solving story problems, the most important technique is to read accurately. Be sure you clearly understand what you are asked to find. Then, evaluate the item in common sense terms to eliminate answer choices. For example, if two people are working together, their combined speed is greater than either individual speed, but not more than twice as fast as the fastest speed. Finally, be alert for the "hidden equation"—some necessary information so obvious that the item assumes that you know it.

Examples:

boys + girls = total class

imported wine + domestic wine = all wine

A wall and a floor intersect to form a right angle (Pythagorean theorem)

Some of the frequently encountered types of problem-solving problems are described in this section, although not every item you may encounter will fall into one of these categories. However, thoroughly familiarizing yourself with the types of problems that follow will help you to develop the skills to translate and solve all kinds of verbal problems. This section covers coin problems, age problems, interest problems, and mixture problems.

Coin Problems

For **coin problems**, change the value of all monies involved to cents before writing an equation. The number of nickels must be multiplied by 5 to give their value in cents; dimes must be multiplied by 10; quarters by 25; half-dollars by 50; and dollars by 100.

Example:

Richard has $3.50 consisting of nickels and dimes. If he has 5 more dimes than nickels, how many dimes does he have?

A. 20   C. 30   E. 40
B. 25   D. 35

Let x equal the number of nickels, $x+5$ equal the number of dimes, $5x$ equal the value of the nickels in cents, $10(x+5)=10x+50$ equal the value of the dimes in cents, and 350 equal the value of the money he has in cents. Thus, $5x+10x+50 = 350 \Rightarrow 15x = 300 \Rightarrow x = 20$. Therefore, Richard has 20 nickels and 25 dimes, (B). Note that (A), 20, is not the correct answer, but if you forget to add 5 to x you could easily choose it as the correct answer. You must be sure to read carefully what you are asked to find and then continue until you have found the quantity sought.

Age Problems

Age problems involve a comparison of ages at the present time, several years from now, or several years ago. A person's age x years from now is found by adding x to his present age. A person's age x years ago is found by subtracting x from his present age.

Examples:

Michelle was 12 years old y years ago. What is her age b years from now?

Michelle's present age is $12 + y$. In b years, her age will be $12 + y + b$.

Logan is 5 years older than Florencia. Three years ago, Logan was twice as old as Florencia. How old is Logan?

If L is Logan's age and F is Florencia's age, $L = F + 5$. Three years ago, Logan was $L - 3$ and Florencia was $F - 3$. So, since 3 years ago, Logan was twice as old as Florencia:

$$L - 3 = 2(F - 3)$$
$$L - 3 = 2F - 6$$
$$L = 2F - 3$$

Substitute $L = F + 5 \Rightarrow F = L - 5$ for F in the equation $L = 2F - 3$ to find Logan's current age:

$$L = 2F - 3$$
$$L = 2(L - 5) - 3$$
$$L = 2L - 13$$
$$L = 13$$

Interest Problems

Simple Interest

Simple interest is computed on the principal (amount of initial investment) only. To calculate the amount of simple interest paid on an investment, multiply the principal invested by the rate (percent) of interest paid and the time of the investment (in years): simple interest income = principal • rate • time.

Examples:

If $4,000 is invested at 3% simple annual interest, how much interest is earned in 4 months?

Since the annual interest is 3%, the interest for 1 year is: $4,000(0.03)(1) = \$120$.

Thus, the interest earned in 4 months, or $\frac{1}{3}$ of a year is $\frac{\$120}{3} = \$40$.

Mr. Krecker invests $4,000, part at 6% and part at 7%; the first year return is $250. Find the amount invested at 7%.

Let x equal the amount invested at 7%. Thus, $4,000 - x$ equals the amount invested at 6%; $0.07x$ equals the income from the 7% investment; and $0.06(4,000 - x)$ equals the income from the 6% investment. Therefore:

$$0.07x + 0.06(4,000 - x) = 250$$
$$7x + 6(4,000 - x) = 25,000$$
$$7x + 24,000 - 6x = 25,000$$
$$x = 1,000 \ (\$1,000 \text{ invested at 7\%})$$

Compound Interest

Compound interest is computed on the principal as well as on any interest already earned. The interest already earned is determined as simple interest for each period that the interest is compounded with the principal increasing to include the previously earned interest. If annual interest is compounded for a given period, the interest rate for that period is only a fraction of the interest rate, as determined by the number of periods for which the interest is compounded.

Example:

If $2,000 is invested at 4% annual interest, compounded quarterly, what is the balance after 9 months?

Since the interest is compounded quarterly, figure the interest for the four periods, with each successive interest computed for the principal plus all prior interest income. Since the interest rate is 4% annually, compounded four times a year, the interest rate for each period is 1%. The balance after the first 3 months (one-quarter of a year) would be $\$2,000 + (\$2,000)(0.01) = \$2,000 + \$20 = \$2,020$. The balance after the second 3 months would be $\$2,020 + (\$2,020)(0.01) = \$2,020 + \$20.20 = \$2,040.20$. The total balance after the final 3 months would be $\$2,040.20 + (\$2,040.20)(0.01) = \$2,040.20 + \$20.40 = \$2,060.60$.

The previous example illustrates how if interest is compounded, the interest is computed on the principal as well as on any interest earned. The general formula for compounded interest follows:

$$\text{Final Balance} = \text{Principal} \cdot \left(1 + \frac{\text{interest rate}}{C}\right)^{(\text{time})(C)}$$

where time is in ***years***, interest rate is an annual rate expressed in decimal form, and C is the number of times the interest is compounded ***annually***.

Example:

If $12,000 is invested at 8% annual interest, compounded semiannually, what is the balance after one year?

The interest is compounded twice a year, so $C = 2$. Therefore, the final balance is

$$12,000\left(1 + \frac{0.08}{2}\right)^{(1)(2)} = 12,000(1.04)^2 = \$12,979.20.$$

Mixture Problems

You should be familiar with two kinds of ***mixture problems***. The first type is sometimes referred to as dry mixture, in which dry ingredients of different values, such as nuts or coffee, are mixed. For this type of problem, always start by writing down what the variable stands for, including units. Doing so will prevent many careless mistakes. Then organize the data in a chart of three rows and three columns labeled as illustrated in the following problem.

Example:

A dealer wishes to mix 20 pounds of coffee selling for $4.50 per pound with some more expensive coffee selling for $6.00 per pound to make a mixture that will sell for $5.00 per pound. How many pounds of the more expensive coffee should he use?

Create a table summarizing the provided information:

	No. of lbs. ×	Price/lb. =	Total Price
Original	20	4.50	4.50(20)
Added	x	6.00	6.00(x)
Mixture	20 + x	5.00	5.00(20 + x)

The value of the original coffee plus the value of the added coffee must equal the value of the mixture:

$$4.50(20) + 6.00(x) = 5.00(20 + x)$$
$$90 + 6x = 100 + 5x$$
$$x = 10$$

Therefore, he should use 10 lbs. of $6.00 coffee.

The second type of mixture item deals with percents and amounts rather than prices and value.

Example:

How much water must be added to 20 gallons of a solution that is 30% alcohol to dilute it to a solution that is only 25% alcohol?

Create a table summarizing the provided information:

	No. of Gals. ×	% Alcohol/100 =	Total Gal. of Alcohol
Original	20	0.30	0.30(20)
Added	x	0	0
Final	20 + x	0.25	0.25(20 + x)

Note that the percentage of alcohol in water is zero. Had pure alcohol been added to strengthen the solution, the percentage would have been 100%. Thus, the amount of alcohol added (none) plus the original amount must equal the amount of alcohol in the new solution:

$$0.30(20) + 0x = 0.25(20 + x)$$
$$30(20) = 25(20 + x)$$
$$600 = 500 + 25x$$
$$100 = 25x$$
$$x = 4 \text{ gallons}$$

EXERCISE 6

DIRECTIONS: Choose the correct answer to each of the following items. Answers are on page 816.

138. Colin and Shaina wish to buy a milkshake. Together they have $4.00, consisting of quarters, dimes, and nickels. If they have 35 coins and the number of quarters is half the number of nickels, how many quarters do they have?

F. 5   H. 20   K. 36
G. 10   J. 23

139. In Juanita's purse, she has 24 coins made up of nickels and dimes. She also knows that she has three times as many dimes as nickels. What is the total value of coins in her purse?

A. $1.50   C. $2.20   E. $2.40
B. $2.10   D. $2.35

140. Leah has been saving quarters and dimes in a jar. If the total value of the 26 coins in her jar is $4.40, how many dimes has she saved?

F. 8   H. 14   K. 18
G. 12   J. 17

141. Robert is 15 years older than Stan. However, y years ago Robert was twice as old as Stan. If Stan is now b years old and $b > y$, find the value of $b - y$.

A. 13   C. 15   E. 17
B. 14   D. 16

142. The sum in years of Sam's and Suzie's ages is 18. If Sam is half as old as Suzie, how old is Suzie?

F. 4   H. 8   K. 12
G. 6   J. 10

143. Jack is 5 years older than his sister, Kate. Six years ago, Jack was twice as old as Kate. How old is Jack now?

A. 11   C. 15   E. 19
B. 13   D. 16

144. How many ounces of pure acid must be added to 20 ounces of a solution that is 5% acid to strengthen it to a solution that is 24% acid?

F. $2\frac{1}{2}$ H. 6   K. 10

G. 5   J. $7\frac{1}{2}$

145. How much water must be added to 30 gallons of a 50% alcohol solution to obtain a 40% alcohol solution?

A. 7.5   C. 10.25   E. 14.5
B. 9   D. 12

146. A baker mixes 10 pounds of dark chocolate selling for $2.00 per pound with some white chocolate selling for $1.50 per pound to make a mixture that sells for $1.80 per pound. Approximately how many pounds of the white chocolate should she use?

F. 4 lbs.   J. 7.67 lbs.
G. 5.33 lbs.   K. 8.33 lbs.
H. 6.67 lbs.

147. A baker produces 400 brownies a day at a cost of 25 cents per brownie. If all the brownies are sold each day, what is the minimum selling price per brownie to make a daily profit of at least $420?

A. $1.00   C. $1.20   E. $1.30
B. $1.10   D. $1.25

148. In a run/walk race, Weber runs x miles in h hours, then walks the remainder of the race route, y miles, in the same number of hours. Which of the following represents Weber's average speed, in miles per hour, for the entire race?

F. $\dfrac{x-y}{h}$ J. $\dfrac{2(x+y)}{2h}$

G. $\dfrac{x-y}{2h}$ K. $\dfrac{x+y}{2h}$

H. $\dfrac{2(x+y)}{h}$

149. If y varies directly with x and the constant of variation is 3, then $y = 12.3$ when $x = 4.1$. If y varies directly with x and $y = 6.72$ when $x = 4.2$, what is the constant of variation?

A. 1.6   C. 2.52   E. 4.2
B. 2.50   D. 3.1

150. At a constant temperature, the resistance of a wire varies directly with length and inversely with the square of the wire diameter. A piece of wire that is 0.1 inch in diameter and 50 feet long has a resistance of 0.1 ohm. What is the resistance, in ohms, of a wire of the same material that is 9,000 feet long and 0.3 inches in diameter?

F. 0.3   H. 2   K. 9
G. 0.9   J. 3

151. The Smith family wanted to make some home improvements. They borrowed $1,500 from a friend at a simple interest rate of 4% per year. Two years later they paid back the $1,500, together with the amount of interest. What was the total amount they paid back?

A. $60   D. $1,560
B. $120   E. $1,620
C. $1,500

152. Riley invests $12,000 in an account that pays 6.5% interest per year compounded quarterly. To the nearest dollar, what is the total amount of money he will have after 4 years?

F. $3,530   J. $13,530
G. $3,531   K. $15,531
H. $12,000

Solve Linear Inequalities

The fundamental rule for working with **linear inequalities** is similar to that for working with equations: treat each side of the inequality exactly the same. However, if you multiply or divide an inequality by a *negative* number, the direction of the inequality sign is reversed. Therefore, remember to change the direction of the inequality sign when multiplying or dividing by a negative number.

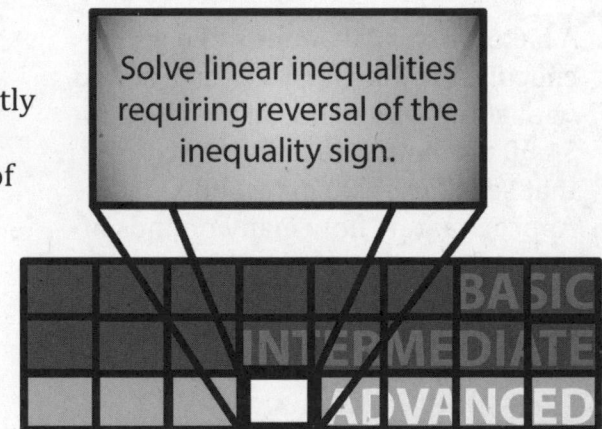

Example:

Multiply both sides by –2:

$$4 > 3$$
$$4(-2) < 3(-2)$$
$$-8 < -6$$

These properties hold true for inequalities containing variables, as the following example illustrates.

Example:

For what values of x is $3(2-x)+x > 30$?

Solve for x: $3(2-x)+x > 30$

$$6 - 3x + x > 30$$
$$6 - 2x > 30$$
$$-2x > 24$$
$$x < -12$$

In the solution, the inequality sign is reversed. Check the solution using $x = -20$ and $x = 0$ to verify the direction of the inequality:

$$3(2 - x) + x > 30$$
$$3(2 - (-20)) + (-20) > 30$$
$$3(22) - 20 > 30$$
$$66 - 20 > 30$$
$$46 > 30$$

$$3(2 - x) + x > 30$$
$$3(2 - 0) + 0 > 30$$
$$3(2) > 30$$
$$6 > 30$$

Only $x = -20$ provides a true statement, so $x < -12$ is correct.

Absolute Value in Algebraic Expressions, Equations, and Inequalities

Algebraic terms involving absolute values are treated the same way as numeric absolute values. Remember that the absolute value of any term is always greater than or equal to zero.

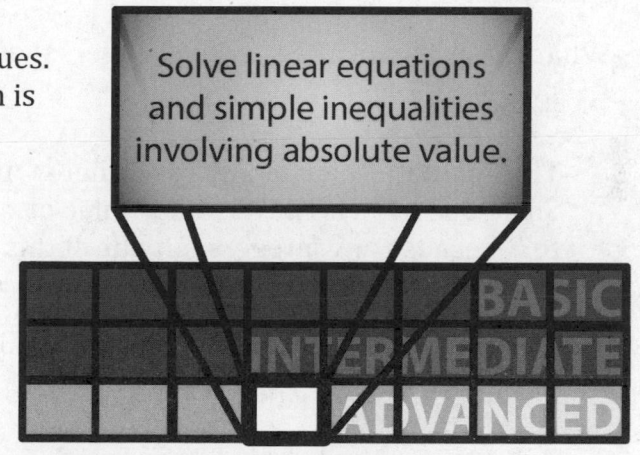

Solve linear equations and simple inequalities involving absolute value.

BASIC
INTERMEDIATE
ADVANCED

PRINCIPLES OF ABSOLUTE VALUE

1. $|x| = x$ if $x \geq 0$; $|x| = -x$ if $x < 0$

2. $|x| = |-x|$

3. $|x| \geq 0$

4. $|x - y| = |y - x|$

Example:

Let x be a member of the following set:

$\{-11, -10, -9, -8, -7, -6, -5, -4, -3, -2, -1, 0, 1, 2, 3, 4\}$. $\dfrac{\left|2x - |x|\right|}{3}$ is a positive integer

for how many different numbers in the set?

If $x < 0$, then $|x| = -x$: $\dfrac{\left|2x - |x|\right|}{3} = \dfrac{\left|2x - (-x)\right|}{3} = \dfrac{\left|2x + x\right|}{3} = \dfrac{\left|3x\right|}{3} = |x|$, which is always a

positive. Therefore, $\dfrac{\left|2x - |x|\right|}{3}$ is a positive integer for all numbers in the set less than

zero. If $x \geq 0$, then $|x| = x$: $\dfrac{\left|2x - |x|\right|}{3} = \dfrac{\left|2x - x\right|}{3} = \dfrac{|x|}{3} = \dfrac{x}{3}$. Thus, the only other number

in the set that returns a positive integer is 3. The total number of values in the set
that satisfy the condition is: 11 + 1 = 12.

Expressions in algebraic equations and inequalities may include absolute values. The same
principles for working with equations and inequalities apply when manipulating absolute
values.

Examples:

What is the sum of all different integers that can be substituted for x such that
$|x| + |x - 3| = 3$?

The absolute value of any real number, including integers, is always zero or more.
Since one term is the absolute value of x, the possible values have to range from –3
to 3 because any integers outside of this range could not yield a true statement.
Only 0, 1, 2, and 3 work in the equality: $|0| + |0 - 3| = 0 + 3 = 3$; $|1| + |1 - 3| = 1 + 2 = 3$;
$|2| + |2 - 3| = 2 + 1 = 3$; $|3| + |3 - 3| = 3 + 0 = 3$. The question asks for the sum of all
possible answers. Thus, 0 + 1 + 2 + 3 = 6.

If x represents an integer, $|x - 3| + |x + 2| < 7$ for how many different values of x?

Temporarily set the two sides of the inequality equal to each other and solve for x:

$$|x - 3| + |x + 2| = 7$$
$$x - 3 + x + 2 = 7$$
$$2x - 1 = 7$$
$$2x = 8$$
$$x = 4$$

or

$$|x - 3| + |x + 2| = 7$$
$$-(x - 3 + x + 2) = 7$$
$$-x + 3 - x - 2 = 7$$
$$-2x + 1 = 7$$
$$-2x = 6$$
$$x = -3$$

Test a value in each region to determine which value(s) cause true inequalities:

Less than –3: $|(-4)-3|+|(-4)+2|<7 \Rightarrow |-7|+|-2|<7 \Rightarrow 9<7$

Between –3 and 4: $|(0)-3|+|(0)+2|<7 \Rightarrow |-3|+|-2|<7 \Rightarrow 5<7$

Greater than 4: $|(5)-3|+|(5)+2|<7 \Rightarrow |2|+|7|<7 \Rightarrow 9<7$

Only the second value returns a true statement. Therefore, $-3 < x < 4$.

Solving Quadratic Equations

You already know how to use the FOIL method to solve a quadratic equation when it is written in standard form. However, for quadratic equations not in standard form, you must first group like terms and rearrange the equation into standard form (i.e. set it equal to zero).

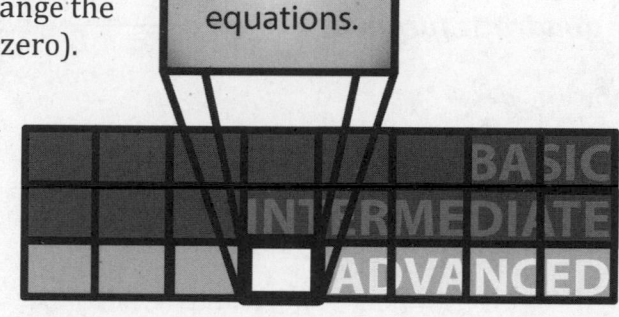

Examples:

Solve for x: $2x^2+12-3x = x^2+2x+18$.

Rewrite the equation by grouping like terms and simplifying:

$$2x^2+12-3x = x^2+2x+18$$
$$\left(2x^2-x^2\right)+(-3x-2x)+(12-18)=0$$
$$x^2-5x-6=0$$
$$(x-6)(x+1)=0$$

Either $x-6=0$ or $x+1=0$. Therefore the set of all possible values for x is $\{-1, 6\}$.

Solve for x: $x(8+x)=2x+36+6x$.

Rewrite the equation by grouping like terms and simplifying:

$$x(8+x)=2x+36+6x$$
$$8x+x^2=8x+36$$
$$x^2=36$$

Since squaring a negative number yields a positive and squaring a positive number yields a positive, $x=\pm 6$.

Some higher degree equations can also be solved if they can be written in quadratic form.

Example:

Solve for x: $x^4 - 13x^2 + 36 = 0$.

Factor: $\left(x^2 - 9\right)\left(x^2 - 4\right) = 0$. Factor again: $(x+3)(x-3)(x+2)(x-2) = 0$. To find the four possible values of x, set each factor equal to zero and solve each for x: $x+3=0 \Rightarrow x=-3$; $x-3=0 \Rightarrow x=3$; $x+2=0 \Rightarrow x=-2$; and $x-2=0 \Rightarrow x=2$. Therefore, the solution set is: {–3, –2, 2, 3}.

In the preceding example, once the original equation had been factored into two quadratic equations ($x^2 - 9$ and $x^2 - 4$), the factors of those quadratic equations were relatively easy to identify. However, not all quadratic equations are easily factorable. In these cases, use the **quadratic formula**, $x = \dfrac{-b \pm \sqrt{b^2 - 4ac}}{2a}$, which is derived from the general quadratic equation $ax^2 + bx + c = 0$.

Example:

Solve for x: $x^2 = 5x + 8$.

$x^2 = 5x + 8 \Rightarrow x^2 - 5x - 8 = 0$. $a = 1$, $b = -5$, $c = -8$. Substitute these values into the quadratic formula and solve for x: $x = \dfrac{-b \pm \sqrt{b^2 - 4ac}}{2a} = \dfrac{5 \pm \sqrt{(-5)^2 - 4(1)(-8)}}{2(1)} = \dfrac{5 \pm \sqrt{25 + 32}}{2} = \dfrac{5 \pm \sqrt{57}}{2}$. So, the solution set for x is $\left\{ \dfrac{5 - \sqrt{57}}{2}, \dfrac{5 + \sqrt{57}}{2} \right\}$.

Solving Systems of Equations

Ordinarily, if an equation has more than one variable, it is not possible to determine the unique numeric solution for any individual variable. For example, the equation $x + y = 10$ does not have one unique solution set for x and y: x and y could be 1 and 9, 5 and 5, –2 and 12, and so on. However, if there are as many equations as there are variables, the equations can be manipulated as a system to determine the unique value of each variable. This technique is called **solving systems of equations** because the equations are taken to be true at the same time, or simultaneously, in

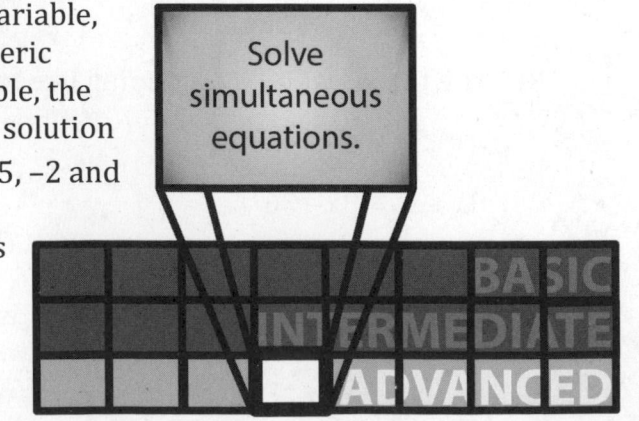

order to determine each variable value. On the exam, systems of equations are typically limited to two equations and two unknowns.

How do you find the specific solution for a given set of equations? There are two methods for solving systems of equations: **substitution** and **linear combination** (**elimination**).

Substitution

The steps for the **substitution method** are as follows:

Step 1: Pick one of the two given equations and define one variable in terms of the other.

Step 2: Substitute the defined variable into the other equation and solve.

Step 3: Substitute the solution back into either equation and solve for the remaining variable.

Examples:

If $2x + y = 13$ and $x - y = 2$, what are the values of x and y?

Redefine one variable in terms of the other. Since y is already a single variable in both equations, define y in terms of x: $y = 13 - 2x$. Substitute $13 - 2x$ for y in the second equation and solve for x: $x - (13 - 2x) = 2 \Rightarrow x - 13 + 2x = 2 \Rightarrow 3x = 15 \Rightarrow x = 5$. Finally, solve for y by substituting 5 for x in either equation: $2x + y = 13 \Rightarrow 2(5) + y = 13 \Rightarrow y = 3$.

If $y = 7 + x$ and $3x + 2y = 4$, what are the values of x and y?

Substitute $7 + x$ for y in the second equation and solve for x: $3x + 2y = 4 \Rightarrow 3x + 2(7 + x) = 4 \Rightarrow 3x + 14 + 2x = 4 \Rightarrow 5x = -10 \Rightarrow x = -2$. Substitute -2 for x in the first equation and solve for y: $y = 7 + x = 7 - 2 = 5$.

Linear Combination (Elimination)

The second method for solving systems of equations is **linear combination** or **elimination**. Eliminate one of the two variables by adding or subtracting the two equations. If necessary, division of one equation by another may eliminate one of two variables.

Examples:

If $2x + y = 8$ and $x - y = 1$, what are the values of x and y?

In this system of equations, there is a "$+y$" term in one equation and a "$-y$" term in the other. Since $+y$ and $-y$ added together yields zero, eliminate the y term by adding the two equations together:

$$2x + y = 8$$
$$\underline{x - y = 1}$$
$$3x = 9$$
$$x = 3$$

Find the value of y by substituting 3 for x in either equation:

$$2x + y = 8$$
$$2(3) + y = 8$$
$$y = 8 - 6$$
$$y = 2$$

If $4x + 3y = 17$ and $2x + 3y = 13$, what are the values of x and y?

In this pair, each equation has a $+3y$ term, which you can eliminate by subtracting the second equation from the first:

$$4x + 3y = 17$$
$$\underline{-(2x + 3y = 13)}$$
$$2x = 4$$
$$x = 2$$

Solve for y by substituting 2 for x in either equation:

$$4x + 3y = 17$$
$$4(2) + 3y = 17$$
$$8 + 3y = 17$$
$$3y = 9$$
$$y = 3$$

If $x^5 = 6y$ and $x^4 = 2y$, x is a real number such that $x \neq 0$, and y is a real number, the $x = ?$

This system of equations is different than the previous examples because they are not linear equations. Since they are not linear, this system is reduced to one equation and one variable by dividing the first equation by the second equation:

$$\frac{x^5}{x^4} = \frac{6y}{2y} \Rightarrow x = 3.$$

If a system of equations has more variables than equations, then probably (though not always) not every variable value can be determined. Instead, you will be asked to solve for one or more variables in terms of another variable.

Examples:

If $y = 2a$ and $3x + 8y = 28a$, find x in terms of a.

Substitute $2a$ for y and solve for x:

$$3x + 8(2a) = 28a \Rightarrow 3x = 28a - 16a \Rightarrow 3x = 12a \Rightarrow x = \frac{12a}{3} = 4a.$$

In terms of a, solve the following pair of equations for x and y: $3x - 4y = 10a$ and $5x + 2y = 8a$.

First, solve for either x or y in terms of a alone. To solve for x, multiply the second equation by 2:

$$2(5x + 2y = 8a)$$
$$10x + 4y = 16a$$

Add the result to the first equation:

$$10x + 4y = 16a$$
$$\underline{+(3x - 4y = 10a)}$$
$$13x = 26a$$
$$x = 2a$$

To find y in terms of a, substitute $2a$ for x in either equation:

$$5x + 2y = 8a$$
$$2y = 8a - 5(2a)$$
$$2y = -2a$$
$$y = -a$$

EXERCISE 7

DIRECTIONS: Choose the correct answer to each of the following items. Answers are on page 816.

153. For what values of x is $8 - 3x > 35$?

- A. $x > 0$
- B. $x \geq 0$
- C. $x > -3$
- D. $x < -9$
- E. $x \geq 9$

154. Solve $6 - 4x \geq 4x - 10$

- F. $x \geq 2$
- G. $x > 2$
- H. $x < 2$
- J. $x \leq 2$
- K. $x \leq -2$

155. Which value of x is in the solution set of $-2x + 4 > 16$?

- A. -9
- B. -6
- C. 6
- D. 9
- E. 12

156. If $\dfrac{2}{3}(6x - 9) + 4 > 5x + 1$, what is the value of x?

- F. $x > -3$
- G. $x < -3$
- H. $x = -3$
- J. $x = 3$
- K. $x \leq -3$

157. For what values of x is $10x - 2(3x + 2) \geq 8x + 2$?

- A. $x < \dfrac{3}{2}$
- B. $x > \dfrac{3}{2}$
- C. $x \leq \dfrac{3}{2}$
- D. $x \leq -\dfrac{3}{2}$
- E. $x \geq -\dfrac{3}{2}$

158. If $|x| + 3 = 10$, then $x = ?$

- F. 6 only
- G. 7 only
- H. $7, -7$ only
- J. 13 only
- K. $13, -13$ only

159. If $2|x - 4| - 3 = -1$, then $x = ?$

- A. $-2, 2$ only
- B. 3 only
- C. $3, -5$ only
- D. $3, 5$ only
- E. 5 only

160. If $|x - 1| < 5$, then which of the following correctly describes all possible values of x?

- F. $x < 4$
- G. $x < 6$
- H. $-4 < x < 6$
- J. $-6 < x < 6$
- K. $-4 < x < 4$

161. If $-5 < x < -1$, and $f(x) = \big|14 - |1 + 2x|\big|$, then $f(x) = ?$

- A. $13 - 2x$
- B. $15 + 2x$
- C. $13 + 2x$
- D. $2x - 13$
- E. $13 + 3x$

162. If $|2x - 3| \geq 7$, then which of the following describes all possible values of x?

- F. $x \geq 5$
- G. $x \geq 2$
- H. $x \leq -2$ or $x \geq 5$
- J. $-2 \leq x \leq 5$
- K. $x \leq 1$ or $x \geq 10$

163. If $x^2 - 3x - 4 = 0$, then $x = ?$

    A. $-4, 1$ only   D. $-1, 4$ only
    B. $-2, 2$ only   E. $-1, 6$ only
    C. $-1, 2$ only

164. If $x^2 + 5x = -4$, then $x = ?$

    F. $-1, -4$ only   J. $1, 4$ only
    G. $-1, -2$ only   K. $2, 6$ only
    H. $1, 2$ only

165. If $3x^2 = 12x$, then $x = ?$

    A. $0, 3$ only   D. $2, 4$ only
    B. $0, 4$ only   E. $3, 12$ only
    C. $-2, 2$ only

166. If $8x + 16 = (x+2)(x+5)$, then $x = ?$

    F. -3 only   J. 2 only
    G. $-3, -2$ only   K. 3 only
    H. $-2, 3$ only

167. Which of the following values for c returns two distinct real solutions to the equation $x^2 - 8x + c = 0$?

    A. -20 C. 18 E. 20
    B. 17 D. 19

168. What are the roots of the equation $(2x+5)(x-4) = 0$?

    F. -2.5 and -4 J. 2.5 and -4
    G. -2.5 and 4 K. 2.5 and 4
    H. 2 and -5

169. If $x + 3y = 5$ and $2x - y = 3$, then $x = ?$

    A. 2 C. 5 E. 9
    B. 4 D. 6

170. If $a + 5b = 9$ and $a - b = 3$, then $a = ?$

    F. 1 H. 5 K. 11
    G. 4 J. 7

171. If $\dfrac{x+y}{2} = 4$ and $x - y = 4$, then $x = ?$

    A. 1 C. 4 E. 8
    B. 2 D. 6

172. If $x + y + z = 6$, $x + y - z = 4$, and $x - y = 3$, then $x = ?$

    F. -2 H. 4 K. 8
    G. 0 J. 6

Graphical Representations

Find the Distance Between Two Points

For simplicity's sake, we will confine the discussion and derivation of the distance formula to the first quadrant of the coordinate plane. This method works for points in all quadrants and for line segments that traverse two or more quadrants.

Use the distance formula.

BASIC
INTERMEDIATE
ADVANCED

Consider the points $P\left(x_1, y_1\right)$ and $Q\left(x_2, y_2\right)$:

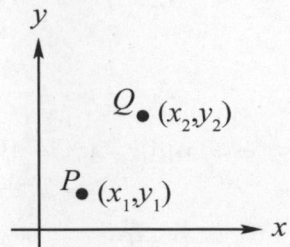

To find the distance between points P and Q, construct a triangle:

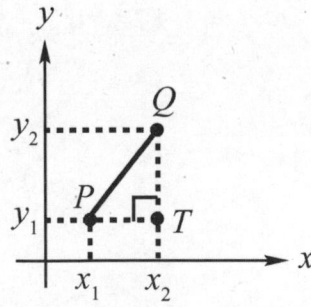

Point T now has the coordinates $\left(x_2, y_1\right)$. To calculate the length of $\overline{PT}$, find the distance moved on the x-axis: $x_2 - x_1$ units. The y-coordinate does not change. Similarly, the length of $\overline{QT}$ will be $y_2 - y_1$ since the distance is purely vertical, moving up from y_1 to y_2, with no change in the x-value.

Now, apply the Pythagorean theorem: $(PQ)^2 = (PT)^2 + (QT)^2 = \left(x_2 - x_1\right)^2 + \left(y_2 - y_1\right)^2 \Rightarrow$

$PQ = \sqrt{\left(x_2 - x_1\right)^2 + \left(y_2 - y_1\right)^2}$.

Example:

In the following figure, what is the length of $\overline{PQ}$?

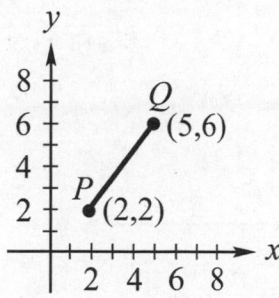

Construct triangle PQR:

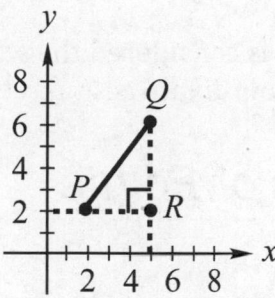

$\overline{QR}$ runs from $(5,6)$ to $(5,2)$, so it must be 4 units long. $\overline{PR}$ runs from $(2,2)$ to $(5,2)$, so it is 3 units long.

Using the Pythagorean theorem: $\left(\overline{PQ}\right)^2 = \left(\overline{QR}\right)^2 + \left(\overline{PR}\right)^2 = 4^2 + 3^2 = 16 + 9 = 25$.
Therefore, $\overline{PQ} = \sqrt{25} = 5$.

You can find the length of any line segment drawn in a coordinate axis system between points (x_1, y_1) and (x_2, y_2) using the derived **distance formula**:

$$d = \sqrt{\left(x_2 - x_1\right)^2 + \left(y_2 - y_1\right)^2}.$$

Remember, distance logically can only be a positive value.

Example:

In the following figure, what is the distance between P and Q?

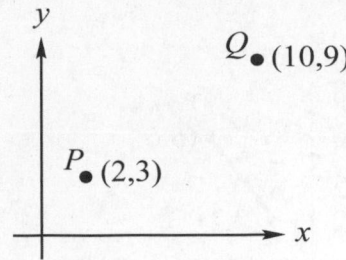

The distance between P and Q is:

$$\sqrt{(x_2-x_1)^2+(y_2-y_1)^2} = \sqrt{(10-2)^2+(9-3)^2} = \sqrt{64+36} = \sqrt{100} = 10.$$

It does not matter which point is considered the start of the line and the end of the line, since the change in each coordinate is squared in the distance formula.

Find Equations of Lines or Points

Parallel Lines

If two parallel lines have slopes m_1 and m_2, then $m_1 = m_2$. Slopes of parallel lines are equal to each other.

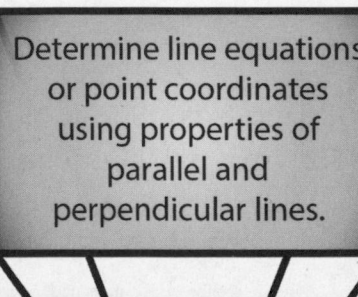

Determine line equations or point coordinates using properties of parallel and perpendicular lines.

Example:

Find the equation for a line that passes through the point $(0,12)$ and is parallel to the line $y = 7x - 15$.

A line has slope-intercept form $y = mx + b$. If the line passes through the y-axis at $(0,12)$, then the y-intercept $b = +12$. If the two lines are parallel, then the slopes are equal and $m = +7$. Therefore, the equation of the line is $y = mx + b \Rightarrow y = 7x + 12$.

Horizontal and Vertical Parallel Lines

The equation of a line that is parallel to the x-axis is $y = k$, where is k is a constant. The equation of a line that is parallel to the y-axis is $x = c$, where c is a constant.

Perpendicular Lines

If two perpendicular lines have slopes m_1 and m_2, then $m_1 = -\dfrac{1}{m_2}$ and vice versa. Slopes of perpendicular lines are opposite reciprocals of each other.

Example:

The equation of a line is $y = \dfrac{x}{4} + 10$. If a second line is perpendicular to the line and passes through point (5,0), what is the equation of this line in slope-intercept form?

> If two lines are perpendicular to one another, their slopes are opposite reciprocals of one another. The first line has a slope of $\dfrac{1}{4}$; thus, the line perpendicular to it has a slope of -4. Substituting the point (5,0) into the equation $y = -4x + b$ gives
>
> $0 = (-4)(5) + b$, $b = 20$. The equation for this line is $y = -4x + 20$.

Inequalities on the Number Line

Linear Inequalities

A linear inequality is similar to a linear equation, except an inequality symbol is used instead of an equals sign. Similar to equations, an inequality may be as simple as $x < 3$, or as complex as $\dfrac{4x-5}{2} + 7 \geq -3(4x+15)$.

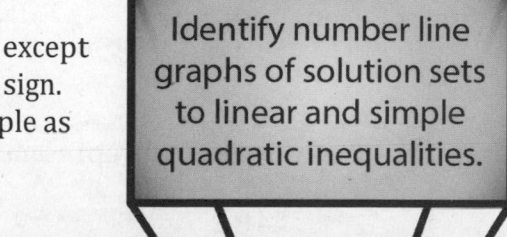

Identify number line graphs of solution sets to linear and simple quadratic inequalities.

The solution set to a linear inequality may be graphed on a number line. In order to graph the solution set, you must first solve the inequality algebraically. Solving a linear inequality is similar to the process of solving a linear equation. As discussed in the previous lesson, there is one important difference: when you multiply or divide an inequality by a negative value, you must switch the direction of the inequality sign.

Examples:

Graph the solution set to $4x - 2 > 6$.

$$4x - 2 > 6$$
$$4x > 8$$
$$x > 2$$

Now graph the solution on the number line. Pay careful attention to the type of inequality symbol. A greater than or less than inequality (>, <) is shown as an open dot (∘) since the value is not included in the solution. A greater than or equal to symbol or a less than or equal to symbol (≥, ≤) is shown as a solid or closed dot (•) since the value is included in the solution. The appropriate side of the number line is shaded.

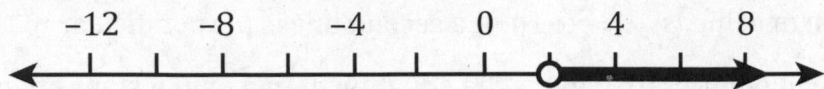

Graph the solution set to $7(x+5) \leq 21$.

Solve the inequality by isolating the variable:

$7(x+5) \leq 21$.

Divide both sides by 7:

$x+5 \leq 3$.

Subtract 5 from both sides:

$x \leq -2$.

Graph a closed dot at –2 to represent equal to:

Shade to the left of the dot to represent less than:

Graph the solution set to $-4(x+5) \leq -24$.

Solve the inequality by isolating the variable. Divide both sides by –4, and remember to switch the inequality symbol since you are dividing by a negative number:

$x+5 \geq 6$.

Subtract 5 from both sides:

$x \geq 1$.

Graph a closed dot at 1 to represent equal to:

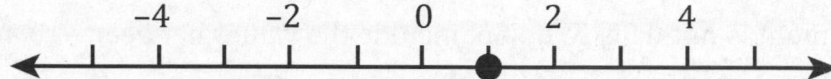

Shade to the right of the dot to represent greater than:

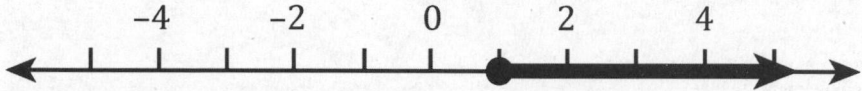

Quadratic Inequalities

A simple quadratic inequality may be simplified to the form of $ax^2 + bx + c \geq 0$ or $ax^2 + bx + c > 0$, where a is any real number such that $a \neq 0$, b is any real number, c is any real number, and any one of the four inequality signs is used. Similar to linear inequalities, quadratic inequalities may be simple, such as $x^2 - 100 \geq 0$ or complex, such as $2x^2 + 5x + 8 < x^2 + 6x + 10$.

The steps to solving and graphing a simple quadratic inequality are similar to those for solving a linear inequality. You must simplify and solve the inequality, graph the points on the number line, and finally shade the appropriate section of the number line.

First, solve the quadratic inequality as if it were a quadratic equation. This will give you the points of intersection on the number line. Remember, when you multiply or divide by a negative value, you must switch the direction of the inequality sign.

Temporarily set the two sides of the inequality equal to each other and solve for x:

$$x^2 - 100 \geq 0$$
$$x^2 - 100 = 0$$
$$(x+10)(x-10) = 0$$
$$x = -10, 10$$

These two solutions create three regions (one to the left of −10, one between −10 and 10, and one to the right of 10). Test a value in each region to determine which value(s) create a true inequality:

Less than –10: $(-20)^2 - 100 \geq 0 \Rightarrow 300 \geq 0$

Between –10 and 10: $(0)^2 - 100 \geq 0 \Rightarrow -100 \geq 0$

Greater than 10: $(20)^2 - 100 \geq 0 \Rightarrow 300 \geq 0$

The second statement is not true, so do not include the values between –10 and 10 in the graph.

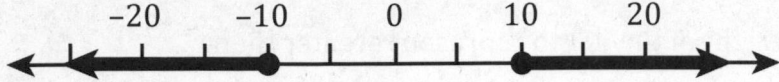

Example:

Graph the solution set to $2x^2 + 5x + 8 < x^2 + 6x + 10$.

Find the roots or solutions of the quadratic inequality by setting the inequality to zero and factoring.

Subtract $x^2 + 6x + 10$ from both sides:

$x^2 - x - 2 < 0$.

Temporarily set the two sides of the inequality equal to each other and factor the resulting quadratic:

$(x - 2)(x + 1) = 0$

$x = 2, -1$

Test a value in each region to determine which value(s) create true inequalities:

Less than –1: $(-2)^2 - (-2) - 2 < 0 \Rightarrow 4 < 0$

Between –1 and 2: $(0)^2 - (0) - 2 < 0 \Rightarrow -2 < 0$

Greater than 2: $(3)^2 - (3) - 2 < 0 \Rightarrow 4 < 0$

Only the second statement is true, so include only those values. To graph the inequality, first graph open dots at –1 and 2:

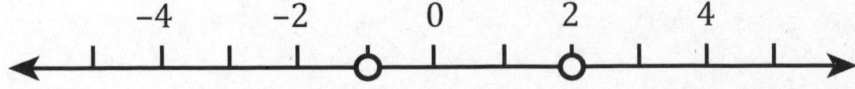

Shade between the dots to identify the interval that solves the inequality:

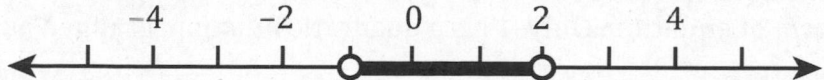

When answering a number line item on a multiple-choice exam, it is sometimes faster to eliminate incorrect choices. A first step is examining the points in each answer choice. Are the points values that make the two sides of the inequality equal? Should the dots be open or closed? Answering these questions may eliminate some of the answer choices. Next choosing a value that is easy to substitute, such as 0, and plugging it into the given equation to see if that point should be included in the graphed solution will eliminate some other choices. This method may allow you to answer the item without taking the time to algebraically solve the inequality.

Parabolas, Circles, and Graphs

Identifying Graphs of Quadratic Functions

A *quadratic function* is expressed in the form $y = ax^2 + bx + c$, where a is any real number such that $a \neq 0$, b is any real number, and c is any real number. Graphs of quadratic functions are called parabolas. The coefficient a determines whether the parabola opens upward (positive a value) or opens downward (negative a value).

You may be asked to identify graphs of simple quadratic functions. The basic quadratic graph that you need to know is $f(x) = x^2$, as illustrated in the following example.

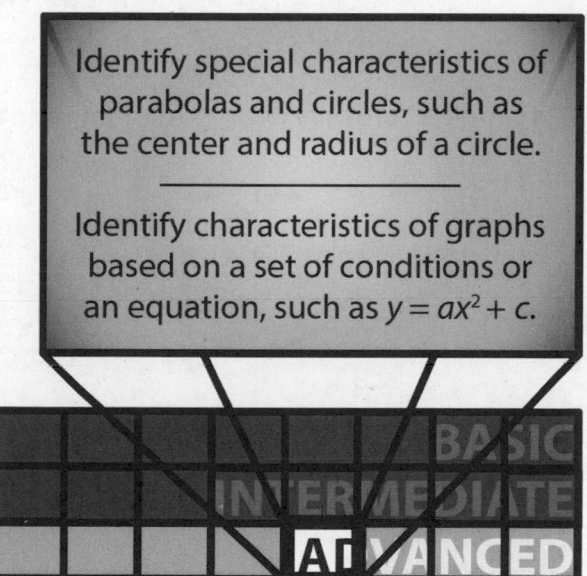

Identify special characteristics of parabolas and circles, such as the center and radius of a circle.

Identify characteristics of graphs based on a set of conditions or an equation, such as $y = ax^2 + c$.

Example:

Which of the following graphs depicts a quadratic function?

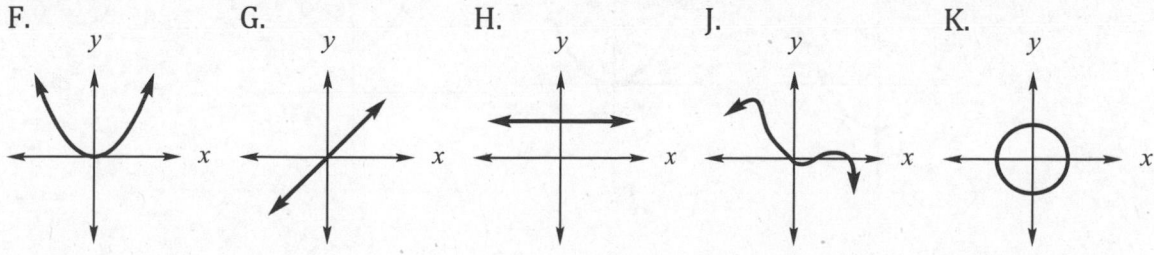

F.   G.   H.   J.   K.

Use the process of elimination to determine the correct answer. (G) and (H) are graphs of lines. (K) is a plot of a circle. (J) is a complicated function without a standard form of equation. Only (F) is a quadratic function, graphed as a parabola: $y = ax^2$.

The general equation for parabolas is $f(x) = a(x - h)^2 + k$ with the vertex, or turning point, at (h,k). Given the equation $f(x) = a(x)^2$, the vertex must be at (0,0) because h and k are both equal to zero. The direction and width of the parabola's opening are determined by the value of a. If $a > 0$, the parabola opens upward, and if $a < 0$, it opens downward.

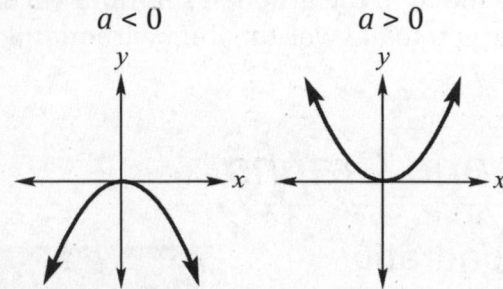

The parabola's width is determined by the absolute value of a.

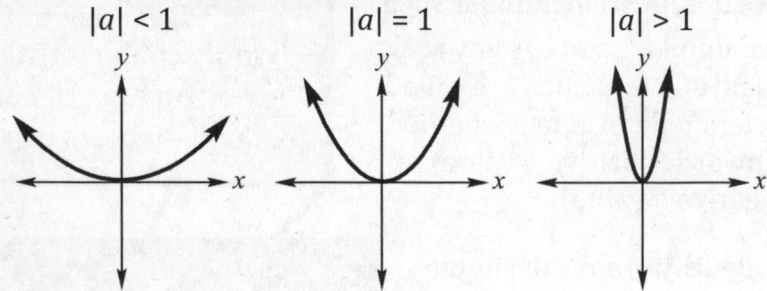

If $f(x) = x^2 + k$, the direction and width of the parabola's opening are fixed because $a = 1$, and the coordinates for the vertex, (h,k), are $(0,k)$ as shown below:

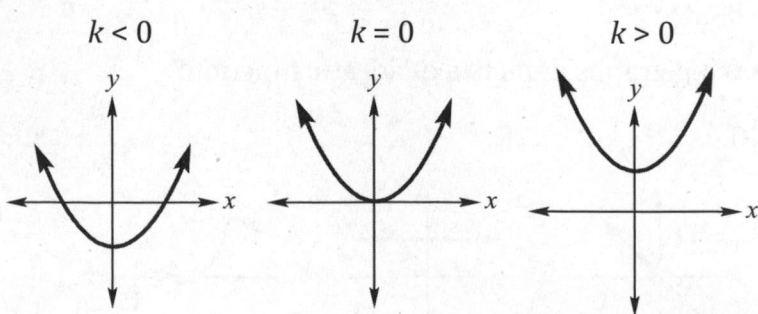

If $f(x) = (x - h)^2$, the direction and width of the parabola's opening are fixed because $a = 1$, and the coordinates for the vertex, (h,k), are $(h,0)$ as shown below:

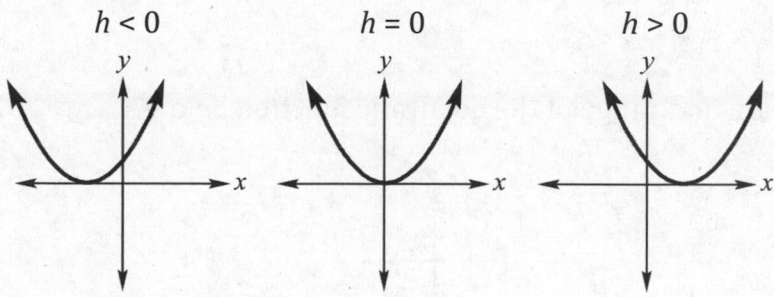

Example:

Which of the following could be the equation for the parabola graphed in the standard (x,y) coordinate plane below?

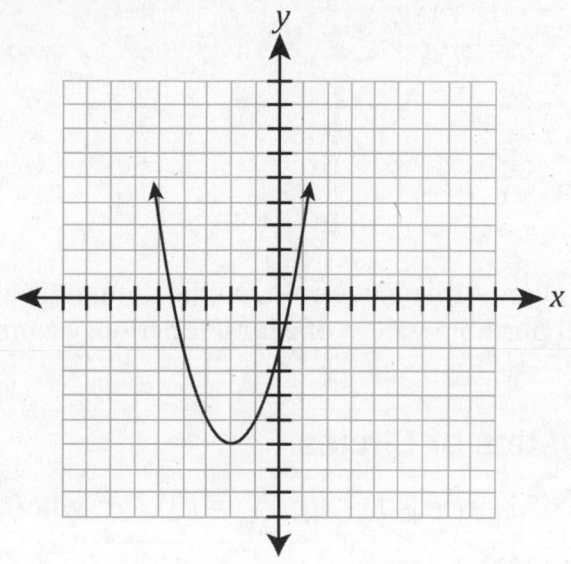

A. $y = (x + 2)^2 - 6$

B. $y = (x - 2)^2 + 6$

C. $y = 2(x - 6)^2 + 2$

D. $y = -(x + 2)^2 - 6$

E. $y = -(x + 6)^2 + 2$

The vertex, (h,k), is $(-2,-6)$, so plug these values into the equation for a parabola: $f(x) = a(x - h)^2 + k = a(x + 2)^2 - 6$. This eliminates (B), (C), and (E). The graph opens upward, so eliminate (D). Therefore, the correct answer is (A).

Domain and Range of Graphed Functions

Domain is the set of all possible values of x in a function. Range is the set of all possible values of y for a function.

Example:

What is the domain and range of the quadratic function below?

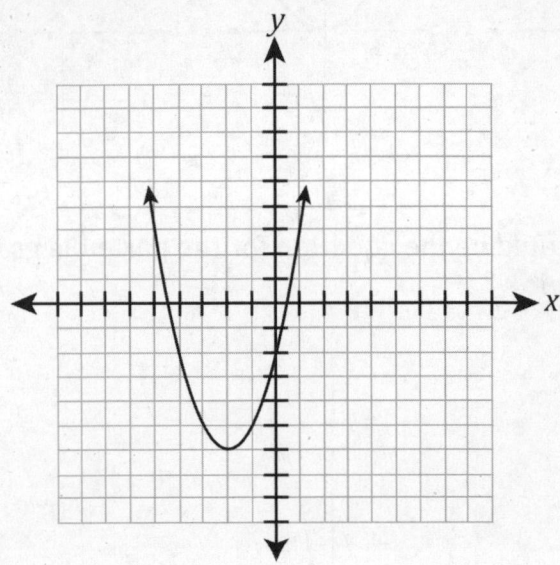

Domain is the set of all possible values of x, so the domain is all real numbers. Range is the set of all possible values of y for a function. y cannot be less than –6, so the range is $y \geq -6$.

Identifying Characteristics of Circles

The standard form equation of a circle is $(x-h)^2 + (y-k)^2 = r^2$ where the center is located at (h,k) and the radius is length r.

Examples:

A circle in the standard (x,y) coordinate plane has center (3,–8) and radius 5 coordinate units. What is the equation of the circle?

The center of (3,–8) gives the first part of the equation: $(x-3)^2 + (y-(-8))^2$, which is simplified to $(x-3)^2 + (y+8)^2$.

The radius is 5 coordinate units, so $5^2 = 25$.

The equation of the circle is $(x-3)^2 + (y+8)^2 = 25$.

An equation of a particular circle in the standard (x,y) coordinate plane is $(x+5)^2 + (y-7)^2 = 50$. What are the coordinates of this circle's center and what is the length, in coordinate units, of this circle's radius?

The equation for the circle is written in standard form: $(x-h)^2 + (y-k)^2 = r^2$, where (h,k) is the center of the circle and r is the radius. Since $h = -5$ and $k = 7$, the center is at $(-5,7)$.

Since $r^2 = 50$, find the radius by taking the square root of the second part of the equation: $\sqrt{50}$, or $5\sqrt{2}$.

Use Coordinate Graphs and Solve Complex Geometry Problems

Graphing Geometric Figures

Items on the exam ask you to combine skills to find information contained in coordinate graphs with your knowledge and understanding of algebraic and geometric concepts. For example, use of the distance formula (p. 594) and midpoint formula (p. 464) can determine the length of line segments that are used in area, perimeter, and circumference calculations.

> Comprehend, analyze, and apply information in coordinate graphs.
>
> ———
>
> Solve problems involving multiple algebraic and/or geometric concepts.

You can also use the coordinate system for graphing geometric figures. The following figure is a graph of a square whose vertices are at coordinates (0,0), (4,0), (4,4), and (0,4).

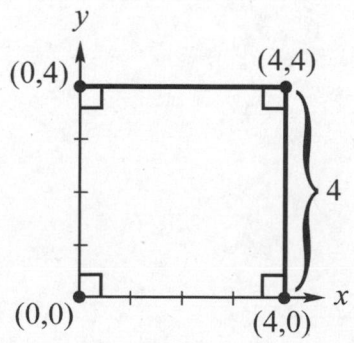

Each side of the square is equal to 4 since each side is 4 units long and parallel to either the x- or y-axis. Note also that every coordinate point is the perpendicular intersection of two line segments.

Example:

In the following figure, what is the area of the circle?

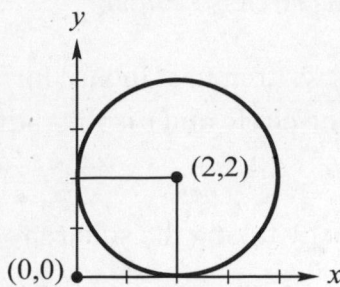

To solve this problem, find the radius of the circle. The center of the circle is located at the intersection of $x = 2$ and $y = 2$, or the point (2,2). Thus, the radius is 2 units long and the area is $\pi r^2 = \pi(2)^2 = 4\pi$.

Interpreting Information from Graphs

You can also use the graphs in the coordinate plane to draw conclusions.

Example:

If the square in the figure below is reflected across the y-axis and then reflected across the x-axis, which of the following graphs shows the resulting position of the square?

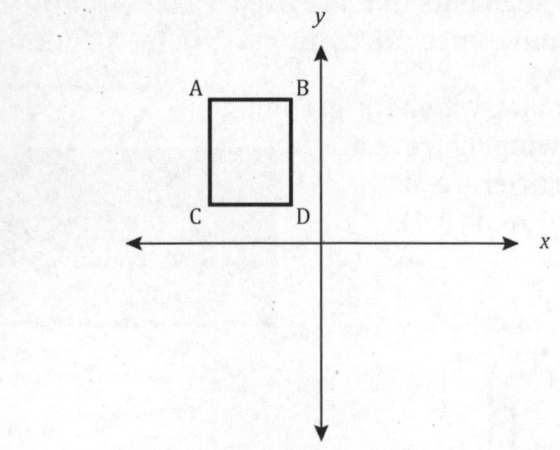

F.　　　　G.　　　　H.　　　　J.　　　　K.

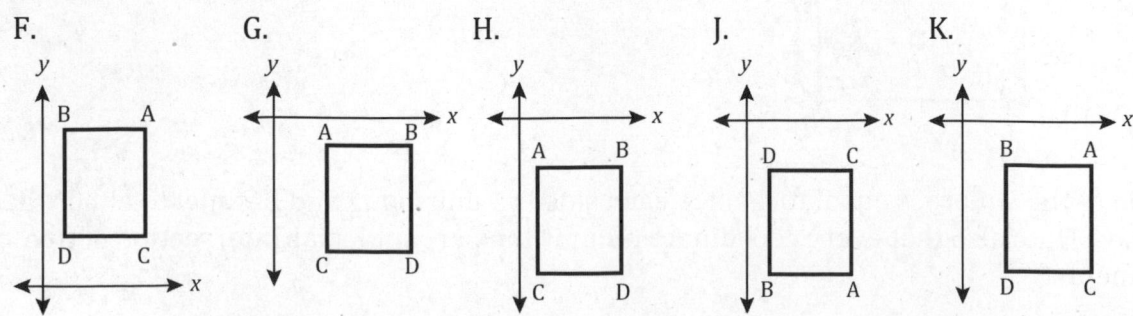

The following graph illustrates the position of the square after the first reflection (across the y-axis), $A'B'C'D'$, and after the second reflection (across the x-axis), $A''B''C''D''$:

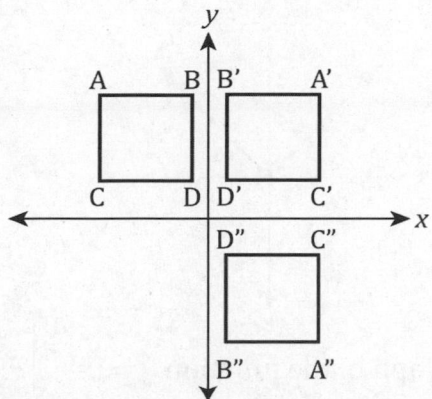

Transformation Effects on Graphs

When you alter a graph, you **transform** it. If you transform a graph without changing its shape, you **translate** it. Vertical and horizontal transformations are translations.

Vertical Translations

To move a function up or down, you add or subtract outside the function. That is, $f(x)+b$ is $f(x)$ moved up b units, and $f(x)-b$ is $f(x)$ moved down b units.

Example:

In order to obtain the graph of $y=(x+2)^2+6$ from the graph of $y=x^2+4x+11$, how should the graph of $y=x^2+4x+11$ be moved?

Rewrite the original in the form $f(x)+b$: $y=x^2+4x+11 \Rightarrow$ $y=x^2+4x+4+7=(x+2)^2+7$. Thus, to obtain the graph of $y=(x+2)^2+6$ from the graph of $y=(x+2)^2+7$, the graph must be moved one unit down.

Horizontal Translations

To shift a function to the left or to the right, add or subtract inside the function. That is, $f(x+b)$ is $f(x)$ shifted b units to the left, and $f(x-b)$ is $f(x)$ shifted b units to the right.

Example:

The following graph is of the function $y = |x|$.

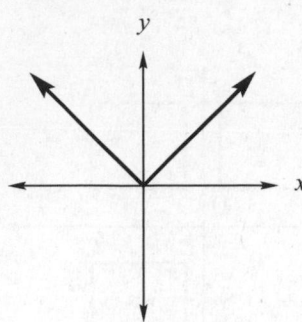

Which of the following is a graph of the function $y = |x+3|$?

A.
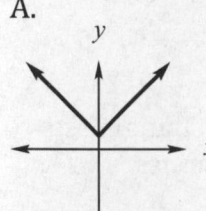

B.
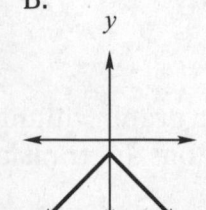

C.
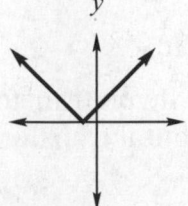

D.
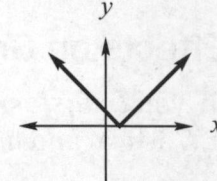

E.
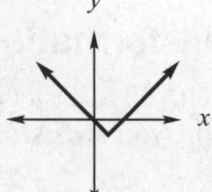

By translation of the original graph from $y = |x|$ to $y = |x+3|$, the original graph is moved three units to the left, (C). Alternatively, substitute values for x and y: for $x = -3, y = 0$. (C) is the only graph that contains the point $(-3,0)$.

EXERCISE 8

DIRECTIONS: Choose the correct answer to each of the following items. Answers are on page 816.

173. If point P has coordinates $(-2,2)$ and point Q has coordinates $(2,0)$, what is the distance from point P to point Q?

A. -4 C. $4\sqrt{5}$ E. 6

B. $2\sqrt{5}$ D. 4

174. If point R has coordinates (x,y) and point S has coordinates $(x+1,y+1)$, what is the distance between point R and point S?

F. $\sqrt{2}$ J. $\sqrt{x^2+y^2+2}$

G. 2   K. $x+y+1$

H. $\sqrt{x^2+y^2}$

175. Will is standing 40 yards due north of point *P*. Grace is standing 60 yards due west of point *P*. What is the shortest distance between Will and Grace?

    A. 20 yards   D. 80 yards
    B. $4\sqrt{13}$ yards   E. $80\sqrt{13}$ yards
    C. $20\sqrt{13}$ yards

176. Find the distance from the point with coordinates $(4,3)$ to the point with coordinates $(8,6)$.

    F.   5   H. $\sqrt{7}$ K. 15
    G. 25   J. $\sqrt{67}$

177. What is the distance from the point $(-2,5)$ to the point $(7,-7)$?

    A.   9   C. 15   E. 24
    B. 12   D. 18

178. What is the equation of the line that passes through the point $(0,13)$ and is parallel to the line $4x + 2y = 17$?

    F. $4x + 2y = 13$
    G. $4x + 2y = -13$
    H. $y = -2x + 13$
    J. $y = 2x + 13$
    K. Cannot be determined from the given information

179. A line passes through the point $(0,-5)$ and is perpendicular to the line $y = -\dfrac{x}{2} + 5$. What is the equation of the line?

    A. $y = -\dfrac{x}{2} - 5$
    B. $y = 2x - 5$
    C. $y = -2x - 5$
    D. $y = -\dfrac{x}{2} + 13$
    E. Cannot be determined from the given information

180. The figure below shows two parallel lines with coordinates of points as shown. What is the slope of the line passing through point $(0,6)$?

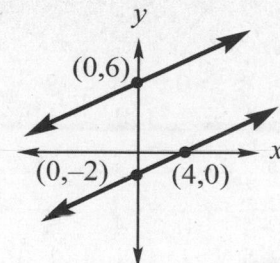

    F. $\dfrac{1}{2}$ H. $\dfrac{1}{4}$ K. $\dfrac{1}{6}$
    G. $\dfrac{1}{3}$ J. $\dfrac{1}{5}$

181. The line that passes through $(1,5)$ and $(-2,17)$ is parallel to the line that passes through $(17,6)$ and $(13,y)$. What is the value of *y*?

    A. 10   C. 16   E. 22
    B. 14   D. 18

182. The equation of a line containing one side of a rectangle in the standard (x,y) coordinate plane is $y = \dfrac{2}{3}x - 5$.

Which one of the following equations is the equation of a line containing an adjacent side of the rectangle?

F. $y = -3x + 2$

G. $y = -\dfrac{2}{3}x + 5$

H. $y = -\dfrac{3}{2}x - 4$

J. $y = \dfrac{2}{3}x + 7$

K. $y = \dfrac{3}{2}x - 8$

183. Which of the following is the graph of the solution set for $2(8 + x) > 4$?

A.

B.

C.

D.

E.

184. The graph shown below is the solution set for $3(9 - x) \geq b$. What values of x make this a true statement for the given values of b?

F. $x \leq 1$

G. $x \leq 3$

H. $x \leq 4$

J. $x \leq 8$

K. $x \leq 32$

185. Which of the following is the graph of the solution set for $\dfrac{-3x + 7}{8} \leq 2$?

A.

B.

C.

D.

E.

186. Which of the following could be the quadratic inequality for the number line graphed below?

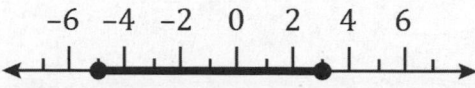

F. $x^2 - 8x - 15 \leq 0$

G. $x^2 - 8x - 15 \geq 0$

H. $x^2 + 2x - 15 \leq 0$

J. $x^2 + 2x - 15 \geq 0$

K. $x^2 - 2x - 8 \leq 0$

187. Which of the following is the graph of the solution set for
$3x^2 + 8x + 12 \geq 2x^2 + 6x + 20$?

A.

B.

C.

D.

E.

188. $\overline{AB}$ is the diameter of a circle whose center is point O. If the coordinates of point A are $(2,6)$ and the coordinates of point B are $(6,2)$, find the coordinates of point O.

F. $(0,0)$ H. $(2,-2)$ K. $(4,4)$

G. $(2,2)$ J. $(4,-4)$

189. In the figure below, $\overline{AB}$ is the diameter of a circle whose center is at point P. What are the coordinates for point B?

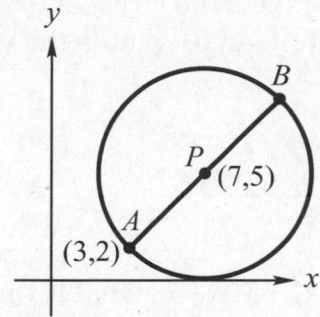

A. $(10,7)$ C. $(12,7)$ E. $(11,7)$

B. $(5,2.5)$ D. $(11,8)$

190. The area of a circle whose center is at $(0,0)$ is 16π. The circle does NOT pass through which of the following points?

F. $(4,4)$ H. $(4,0)$ K. $(0,-4)$

G. $(0,4)$ J. $(-4,0)$

191. The figure below shows a circle with an area of 9π.

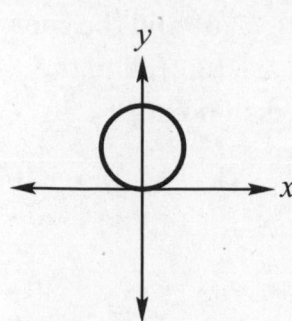

The circle is tangent to the x-axis at $(0,0)$ and the center of the circle lies on the y-axis. The constant function $y = k$ intersects the circle at exactly one point. If $k > 0$, what is the value of k?

A. 1   C. 3   E. 9
B. 2   D. 6

192. If $y = -2x^2 + 16x - 1$, what is the largest possible value for y?

F. −1
G. 13
H. 31
J. 32
K. Cannot be determined from the given information

193. Which of the following graphs depicts the quadratic functions $y = \dfrac{x^2}{2}$ and $y = -\dfrac{x^2}{2}$?

A.

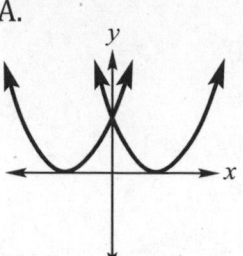

D.

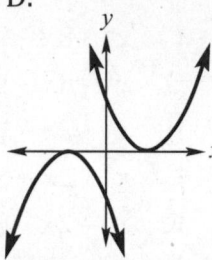

B.

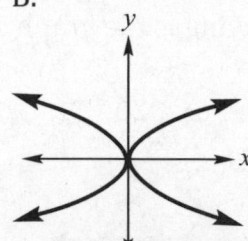

E.

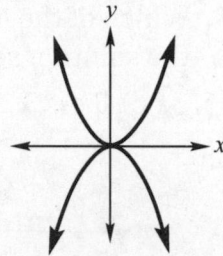

C.

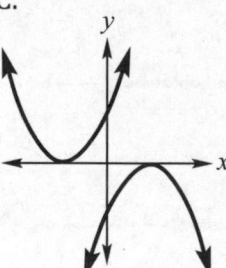

194. The equation, $y = G(x)$ is graphed in the standard (x,y) coordinate plane. If $G(x)$ is a 7th degree polynomial, which of the following CANNOT be the number of times the graph intersects the x-axis?

F. 0   H. 3   K. 7
G. 1   J. 5

195. The *domain* of a function *f* is the set of all values of *x* for which *f*(*x*) is defined. Which one of the following sets represents the domain of the function graphed below?

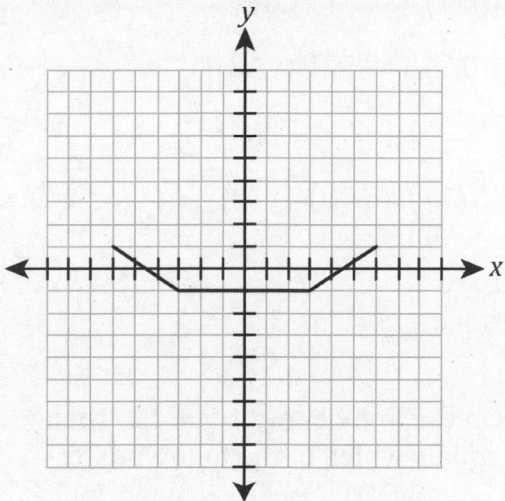

A. $\{-1 \le y \le 1\}$

B. $\{-4.5 \le y \le 4.5\}$

C. $\{-4 \le x \le 4\}$

D. $\{-6 \le x \le 6\}$

E. $\{-1 \le x \le 3\}$

196. The graph of a certain hyperbola *y* = *f*(*x*), is shown in the standard (*x,y*) coordinate plane below.

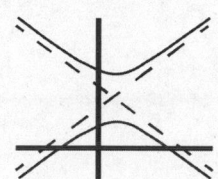

Among the following graphs, which best represents *y* = –*f*(*x*)?

F.
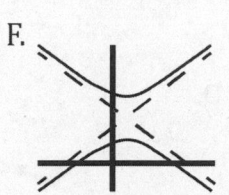

J.
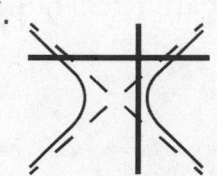

G.
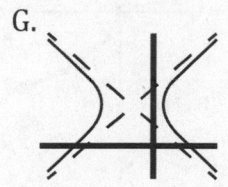

K.
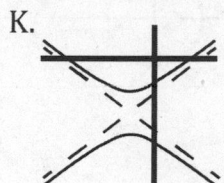

H.
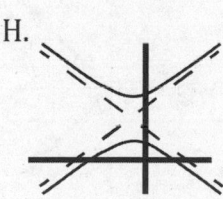

197. The equation *y* = P(*x*) is graphed in the standard (*x,y*) coordinate plane. If P(*x*) is a parabola as shown below, which of the following would move the parabola up 3 units?

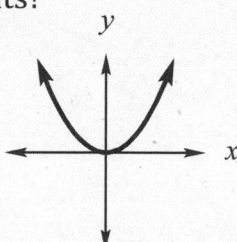

A. P(*x*)   C. P(*x*) + 3   E. 3(P(*x*))

B. –P(*x*)   D. P(*x*) – 3

198. The graph of $y = 4x^2$ intersects the graph of $y = x^2 + 3x$ at how many points?

F. 0   H. 2   K. 4
G. 1   J. 3

199. Which of the following graphs represents a relation of which the domain is the set of all real numbers and the range is the set of all non-negative real numbers?

A.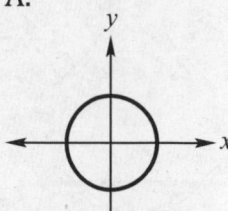

D.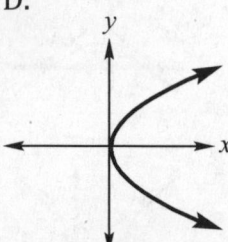

B.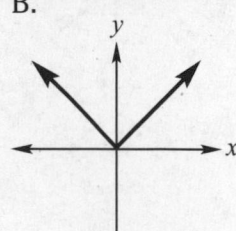

E.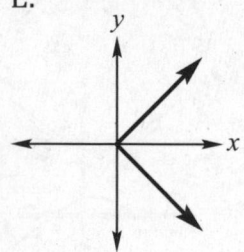

C.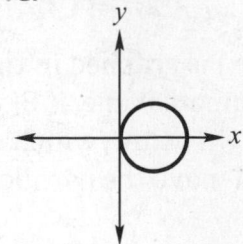

200. In each of the following four sets, the three ordered pairs belong to a linear function. In how many of the four sets is the value of the variable x less than zero?

$\{(0,1), (-4,7), (x,0)\}$

$\{(0,2), (-5,52), (x,12)\}$

$\{(2,-5), (-2,-17), (x,13)\}$

$\{(6,17), (8,25), (x,4)\}$

F. 0   H. 2   K. 4
G. 1   J. 3

201. On the line below, if $x = 4.2$, then y equals which of the following?

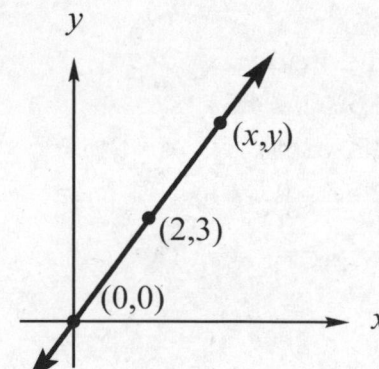

A. 2.8   C. 4.8   E. 6.3
B. 3.4   D. 6.2

202. In the standard (x,y) coordinate plane shown below, $\triangle RST$ has vertices at $R(5,-3)$, $S(4,-3)$ and $T(2,2)$. A translation is performed on $\triangle RST$, and the image of each point P with coordinates (x,y) is the point P' with coordinates (x',y') where $x' = x - 1$ and $y' = y + 5$. The vertices of $\triangle R'S'T'$ are in which quadrant(s)?

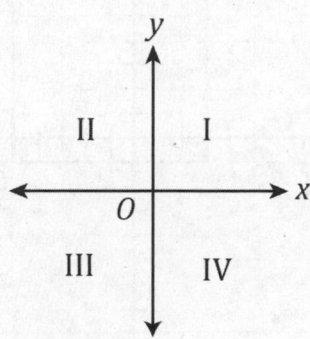

F. Quadrant I only
G. Quadrant II only
H. Quadrants I and IV only
J. Quadrant I and II only
K. Quadrant IV only

203. If point B (not shown in the figure below) lies below the x-axis at point $(4,-4)$, what is the area of $\triangle ABC$?

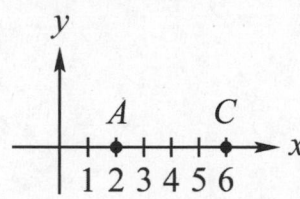

A. 2   C. 6   E. 16
B. 4   D. 8

204. The vertices of a triangle are $(2,1)$, $(2,5)$, and $(5,1)$. What is the area of the triangle?

F. 12   H. 8   K. 5
G. 10   J. 6

205. In the figure below, which is not necessarily drawn to scale, $ABCD$ is a square and $\angle FGH \cong \angle A$.

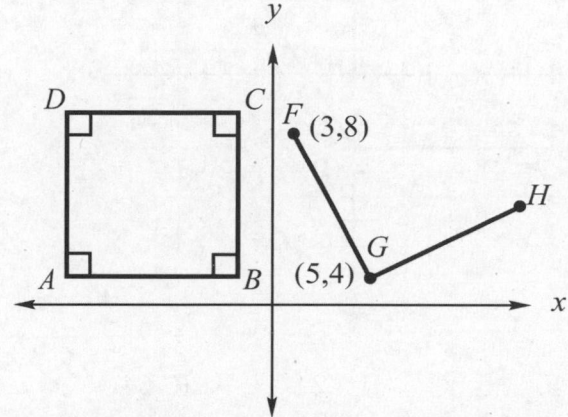

If points F and G have the coordinates as indicated in the figure, how many of the following four ordered pairs could possibly represent point H?

$(8,6), (9,6), (11,7), (13,8)$

A. 0   C. 2   E. 4
B. 1   D. 3

206. What is the area, in square coordinate units, of the parallelogram with vertices as shown in the standard (x,y) coordinate plane below?

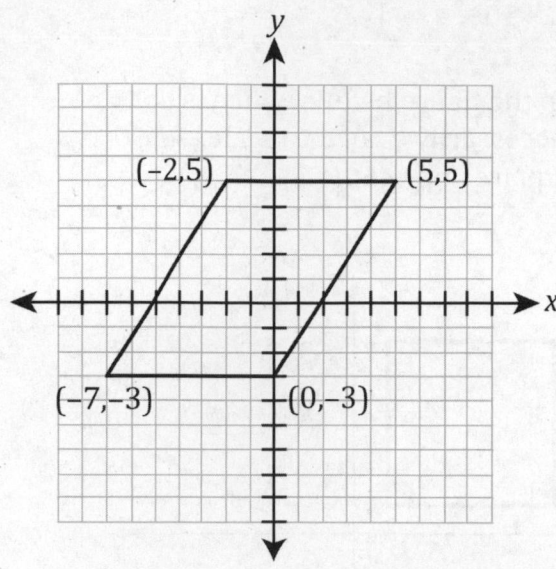

F. 10   H. 21   K. 64
G. 14   J. 56

207. What is the area, in square coordinate units, of the largest circle to fit inside the square shown in the standard (x,y) coordinate plane below?

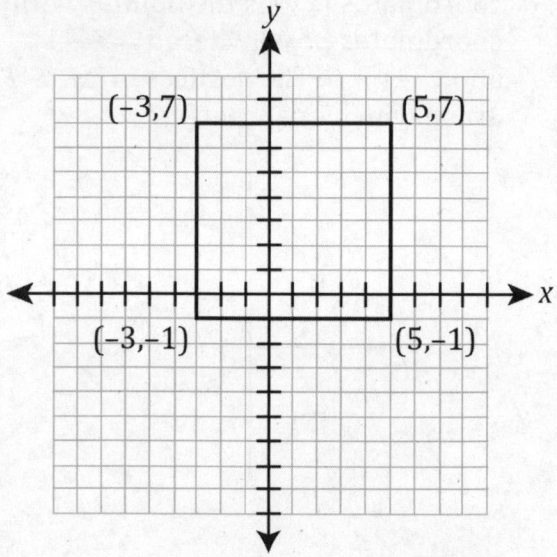

A. 8   C. 16π E. 64
B. 8π D. 64π

Plane Figures

Triangles

Pythagorean Theorem

The sides of every right triangle fit a special relationship called the **Pythagorean theorem**: $c^2 = a^2 + b^2$.

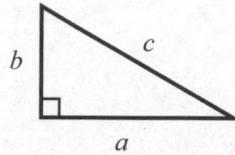

Example:

If the legs of a right triangle are 3 and 8, what is the hypotenuse?

$$h^2 = l_1^2 + l_2^2 = 3^2 + 8^2 = 9 + 64 = 73 \Rightarrow$$
$$h = \sqrt{73}$$

Use the Pythagorean theorem.

_____

Apply properties of special triangles such as 30°-60°-90°, 45°-45°-90°, similar, and congruent.

Special Properties of 45°-45°-90° Triangles

The sides of **45°-45°-90° triangles** share special relationships. In a triangle with angles of 45°-45°-90°, the length of the hypotenuse is equal to the length of either side multiplied by the square root of two. Conversely, the length of each of the two sides is equal to one-half the length of the hypotenuse multiplied by the square root of two. 45°-45°-90° triangles are also isosceles right triangles.

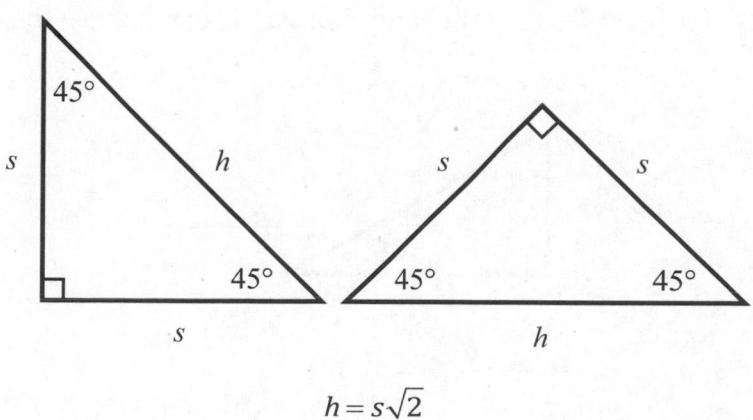

$$h = s\sqrt{2}$$

Example:

In $\triangle ABC$, both $\angle A$ and $\angle C$ are 45°. If the length of $\overline{AB}$ is 3, what is the length of $\overline{AC}$?

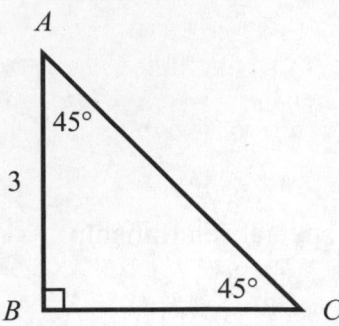

$$h = s\sqrt{2} \Rightarrow AC = AB\left(\sqrt{2}\right) = 3\sqrt{2}$$

Special Properties of 30°-60°-90° Triangles

Similarly, the sides of **30°-60°-90° triangles** also share special relationships. In triangles with angles of 30°-60°-90°, the length of the side opposite the 30° angle is equal to one-half the length of the hypotenuse, and the length of the side opposite the 60° angle is equal to one-half the length of the hypotenuse multiplied by $\sqrt{3}$.

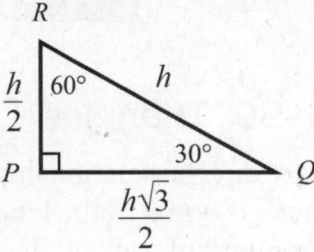

Example:

In $\triangle ABC$, $\angle A = 60°$ and $\angle C = 30°$. If the length of $\overline{AC}$ is 6, what are the lengths of $\overline{AB}$ and $\overline{BC}$?

$$AB = \frac{AC}{2} = \frac{6}{2} = 3 \Rightarrow BC = \frac{AC\sqrt{3}}{2} = \frac{6\sqrt{3}}{2} = 3\sqrt{3}$$

Similar Triangles

"Real world" items such as blueprints, scale drawings, microscopes, and photo enlargements involve similar figures. **Similar triangles** are frequently encountered on the exams. The symbol for similarity is "~." If two triangles are similar, the corresponding sides have the same ratio, and their corresponding angles are **congruent**; that is, they have the same number of degrees. Again, the symbol for congruency is "$\cong$."

Examples:

In the following figure, $\triangle ABC \sim \triangle DEF$. Find the length of $\overline{AC}$.

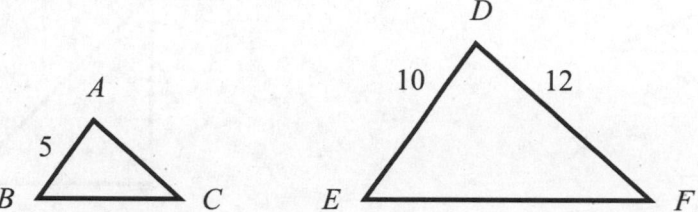

The triangles are similar, so create a proportion relating the similar sides:

$$\frac{AC}{5} = \frac{12}{10} \Rightarrow 10(AC) = 5(12) \Rightarrow 10AC = 60 \Rightarrow AC = 6.$$

Right triangle PQR is similar to right triangle STV. The hypotenuse of $\triangle PQR$ is 12 units long and one of the legs is 6 units long. Find the degree measure of the smallest angle of $\triangle STV$.

Any right triangle in which one leg is equal to one-half the hypotenuse must be a 30°-60°-90° triangle. Since the two triangles are similar, the matching angles are congruent. Therefore, the smallest angle of $\triangle STV$ is 30°.

EXERCISE 9

DIRECTIONS: Choose the correct answer to each of the following items. Answers are on page 816.

208. In the figure below, what is *x* equal to?

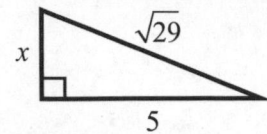

F. $\sqrt{29} - 5$ H. 2   K. 24
G. $\sqrt{2}$ J. $\sqrt{24}$

209. An umbrella 50" long can lie diagonally on the bottom of a trunk with a length and width that are which of the following, respectively?

A. 26", 30"   D. 40", 21"
B. 30", 36"   E. 40", 30"
C. 31", 31"

210. If the legs of a right triangle are 3 and 6, what is the hypotenuse?

F. $\sqrt{42}$ H. $3\sqrt{6}$ K. 9
G. $3\sqrt{5}$ J. $5\sqrt{3}$

211. In the figure below, what is the length of $\overline{AB}$?

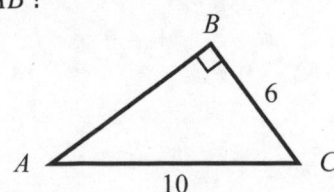

A. 4   C. 12   E. 24
B. 8   D. 16

212. In the figure below, what is the length of $\overline{AC}$?

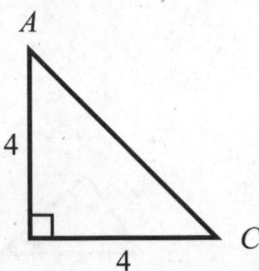

F. 2   H. 4   K. 8
G. $2\sqrt{2}$ J. $4\sqrt{2}$

213. In the figure below, what are *a* and *b*?

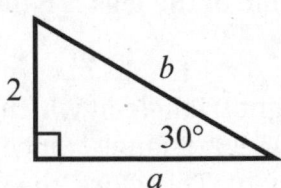

A. $a = \sqrt{3}, b = 2$
B. $a = 2\sqrt{3}, b = 4$
C. $a = 2, b = 4$
D. $a = 4, b = 2\sqrt{3}$
E. $a = 4, b = 4\sqrt{3}$

214. In the figure below, what are
e and f?

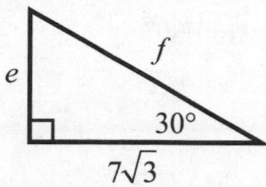

F. e = 2, f = 6
G. e = √2, f = 8
H. e = 4, f = 3√5
J. e = 7, f = 10
K. e = 7, f = 14

215. In the figure below, what is the length
of $\overline{JK}$?

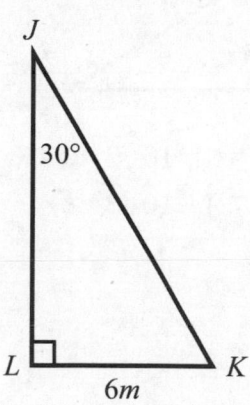

A. 9m   C. 12m   E. 12m√3
B. 6m√3   D. 14m

216. If the longest side of a 30°-60°-90°
triangle is 2√3, what is the area of
the triangle?

F. 8   H. 1.5√3   K. 1
G. 4   J. 2

217. In the figure below, what is the length
of $\overline{JK}$?

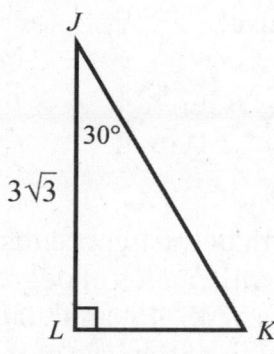

A. 3   C. 6   E. 6√3
B. $4\frac{1}{2}$ D. 3√6

218. In the figure below, what are k and m?

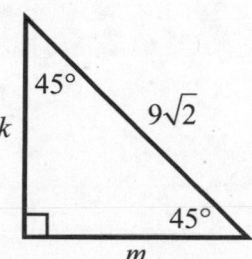

F. k = 3, m = 3
G. k = 2√3, m = 3
H. k = 4, m = 6
J. k = 9, m = 9
K. k = 3, m = 9

219. Two congruent legs of a triangle with angles of degree measures of 45, 45, and 90 are 5. What is the length of the hypotenuse?

A. 5   C. $5\sqrt{3}$ E. $6\sqrt{3}$

B. $5\sqrt{2}$ D. $6\sqrt{2}$

220. The length of the hypotenuse of a triangle with angles of degree measures of 45, 45, and 90 is 6. What is the length of the legs of the triangle?

F. 3   H. $3\sqrt{3}$ K. $4\sqrt{2}$

G. $3\sqrt{2}$ J. 4

221. The length of the hypotenuse of a triangle of degree measures 45, 45, and 90 is 7. What is the length of the legs of the triangle?

A. $\dfrac{7\sqrt{3}}{3}$ C. $7\sqrt{2}$ E. 8

B. $\dfrac{7\sqrt{2}}{2}$ D. $7\sqrt{3}$

222. In the figure below, which is not necessarily drawn to scale,

$$\angle ABC = 90°,\ \overline{AB} = 10,\text{ and } \dfrac{\overline{AB}}{\overline{BC}} = 1.$$

What is the length of $\overline{AC}$?

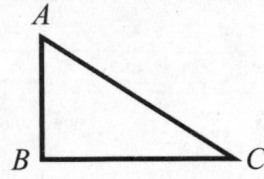

F. 10   H. $10\sqrt{2}$ K. $20\sqrt{3}$

G. 20   J. $10\sqrt{3}$

223. In the figures below, what is the ratio of the perimeter of $\triangle ABC$ to the perimeter of $\triangle DEF$?

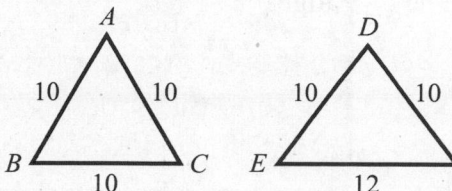

A. 1:1 C. 15:16 E. 7:3
B. 5:6 D. 6:5

224. A triangle with sides of 12, 14, and 20 is similar to a second triangle that has one side with a length of 40. What is the smallest possible perimeter of the second triangle?

F. 48 H. 120 K. 180
G. 92 J. 160

225. $\triangle ABC$ is similar to $\triangle XYZ$. $\overline{AB} = 4$, $\overline{XY} = 12$, and $\overline{AC} = 6$. What is the length of $\overline{XZ}$?

A. 8 C. 12 E. 18
B. 10 D. 16

226. $\triangle ABC$ is similar to $\triangle XYZ$. $\overline{AC} = 10$, $\overline{XZ} = 30$, and $\overline{BC} = 5$. What is the length of $\overline{YZ}$?

F. $1\dfrac{1}{3}$ H. 10 K. 20
G. 5   J. 15

227. $\triangle ABC$ is similar to $\triangle XYZ$. $\overline{AB} = 3s$, $\overline{XY} = 9s$, and $\overline{BC} = s$. What is the length of $\overline{YZ}$?

A. $\dfrac{s}{3}$ C. 3s E. 12s
B. 3   D. 6s

Circle Properties and Formulas

A **chord** is a line segment that connects any two points on a circle. A **secant** is a chord that extends in either one or both directions. A **tangent** is a line that touches a circle at one and only one point. A line that is tangent to a circle is perpendicular to a radius drawn to the point of tangency. An **arc** of a circle is any part of the **circumference**. The symbol for arc is " ⌒ ."

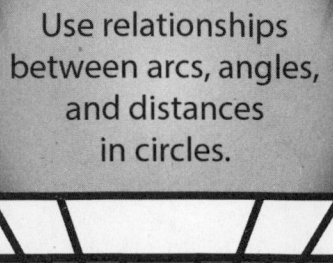

Use relationships between arcs, angles, and distances in circles.

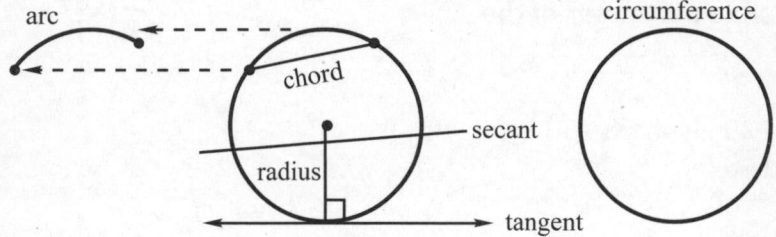

Example:

Two different circles lie in a flat plane. The circles may or may not intersect, but neither circle lies entirely within the other. What is the difference between the minimum and maximum number of lines that could be common tangents to both circles?

Three cases are possible for the orientation of the two circles:

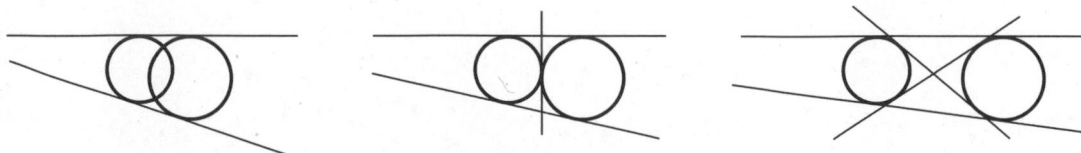

The difference between the minimum and maximum number of tangents that could be common to both circles is: $4 - 2 = 2$.

A *central angle*, such as ∠AOB in the next figure, is an angle with a vertex at the center of the circle and with sides that are radii. A central angle is equal to, or has the same number of degrees as, its intercepted arc. An *inscribed angle*, such as ∠MNP, is an angle with a vertex on the circle and with sides that are chords. An inscribed angle has half the number of degrees of its intercepted arc. For example, in the figure below, ∠MNP intercepts $\overset{\frown}{MP}$ and has half the degrees of $\overset{\frown}{MP}$.

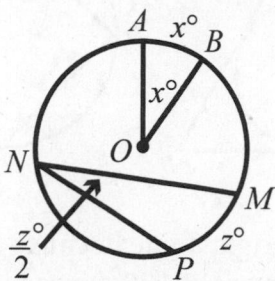

Since the number of degrees of arc in an entire circle is 360, the length of the intercepted arc of a central angle is $\dfrac{x}{360}$ of the circumference of the circle, where x is the degree measure of the central angle.

Example:

In the following circle with center O, if $x = 60$ and the diameter of the circle is 12, what is the length of $\overset{\frown}{MN}$?

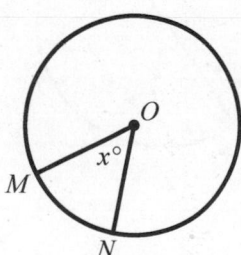

Since ∠MON is a central angle, it has the same number of degrees as the intercepted arc $\overset{\frown}{MN}$. Thus, the length of $\overset{\frown}{MN}$ is $\dfrac{x}{360} = \dfrac{60}{360} = \dfrac{1}{6}$ of the circumference of the circle. The circumference of the circle is $2\pi r = 2\pi \cdot \dfrac{d}{2} = \pi d = 12\pi$. Therefore, the length of $\overset{\frown}{MN}$ is $\dfrac{12\pi}{6} = 2\pi$.

If each side of a polygon is tangent to a circle, the polygon is *circumscribed* about the circle and the circle is *inscribed* in the polygon. Conversely, if each vertex of a polygon lies on a circle, then the polygon is *inscribed* in the circle and the circle is *circumscribed* about the polygon.

Example:

In the following figure, $\triangle ABC$ is circumscribed about a circle and square $DEFG$ is inscribed in a circle.

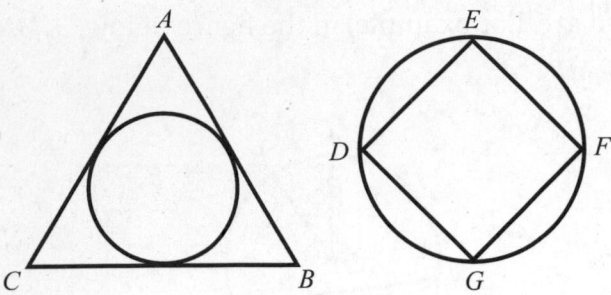

An angle inscribed in a semicircle is a right angle because the semicircle has a measure of 180°: the inscribed angle intercepts an arc of 180 degrees, and since the inscribed angle is half the measure of its intercepted arc, its measure is 90°.

Example:

In the following figure with center O, $\overset{\frown}{NP}$ has a degree measure of 180°; therefore, the degree measure of $\angle NMP$ must be 90°.

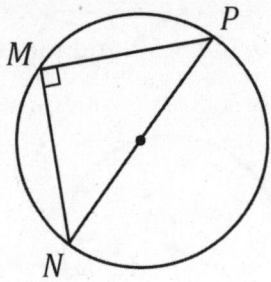

Solve Multi-Step Geometric Problems

Some geometry problems require you to complete multiple steps involving different mathematical concepts. To solve these types of problems, you will need to utilize a combination of the skills and properties that you have learned in order to derive the correct answer.

Examples:

In the figure below, *BCEF* is a square with an area of 16. What is the perimeter of the polygon *ABCDEF*?

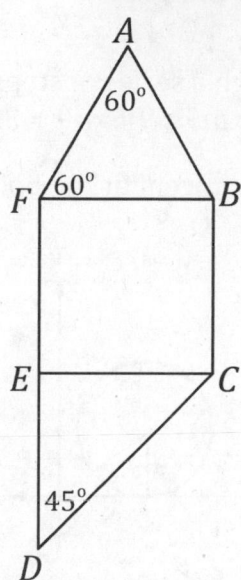

This item can be solved through a series of steps. First, find the length of the sides of the square. Since the square's area is 16, each side of the square has a length of 4 ($\text{area}_{\text{square}} = s^2 = 16 \Rightarrow s = 4$).

Next, find the lengths of the sides of $\triangle ABF$. Since it has two 60° angles, the third angle is also 60°, and it is an equilateral triangle. The lengths of each side of an equilateral triangle are the same. Since $\overline{FB} = 4$, $\overline{FA} = 4$ and $\overline{AB} = 4$.

Then, find the lengths of the sides of $\triangle CED$. Since it has one 45° angle and one 90° angle, it is a 45°-45°-90° triangle, and sides $\overline{CE}$ and $\overline{DE}$ are the same length. Since $\overline{CE} = 4$, $\overline{DE} = 4$. And using the properties of a 45°-45°-90° triangle, $\overline{CD} = 4\sqrt{2}$.

Now, add up all the sides of the polygon to determine the perimeter:

$$\overline{AB} + \overline{BC} + \overline{CD} + \overline{DE} + \overline{EF} + \overline{AF} = 4 + 4 + 4\sqrt{2} + 4 + 4 + 4 = 20 + 4\sqrt{2}$$

The figure below shows a circle with an area of 9π square inches and a radius drawn to the point of tangency of the circle on the x-axis. If the point of tangency is 4 inches from the origin, what is the number of inches from the origin to the center of the circle?

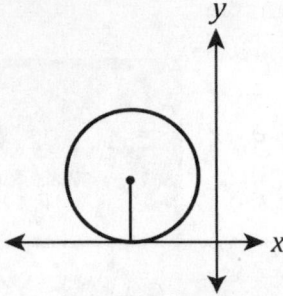

This item can be solved through a series of steps. First, determine the radius of the circle from the area of a circle: $\pi r^2 = 9\pi \Longrightarrow r = 3$.

A radius is perpendicular to a tangent at the point of tangency, so draw a right triangle:

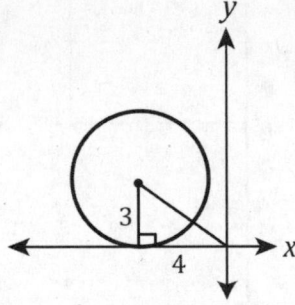

Since the radius is 3 and the distance from the point of tangency to the origin is 4, use the Pythagorean theorem to find the length of the hypotenuse of this right triangle: $h^2 = x^2 + y^2 = 3^2 + 4^2 \Longrightarrow h = 5$.

EXERCISE 10

DIRECTIONS: Fill in the rows in the following tables, working across each row. Use the values provided and your knowledge about the properties of angles, squares, and circles to calculate the missing values in each row. Answers are on page 817.

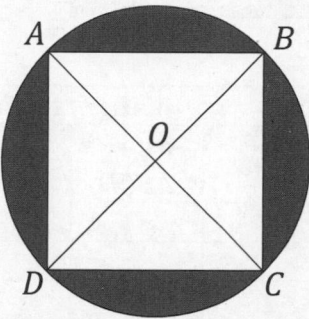

Assumed Values	Values to Deduce					
	AB	Radius	Area of $ABCD$	Circumference of Circle	Area of Circle	Shaded Area
$AB = 1$	1					
Radius = 1		1				
Area of $ABCD$ = 4			4			
Circumference of Circle = 2π				2π		
Area of Circle = 4π					4π	

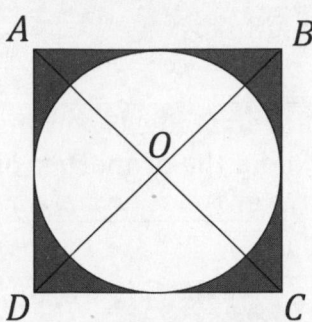

Assumed Values	Values to Deduce						
	AB	AO	Radius	Area of $ABCD$	Circumference of Circle	Area of Circle	Shaded Area
$AB = 1$	1						
$AO = 1$		1					
Radius = 1			1				
Area of $ABCD$ = 16				16			
Circumference of Circle = 8π					8π		
Area of Circle = 9π						9π	

DIRECTIONS: Choose the correct answer to each of the following items. Answers are on page 817.

228. In the circle below, $\overline{RS}$ is parallel to diameter $\overline{PQ}$, and $\overline{PQ}$ has a length of 12. What is the length of $\overset{\frown}{RS}$?

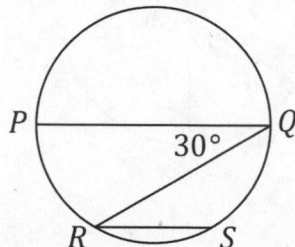

F. $\dfrac{\pi}{2}$ H. $\dfrac{3\pi}{2}$ K. $\dfrac{7\pi}{2}$

G. π J. 2π

229. In the circle below with center O, $\overline{MO}$ has a length of 5. What is the length of $\overset{\frown}{MN}$?

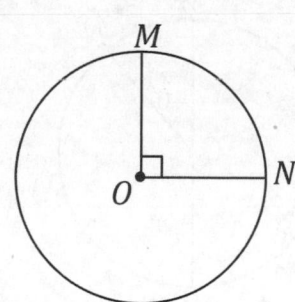

A. $\dfrac{3\pi}{2}$ C. $\dfrac{5\pi}{2}$ E. 10π

B. 2π D. 5π

230. In the circle below with center O, the measure of $\angle POQ$ is 36° and the length of $\overline{NP}$ is 6. What is the length of $\overset{\frown}{MN}$?

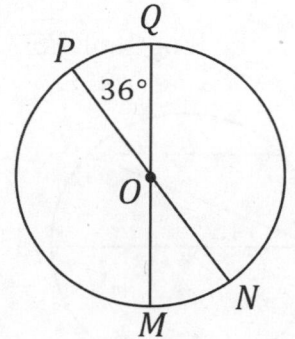

F. $\dfrac{3\pi}{10}$ H. $\dfrac{3\pi}{4}$ K. 3π

G. $\dfrac{3\pi}{5}$ J. $\dfrac{6\pi}{5}$

Questions 231–232 refer to the following figure.

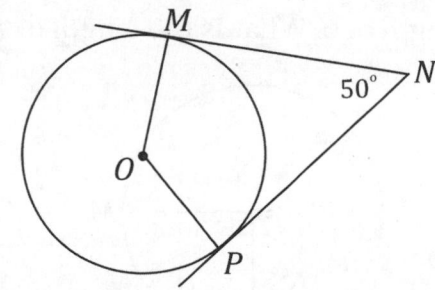

231. In the circle below with center O, $\overline{NM}$ is tangent to the circle at point M, and $\overline{NP}$ is tangent to the circle at point P. $\angle MNP$ is 50°. What is the degree measure of $\overset{\frown}{MP}$?

A. 65°   C. 120°   E. 180°

B. 80°   D. 130°

232. In the same figure, if $\overline{MO}$ equals 18, what is the length of $\overarc{MP}$?

F. 9π H. 13π K. 36π
G. 12π J. 18π

233. In the circle below, $\overline{RS}$ is parallel to diameter $\overline{PQ}$, and $\overline{PQ}$ has a length of 16. What is the length of $\overarc{RS}$?

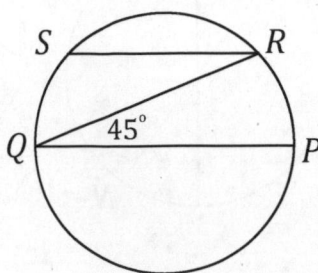

A. $\dfrac{\pi}{2}$ C. 4π E. 16π
B. 2π D. 8π

234. In the circle below with center O, $\angle MOP$ is a right angle and $\overline{MO}$ has a length of 6. What is the length of $\overarc{NP}$?

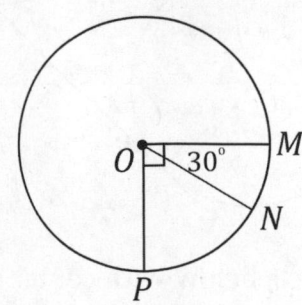

F. 2π H. 4π K. 12π
G. 3π J. 6π

235. A circle is divided into 6 equal pieces as shown in the figure below. If the circumference of the circle is 18π, what is the length of $\overarc{MN}$?

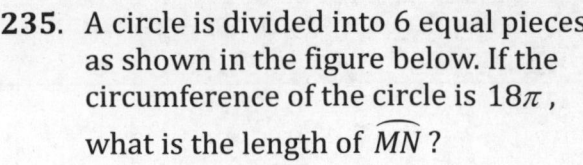
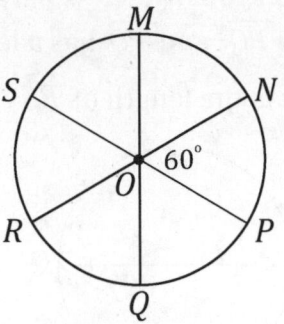

A. $\dfrac{\pi}{3}$ C. 3π E. 18π
B. 3 D. 6π

236. In the circle below with center O, $\angle MON$ is 40° and the measure of $\overarc{PN}$ is 7π. What is the length of the diameter of the circle, $\overline{MP}$?

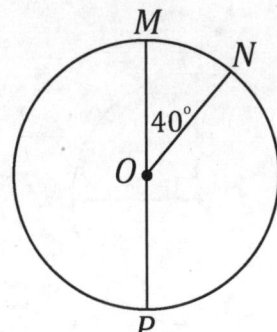

F. $\dfrac{7}{18}$ H. 18 K. 18π
G. $\dfrac{31}{2}$ J. 36

237. In the figure below, a circle is inscribed in square *ABCD*. If the lengths of the sides of the square are 10, what is the circumference of the circle?

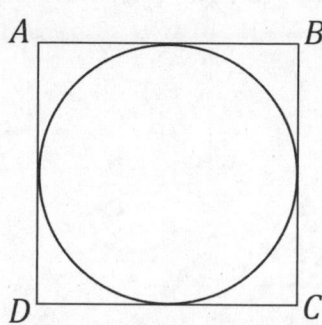

A. 10
B. 5π
C. 10π
D. 40
E. 20π

238. In the diagram below, $\overline{AD} \cong \overline{AE}$ and $\overline{AB} \cong \overline{BF} \cong \overline{CE} \cong \overline{CF} \cong \overline{DE}$.

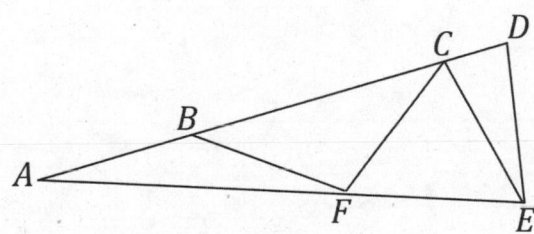

What is the degree measure of $\angle DAE$?

F. 20°
G. 24°
H. 25°
J. 30°
K. 35°

239. The figure below shows a circle of area 144π square inches with a radius drawn to the point of tangency of the circle on the *x*-axis.

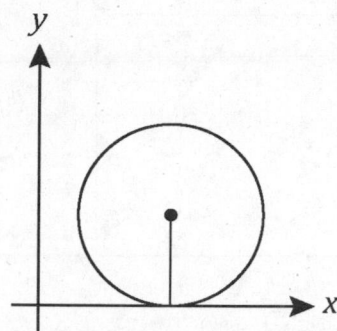

If this point of tangency is 16 inches from the origin, what is the number of inches from the origin to the center of the circle?

A. 12
B. 16
C. $12\sqrt{2}$
D. 20
E. $16\sqrt{2}$

240. At 12 cents per square foot, how much will it cost to paint the rectangular slab in the figure below?

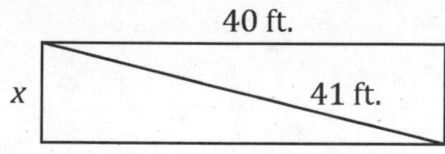

F. $43.20
G. $46.40
H. $98.40
J. $196.80
K. $201.50

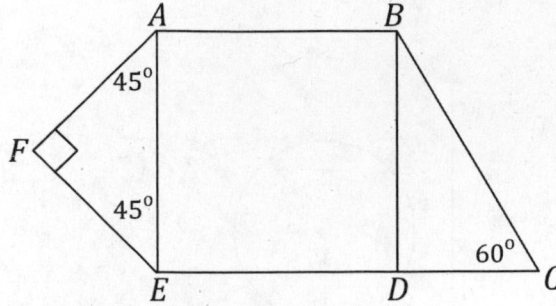
241. In the figure below, if *ABDE* is a square and the length of $\overline{AF}$ is $9\sqrt{2}$, what is the length of $\overline{BC}$?

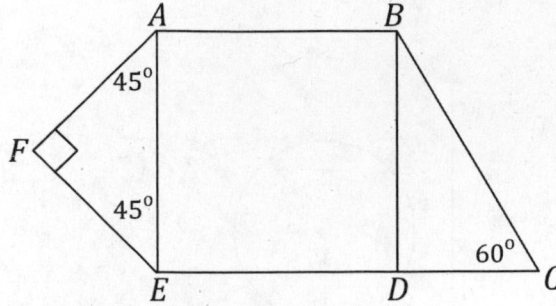

A. 6   C. $9\sqrt{3}$ E. $12\sqrt{3}$
B. 12   D. 18

242. What is the <u>maximum</u> number of non-overlapping sections that can be created when a circle is crossed by four straight lines?

F. 8   H. 10   K. 12
G. 9   J. 11

Measurement

Area, Perimeter, and Volume

Advanced level items testing measurement concepts often require you to use more than one geometric formula. We've already covered perimeter and area in Intermediate Level (p. 488), so let's start with a brief review of volume and surface area of the basic three-dimensional shapes. As with two-dimensional measurements, such as perimeter and area, questions about surface area and volume can be presented as direct application items or word problems.

Compute a measure using relationships between perimeter, area, and volume of geometric figures.

In a three-dimensional figure, the total space contained within the figure is called the **volume**; it is expressed in **cubic units** (e.g., cubic meters, cubic inches, cm^3). The total outside surface is called the **surface area**; it is expressed in **square units** (e.g., square meters, square feet, cm^2).

A **rectangular solid** is a figure of three dimensions having six rectangular faces that meet each other at right angles. The three dimensions are length, width, and height.

A **cube** is a rectangular solid whose edges are equal.

A **cylinder** is a solid composed of two circular, parallel planes joined at the edges by a curved surface. The centers of the circular planes both lie in a line perpendicular to both planes.

To find the volume of a rectangular solid or cube, multiply together the three dimensions. To find the volume of a cylinder, multiply the cylinder's height by the area of its circular base.

VOLUME OF RECTANGULAR SOLIDS, CUBES, AND CYLINDERS

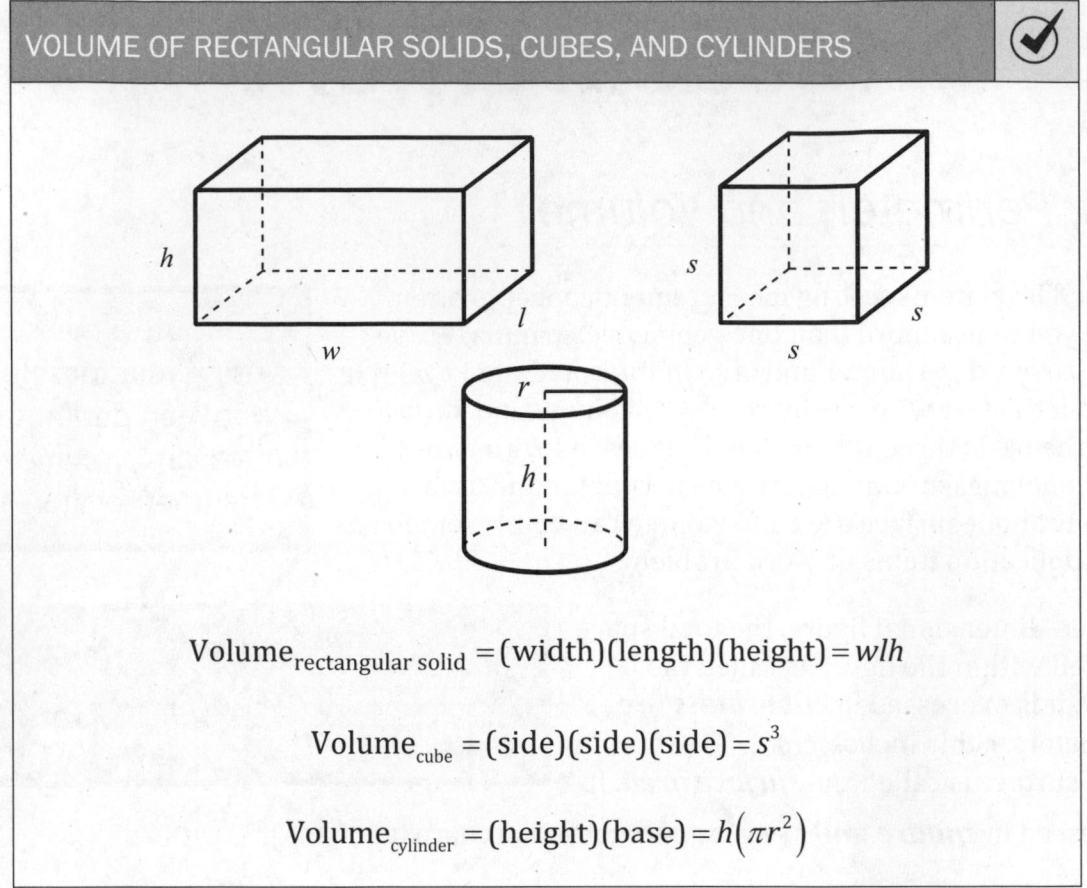

$$Volume_{rectangular\ solid} = (width)(length)(height) = wlh$$

$$Volume_{cube} = (side)(side)(side) = s^3$$

$$Volume_{cylinder} = (height)(base) = h(\pi r^2)$$

Examples:

The figure below shows a cube with edges equal to 2.5. What is the volume of the cube?

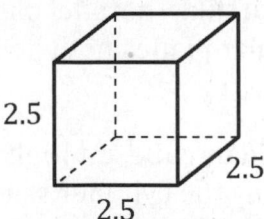

A. 2.5   C. 7.5   E. 37.5
B. 6.25   D. 15.625

To find the volume of a rectangular solid, multiply the three dimensions:

$$s^3 = (2.5)^3 = 15.625$$

A fish tank has inner dimensions of 2 feet by $\frac{3}{2}$ feet by 3 feet. What is the volume, in cubic feet, of the interior of the fish tank?

F. 64.5   H. 13   K. 27

G. 9   J. 13.5

To calculate the interior volume of the tank, multiply the three dimensions together:

$$2 \text{ feet} \cdot \frac{3}{2} \text{ feet} \cdot 3 \text{ feet} = 9 \text{ cubic feet}$$

And to find the surface area of rectangular solids, cubes, and cylinders, simply find the area of each surface and add them together. Notice that for a cylinder, this is equal to the circumference of the end of the cylinder times the height plus twice the area of the cylinder's base.

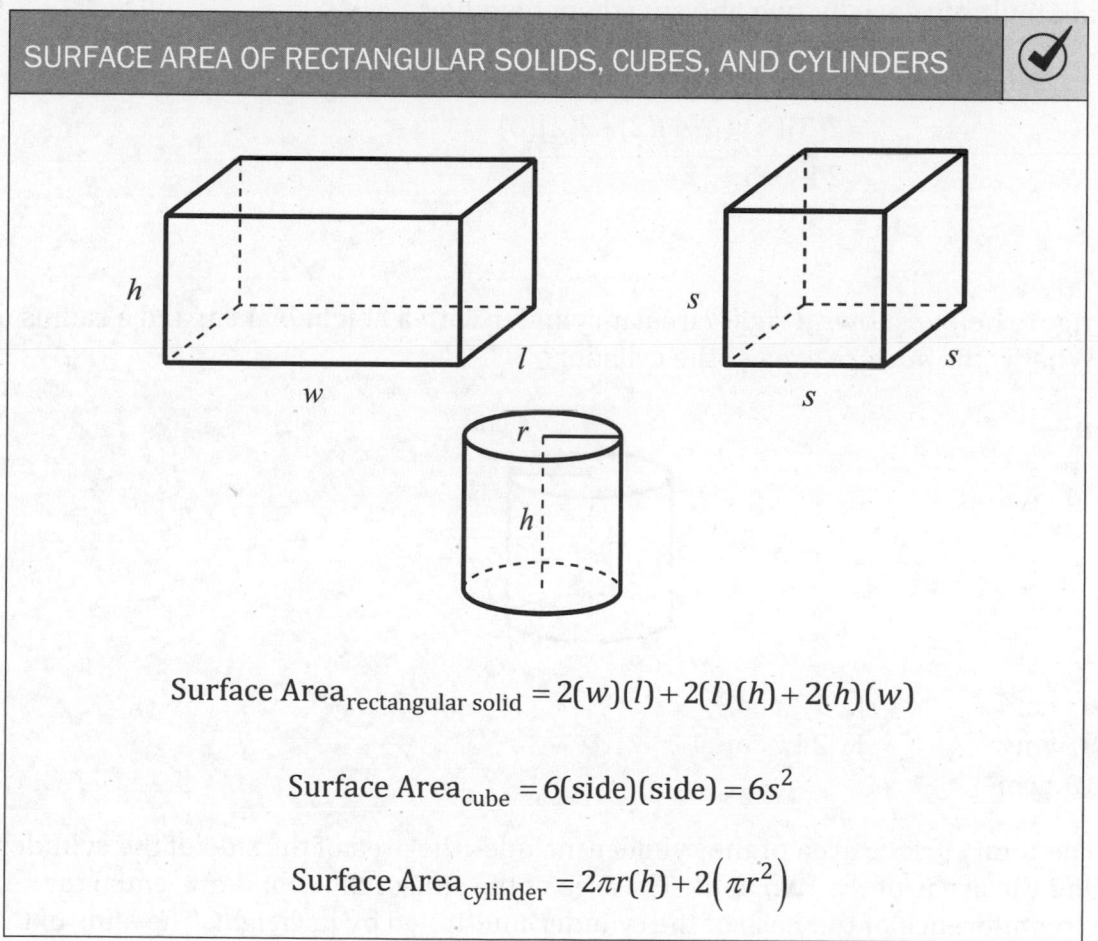

SURFACE AREA OF RECTANGULAR SOLIDS, CUBES, AND CYLINDERS

$$\text{Surface Area}_{\text{rectangular solid}} = 2(w)(l) + 2(l)(h) + 2(h)(w)$$

$$\text{Surface Area}_{\text{cube}} = 6(\text{side})(\text{side}) = 6s^2$$

$$\text{Surface Area}_{\text{cylinder}} = 2\pi r(h) + 2\left(\pi r^2\right)$$

Examples:

The figure below shows a rectangular solid. What is the surface area of the rectangular solid?

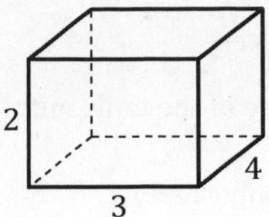

A. 23   C. 52   E.   576
B. 24   D. 104

To find the surface area, determine the area of the three different faces of the solid and multiply each by two and sum them together:

$$
\begin{aligned}
\text{Surface Area} &= 2(w)(l) + 2(l)(h) + 2(h)(w) \\
&= 2(3)(4) + 2(4)(2) + 2(2)(3) \\
&= 24 + 16 + 12 \\
&= 52
\end{aligned}
$$

The figure below shows a right circular cylinder with a height of 4 cm and a radius of 2 cm. What is the surface area of the cylinder?

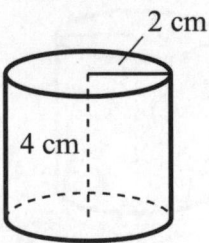

F. $6\pi\,\text{cm}^2$ J. $12\pi\,\text{cm}^2$
G. $8\pi\,\text{cm}^2$ K. $24\pi\,\text{cm}^2$
H. $10\pi\,\text{cm}^2$

The total surface area of the cylinder includes the area of the side of the cylinder and the areas of the two ends. The area of the side of the cylinder is equal to the circumference of the base of the cylinder multiplied by its height. The ends of the cylinder are circles. Thus, the surface area is:

$$
2\pi rh + 2\pi r^2 = 2\pi(2)(4) + 2\pi(2)^2 = 16\pi + 8\pi = 24\pi\,\text{cm}^2
$$

Finally, the volume of a sphere is $\dfrac{4\pi}{3}$ multiplied by the radius cubed. The surface area of a sphere is 4π multiplied by the radius squared.

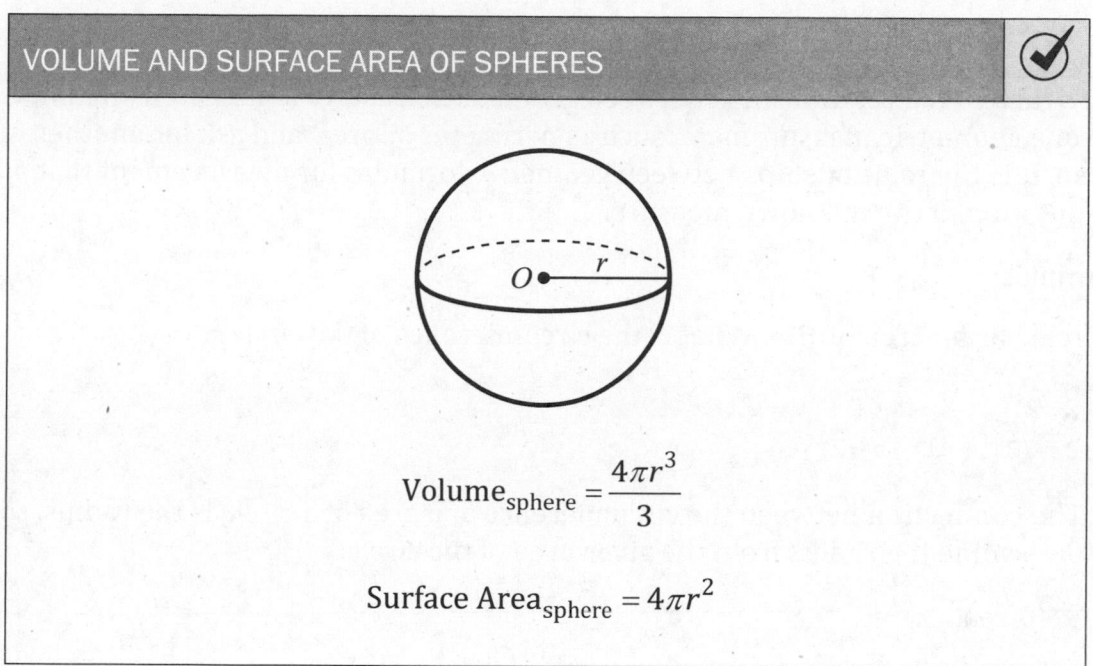

VOLUME AND SURFACE AREA OF SPHERES

$$\text{Volume}_{\text{sphere}} = \frac{4\pi r^3}{3}$$

$$\text{Surface Area}_{\text{sphere}} = 4\pi r^2$$

Examples:

What is the volume, in cubic inches, of a sphere of radius 6 inches?

A. 8π cubic inches
B. 144π cubic inches
C. 216π cubic inches
D. 288π cubic inches
E. 864π cubic inches

The volume of the sphere is:

$$\frac{4\pi r^3}{3} = \frac{4\pi(6)^3}{3} = \frac{4\pi(216)}{3} = 288\pi \text{ cubic inches}$$

What is the total surface area, in square inches, of a ball with a diameter of 1 foot?

F. π square inches
G. 4π square inches
H. 144π square inches
J. 288π square inches
K. 576π square inches

The surface area of a sphere is equal to $4\pi r^2$. The item stem asks for the surface area in square inches, but the dimension is given in feet. A diameter of 1 foot equals a radius of one-half foot, or 6 inches. Thus, the surface area of the ball is:

$$4\pi r^2 = 4\pi(6)^2 = 144\pi \text{ square inches}$$

Now, let's turn to the relationships between geometric measurements. Often an item will provide one geometric measurement, such as perimeter or area, and ask for another, such as volume. It is the relationships between geometric formulas for measurement that allows the computation of the unknown measure.

Examples:

A circle has an area of 8π. What is the circumference of the circle?

A. $2\sqrt{2}$ C. $4\sqrt{2}$ E. $8\pi\sqrt{2}$
B. $2\pi\sqrt{2}$ D. $4\pi\sqrt{2}$

The connection between the circumference and area of a circle is the radius, so determine the radius from the given area of the circle:

$$\text{Area} = \pi r^2$$
$$8\pi = \pi r^2$$
$$2\sqrt{2} = r$$

So, the circumference of the circle is:

$$2\pi r = 2\pi(2\sqrt{2}) = 4\pi\sqrt{2}$$

If the perimeter of an equilateral triangle is 18, what is the area of the triangle?

F. $\dfrac{9\sqrt{3}}{2}$ H. 36   K. Cannot be determined from the given information

G. $9\sqrt{3}$ J. 216

An equilateral triangle has three equal sides:

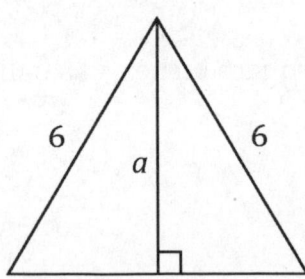

The altitude, a, bisects the base of the equilateral triangle, so half the base is 3. Find the altitude using the Pythagorean theorem:

$$a^2 + 3^2 = 6^2$$
$$a^2 = 36 - 9 = 27$$
$$a = \sqrt{27} = 3\sqrt{3}$$

Thus, the area of the equilateral triangle is:

$$\frac{ab}{2} = \frac{3\sqrt{3} \cdot 6}{2} = 9\sqrt{3}$$

The length of a rectangle is one and a half times its width. If the area of the rectangle is 24, what is the perimeter of the rectangle?

A. 16   C. 20   E. 24
B. 18   D. 22

If the width of the rectangle is w, then the length, l, is $\dfrac{3w}{2}$. Now, find w from the given area of the rectangle:

Area=wl

$$24 = w\left(\frac{3w}{2}\right)$$
$$24\left(\frac{2}{3}\right) = w^2$$
$$16 = w^2$$
$$4 = w$$

And since the width is equal to 4, the length is $\dfrac{3w}{2} = \dfrac{3(4)}{2} = 6$. Thus, the perimeter of the rectangle is:

$$2w + 2l = 2(4) + 2(6) = 20$$

And like all geometric measurement concepts tested, the ability to use one formula to solve for the measurements needed in another can be presented in word problem format.

Example:

A rectangular swimming pool is 32 feet long and 16 feet wide and has a depth of 6 feet. If the pool contains 20,000 gallons of water, what is the approximate depth, in feet, of the water? (1 cubic foot = 7.5 gallons)

F. 2.6   H. 3.6   K. 5.2
G. 3.2   J. 4.0

First, convert the volume of water to cubic feet:

$$20{,}000 \text{ gallons} \cdot \frac{1 \text{ cubic foot}}{7.5 \text{ gallons}} \approx 2{,}667 \text{ cubic feet}$$

Now, use the volume formula for a rectangular solid to determine the depth of the water:

$$\text{Volume} = \text{length} \cdot \text{width} \cdot \text{depth}$$
$$2{,}667 \text{ cubic feet} = (32 \text{ feet})(16 \text{ feet})(d \text{ feet})$$
$$\frac{2{,}667}{512} = d$$
$$5.2 \approx d$$

Scale Factors

Advanced measurement items involving scale factors require you to rewrite geometric formulas in terms of the given measurements after being scaled by the appropriate factor. Simply apply the scale factor to the given measurements and solve for the missing value.

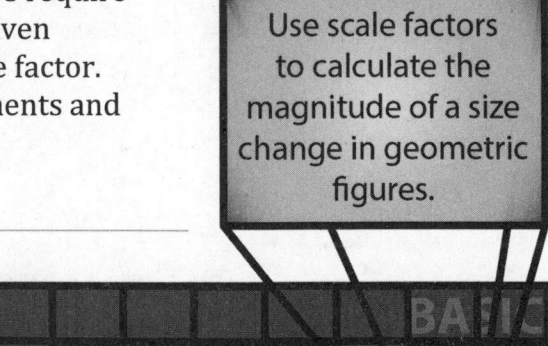

Use scale factors to calculate the magnitude of a size change in geometric figures.

Example:

The width of a rectangle is increased by 250% while the length is decreased by 50%. Which of the following equations correctly expresses the relationship of the new area, A', to the old area, A?

A. $A' = 0.25A$ D. $A' = 1.5A$
B. $A' = 0.5A$ E. $A' = 2.5A$
C. $A' = 1.25A$

Let w' equal the new width and l' the new length, so $w' = 2.5w$ and $l' = 0.5l$. Solve for the new area in terms of the old area:

$$A' = w'l' = (2.5w)(0.5l) = 1.25wl = 1.25A$$

Therefore, the new rectangle is 25% larger than the old rectangle, (C).

Like all geometry measurement items, problems involving scale factors can be presented as a word problem. The strategy is the same: rewrite the new measurement in terms of the old measurement.

Example:

A scale model of a famous landmark building is 12 inches tall and has columns on each corner that are 3 inches tall. If the actual columns are 36 feet tall, what is the height, in feet, of the actual building?

F. 12   H. 72   K. 432
G. 48   J. 144

In the model, 1 inch represents 12 feet, so the height of the building is

$$12 \text{ inches} \cdot \frac{12 \text{ feet}}{1 \text{ inch}} = 144 \text{ feet, (J)}.$$

Composite Figures

Advanced measurement items often ask for the area of geometric figures comprised of two or more of the basic geometric shapes already reviewed. The strategy for these items is always the same: break down the composite figure into basic shapes, use a known measurement to deduce other measurements, and then add or subtract the pieces to find the area of the composite shape.

Determine the area of composite geometric figures when planning or visualization is required.

Example:

A carpenter is building the enclosed staircase shown in the figure below. All lines intersect at right angles and each step has identical dimensions. Decorative paneling is to be applied to the entire area using an adhesive. What is the area, in square inches, that the adhesive must cover?

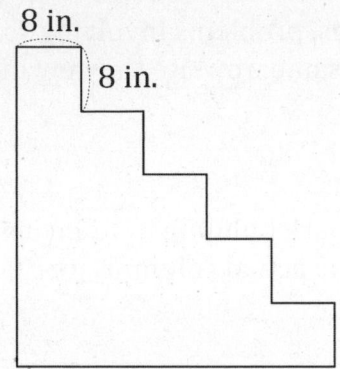

A. 64   C. 512   E. 960
B. 320   D. 768

The key to solving this item is to notice that the wall is actually composed of 15 squares, each 8 inches by 8 inches:

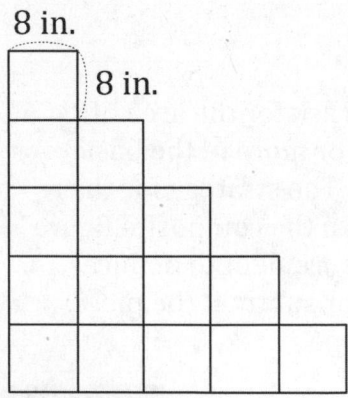

So, the total area the adhesive must cover is:

$$15(\text{Area}_{8"x8"}) = 15(8)(8) = 960 \text{ square inches}$$

Items involving composite geometric figures aren't limited to two dimensions.

Examples:

A shipment of toy puzzle cubes are to be packed in a cardboard box that measure 0.4 meters by 0.5 meters by 0.25 meters. If a single puzzle cube measures 6 centimeters per side, what is the maximum number of cubes that can be shipped in one cardboard box? (1 meter = 100 centimeters)

A. 18   C. 96   E. 192
B. 72   D. 144

This item requires visualization to solve. First, convert the dimensions of the cardboard box to centimeters: 40 centimeters by 50 centimeters by 25 centimeters. Next, draw a quick sketch of the box:

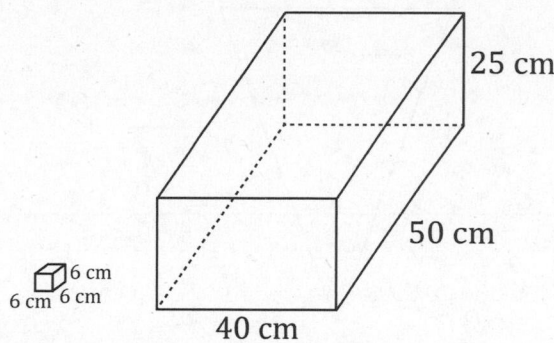

Since each cube is 6 centimeters on a side, divide each dimension of the box by 6:

$40 \div 6 = 6$ plus a remainder of 4

$50 \div 6 = 8$ plus a remainder of 2

$25 \div 6 = 4$ plus a remainder of 1

So, the first layer of cubes in the box is (6)(8) = 48 cubes. And the box allows for 4 layers, so a total of (48)(4) = 192 cubes in the box:

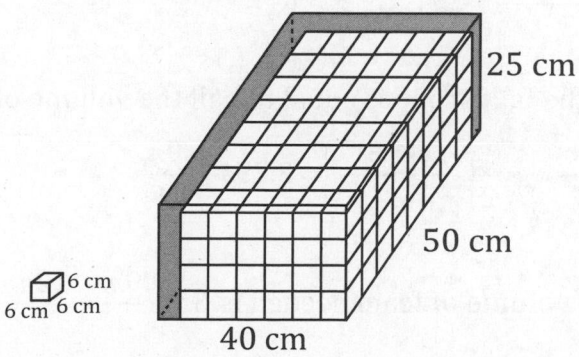

The figure below shows a sign being fabricated for an ice cream shop. The base of the sign is a cone, and the top is half a sphere. Once the top has been welded to the base, the interior of the sign will be filled with a stabilizing foam using the fill port. What is the total volume of stabilizing foam needed to completely fill the sign? (Note: For a cone of radius r at the base and height h, the volume is $\dfrac{\pi r^2 h}{3}$; and for a sphere of radius r, the volume is $\dfrac{4\pi r^3}{3}$.)

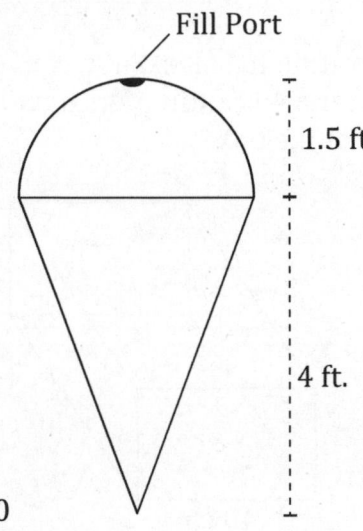

Fill Port

1.5 ft.

4 ft.

0

F. $\dfrac{21\pi}{4}$ H. $\dfrac{3\pi}{2}$ K. $\dfrac{3\pi}{4}$

G. $\dfrac{15\pi}{2}$ J. π

The radius of the half scoop of ice cream is 1.5 feet, so the radius of the base of the cone is also 1.5 feet. And the height of the cone is 4 feet. Thus, the volume of the cone is $\dfrac{\pi r^2 h}{3} = \dfrac{\pi (1.5)^2 (4)}{3} = 3\pi$.

And the volume of the half scoop is equal to half the volume of a sphere with the same radius $\dfrac{1}{2}\left(\dfrac{4\pi r^3}{3}\right) = \dfrac{1}{2}\left(\dfrac{4\pi (1.5)^3}{3}\right) = 2.25\pi = \dfrac{9\pi}{4}$.

Therefore, the total volume of foam needed is $3\pi + \dfrac{9\pi}{4} = \dfrac{12\pi}{4} + \dfrac{9\pi}{4} = \dfrac{21\pi}{4}$, (F).

Now, whereas composite problems require you to add areas together, shaded area problems require you to find the difference in areas. This type of problem is fairly common. To successfully solve shaded area problems, recognize that the area in question is typically the difference between the areas of other known shapes. And, as with composite problems, shaded area problems can be presented in both two and three dimensions.

Examples:

The figure below shows a rectangular piece of glass 3 feet by 6 feet in size that is to be cut into the shape of a rectangle topped by a semicircle. If the shaded portion of the figure is waste, what is the area, in square feet, of the waste?

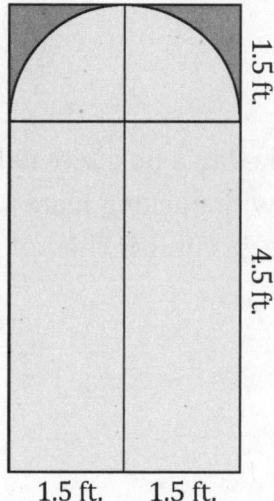

1.5 ft.   1.5 ft.

F. $\dfrac{9}{2} - \dfrac{9}{4}\pi$ J. $\dfrac{9}{2} + \dfrac{9}{4}\pi$

G. $\dfrac{9}{2} - \dfrac{9}{8}\pi$ K. 27π

H. $\dfrac{9}{2} + \dfrac{9}{8}\pi$

The shaded portion of the figure is the difference between a rectangle and a semicircle:

1.5 ft. | Area_{Rectangle} | minus | Area_{Semicircle}

3 ft.   1.5 ft.   1.5 ft.

Shaded Area = Area$_{Rectangle}$ − Area$_{Semicircle}$

$$= wl - \frac{\pi r^2}{2}$$

$$= \left(\frac{3}{2}\right)(3) - \frac{\pi \left(\frac{3}{2}\right)^2}{2}$$

$$= \frac{9}{2} - \frac{\frac{9}{4}\pi}{2}$$

$$= \frac{9}{2} - \frac{9}{8}\pi$$

A ball of diameter 10 inches is packed in a box with sides of 10 inches. If the extra space in the box needs to be filled with packing material, which of the following expressions represents the volume, in cubic inches, of required packing material?

F. $\dfrac{500\pi}{3} - 1{,}000$

G. $1{,}000 - \dfrac{500\pi}{3}$

H. $1{,}000\pi + \dfrac{500}{3}$

J. $1{,}000\pi - \dfrac{500}{3}$

K. $1{,}000 + \dfrac{500\pi}{3}$

Since a figure isn't provided, draw one:

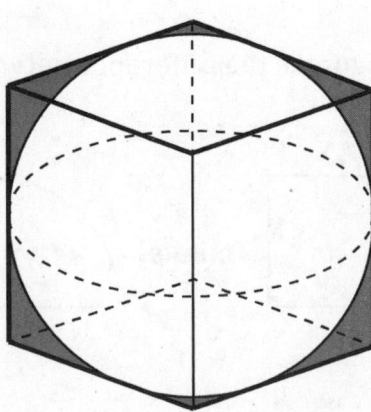

So, the required volume of packing material is the difference between the volume of a cube of side 10 inches and a sphere of radius 5 inches:

$$\text{Volume}_{\text{packing material}} = \text{Volume}_{\text{cube}} - \text{Volume}_{\text{sphere}}$$

$$= s^3 - \frac{4\pi r^3}{3}$$

$$= 10^3 - \frac{4\pi(5)^3}{3}$$

$$= 1,000 - \frac{500\pi}{3}$$

EXERCISE 11

DIRECTIONS: Choose the correct answer to each of the following items. Answers are on page 817.

243. What is the volume of the rectangular solid shown below?

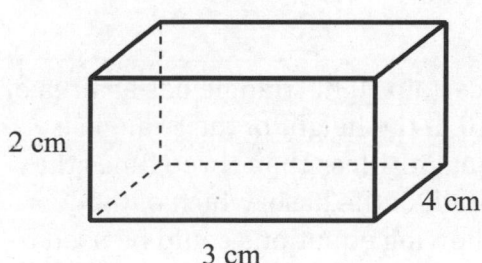

2 cm

4 cm

3 cm

A. 9 cm³   C. 24 cm³   E. 52 cm³
B. 14 cm³   D. 30 cm³

244. If $2\sqrt{12}$, $3\sqrt{6}$, and $4\sqrt{3}$ are the dimensions of a rectangular solid, what is the volume of the solid?

F. $\sqrt{24}$ J. $216\sqrt{24}$
G. $\sqrt{5,184}$ K. $5,184$
H. $144\sqrt{6}$

245. What is the surface area of the cube shown below?

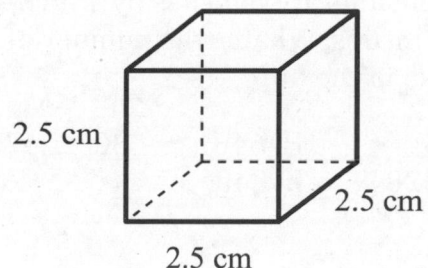

2.5 cm

2.5 cm

2.5 cm

A. 15.5 cm²   D. 37.5 cm²
B. 20.0 cm²   E. 93.75 cm²
C. 25.0 cm²

246. If wrapping paper costs $0.50 per square foot, how much does it cost to wrap a gift box that is 6 inches per side? Assume you only need to buy enough paper to exactly cover the box on all sides.

F. $0.75   J. $27.00
G. $9.00   K. $30.00
H. $18.00

247. The figure below shows a small alloy cylinder used by a jeweler in the assembly of a necklace. What is the approximate volume of the alloy, in cubic centimeters, in the cylinder?

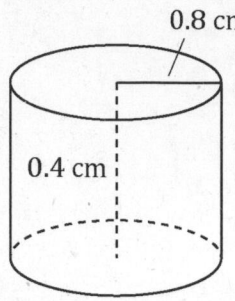

0.8 cm

0.4 cm

A. 0.2 cm³   D. 0.8 cm³
B. 0.4 cm³   E. 1.0 cm³
C. 0.6 cm³

248. A rectangular bin 4 feet long, 3 feet wide, and 2 feet high is solidly packed with bricks whose dimensions are 8 inches by 4 inches by 2 inches. What is the number of bricks in the bin?

F. 54   H. 648   K. 41,472
G. 320   J. 848

249. A box is 12 inches in width, 16 inches in length, and 6 inches in height. How many square inches of paper would be required to cover it on all sides?

A. 192   C. 720   E. 1,440
B. 360   D. 900

250. What is the length of the altitude of an equilateral triangle with a perimeter of 24?

F. $2\sqrt{3}$ H. $4\sqrt{3}$ K. $4\sqrt{5}$
G. 6   J. 8

251. A triangle with sides of 4, 6, and 8 has the same perimeter as an equilateral triangle with sides of length equal to which of the following?

A. 2   C. 3   E. 8
B. $\dfrac{3}{2}$ D. 6

252. If the perimeter of a square is equal to 40, what is the length of the diagonal?

F. $10\sqrt{2}$ H. 10   K. $3\sqrt{5}$
G. 14   J. $5\sqrt{3}$

253. A certain right triangle has an area of 210. If the height of the triangle is equal to 1 less than three times the length of the base, which of the following equations could be used to find the height, h, of the triangle?

A. $h^2 - \dfrac{h}{3} = 70$

B. $h^2 - h = 1,260$

C. $h - h^2 = 1,260$

D. $h(2h + 1) = 1,260$

E. $h^2 + h = 1,260$

254. The area of a circle is 49π. What is its circumference?

F. 14π H. 49π K. 147π
G. 28π J. 98π

255. Each side of a cube is a square with an area of 49 square centimeters. What is the volume of the cube, in cubic centimeters?

A. 49   C. 7^4 E. 7^{49}
B. 7^3 D. 49^7

256. In the figure below, a circle is inscribed in a square. If the radius of the circle is equal to 3, what is the area of the square?

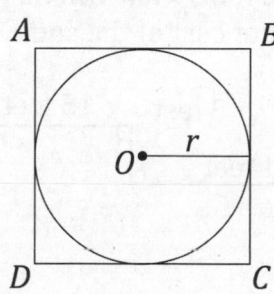

F. 12   H. 9π K. 36π
G. 24   J. 36

257. If the ratio of the volumes of two spheres is 3:8, what is the ratio of their radii?

A. $\sqrt{3}:2$ D. 3:8
B. $\sqrt[3]{3}:2$ E. $\sqrt{3}:2\sqrt{2}$
C. $\sqrt[3]{3}:2\pi$

258. A sphere of volume 36π cm³ is inscribed in a cube. What is the length, in centimeters, of one side of the cube?

F. 2   H. $3\sqrt{3}$ K. $6\sqrt{3}$
G. 3   J. 6

259. A certain triangle has side lengths of 6, 8, and 10. A rectangle equal in area to that of the triangle has a width of 3. What is the perimeter of the rectangle?

A. 11   C. 22   E. 30
B. 16   D. 24

260. In the figure below, the radius of the circle with center O is equal to one-fourth the side of square $ABCD$. If the area of circle O is 16π, what is the perimeter of square $ABCD$?

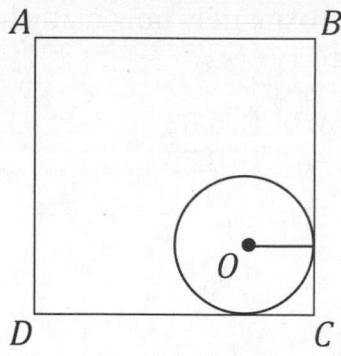

F. 4π H. 32   K. 128
G. 16   J. 64

261. If the surface area of the sphere is 324π, what is the sphere's volume?

A. 243π C. 729π E. $1,296\pi$
B. 324π D. 972π

262. A piece of wire is shaped to enclose a square, whose area is 121 square inches. It is then reshaped to enclose a rectangle whose length is 13 inches. What is the area of the rectangle, in square inches?

F. 64   H. 117   K. 234
G. 96   J. 144

263. If the radius of a circle increases by 50%, by how much does the area of the circle increase?

A. 50%   C. 100%   E. 225%
B. 75%   D. 125%

264. For HO scale railcar models, the ratio of linear measure of model to actual length is 1:87. A hobbyist designed a model of a locomotive that was exactly 41 feet in length, erroneously calculating that the model should be 6.22 inches. The hobbyist's model was approximately how many inches too long?

F. 0.47   H. 0.62   K. 41.40
G. 0.56   J. 8.70

265. What is the area of the figure below?

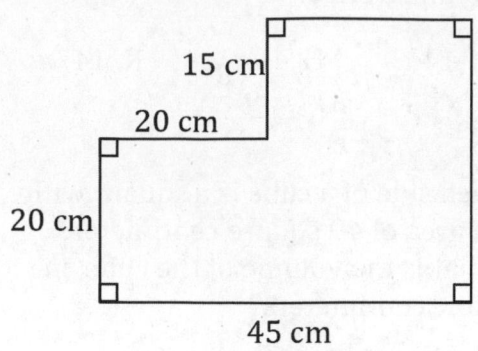

A. 1,275 cm²   D. 195 cm²
B. 995 cm²   E. 135 cm²
C. 450 cm²

266. A yard with the dimensions shown below is to be sodded. If sod costs $3 per square foot, what will be the total approximate cost of the sod needed?

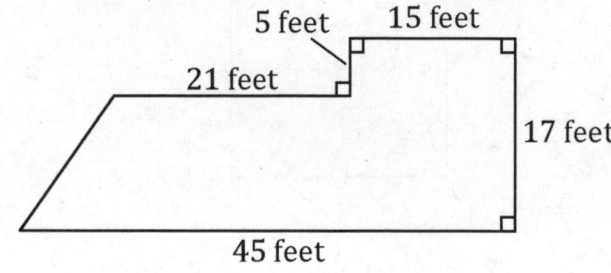

F. $185   J. $1,700
G. $560   K. $2,300
H. $770

267. In the figure below, the area of △*ABC* is 24. What is the area of △*DBC*?

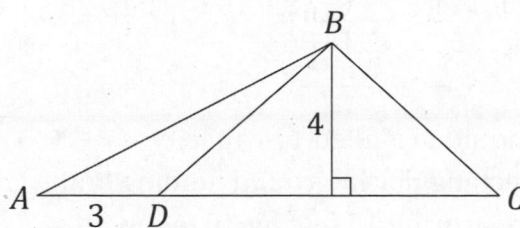

A. 20   C. 16   E. 12
B. 18   D. 14

268. In the figure below, square *ABCD* is inscribed in square *EFGH* and $\overline{AB} = 2$. What is the area of the shaded portion?

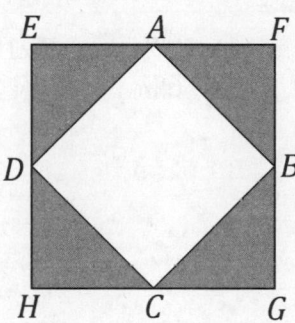

F. $4 - 2\sqrt{2}$

G. $2\sqrt{2}$

H. 4

J. 8

K. Cannot be determined from the given information

269. The figure below shows a circle with center *O*. If the circle is tangent to the *x*-axis and *y*-axis at points *A* and *B*, respectively, what is the area of the shaded region?

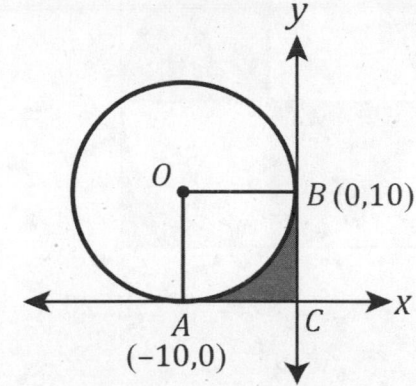

A. $100\pi - 100$ D. $25\pi - 25$
B. $100\pi - 50$ E. $100 - 25\pi$
C. $50\pi - 50$

270. In the figure below, if $\overset{\frown}{BC}$ equals 60°, then what is the area of △*ABC*?

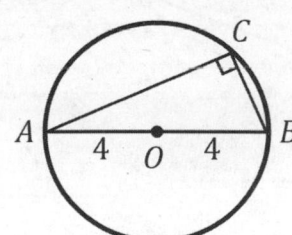

F. 16   H. $8\sqrt{3}$ K. $4\sqrt{3}$
G. $10\sqrt{2}$ J. 12

271. In the figure below, a circle with center O has an area of 4π and is inscribed in a square. What is the total area of the shaded regions?

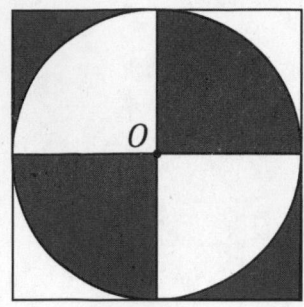

A. 2 C. 8 E. 20
B. 4 D. 16

Questions 272–273 refer to the following information.

The figure below shows a pitched roof and the attic floor beneath it.

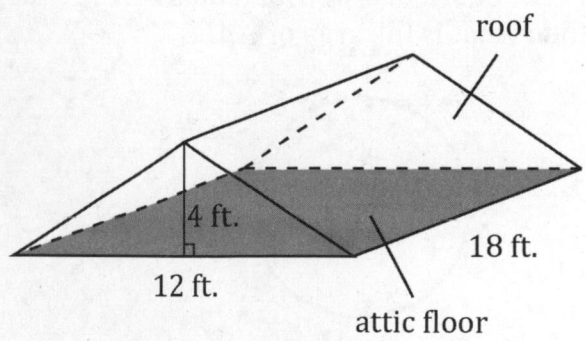

roof
4 ft.
18 ft.
12 ft.
attic floor

272. What is the combined surface area, in square feet, of the two sides of the pitched roof?

F. $36\sqrt{13}$ J. 468
G. 212 K. 864
H. $72\sqrt{13}$

273. What is the volume, in cubic feet, of the attic beneath the roof?

A. 144 C. 432 E. 1,728
B. 360 D. 864

274. Liquid in a filled-to-capacity rectangular in-ground holding tank measuring 15 feet by 20 feet with a uniform depth of 8 feet is pumped into an empty above-ground cylindrical storage tank with a diameter of 20 feet and a height of 10 feet. Once all of the liquid from the holding tank is in the storage tank, the storage tank will be filled to approximately what percentage of its capacity?

F. 4% H. 48% K. 100%
G. 30% J. 76%

Functions

Composite Functions

The term **composite function** refers to the combining of functions such that the output from, one function is used as the input for another function.

To evaluate composite functions at integer values, simply start with the innermost value: substitute that value into the given function, find the resulting value, and substitute that resulting value into the outer function. So, $f(g(x))$, read "f of g of x," is evaluated by first solving $g(x)$ for a given value, then using the resulting value to solve function f.

> Evaluate composite functions using integer values.
>
> ———
>
> Create an expression for the composite of two simple functions.

Examples:

If $f(x) = -4x + 1$ and $g(x) = -2x^2 + 3$, then $f(g(2)) = ?$

A. −7 C. 2 E. 35
B. −5 D. 21

First, evaluate $g(x)$ for $x = 2$: $g(2) = -2(2)^2 + 3 = -8 + 3 = -5$. Now, evaluate $f(x)$ for $x = -5$: $f(x) = -4(-5) + 1 = 20 + 1 = 21$, (D).

If $f(x) = 5x + 3$, then $f(f(x)) = ?$

F. $5x + 3$ J. $25x + 30$
G. $10x + 6$ K. $25x^2 + 30x + 9$
H. $25x + 18$

Substitute $5x + 3$ for x in $f(x)$ and evaluate: $f(f(x)) = f(5x + 3) = 5(5x + 3) + 3 = 25x + 15 + 3 = 25x + 18$, (H).

If $f(x) = 5x + 3$ and $g(x) = 2x^2 + x - 4$, then $f(g(x)) = ?$

A. $2x^2 + x - 4$

B. $5x + 3$

C. $10x^2 + 5x - 17$

D. $12x^2 + 6x - 21$

E. $10x^2 + x - 12$

Substitute $2x^2 + x - 4$ for x in $f(x)$ and evaluate: $f(g(x)) = f(2x^2 + x - 4) =$
$5(2x^2 + x - 4) + 3 = 10x^2 + 5x - 20 + 3 = 10x^2 + 5x - 17$, (C).

If $f(x) = 5x + 3$ and $g(x) = 2x^2 + x - 4$, then $g(f(x)) = ?$

F. $10x^2 + 5x - 17$

G. $25x^2 + 30x + 9$

H. $50x^2 + 55x + 18$

J. $50x^2 + 60x + 18$

K. $50x^2 + 65x + 17$

Substitute $5x + 3$ for x in $g(x)$ and evaluate: $g(f(x)) = g(5x + 3) = 2(5x + 3)^2 +$
$(5x + 3) - 4 = 2(25x^2 + 30x + 9) + 5x - 1 = 50x^2 + 60x + 18 + 5x - 1 = 50x^2 + 65x + 17$,
(K).

Trigonometry

Several trigonometric values are very helpful when solving a right triangle. (For a review of trigonometric relationships, see page 506.)

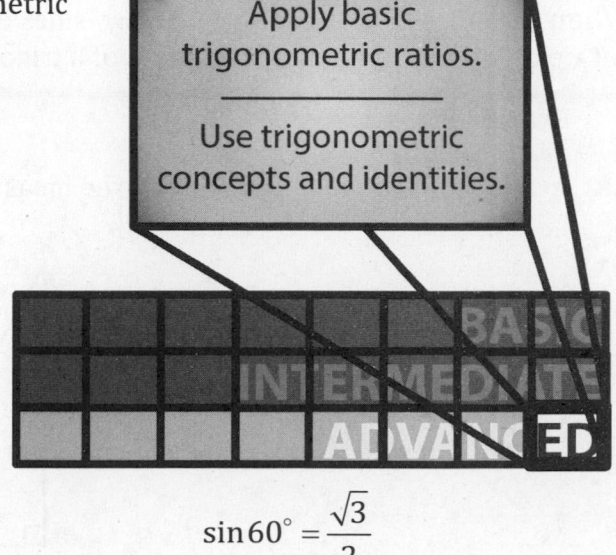

Apply basic trigonometric ratios.

Use trigonometric concepts and identities.

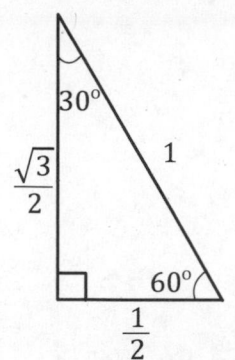

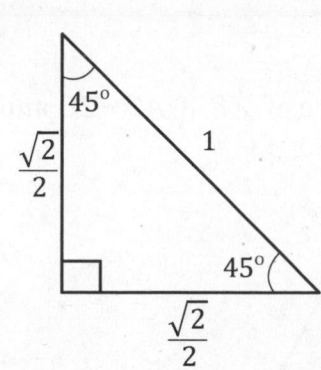

$$\sin 30° = \frac{1}{2}$$

$$\cos 30° = \frac{\sqrt{3}}{2}$$

$$\tan 30° = \frac{\sqrt{3}}{3}$$

$$\sin 45° = \frac{\sqrt{2}}{2}$$

$$\cos 45° = \frac{\sqrt{2}}{2}$$

$$\tan 45° = 1$$

$$\sin 60° = \frac{\sqrt{3}}{2}$$

$$\cos 60° = \frac{1}{2}$$

$$\tan 60° = \sqrt{3}$$

You do not have to memorize all the values above. It's easier to learn the lengths of the sides of the 60°-60°-90° and 45°-45°-90° triangles above so you can derive the values when needed. Eventually, you will know the values without using the triangles.

Example:

In the right triangle below, the length of $\overline{AB}$ is 20 centimeters and $\angle A$ measures 30°. What is the length, in centimeters, of $\overline{BC}$?

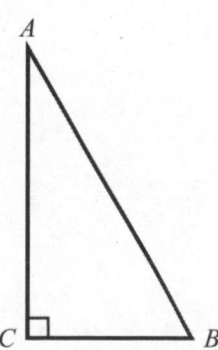

F. 5

G. $5\sqrt{2}$

H. 10

J. $10\sqrt{3}$

K. 20

$$\sin 30° = \frac{\overline{BC}}{20} \Rightarrow \frac{1}{2}(20) = 10 \, .$$

When you are given the lengths of two sides of a triangle and asked to find a missing angle, set up an equation using the inverse of a trigonometric function.

Example:

In the figure below, find the degree measure of $\angle B$ if $\overline{AC} = 26$ and $\overline{BC} = 15$.

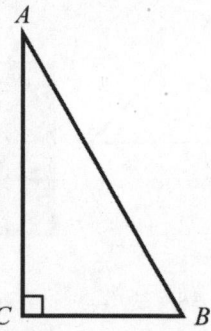

To find $\angle B$, first choose your function in relation to $\angle B$ with the given sides. $\overline{AC}$ is opposite $\angle B$, $\overline{BC}$ is adjacent to $\angle B$, and the tangent function is defined using the opposite and adjacent sides. So, set up your equation and find $\angle B$.

$$\tan B = \frac{26}{15} \Rightarrow B = \tan^{-1}\left(\frac{26}{15}\right) \approx 60.02°$$

We can also use the reciprocal of the sine, cosine, and tangent functions to solve right triangles and derive more identities. The reciprocal functions are the cosecant (csc), secant (sec), and cotangent (cot).

$$\csc A = \frac{1}{\sin A}$$

$$\sec A = \frac{1}{\cos A}$$

$$\cot A = \frac{1}{\tan A}$$

Another helpful identity is the Pythagorean identity, $\sin^2\theta + \cos^2\theta = 1$. If we divide both sides of the equation by $\sin^2\theta$ and $\cos^2\theta$, we find two additional identities:

$$1 + \cot^2\theta = \csc^2\theta.$$

$$\tan^2\theta + 1 = \sec^2\theta.$$

Example:

What is the value of $\sin^2 30° + \cos^2 30°$?

A. $\dfrac{\sqrt{3}+1}{2}$ C. $\dfrac{\sqrt{5}}{2}$ E. 1

B. $\sqrt{5}$ D. $\dfrac{3}{4}$

Substitute the values of each of the terms: $\sin^2 30° + \cos^2 30° =$

$(\sin 30°)^2 + (\cos 30°)^2 = \left(\dfrac{1}{2}\right)^2 + \left(\dfrac{\sqrt{3}}{2}\right)^2 = \dfrac{1}{4} + \dfrac{3}{4} = 1$. Alternatively, use the

Pythagorean identity, $\sin^2 x + \cos^2 x = 1$.

Unit Circle Trigonometry

We can easily find the sine, cosine, and tangent of angles using a graphic organizer, the unit circle. The unit circle is simply a circle with radius 1 with values for the six trigonometric functions easily identifiable.

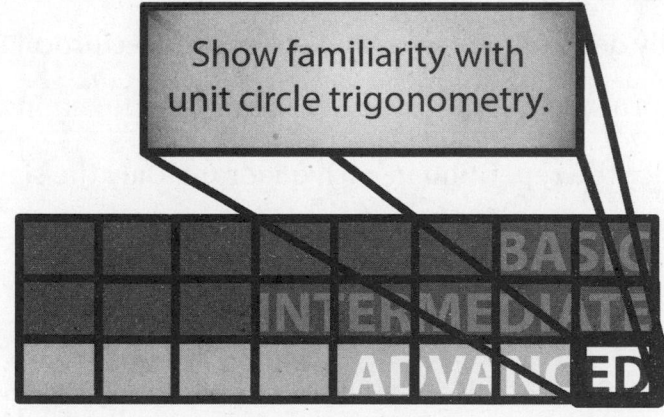

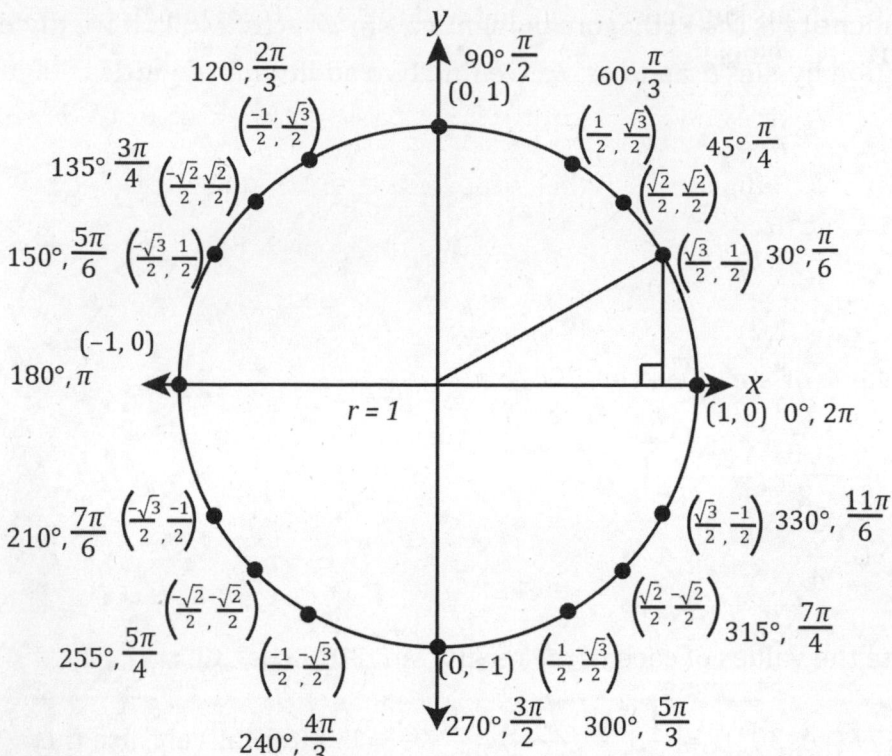

Note that an angle measured in degrees can be converted to radians using the conversion factor $\pi(\text{radians}) = 180°$. For example, $45° = \dfrac{180°}{4} = \dfrac{\pi}{4}$.

Ordered pairs in a unit circle at each angle state the values for $(\cos\theta, \sin\theta)$. The $\tan\theta$ is easily derived by $\dfrac{\sin\theta}{\cos\theta}$, and each of the reciprocal functions are found by taking the reciprocal of the sine, cosine, and tangent functions.

Notice the repetition in each quadrant. Only the signs change for angles with the same reference angle. For example, $\sin 30° = \dfrac{1}{2}$, $\sin 150° = \dfrac{1}{2}$, $\sin 210° = -\dfrac{1}{2}$, and $\sin 330° = -\dfrac{1}{2}$.

y

sin	sin, cos, tan
II	I
(−,+)	(+,+)

x

(−,−)	(+,−)
III	IV
tan	cos

In quadrant I, all functions sine, cosine, tangent and the reciprocal functions, cosecant, secant, and cotangent are positive.

In quadrant II, only the sine and its reciprocal function, cosecant, are positive.

In quadrant III, only the tangent and its reciprocal function, cotangent, are positive.

In quadrant IV, only the cosine and its reciprocal function, secant, are positive.

Identify Trigonometric Graphs

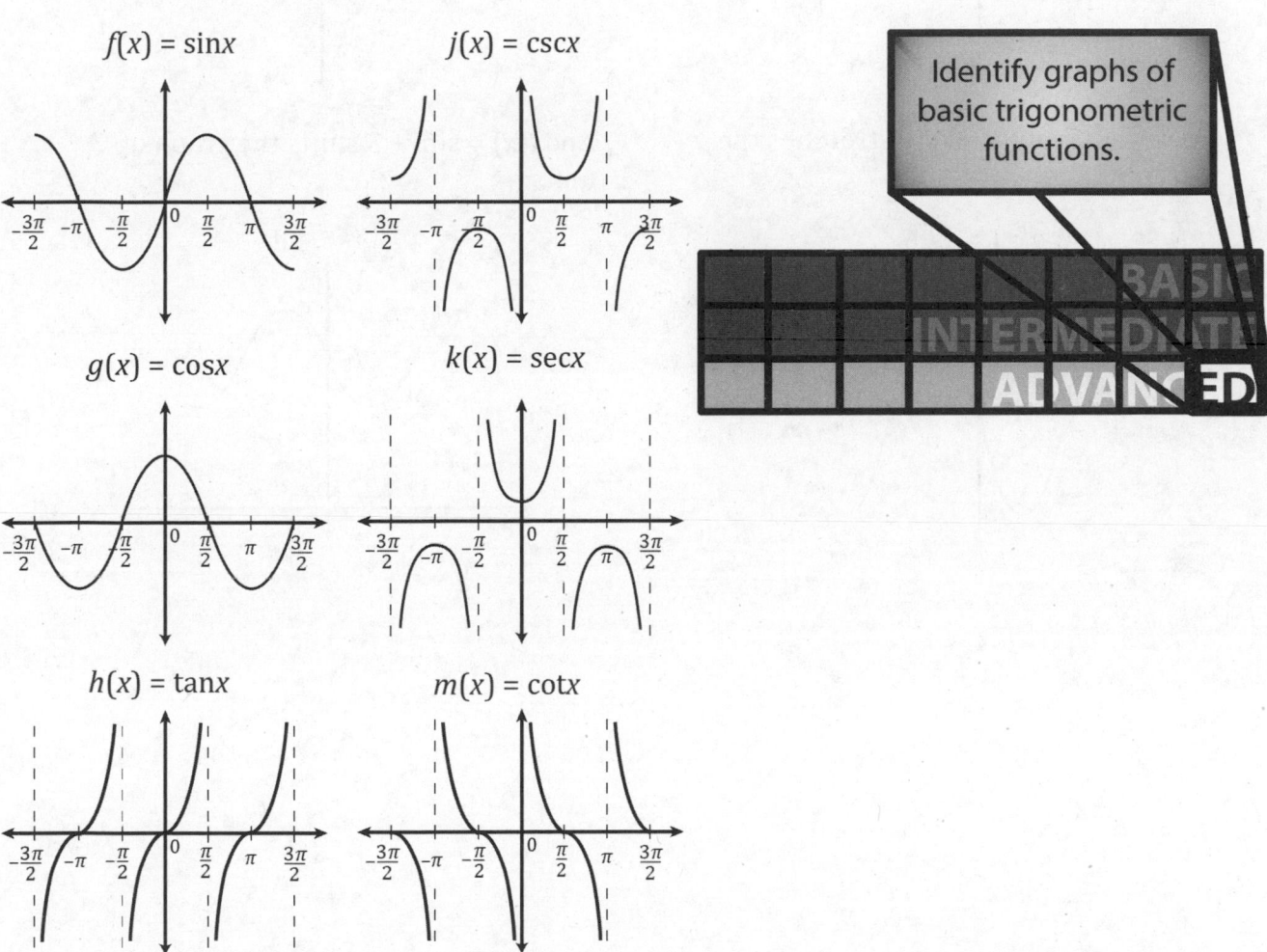

Identify graphs of basic trigonometric functions.

Graphs of trigonometric functions can be transformed by adding, subtracting, multiplying, and dividing the function with real numbers. The transformations include shifting graphs up, down, left, and right and stretching and shrinking graphs horizontally and vertically.

Examples:

$f(x) = \sin x$ is the parent function:

$$f(x) = \sin x$$

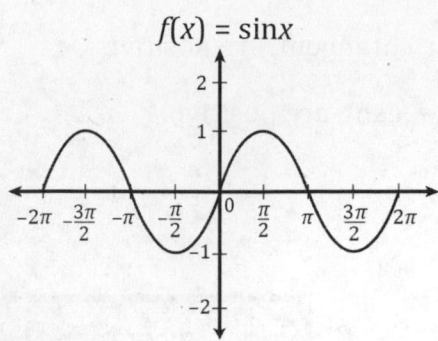

$h(x) = \dfrac{1}{2}\sin x$ vertically shrinks the graph:

$$h(x) = \dfrac{1}{2}\sin x$$

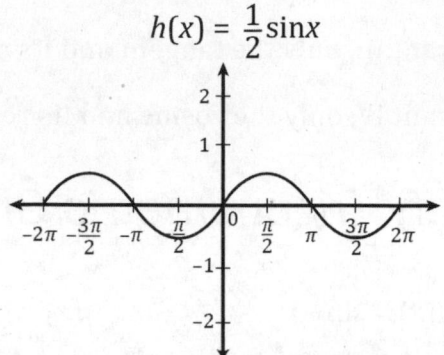

$g(x) = 2\sin x$ vertically stretches the graph:

$$g(x) = 2\sin x$$

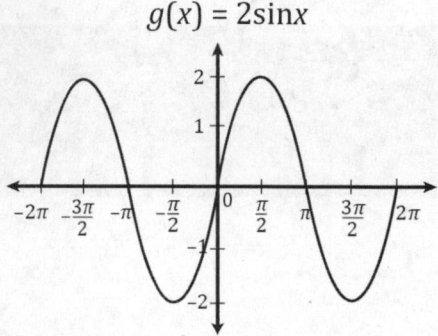

And $j(x) = \sin x + 3$ shifts the graph up 3 units:

$$j(x) = \sin x + 3$$

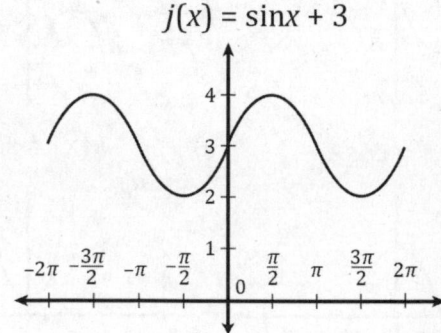

Examples:

The figure below is a possible graph of which of the following equations?

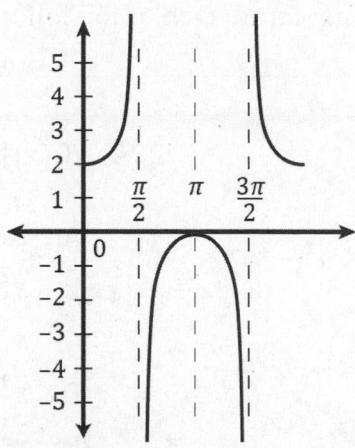

A. $y = 2(\sin x)$ D. $y = \csc x - 1$

B. $y = \sin x + 2$ E. $y = \sec x + 1$

C. $y = \csc x + 1$

The figure is the graph of the secant function displaced one unit up on the coordinate axes, which is represented by adding 1 to the secant function: $y = \sec x + 1$, (E).

The figure below is a graph of which of the following functions?

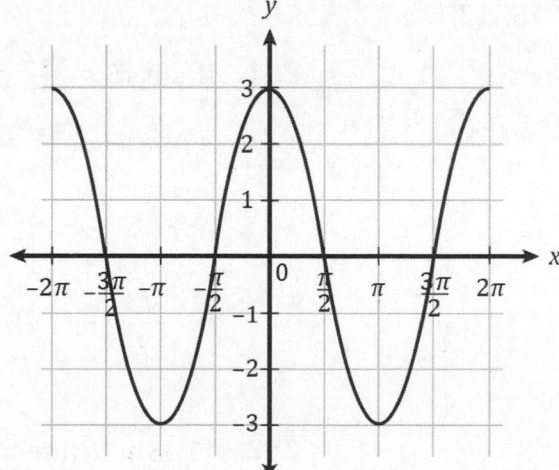

F. $f(x) = \dfrac{\cos x}{3}$ J. $f(x) = 3 \cos x$

G. $f(x) = \sin x + 3$ K. $f(x) = 5 \sec x$

H. $f(x) = \cos x + 3$

The figure is the graph of the cosine function stretched vertically by a factor of 3, (J).

EXERCISE 12

> **DIRECTIONS:** Choose the correct answer to each of the following items. Answers are on page 818.

Questions 275–280 refer to the following information.

$$f(x) = x^2 + 3x$$
$$g(x) = 4x - 2$$

275. $f(g(2)) = ?$

    A. 6   C. 16   E. 60

    B. 10   D. 54

276. $f(f(-3)) = ?$

    F. −14   H. 0   K. 18

    G. −2   J. 9

277. $g(f(-1)) = ?$

    A. −10   C. −6   E. 12

    B. −8   D. −2

278. $f(g(x)) = ?$

    F. $4x - 2$

    G. $4x^2 + 3x + 4$

    H. $16x^2 + 12x - 2$

    J. $16x^2 - 4x - 2$

    K. $8x^2 + 3x + 4$

279. $f(f(x)) = ?$

    A. $2x^2 + 6x$

    B. $x^2 + 3x$

    C. $x^4 + 9x^2 + 3x$

    D. $x^4 + 6x^3 + 9x^2$

    E. $x^4 + 6x^3 + 12x^2 + 9x$

280. $g(f(x)) = ?$

    F. $x^2 + 7x - 2$

    G. $4x^2 + 12x - 2$

    H. $4x^3 + 10x^2 - 6x$

    J. $4x^2 + 7x - 2$

    K. $4x^3 + 10x^2 + 12x - 2$

281. If $\sin 45° = \dfrac{\sqrt{2}}{2}$, then

    $\sin^2 x + \cos^2 x = ?$

    A. $\dfrac{1}{2}$ C. 1   E. 4

    B. $\dfrac{\sqrt{3}}{2}$ D. 2

282. $(1 - \sin^2 \theta)(\sec \theta) = ?$

    F. $\sin^2 \theta$ H. $\tan \theta$ K. $\csc \theta$

    G. $\cot^2 \theta$ J. $\cos \theta$

283. $\cos x - (\cos x)(\sin^2 x) = ?$

    A. $\cos^3 x$ C. $-\sin^2 x$ E. $2\cos^2 x$

    B. $\sin^2 x$ D. 0

284. $(\csc A)(\sin A) - \sin^2 A = ?$

    F. $\csc A - \sin A$ J. $\sin A$

    G. $\cot^2 A$ K. $\cos^2 A$

    H. $\cot A$

285. If $\tan x = 1$ and $0° < x < 360°$, then $x = ?$

    A. $45°, 135°$ D. $45°, 315°$

    B. $45°, 225°$ E. $135°, 315°$

    C. $135°, 225°$

286. If $\sin\theta = -\dfrac{\sqrt{3}}{2}$ and $\pi < \theta < \dfrac{3\pi}{2}$, then $\cos\theta = ?$

    F. $-\dfrac{\sqrt{3}}{2}$ H. $-\dfrac{1}{2}$ K. $\dfrac{\sqrt{3}}{2}$

    G. $-\dfrac{\sqrt{2}}{2}$ J. $\dfrac{1}{2}$

287. What is the equation for the function below?

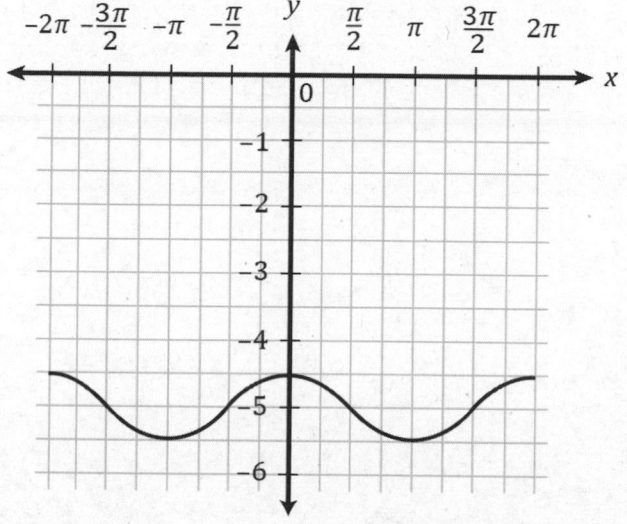

    A. $\dfrac{1}{2}\cos\theta - 5$ D. $2\sin\theta - 5$

    B. $\dfrac{1}{2}\sin\theta + 5$ E. $2\cos\theta - 5$

    C. $-5\cos\theta$

288. What is the equation for the function below?

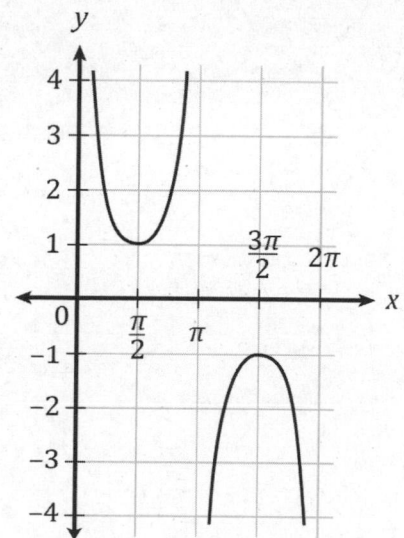

    F. $\sec 2x$ H. $\csc 2x + 4$ K. $\csc x$

    G. $4\csc x$ J. $\sin 2x$

Science Skills Review

Course Concept Outline

	Interpretation of Data (ID)	Scientific Investigation (SI)	Evaluation of Models, Inferences, and Experimental Results (EM)
Basic	Recognize features of basic data presentations, such as headings and units. Use a simple presentation of data to identify one, two, or more pieces of data, either numerical or non-numerical. Find information in a body of scientific text. Determine direct and inverse relationships of variables in a data presentation.		
Intermediate	Understand basic scientific terms. Read and interpret data in more complex data presentations. Understand the relationship between variables in more complex data presentations.	Understand tools and methods in an experiment. Understand an experimental design. Identify a control in an experiment. Compare and contrast experiments. Predict the results of an additional step in an experiment. Determine what would cause a specific result in an experiment.	Select a hypothesis, prediction, or conclusion supported by a data presentation or a model.
Advanced		Select an alternative method to test a hypothesis. Evaluate the precision and/or accuracy of an experiment or model.	Identify key issues or assumptions in a model. Determine whether information supports or contradicts a hypothesis or conclusion. Compare and contrast models. Determine the effect of new information on a model.

BASIC

At this level, science passages feature data presentations and ask questions based on the provided data. This section discusses common types of data presentations, how to locate and read data, and how to interpret data.

Purpose of Data Presentations

Science is concerned with numbers, which are called data. Data answer questions such as:

> How many are there?
>
> How tall are they?
>
> How much do they weigh?
>
> What are their volumes?

By observing phenomena in the world and by conducting experiments in controlled environments, scientists accumulate data about the objects they are studying:

> There are 24 unmarked butterflies.
>
> The bean seedling is 12 inches tall.
>
> The sample is 5 grams.
>
> The sample is 25 milliliters.

After collecting data, a scientist must determine the most appropriate way to present the information so that it can be easily interpreted and analyzed. Most commonly, scientists report their data using tables and graphs. These pictorial representations are easy ways to show where a pattern, trend, or relationship exists. The tables and graphs can be organized in a variety of ways, but there are some generally accepted basic guidelines.

Recognize features of basic data presentations, such as headings and units.

Use a simple presentation of data to identify one, two, or more pieces of data, either numerical or non-numerical.

Find information in a body of scientific text.

Determine direct and inverse relationships of variables in a data presentation.

BASIC
INTERMEDIATE
ADVANCED

Common Types of Data Presentations

Tables

A **table** presents data in the form of rows and columns. The number of vertical columns and horizontal rows depends on the kind and amount of data collected. A heading or title is included to communicate the purpose of the experiment. The data needed to answer questions are located by referencing column and row. The descriptive information is always very important.

Example:

A student visiting a national historic site used the car's odometer to measure the distance he traveled for one hour. His mother set the car in cruise control and was driving at a constant speed of 45 miles per hour, and they did not stop during the hour he took measurements. The student's measurements are recorded in the table below.

Miles Traveled over a One Hour Period	
Time (minutes)	Total Miles Traveled
0	0.0
10	7.5
20	15.0
30	22.5
40	30.0
50	37.5
60	45.0

The title of this table tells us that it is a summary of miles traveled over a one hour period. The first column indicates that the distance is measured every 10 minutes. The second column shows the distance at every 10 minute measurement. Based on the information given in the table, we can see a general trend: the distance traveled increased over time.

A laboratory investigation was performed to determine the length of time necessary to digest starch (carbohydrates). Ten grams of potato were added to 15 milliliters of an enzyme solution in a test tube. The percentage of starch digested was recorded over a 24 hour period, as summarized in the table below.

Carbohydrate Digestion over a 24 Hour Period	
Time (hours)	Percentage of Carbohydrates Digested
0	0
4	5
8	15
12	50
16	75
20	85
24	90

The title of this table tells us that it is a summary of carbohydrate digestion over a 24-hour period. The first column indicates that the digestion is measured every 4 hours. The second column shows the percentage of carbohydrates digested at each 4 hour measurement. Based on the information given in the table, we can see a general trend: the percentage of carbohydrates digested increased over time.

Graphs

Scientists often collect large amounts of data while performing experiments. It may not be possible to clearly present the data in the form of a table. The arrangement of the data in a table may not easily or adequately show a pattern, trend, or relationship. Usually, a well-constructed **graph** can communicate experimental results more clearly than a data table. Generally, when data are arranged in a graph, the patterns, trends, and relationships are more apparent than when those same values are arranged in a table.

Four of the most common kinds of graphs are line, bar, cumulative bar, and circle graphs. A line graph is just what the name implies: a line or lines plotted in the x-y plane to show the relationship between variables, one measured along the horizontal axis and the other by the vertical axis. A bar graph is easy to identify because it uses bars to represent value. In a cumulative bar graph, each bar portion represents a part or percentage of the whole bar, so the appearance is that of bar parts stacked on top of one another to reach a total. A circle graph is easy to recognize and commonly called a pie chart because the division of the circle into sectors resembles a pie cut into pieces.

Line Graphs

A **line** graph has four basic parts: **horizontal** or **x-axis** (A), **vertical** or **y-axis** (B), **line** (C), and **heading** or **title** (D). A line graph is used to show the relationship between two values. The variables being compared are positioned on the two axes of the graph. As with a table, the heading or title communicates the purpose of the experiment.

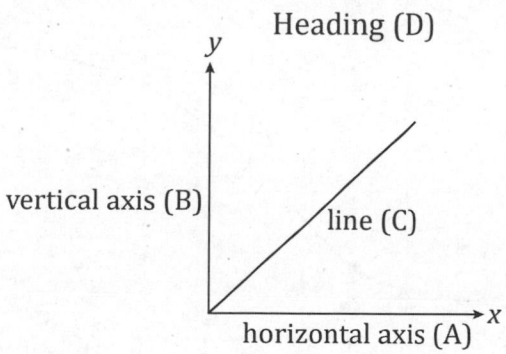

Data appear on a graph as dots. Each dot, or point, represents the relationship that exists between a measurement on the horizontal axis and a measurement on the vertical axis. The various points are connected to form a line, and the slope of that line represents the relationship between the two values. A line may be straight or curved.

Example:

The graph below shows the data points in the "Miles Traveled over a One Hour Period" table.

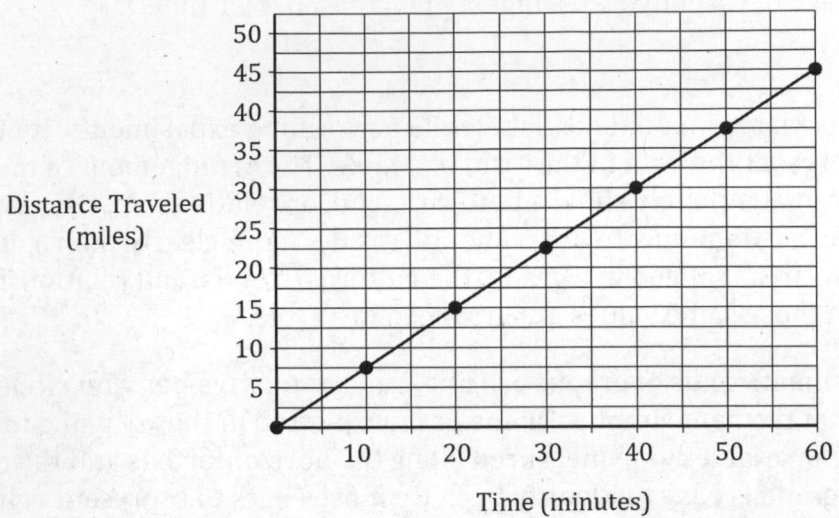

The *x*-axis represents time (in minutes), and the *y*-axis represents the distance traveled (in miles). Each point matches the earlier table, but this time the points are represented on a graph so that it is easy to see the relationship between the points. Based on the information given in the graph, we can easily see the trend: the distance traveled increased at a steady rate.

The graph below shows the data points in the "Carbohydrate Digestion over a 24 Hour Period" table.

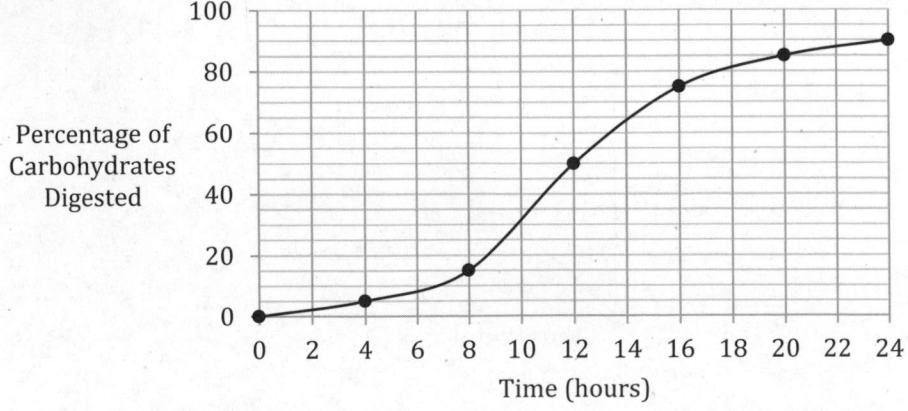

The *x*-axis represents time (in hours), and the *y*-axis represents the percentage of carbohydrates digested. Each point matches the earlier table, but this time the points are represented on a graph so that it is easy to see the relationship between the points. Based on the information given in the graph, we can expand on the earlier trend that the percentage of carbohydrates digested increased over time. Notice that the percentage of carbohydrates digested increased rapidly between 8 hours and 16 hours and more slowly between 0 hours and 8 hours and between 16 hours and 24 hours. This is evident in the changing slope of the line at various points.

Bar Graphs

A **bar graph** is similar to a line graph, but it is better for making simple comparisons. This type of graph is typically used to display data that does not continuously change. Bar graphs present related data side by side so the data can be easily compared.

The basic setup of a bar graph is similar to a line graph in that there is a horizontal x-axis, a vertical y-axis, and a heading describing the presented data. However, thick bars rather than data points show relationships among data. The bars on the x-axis are drawn up to an imaginary point where they would intersect with the values of the y-axis if these values were extended. Generally, the taller the bar, the greater the value it represents.

Example:

The following bar graph shows the percentage of the human population having each of the four blood types:

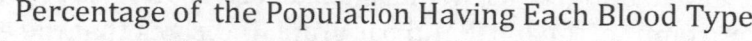

Percentage of the Population Having Each Blood Type

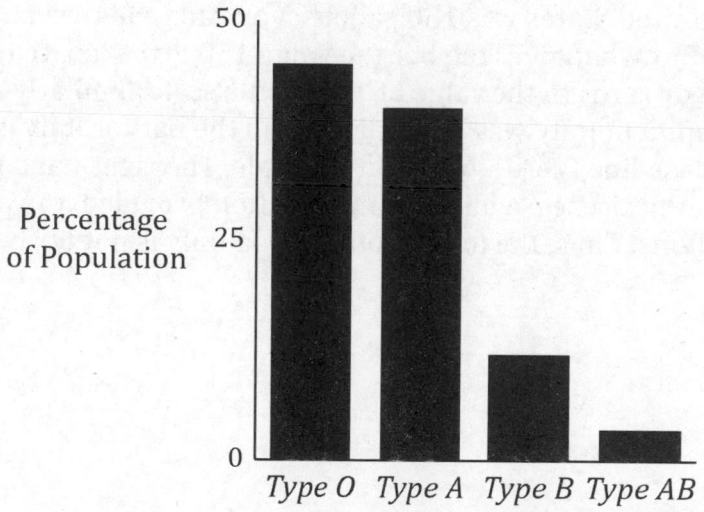

The x-axis represents the different blood types found in the population. The y-axis represents the percentage of each blood type. The graph shows that the most common blood type is Type O, while the least common is Type AB.

Note that the bars in a graph do not necessarily have to be oriented vertically. They can be oriented horizontally with the base line on the left or the right. As with vertical bars, in a horizontal configuration, the longer the bar, the greater the value it represents.

Example:

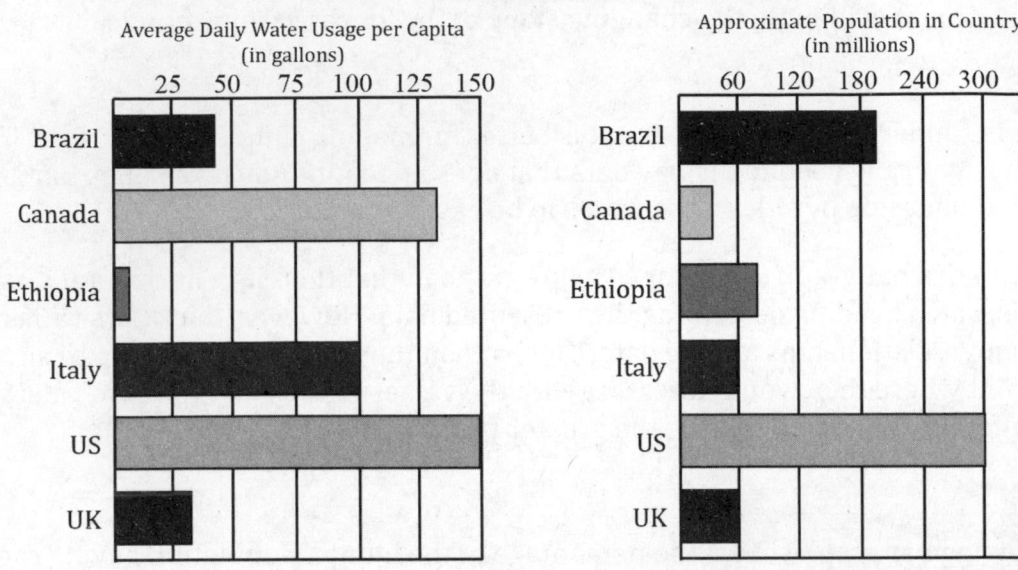

In each of the above bar graphs, the magnitude of a reading is represented by the length of the bar. For example, the left-hand bar graph indicates that the average daily water usage per capita in the United States was 150 gallons: you can read the value "150" from the scale above the bar. But what gives the bar the value 150 is the length of the bar: it runs from the base line (or zero) to the value of 150 on the scale. Similarly, the average daily water usage per capita in Italy was 100 gallons, and the bar for Italy is 100 units long, running from the base line (zero) to 100 on the scale. The right-hand bar graph is read in the same way, but notice the additional information provided: the populations are graphed in terms of millions. Thus, the total population in Italy is not 60, but 60,000,000.

Cumulative Bar Graphs

The key feature of the cumulative bar graph is that only the bottom component and the total are read from the base line. All other components are read from the top of the component immediately below to the bottom of the component immediately above (or the top of the bar in the case of the topmost component).

Example:

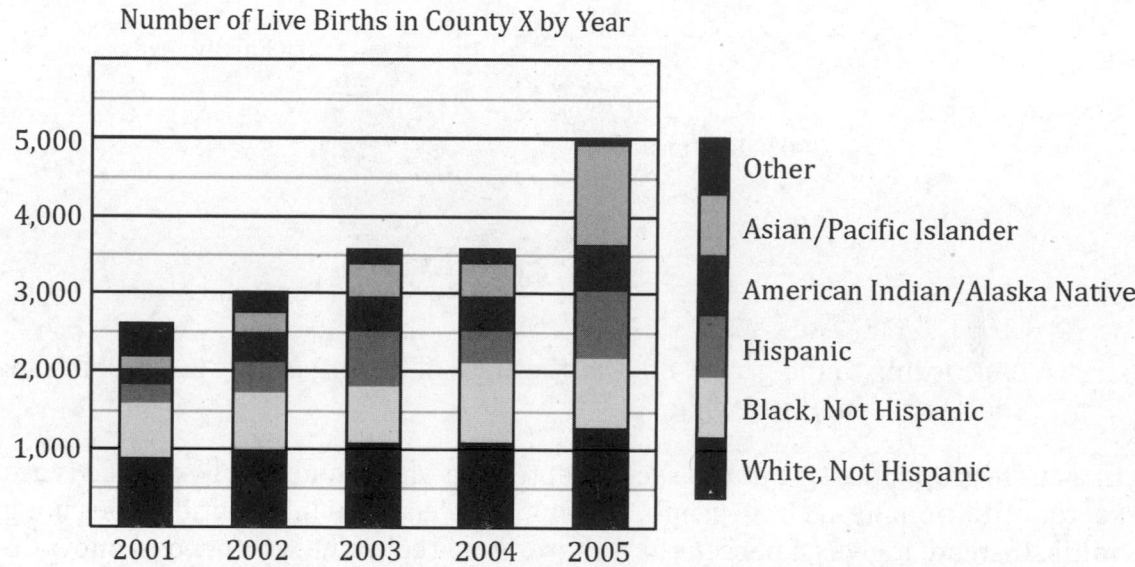

Number of Live Births in County X by Year

In this graph, the number of "white (not Hispanic)" live births in County X can be read directly from the scale: 800 in 2001, 1,000 in 2002, and so on. And the total number of live births in County X can be read from the scale: 2,600 in 2001 and 3,000 in 2002. But you *cannot* read the value of the other components directly from the scale. The number of "black (not Hispanic)" births in 2001 was about $1,600 - 800 = 800$, not 1,600; and the number of "other" live births in 2005 was about $5,000 - 4,900 = 100$, not 5,000.

Note that for questions based on cumulative bar graphs, you can make the mistake of attempting a reading directly from the scale rather than correctly finding the length of that component of the bar.

Circle Graphs

Circle graphs use a circle divided into sections to display data. A circle graph is sometimes called a pie graph or pie chart because it looks like a pie cut up into pieces. Each section of the graph represents one of the categories of a particular subject. The whole circle represents 100% of the data for all of the categories. The bigger the section, the larger the value it represents. Circle graphs are typically used to illustrate information that is collected by observation rather than by experimentation.

Example:

The following circle graph represents the mass of organisms in a sample of soil:

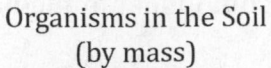

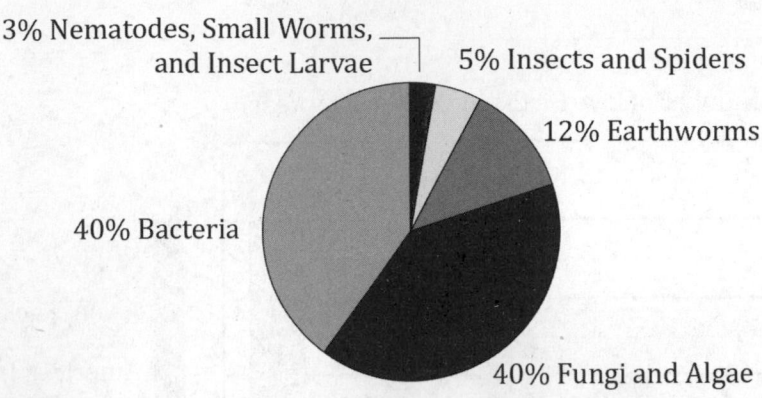

According to the graph, 80% of the mass of the organisms in the soil is made up of bacteria, fungi, and algae.

In a circle graph, the size of the sector represents value, and usually a value is attached to each sector. Additionally, a circle graph, without supplemental information, does not give a real value. Instead, it gives a percent or a share. For a real value, you need to know the total value represented by the graph, and this is often given in a note.

Example:

Composition of Wetland Area, 2004
(Total area = 108 million acres)

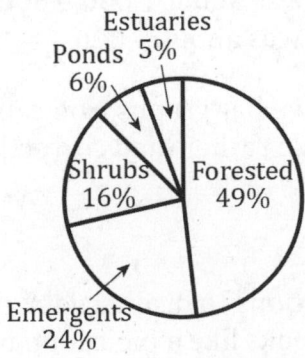

In this case, the percentages are given and you could, if asked, compare those directly, e.g., there is a little more than twice as much forested wetlands (49%) as emergent wetlands (24%). And because you have the total area of wetlands for the entire graph (108 million acres), you can calculate values for each sector. For example, the total number of acres of estuary wetlands is 5% of 108 million, or 5.4 million acres.

Note that a single circle graph can only show one time period, size, source, etc. (e.g., year, acreage, country, etc.). Some science passages include multiple elements such as both a bar graph and a circle graph. Often, the circle graph will apply to only one of the bars in the bar graph—not to all of them.

Example:

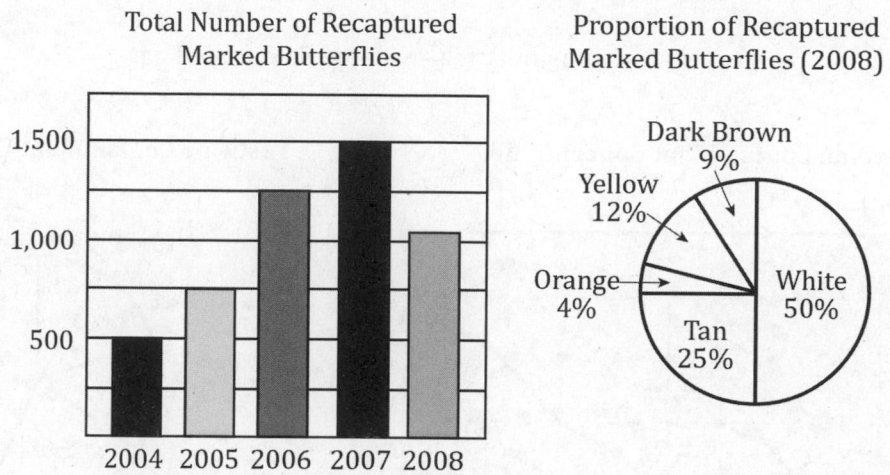

In this case, inclusion of the bar and circle graphs allows for the question: "Of the recaptured marked butterflies in 2008, about how many more were marked white than tan?" The bar graph indicates that the total number of recaptured butterflies is a little more than 1,000. Based on the circle graph, 50% of the total, or a little more than 500, were marked white; and 25% of the total, or a little more than 250, were marked tan. Therefore, approximately $500 - 250 = 250$ more of the recaptured butterflies were marked white than tan.

Locating and Reading Data

Often questions based on tables and graphs require you to gather the data from the graph. These types of the questions fall into one of three major categories: reading values, manipulating values, and drawing inferences.

We'll look at examples of each category, but we'll need a graph for the examples:

Contaminant Levels in Maine Bald Eagle Eggs

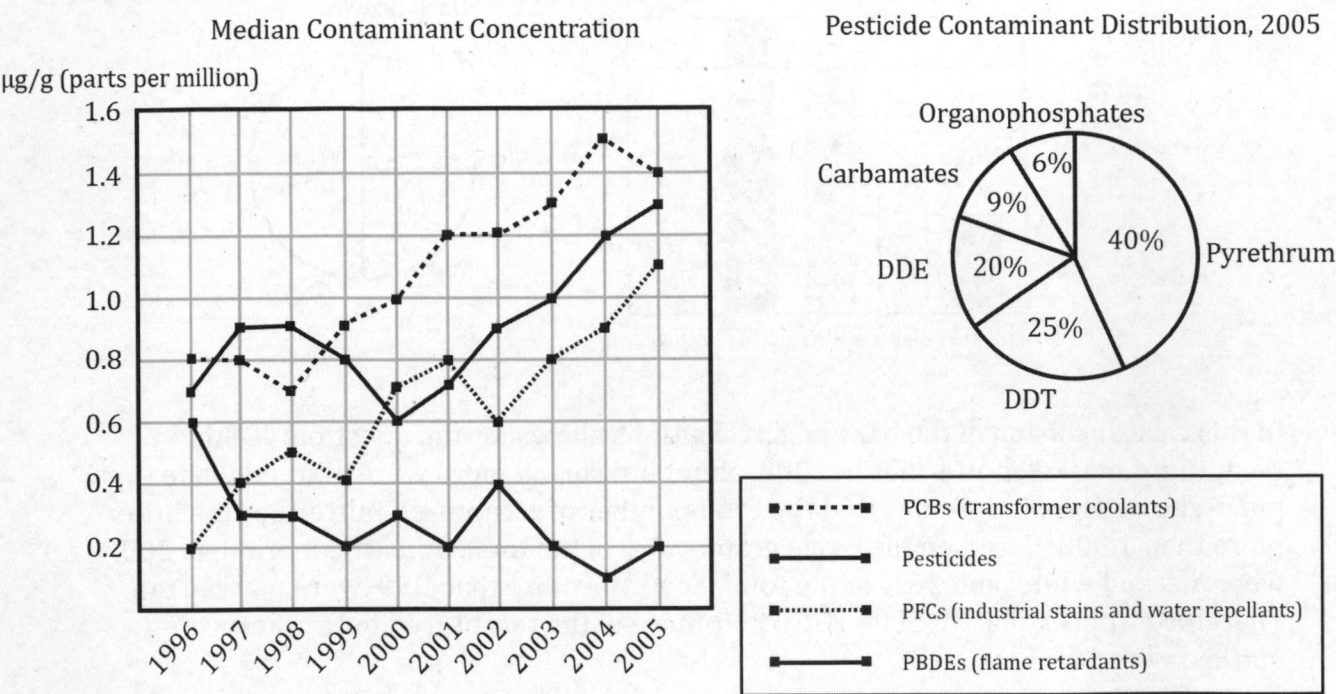

Reading Values

Questions that ask about values ask for one of two things: a specific value or a comparison of values. Typically, no calculations are required.

Examples:

1. What was the median contaminant concentration of PCBs (transformer coolants) found in Maine bald eagle eggs in 2002?

   A. 0.2 µg/g
   B. 0.7 µg/g
   C. 0.8 µg/g
   D. 1.2 µg/g

   Read the value of average contaminant concentration of PCBs for the year 2002: 1.2 µg/g, (D).

2. In which year did the median contaminant concentration of PFCs (industrial stains and water repellants) found in Maine bald eagle eggs first exceed 0.6 µg/g (parts per million)?

F. 1998
G. 1999
H. 2000
J. 2001

Locate the line for PFCs and find the first year for which the line broke across the 0.6 mark: 2000, (H).

3. For how many years shown was the median contaminant concentration of pesticides found in Maine bald eagle eggs less than that of PFCs (industrial stains and water repellants)?

A. One
B. Two
C. Three
D. Four

The line for pesticides falls below the line for PFCs for two years, (B): 2000 and 2001.

It's possible for reading values questions to be more complicated, but only because the question stem asks you to retrieve more data from the graph.

Example:

1. For how many years in which the median contaminant concentration of PCBs (transformer coolant) found in Maine bald eagle eggs was greater than that of pesticides was the contaminant concentration of PFCs (industrial stains and water repellants) greater than that of PBDEs (flame retardants)?

F. Six
G. Seven
H. Eight
J. Nine

This question requires you to first identify those years in which contaminant concentration of PCBs was greater than that of pesticides: 1996, 1999, 2000, 2001, 2002, 2003, 2004, 2005. Next, identify those years in which contaminant concentration of PFCs was greater than that of PBDEs: 1997, 1998, 1999, 2000, 2001, 2002, 2003, 2004, 2005. There is a total of seven years, (G), that satisfy both: 1999, 2000, 2001, 2002, 2003, 2004, 2005.

Manipulating Values

The second group of questions require a calculation of some sort. Simple calculations involve basic manipulations such as addition and subtraction.

Examples:

1. What was the difference in median contamination due to PFCs (industrial stains and water repellants) from 2000 to 2005?

    A. 2.2 µg/g
    B. 1.8 µg/g
    C. 0.5 µg/g
    D. 0.4 µg/g

    Read the value of contaminant concentration of PCBs for the years 2000 (0.7 µg/g) and 2005 (1.1 µg/g): 1.1 µg/g – 0.7 µg/g = 0.4 µg/g, (D).

2. How much was contamination from PBDEs (flame retardants) reduced in Maine bald eagle eggs between the beginning and end of the study (first and last dates shown)?

    F. 0.1 µg/g
    G. 0.3 µg/g
    H. 0.4 µg/g
    J. 1.2 µg/g

    The first measurement of PDBEs (flame retardants) was taken in 1996 at 0.6 µg/g. The last measurement of PDBEs was taken in 2005 at 0.2 µg/g. Subtract the measurement in 2005 from the measurement in 1996: 0.6 µg/g – 0.2 µg/g = 0.4 µg/g (H).

More difficult manipulation questions require you to express some value as a fraction, a percentage, or in terms of a ratio.

Examples:

1. PBDEs (flame retardants) accounted for what approximately percent of the total median contaminant concentration found in Maine bald eagle eggs in 2002?

    A. 4%
    B. 13%
    C. 18%
    D. 23%

    In 2002, PBDEs had a median contaminant concentration of 0.4 µg/g and the total median contaminant concentration was: $1.2 + 0.9 + 0.6 + 0.4 = 3.1$ µg/g. And $\frac{0.4}{3.1} = 0.13 = 13\%$, (B).

2. What was the ratio of median contaminant concentration of pesticides in 2000 to median contaminant concentration of pesticides in 2004 as found in Maine bald eagle eggs?

F. 3:1
G. 2:1
H. 1:2
J. 1:3

In 2000, pesticides had a median contaminant concentration of 0.6 µg/g. In 2004, pesticides had a median contaminant concentration of 1.2 µg/g. And

$$\frac{0.6}{1.2} = \frac{1}{2} = 1:2, \text{(H)}.$$

For questions that require manipulations, analyze the question stem to determine what data you need and make a note on your scratch paper. Then find the data on the graph and enter it on your note. Finally, do the required manipulation.

Drawing Inferences

The third common type of table and graph data analysis question requires you to draw an inference from the data. In other words, the first question type (reading values) asks you to demonstrate that you know how to read the graph. The second question type (manipulating values) requires you to manipulate the data in order to arrive at a solution. For this third question type (drawing inferences), you have to draw further conclusions based on the data explicitly given.

Example:

1. In 2005, what percentage of the total median contaminant concentration found in Maine bald eagle eggs was due to DDE?

A. 2.5%
B. 3.0%
C. 6.5%
D. 9.0%

According to the line graph, in 2005, the total median contaminant concentration was $1.4 + 1.3 + 1.1 + 0.2 = 4.0$ µg/g. According to the circle graph, in 2005, DDE was responsible for 20% of the pesticide contaminants, or $(0.2)(1.3) = 0.26$ µg/g. Therefore, DDE was responsible for $\frac{0.26}{4.0} = 0.065 = 6.5\%$, (C), of the total median contaminant concentration found in Maine bald eagle eggs in 2005.

Interpreting Data

Data analysis of tables and graphs can be time-consuming, so fortunately there are three general shortcuts: approximation, simplification, and "meastimation," a combination of measurement and estimation.

Approximation

As you have already seen, some graph questions explicitly invite you to approximate. Question stems are particularly likely to include words such as "approximately" or "about" or "most nearly" when the graph uses large values and an exact value cannot reliably be read from the graph.

Example:

A graph entitled "Total Microbial Bacteria Count by Elapsed Time" with values in the millions of cells/mL is not going to permit a reading of 1,197,268. Round off, usually to the nearest integer or tenth: 1.2 million.

Simplification

A second way to avoid doing arithmetic is to set up your solution and then simplify the numbers before doing the calculation.

Example:

Suppose that you are asked to find the difference between two populations, one that is 25% of the total population, and the other 40%, when the total population is 14,356,341. Round off the population to 14 million and set up your solution (40% of 14) – (25% of 14) = ? Instead of doing two multiplications and then a subtraction, you can subtract first (40% – 25% = 15%) and then do one multiplication: 15% of 14 is 0.15(14) = 2.1 million, or 2,100,000.

"Meastimation"

A third shortcut is to use the picture itself to "meastimate" quantities. "Meastimate" is a made-up word that just indicates a combination of measuring and estimating.

Examples:

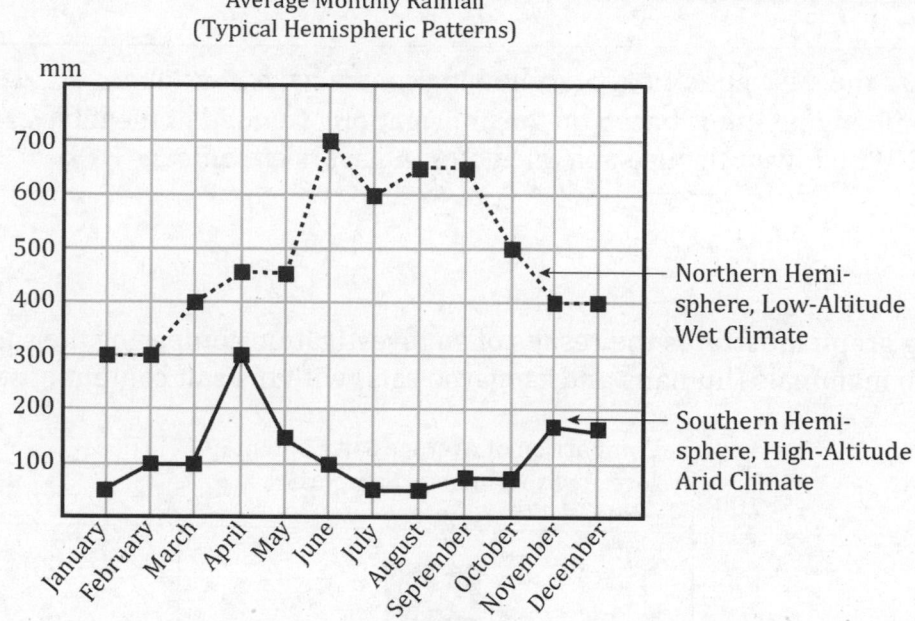

Average Monthly Rainfall
(Typical Hemispheric Patterns)

Northern Hemi-sphere, Low-Altitude Wet Climate

Southern Hemi-sphere, High-Altitude Arid Climate

1. In which of the following months was the difference in rainfall between the low-altitude wet climate and the high-altitude arid climate the greatest?

   A. January
   B. June
   C. July
   D. December

   You can "meastimate" the answer just by looking at the difference between the two lines: of the four months given, the difference between the two lines is greatest in June, (B).

2. What was the difference between the northern climate rainfall and the southern climate rainfall in November?

   F. 150 mm
   G. 200 mm
   H. 220 mm
   J. 300 mm

   You can "meastimate" the answer just by looking at the difference between the two lines: for November, the different is slightly more than 200, or 220 mm, (H).

The point here is that you can't answer a graph question with greater precision than the graph itself, so questions often invite you to approximate. And even when the question doesn't specifically call for an approximation, you'll save time if you use one of these shortcuts.

EXERCISE

DIRECTIONS: Read the descriptions of the following controlled experiments and data sets. Answer the accompanying items based on the information provided in the tables and graphs. You are NOT allowed the use of a calculator. Answers are on page 818.

Passage I

The following graph illustrates the results of an investigation comparing the salt content in the urine of two mammals (humans and kangaroo rats) with the salt content of seawater:

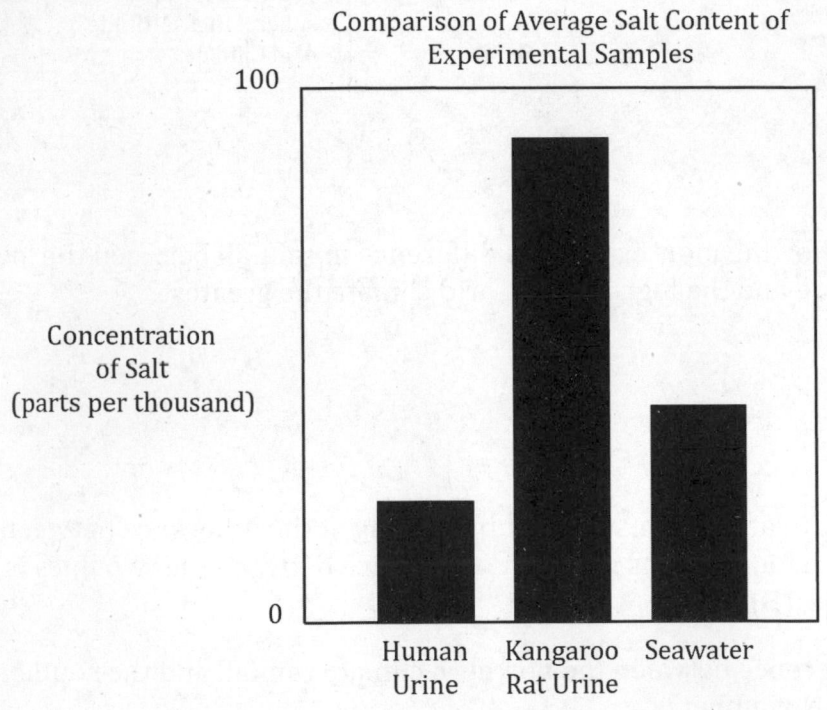

Comparison of Average Salt Content of Experimental Samples

1. The *x*-axis represents:

_____

_____.

2. The *y*-axis represents:

_____

_____.

3. The mammal with a concentration of salt in its urine closest to the concentration of salt in seawater is the:

_____

_____.

Passage II

A scientist wanted to determine the effects of different doses of an experimental drug called PCH. This drug was believed to help control weight gain. To test this hypothesis, four experimental groups of 100 rats each were all given a daily dose of sugar. Three of the four experimental groups were also given a daily dose of PCH, with each group receiving a different amount of the drug. The rats were all fed the same kind and amount of food. After four months, the percentage of rats gaining weight was determined. The results of this experiment are presented in Table 1.

Table 1: The Effects of Weight Gain in Rats		
Group	Contents of Dose	% of Rats Gaining Weight
1	5 grams of sugar	17%
2	5 grams of sugar 1 gram of PCH	23%
3	5 grams of sugar 5 grams of PCH	19%
4	5 grams of sugar 10 grams of PCH	21%

4. Which was the control group in this experiment?

F. Group 1
G. Group 2
H. Group 3
J. Group 4

5. As the dose of PCH increases, the percentage of rats gaining weight:

A. increases.
B. decreases.
C. remains constant.
D. varies.

6. In order to further investigate the results of this experiment, it would be most useful to know the:

   F. characteristics of the rats in each group.
   G. chemical composition of PCH.
   H. kind of sugar used in the doses.
   J. kind of food fed to the rats.

7. From the data showing the percentage of rats gaining weight, it could be concluded that:

   A. PCH was effective in helping control the weight gain of the rats.
   B. sugar was required for the PCH to be effective.
   C. sugar alone was responsible for the weight gain of the rats.
   D. PCH had no significant effect in helping control the weight gain of the rats.

Passage III

Atoms are considered the basic building blocks of matter. The atom consists of a positively charged center, or nucleus, surrounded by negatively charged electrons. The major kinds of particles in the nucleus are protons, which are positively charged, and neutrons, which have no charge. The number of protons in one atom of an element, called the atomic number, identifies the element. The mass number of the atom represents the total number of protons and neutrons. Not all of the atoms of an element are identical. The different atoms of an element are called isotopes. The three carbon-isotopes are shown in Table 2.

Table 2: Some Isotopes of Carbon				
Name	Protons	Neutrons	Electrons	Mass Number
Carbon-12	6	6	6	12
Carbon-13	6	7	6	13
Carbon-14	6	8	6	14

8. The atomic number of the element carbon is:

   F. 6.
   G. 7.
   H. 12.
   J. 34.

9. The three carbon-isotopes all have:

   A. the same number of neutrons.
   B. the same mass number.
   C. an equal number of protons and electrons.
   D. an equal number of neutrons and protons.

10. Carbon-13 has:

   F.   6 protons and 7 electrons.
   G. 7 protons and 6 electrons.
   H. 6 protons and 7 neutrons.
   J.   13 protons.

11. If the isotope of an element contains 8 protons, 9 neutrons, and 8 electrons, the atomic number and mass number would be, respectively:

   A. 8 and 17.
   B. 9 and 17.
   C. 8 and 26.
   D. 9 and 26.

Passage IV

The following table summarizes the estimated population exposed to five major earthquakes. The moment magnitude and Modified Mercalli scales are used to rate and compare the intensity of earthquakes. The moment magnitude is a measure of the motion of the ground on either side of the earthquake fault; each increase of 1 represents approximately a 32-fold increase in the energy released by the earthquake. The Modified Mercalli scale is from I (not felt) to XII (extreme). It is subjective, as it describes and rates earthquakes in terms of human reactions and observations.

Table 3: Estimated Population Exposed to Earthquake Shaking											
Location (Date)	Moment Magnitude Scale	Estimated Population Exposure (thousands)									
		Estimated Modified Mercalli Intensity									
		I	II–III	IV	V	VI	VII	VIII	IX	X+
Coast of Central Peru (8/15/07)	8.0	—	348	527	2,285	7,875	1,297	449	0	0
Eastern Sichuan, China (5/12/08)	7.9	—	67,275	190,360	89,674	15,469	11,873	4,684	707	605
Pakistan (10/28/08)	6.4	—	4,308	10,340	2,308	332	98	42	7	0
Sulawesi, Indonesia (11/16/08)	7.3	—	1,272	2,242	835	611	120	0	0	0
Coast of Central Peru (2/2/09)	6.0	—	2,386	7,538	371	198	110	0	0	0

12. In 2008, what was the approximate total population exposed to earthquake shaking in Eastern Sichuan, China?

F.   380,647
G.   3,806,470
H.   38,064,700
J.   380,647,000

13. In 2009, what was the approximate total population exposed to earthquake shaking on the coast of central Peru?

A.   5,080,000
B.   10,603,000
C.   18,433,000
D.   29,036,000

14. According to the table, what was the approximate total population exposed to earthquake shaking of Mercalli intensity VIII or higher in 2008?

F. 6,045,000
G. 4,996,000
H. 2,684,000
J. 1,319,000

15. Which of the following earthquakes resulted in the greatest population exposed to earthquake shaking of Mercalli intensity V?

A. Coast of central Peru, 2007
B. Pakistan, 2008
C. Sulawesi, Indonesia, 2008
D. Coast of central Peru, 2009

16. What was the approximate total population exposed to earthquake shaking of Mercalli intensity III or lower for all five earthquakes listed in the table?

F.   75,600
G. 67,300,000
H. 70,000,000
J. 75,600,000

17. For which of the following pairs of earthquakes was the ratio of moment magnitude scale ratings the greatest?

A. China (2008) : Pakistan (2008)
B. Peru (2007) : Peru (2009)
C. China (2009) : Indonesia (2008)
D. Indonesia (2008) : Pakistan (2008)

Passage V

Soil is made up of rock and mineral particles, water, gases (air), dead plant and animal matter, and tiny living organisms. Water soaks into the ground from rain (and other forms of precipitation). Gases come from the air, plants, and animals. Soil also contains living organisms (such as bacteria, fungi, insects, etc.) that break down organic plant and animal matter in the soil, making it rich and healthy for plants to grow in. An experiment was conducted on soil samples collected from two different geological locations. The following graphs summarize the soil sample compositions by content, shown in volume percent.

Soil Composition by Sample Location
(Soil Sample Sizes = 100 mL)

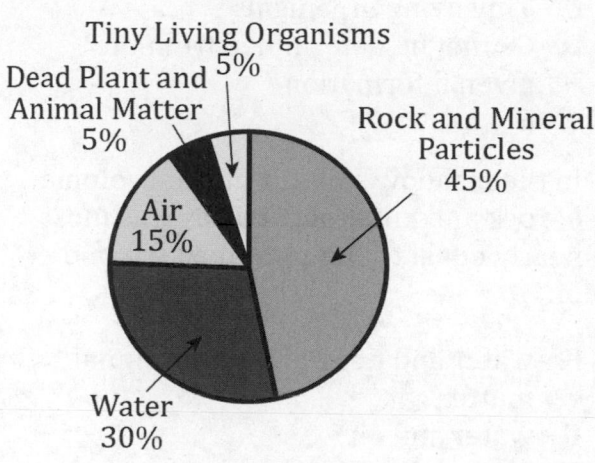

Woodland

Tiny Living Organisms
5%

Dead Plant and
Animal Matter
10%

Rock and Mineral
Particles
40%

Air
20%

Water
25%

Meadow

Tiny Living Organisms
5%

Dead Plant and
Animal Matter
5%

Rock and Mineral
Particles
45%

Air
15%

Water
30%

18. What was the total volume of rock and mineral particles in the meadow soil sample?

  F. 45 mL
  G. 40 mL
  H. 30 mL
  J. 25 mL

19. What component had the same volume in both of the soil samples?

  A. Rock and mineral particles
  B. Water
  C. Tiny living organisms
  D. Cannot be determined from the given information

20. In the meadow soil sample, the volume of rock and mineral particles was most nearly equal to the combined volume of:

  F. water and dead plant and animal matter.
  G. water and air.
  H. air and dead plant and animal matter.
  J. air and tiny living organisms.

21. What is the ratio of the percentage of water in the woodland soil sample to the percentage of water in the meadow soil sample?

  A. $\frac{6}{5}$
  B. 1
  C. $\frac{5}{6}$
  D. $\frac{3}{4}$

22. The dead plant and animal matter had how much more volume in the woodland soil sample than in the meadow soil sample?

  F. 5 mL
  G. 10 mL
  H. 15 mL
  J. Cannot be determined from the given information

Passage VI

The following graph summarizes the results of an experiment conducted to investigate the role that light plays in the growth and development of bean seedlings. Seedlings were grown in two conditions: constant light and partial darkness (regular alternating intervals of light and darkness). Seedling heights were measured at five-day intervals following planting and the median height of the seedlings in each group was determined.

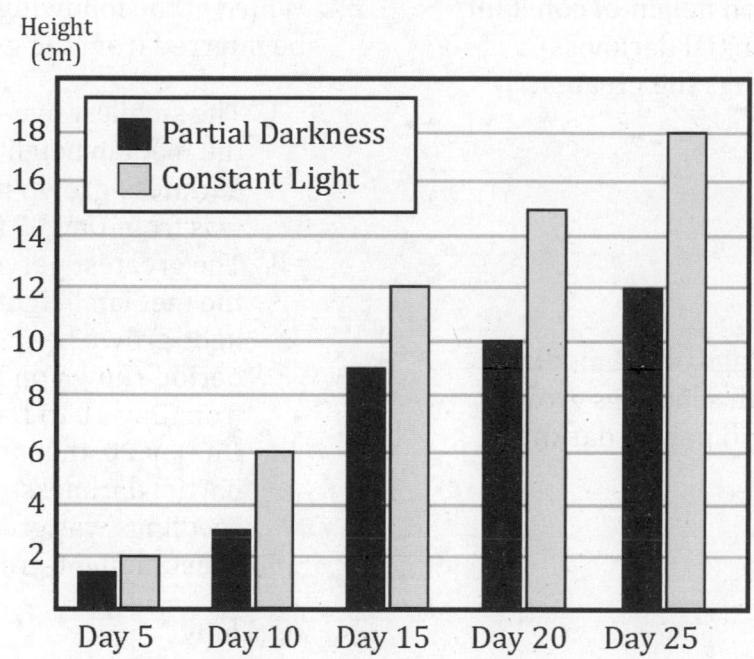

Median Height of Bean Seedlings
(Phaseolus vulgaris)

23. What was the median height for the bean seedlings grown in partial darkness after 20 days?

A. 3 cm
B. 8 cm
C. 10 cm
D. 12 cm

24. For which day was the difference between the median height of constant light-grown and partial darkness-grown bean seedlings the greatest?

F. Day 10
G. Day 15
H. Day 20
J. Day 25

25. What was the average of the median heights for the bean seedlings grown in constant light and partial darkness on Day 25?

A. 12 cm
B. 15 cm
C. 18 cm
D. 30 cm

26. For which day was the ratio of the median height of constant light-grown to partial darkness-grown seedlings the greatest?

F. Day 5
G. Day 10
H. Day 15
J. Day 20

27. Which of the following statements can be inferred from the graph?

I. The smallest five-day increase in the median height of partial darkness-grown bean seedlings was from Day 15 to Day 20.
II. The greatest percent increase in the median height of constant light-grown bean seedlings for the period shown on the graph was from Day 10 to Day 15.
III. On Day 20, the median height of partial darkness-grown bean seedlings was greater than that of constant light-grown seedlings.

A. I only
B. II only
C. I and II only
D. I and III only

Passage VII

Amphibians (frogs, toads, and salamanders) are sometimes found in areas where fresh water breeding sites are susceptible to acidification (a reduction in pH to acidic levels) from man-made sources via acid rain, acid snowmelt, or other modes of pollution. Some species are more tolerant of acid conditions than others. Thus, depending on the species, the amount of acidity, and other environmental variables, amphibians may experience developmental deformities and increased mortality due to acidification. The following graph summarizes the results of an experiment studying the survival rate of two species of amphibian larvae (tadpoles) at varying pH levels. The experiment studied sample sets of the two species at each pH level, varying only the pH level in each sample set.

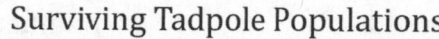

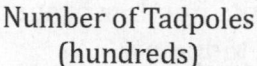

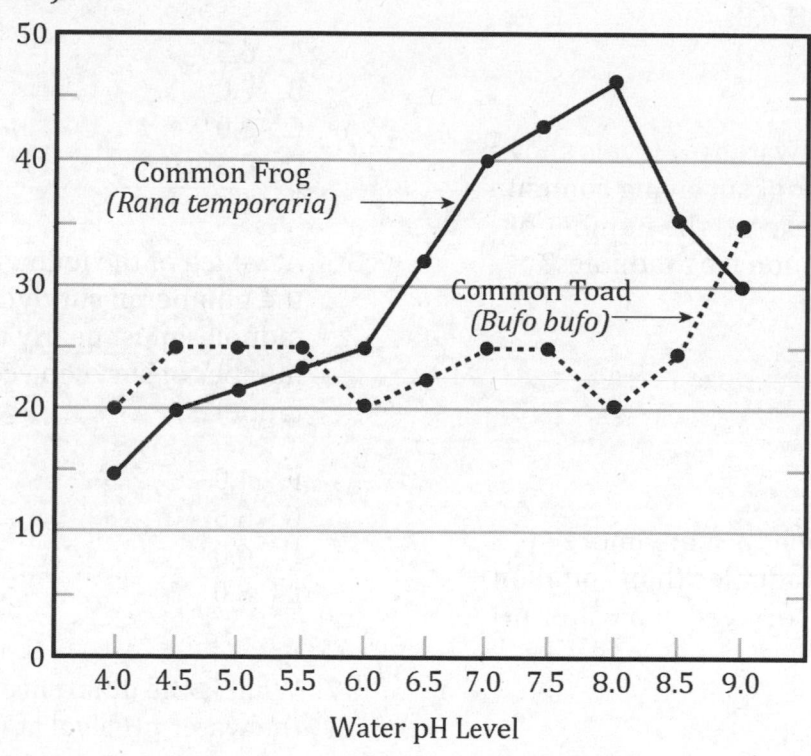

28. Approximately how many common frog tadpoles survived at a water pH level of 7.0?

    F.   25
    G.   40
    H. 2,500
    J.   4,000

29. Approximately how many common toad tadpoles survived at a water pH level of 4.0?

    A. 2,000
    B. 1,500
    C.   20
    D.   15

30. At a water pH level of 9.0, what was the approximate total surviving tadpole population?

    F. 6,500
    G. 3,500
    H. 3,000
    J.   500

31. The smallest percent increase in the number of surviving common frog tadpoles occurred from:

    A. pH 4.0 to pH 4.5.
    B. pH 4.5 to pH 5.0.
    C. pH 6.0 to pH 6.5.
    D. pH 6.5 to pH 7.0.

32. For how many water pH levels shown did the number of surviving common toad tadpoles exceed the number of surviving common frog tadpoles?

    F. Three
    G. Four
    H. Five
    J. Six

33. Approximately how many more common frog tadpoles than common toad tadpoles survived at a water pH level of 7.5?

    A. 1,700
    B. 2,500
    C. 4,500
    D. 7,000

34. What is the ratio of surviving common toad tadpoles to surviving common frog tadpoles at a water pH level of 8.5?

    F. 1 : 2
    G. 5 : 7
    H. 7 : 5
    J. 14 : 5

35. At which pH level was there the greatest difference between the number of surviving common frog tadpoles and the number of surviving common toad tadpoles?

    A. 6.5
    B. 7.0
    C. 8.0
    D. 8.5

36. At which of the following pH levels was the number of surviving common toad tadpoles most nearly equal to the number of surviving common frog tadpoles?

    F. 4.0
    G. 5.5
    H. 6.0
    J. 8.0

37. What is the difference in pH between the water pH level at which the greatest number of common frog tadpoles survived and the water pH level at which the greatest number of common toad tadpoles survived?

    A. 0.0
    B. 0.5
    C. 1.0
    D. 2.0

Passage VIII

The ionization energy of an atom is the minimum energy required to remove an electron from the ground state of the isolated gaseous atom. The first ionization energy, I_1, is the energy needed to remove the first electron from the atom, the second ionization energy, I_2, is the energy needed to remove the next (i.e., the second) electron from the atom, and so on. The higher the value of the ionization energy, the more difficult it is to remove the electron. The following table summarizes the first five ionization energies for five consecutive elements in the periodic table.

Table 4: Ionization Energies by Element							
			Ionization Energy in kilojoules per mole (kJ/mol)				
Number	Symbol	Name	I_1	I_2	I_3	I_4	I_5
11	Na	Sodium	496	4,562	6,910	9,543	13,354
12	Mg	Magnesium	738	1,451	7,733	10,543	13,630
13	Al	Aluminum	578	1,817	2,749	11,577	14,842
14	Si	Silicon	787	1,577	3,232	4,356	16,091
15	P	Phosphorus	1,012	1,907	2,914	4,964	6,274

38. According to Table 4, what is the approximate total ionization energy required for removing the first five electrons of a phosphorus atom?

    F.   1,000 kJ/mol
    G.   4,000 kJ/mol
    H. 17,000 kJ/mol
    J.   26,000 kJ/mol

39. The first ionization energy is most nearly equal for which two elements?

    A. Sodium and magnesium
    B. Magnesium and silicon
    C. Sodium and aluminum
    D. Aluminum and silicon

40. For sodium, the first ionization energy is approximately what percentage of the second ionization energy?

    F.   5%
    G. 11%
    H. 33%
    J.   50%

41. The first ionization energy of phosphorus is approximately what fraction of the total ionization energy required for removing the first three electrons of a phosphorus atom?

    A. $\dfrac{1}{6}$

    B. $\dfrac{1}{4}$

    C. $\dfrac{1}{3}$

    D. $\dfrac{1}{2}$

42. In Table 4, which element has smallest difference between the first and fifth ionization energies?

    F. Sodium
    G. Magnesium
    H. Silicon
    J. Phosphorus

Passage IX

Greenhouse gas emissions come primarily from energy-related carbon dioxide emissions, resulting from the combustion of fossil fuels in energy use. Additional carbon dioxide emissions result from deforestation and decay of biomass. Another greenhouse gas, methane, comes from landfills, coal mines, oil and natural gas operations, and agriculture. Nitrous oxide is emitted through the use of nitrogen fertilizers and from industrial and waste management processes. Several anthropogenic (human-made) gases—hydrofluorocarbons (HFCs), perfluorocarbons (PFCs), and sulfur hexafluoride (SF_6)—are released as byproducts of industrial processes and through leakage. In the charts below, greenhouse gas emissions are measured in carbon dioxide equivalents, or the amount of carbon dioxide that would have the same warming potential in the atmosphere.

Greenhouse Gas Emissions, 2004

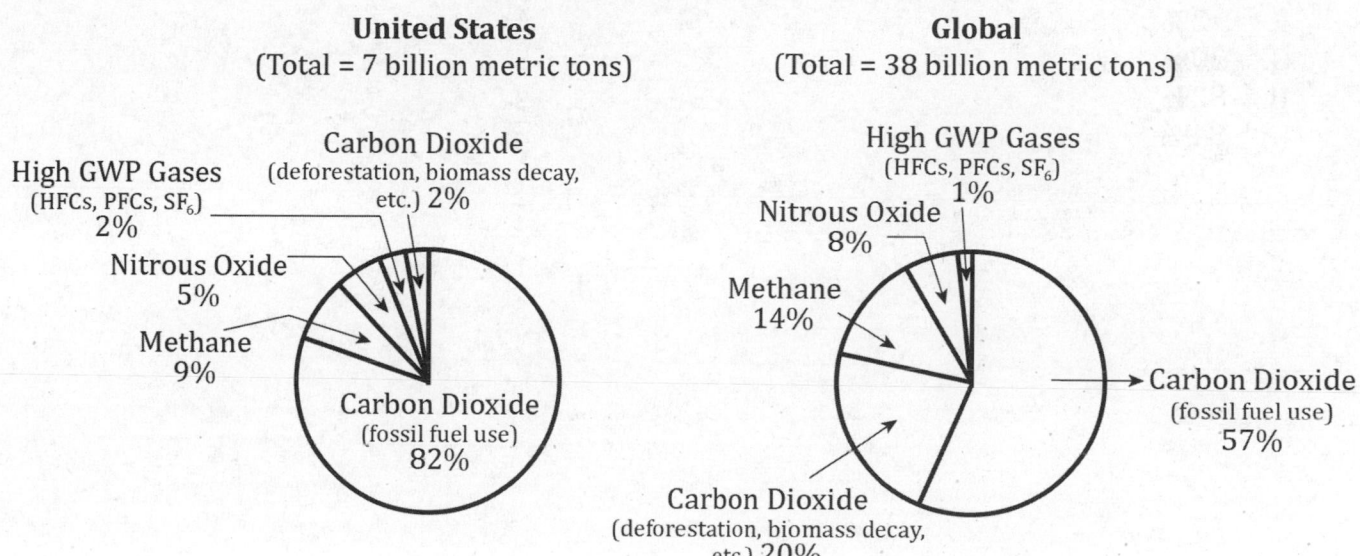

United States
(Total = 7 billion metric tons)

High GWP Gases
(HFCs, PFCs, SF_6)
2%

Carbon Dioxide
(deforestation, biomass decay, etc.) 2%

Nitrous Oxide
5%

Methane
9%

Carbon Dioxide
(fossil fuel use)
82%

Global
(Total = 38 billion metric tons)

High GWP Gases
(HFCs, PFCs, SF_6)
1%

Nitrous Oxide
8%

Methane
14%

Carbon Dioxide
(fossil fuel use)
57%

Carbon Dioxide
(deforestation, biomass decay, etc.) 20%

43. In terms of percentage, emissions from methane gas in the United States was most nearly equal to emissions from which greenhouse gas globally?

A. Methane
B. Nitrous oxide
C. Carbon dioxide (fossil fuel use)
D. High GWP gases

44. How much of the greenhouse gases in the United States came from carbon dioxide emissions that did not involve fossil fuel use?

F. 2%
G. 20%
H. 82%
J. 84%

45. Global greenhouse gas emissions from sources other than carbon dioxide constituted approximately what percentage of the total?

A. 20%
B. 23%
C. 43%
D. 57%

46. What was the approximate fraction of total global greenhouse gas emissions from carbon dioxide emissions that did not involve fossil fuel use?

F. $\dfrac{4}{5}$

G. $\dfrac{3}{5}$

H. $\dfrac{1}{4}$

J. $\dfrac{1}{5}$

Passage X

Cellular respiration refers to the process of converting the chemical energy of organic molecules into a form immediately usable by organisms. Glucose may be oxidized completely if sufficient oxygen is available according to the following equation:

$$C_6H_{12}O_6 + 6\ O_2(g) \rightarrow 6\ H_2O + 6\ CO_2(g) + energy$$

The following graph summarizes the results of an experiment conducted to monitor the carbon dioxide produced by cellular respiration of peas during germination at two different temperatures.

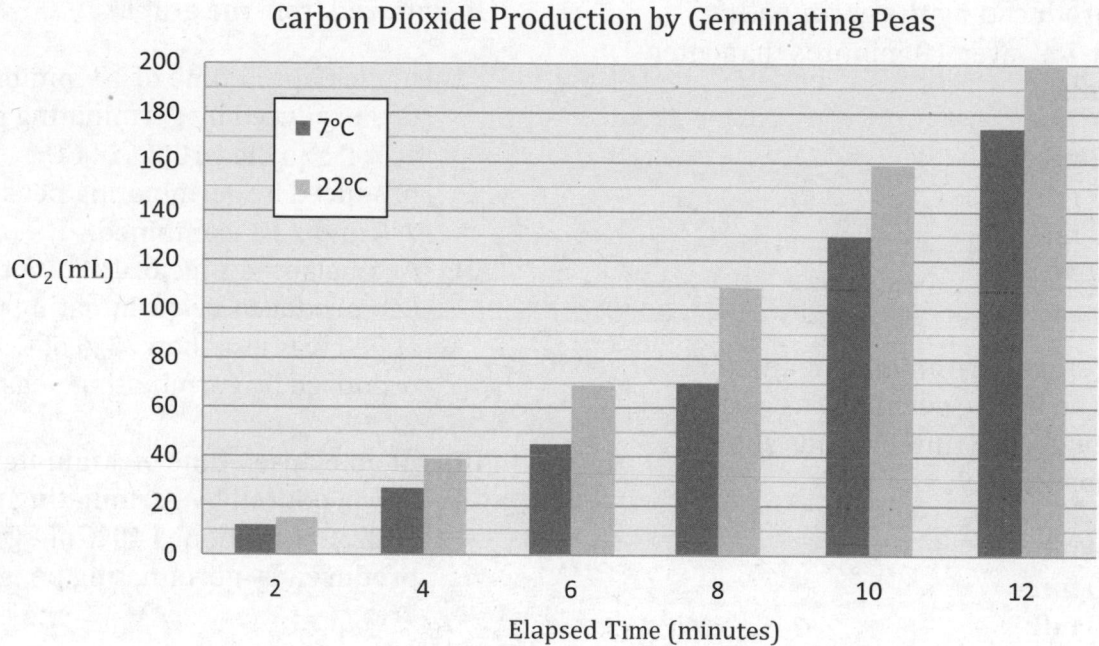

Carbon Dioxide Production by Germinating Peas

47. For which of the following elapsed times was the ratio of CO_2 produced by germinating peas at 22°C to that produced by germinating peas at 7°C the greatest?

    A.   2 minutes
    B.   6 minutes
    C.   8 minutes
    D. 10 minutes

48. How much more carbon dioxide had been produced by the germinating peas at 7°C after 10 minutes than after 2 minutes?

    F.   12 mL
    G.   45 mL
    H. 118 mL
    J. 130 mL

49. The average (arithmetic mean) of CO_2 produced by the germinating peas at 22°C for the six time periods shown was most nearly:

    A.   70 mL.
    B. 100 mL.
    C. 110 mL.
    D. 200 mL.

50. For how many of the elapsed time periods shown did CO_2 produced by germinating peas at 22°C exceed that produced by germinating peas at 7°C by more than 20 ppt?

    F. Five
    G. Four
    H. Three
    J. Two

51. Which of the following statements can be inferred from the graph?

    I.   At an elapsed time of 12 minutes, CO_2 produced by germinating peas at 7°C equalled 100% of CO_2 produced by germinating peas at 7°C and 22°C combined.
    II. At an elapsed time of 10 minutes, CO_2 produced by germinating peas at 7°C was less than 75% of CO_2 produced by germinating peas at 22°C.
    III. At an elapsed time of 4 minutes, CO_2 produced by germinating peas at 22°C was about 140% of CO_2 produced by germinating peas at 7°C.

    A. I only
    B. III only
    C. I and III only
    D. II and III only

Passage XI

Insects are the most numerous group of animals on the planet, making up about 80% of all animals. They play essential roles in the balance of nature as predators, food for other animals, and scavengers. The following graph summarizes the results of a backyard inventory of five general insect populations in five different locations, each measuring five square meters.

Backyard Inventory of Insect Populations (by Location)

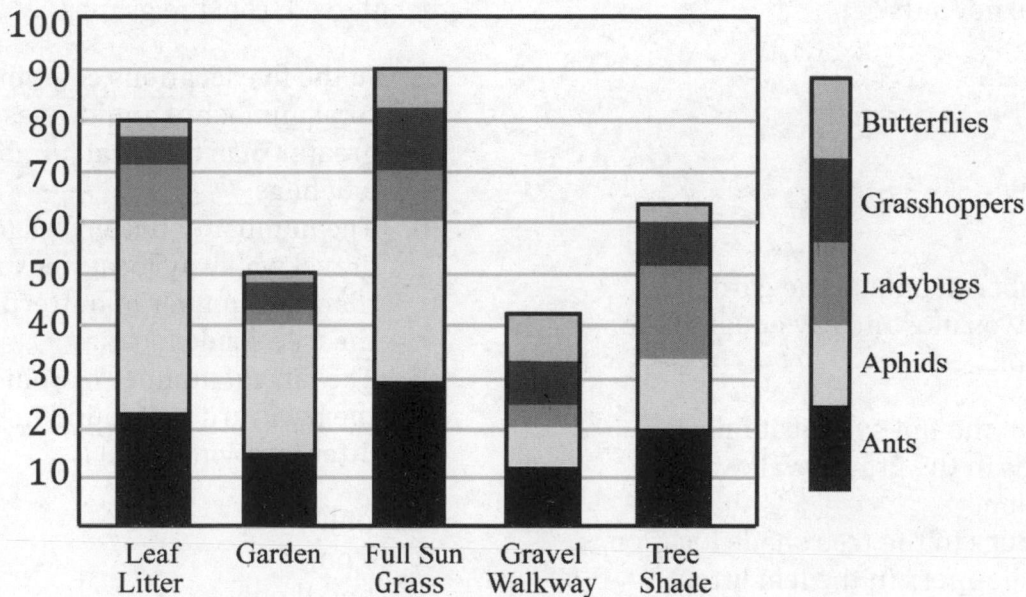

52. What was the approximate number of ladybugs in the tree shade location?

F. 51
G. 36
H. 21
J. 17

53. In the full sun location, what was the approximate total number of insects that were not ants?

A. 51
B. 61
C. 77
D. 119

54. The number of ants in the garden location was most nearly equal to the number of:

F. ants in the full sun location.
G. aphids in the gravel walkway location.
H. ladybugs in the tree shade location.
J. grasshoppers in the leaf litter location.

55. What was the approximate total number of grasshoppers in the five backyard locations combined?

A. 37
B. 44
C. 52
D. 60

56. Which of the following statements can be inferred from the graph?

I. In the five locations combined, the total number of aphids was greater than the total number of ladybugs.
II. The number of butterflies in the gravel walkway location was less than the number of butterflies in the tree shade location.
III. The largest number of aphids in the backyard was found in the leaf litter location.

F. I only
G. III only
H. I and II only
J. I and III only

Passage XII

Harmful algal blooms caused by the rapid growth of algae, such as blue-green algae (cyanobacteria), can present problems for ecosystems and be extremely toxic to animals and humans. Daily water samples taken from a lake with algal bloom were analyzed for potentially toxin-producing cyanobacteria. The following graph presents the results.

Densities of Potentially Toxigenic Cyanobacteria in Water Samples

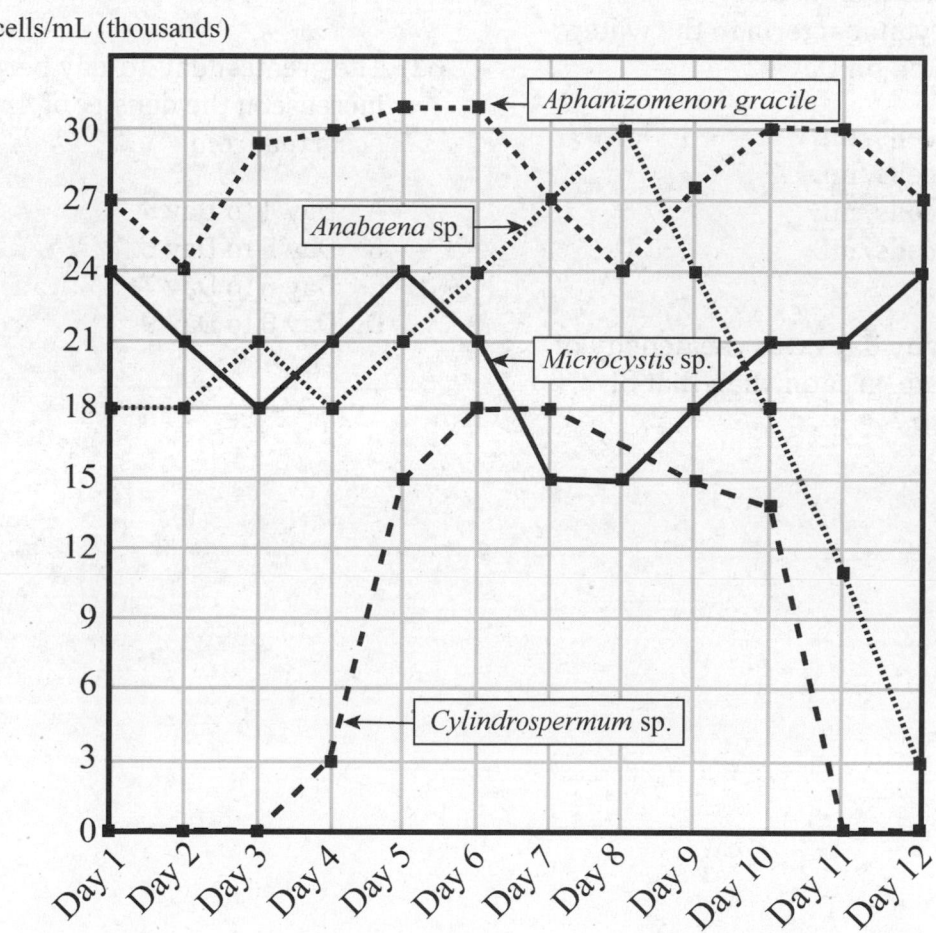

57. Water samples from which of the following days had the greatest density of *Microcystis* sp.?

    A. Day 3
    B. Day 5
    C. Day 6
    D. Day 8

58. What was the total density of measured cyanobacteria in the water samples taken on Day 4?

    F. 75,000 cells/mL
    G. 72,000 cells/mL
    H. 58,000 cells/mL
    J. 30,000 cells/mL

59. For how many days was the density of *Microcystis* sp. greater than that of *Anabaena* sp.?

    A. Three
    B. Five
    C. Seven
    D. Nine

60. The difference between the densities of *Aphanizomenon gracile* and *Microcystis* sp. was greatest in the water samples taken on which of the following days?

    F. Day 3
    G. Day 4
    H. Day 6
    J. Day 7

61. The greatest day-to-day percent increase in the density of *Anabaena* sp. occurred from:

    A. Day 4 to Day 5.
    B. Day 5 to Day 6.
    C. Day 6 to Day 7.
    D. Day 8 to Day 9.

Passage XIV

An entomologist studied the butterfly population of vacant land located around a small city. Each year from 2004 to 2008, the researcher netted butterflies, affixed to each butterfly a small adhesive tag with the date and location of capture, and then released them. Later that year, if the butterflies were recaptured, the information on the tag and the new information on the recapture were entered into a data base. The researcher followed the same procedure each year with a new population of butterflies. Early in 2008, a construction project destroyed 40 acres of butterfly habitat, and the project was discontinued after that year's research.

Total Number of Recaptured
Marked Butterflies

Distance of Recapture
from Release (2007)

Total = 1,500

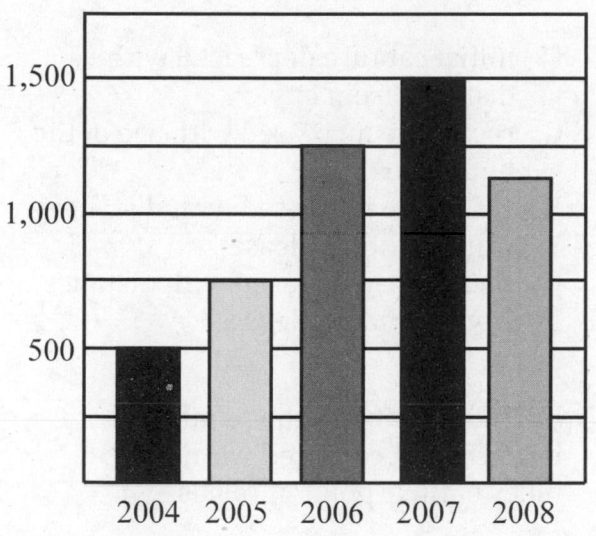

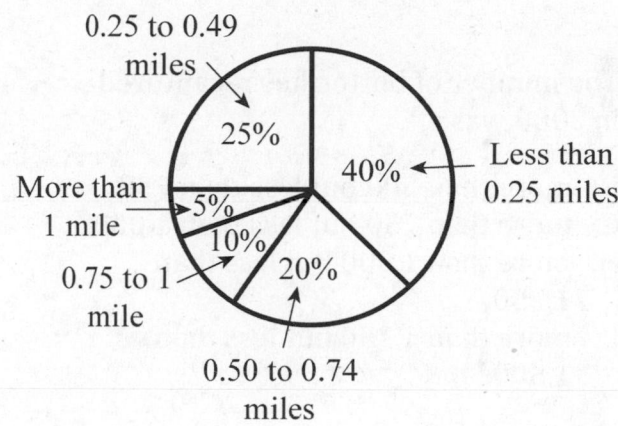

62. The *x*-axis of the bar graph shows the:

  F. number of butterflies tagged.
  G. number of butterflies recaptured.
  H. butterfly population of the area.
  J.   the years the research was done.

63. The large drop from 2007 to 2008 in the number of butterflies recaptured was probably due to:

  A. poor experimental technique.
  B. the abandonment of the project.
  C. excessive netting in prior years.
  D. a drop in butterfly population.

64. The number of butterflies recaptured in 2008 was:

  F. more than 500 but less than 750.
  G. more than 750 but less than 1,000.
  H. more than 1,000 but less than 1,250.
  J.   more than 1,250 but less than 1,500.

65. Which of the following variables is the subject of the circle graph?

  A. Distance of recapture from point of release
  B. Distance of release from point of capture
  C. Number of butterflies initially captured
  D. Number of butterflies initially released

66. The data provided by the circle graph suggest that the frequency of:

  F. initial capture decreased with distance from city.
  G. recapture increased with age of the butterflies.
  H. recapture increased with distance from point of release.
  J.   recapture decreased with distance from point of release.

67. In 2007, what was the number of butterflies recaptured within 0.25 miles of their point of release?

  A.   250
  B.   400
  C.   600
  D. 1,500

Passage XV

An asteroid, also called a planetoid, is a small celestial body which orbits the Sun along with other objects in the solar system such as planets. However, asteroids are typically much smaller than planets.

Since it formed over 4.5 billion years ago, Earth has been hit many times by asteroids with orbits that brought them into the inner solar system. Such objects, collectively known as Near Earth Objects, still pose a danger to Earth today. Depending on the size of the impacting object, such a collision could cause massive catastrophes on a global scale.

An impact by an asteroid 10 kilometers in diameter is widely viewed as an extinction-level event likely to cause catastrophic damage to the biosphere. If traveling fast enough, objects as small as 100 meters in diameter can be extremely destructive. The largest asteroids would cause the most damage, but there are fewer of them. Using historical data, astronomers have created mathematical models to estimate the probability of an asteroid of a given size hitting Earth (see Table 5).

Table 5: Impact Probability of Earth-Bound Asteroids		
Approximate Asteroid Diameter (kilometers)	Estimated Number Near Earth	Impact Probability (in one year)
0.001 (1 meter)	10,000,000	2 (1 or more every year)
0.1 (100 meters)	100,000	0.0002 (1 every 5,000 years)
1	1,000	0.000002 (1 every 500,000 years)
10	10	0.00000001 (1 every 100 million years)

68. According to the passage, which of the following pairs of terms can be used interchangeably?

    F. Planet and planetoid
    G. Near Earth Object and planet
    H. Earth and planetoid
    J. Asteroid and planetoid

69. According to the passage, asteroids are celestial bodies that:

    A. orbit Earth.
    B. collide with the Sun.
    C. orbit the Sun.
    D. are larger than Earth.

70. According to the passage, the destructive effect of an asteroid striking Earth would depend on its:

    F. size only
    G. speed only
    H. size and speed only
    J. size, speed, and shape

71. According to Table 5, the estimated number of asteroids near Earth with diameters of approximately 1,000 meters is:

    A.   10
    B.   1,000
    C.   100,000
    D. 1,000,000

72. According to Table 5, the probability in any given year of Earth's being struck by an asteroid with a diameter of approximately 100 meters is:

    F. 0.02.
    G. 0.0002.
    H. 0.000002.
    J. 0.00000001.

73. It can be inferred from Table 5 that a 0.002 probability of an event's occurring in any given year is approximately equivalent to:

    A. once every 10 years.
    B. once every 500 years.
    C. once every 1,000 years.
    D. once every 50,000 years.

74. According to the passage, a collision between Earth and an asteroid with a diameter of 10 kilometers:

    F. has not happened since Earth's formation.
    G. would be an extinction-level event.
    H. would have little effect on the biosphere.
    J. occurs every 10 years.

75. It can be inferred from Table 5 that the probability in any given year of Earth being struck by an asteroid with a diameter of approximately 10 meters is:

    A. less than 0.000002.
    B. less than 0.0002 but greater than 0.000002.
    C. greater than 2.
    D. less than 2 but greater than 0.0002.

76. It can be inferred from Table 5 that the probability of Earth being struck by an asteroid of any given size varies:

    F. directly with the diameter of the asteroid.
    G. inversely with the diameter of the asteroid.
    H. inversely with the number of asteroids.
    J. inversely with the number of years.

INTERMEDIATE

Understand tools and methods in an experiment.

Understand an experimental design.

Identify a control in an experiment.

Compare and contrast experiments.

Predict the results of an additional step in an experiment.

Determine what would cause a specific result in an experiment.

Understand basic scientific terms.

Read and interpret data in more complex data presentations.

Understand the relationship between variables in more complex data presentations.

Select a hypothesis, prediction, or conclusion supported by a data presentation or a model.

BASIC

INTERMEDIATE

ADVANCED

Science passages describe scientific methods that may be unfamiliar to you but are commonly used by scientists to interpret and analyze scientific information. Familiarity with these basics of experimental design will help you understand science passages and items.

Science Vocabulary List

The following list consists of terms that are commonly found in Science passages and corresponding items. Understanding the definitions and uses of these terms will help you to better understand the material in which they are used. Review the following list and highlight or circle any unfamiliar words or terms.

absolute—existing independent of any other cause

accuracy—freedom from mistake; exactness

adverse—acting against or in an opposite direction

analogous—similar or comparable in some way

analyze—to study the relationship of the parts of something by analysis

application—ability to put to a practical use

approximately—nearly; an estimate or figure that is almost exact

argument—a reason for or against something

assumption—something accepted as true

comprehend—to understand fully

concentration—the ratio of the amount of solute to the amount of solvent or solution

conclusion—a final decision based on facts, experience, or reasoning

confirm—to make certain something is true

consequence—something produced by a cause or condition

consistent—in agreement; firm; changeless

constant—remaining steady and unchanged

contradiction—a statement in opposition to another statement

control group—experimental group in which conditions are controlled

controlled experiment—one in which the condition suspected to cause an effect is compared to one without the suspected condition

controlled variable—a factor in an experiment that remains constant

correlation—a close connection between two ideas or sets of data

criticism—a finding of fault; disapproval

definitive—accurate or sure

demonstrate—use examples or experiments to explain something

dependence—a state of being controlled by something else

dependent variable—result or change that occurs due to the part of an experiment being tested (positioned on the vertical y-axis)

diminish—to make smaller or less; decrease in size

direct relationship—the connection between two variables that show the same effect (i.e., both increase or both decrease)

effective—producing or able to produce a desired condition

estimation—formation of calculation based on incomplete data

ethical—following accepted rules of behavior

evaluation—the result of a finding; estimating the value of something

evidence—that which serves to prove or disprove something

examine—to look at or check carefully

expectation—the extent of a chance that something will occur

experiment—a test made to find something out

experimental design—the plan for a controlled experiment

experimental group—the experimental part in which all conditions are kept the same except for the condition being tested

explanation—a statement that makes something clear

extrapolation—estimation of a value for one characteristic that is beyond the range of a given value of another characteristic

figure—a picture that explains

fundamental—a basic part

generalization—something given as a broad statement or conclusion

hypothesis— a testable explanation of a question or problem

illustrate—to make clear by using examples

imply—to suggest rather than to say plainly

inconsistent—not in agreement

incorporate—to join or unite closely into a single body

independent variable—in a controlled experiment, the variable that is being changed (positioned on the horizontal *x*-axis)

indication—the act of pointing out or pointing to something

indicator—any device that measures, records, or visibly points out; any of various substances used to point out a cause, treatment, or outcome on an action

ingredient—any of the components of which something is made

interpolation—estimation of a value that falls between two known values; a "best-fit line" on a graph

interpretation—the act of telling the meaning of; explanation

inverse (indirect) relationship—the connection between two variables that shows the opposite effect (i.e., when the value of one variable increases, the value of the other variable deceases)

investigate—to study by close and careful observation

irregular—not continuous or coming at set times

issue—something that is questioned

judgment—an opinion formed by examining and comparing

justify—to prove or show to be right or reasonable

legend—a title, description, or key accompanying a figure or map

maximum—as great as possible in amount or degree

measurement—the act of finding out the size or amount of something

mechanism—the parts or steps that make up a process or activity

minimum—as small as possible in amount or degree

model—a pattern or figure of something

modify—to make changes in something

observation—the act of noting and recording facts and events

opinion—a personal belief based on experience and on certain facts

optimum—the best or most favorable degree, condition, or amount

pattern—a model, guide, or plan used in making things; definite direction, tendency, or characteristics

perform—to carry out; accomplish

phenomenon—an observable fact or event

precision—the quality of being exactly stated; exact arrangement

predict—to figure out and tell beforehand

preference—a choosing of or liking for one thing rather than another

probability—the quality of being reasonably sure but not certain of something happening or being true

procedure—the way in which an action or actions is carried out

proponent—one who supports a cause

proportional—any quantities or measurements having the same fixed relationship in degree or number

reasonable—showing or containing sound thought

refute—to prove wrong by argument or evidence

relationship—the state of being connected

replicate—to copy or reproduce

revise—to look over again; to correct or improve

simulation—the act or process of simulating a system or process

study—a careful examination and investigation of an event

suggest—to offer as an idea

summarize—to state briefly

support—to provide evidence

theory—a general rule offered to explain experiences or facts

translate—to change from one state or form to another

treatment—an exposure to some action

underlying—something which forms the support for something else

unit—a fixed quantity used as a standard of measurement

validity—the quality of being based on evidence that can be supported

value—the quantity or amount for which a symbol stands

variable—that which can be changed

viewpoint—opinion; judgment

Types of Research

Scientists regularly attempt to identify and solve problems by investigating the world around them. Different scientists may use different approaches to conduct their investigations. *Qualitative*, or descriptive, research is based generally on observable data only.

Example:

A field biologist may observe coral reefs in order to determine if the loss of this habitat would threaten the extinction of many species that live in the coral reefs.

Quantitative research is based on the collection of numerical data—usually by counting or measuring.

Example:

A laboratory biologist may investigate the factors that affect the flow of substances across cell membranes. Numerical data is collected by measuring the change in mass of a cellophane bag that is filled with a sugar solution and then placed in a beaker of pure water.

Forming and Testing Hypotheses

Scientists normally ***form a hypothesis*** and then test it through observation, experimentation, and/or prediction. A hypothesis is defined as a possible explanation for a question or problem that can be formally tested. A hypothesis can be thought of as a prediction about why something occurs or about the relationship between two or more variables.

Scientists describe an experiment as a procedure that ***tests a hypothesis*** by collecting information under controlled conditions. Based on the experimental results, scientists can determine whether the hypothesis is correct or must be modified and re-tested. Testing hypotheses through experiments is at the core of scientific investigations and studies.

An important part of testing a hypothesis is identifying the ***variables*** that are part of an experiment. A variable is any condition that can change in an experiment. The variable that the experimenter thinks is the cause is the ***independent variable***. It is controlled by the experimenter. The effect is the ***dependent variable.*** The experimenter measures it. The variables that are not changed (***controlled variables***) are used to isolate the condition(s) that affect(s) the outcome of the experiment.

Example:

Scientists conduct a controlled experiment to determine how a high protein diet affects the growth rate of rats.

Independent variable: exposure to a high protein diet

Dependent variable: the rats' growth rates

Possible hypothesis: When the amount of protein is increased in the diet of rats, their growth rate will increase.

Design of Controlled Experiments

The design of controlled experiments involves two groups: the **control group** and the **experimental group**. The control group receives either the standard treatment or no treatment at all. The experimental group receives the experimental treatment. In the example above, the control group of rates would receive their usual food. The experimental group of rats would receive high-protein food.

The control group and the experimental group must be similar in all ways except for the independent variable that is being tested in the experimental group. It is common in a controlled experiment to have more than one experimental group to represent the possible variations in the conditions of the independent variable. All other variables that could affect the outcome of the experiment are held constant.

Example, continued:

In the previous experiment about the effect of a high protein diet on the growth rate of rats, a large test population of similar rats would be randomly divided into two smaller groups of equal number—the control group and the experimental group.

In the example experiment, the rats are randomly divided to ensure that both groups are representative samples of the original population. If the test group is not representative of the original population, other uncontrolled conditions could affect the outcome of the experiment. If there are any uncontrolled conditions in either group, it could be argued that any experimental results would be due to differences in the composition of the different test groups instead of a result of the independent variable.

Example, continued:

The rats in the control group are exposed to the same environmental conditions as the rats in the experimental group, except for the amount of protein in their diet. The control group rats are given a diet with the normal amount of protein. The rats in the experimental group are exposed to a high protein diet (independent variable). (It would be possible to have more than one experimental group with each having a greater amount of protein.) The other conditions that could change, such as the temperature, amount of food and water, and amount of living space, are held constant for both groups of rats. The data collected can be used to determine if the hypothesis is correct. The following table summarizes the design of the experiment:

Test Population (number of test subjects)	Controlled Variables (conditions that are kept the same in both groups)	Independent Variables (conditions that vary between the two groups)	Dependent Variables (conditions that result from the experiment)
Control Group (50 rats)	sunlight, temperature, amount of water and food, amount of living space	normal protein diet	growth rate
Experimental Group (50 rats)	sunlight, temperature, amount of water and food, amount of living space	high protein diet	growth rate

Representing Experimental Relationships

Relationships between variables may be direct, indirect (inverse), or constant, and those relationships can be plotted on a graph or organized in a table. A **direct relationship** occurs when one variable increases as the other increases, or when one variable decreases as the other decreases. An **indirect**, or inverse, **relationship** occurs when one variable increases as the other decreases. A **constant relationship** occurs when a change in one variable has no effect on the other variable.

Example:

The slopes of the lines in the following three graphs illustrate the typical kinds of relationships between variables shown in a line graph:

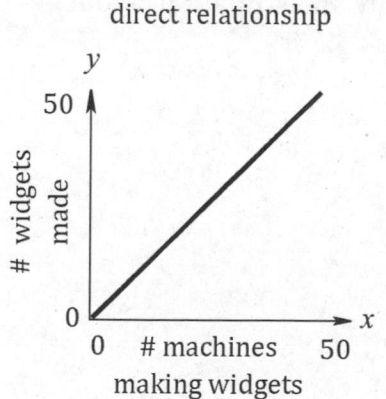

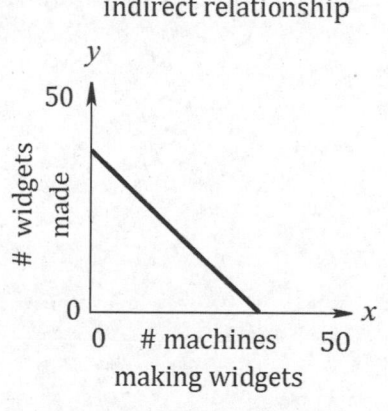

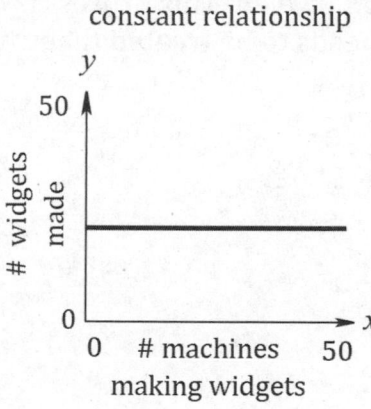

The first graph illustrates a **direct relationship**—as the number of machines increases, the number of widgets made increases. The second graph illustrates an **indirect relationship**—as the number of machines increases, the number of widgets made decreases. The third graph illustrates a **constant relationship**—as the number of machines increases, the number of widgets made does not change.

Since the collection of experimental data is often subject to error, data points plotted on a graph may show only scattered points without a clear, smooth line. As a result, another type of line graph is required to illustrate an estimate of a value that falls among the known values on the graph. A ***best-fit*** line, a line that comes close to all of the points, must be calculated. This process is called ***interpolation***.

Example:

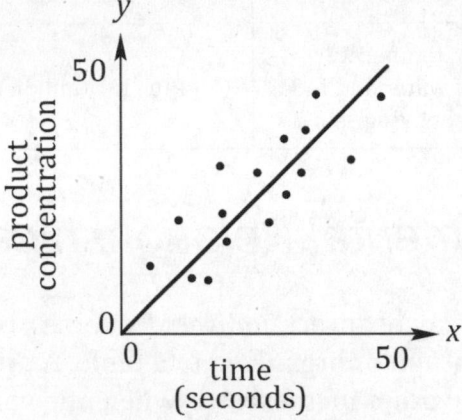

The scattered points in the graph above plot data collected from a progressing chemical reaction. To determine the relationship between time and concentration of products, a line is drawn so that an approximately equal number of points fall on either side of the line. This graph indicates a direct relationship between the product concentration and time (as time progresses, more product is formed).

Sometimes, it is necessary for a scientist to estimate a value beyond the limits of the available data shown on the graph. The scientist must then extend the line on the graph based on the data given. This process is called ***extrapolation***. An extrapolation is only an estimation, and it needs to be treated that way.

Example, continued:

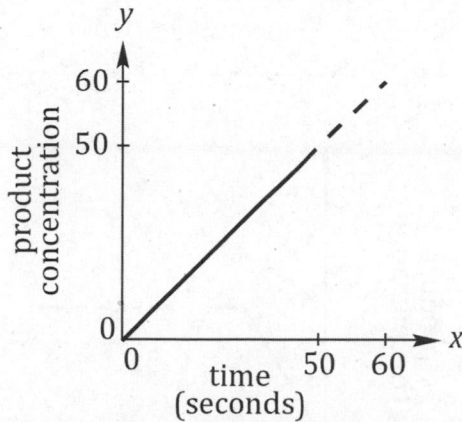

If the line is relatively straight, as shown in the graph above, the line can be extended far enough so that the values called for can be included. Suppose the scientist wanted to determine the reaction rate at a time of 60 seconds. By extending the line to follow the apparent pattern, it is possible to predict product concentration at a time on measured in the experiment.

When using the technique of extrapolation, a scientist must be careful not to make the possible false assumption that the relationship will continue unchanged indefinitely. It is possible that beyond a certain time, an unexpected change in the independent variable will result in an unpredicted change in the dependent variable. For example, in a chemical reaction, as the reactants are used up, the concentration of product will plateau.

Example, continued:

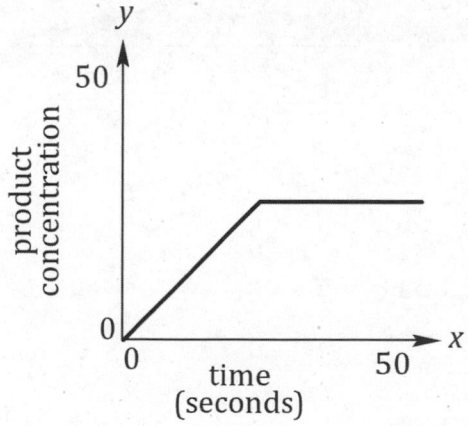

In the graph above, if the data collection had stopped after about 15 seconds, the scientist may have inaccurately predicted that the product concentration would continue to increase.

Occasionally a line graph will show a "break" in the scale to conserve space when no values fall into the deleted part.

Example, continued:

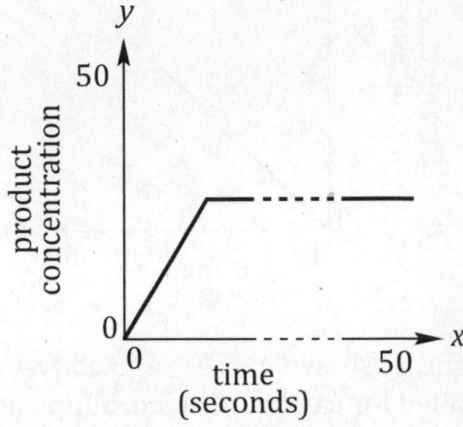

An open circle, however, shows missing data that has been extrapolated.

Example:

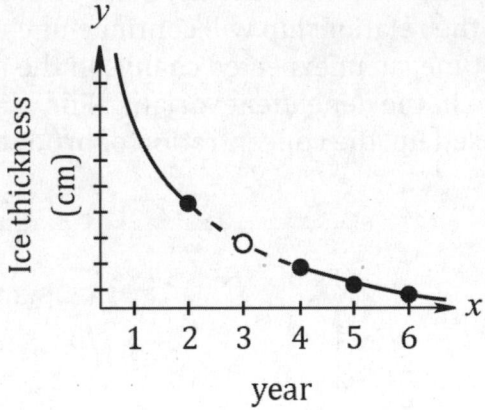

EXERCISE

DIRECTIONS: Read the description of the following controlled experiment and answer the accompanying items. You are NOT allowed the use of a calculator. Answers are on page 819.

Passage I

An experiment was carried out to determine the effect of temperature on the heart rate of frogs. In the experiment, 100 frogs were removed from a large 25°C enclosure and separated randomly into four equal groups: A, B, C, and D. Each group was maintained in a separate container at a different constant temperature: Group A at 5°C; Group B at 15°C; Group C at 25°C; and Group D at 35°C. All other conditions, such as the size, type, age, and number of the frogs, as well as the size of the container and the amount of light, were the same for all groups of frogs.

1. The purpose of the experiment is to:

   _____

   _____

   _____

   _____

2. The independent variable is:

   _____

   _____

3. The dependent variable is:

   _____

   _____

4. The controlled variables are:

   _____

   _____

5. The control group(s) is (are):

   _____

   _____

6. The experimental group(s) is (are):

   _____

   _____

7. Write a possible hypothesis by filling in the blanks in the following sentence:

   When the _____
   (independent variable)

   is _____,
   (describe how it is changed)

   then the _____
   (dependent variable)

   will _____.
   (describe the effect)

Passage II

Sodium chloride (table salt) is a crystalline solid made up of sodium ions (Na^+) and chloride ions (Cl^-). Ions are atoms that are electrically charged. When sodium chloride is dissolved in water, it separates into its ions. The sodium ions and chlorine ions are released from their positions in the crystal pattern, and they move about freely. Other crystalline substances, such as sugar, do not produce ions when dissolved in water. When substances react with water to form ions, they are said to be ionized. The charged ions in the water are responsible for the conduction of electricity. Substances that conduct an electrical current when dissolved are called electrolytes. Substances that do not conduct an electrical current are called non-electrolytes.

To study the electrical conductivity of sodium chloride, an apparatus that measures the ability of substances to conduct electricity was used.

Experiment 1

Solid sodium chloride was tested and found to be a non-conductor. Pure water was also tested and found to be a non-conductor. When a teaspoon of sodium chloride was added to 50 mL of water, the solution was found to be a good conductor of electricity. Sugar did not conduct electricity as a solid or when dissolved in water.

Experiment 2

When a few crystals of sodium chloride were added to 50 mL of water, the solution showed a weak conduction of electricity. As additional sodium chloride was added, the ability of the solution to conduct electricity increased. After a certain point, adding more sodium chloride to the solution did not change the conduction of electricity.

8. Experiment 1 indicates that sodium chloride conducts electricity when it is:

    F. dissolved in alcohol.
    G. tested as a solid.
    H. dissolved in water.
    J. combined with sugar.

9. Which of the following is NOT a characteristic of sugar?

    A. Solid sugar is an electrolyte.
    B. Solid sugar is a non-electrolyte.
    C. Solid sugar dissolves in water.
    D. Sugar solutions do not conduct electricity.

10. In order for a substance to be a conductor of electricity, the substance must have:

    F. rapidly moving molecules.
    G. charged particles that are free to move.
    H. ions in a crystalline form.
    J. been dissolved.

11. Which of the following graphs could represent the relationship between the amount of sodium chloride dissolved in water and its conductivity?

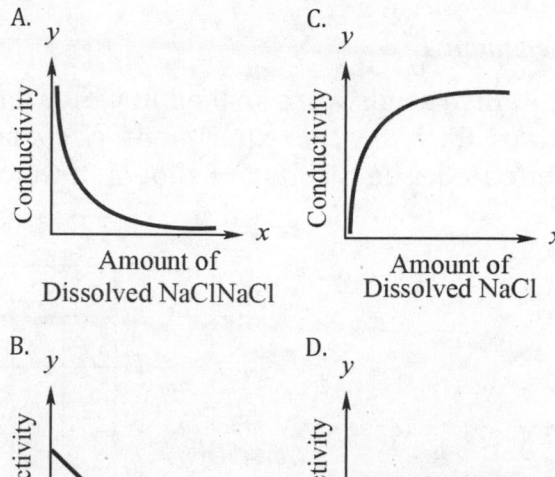

Passage III

Germination is the beginning of the growth of a seed after a period of inactivity. The following experiments were designed to compare the amount of time it takes for seeds of different vegetables to germinate.

Experiment 1

Radish seeds were soaked in water for 24 hours and then planted and kept at 25°C for 10 days. Each day the experimenters counted the total number of seeds that had germinated. The results are shown in Graph 1.

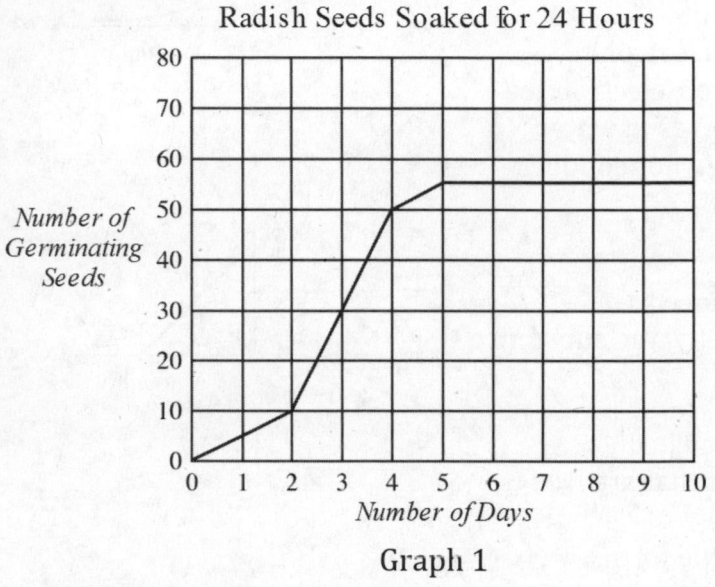

Radish Seeds Soaked for 24 Hours

Graph 1

Experiment 2

Bean seeds were soaked in water for 24 hours and then planted and kept at 25°C for 10 days. Each day the experimenters counted the total number of seeds that had germinated. The results are shown in Graph 2.

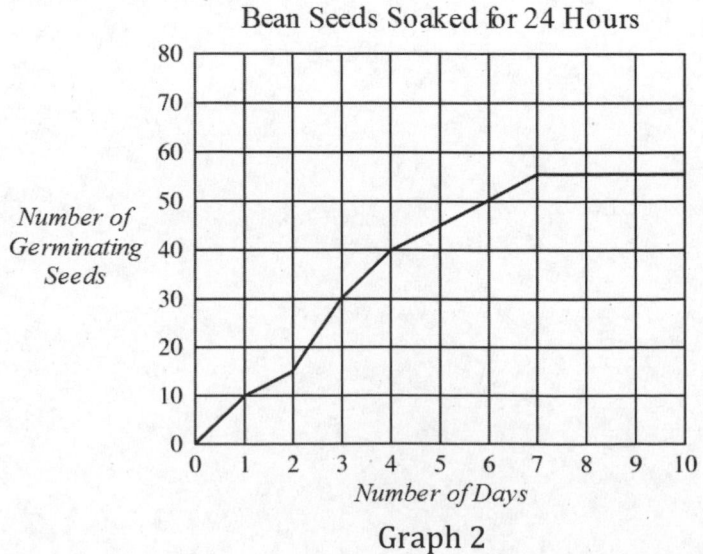

Bean Seeds Soaked for 24 Hours

Graph 2

12. Graphs 1 and 2 show that by the end of Day 3:

   F. more radish seeds had germinated than been seeds.
   G. more bean seeds had germinated than radish seeds.
   H. equal numbers of radish seeds and bean seeds had germinated.
   J. no radish seeds or bean seeds had germinated.

13. Based on the experimental results, which of the following conclusions is true?

   A. Twenty-four hours is the best soaking period for both radish seeds and bean seeds.
   B. Radish seeds and bean seeds germinate at different rates.
   C. The bean seeds had a steady rate of germination.
   D. Bean seeds of this kind require seven days to germinate.

14. Which factor is the independent variable in set of experiments?

   F. The period of the soaking
   G. The dishes in which the seeds were planted
   H. The rate of germination
   J. The kind of seeds used

15. To test the hypothesis that ultraviolet radiation affects bean seed germination, which of the following experimental designs would be the best to use?

   A. Plant 100 normal bean seeds and 100 normal radish seeds and monitor the health of all plants for one month.
   B. Plant 100 bean seeds that have been exposed to ultraviolet radiation; at the same time, plant 100 normal bean seeds, and compare the results.
   C. Use 100 radish seeds and 100 bean seeds that have been exposed to ultraviolet violation, and compare the results.
   D. Plant 100 bean seeds that have been exposed to ultraviolet radiation, and note the effects of the radiation.

Passage IV

When one end of a cord under tension is disturbed, the displacement moves down the cord in the form of a *transverse wave.* If the other end of the cord is fixed, the wave is reflected and moves back in the opposite direction encountering other waves moving toward the fixed point. Certain frequencies produce *standing waves*, which are characterized by motionless nodes separating oscillating segments of cord (see Figure 1). For a cord of a given length and density, only certain frequencies will produce standing waves.

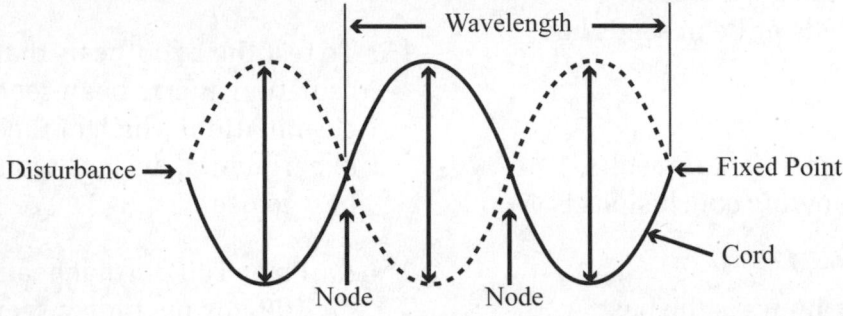

Figure 1

A group of students performed three investigations using the setup shown in Figure 2. One end of a cord was fastened to the reciprocating blade of a jig saw and the other was hung over a pulley and attached to a block. A stroboscope measured the frequency of the vibrations in the cord. The length of the cord from the jig saw blade to the pulley was 2 meters, and the length of the standing waves was measured using the meter stick attached to the lab table.

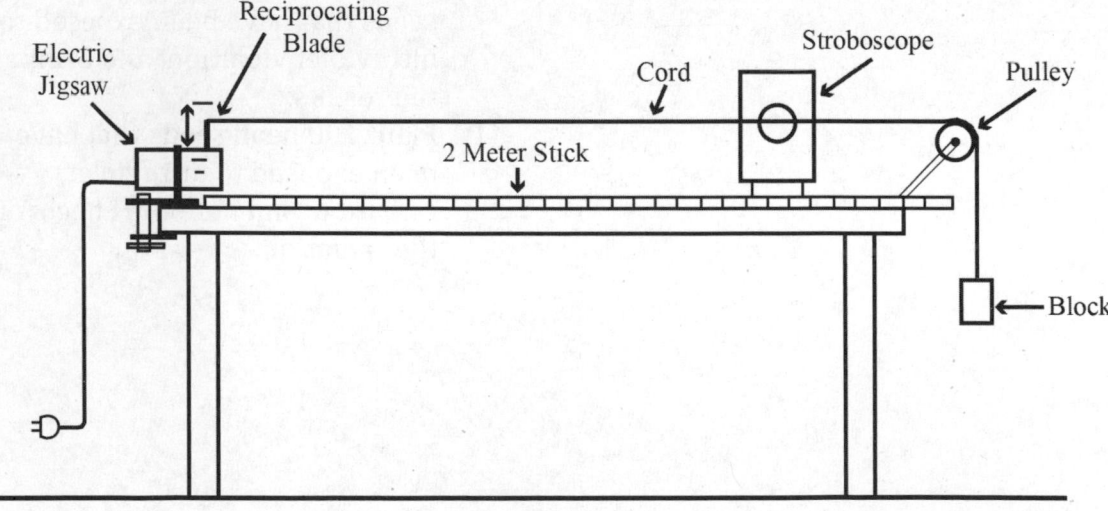

Figure 2

Experiment 1

The students conducted five trials using the same cord of density 0.0076 kilograms per meter and block while adjusting the frequency to produce standing waves at pre-determined wavelengths. The cord tension in all five trials was 2 newtons. They recorded the length and frequency of the waves (see Table 1).

Table 1		
Trial	Wavelength (meters)	Frequency (hertz)
1	4	4.05
2	2	8.05
3	1.3	12.33
4	1	16.3
5	0.8	20.25

Experiment 2

Using the same cord, the students decreased the tension to 1 newton and conducted five more trials, adjusting the frequency to produce standing waves at pre-determined wavelengths (see Table 2).

Table 2		
Trial	Wavelength (meters)	Frequency (hertz)
1	4	2.87
2	2	5.74
3	1.3	8.62
4	1	11.47
5	0.8	14.34

Experiment 3

The students kept the tension at 1 newton but used five different cords of different densities. Again, they conducted five trials, adjusting the frequency to produce standing waves at pre-determined wavelengths and then recording the lengths of the waves and the frequencies (see Table 3).

Table 3			
Trial	Cord Density (kilogram per meter)	Wavelength (meters)	Frequency (hertz)
1	0.0076	4	2.87
2	0.011	2	4.77
3	0.018	1.3	5.60
4	0.025	1	6.32
5	0.032	0.8	6.99

16. In the experimental setup shown in Figure 2, the frequency of the standing wave was equal to:

    F. the speed the wave travels along the cord.
    G. the density of the cord.
    H. the length of the standing wave.
    J. the rate of movement of the reciprocating saw blade.

17. For all three experiments, which of the following remained constant?

    A. Lengths of the standing waves obtained
    B. Tension placed on the cord
    C. Length of the cord from saw blade to pulley
    D. Frequency of the disturbance applied to the cord

18. In the experimental setup shown in Figure 2, the electric jig saw was used to control:

    F. the vibrations of the cord.
    G. the tension on the cord.
    H. the length of the cord.
    J. the direction of the wave.

19. In the experimental setup shown in Figure 2, the block was attached to the cord in order to:

    A. place tension on the cord.
    B. measure wavelengths.
    C. change the cord density.
    D. vibrate the cord.

20. The density of the cord was held constant in which of the experiments?

    F. Experiment 1 only
    G. Experiment 2 only
    H. Experiments 1 and 2 only
    J. Experiments 1, 2, and 3

21. The students learned that increasing the density of the cord required:

    A. no change in the frequency needed to produce standing waves of a certain length.
    B. an increase in the frequency needed to produce standing waves of a certain length.
    C. a decrease in the frequency needed to produce standing waves of a certain length.
    D. an increase in tension in order to produce standing waves of a certain length.

22. What frequency was required to produce a standing wave of length 1 meter in a cord with density of 0.025 kilograms per meter at 1 newton of tension?

    F. 2.87 hertz
    G. 6.32 hertz
    H. 11.47 hertz
    J. 16.30 hertz

Passage V

A projectile is any object that is thrown or otherwise projected into the air. Once in the air, the only force assumed to be acting on the projectile is gravity. The effect of air resistance is assumed to be negligible. The path followed by a projectile is the trajectory.

A student performs a series of experiments using a spring launch (see Figure 3).

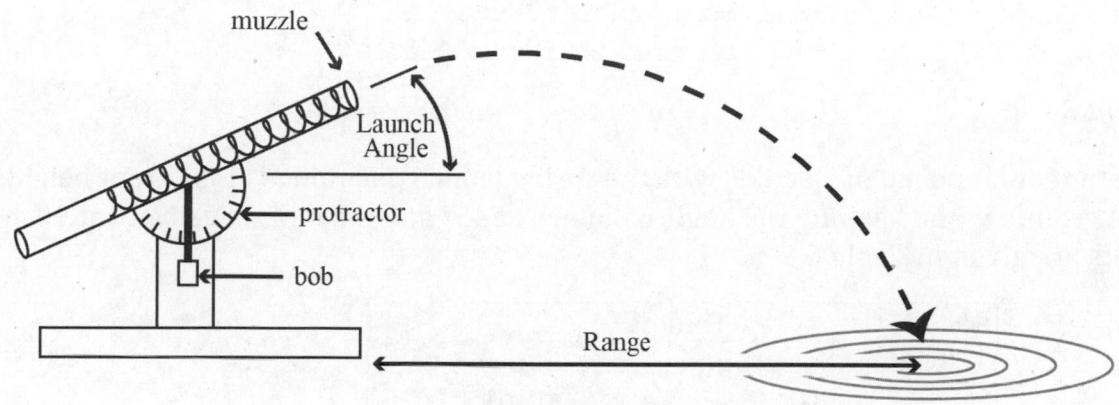

Figure 3

Experiment 1

The student launched the projectile at various angles, using the protractor to measure the angle degree, while the muzzle velocity of the projectile was held constant at 10.0 meters per second (m/s). Both the spring launch and the point of impact of the projectile were at ground level. Range was measured horizontally from a point at ground level directly below the spring launch to the point of impact at ground level. The results are given in Table 4.

Table 4	
Launch Angle (degrees above horizontal)	Range (m)
10°	3.5
20°	6.6
30°	8.8
45°	10.2
60°	8.8
70°	6.6
80°	3.5

Experiment 2

In a second experiment, the student varied the muzzle velocity while keeping the angle of launch constant at 45°. The results are given in Table 5.

Table 5	
Muzzle Velocity (m/s)	Range (m)
10	10.2
15	23.0
20	40.8
25	63.8

Experiment 3

The student launched projectiles with the spring launch positioned at different heights above the ground while keeping the angle of launch at 45° and the muzzle velocity at 10 m/s. The results are given in Table 6.

Table 6	
Height above ground (m)	Range (m)
1	11.1
2	11.9
3	12.6
4	13.3

23. Which of the following is a controlled variable in Experiment 1?

A. Launch angle only
B. Range of projectile only
C. Muzzle velocity only
D. Launch angle and muzzle velocity

24. In which experiment was the height of the spring launch varied?

F. Experiment 1 only
G. Experiment 3 only
H. Experiments 1 and 2 only
J. Experiments 2 and 3 only

25. According to Table 4, the launch angle that produces the greatest range is:

A. 10°.
B. 45°.
C. 60°.
D. 80°.

26. The results of Experiment 2 support which of the following conclusions?

   F. The greater the muzzle velocity, the less the range.
   G. Varying muzzle velocity has no effect on range.
   H. Doubling the muzzle velocity doubles the range.
   J. The greater the muzzle velocity, the greater the range.

27. Experiment 3 was designed to determine whether changes in:

   A. the position of the spring launch affect range.
   B. range affect the position of the spring launch.
   C. maximum height of the trajectory affect muzzle velocity.
   D. muzzle velocity affect the height of the projectile.

28. According to the information provided, the trajectory is the:

   F. distance between the launch site and the point of impact.
   G. angle at which the projectile strikes the ground.
   H. path followed by the projectile after launch.
   J. maximum height of the projectile attained during flight.

29. Which of the following is a controlled variable in Experiment 2?

   A. Muzzle velocity only
   B. Position of the spring launch only
   C. Launch angle only
   D. Position of the spring launch and launch angle

30. In Experiment 2, the muzzle velocity of the spring launch is measured in:

   F. meters per second.
   G. meters.
   H. degrees.
   J. meters per degree.

31. The results of all three experiments support the conclusion that the maximum range of the projectile is achieved by:

   A. setting the launch angle to 45°, maximizing muzzle velocity, and maximizing the height of the vertical placement of spring launch.
   B. setting the launch angle to 80°, maximizing muzzle velocity, and maximizing the height of the vertical placement of spring launch.
   C. setting the launch angle to 45°, maximizing muzzle velocity, and minimizing the height of the vertical placement of spring launch.
   D. setting the launch angle to 20°, minimizing muzzle velocity, and minimizing the height of the vertical placement of spring launch.

32. In Figure 3, the function of the protractor on the spring launch is to:

   F. control the muzzle velocity.
   G. measure the mass of the projectile.
   H. determine the launch angle.
   J. measure the wind velocity.

Passage VI

The energy, as measured in joules (J), that an object has by virtue of its position with respect to nearby masses is called *gravitational potential energy* (GPE), while energy of motion is called *kinetic energy* (KE). An object falling toward the earth has both gravitational potential energy and kinetic energy. An object's *total mechanical energy* (TME) is the sum of GPE and KE. Objects in motion lose total mechanical energy because of friction.

Experiment 1

A steel marble weighing 1 kilogram (kg) was placed on a track and allowed to roll as shown in Figure 4. A series of photogates (timing devices useful for measuring events which happen faster than can be timed by hand) measured the speed of the marble at various positions on the track. The speed of the marble was used to calculate its kinetic energy. The results are given in Table 7.

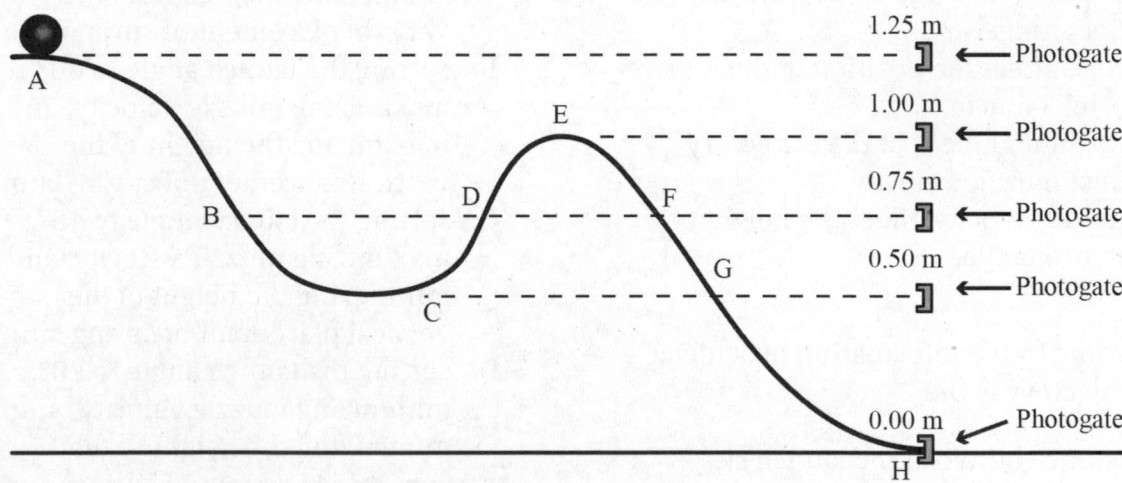

Figure 4

	Table 7			
	Height (m)	GPE (J)	KE (J)	TME (J)
A	1.25	12.5	0.0	12.5
B	0.75	7.5	4.8	12.3
C	0.50	5.0	7.2	12.2
D	0.75	7.5	4.5	12.0
E	1.00	10.0	1.9	11.9
F	0.75	7.5	4.3	11.8
G	0.50	5.0	7.2	12.2
H	0.00	0.0	11.5	11.5

Experiment 2

Students constructed a pendulum by hanging a 1 kg mass ("pendulum bob") from the end of a cord 2 meters long. The bob was pulled to the side and released at a height of 0.2 meters.

The students allowed the bob to swing through ten cycles before stopping its motion. Using a photogate and timer, the students determined the speed of the bob at five selected points along its path for both the first (Figure 5) and tenth swings.

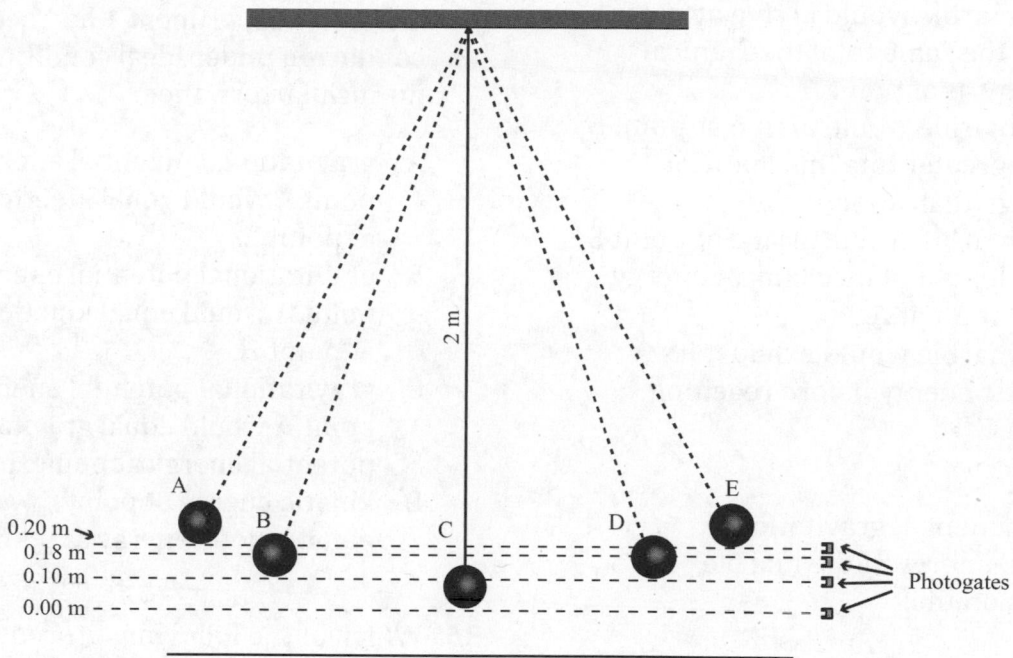

Figure 5

Note: Points A and E are the end points of the swing of the pendulum where height (h) has its maximum value. As the pendulum continues to swing, h values for points A and E will decrease because of frictional effects.

	Height (m)	GPE (J)	KE (J)	TME (J)
Table 8				
First Swing of Pendulum				
A	0.2	1.96	0.00	1.96
B	0.1	0.98	0.98	1.96
C	0.0	0.00	1.96	1.96
D	0.1	0.98	0.98	1.96
E	0.2	1.96	0.00	1.96
Tenth Swing of Pendulum				
	Height (m)	GPE (J)	KE (J)	TME (J)
A	0.18	1.76	0.00	1.76
B	0.10	0.98	0.78	1.76
C	0.00	0.00	1.76	1.76
D	0.10	0.98	0.78	1.76
E	0.18	1.76	0.00	1.76

33. In Experiment 1, if point E of the track were raised to the same height as point A, what would be the probable result?

    A. The marble would arrive at point E with the same total mechanical energy as at point A.
    B. The marble would arrive at point E with greater total mechanical energy than at point A.
    C. The marble would arrive at point E with less total mechanical energy than at point A.
    D. The marble would exhaust its kinetic energy before reaching point E.

34. In Experiment 1, gravitational potential energy of the marble depends on the:

    F. height of the marble on the track at any given point.
    G. speed of the marble at any given point along the track.
    H. horizontal distance between the points along the track.
    J. physical composition of the marble used.

35. In Experiment 1, total mechanical energy of the system is lost to air resistance, friction between the marble and the surface of the track, and other factors. If Experiment 1 had been conducted under ideal conditions with no such factors, then:

    A. gravitational potential energy at point A would equal kinetic energy at point E.
    B. gravitational potential energy at point A would equal kinetic energy at point H.
    C. gravitational potential energy at point A would equal gravitational potential energy at point H.
    D. kinetic energy at point C would equal kinetic energy at point H.

36. Which of the following procedures could be used to determine whether friction might have affected the results of Experiment 1?

    F. Recalculate and verify the results using the data already collected.
    G. Move the photogate at height 1.25 meters to 0.25 meters and run the experiment again.
    H. Coat the surface of the track with a sticky substance and conduct the experiment again.
    J. Add horizontal track to point H and run the experiment again to measure kinetic energy at the new end.

37. In Experiment 2, the height for points A and E is less for the tenth swing of the bob than the first swing of the bob. This is because the:

   A. 2 meter cord holding the 1 kilogram weight contracted.

   B. system lost total mechanical energy due to friction.

   C. mass of the 1 kilogram bob increased.

   D. time needed to complete the swing of the bob increased.

38. The students who conducted Experiment 2 want to determine how many swings would be completed before the system loses one-half of its original total mechanical energy. Which of the following changes to the experimental conditions would allow them to collect this data?

   F. Substitute a 2 kilogram bob for the 1 kilogram bob.

   G. Lengthen the cord from 2 meters to 4 meters.

   H. Increase the release height from 0.2 meters to 0.4 meters.

   J. Continue the experiment until the bob reaches a height of 0.1 m at points A and E.

39. According to Table 8, the pendulum system had its greatest kinetic energy at point:

   A. B on the first swing of the bob.

   B. C on the first swing of the bob.

   C. C on the tenth swing of the bob.

   D. E on the tenth swing of the bob.

40. The steel marble in Experiment 1 and the pendulum bob in Experiment 2:

   F. both gain kinetic energy as they move from point A to point B.

   G. both lose kinetic energy as they move from point A to point B.

   H. gain potential energy as they move from point A to point B.

   J. gain total mechanical energy as they move from point A to point B.

41. In Experiment 1, the total mechanical energy at point C is:

   A. equal to potential energy at point C.

   B. equal to kinetic energy at point C.

   C. less than potential energy at point C.

   D. greater than kinetic energy at point C.

42. The results of Table 7 and Table 8 best support the conclusion that:

   F. kinetic energy in a system is constant.

   G. potential energy in a system is constant.

   H. systems lose total mechanical energy due to frictional effects.

   J. a decrease in potential energy in a system is accompanied by a decrease in kinetic energy.

Passage VII

A Hertzsprung-Russell (H-R) diagram is used to plot the luminosity (or true brightness) of a star versus its surface temperature. Luminosity is typically expressed in relation to the luminosity of the Sun (solar units). For example, a star with a luminosity of 2 solar units would emit twice as much energy as does our Sun. Surface temperatures of stars are expressed in kelvins (K).

Stars plotted on an H-R diagram generally fall into four main regions: main sequence, red giants, supergiants, and white dwarfs. All main sequence stars (which comprise approximately 90% of all stars) undergo hydrogen fusion in their cores. The heat and pressure created by fusion prevent gravitational forces acting inward from crushing the star.

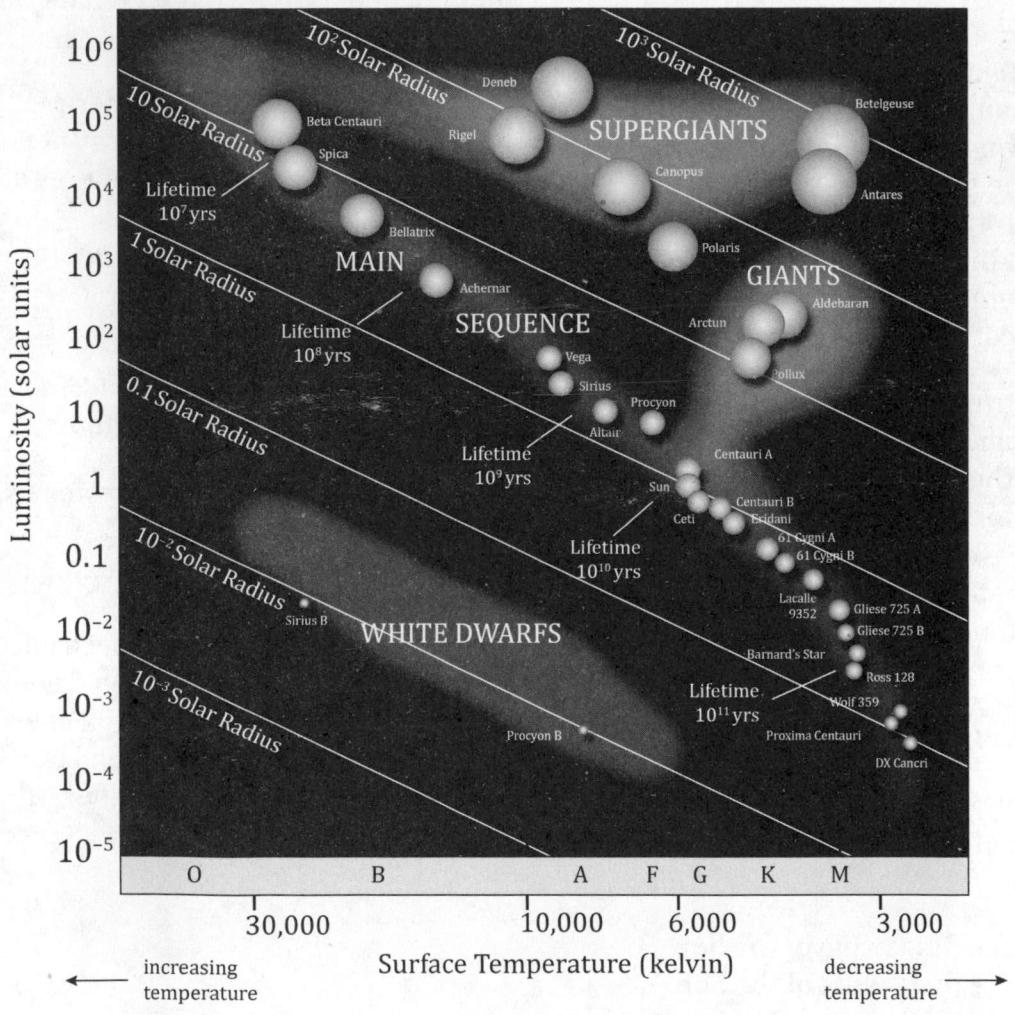

Figure 6

The evolutionary fate of main sequence stars depends on their mass. When mid-mass main sequence stars, such as the Sun, run out of hydrogen in their cores, other fusion reactions occur; and the stars expand to become red giants. When fusion stops altogether, after a brief transitory phase called a planetary nebula, the cores of mid-size stars remain as planet-sized, very hot objects called white dwarfs. From birth to death, mid-mass stars exist on the order of billions of years.

Main sequence stars with much more mass than the Sun appear in the upper left of the H-R diagram. When hydrogen fusion ceases in the cores of these rare stars, other fusion reactions support the star, and they evolve into red supergiants. Eventually, when fusion reactions in their cores cease altogether, gravity begins to crush the stars and runaway thermonuclear reactions cause the outer layers to explode in an event called a supernova. The spent cores of these stars become either neutron stars or black holes. Neither neutron stars nor black holes appear on the H-R diagram. Large mass stars exist for the shortest amount of time—just millions of years—because they burn through their fuel quickly.

Finally, the majority of all main sequence stars have much less mass than the Sun. Fusion reactions in their cores take place at a much slower rate. In fact, these stars will remain on the main sequence for trillions of years. Since the universe is only 13.8 billion years old, not a single low-mass star has yet to evolve off the main sequence.

The diagram below shows the Sun's future evolutionary journey on the H-R diagram.

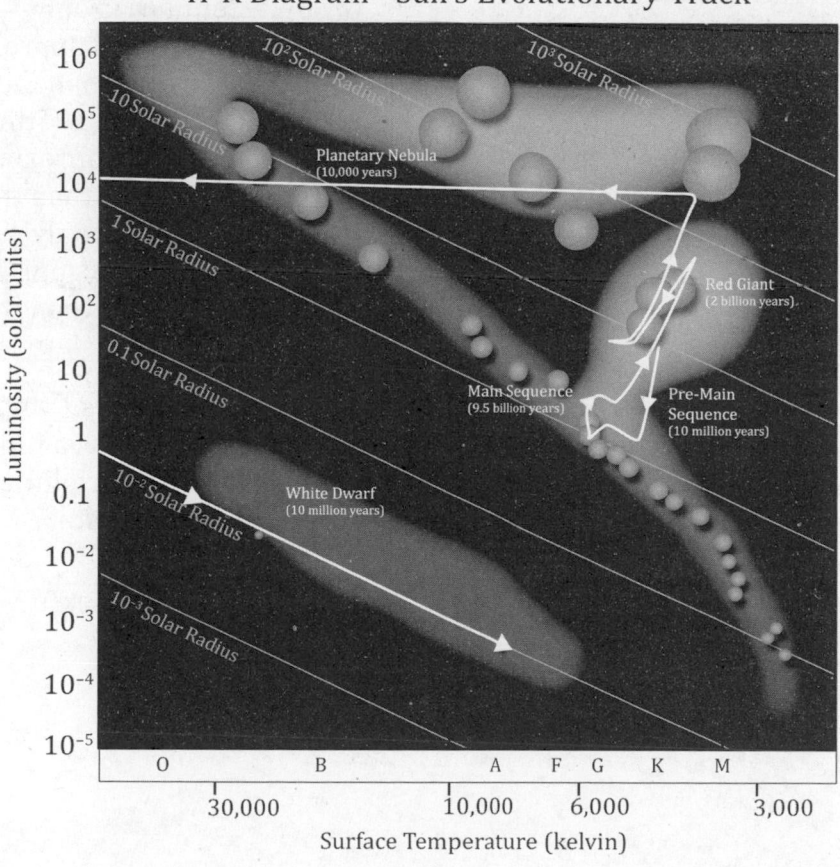

H-R Diagram - Sun's Evolutionary Track

Figure 7

43. According to the information provided, the Sun is currently a:

   A. main sequence star.
   B. red giant.
   C. supergiant.
   D. white dwarf.

44. According to the information provided in the passage, when the fusion reactions in a mid-mass star cease altogether, it becomes a:

   F. red giant.
   G. supergiant.
   H. white dwarf.
   J. neutron star.

45. According to the information provided, what is the current surface temperature of the Sun?

   A. 20,000 K
   B. 8,300 K
   C. 5,800 K
   D. 3,400 K

46. According to Figure 7, the Sun's total time on the main sequence will be about:

   F. 9.5 million years.
   G. 11.5 million years.
   H. 9.5 billion years.
   J. 11.5 billion years.

47. According to Figure 6, which of the following statements is true?

   A. The star Rigel is cooler and brighter than Aldebaran.
   B. Betelgeuse is cooler and brighter than Sirius.
   C. Proxima Centauri is brighter and hotter than the Sun.
   D. Sirius is dimmer and hotter than the Sun.

48. According to Figure 6, which statement contains a correct comparison of Beta Centauri and the Sun?

   F. Beta Centauri is 10^2 times more luminous and approximately 2,000 K hotter than the Sun.
   G. Beta Centauri is only $1/10^2$ times as luminous and approximately 2,000 K cooler than the Sun.
   H. Beta Centauri is 10^5 times more luminous and approximately 20,000 K hotter than the Sun.
   J. Beta Centauri is only $1/10^5$ times as luminous and approximately 20,000 K cooler than the Sun.

49. According to Figures 6 and 7, the Sun's luminosity when it is a red giant will closely match the brightness of what current prominent star?

   A. Antares
   B. Betelgeuse
   C. Aldebaran
   D. Barnard's star

50. According to Figure 7, how does the luminosity and surface temperature of the present Sun compare to its luminosity and surface temperature when it evolves into a white dwarf?

F. The white dwarf is hotter and brighter than the current Sun.
G. The white dwarf is hotter and dimmer than the current Sun.
H. The white dwarf is cooler and brighter than the current Sun.
J. The white dwarf is cooler and dimmer than the current Sun.

51. According to the information provided, most stars in the universe are:

A. red giants.
B. main sequence stars with about the same mass as the Sun.
C. main sequence stars with more mass than the Sun.
D. main sequence stars with less mass than the Sun.

Passage VIII

When an object from space strikes the surface of a solid planet or moon, the result is a crater. The edges of the crater are called the rim of the crater. Surrounding the crater is material called ejecta, which is thrown from the point of impact by the impactor (object striking the surface) (see Figure 8). The size of the crater is a function of both the velocity and mass of the impactor.

Cross-Sectional View of a Crater

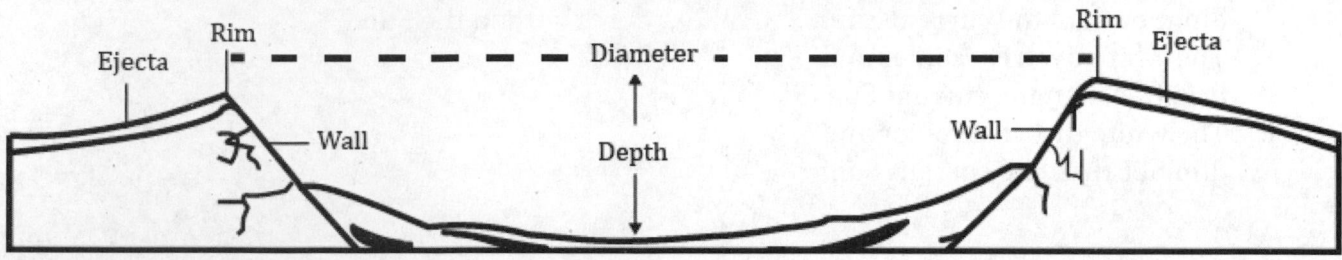

Figure 8

A team of students conducted experiments to determine how mass and velocity affect crater formation.

Experiment 1

The students filled a box with sand. They then dropped smooth spheres made of different materials but with identical diameters into the box. The objects were all dropped from a height of 1.0 meter and therefore had approximately the same velocity upon impact with the sand. The students measured the diameter of each crater formed in the sand from rim to rim. The students conducted multiple trials for each sphere, leveling the sand after each trial, and recorded the data in Table 9.

Table 9					
Material/ Mass of Impactor (grams)	Crater Diameter (centimeters)				
	Trial 1	Trial 2	Trial 3	Trial 4	Average
Cork (1.8 g)	3.8	3.7	3.9	3.8	3.8
Wood (5.7 g)	5.1	5.1	5.4	4.7	5.1
Glass (21.4 g)	6.2	6.3	6.1	6.5	6.3
Aluminum (27.1 g)	6.5	6.1	6.5	6.4	6.4
Steel (64.1 g)	8.0	8.6	8.5	8.6	8.4

Experiment 2

To determine how velocity affects crater diameter, the students used only the steel sphere, dropped from four different heights. The velocity of the sphere at each height was determined using the equation:

$$v = \sqrt{2gh}$$

Equation 1

where *v* is the velocity of the impactor in meters/second as it hits the sand, *g* is the acceleration due to gravity (9.8 meters/second-squared) and *h* is the drop height in meters. The data from this experiment are recorded in Table 10.

Table 10						
Drop Height (meters)	Velocity of Impactor (meters/second)	Crater Diameter (centimeters)				
		Trial 1	Trial 2	Trial 3	Trial 4	Average
0.5	3.1	5.4	5.6	5.5	5.5	5.5
1.0	4.4	8.4	8.6	8.1	8.5	8.4
1.5	5.4	10.1	9.3	9.9	9.9	9.8
2.0	6.3	11.0	11.3	10.9	10.9	11.0

52. According to the passage, ejecta is:

    F. the composition of the impactor.
    G. material thrown out of the impact site.
    H. the top of the crater wall.
    J. a solid planet or moon.

53. In Experiment 1, the masses of the spherical objects were measured in:

    A. meters.
    B. grams.
    C. centimeters.
    D. meters/second.

54. In Experiment 2, the impact velocity of the spherical object dropped for each trial was reported in:

    F. centimeters.
    G. meters.
    H. meters/second.
    J. meters/second-squared.

55. Which of the following is the independent variable in Experiment 1?

    A. Mass of the impactor
    B. Initial velocity of the impactor
    C. Diameter of the impactor
    D. Drop height of the impactor

56. Which of the following is the independent variable in Experiment 2?

    F. Material of the impactor
    G. Mass of the impactor
    H. Drop height of the impactor
    J. Acceleration of the impactor

57. In Experiment 2, which trial for a drop height of 2 meters produced the crater with the greatest diameter?

    A. Trial 1
    B. Trial 2
    C. Trial 3
    D. Trial 4

58. According to the information provided, the velocity of the impactor as it hit the sand was a function of:

F. drop height only.

G. acceleration due to gravity only.

H. drop height and acceleration due to gravity.

J. mass and drop height.

59. Which of the following graphs represents the relationship between the mass of the impactor and the average crater diameter in Experiment 1?

A.

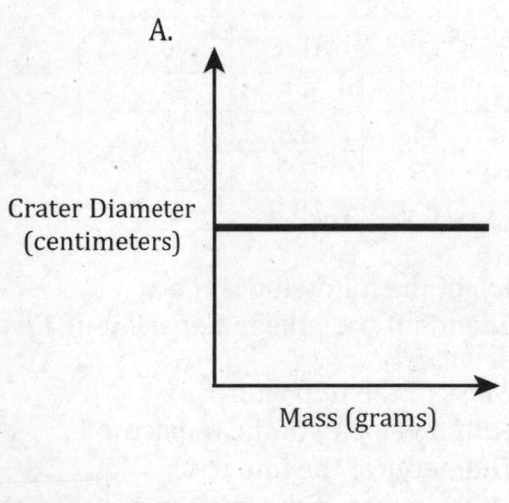

B.

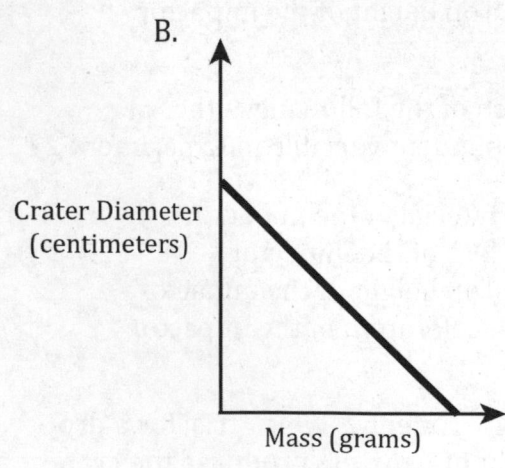

C.

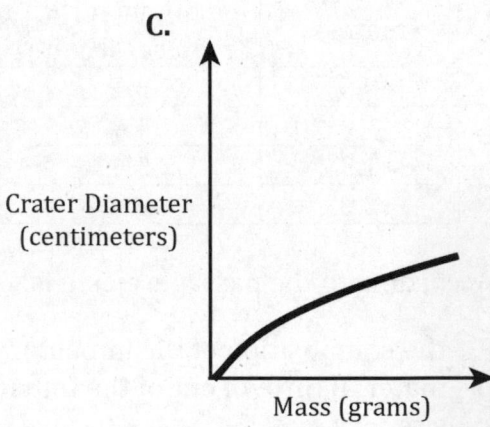

D.

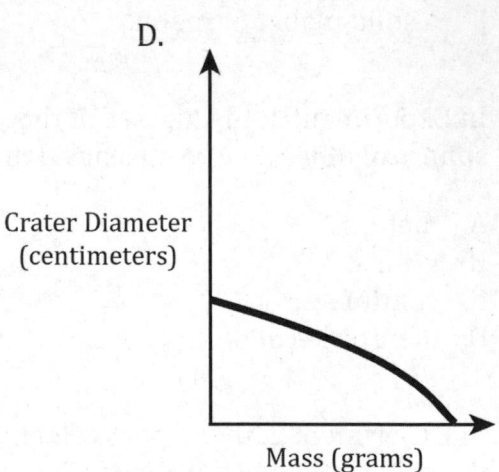

60. If Experiment 2 were conducted on the moon where the acceleration due to gravity is approximately 1.6 meters/second-squared, the most likely difference in the result would be:

    F. a crater of smaller diameter.
    G. a crater of larger diameter.
    H. a crater of similar diameter.
    J. greater velocity on impact.

Passage IX

A team of safety experts conducted experiments to determine the distance required to stop a vehicle traveling at different speeds. The experiments were all conducted along a stretch of flat, straight, paved roadway. A series of traffic signals was set up near the middle of the roadway. At the start of each experiment, the vehicle accelerated until it reached a pre-determined speed. The driver then continued traveling at that speed until one of the traffic signals was triggered. (The timing for the trigger was not known by the driver).

A driver always takes a small amount of time to react to seeing a traffic light before applying the brakes. The distance the car traveled during this interval is called the reaction distance. In the experiments, the team measured the reaction distance by recording the position of the vehicle when the traffic light was triggered and the position of the car when a sensor attached to the brakes indicated that the brakes had been applied. The team measured the additional distance the car traveled until it reached a full stop.

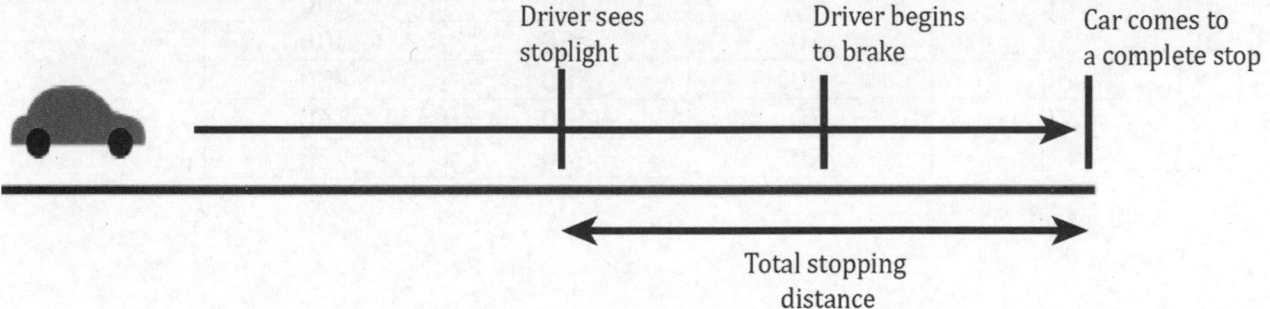

Figure 9

The team conducted seven runs on dry pavement and recorded their findings in Table 11.

Table 11: Stopping Distance on Dry Pavement			
Initial Speed (miles per hour)	Reaction Distance (feet)	Braking Distance (feet)	Total Stopping Distance (feet)
20	20	20	40
30	30	45	75
40	40	80	120
50	50	125	175
60	60	180	240
70	70	245	315
80	80	320	400

Next, the team soaked the entire course with ordinary water using a fire hose. They conducted seven runs on wet pavement and recorded their findings in Table 12.

Table 12: Stopping Distance on Wet Pavement			
Initial Speed (miles per hour)	Reaction Distance (feet)	Braking Distance (feet)	Total Stopping Distance (feet)
20	20	40	60
30	30	90	120
40	40	160	200
50	50	250	300
60	60	360	420
70	70	490	560
80	80	640	720

61. According to the description of the experiment, total stopping distance is the sum of:

A. reaction distance and braking distance.
B. initial speed and reaction distance.
C. initial speed and braking distance.
D. reaction distance, braking distance, and initial speed.

62. According to the description of the experiment, the sensor was attached to the brakes to mark the point at which:

F. the traffic signal was triggered.
G. the driver applied the brakes.
H. the vehicle came to a full stop.
J. the vehicle reached a constant speed.

63. In Tables 11 and 12, the initial speed of the vehicle is given in the tables in units of:

A. miles.
B. meters per second.
C. hours.
D. miles per hour.

64. The braking distance for the vehicle traveling at 40 miles per hour on dry pavement was:

F. 40 feet.
G. 80 feet.
H. 120 feet.
J. 160 feet.

65. The Total Stopping Distance for the vehicle traveling at 60 miles per hour on wet pavement was:

A. 60 feet
B. 240 feet
C. 360 feet
D. 420 feet

66. Which of the following distances recorded by the team was the greatest?

F. Braking distance at 60 miles per hour on dry pavement
G. Reaction distance at 60 miles per hour on wet pavement
H. Total stopping distance at 20 miles per hour on dry pavement
J. Braking distance at 80 miles per hour on wet pavement

67. Which of the following measurements was not affected by the condition of the pavement (dry versus wet)?

A. Total stopping distance
B. Braking distance
C. Reaction distance
D. Length of skid marks

68. Which of the following graphs represents the relationship between total stopping distance on dry pavement and initial speed?

F.

Total Stopping
Distance on Dry
Pavement
(feet)

Initial Speed
(miles per hour)

H.

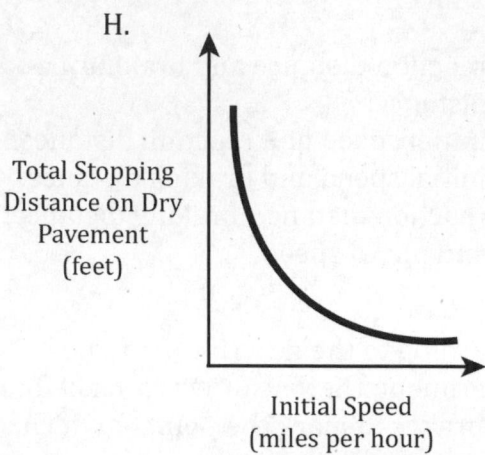

Total Stopping
Distance on Dry
Pavement
(feet)

Initial Speed
(miles per hour)

G.

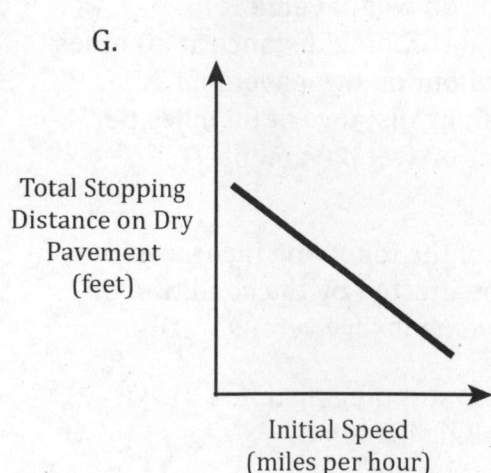

Total Stopping
Distance on Dry
Pavement
(feet)

Initial Speed
(miles per hour)

J.

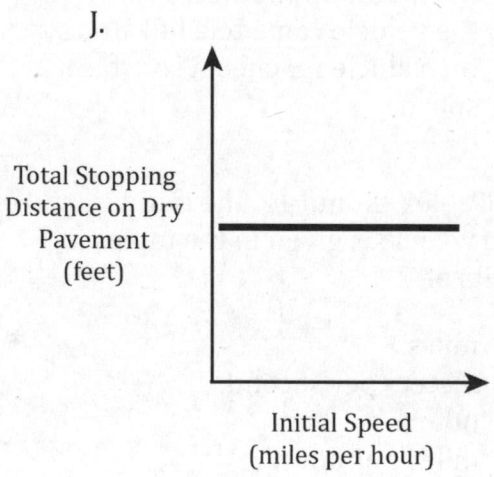

Total Stopping
Distance on Dry
Pavement
(feet)

Initial Speed
(miles per hour)

69. The timing for triggering the traffic light was unknown to the driver. It can be inferred that this step was taken in order to:

A. increase the total stopping distance.
B. equalize initial speed from run to run.
C. prevent the driver from anticipating when to brake.
D. ensure that no signal wore out prematurely.

70. Upon reviewing the results of the experiments, the team realized that sometimes, after the sensor indicated application of the brakes, the driver did not immediately fully apply the brakes (in order to avoid skidding). This delay would raise doubts about the accuracy of which data?

F. Initial speed
G. Reaction distance
H. Braking distance
J. Final speed

Passage X

The ocean is salty because of the gradual concentration of dissolved chemicals eroded from Earth's crust and washed into the ocean. Solid and gaseous ejections from volcanoes, suspended particles swept to the ocean from the land by onshore winds, and materials dissolved from sediments deposited on the ocean floor also contribute salts.

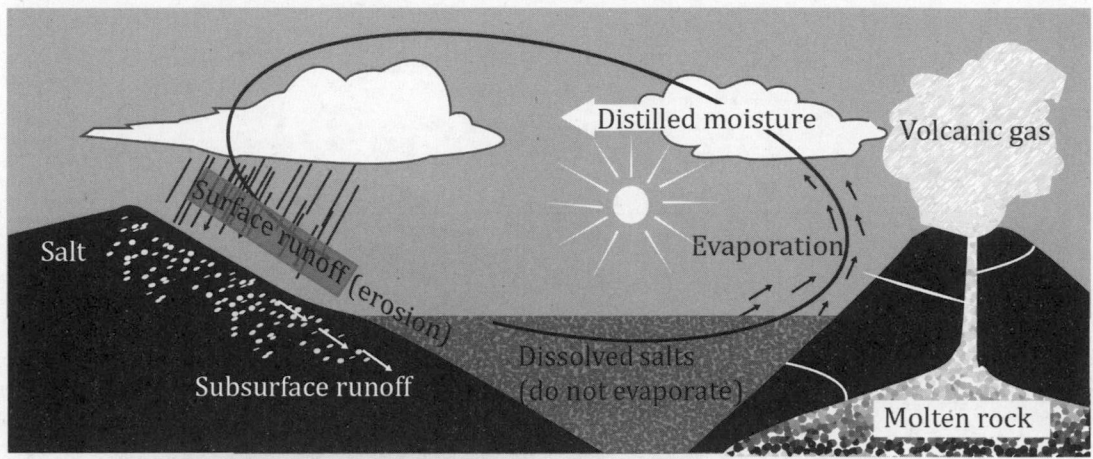

Figure 10

Salts become concentrated in the ocean because the Sun's heat distills or vaporizes almost pure water from the surface of the ocean, leaving the salts behind. In the hydrologic cycle (see Figure 10), water vapor rises from the ocean surface and is carried landward by the winds. When the vapor collides with a colder mass of air, it condenses (changes from a gas to a liquid) and falls to Earth as rain. The rain runs off into streams which in turn transport water to the ocean. Evaporation from both the land and the ocean again causes water to return to the atmosphere as vapor and the cycle starts anew. Because salts are continually added to the ocean basic and do not evaporate, the salinity of ocean water has increased over time.

Oceanographers report salinity (total salt content) and the concentrations of individual chemical constituents in seawater— for example, chloride, sodium, or magnesium—in parts per thousand (‰). That is, a salinity of 35 ‰ means 35 units of salt per 1,000 units of seawater. Similarly, a sodium concentration of 10 ‰ means 10 units of sodium per 1,000 units of seawater.

The salinity of surface seawater varies from one location to another in the world's oceans. The average salinity of surface seawater worldwide is 35 ‰, a value found at the equator. Maximum salinity values are found near the Tropics of Cancer and Capricorn (23.5° N and 23.5° S, respectively). As shown in Figure 11, at these locations, evaporation rates are higher and precipitation amounts are less than those found at the equator. High winds and high temperatures are responsible for the higher evaporation rates at these latitudes.

At still higher latitudes (45° N and 45° S), surface salinity values lower than average are found (34–34.5 ‰) because cooler temperatures result in much lower evaporation rates. Figure 11 does not show salinity values for polar waters (found at latitudes 60° N and 60° S and all locations poleward). At these locations, surface salinity values undergo significant seasonal variations. Values are higher in the autumn as sea ice forms (a process that removes water from seawater). In the spring, the melting of sea ice lowers salinity values as freshwater is once again added to the oceans (see Figure 11).

Longitudinal Variations in Evaporation and Precipitation

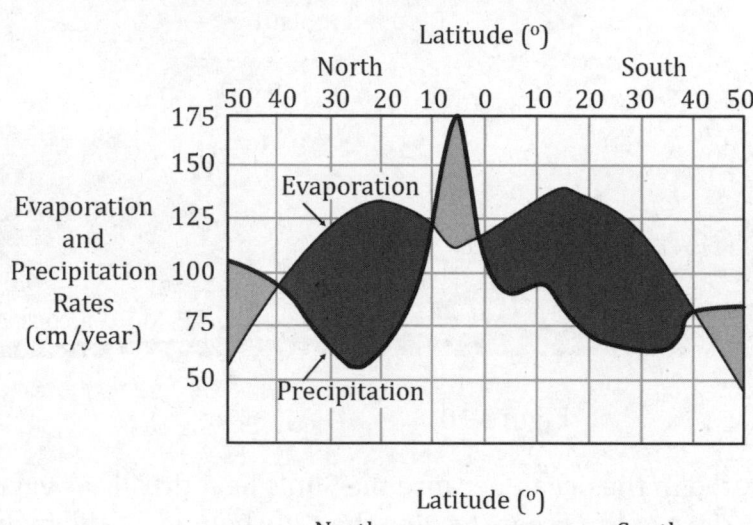

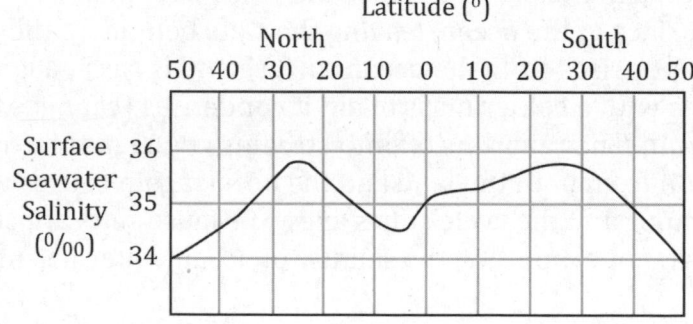

Figure 11

| Table 13: Principal Constituents of Seawater ||
Chemical Constituent	Concentration (parts per thousand)
Calcium (Ca)	0.419
Magnesium (Mg)	1.304
Sodium (Na)	10.710
Potassium (K)	0.390
Bicarbonate (HCO_3)	0.146
Sulfate (SO_4)	2.690
Chloride (Cl)	19.350
Bromide (Br)	0.070
Total dissolved solids (salinity)	35.079

Table 14: Comparison between Seawater and River Water		
Chemical Constituent	Percentage of Total Salt Content	
	Seawater	River Water
Silica (SiO_2)	—	14.51
Iron (Fe)	—	0.74
Calcium (Ca)	1.19	16.62
Magnesium (Mg)	3.72	4.54
Sodium (Na)	30.53	6.98
Potassium (K)	1.11	2.55
Bicarbonate (HCO_3)	0.42	31.90
Sulfate (SO_4)	7.67	12.41
Chloride (Cl)	55.16	8.64
Nitrate (NO_3)	—	1.11
Bromide (Br)	0.20	—
Total	100.00	100.00

71. According to the provided information, which of the following contribute salts that make the ocean saline?

  I. Surface run-off
 II. Volcanic action
III. Subsurface run-off

A. I only
B. II only
C. I and III only
D. I, II, and III

72. According to the passage, the symbol "‰" means parts per:

F. hundred.
G. thousand.
H. one-hundredth.
J. one-thousandth.

73. According to the passage, surface seawater in the Tropics of Cancer and Capricorn have a greater than average salinity because:

A. evaporation is greater and precipitation is less than at the equator.
B. both evaporation and precipitation are greater than at the equator.
C. both evaporation and precipitation are less than at the equator.
D. evaporation is less and precipitation is greater than at the equator.

74. According to the passage, surface seawater at the equator has a salinity:

F. greater than the worldwide average.
G. less than the worldwide average.
H. equal to the worldwide average.
J. that cannot be measured.

75. According to Figure 11, from the equator southward, the salinity of the surface seawater:

A. first decreases, then increases.
B. first increases, then decreases.
C. decreases at a constant rate.
D. remains approximately the same.

76. According to the provided information, average surface seawater salinity is approximately the same at:

F. the equator and the poles.
G. the Tropics of Cancer and Capricorn.
H. latitude 40° N and 25° S.
J. the equator and latitude 50° S.

77. Which of the following chemicals is found at the highest concentration in seawater?

A. Calcium
B. Magnesium
C. Sodium
D. Sulfate

78. Which of the following chemicals comprises a greater percentage of total salt content in river water than in sea water?

F. Sodium
G. Chloride
H. Bicarbonate
J. Bromide

79. The shaded areas of the top graph in Figure 11 indicate the:

A. difference between precipitation and evaporation.
B. excess of evaporation over precipitation.
C. difference in salinies of evaporation and precipitation.
D. overlap in the chemical composition of evaporation and precipitation.

80. The data in Figure 11 supports which of the following conclusions?

F. A high evaporation rate and low precipitation are associated with high surface seawater salinity.
G. A high evaporation rate and low precipitation are associated with low surface seawater salinity.
H. The greatest surface seawater salinity is recorded at latitude 5° N.
J. The lowest surface seawater salinity is recorded at latitude 25° N.

81. According to Figure 11, the latitude with equal evaporation and precipitation rates having the lowest surface seawater salinity is:

A. 40° N.
B. 10° N.
C. 2° N.
D. 40° S.

82. According to Table 14, which of the following chemical constituents is present in seawater but not in river water?

F. SiO_2
G. Fe
H. NO_3
J. Br

ADVANCED

The Basic and Intermediate chapters of this science skills review introduced two types of science passages—passages featuring scientific data and passages featuring scientific experiments. The third type of scientific passage you will encounter on standardized tests features conflicting viewpoints, such as an exchange between two scientists with differing views or an explanation of two scientific theories.

Example*:*

In the United States, there are millions of cases of food poisoning reported each year. Food poisoning is due to deadly bacteria, such as *Salmonella*. Since the mid-1980s, the United States Food and Drug Administration has approved irradiation of a variety of foods. Food is irradiated to destroy the harmful bacteria. During irradiation, gamma rays passing through food break chemical bonds among atoms and destroy the genetic material of the bacteria, which prevents them from reproducing. Although the irradiation of food is becoming more widespread, the practice continues to be a controversial topic.

Select an alternative method to test a hypothesis.

Evaluate the precision and/or accuracy of an experiment or model.

Identify key issues or assumptions in a model.

Determine whether information supports or contradicts a hypothesis or conclusion.

Compare and contrast models.

Determine the effect of new information on a model.

BASIC

INTERMEDIATE

ADVANCED

Viewpoint 1

Proper preparation of food kills harmful bacteria in or on food. This means that irradiation is not necessary. According to some scientists, there is evidence that irradiation lessens the nutritional value of food by causing the loss of vitamins. Foods exposed to gamma rays have lost such vitamins as A, C, and E. One study found that animals that were fed irradiated food lost weight. Some chemicals in the food may be changed, resulting in the production of toxic by-products. While these unidentified toxic substances occur in small amounts, no one is certain what effect they will have as they accumulate in the body over a lifetime of consuming irradiated food.

Viewpoint 2

Food irradiation has significant value in destroying the bacteria that infect the food. Irradiated food has a much longer shelf life than traditionally treated food. Irradiation destroys nutrients but no more than is normally destroyed by cooking food. Food irradiated with 10,000 rads or less of gamma rays show little or no nutrient loss. According to the FDA, food exposed to greater than 10,000 rads exhibits nutrient loss that is generally no more than the loss that occurs in frozen and canned food. FDA scientists also admit that some by-products of the alteration of chemicals in the food are cancer-causing agents. However, they occur in very small amounts in irradiated food. Most of these by-products are identical to naturally occurring food substances.

1. One of the principal differences between the viewpoints concerns:

   A. loss of nutritional value of food caused by irradiation.
   B. the effectiveness of food irradiation in destroying harmful bacteria.
   C. the accumulation of by-products of food irradiation in the body.
   D. the effect of gamma rays on the breakdown of vitamin A.

   Viewpoint 1 states that irradiation lessens the nutritional value of food as demonstrated by weight loss in animals, but Viewpoint 2 states that the effects of irradiation on nutrients are nominal and equivalent to cooking and preservation effects on food. Therefore, (A) is the best choice. (B) and (C) are concerns with which both viewpoints share a common opinion. (D) is mentioned by Viewpoint 1 but not by Viewpoint 2.

2. According to Viewpoint 1:

   F. the by-products of food irradiation are cancer-causing.
   G. the irradiation of food increases the nutritional value of food.
   H. the by-products of food irradiation are identical to naturally occurring food substances.
   J. the irradiation of food lessens the nutritional value of food.

   Viewpoint 1 states that irradiation lessens the nutritional value of food, (J). (F) is wrong because Viewpoint 1 uses the term "toxic" to describe by-products while Viewpoint 2 uses the term "cancer-causing." (G) is wrong because it contradicts Viewpoint 1's position. (H) is wrong because Viewpoint 2 holds this position, not Viewpoint 1.

3. These viewpoints are similar because they both suggest that food irradiation:

   A. is necessary to destroy harmful bacteria in food.
   B. is not necessary to destroy harmful bacteria in food.
   C. can lessen the nutritional value of food.
   D. can improve the nutritional value of food.

   Both viewpoints state that irradiation lessens the nutritional value of food, (C). The distinction that is made between the two viewpoints is as to the amount of loss. Viewpoint 1 suggests the opposite of (A), Viewpoint 2 suggests the opposite of (B), and (D) is wrong because neither viewpoint suggests that irradiation can improve the nutritional value of food.

4.   Which experimental information would NOT support Viewpoint 1?

F.   Food exposed to gamma rays loses much of its vitamins A, C, and E content.
G.   Food exposed to gamma rays does not lose much of its vitamins A, C, and E content.
H.   Toxic by-products of food alteration by gamma rays are accumulated in the body over a period of time.
J.   Irradiated food has a shelf life twice that of non-irradiated food.

Eliminate (F) because it is stated by (and therefore supports) Viewpoint 1. Eliminate (H) because it supports Viewpoint 1. Eliminate (J) because, while it supports Viewpoint 2, it does not necessarily provide information that would not support Viewpoint 1. Therefore, by the process of elimination, (G) is the correct choice.

The following exercise includes all three types of scientific passages— conflicting viewpoints, data, and experiments—at an advanced level.

EXERCISE

DIRECTIONS: Read each of the following passages and answer the accompanying items. You are NOT allowed the use of a calculator. Answers are on page 820.

Passage I

Nuclear reactors release great amounts of nuclear energy through controlled chain reactions. For this reason, nuclear power has been considered a source of abundant energy. Nuclear power, however, poses several problems. The most serious problem is the radioactive waste produced by the use of nuclear energy. The waste is very dangerous and remains so for thousands of years. How and where to dispose of this waste safely is a dilemma that has not been resolved. In 1987, the US Congress authorized the Department of Energy to study Yucca Mountain in the southern desert of Nevada as a place to bury the highly radioactive nuclear fuel rods from nuclear power plants.

Geologist 1

The most feasible and safe method for disposing of highly radioactive material is to store it underground. Yucca Mountain was chosen because it is believed that the rock type under the mountain (comprised of a thick layer of volcanic rock) could keep the radioactive waste isolated for thousands of years. Other factors that make the Yucca mountain region a good candidate as a disposal site include the fact that it is very remote and sparsely populated. Also, there is little rainfall in the area, thus reducing the likelihood of seepage into and out of the disposal area. The last volcanic activity in the area is thought to have occurred several hundred to several thousand years ago. Research conducted in 2002 suggested that the probability of volcanic activity occurring near the Yucca Mountain site during the next 10,000 years is between 1 in 1,000 and 1 in 10,000.

Geologist 2

Burial of radioactive waste is the best disposal method. Yucca Mountain, however, is not the best site because it is hydrologically and geologically active. Burial at this site poses the risk of radioactive materials leaking out and contaminating surrounding soil and ground water. If a leak did occur, ground water contamination would be a major problem. Many of the surrounding cities, including parts of Las Vegas, receive some of their water from the aquifers in the area. The area around Yucca Mountain has numerous faults and even a small volcano nearby. Any significant geological activity could disturb waste containers. If earthquakes or volcanic eruptions occurred, the radioactive material at the site could be carried to the surface, threatening the entire region.

1. According to Geologist 1:

   A. radioactive waste should not be buried underground.
   B. the geologic structure of Yucca Mountain would minimize potential contaminates.
   C. earthquake or volcanic activity is likely to occur near Yucca Mountain.
   D. the radioactive waste should be buried somewhere other than Yucca Mountain.

2. Which of the following would provide the strongest evidence for the position of Geologist 2?

   F. The site is both geologically stable and safe from the entry of water.
   G. Construction at the site has been found to be destructive to animal habitats.
   H. The rock formations of Yucca Mountain will keep the waste sufficiently isolated for thousands of years.
   J. There is a periodic upwelling of ground water at Yucca Mountain.

3. Both geologists agree that:

   A. the radioactive waste should be buried somewhere other than Yucca Mountain.
   B. hydrological and geological activity near Yucca Mountain is minimal.
   C. the best way to store radioactive waste is to bury it underground.
   D. the radioactive waste is likely to leak into ground water.

4. Which of the following would provide the strongest evidence for the position of Geologist 1?

   F. Previous earthquake activity near the Yucca site was minor in nature.
   G. There is a large aquifer underneath Yucca Mountain.
   H. The Yucca Mountain site is affected by 32 known earthquake faults.
   J. The volcanic tuff in the area is riddled with fractures that allow for the passage of water.

Passage II

Many scientists believe that comets form in frigid temperatures at the edge of our solar system or beyond and consist of rocky material, dust, and water ice. This theory is called the dirty snowball theory. According to the dirty snowball theory, a comet is a dense nucleus, about 50 percent to 80 percent of which is water ice, surrounded by a cloud of diffuse material called a coma (see Figure 1). A few comets have highly elliptical orbits that bring them very close to the Sun. As comets approach within a few AU of the sun (an AU or astronomical unit is equal to the mean distance between the Earth and the Sun or about 92,960,000 miles), the surface of the nucleus heats up, and volatile materials boil off carrying along small solid particles that reflect sunlight. Comets develop long tails of luminous material extending for millions of miles from the comet head. The theory, which virtually all astronomers accepted for years, explained the "outgassing" of comets as the effect of heating by the Sun. When a comet moves closer to the Sun, ices in the nucleus "sublimate," or evaporate into space, simultaneously ejecting dusty material held within the ices.

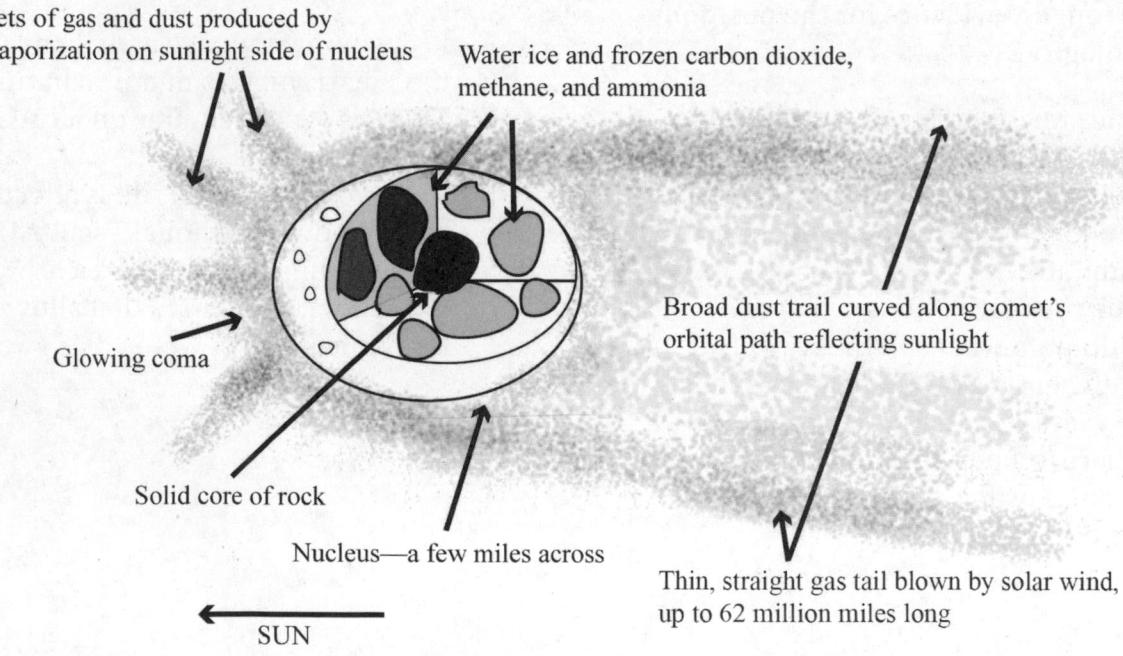

Figure 1

Scientist 1

In 1986, visits to Halley's Comet by the European *Giotto* and Russian *Vega* probes failed to locate surface water and raised the distinct possibility that the nucleus might not be ejecting water into space. In 2001, the *Deep Space 1* craft did a close flyby of the Comet Borrelly and detected no frozen water on the surface. Instead, a spectrum analysis suggests that the surface of the comet is dry. In 2004, the *Stardust* spacecraft passed by Comet Wild 2 and could not find even a trace of water on the surface. In 2005, the NASA *Deep Impact* mission found a smattering of water ice on the surface of comet Tempel 1. The problem is that, to account for the water supposedly being "exhaled" by Tempel 1, the investigators needed 200 times more exposed water ice than was found. So far, it has not been possible to find very much ice in these so-called dirty snowballs.

Scientist 2

The dirty snowball model is still the best theory we have. It is not surprising that very little ice has been observed on the surfaces of comets. Readings are taken when the comets are in the inner solar system would have vaporized any water ices on the surface, due to solar heating, leaving behind a crust of dark dust and rock particles. The majority of a comet's water ice is below the surface, and it is these reservoirs that feed the jets of vaporized water that form the coma.

Scientist 1

If a thin crust of dust hides the water below the surface of the nucleus, one would think that a newly formed crater would be exactly what was needed to stimulate the comet to produce water. In the case of Deep Impact and Comet Tempel 1, the probe crashed into the comet and removed many thousands of tons of material. Prior to impact, the calculated "water" output was 550 pounds per second; and not long after the impact, the calculated output was, once again, 550 pounds per second. So despite the impressive explosion, the hypothesized sub-surface water was never observed.

Scientist 2

The scientific instruments used to study comets do not observe water directly. Instead, they detect the most abundant companion of cometary dust: the "hydroxyl" radical, OH. The coma's water has been broken down by the Sun's ultraviolet radiation, forming the hydroxyl radical along with atomic hydrogen and oxygen. The abundance of OH in a comet nucleus is a direct pointer to the abundance of water held by the nucleus.

Scientist 1

In their analysis of the coma, conventional astronomers begin with the assumption that water is evaporating in the heat of the Sun off the surface ices of the nucleus. They do not observe the water, but cite the effects of solar radiation on assumed water to account for the abundant hydroxyl radical in the coma. The OH is more likely the result of electrical activity. The role of electricity also explains the cometary coma, the spherical envelope around the nucleus. It could not be maintained by gravity because gravity is too weak. As the comet speeds around the Sun, the nucleus continues to hold in place the giant spherical cloud, up to 16 million miles or more in diameter.

5. According to the information provided, the nucleus of a comet is about how large?

   A. A few miles across
   B. 16 million miles across
   C. 62 million miles across
   D. 93 million miles across

6. Scientist 1 and Scientist 2 disagree primarily about whether:

   F. comets are formed at the edge of the solar system.
   G. comets contain significant amounts of frozen water.
   H. comets follow long elliptical orbits that approach the Sun.
   J. the majority of a comet's ice is on the surface.

7. The dirty snowball theory predicts that a comet located in the outer regions of the solar system would:

   A. have no surface ice.
   B. be strongly affected by the Sun's radiation.
   C. not follow an elliptical orbit.
   D. not show evidence of outgassing.

8. According to Scientist 1, the amount of water observed on the surface of Tempel 1 was:

   F. sufficient to explain the water exhaled.
   G. too great to be the source of the exhaled water.
   H. evidence of additional ice trapped in the nucleus.
   J. too small to account for the gases exhaled.

9. According to the information provided, the cloud of diffuse gases that surround the nucleus of a comet is called the:

   A. coma.
   B. gas tail.
   C. core.
   D. dust trail.

10. Which of the following best summarizes the positions of the two scientists on the significance of the hydroxyl radical, OH:

	Scientist 1	Scientist 2
F.	OH cannot be directly observed but is evidence of water in comets.	OH can be directly observed as can the frozen water that is trapped in comets.
G.	OH can be directly observed but is not produced by the breakdown of water in comets.	OH is a pointer to the frozen water contained by comets, but the ice cannot be directly observed.
H.	OH can be directly observed and is the product of the breakdown of water in comets.	OH cannot be directly observed and is not related to the breakdown of ice in comets.
J.	OH can be directly observed as can the presence of ice in the nucleus of a comet.	OH cannot be directly observed, but the water in comets has been directly observed.

11. According to Scientist 1, if Tempel 1 contained significant reservoirs of water, then following the crash of the *Deep Impact* probe, the comet should have produced:

A. no water at all.
B. some water but less than 550 pounds per second.
C. exactly 550 pounds of water per second.
D. more than 550 pounds of water per second.

Passage III

Relative humidity is a measure of how much water vapor is in the air relative to the total amount of water vapor that the air is capable of holding at a given temperature. Heat index is a combined measure of relative humidity and air temperature. The heat index provides a more accurate indication of the perceived—that is, felt—temperature than is provided by the air temperature alone.

A psychrometer is used to monitor heat index and consists of two traditional bulb thermometers: one "dry" and one "wet." The dry-bulb thermometer indicates the ambient temperature (current air temperature without regard to humidity or wind). The wet-bulb thermometer is covered with a wet cloth, or wick, and is exposed to moving air for a period. The moisture from the wick evaporates and cools the bulb, lowering its temperature. Once both bulb temperatures are stable, the readings are recorded. A small difference between bulb temperatures—due to a low evaporation rate on the wet-bulb wick—indicates a high relative humidity. A large difference between bulb temperatures—due to a high evaporation rate on the wet-bulb wick—indicates low relative humidity.

To determine the measure of relative humidity, the intersection of the dry-bulb and wet-bulb temperatures is located on a psychrometric graph (Figure 2). Absolute humidity is the amount of water carried in the air, as measured in grams of water per kilogram of air. The ratio of the absolute humidity to the maximum amount of water that the air can hold gives the relative humidity, expressed as a percent.

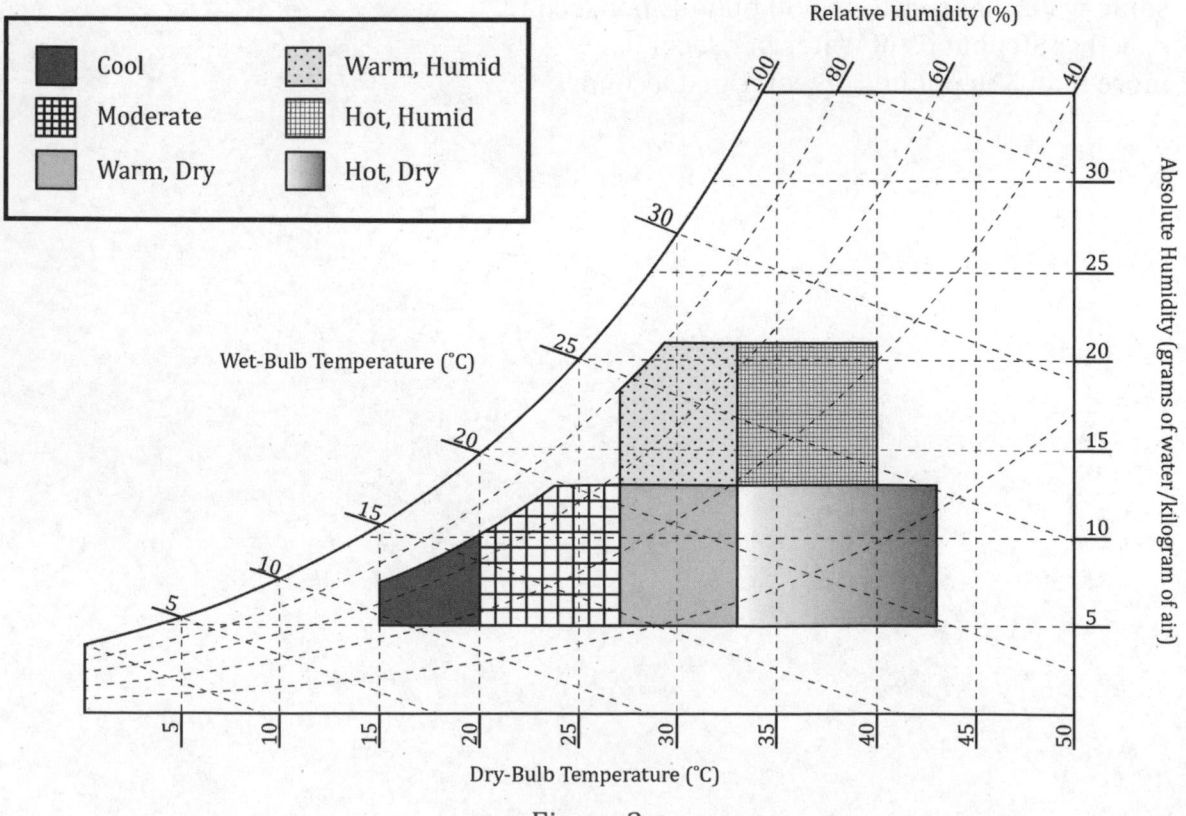

Figure 2

To determine the heat index, the intersection of the dry-bulb temperature and the relative humidity is located on a heat index graph (Figure 3). Certain ranges of heat indices correspond to warning level categories regarding sunstroke and heat exhaustion. There are four main warning levels as indicated in Table 1.

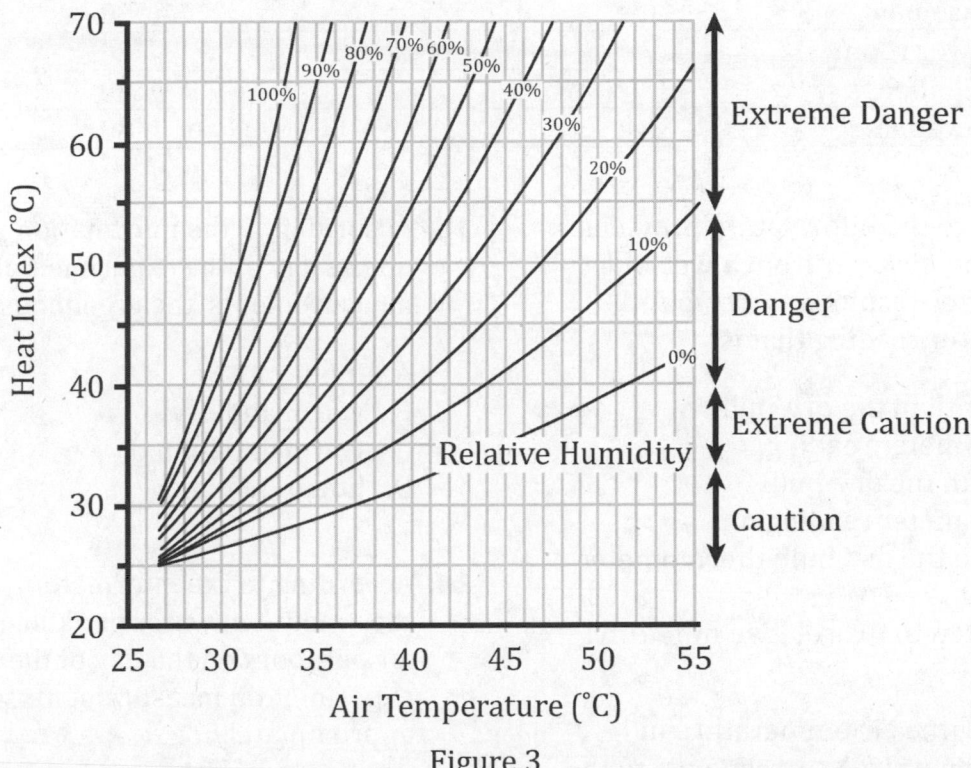

Figure 3

Table 1: Heat Index Warning Categories	
Caution	Fatigue is possible with prolonged exposure and/or physical activity.
Extreme Caution	Sunstroke, heat cramps, and heat exhaustion are possible with prolonged exposure and/or physical activity.
Danger	Sunstroke, heat cramps, and heat exhaustion are likely. Heatstroke is possible with prolonged exposure and/or physical activity.
Extreme Danger	Heatstroke/sunstroke is highly likely with continued exposure.

A group of students used a psychrometer to conduct dry- and wet-bulb measurements at several locations in and around their school. The results are summarized in Table 2.

Table 2: Experimental Measurements			
Measurement Location	Dry-Bulb Temperature (°C)	Wet-Bulb Temperature (°C)	Relative Humidity (%)
Classroom	23	13	30
Basement	16	11	50
Shower room	27	24	80
Greenhouse	32	26	60
Outdoors	30	27	80

12. According to the information provided, evaporation of water from a wet-bulb thermometer results in a wet-bulb thermometer reading that is:

    F. greater than the dry-bulb thermometer reading.
    G. less than the dry-bulb thermometer reading.
    H. equal to the dry-bulb thermometer reading.
    J. unrelated to the relative humidity.

13. In Figure 3, the air temperature in degrees Celsius (°C) corresponds to the:

    A. dry-bulb measurement.
    B. wet-bulb measurement.
    C. difference between the dry- and wet-bulb measurements.
    D. difference between the relative humidity and the absolute humidity.

14. According to the information provided, the heat index depends on:

    F. dry-bulb temperature only.
    G. wet-bulb temperature only.
    H. relative humidity only.
    J. dry-bulb temperature and relative humidity.

15. According to the information provided, on the day of the experimental measurements, the greenhouse was:

    A. moderate.
    B. warm and dry.
    C. warm and humid.
    D. hot and humid.

16. According to the information provided, the amount of water per kilogram of air outdoors on the day of the experimental measurements was approximately:

    F. 10 grams.
    G. 22 grams.
    H. 80 grams.
    J. Cannot be determined from the given information

17. According to the information provided, the heat index outdoors on the day of the experimental measurements was approximately:

    A. 25°C.
    B. 30°C.
    C. 38°C.
    D. 45°C.

18. Based on the information provided, the heat index warning for outdoor activities on the day of the experimental measurements was:

   F. Caution.
   G. Extreme Caution.
   H. Danger.
   J. Extreme Danger.

19. According to Table 2, which of the following two locations had the same relative humidity on the day of the experimental measurements?

   A. The shower room and outdoors
   B. The basement and the greenhouse
   C. The classroom and the basement
   D. The shower room and the greenhouse

20. Located in the students' classroom is a terrarium. If the terrarium habitat is maintained at a relative humidity of 80%, how many percentage points higher is the terrarium's relative humidity than the classroom's relative humidity?

   F. 30%
   G. 40%
   H. 50%
   J. 80%

21. According to Figure 2 and Table 2, which one of the following locations had the greatest absolute humidity on the day of the experimental measurements?

   A. Basement
   B. Shower room
   C. Greenhouse
   D. Outdoors

22. The students determine at the conclusion of their data collection that the wet-bulb thermometer did not properly measure temperature. It gave readings that were approximately 1.5°C lower than the actual temperatures. How did the faulty thermometer affect the relative humidity values reported in Table 2?

   F. No impact
   G. Actual relative humidity values would be higher than reported values
   H. Actual relative humidity values would be lower than the reported values
   J. Some values would be higher, some would be lower

23. The ambient temperature in the classroom drops several degrees during the night, with no change in absolute humidity. Which of the following values would change from the reported values if the students repeated their measurements the following morning?

   A. Dry-bulb and wet-bulb temperatures only
   B. Relative humidity only
   C. Dry-bulb temperature and relative humidity only
   D. Dry-bulb temperature, wet-bulb temperature, and relative humidity

24. After heavy use of the showers, a condensation fog develops in the shower room (indicating a relative humidity of 100%). The dry-bulb temperature in the shower room is 28°C. According to Figure 2, the wet-bulb temperature would be:

   F. 18°C.
   G. 22°C.
   H. 25°C.
   J. 28°C.

25. After heavy use of the showers, a condensation fog develops in the shower room (indicating a relative humidity of 100%). In an attempt to clear the fog, the temperature in the shower room is lowered by 5°C. What will be the consequence of the temperature change?

   A. The fog will dissipate and the relative humidity will drop to approximately 80%.
   B. The fog will dissipate and the relative humidity will drop to approximately 60%.
   C. The fog will dissipate and the relative humidity will drop to approximately 40%.
   D. The fog will thicken.

26. How much more water vapor is air holding on a day when the outside air temperature is 38°C and the heat index is 55°C versus a day when the outside air temperature is 30°C and the heat index is 45°C?

   F. 38°C air is holding approximately 5 g/kg more water vapor
   G. 30°C air is holding approximately 5 g/kg more water vapor
   H. 38°C air is holding approximately 10 g/kg more water vapor
   J. Samples of both air parcels are holding approximately the same amount of water vapor

Passage IV

A charged particle experiences a force when moving through a magnetic field. If a magnet is placed in the vicinity of a current-carrying wire of conducting material, the wire will experience a force due to the interaction between the magnetic field and the charged particles moving through the wire.

To study the interaction between a current-carrying wire and a magnetic field, a group of students conducted a series of experiments using a current balance (Figure 4), in which a current passing through a conducting loop of wire, or current loop, is acted on by the magnetic field produced by a permanent magnet. The current in the loop is produced using a variable power supply connected to the loop. The magnet, with a channel in its center, is placed on a digital electronic scale.

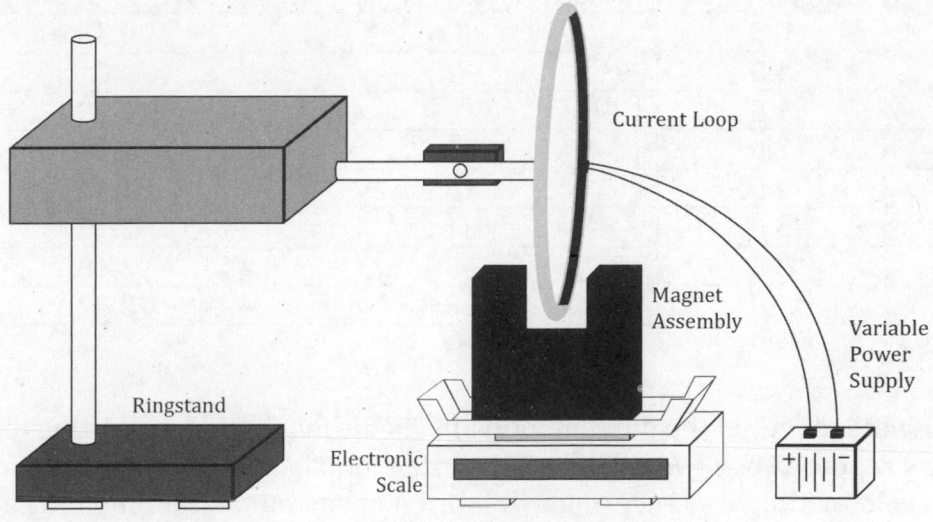

Figure 4

When lowered into the channel of the magnet, the current loop experiences a force due to the magnetic field produced by the magnet, as given by:

$F = ILB$ (Equation 1)

where I is the current in the wire in amperes (A), L is the length of the current loop in meters (m), and B is the magnetic field strength in teslas (1 T = 1 kg/A/s^2). The standard unit of force is the newton (1 N = 1 kg • m/s^2).

Newton's third law of motion, or the law of action-reaction, states that the force on the current loop is equal to the force on the scale. According to Newton's second law of motion, the force on the scale is:

$F = ma$ (Equation 2)

where m is the scale reading in kilograms (kg) and a is the acceleration due to gravity (9.8 m/s^2).

Experiment 1

To demonstrate how currents through the loop are affected by a magnetic force, the students applied different currents to a loop of length 2.4 cm. First, with the magnet in place and no current loop, the scale was zeroed so that scale readings with the current loop in the magnet channel correspond solely to the force acting on the current loop. Then the current loop was placed in the magnet channel without any part of the loop touching the magnet. The power supply was set to 0.5 A and the scale reading was recorded. This was repeated for increased current in steps of 0.5 A up to a maximum of 4.0 A. The students used Newton's second law of motion to calculate the force on the scale and thus the force on the current loop. The results are summarized in Table 3.

Table 3: Experiment 1 Data and Calculations			
Trial	Current, I (A)	Scale Reading, m (10^{-4} kg)	Force, F (10^{-2} N)
1	0.5	3.6	0.35
2	1.0	7.2	0.71
3	1.5	10.7	1.05
4	2.0	14.3	1.41
5	2.5	18.0	1.76
6	3.0	21.6	2.12
7	3.5	25.1	2.46
8	4.0	28.8	2.82

Experiment 2

To determine how the length of the current loop affects the magnetic force acting on it, Experiment 1 was repeated using four different current loop lengths: 1.2 cm, 2.4 cm, 3.6 cm, and 4.8 cm. The scale reading was recorded while 1.5 A of current was applied to each current loop length lowered into the magnet channel. The results are summarized in Table 4.

Table 4: Experiment 2 Data and Calculations			
Trial	Loop Length, L (10^{-2} m)	Scale Reading, m (10^{-4} kg)	Force, F (10^{-2} N)
1	1.2	5.4	0.53
2	2.4	10.7	1.05
3	3.6	15.9	1.56
4	4.8	21.6	2.12

Experiment 3

To determine how the strength of the magnetic field affects the magnetic force acting on the current loop, Experiment 1 was repeated using different numbers of parallel magnets. Each time a magnet was added, the scale was zeroed. For each magnet arrangement, the scale reading was recorded while 1.5 A of current was applied to a 2.4 cm loop lowered into the center magnet channel. The results are summarized in Table 5.

Table 5: Experiment 3 Data and Calculations			
Trial	Number of Magnets	Scale Reading, m (10^{-4} kg)	Force, F (10^{-2} N)
1	1	10.7	1.05
2	2	21.6	2.12
3	3	32.3	3.17
4	4	42.9	4.20

27. According to the experimental results, for one magnet and a 2.4 cm loop carrying a 2.5 A current, the electronic scale showed a reading of:

A. 0 kg.
B. 18.0×10^{-2} kg.
C. 1.76×10^{-2} kg.
D. 18.0×10^{-4} kg.

28. According to the experimental results, the strength of the magnetic force of one magnet acting on a 4.8 cm loop carrying a 1.5 A current was:

F. 21.6×10^{-4} N.
G. 1.05×10^{-2} N.
H. 2.12×10^{-2} N.
J. not determined by any of the experimental trials conducted.

29. According to the information provided, which one of the following is NOT true for the current balance in these experiments?

A. The magnetic force on the current loop increases for increasing current.
B. The magnetic force on the current loop decreases for decreasing loop length.
C. The magnetic force on the current loop increases for increasing magnetic field.
D. The scale reading increases for decreasing magnetic force on the current loop.

30. According to the experimental results, for a fixed number of magnets and current, if the current loop length is doubled, then the magnetic force on the current loop:

F. decreases by approximately half.
G. remains constant.
H. increases by approximately one-third.
J. approximately doubles.

31. Which of the following graphs best represents the results from both Experiments 1 and 2?

A.

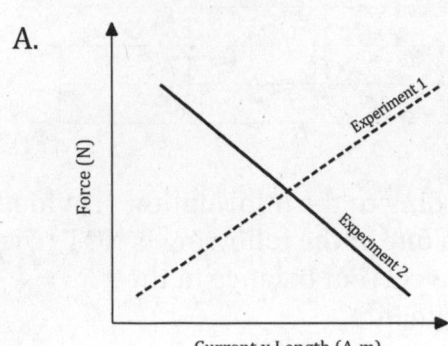

B.

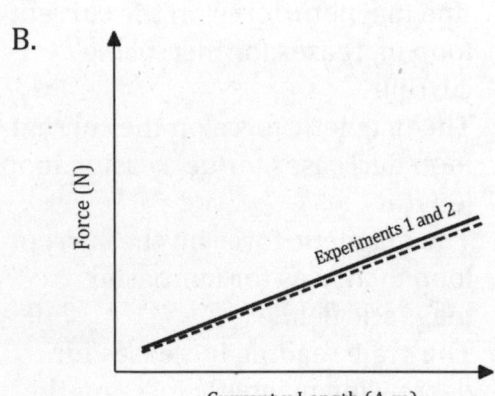

C.

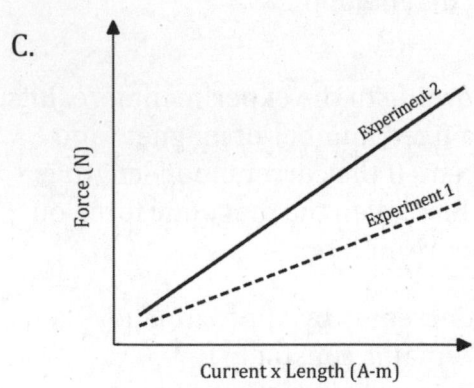

D.

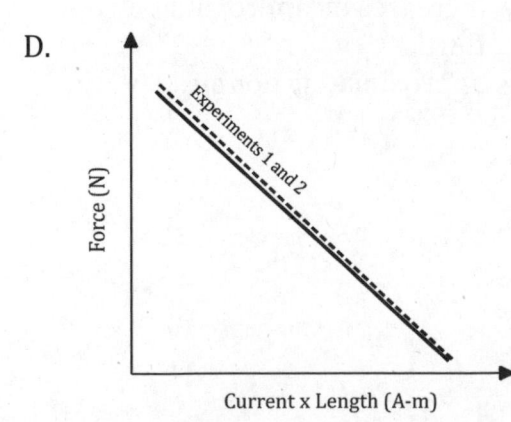

32. According to the experimental setups, the electronic scale was zeroed without the current loop in place for each magnet arrangement. If the students had forgotten this step in each experiment, how do they adjust the data once the experiments are over?

F. Add the mass of each magnet arrangement to the corresponding scale readings.
G. Subtract the mass of each magnet arrangement from the force calculations.
H. Subtract the mass of each magnet arrangement from the corresponding scale readings.
J. It is not possible to correct for failing to zero the scale once the experiments are over.

33. According to the information provided and Table 4, which of the following expressions correctly calculates the experimental magnetic force on the 3.6 cm current loop in Experiment 2?

A. $F = 1.5 \times 0.036 \times 1.56$
B. $F = 0.00159 \times 9.8$
C. $F = 5.4 \times 9.8$
D. $F = 15.9 \times 9.8$

34. According to the experimental results, how much current through a 2.4 cm loop placed in the channel of four parallel magnets is needed to create a magnetic force equal to 4.20×10^{-2} N?

F. 1.5 A
G. 4.0 A
H. 8.0 A
J. Cannot be determined from the provided information.

35. According to the experimental results, the strength of the magnetic force of two magnets acting on a 2.4 cm loop carrying a current of 2.5 A was:

A. 18.0×10^{-4} N.
B. 1.76×10^{-2} N.
C. 2.12×10^{-2} N.
D. not determined by any of the experiment trials conducted.

36. According to the information provided, which trials in the three experiments had identical setups?

F. Experiment 1: Trial 3; Experiment 2: Trial 1; and Experiment 3: Trial 1
G. Experiment 1: Trial 3; Experiment 2: Trial 2; and Experiment 3: Trial 1
H. Experiment 1: Trial 3; Experiment 2: Trial 2; and Experiment 3: Trial 2
J. Experiment 1: Trial 6; Experiment 2: Trial 4; and Experiment 3: Trial 1

37. According to the experimental results, which of the following two experimental setups produced approximately the same magnetic force as one magnet with a 2.4 cm loop length carrying a 3.0 A current?

A. One magnet with a 2.4 cm loop length carrying a 1.5 A current and two magnets with a 2.4 cm loop length carrying a 1.5 A current
B. One magnet with a 1.2 cm loop length carrying a 1.5 A current and three magnets with a 2.4 cm loop length carrying a 1.5 A current
C. One magnet with a 4.8 cm loop length carrying a 1.5 A current and two magnets with a 2.4 cm loop length carrying a 1.5 A current
D. Two magnets with a 4.8 cm loop length carrying a 1.5 A current and three magnets with a 2.4 cm loop length carrying a 1.0 A current

38. If the students conducted a new trial using a loop length of 4.8 cm, a current of 3.0 A, and two magnets, the expected force would be:

F. $2 \times 1.05 \times 10^{-2}$ N.
G. $4 \times 1.05 \times 10^{-2}$ N.
H. $6 \times 1.05 \times 10^{-2}$ N.
J. $4 \times 2.12 \times 10^{-2}$ N.

39. Over time, current-carrying wires experience increases in temperature. Increased temperature, in turn, decreases the current because the atoms in the wire become more energetic and decrease the flow of electrons. Based on this information, if the students extended the time for any of the trials in Experiment 3, what changes in values would be noted?

A. Scale readings would slowly decrease and force values would increase
B. Scale readings would slowly decrease and force values would decrease
C. Scale readings would slowly increase and force values would increase
D. Scale readings would slowly increase and force values would decrease

40. The students are in search of a new variable to test related to Equation 1. Which of the following independent variables would be the best choice if the students wish to address a novel scientific question not covered by their previous experiments?

F. Material of conducting wire
G. Shape of loop
H. Brand of power supply
J. Size of magnets

41. The following errors were discovered after the experiments were completed. Which error will require the students to repeat all or part of an experiment (as opposed to simply recalculating the collected data)?

A. The power source used in Experiment 2 provided 0.1 A more current than indicated on its dial.
B. The larger loops (3.6 cm and 4.8 cm) in Experiment 2 were touching the magnet.
C. The magnet used in all four of the trials for Experiment 3 had only 90% the strength of the other three magnets used in trials 2, 3, and 4.
D. A small paper clip was found on the bottom of the magnet used in all trials for Experiment 1.

Passage V

The electrical resistance of a conductor represents its opposition to the flow of electrons and is defined by the relationship known as Ohm's law:

$$R = \frac{V}{I}$$

(Equation 3)

where R is the conductor's resistance in ohms (Ω), V is the potential difference across the conductor, or voltage, measured in volts (V), and I is the electrical current applied to the conductor in amps (A). The material from which a conductor is made, the length of the conductor, the diameter of the conductor, and the temperature of the conductor are all things that impact its resistance.

Using a simple circuit (Figure 5), a group of students investigated the dependence of a conductor's electrical resistance on its length, material, and diameter. The ammeter measures the current produced by a variable power supply. The voltmeter measures the potential voltage across the conductor.

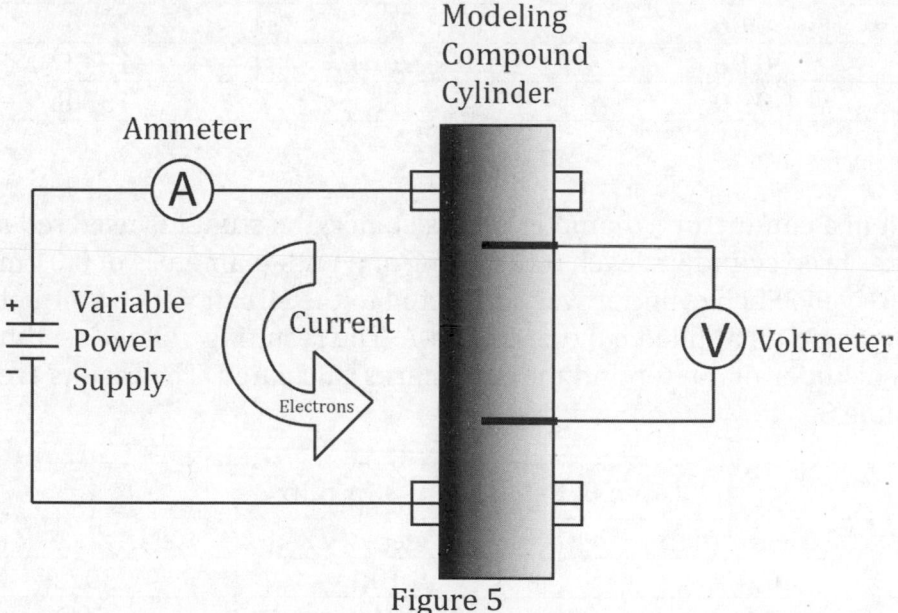

Figure 5

Experiment 1

To study the effect of a conductor's length on its resistance, the students used red modeling compound to make a cylinder 0.01 m in diameter and slightly longer than 0.1 m in length. The cylinder was connected to the circuit and a current of 0.04 A was applied. The voltmeter probes were inserted in the cylinder with a separation of 0.02 m and the voltage reading recorded. The separation distance between the probes is the conductor length. The separation was then increased by 0.02 m and the voltage recorded again. This was repeated until a total separation (conductor length) of 0.10 m was reached. The students calculated the resistance for each conductor length using Ohm's law. The results are summarized in Table 6.

Table 6: Experiment 1 Results			
Trial	Conductor Length (m)	Voltage, V (V)	Resistance, R (Ω)
1	0.02	1.58	39.5
2	0.04	3.15	78.8
3	0.06	4.79	119.8
4	0.08	6.34	158.5
5	0.10	8.10	202.5

Experiment 2

To study the effect of a conductor's material on resistance, the students repeated Experiment 1 for an identical cylinder made of blue modeling compound. The results are summarized in Table 7.

Table 7: Experiment 2 Results			
Trial	Conductor Length (m)	Voltage, V (V)	Resistance, R (Ω)
1	0.02	1.22	30.5
2	0.04	2.43	60.8
3	0.06	3.76	94.0
4	0.08	4.96	124.0
5	0.10	6.15	153.8

Experiment 3

To study the effect of a conductor's diameter on resistance, the students used red modeling compound to make three cylinders, each 0.12 m long and with diameters of 0.01 m, 0.02 m, and 0.03 m, respectively. Each cylinder was connected to the circuit with a voltmeter probe separation of 0.10 m and an applied current of 0.04 A. The resulting voltage reading was recorded for each cylinder diameter and the resistances calculated. The results are summarized in Table 8.

Table 8: Experiment 3 Results			
Trial	Conductor Diameter (m)	Voltage, V (V)	Resistance, R (Ω)
1	0.01	8.10	202.5
2	0.02	2.04	50.9
3	0.03	1.02	25.5

42. According to the experimental results, what was the voltage measured across the 0.01 m diameter conducting cylinder made of red modeling compound when the distance between the voltmeter probes was 0.08 m?

   F. 8.10 V
   G. 6.34 V
   H. 4.96 V
   J.   1.58 V

43. According to the experimental results, increased conductor length resulted in:

   A. decreased voltage.
   B. decreased resistance.
   C. increased resistance.
   D. increased current.

44. According to the experimental results, increased conductor diameter resulted in:

   F. decreased voltage.
   G. increased resistance.
   H. increased voltage.
   G. increased current.

45. According to the experimental results, conductor resistance:

   A. increases with increased conductor length, decreases with increased conductor diameter, and is independent of conductor material.
   B. decreases with increased conductor length, increases with increased conductor diameter, and is dependent on conductor material.
   C. increases with increased conductor length, decreases with increased conductor diameter, and is dependent on conductor material.
   D. increases with increased conductor length, increases with increased conductor diameter, and is independent of conductor material.

46. According to the experimental results, which one of the following is true?

   F. Red modeling compound has the same electrical resistance as blue modeling compound.
   G. Red modeling compound has less electrical resistance than blue modeling compound.
   H. Red modeling compound has less electrical resistance than blue modeling compound for low currents and greater electrical resistance for high currents.
   J. Red modeling compound has greater electrical resistance than blue modeling compound.

47. Which of the following graphs correctly represents how the electrical resistance of the conductor in Experiment 1 changed as a function of voltage across the conductor?

A.
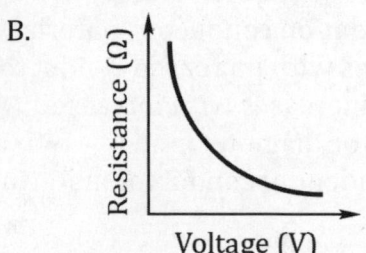

B.
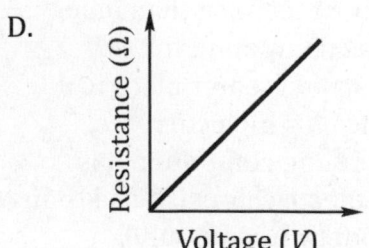

C.

D.

48. According to the information provided, which of the following were used in all three experiments?

F.   Voltmeter, ammeter, and galvanometer
G.   Voltmeter, ammeter, and red modeling compound
H.   Voltmeter, ammeter, and blue modeling compound
J.   Voltmeter, ammeter, and variable power supply

49. Which of the following describes the trial that tested a conducting cylinder made of red modeling compound that had a length of 0.12 m and a diameter of 0.02 m?

A.   Current, voltage, and resistance were 4 A, 2.04 V, and 50.9 Ω, respectively.
B.   Current, voltage, and resistance were 0.04 A, 2.04 V, and 50.9 Ω, respectively.
C.   Current, voltage, and resistance were 0.04 A, 8.10 V, and 202.5 Ω, respectively.
D.   Current, voltage, and resistance were 0.04 A, 6.15 V, and 153.8 Ω, respectively.

50. According to the information provided, which of the following had identical experimental setups?

    F. Trial 1 in Experiment 1 and Trial 2 in Experiment 3

    G. Trial 4 in Experiment 1 and Trial 5 in Experiment 2

    H. Trial 5 in Experiment 1 and Trial 1 in Experiment 3

    J. None of the trials in any experiment have identical setups.

51. According to the information provided, which one of the following was a controlled variable in all three experiments?

    A. Voltage

    B. Current

    C. Conductor length

    D. Conductor diameter

52. The students wish to use the calculated resistance values to predict the results of other hypothetical trials. Based on the data obtained, extrapolation would be most difficult for which of the following situations?

    F. Red modeling compound with 0.20 m conductor length

    G. Blue modeling compound with 0.20 m conductor length

    H. Red modeling compound with 0.06 m conductor diameter

    J. Extrapolation would be equally difficult for all these situations.

53. After all trials were completed, the students discovered that the ammeter used in the circuit was faulty. Actual current readings were 0.02 A rather than 0.04 A. Which of the following is the best way for the students to address this discrepancy?

    A. Conductor length values should be recalculated.

    B. Voltage drop values should be recalculated.

    C. Resistance values should be recalculated.

    D. It will be necessary to repeat the entire experiment.

54. After all trials were completed, the students discovered that the ammeter used in the circuit was faulty. Actual current readings were 0.02 A rather than 0.04 A. What impact will this discrepancy have on the values reported in Table 8?

    F. Voltage values will be smaller than reported in the table.

    G. Resistance values will be smaller than reported in the table.

    H. Resistance values will be larger than reported in the table.

    J. None of the values will be affected by the discrepancy.

55. The data from all three experiments closely adhere to Ohm's law. Which of the following offers the best explanation for this fact?

   A. Resistance values were computed using Ohm's law.

   B. The red and blue modeling compound are good conductors.

   C. The ammeter and voltmeter were correctly added to the circuit.

   D. Voltage and resistance are directly proportional in all three experiments.

56. Based on the experimental results, the students hypothesize that the resistance of all conductors decreases with increasing diameter. Which of the following proposed experiments would offer the best way to test the general applicability of this hypothesis?

   F. Repeat Experiment 1 with blue modeling compound.

   G. Repeat Experiment 1 with red modeling compound.

   H. Repeat Experiment 3 with green modeling compound.

   J. Repeat Experiment 3 with a metallic conductor.

Passage VI

Capacitors are electrical devices used to store energy in an electric field. A simple capacitor consists of two conducting metal parallel plates, separated by an insulating material, or dielectric, such as plastic, paper, glass, or mica. When the plates of the capacitor are connected to the terminals of a voltage source, such as a battery, there is a potential difference (voltage) across the plates. A static electric field develops across the dielectric, causing positive charge to collect on one plate and negative charge on the other plate (Figure 6).

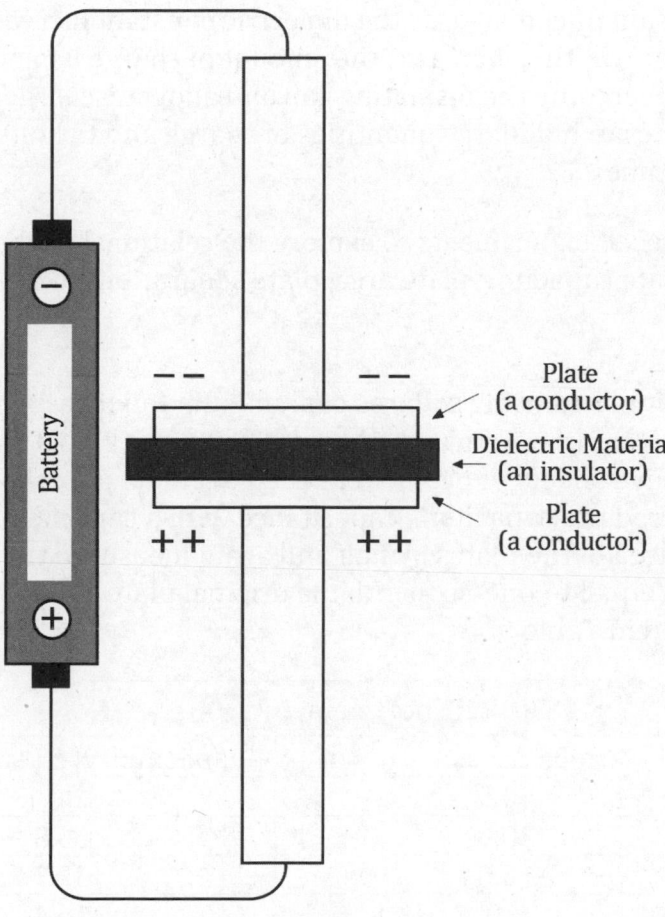

Figure 6

A capacitor's ability to store electric charge is called capacitance and is measured in farads (F). Capacitance (C) is the ratio of the electric charge (Q) on each conductor, in coulombs, to the potential difference (V) between them, in volts:

$$C = \frac{Q}{V}$$

(Equation 4)

For a parallel plate capacitor in which the plates extend uniformly over an area (A) and the width of the plates is much greater than their separation (d), the capacitance is given by:

$$C = \frac{k\varepsilon_0 A}{d}$$
(Equation 5)

The dielectric constant (k) describes the effect of the insulating material on capacitance. It is defined as the ratio of the permittivity of the material (ε) to the permittivity of free space (ε_0). Permittivity relates to the extent to which the material (or free space) concentrates electric flux. If all other factors remain unchanged, as the dielectric constant increases, the electric flux density increases. In a capacitor, this increases the amount of charge it can withstand before there is enough charge to overcome the insulating gap and allow discharge. This quality enables the capacitor's plates to hold large quantities of charge and to hold their electric charge for long periods of time.

A student conducted a series of experiments to explore the relationships between the capacitance of a parallel plate capacitor, plate area, plate separation, and dielectric constant.

Experiment 1

The student made capacitor plates using squares of aluminum foil measuring 20 cm per side. Paper with a dielectric constant of 3.7 and a thickness of 0.02 cm (2×10^{-4} m) was used to make insulating material. Five sheets of paper were used to create a total plate separation of 0.1 cm. The student measured the capacitor's capacitance with a capacitance meter. The student then reduced the area of the plates by half and again measured the capacitance. This was repeated until an area equal to one-sixteenth the original plate size had been reached. The results are summarized in Table 9.

Table 9: Experiment 1 Results		
Trial	Plate Surface Area, A (10^{-3} m^2)	Capacitance, C (10^{-12} F)
1	40.0	130.1
2	20.0	65.5
3	10.0	32.7
4	5.0	16.4
5	2.5	8.2

Experiment 2

The student made another capacitor identical to the original capacitor in Experiment 1. The student removed one sheet of paper at a time and measured the capacitance for each separation until a separation of 0.02 cm was reached. The results are summarized in Table 10.

Table 10: Experiment 2 Results		
Trial	Plate Separation, d (10^{-4} m)	Capacitance, C (10^{-12} F)
1	10	130.1
2	8	163.7
3	6	218.3
4	4	327.5
5	2	654.9

Experiment 3

The student made four capacitors identical to the original capacitor in Experiment 1, but each with a different insulating material of the same thickness (0.1 cm): paper, glass, mica, and polystyrene plastic. The capacitance of each capacitor was measured. The results are summarized in Table 11, including each material's dielectric constant.

Table 11: Experiment 3 Results		
Dielectric	Dielectric Constant, k	Capacitance, C (10^{-12} F)
Paper	3.7	130.1
Glass	4.8	169.8
Mica	7.5	265.5
Polystyrene plastic	2.4	84.9

57. In Experiment 1, what was the capacitance when the capacitor's plate area had been decreased to one-eighth its original size?

    A. 327.5×10^{-12} F
    B. 65.5×10^{-12} F
    C. 32.7×10^{-12} F
    D. 16.4×10^{-12} F

58. According to the experimental results, what was the capacitance when the capacitor had four sheets of paper acting as insulating material?

    F. 130.1×10^{-12} F
    G. 163.7×10^{-12} F
    H. 327.5×10^{-12} F
    J. 654.9×10^{-12} F

59. In Experiment 1, an increase in capacitance was a result of:

    A. the separation between the plates decreases.
    B. the separation between the plates increases.
    C. the surface area of the plates decreases.
    D. the surface area of the plates increases.

60. In Experiment 2, reducing the separation between plates resulted in:

    F. an increase in capacitance.
    G. a decrease in capacitance.
    H. no change in capacitance.
    J. an increase in dielectric constant.

61. According to the information provided, if all other factors are unchanged, increasing the permittivity of an insulating material results in the electric flux density:

A. decreasing in the insulating material.
B. decreasing in the parallel plates.
C. increasing in the insulating material.
D. increasing in the parallel plates.

62. In Experiment 3, the greatest capacitance resulted from the use of which of the following dielectrics?

F. glass
G. mica
H. paper
J. polystyrene plastic

63. According to the information provided and the experimental results, doubling the dielectric constant of the capacitor's insulating material results in the capacitance:

A. decreasing by half.
B. doubling.
C. being squared.
D. remaining constant.

64. According to the information provided and the experimental results, which of the following correctly lists the dielectrics used in Experiment 3 in increasing order of permittivity relative to the permittivity of free space?

F. mica, glass, paper, polystyrene plastic
G. paper, glass, polystyrene plastic, mica
H. polystyrene plastic, paper, glass, mica
J. Cannot be determined from the given information

65. Based on the information provided and the experimental results, which one of the following graphs represents the relationship between capacitance and dielectric constant, if all other factors remain unchanged?

A.
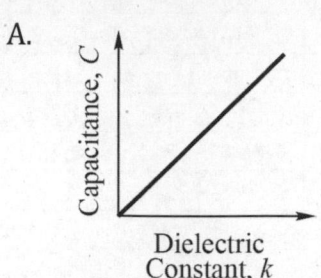

B.
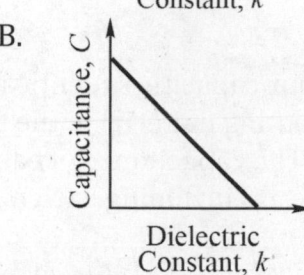

C.
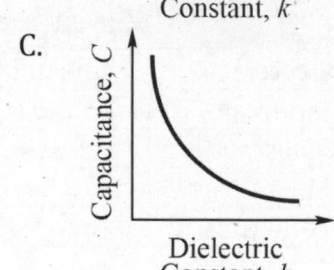

D.
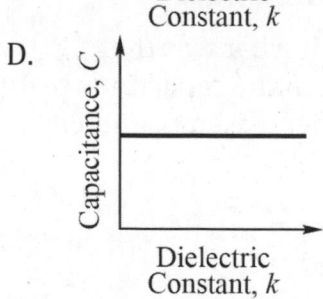

66. By the end of all three experiments, the student had tested how many different capacitor designs with a dielectric constant of 3.7?

F. 1
G. 9
H. 12
J. 14

67. According to the experimental setup, the parallel plates in each of the capacitors tested in Experiment 3 were made with:

    A. polystyrene plastic, paper, glass, and mica that measured 0.02 cm × 0.02 cm.

    B. polystyrene plastic, paper, glass, and mica that measured 20 cm × 20 cm.

    C. aluminum foil that measured 20 cm × 20 cm.

    D. paper that measured 20 cm × 20 cm.

68. According to the experimental setups, which of the following correctly lists the independent variable in each experiment?

    F. Experiment 1: plate surface area; Experiment 2: plate separation; Experiment 3: capacitance

    G. Experiment 1: plate surface area; Experiment 2: plate separation; Experiment 3: dielectric material

    H. Conductor material is the independent variable for all three experiments.

    J. Capacitance is the independent variable for all three experiments.

69. According to the experimental setups, which of the following are controlled and dependent variables in all three experiments?

    A. conductor material = controlled; capacitance = dependent

    B. dielectric = controlled; capacitance = dependent

    C. dielectric = controlled; voltage = dependent

    D. conductor material = controlled; dielectric = dependent

70. According to the experimental results, which of the following best describes the capacitor that had the greatest ability to store charge?

    F. Dielectric constant = 3.7; plate surface area = 2.5×10^{-3} m^2; plate separation = 2×10^{-4} m

    G. Dielectric constant = 2.4; plate surface area = 2×10^{-3} m^2; plate separation = 2×10^{-4} m

    H. Dielectric constant = 2.4; plate surface area = 40×10^{-3} m^2; plate separation = 2×10^{-4} m

    J. Dielectric = 3.7; plate surface area = 40×10^{-3} m^2; plate separation = 2×10^{-4} m

71. According to the information provided, which of the following must be true if Equation 5 is to apply to a parallel plate capacitor?

    I. The plates are uniform.

    II. The separation of the plates is much greater than their width.

    III. The width of the plates is much greater than their separation.

    A. I only

    B. I and II only

    C. I and III only

    D. I, II, and III

72. Based on the information provided, which of the following equations is equivalent to Equation 5?

    F. $C = \varepsilon A$

    G. $C = \dfrac{\varepsilon A}{\varepsilon_0 d}$

    H. $C = \dfrac{kA}{\varepsilon_0 d}$

    J. $C = \dfrac{\varepsilon A}{d}$

Passage VII

A vacuum tube is an electronic device consisting of two or more electrodes encased in an evacuated glass envelope. The simplest vacuum tube, or diode (Figure 7), contains two electrodes: a filament (cathode) and a plate (anode). A variable power source, such as a battery, is used to heat the filament and supply the plate voltage. When the tube's filament is heated sufficiently, electrons are emitted from its surface and are attracted to the positively charged anode. Since the electrons flow only one way—from the hot filament to the cool plate—diodes are commonly used in electronic circuits to prevent current flow in the wrong direction.

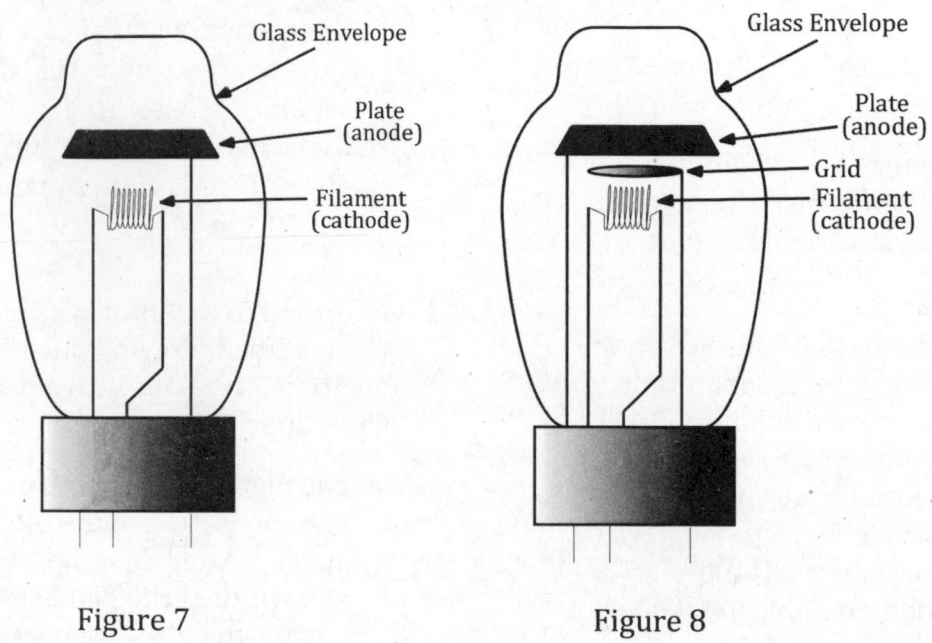

Figure 7   Figure 8

In a triode (Figure 8), the introduction of a third electrode, a wire mesh grid between the filament and the plate, yields another function. Applying a negative voltage to the grid slows the current flowing from the filament to the plate. Thus, it allows the device to be used as an electronic amplifier.

Experiment 1

Students conducted an experiment to see how the current flow in a diode depends on filament temperature and plate voltage. Using a variable power supply and infrared thermometer, the filament temperature was set to 800°C. An ammeter was used to measure the plate current as a function of voltage applied to the plate, which was measured using a voltmeter. The experiment was repeated for four additional filament temperatures: 850°C, 900°C, 950°C, and 1,000°C. The results are presented in Graph 1.

Graph 1: Diode Experimental Results

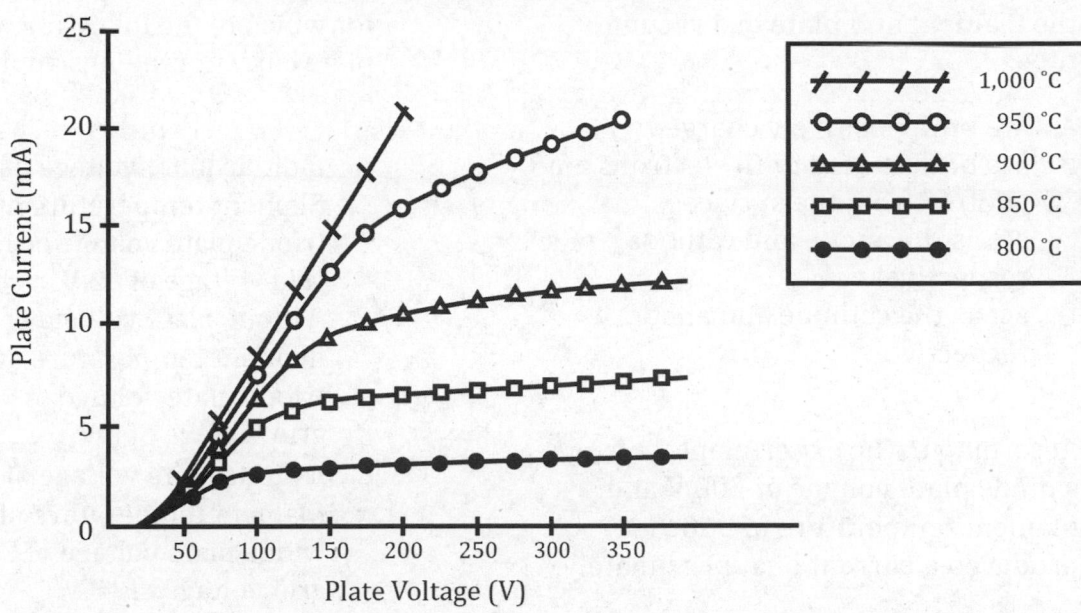

Experiment 2

Students conducted an experiment to see how the current flow in a triode depends on grid voltage and plate voltage. Using a variable power supply and infrared thermometer, the filament temperature was set to 800°C. The grid voltage (V_G) was set to 0 V. An ammeter was used to measure the plate current. Voltage applied to the plate was measured using a voltmeter. The experiment was repeated for four additional grid voltages: −2 V, −4 V, −6 V, and −8 V. The results are presented in Graph 2.

Graph 2: Triode Experimental Results

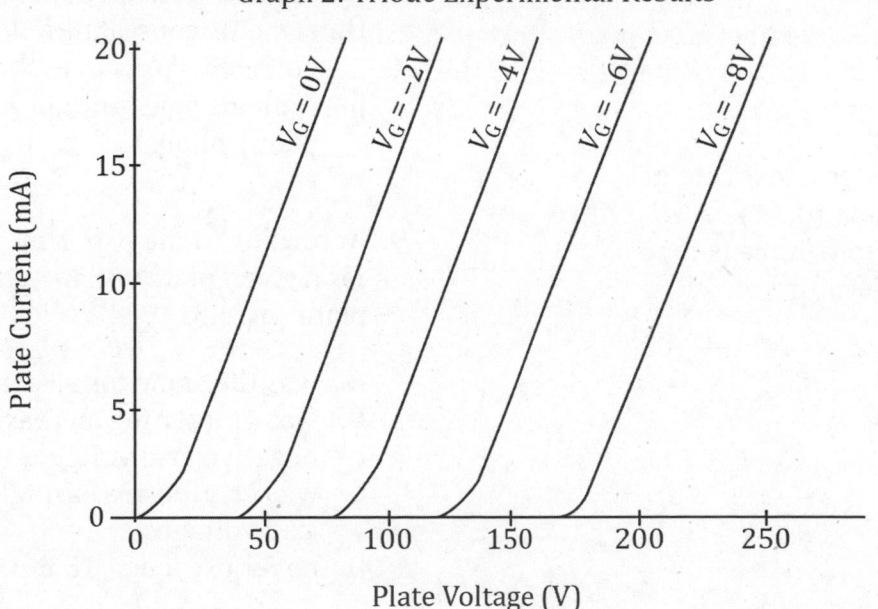

73. According to the information provided, the filament and plate in a vacuum tube:

    A. are both positively charged.
    B. are both heated until electrons are emitted from the surfaces.
    C. act as the anode and cathode, respectively.
    D. act as the cathode and anode, respectively.

74. According to the experimental results, a diode plate voltage of 200 V and filament temperature of 950°C produced a current of approximately:

    F. 5 mA.
    G. 10 mA.
    H. 15 mA.
    J. 20 mA.

75. According to Graph 2, the grid voltage that resulted in a current of 15 mA for a plate voltage of 175 V was:

    A. −2 V.
    B. −4 V.
    C. −6 V.
    D. −8 V.

76. In Graph 1, the greatest rate of increase in diode plate current with increasing plate voltage is for a filament temperature of:

    F. 80°C.
    G. 900°C.
    H. 950°C.
    J. 1,000°C.

77. According to the experimental results, for which of the following were the plate current readings approximately equal?

    A. A diode plate voltage of 125 V and filament temperature of 950°C; a triode plate voltage of 100 V and grid voltage of −2 V.
    B. A diode plate voltage of 175 V and a filament temperature of 900°C; a triode plate voltage of 45 V and a grid voltage of 0 V.
    C. A diode plate voltage of 250 V and filament temperature of 950°C; a triode plate voltage of 200 V and a grid voltage of −8 V.
    D. A diode plate voltage of 100 V and a filament temperature of 1,000°C; a triode plate voltage of 25 V and a grid voltage of 0 V.

78. According to the experimental results, as the filament temperature of a diode increases, the plate current:

    F. decreases for all plate voltages.
    G. increases for all plate voltages.
    H. remains constant for all plate voltages.
    J. remains constant for only certain plate voltages.

79. According to the experimental results, for a given plate voltage, the triode's plate current:

    A. was the same for all grid voltages.
    B. was greater for increasingly negative grid voltages.
    C. was less for increasingly negative grid voltages.
    D. never exceeded 15 mA.

80. According to the experimental setups, the current, the voltage, and the filament temperature were measured with:

    F. an ammeter, a voltmeter, and an infrared thermometer, respectively.

    G. an ammeter, an infrared thermometer, and a voltmeter, respectively.

    H. an infrared thermometer, an ammeter, and a voltmeter, respectively.

    J. a voltmeter, an ammeter, and an infrared thermometer, respectively.

81. For each of the curves in Graph 1, the controlled variable was the:

    A. plate voltage.
    B. plate current.
    C. grid voltage.
    D. filament temperature.

82. For both Experiments 1 and 2, the dependent variable was the:

    F. plate voltage.
    G. plate current.
    H. grid voltage.
    J. filament temperature.

83. Based on the information provided and the experimental results, which of the following conclusions is correct?

    A. In a vacuum tube, increasing filament temperature increases current flow from the anode to the cathode.

    B. In a diode, positive plate voltages increase current flow from the anode to the cathode.

    C. In a triode, negative grid voltages decrease current flow from the cathode to the anode.

    D. In a triode, positive plate voltages decrease current flow from the anode to the cathode.

84. Based on the relationship between current and filament temperature observed with the diode, an increase in the triode's filament temperature might be expected to:

    F. decrease the current in the triode for all plate voltages.

    G. increase the current in the triode for all plate voltages.

    H. have no effect on the current for all plate voltages.

    J. have no effect on the current for only certain plate voltages.

85. Based on the results of Experiment 2, applying positive voltages to the triode grid while keeping the plate voltage constant would cause the plate current to:

    A. decrease only.
    B. increase only.
    C. remain constant.
    D. increase, then remain constant.

86. For any given filament temperature, there will be a point at which all the electrons emitted by the filament will be drawn to the plate and a further increase in plate voltage will not increase plate current. Based on Graph 1, for which filament temperature is this phenomena most pronounced?

    F. 800°C

    G. 950°C

    H. 1,000°C

    J. This effect is not observed for any filament temperature.

87. At a given plate voltage, when the grid voltage is sufficiently negative, the plate current becomes zero and the triode is "cut-off." The negative grid voltage for which the plate current just becomes zero for a given plate voltage is called the cut-off grid voltage. Based on Graph 2, the cut-off grid voltage for the triode at a plate voltage of 100 V is approximately:

    A. −3 V.

    B. −4 V.

    C. −5 V.

    D. −6 V.

Passage VIII

The photoelectric effect is the emission of electrons from a metal surface when illuminated with sufficiently energetic photons of electromagnetic radiation. Photons are massless particles traveling in a wave-like pattern at the speed of light. The energy of each photon, E, is proportional to its frequency, v, in hertz (1 Hz = 1 cycle/second):

$$E = hv \qquad \text{(Equation 6)}$$

where the constant of proportionality, h, is Planck's constant $(4.14 \times 10^{-15} \text{ eV·s})$. From the relationship of frequency to wavelength, λ (m), and the speed of light, c $(3 \times 10^8 \text{ m/s})$, this energy can also be expressed as:

$$E = \frac{hc}{\lambda} \qquad \text{(Equation 7)}$$

In order for the photoelectric effect to occur, the incoming photon must have sufficient energy to eject a bound electron from the metal surface. This threshold energy, known as the work function, W, depends on the atoms that make up the metal. If the photon energy is equal to or greater than the work function, the energy is absorbed by an electron bound to the metal surface and it is ejected. Thus, the work function can be denoted as:

$$W = hv_0 \qquad \text{(Equation 8)}$$

where v_0 is the threshold light frequency required for an electron to be emitted from the metal surface. If the light frequency is higher than the threshold frequency, the excess energy will give the emitted electron a certain kinetic energy, KE:

$$KE = hv - W \qquad \text{(Equation 9)}$$

An apparatus for observing the photoelectric effect consists of an evacuated glass tube, that is, a gas tube empty of all gases, with an anode at one end and a cathode at the other (Figure 9). When radiation of sufficient energy hits the anode target material, electrons are released and move through the vacuum to the cathode. This creates an electric current, or photocurrent, in an exterior circuit that can be measured with an ammeter.

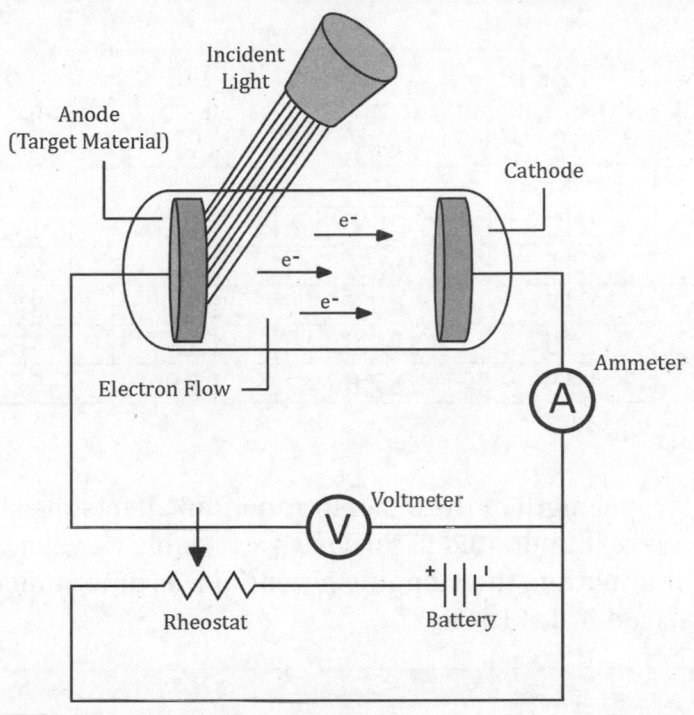

Figure 9

A negative voltage, supplied to the cathode by a battery and controlled by a rheostat, can be used to oppose the motion of the electrons through the vacuum. If enough negative voltage is applied, even the most energetic electrons do not make it to the cathode and no photocurrent is produced. The relationship between the maximum kinetic energy of the electrons, KE_{max}, and this voltage, known as the stopping potential, V_s, is:

$$V_s e = KE_{max}$$

(Equation 10)

where e is the charge on one electron. Therefore, the stopping potential in volts (V) translates to kinetic energy in electron volts (eV). Substitution of Equation 10 into Equation 9 indicates that a graph of the stopping potential as a function of radiation frequency is linear with the magnitude of the y-intercept equal to the work function of the metal surface.

Experiment 1

To demonstrate how the intensity of the incident radiation affects the photocurrent and stopping potential, a photoelectric apparatus with a sodium anode was illuminated with an ultraviolet laser of wavelength 360 nanometers (1 nm = 10^{-9} m). The photocurrent, expressed in microamperes (1 μA = 10^{-6} A), was measured as the light intensity was increased in steps of

20% of the source's rated total output. At each light intensity, the stopping potential was determined by applying a voltage to the cathode and increasing it until the photocurrent just barely stopped. The experiment was repeated for a potassium anode and a cesium anode. The results are summarized in Table 12.

Table 12: Experiment 1 Results						
Relative Light Intensity (%)	Sodium		Potassium		Cesium	
	Photocurrent (µA)	Stopping Potential (V)	Photocurrent (µA)	Stopping Potential (V)	Photocurrent (µA)	Stopping Potential (V)
0	0	-	0	-	0	-
20	54.7	1.15	45.9	1.25	115.7	1.55
40	109.4	1.15	96.5	1.25	231.4	1.55
60	164.1	1.15	149.7	1.25	374.1	1.55
80	218.8	1.15	195.6	1.25	462.8	1.55
100	271.0	1.15	257.8	1.25	574.4	1.55

Experiment 2

To demonstrate how the wavelength of the incident radiation affects the stopping potential, each of the three anodes were illuminated in turn with a variable wavelength laser. For each wavelength and anode combination, the stopping potential was determined as in Experiment 1. The results are summarized in Table 13.

Table 13: Experiment 2 Results				
Incident Light		Stopping Potential (V)		
Color	Wavelength (nm)	Sodium	Potassium	Cesium
Red	700	0	0	0
Yellow	580	0	0	0.24
Green	525	0.07	0.17	0.47
Blue	420	0.66	0.76	1.06
Violet	400	0.81	0.91	1.21
Ultraviolet	360	1.15	1.25	1.55

88. According to the information provided, in a photoelectric effect experiment, the stopping potential is a measure of the:

F. photon energy of the radiation incident on the metal surface of the anode.

G. energy required to eject an electron from the metal surface of the anode.

H. average kinetic energy of the electron emitted from the metal surface of the anode.

J. maximum kinetic energy of the most energetic electron emitted from the metal surface of the anode.

89. According to the experimental results, the stopping potential of potassium when illuminated with a 360 nm laser is:

A. 0 V.

B. 1.25 V.

C. 2.2 V.

D. 257.8 V.

90. According to the information provided, the photocurrent for the potassium anode when illuminated with a 360 nm laser at 100% intensity is:

F. 0 μA.

G. 271.0 μA.

H. 257.8 μA.

J. 574.4 μA.

91. According to the experimental results, what was the measured photocurrent for the cesium anode when illuminated with the ultraviolet laser at a relative light intensity of 80%?

A. 1.55 μA

B. 218.8 μA

C. 462.8 μA

D. 574.4 μA

92. According to the information provided, the negative voltage (supplied to the cathode of a photoelectric apparatus):

F. is measured with an ammeter.

G. has no effect on the motion of the electrons through the tube.

H. is used to increase the number of electrons moving through the tube as a measure of the photocurrent.

J. is increased until the photocurrent reaches zero as a measure of the anode target material stopping potential.

93. According to the information provided, the purpose of the rheostat shown in Figure 9 is to:

A. measure the amount of negative voltage applied to the cathode from the battery.

B. measure the photocurrent produced by electrons moving from the anode to the cathode in the glass tube.

C. control the amount of negative voltage applied to the cathode from the battery.

D. supply negative voltage to the cathode for stopping electrons from moving from the anode to the cathode in the glass tube.

94. According to the information provided, the glass tube in a photoelectric apparatus:

  F. is coated with metal target material.

  G. is empty of all gases.

  H. emits light of sufficient energy to cause a photoelectric effect.

  J. causes a flow of electron between the anode and the cathode, which in turn creates a photocurrent.

95. Based on the results from Experiment 1, it can be concluded that the photocurrent:

  A. increases as the relative light intensity increases.

  B. depends on the type of metal being illuminated.

  C. Neither (A) nor (B)

  D. Both (A) and (B)

96. The experimental results support which of the following conclusions?

  F. A decrease in the frequency of the incident light results in an increase in the kinetic energy of the emitted electrons and a decrease in the work function of the metal decreases the kinetic energy of the emitted electrons.

  G. An increase of the frequency of the incident light results in a decrease in the kinetic energy of the emitted electrons and an increase in the work function of the metal increases the kinetic energy of the emitted electrons.

  H. Both a decrease in the work function of the metal and an increase of the frequency of the incident light result in an increase in the kinetic energy of the emitted electrons.

  J. Neither a change in the frequency of the incident light nor a change in the work function of the metal affects the kinetic energy of the emitted electrons.

97. Based on the information provided, it can be concluded that the work function of a metal depends on:

  A. the frequency of the incident radiation.

  B. the maximum kinetic energy of the electrons.

  C. its stopping potential.

  D. the atoms that make up the metal.

98. According to the experimental results, which of the following conclusions is NOT true?

F. The stopping potential of the anode metal was dependent on the frequency of the light incident on the anode.

G. The stopping potential of the anode metal was independent of the relative intensity of the light incident on the anode.

H. The work function of the anode metal was independent of the frequency of the light incident on the anode.

J. The stopping potential of the anode metal is dependent on the relative intensity of the light incident on the anode.

99. According to the information provided, if the surfaces of both potassium and sodium are irradiated with photons of the same wavelength, the electrons emitted from the potassium surface will:

A. have a lower maximum kinetic energy than the electrons emitted from the sodium surface.

B. move with the same average velocity as the electrons emitted from the sodium surface.

C. have a greater maximum kinetic energy than the electrons emitted from the sodium surface.

D. move with a slower maximum velocity than the electrons emitted from the sodium surface.

100. According to the information provided, which of the following must be true in order for an electron to be emitted from the metal surface of the anode in the photoelectric apparatus?

F. The energy of an incident photon must be equal to or greater than the work function of the metal.

G. The energy of an incident photon must be less than the work function of the metal.

H. The stopping potential of the metal must be equal to or greater than the energy of the incident photons.

J. The energy of the emitted electron must be equal to or less than the work function of the metal.

Passage IX

Ionizing radiation is composed of subatomic particles and electromagnetic radiation with enough energy to remove tightly bound electrons from atoms, thus creating ions. Radioactive materials release ionizing radiation, typically in the form of alpha particles, beta particles, and gamma rays. Alpha particles are positively charged helium nuclei consisting of two protons and two neutrons. Beta particles are fast-moving, negatively charged electrons. Gamma rays are a form of high-energy electromagnetic radiation with wavelengths slightly shorter than x-rays.

A variety of materials may serve as shields against ionizing radiation. As the radiation enters the shield, it ionizes atoms in the material, losing energy with each ionization. If the shield is thick enough, the radiation will lose all its energy and not emerge from the shield.

A Geiger counter is a device used for detecting ionizing radiation. At the heart of a Geiger counter is a gas-filled sensing element known as a Geiger-Müller tube (Figure 10). Ionizing radiation enters the tube through a thin mica window, interacts with the gas molecules in the tube, and produces electrons and positively charged ions. A high-voltage power supply establishes a constant potential difference between a positively charged central wire electrode and a negatively charged outer casing. Electrons are attracted to the central electrode and positively charged ions are attracted to the outer casing, resulting in an electrical pulse relayed to an external counting circuit. Each counted pulse reflects the entrance into the tube of one subatomic particle or photon of ionizing radiation.

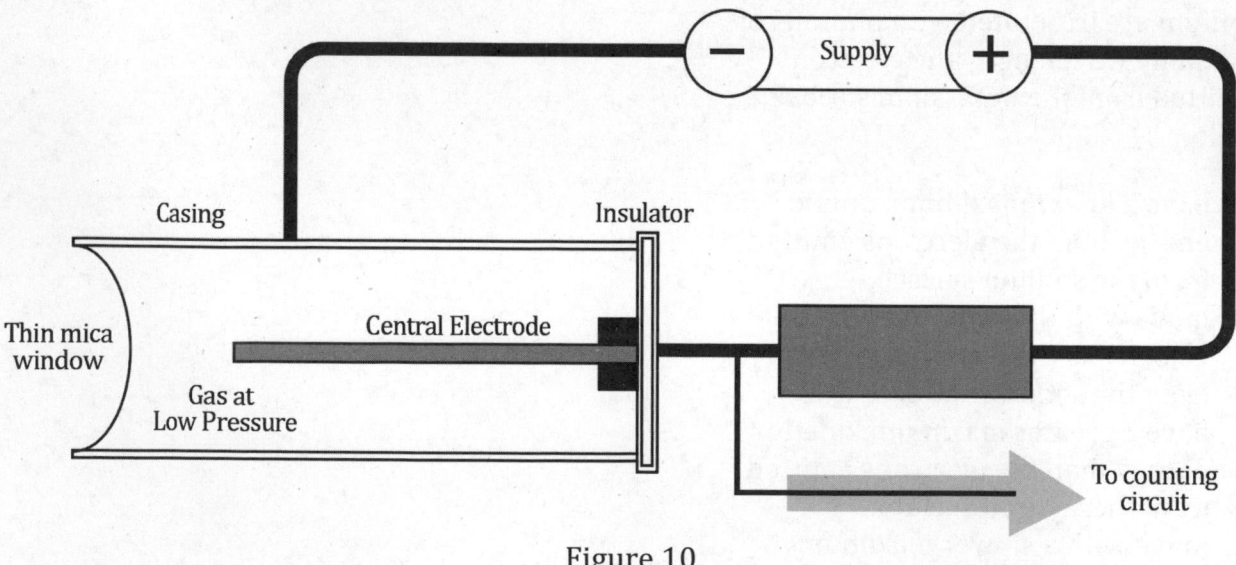

Figure 10

Radioactive decay is a random process resulting in inherent fluctuation in detector readings. In addition, Geiger counters are sensitive to background radiation, that is, radiation originating from sources present in the earth's environment other than the particular source being observed. Thus, any Geiger counter reading includes this background radiation.

Using alpha, beta, and gamma radiation sources, a group of students investigated how detection of ionizing radiation with a Geiger counter is affected by the distance between the source and the tube window and the use of shields between the source and the tube window.

Experiment 1

Using a Geiger counter, the students measured the background radiation. To ensure accuracy, all radioactive sources were removed from the room. Five one-minute trials were conducted and the average count rate calculated. The results are summarized in Table 14.

Table 14: Experiment 1 Results	
Trial	Count Rates (counts/minute)
1	15
2	13
3	16
4	17
5	14
Average	15

Experiment 2

The students placed the alpha source 1.0 cm from the Geiger counter tube window and took three measurements, each of one-minute duration. Measurements were repeated after increasing the source distance to 2.0 cm and to 3.0 cm. The experiment was repeated for the beta source and the gamma source. The average total count rates were calculated and corrected by subtracting the average background radiation count rate from Experiment 1. The results are summarized in Table 15.

Table 15: Experiment 2 Results						
Source	Source Distance (cm)	Count Rates (counts/minute)				
		Trial			Average	
		1	2	3	Total	Corrected
Alpha	1.0	272	273	275	273	258
	2.0	79	80	81	80	65
	3.0	42	43	44	43	28
Beta	1.0	331	335	332	333	318
	2.0	94	95	93	94	79
	3.0	49	51	50	50	35
Gamma	1.0	501	498	505	501	486
	2.0	136	136	137	136	121
	3.0	70	69	70	70	55

Experiment 3

The students used paper, aluminum, and lead, all of the same thickness, to measure the effectiveness of each material as a shield. They conducted three one-minute trials for each source with each shield. In each trial, the source was placed 1.0 cm from the Geiger counter tube window and the shield was placed between the source and the tube window. The average total count rates were calculated and corrected by subtracting the average background radiation count rate from Experiment 1. The results are summarized in Table 16.

Table 16: Experiment 3 Results						
		Count Rates (counts/minute)				
		Trial			Average	
Source	Shield	1	2	3	Total	Corrected
Alpha	Paper	15	15	17	16	1
	Aluminum	15	14	17	15	0
	Lead	15	15	16	15	0
Beta	Paper	330	333	334	332	317
	Aluminum	17	13	15	15	0
	Lead	14	15	16	15	0
Gamma	Paper	497	498	501	499	484
	Aluminum	478	473	475	475	460
	Lead	267	263	268	266	251

101. According to the experimental results, paper was the most effective in shielding:

A. alpha particles.
B. beta particles.
C. gamma rays.
D. Cannot be determined from the given information

102. Which of the following best represents the results from Experiment 2?

F.
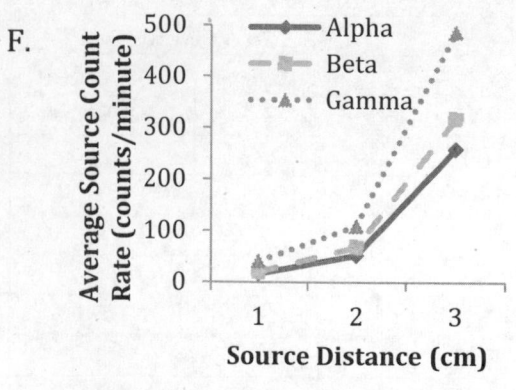

H.
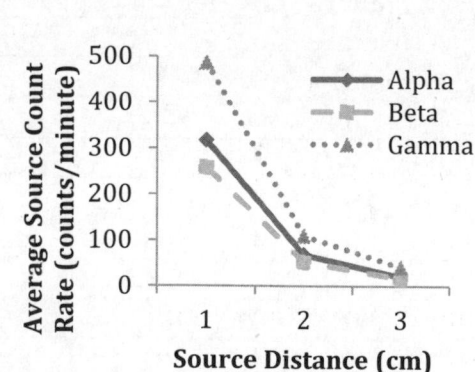

G.
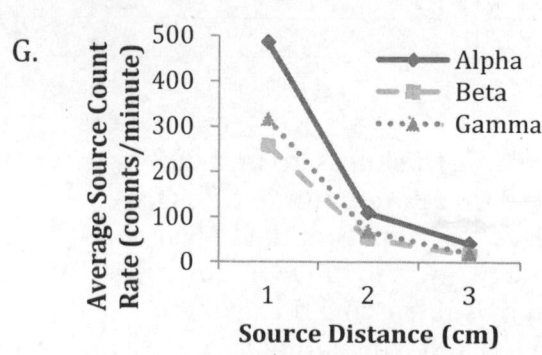

J.
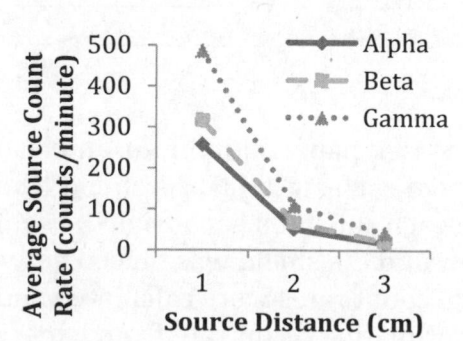

103. Based on the information provided, which of the following correctly represents where gamma rays fall on the electromagnetic spectrum?

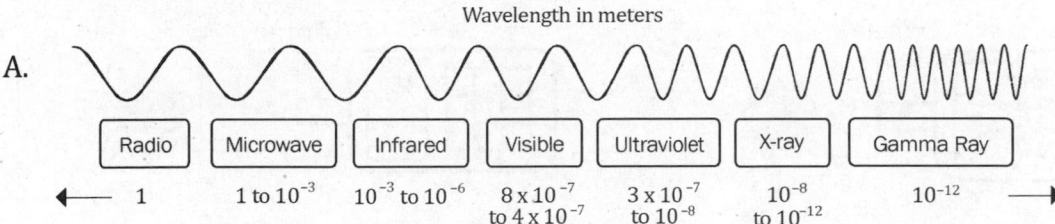

A.

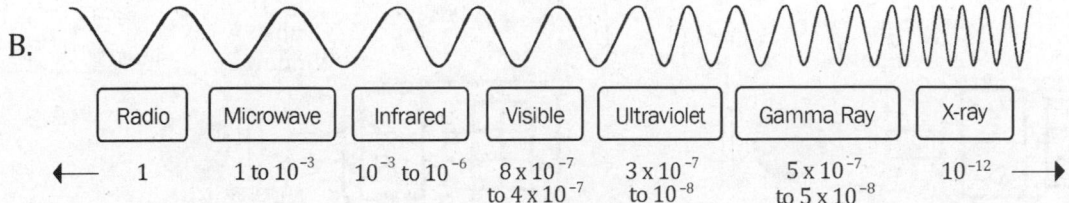

B.

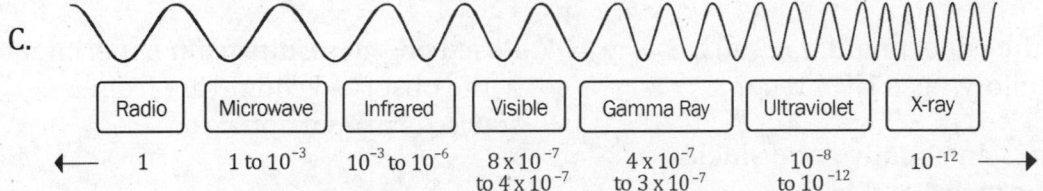

C.

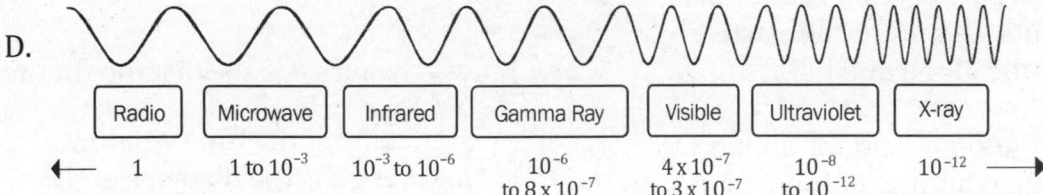

D.

104. Which of the following expressions represents the calculation used to determine the actual count rate, R_a, of the radioactive sources?

F. $R_a = R_{observed} - R_{background}$

G. $R_a = R_{observed} + R_{background}$

H. $R_a = \dfrac{R_{observed}}{R_{background}}$

J. Cannot be determined from the given information

105. Which of the following best represents the experimental setup in Experiment 3?

A.
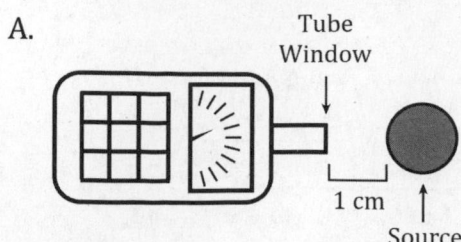

C.
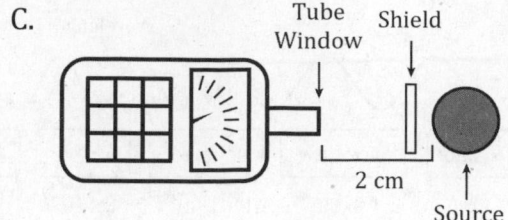

B.
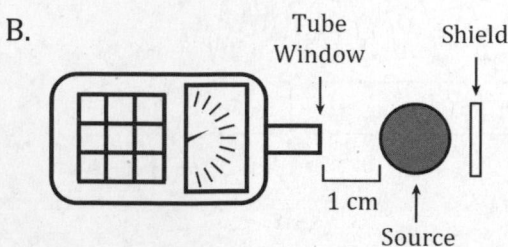

D.
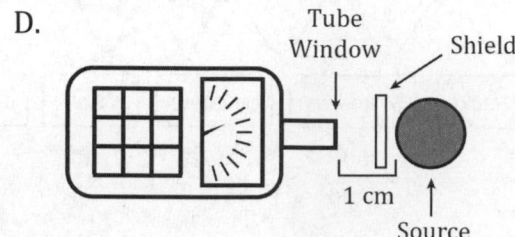

106. According to the experimental results, which of the following is NOT true?

   F. Aluminum is an equally good shield for alpha particles and beta particles.

   G. The gamma source used in the experiments was more radioactive than both the alpha and beta sources.

   H. Paper is a better shield for alpha particles than both aluminum and lead.

   J. Both aluminum and paper have a minimal effect on shielding of gamma rays.

107. Based on the results from Experiment 2, the observed count rate from a source is proportional to:

   A. $\frac{1}{r^2}$, where r is the radius of the tube window.

   B. $\frac{1}{d^2}$, where d is the distance of the source from the tube window.

   C. d, where d is the distance of the source from the tube window.

   D. d^2, where d is the distance of the source from the tube window.

108. Based on the experimental results, you can most effectively reduce your exposure to an ionizing radiation source by:

    F. increasing your distance from the source.
    G. decreasing your distance from the source.
    H. placing shielding between yourself and the source.
    J. both increasing distance from the source and placing shielding between yourself and the source.

109. For a given source at a given distance, there were fluctuations in count values in the different trials. This was true for both Experiment 2 and Experiment 3. Based on the information provided, this fluctuation is likely the result of:

    A. the random nature of radioactivity.
    B. faulty apparatus.
    C. experimental error.
    D. the time of day when the experiment was performed.

110. The background radiation of an environment is defined as the total number of emissions per second in all directions. Based on the information provided, if a Geiger counter is placed on a student desk in a classroom and allowed to collect measurements for a few minutes, why will it only detect a small fraction of the total amount of background radiation in the classroom?

    F. Source count rates are given in counts per minute.
    G. Source count rates include the background radiation.
    H. The Geiger counter is not equally sensitive to all types of radioactivity.
    J. The Geiger counter only detects radiation that enters through the mica window.

111. Using the results from Experiments 2 and 3, if a new trial were conducted for Experiment 3, using a paper shield, but where the distance from the gamma source to the Geiger counter is changed from 1.0 cm to 2.0 cm, what would be a credible value for the corrected count rate?

    A. 110 counts/min
    B. 256 counts/min
    C. 504 counts/min
    D. Cannot be determined from the information given

112. Using the results from Experiments 2 and 3, if a new trial were conducted for Experiment 3, using an aluminum shield, but where the beta source is moved from 1.0 cm to 3.0 cm from the Geiger counter, what would be a credible range for the total count rate?

 F. 1–2 counts/minute
 G. 12–15 counts/minute
 H. 33–335 counts/minute
 J. Cannot be determined from the information given

113. A new trial is conducted for Experiment 3, using a glass shield of the same thickness as the other shields, and where all other variables remain the same. What would be a credible value for the gamma source?

 A. 465 counts/minute
 B. 272 counts/minute
 C. 15 counts/minute
 D. Cannot be determined from the information given

114. After completing all measurements, the students determined that the Geiger counter was not perfectly lined up with the radioactive sources for any of the trials. For which experiment is the validity of the data NOT affected by the alignment error?

 F. Experiment 1
 G. Experiment 2
 H. Experiment 3
 J. All three experiments are affected

115. After completing Experiment 3, the students determined that the alpha source had been placed on a shelf in direct alignment with the Geiger counter and approximately 350 cm behind the beta and gamma sources. What is the likely impact of this error on trial results for the beta and gamma sources?

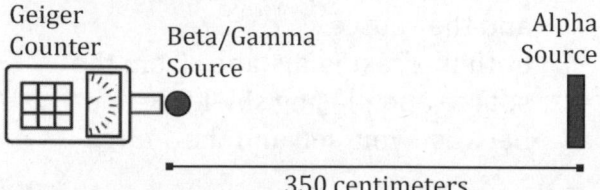

Geiger Counter   Beta/Gamma Source   Alpha Source

350 centimeters

 A. All values are invalid.
 B. All values remain valid.
 C. Paper shield values are invalid and all other values are valid
 D. Beta source values are valid and gamma source values are invalid.

Answer Key

Outline

English and Writing

English Basic

Exercise 1
(p. 6)

1. C
2. H
3. C
4. F
5. B
6. G
7. A
8. G
9. D
10. J
11. C
12. F
13. A
14. H
15. A
16. G
17. A
18. J
19. A
20. F

Exercise 2
(p. 10)

21. C
22. J
23. D
24. G
25. B
26. J
27. B
28. G
29. A
30. G
31. A
32. G
33. B
34. H
35. C

Exercise 3
(p. 20)

36. H
37. C
38. J
39. C
40. J
41. B
42. H
43. C
44. F
45. D
46. J
47. A
48. H
49. C
50. H

Exercise 4
(p. 24)

51. C
52. G
53. C
54. J
55. C
56. H
57. C
58. J
59. D
60. H
61. C
62. H
63. B
64. J
65. C
66. J
67. B
68. G
69. C
70. J

Exercise 5
(p. 29)

71. C
72. J
73. D
74. J
75. D
76. J
77. C
78. J
79. C
80. J
81. C
82. F
83. C
84. H
85. B
86. H
87. B
88. H
89. C
90. J

Exercise 6
(p. 34)

91. D
92. G
93. D
94. G
95. A
96. H
97. D
98. J
99. C
100. H
101. C
102. J
103. A
104. J

105. B
106. J
107. B
108. J
109. A
110. H

Exercise 7
(p. 40)

111. C
112. G
113. A
114. H
115. D
116. F
117. A
118. F
119. C
120. F
121. A
122. F
123. D
124. H
125. C
126. H
127. B
128. J
129. D
130. H

Exercise 8
(p. 46)

131. principal
132. accept
133. weather
134. into
135. advise
136. than
137. all ready
138. stationery
139. effect
140. sit
141. lie
142. altogether
143. passed
144. dessert
145. lose
146. affect
147. you're
148. used
149. rise
150. supposed
151. its
152. conscious
153. seem
154. allusions
155. complement
156. later
157. build
158. knew
159. personal
160. course
161. cloth

162. elude
163. no
164. ante
165. morale
166. capital
167. faze
168. excess
169. proceed
170. forte
171. disperse
172. formally
173. averse
174. incidence
175. dual
176. expend
177. discomfort
178. idol
179. emigrate
180. clique

Exercise 9
(p. 50)

181. C
182. F
183. C
184. F
185. C
186. F
187. A
188. H
189. A
190. F
191. C

192. F
193. B
194. H
195. C
196. F
197. D
198. F
199. B
200. H

Exercise 10
(p. 55)

201. D
202. H
203. D
204. H
205. D
206. H
207. D
208. F
209. D
210. G
211. A
212. H
213. D
214. F
215. B
216. H
217. C
218. J
219. A
220. H

English Intermediate

Exercise 1
(p. 60)

1. A
2. H
3. D
4. F
5. C
6. H
7. B
8. F
9. C
10. H
11. B
12. F
13. C
14. J
15. A
16. G
17. D
18. J
19. A
20. G

Exercise 2
(p. 66)

21. D
22. G
23. A
24. H
25. C
26. G
27. B
28. J
29. A
30. H
31. C
32. J
33. A
34. G
35. A
36. J
37. C
38. F
39. B
40. J

Exercise 3
(p. 75)

41. D
42. G
43. B
44. J
45. B
46. J
47. C
48. F
49. C
50. G
51. B
52. F
53. B
54. H
55. A
56. H
57. C
58. H
59. D
60. H

Exercise 4
(p. 80)

61. C
62. J
63. D
64. H
65. B
66. H
67. D
68. G
69. B
70. H
71. C
72. H
73. C
74. J
75. D

Exercise 5
(p. 85)

76. H
77. D
78. G
79. C
80. G
81. D
82. F
83. D
84. H
85. A
86. H
87. C
88. J
89. B
90. G

Exercise 6
(p. 91)

91. A
92. F
93. A
94. J
95. B
96. F
97. B
98. J
99. C
100. G
101. A
102. G
103. D
104. J
105. B

Exercise 7
(p. 97)

106. F
107. C
108. H
109. D
110. H
111. C
112. G
113. B
114. J
115. B
116. G
117. C
118. J
119. C
120. J
121. D
122. G
123. C
124. J
125. B

Exercise 8
(p. 103)

126. J
127. C
128. F
129. D
130. G
131. C
132. F
133. D
134. J
135. B
136. J
137. D
138. H
139. D
140. H
141. C

142. J
143. D
144. G
145. D

Exercise 9
(p. 108)

146. G
147. A
148. F
149. B
150. G
151. B
152. G
153. B
154. H
155. B

156. H
157. C
158. H
159. D
160. H
161. C
162. J
163. A
164. H
165. D

Exercise 10
(p. 112)

166. J
167. C
168. F
169. B

170. H
171. A
172. J
173. A
174. G
175. D
176. H
177. C
178. H
179. C
180. G
181. B
182. J
183. B
184. F
185. C

Exercise 11
(p. 117)

186. J
187. B
188. H
189. A
190. F
191. B
192. H
193. D
194. G
195. D
196. F
197. A
198. G
199. B
200. H

English Advanced

Exercise 1
(p. 122)

1. A
2. F
3. C
4. J
5. A
6. G
7. D
8. G
9. A
10. H
11. B
12. D
13. A
14. G
15. A
16. F
17. C
18. H
19. A
20. F

Exercise 2
(p. 127)

21. D
22. G
23. A
24. G
25. C
26. F
27. D
28. G
29. D
30. F

Exercise 3
(p. 133)

31. B
32. H
33. C
34. G
35. D
36. H
37. C
38. F

39. B
40. J
41. D
42. G
43. B
44. J
45. B

Exercise 4
(p. 137)

46. G
47. A
48. J
49. B
50. J
51. C
52. H
53. B
54. H
55. D
56. J
57. D
58. J
59. D

60. H

Exercise 5
(p. 143)

61. B
62. J
63. B
64. F
65. A
66. F
67. B
68. G
69. D
70. H

Exercise 6
(p. 147)

71. A
72. H
73. A
74. J
75. C
76. F
77. A

78.	J	87.	C	96.	H	105.	B
79.	A	88.	F	97.	B	106.	H
80.	G	89.	B	98.	F	107.	C
		90.	J	99.	B	108.	G
				100.	J	109.	B
						110.	J

Exercise 7
(p. 151)

Exercise 8
(p. 154)

81. D
82. F
83. C
84. G
85. B
86. G

91. C
92. G
93. A
94. G
95. D

Exercise 9
(p. 160)

101. B
102. G
103. B
104. J

Exercise 10 (p. 164)

111. William Faulkner, a great American author, writes books that are both poetic and grotesque.
112. After the bubble burst, many dot-com owners, who were briefly worth millions on paper, almost overnight found themselves looking for jobs.
113. Sergeant Rodriguez, who served two tours of duty in Iraq, was hard on new recruits because he wanted them to be well-prepared when they were finally deployed.
114. The naturally occurring grasslands of the southern Great Plains, which includes large parts of South Dakota and Nebraska, were replaced with cultivated fields.
115. Professional racecar driver Dale Earnhardt, Sr., who won 76 races in his career, was killed on the final lap of the 2001 Daytona 500 after making contact with another car and hitting the outside wall nose first.
116. Jack the Ripper is the best-known name given to an unidentified serial killer who was criminally active in the impoverished areas in and around the Whitechapel district of London in 1888.
117. During the Great Depression, the term "Okies" referred to very poor migrants from Oklahoma and surrounding states, who moved to California in search of jobs after the ecological disaster called the "Dust Bowl."
118. Professional athletes, because of the wear and tear on various joints, are prone to develop arthritis in later life.
119. The moon, which was not quite full, cast eerie shadows on the lawn and the side of the house.
120. Jules Verne, who is considered a major literary author in France and most of the rest of Europe, is usually regarded by English readers as a writer of fiction and children's books.
121. The first electric chair was built for the state of New York by Harold P. Brown, who was secretly paid by Edison to demonstrate that alternating current was more dangerous than direct current.

122. After placing his pregnant wife into Lifeboat #4, Colonel Astor stood on the starboard bridge wing smoking a cigarette with Jacques Futrelle, an American writer of detective fiction; 30 minutes later the ship slipped into the icy waters of the North Atlantic.

123. *The Constitution,* as *The Atlanta Constitution* originally was known, was first published on June 16, 1868, and was so successful that by 1871 it had killed off the *Daily Intelligencer,* the only Atlanta paper to survive the American Civil War.

124. At 11:30 a.m. local time on May 29, 1953, Edmund Hillary and Tenzing Norgay, a Nepali Sherpa climber from Darjeeling, reached the summit of Mount Everest, the first climbers to do so.

125. The Hope Diamond, also known as the Tavernier Blue, is a large, 45.52-carat diamond with trace amounts of boron within its crystal structure that makes it appear blue to the naked eye.

126. A cummerbund is a broad, pleated waist sash often worn with tuxedos, single-breasted dinner jackets first adopted by British military officers in colonial India as an alternative to a waistcoat.

127. Unlike other modes of diving, which rely either on breath-hold or on air pumped from the surface, scuba divers carry their own source of oxygen, a system that allows greater freedom of movement.

128. Hypothermia, a condition in which core body temperature drops below that required for normal metabolism and other bodily functions, is the opposite of hyperthermia, which is present in heat exhaustion and heat stroke.

129. The *Ride of the Valkyries,* the popular title for the beginning of Act III of the opera of *Die Walküre* by Richard Wagner, was used in *Apocalypse Now*, a 1979 war film.

130. Kate Chopin, born Katherine O'Flaherty, was an American author of short stories and novels who is now considered by some to have been a forerunner of feminist authors of the twentieth century.

Exercise 11
(p. 167)

131. A
132. J
133. C
134. J
135. C

Exercise 12
(p. 169)

136. F
137. A
138. G
139. B
140. F

Writing an Essay

Exercise 1 (p. 187)

Above Average Response

Parents, educators, and government leaders are increasingly concerned about the quality of education in our schools. Recently, the government instituted a policy of comprehensive testing to ensure that all students are getting a quality education and that no child is left behind. The theory is that these tests show what students have learned. If the students in a particular school don't score high enough, then that school is deemed to be failing its students. At that point, special programs are made available to provide additional instruction and tutoring to the school's students. The additional opportunities are supposed to help students learn and then perform better on the tests.

If you think about the structure of education, you'll see that it involves teachers and students in a school setting. Teachers have always evaluated students. Periodically, teachers give us tests, and we get report cards to tell our parents how we are doing in school. The new government testing is designed to find out whether schools are doing a good job. But in all of this, no one is testing the teachers. I think that if everyone is serious about improving the quality of education, then it would be a good idea to have students give their teachers report cards. These report cards would help administrators evaluate teachers, improve the quality of teaching by addressing problems, and ensure that students receive the best possible education.

From a school improvement standpoint, teacher evaluations would help administrators learn which teachers are doing a good job and which teachers are not. When a student performs poorly in math, everyone assumes that it is the student who is at fault. And with the new testing program, if the average math score is low, then it must be the school that is failing. But it might also be the case that a single bad teacher is the real cause. A teacher who can't make math concepts clear to students could easily have an entire class with students getting poor marks on their report cards. Parents will lecture their children but never realize that the whole class has the same problem. The school may get blamed for not providing a quality education, but maybe there are other classes in the school that don't have this problem. In other words, student evaluations could be a valuable tool for identifying the real problem.

Another advantage of student evaluations would be improving the quality of teaching. Let's say, for example, that a particular teacher speaks softly and is hard to hear. Students might not want to say anything about the teacher. If only one or two students complain, they may be considered trouble-makers. But if the entire class fills out an evaluation form and under "Ability to Communicate" says "The teacher is hard to hear," then the problem can be addressed. Administrators could meet with the teacher and go over the evaluations. They could suggest to the teacher to speak up more clearly.

The objection that students might retaliate personally is really just a red herring. Students are already permitted to vote for the "Outstanding Teacher" award (or similar awards) given by most schools. Additionally, it would be obvious from the tone of the evaluations if the teacher had been unfairly criticized. Statements like "A rotten teacher" or "Can't really help us" wouldn't carry much weight. Statements like "Speaks too softly" or "Doesn't answer questions about difficult topics" are useful.

Finally, a structured evaluation would make it less likely that students would comment on irrelevant factors like a teacher's personal habits.

If you listen to the debate about education, you can't help but notice that the issues are complicated. A quality education is not a simple matter. You need the right setting, the proper tools, motivated students, effective teachers, and good administration. It's like a complex recipe that calls for good ingredients mixed up in the right proportions and cooked at the right temperature for the correct length of time. Student evaluations of teachers is not going to solve all of the education world's problems. But student evaluations could be an important part of a successful recipe.

ESSAY SCORE QUALIFICATIONS	
POSITION ON ISSUE	The writer clearly states the position at the end of the second paragraph.
TOPIC DEVELOPMENT AND ESSAY ORGANIZATION	Although the structure of the essay isn't articulated in outline form (such as "Point 1," "Point 2," etc.), the structure is evident. The writer uses paragraphing and transitional phrases, such as "another advantage," to help the reader follow the train of thought. The writer develops the points within each paragraph. In the next-to-the-last paragraph, for example, the writer offers three reasons for believing that the danger of personal retaliation is not very significant.
LANGUAGE USAGE, SENTENCE STRUCTURE, AND PUNCTUATION	The essay might be subjected to two related criticisms. One, sometimes the examples seem to be a little abstract. The example of "math scores" never really gets very specific, though it is difficult to say exactly how the writer could improve on what is written. Additionally, the prose, while effective, seems a little dry. It lacks zip. Even the recipe analogy in the last paragraph seems flat. Maybe the writer could have mentioned a specific dish, say gumbo, in which several ingredients have to be mixed together to get the desired result. Even that little flair would have lightened up the writing style.
SUMMARY AND CONCLUSIONS	This is a very strong response. Most readers would say it fits the qualifications of a "Superior" or "Excellent" essay (see the "Essay Score Qualifications" table on page 185 of the student text).

Below Average Response

In my opinion, students should not get to evaluate teachers because it wouldn't mean anything, and it would just be a chance for some students to dump on teachers they don't like.

Teachers give students grades for a reason. Teachers know more than the students do because they've been to college. So when a teacher gives a test, that teacher knows the right answer and can mark the papers accordingly. This system makes sense. Students have not been to college. They don't have experience teaching classes. Most, if not all, students couldn't make up an exam to test a teacher's ability to teach. They wouldn't know which questions to ask on the exam and wouldn't know what the right answers are. So students really don't know how to grade a teacher on ability to teach.

Also, some, maybe even many, students would use the evaluation to take pot shots at teachers they don't like or have a grudge about. This would be especially dangerous if students got together to say the same thing. If only one student says a teacher is rude, then no one might care. If half the class says a teacher is rude, the principal would figure where there's smoke there's fire.

The evaluations could also be unfair to hard teachers. No students like to have a lot of homework, but homework is important. It's a given fact that some teachers give more homework than others. So would students give low marks to the teachers who gave the most homework? That seems like it might happen.

Even if there were an evaluation form with categories, this would still be a problem. Everyone could agree to mark low on "Preparedness" and "Ability to Communicate." That way, there wouldn't be any question asked about retribution. The students would be using the form.

Student evaluations of teachers is not a good idea. The whole thing won't help and it could really hurt some good teachers.

ESSAY SCORE QUALIFICATIONS	
POSITION ON ISSUE	The writer conveys the position in the first sentence. Although the position is clearly stated, the prose used is not an effective manner in which to start the essay.
TOPIC DEVELOPMENT AND ESSAY ORGANIZATION	This essay is pretty rough, but it does contain some relevant ideas. The writer explains that the evaluations would have limited utility and, further, that the system could be abused. The second point is developed in greater detail than the first. The writer argues that students might conspire against an unpopular teacher and that the evaluations might be used to retaliate against taskmasters. The final point in this development—that the evaluation form itself might mask this phenomenon—is particularly interesting.
	The essay lacks coherent structure. The writer fails to outline her ideas in the introductory paragraphs and does not use helpful transitional phrases.
LANGUAGE USAGE, SENTENCE STRUCTURE, AND PUNCTUATION	The essay suffers from informal language and glaring grammar errors.
SUMMARY AND CONCLUSIONS	The prose is not polished. Nonetheless, it is an honest effort and addresses the topic. This essay would likely fit the qualifications of an "Average" essay (see the "Essay Score Qualifications" table on page 185 of the student text). Some readers might not score it quite that high, and it would be surprising if it were categorized as "Good."

Reading

Reading Basic

Exercise 1 (p. 214)

1.	C	18.	F	35.	B	52.	J
2.	F	19.	D	36.	J	53.	C
3.	C	20.	F	37.	C	54.	J
4.	J	21.	A	38.	F	55.	C
5.	D	22.	H	39.	C	56.	G
6.	G	23.	C	40.	F	57.	C
7.	D	24.	J	41.	B	58.	G
8.	F	25.	B	42.	F	59.	A
9.	D	26.	J	43.	A	60.	F
10.	J	27.	D	44.	H	61.	B
11.	B	28.	F	45.	D	62.	H
12.	J	29.	B	46.	G	63.	D
13.	C	30.	F	47.	B	64.	F
14.	G	31.	A	48.	F	65.	B
15.	D	32.	J	49.	D	66.	J
16.	F	33.	B	50.	J	67.	B
17.	A	34.	G	51.	D		

Reading Intermediate

Exercise 1 (p. 256)

1.	A	18.	F	35.	D	52.	J
2.	G	19.	D	36.	F	53.	A
3.	D	20.	F	37.	D	54.	G
4.	G	21.	B	38.	G	55.	D
5.	D	22.	J	39.	C	56.	F
6.	G	23.	A	40.	J	57.	D
7.	B	24.	F	41.	A	58.	J
8.	H	25.	D	42.	F	59.	A
9.	C	26.	J	43.	D	60.	H
10.	F	27.	B	44.	F	61.	B
11.	A	28.	G	45.	D	62.	F
12.	G	29.	A	46.	F	63.	B
13.	B	30.	F	47.	B	64.	J
14.	G	31.	B	48.	H	65.	A
15.	A	32.	F	49.	A	66.	G
16.	J	33.	B	50.	G	67.	C
17.	D	34.	F	51.	C	68.	H

69.	B	76.	F	83.	C	90.	F
70.	F	77.	D	84.	G	91.	B
71.	D	78.	H	85.	A	92.	J
72.	G	79.	C	86.	G	93.	D
73.	A	80.	F	87.	C	94.	G
74.	F	81.	D	88.	H	95.	A
75.	A	82.	F	89.	A		

Reading Advanced

Exercise 1 (p. 305)

1.	D	16.	J	31.	A	46.	F
2.	J	17.	A	32.	G	47.	A
3.	B	18.	H	33.	D	48.	G
4.	F	19.	C	34.	H	49.	C
5.	A	20.	G	35.	B	50.	J
6.	F	21.	B	36.	F	51.	B
7.	D	22.	F	37.	C	52.	H
8.	G	23.	D	38.	H	53.	A
9.	A	24.	H	39.	A	54.	F
10.	J	25.	C	40.	H	55.	D
11.	B	26.	F	41.	B	56.	F
12.	F	27.	C	42.	J	57.	B
13.	A	28.	J	43.	A	58.	F
14.	H	29.	B	44.	H		
15.	A	30.	G	45.	A		

Mathematics

Mathematics Basic

Exercise 1
(p. 341)

1. C
2. J
3. D
4. K
5. A
6. H
7. D
8. H
9. A
10. H
11. D
12. G
13. E
14. F
15. E
16. J
17. B
18. F
19. B
20. F
21. B
22. G
23. C
24. K
25. B
26. G
27. E
28. J
29. B
30. J

Exercise 2
(p. 347)

31. B
32. G
33. C
34. G
35. E
36. J
37. D
38. G
39. E
40. H
41. D
42. J
43. D
44. H
45. E
46. F
47. A
48. J
49. C
50. H
51. C
52. F
53. D
54. H
55. B

Exercise 3
(p. 355)

56. H
57. B
58. H
59. E
60. F
61. E
62. G
63. B
64. H
65. B
66. K
67. B
68. H
69. A
70. F
71. D
72. J
73. A
74. H
75. B
76. H
77. A
78. G
79. C
80. G

Exercise 4
(p. 363)

81. C
82. G
83. B
84. G
85. E
86. J
87. A
88. H
89. C
90. G
91. C
92. K
93. D
94. J
95. B
96. K
97. B
98. H
99. B
100. J

Exercise 5
(p. 369)

101. A
102. J
103. C
104. F
105. B
106. H
107. C
108. H
109. E
110. J
111. D
112. F
113. D
114. K
115. C

Exercise 6
(p. 373)

116. H
117. B
118. J
119. A
120. F
121. C
122. J
123. B
124. J
125. E
126. F
127. D
128. K
129. B
130. H
131. B
132. K
133. C
134. F
135. D

Exercise 7
(p. 378)

136. K
137. D
138. F
139. D
140. H
141. A
142. H
143. E
144. G
145. B

Exercise 8
(p. 385)

146. H
147. D
148. G
149. A
150. H
151. A
152. K
153. C
154. J
155. D
156. H
157. D
158. H
159. E
160. H

Mathematics Intermediate

Exercise 1
(p. 395)

1. D
2. F
3. D
4. J
5. C
6. J
7. B
8. F
9. B
10. H
11. B
12. J
13. B
14. J
15. D
16. G
17. C
18. G
19. C
20. G
21. A
22. J
23. C
24. J
25. B

Exercise 2
(p. 406)

26. J
27. A
28. G
29. B
30. H
31. C
32. G
33. A
34. K
35. C
36. J
37. D
38. J
39. C
40. K
41. D
42. H
43. C
44. G
45. A
46. H
47. D
48. H
49. D
50. G

Exercise 3
(p. 421)

51. C
52. K
53. B
54. F
55. B
56. J
57. A
58. J
59. B
60. G
61. C
62. K
63. D
64. H
65. E
66. F
67. C
68. F
69. D
70. J
71. C
72. J
73. C
74. K
75. D
76. H
77. C
78. G
79. C
80. H

Exercise 4
(p. 438)

81. E
82. K
83. A
84. H
85. A
86. F
87. E
88. G
89. D
90. H
91. B
92. J
93. E
94. H
95. D
96. K
97. C
98. J
99. E
100. F
101. D
102. J
103. C
104. J
105. E
106. H
107. B
108. F
109. E
110. F

Exercise 5
(p. 456)

111. D
112. F
113. D
114. H
115. E
116. K
117. C
118. J
119. E

120. F
121. D
122. J
123. E
124. J
125. A
126. G
127. D
128. H
129. C
130. J
131. A
132. H
133. B
134. G
135. A
136. J
137. D
138. F
139. B
140. H
141. A
142. G
143. B
144. F
145. E
146. F
147. C
148. G
149. C
150. F
151. C
152. K
153. A
154. K
155. A

Exercise 6
(p. 469)

156. J
157. E
158. G
159. A
160. K
161. C

162. H
163. B
164. J
165. E
166. G
167. A
168. H
169. D
170. H
171. D
172. J
173. E
174. K
175. B
176. F
177. E
178. G
179. C
180. F
181. B
182. J
183. D
184. F
185. D

Exercise 7
(p. 479)

186. F
187. E
188. J
189. A
190. J
191. C
192. H
193. E
194. K
195. B
196. K
197. B
198. G
199. C
200. G

Exercise 8
(p. 485)

201. D
202. H
203. B
204. H
205. E
206. J
207. B
208. J
209. B
210. J

Exercise 9
(p. 498)

211. C
212. J
213. B
214. F
215. C
216. J
217. B
218. G
219. E
220. H
221. B
222. J
223. A
224. H
225. B
226. H
227. D
228. J
229. B
230. K
231. E
232. K
233. E
234. H
235. C
236. H
237. C

Exercise 10
(p. 508)

238. F
239. B

240.	J
241.	C
242.	J
243.	B

244.	J
245.	A
246.	K
247.	A

248.	H
249.	A
250.	G

Mathematics Advanced

Exercise 1
(p. 517)

1. D
2. H
3. D
4. H
5. C
6. G
7. D
8. J
9. B
10. J
11. D
12. K
13. D
14. H
15. D
16. F
17. C
18. G
19. A
20. F
21. E
22. J
23. D
24. J
25. B

Exercise 2
(p. 535)

26. J
27. E
28. G
29. E

30. K
31. D
32. J
33. C
34. J
35. A
36. K
37. D
38. G
39. C
40. K
41. D
42. H
43. C
44. G
45. A
46. K
47. E
48. H
49. B
50. F
51. D
52. K
53. D
54. K
55. A

Exercise 3
(p. 549)

56. J
57. E
58. J
59. C
60. F
61. D

62. H
63. D
64. J
65. B
66. G
67. D
68. H
69. A
70. F
71. E
72. F
73. E
74. G
75. D
76. J
77. D
78. H
79. E
80. J
81. D

Exercise 4
(p. 560)

82. G
83. E
84. J
85. B
86. K
87. C
88. H
89. C
90. H
91. B
92. G
93. D

94. G
95. C
96. J
97. C
98. J
99. C
100. F
101. C
102. K
103. D
104. J
105. D
106. K
107. B
108. H
109. D
110. F
111. C
112. J

Exercise 5
(p. 572)

113. C
114. F
115. B
116. H
117. C
118. H
119. E
120. H
121. D
122. G
123. E
124. J
125. B

126.	F	152.	K	175.	C	204.	J
127.	D			176.	F	205.	D
128.	G	**Exercise 7**		177.	C	206.	J
129.	E	(p. 592)		178.	H	207.	C
130.	J			179.	B		
131.	D	153.	D	180.	F	**Exercise 9**	
132.	K	154.	J	181.	E	(p. 620)	
133.	A	155.	A	182.	H		
134.	H	156.	G	183.	B	208.	H
135.	C	157.	D	184.	J	209.	E
136.	G	158.	H	185.	E	210.	G
137.	E	159.	D	186.	H	211.	B
		160.	H	187.	A	212.	J
Exercise 6		161.	B	188.	K	213.	B
(p. 582)		162.	H	189.	D	214.	K
		163.	D	190.	F	215.	C
138.	G	164.	F	191.	D	216.	H
139.	B	165.	B	192.	H	217.	C
140.	H	166.	H	193.	E	218.	J
141.	C	167.	A	194.	F	219.	B
142.	K	168.	G	195.	D	220.	G
143.	D	169.	A	196.	K	221.	B
144.	G	170.	G	197.	C	222.	H
145.	A	171.	D	198.	H	223.	C
146.	H	172.	H	199.	B	224.	G
147.	E			200.	G	225.	E
148.	K	**Exercise 8**		201.	E	226.	J
149.	A	(p. 608)		202.	F	227.	C
150.	H			203.	D		
151.	E	173.	B				
		174.	F				

Exercise 10
(p. 629)

Assumed Values	Values to Deduce					
	AB	Radius	Area of $ABCD$	Circumference of Circle	Area of Circle	Shaded Area
$AB = 1$	1	$\dfrac{\sqrt{2}}{2}$	1	$\pi\sqrt{2}$	$\dfrac{\pi}{2}$	$\dfrac{\pi}{2}-1$
Radius = 1	$\sqrt{2}$	1	2	2π	π	$\pi-2$
Area of $ABCD$ = 4	2	$\sqrt{2}$	4	$2\pi\sqrt{2}$	2π	$2\pi-4$
Circumference of Circle = 2π	$\sqrt{2}$	1	2	2π	π	$\pi-2$
Area of Circle = 4π	$2\sqrt{2}$	2	8	4π	4π	$4\pi-8$

Assumed Values	Values to Deduce						
	AB	AO	Radius	Area of $ABCD$	Circumference of Circle	Area of Circle	Shaded Area
$AB = 1$	1	$\dfrac{\sqrt{2}}{2}$	$\dfrac{1}{2}$	1	π	$\dfrac{\pi}{4}$	$1-\dfrac{\pi}{4}$
$AO = 1$	$\sqrt{2}$	1	$\dfrac{\sqrt{2}}{2}$	2	$\pi\sqrt{2}$	$\dfrac{\pi}{2}$	$2-\dfrac{\pi}{2}$
Radius = 1	2	$\sqrt{2}$	1	4	2π	π	$4-\pi$
Area of $ABCD$ = 16	4	$2\sqrt{2}$	2	16	4π	4π	$16-4\pi$
Circumference of Circle = 8π	8	$4\sqrt{2}$	4	64	8π	16π	$64-16\pi$
Area of Circle = 9π	6	$3\sqrt{2}$	3	36	6π	9π	$36-9\pi$

228. J
229. C
230. G
231. D
232. H
233. C
234. F
235. C
236. H
237. C
238. F
239. D
240. F

241. E
242. J

Exercise 11
(p. 649)

243. C
244. H
245. D
246. F
247. B
248. H
249. C
250. H

251. D
252. F
253. E
254. F
255. B
256. J
257. B
258. J
259. C
260. J
261. D
262. H
263. D

264. G
265. A
266. J
267. B
268. H
269. E
270. H
271. C
272. H
273. C
274. J

Exercise 12
(p. 664)

275. D
276. H
277. A
278. J
279. E
280. G

281. C
282. J
283. A
284. K
285. B
286. H
287. A
288. K

Science

Science Basic

Exercise (p. 686)

1. the experimental samples
2. salt content
3. human
4. F
5. D
6. F
7. D
8. F
9. C
10. H
11. A
12. J
13. B
14. F
15. B
16. J
17. B
18. F
19. C
20. G
21. C
22. F
23. C
24. J

25. B
26. G
27. A
28. J
29. A
30. F
31. B
32. H
33. A
34. G
35. C
36. G
37. C
38. H
39. B
40. G
41. A
42. J
43. B
44. F
45. B
46. J
47. C
48. H
49. B
50. G

51. B
52. J
53. B
54. H
55. A
56. J
57. B
58. G
59. C
60. J
61. A
62. J
63. D
64. H
65. A
66. J
67. C
68. J
69. C
70. H
71. B
72. G
73. B
74. G
75. D
76. G

Science Intermediate

Exercise (p. 721)

1. determine the effect of temperature on the heart rate of frogs
2. temperature
3. heart rate
4. size, type, age, and number frogs, as well as container size and amount of light
5. Group C
6. Groups A, B, and D
7. temperature, increased, heart rate of the frogs, increase

8.	H	27.	A	46.	H	65.	D
9.	A	28.	H	47.	B	66.	J
10.	G	29.	D	48.	H	67.	C
11.	C	30.	F	49.	C	68.	F
12.	H	31.	A	50.	G	69.	C
13.	B	32.	H	51.	D	70.	H
14.	J	33.	D	52.	G	71.	D
15.	B	34.	F	53.	B	72.	G
16.	J	35.	B	54.	H	73.	A
17.	C	36.	H	55.	A	74.	H
18.	F	37.	B	56.	H	75.	B
19.	A	38.	J	57.	B	76.	G
20.	H	39.	B	58.	H	77.	C
21.	C	40.	F	59.	C	78.	H
22.	G	41.	D	60.	F	79.	A
23.	C	42.	H	61.	A	80.	F
24.	G	43.	A	62.	G	81.	A
25.	B	44.	H	63.	D	82.	J
26.	J	45.	C	64.	G		

Science Advanced

Exercise (p. 754)

1.	B	42.	G	83.	C
2.	J	43.	C	84.	G
3.	C	44.	F	85.	B
4.	F	45.	C	86.	F
5.	A	46.	J	87.	C
6.	G	47.	D	88.	J
7.	D	48.	J	89.	B
8.	J	49.	B	90.	H
9.	A	50.	H	91.	C
10.	G	51.	B	92.	J
11.	D	52.	H	93.	C
12.	G	53.	C	94.	G
13.	A	54.	H	95.	D
14.	J	55.	A	96.	H
15.	C	56.	J	97.	D
16.	G	57.	D	98.	J
17.	C	58.	G	99.	C
18.	G	59.	D	100.	F
19.	A	60.	F	101.	A
20.	H	61.	C	102.	J
21.	D	62.	G	103.	A
22.	G	63.	B	104.	F
23.	D	64.	H	105.	D
24.	J	65.	A	106.	H
25.	D	66.	G	107.	B
26.	J	67.	C	108.	J
27.	D	68.	G	109.	A
28.	H	69.	A	110.	J
29.	D	70.	J	111.	A
30.	J	71.	C	112.	F
31.	B	72.	J	113.	D
32.	H	73.	D	114.	F
33.	B	74.	H	115.	B
34.	F	75.	C		
35.	D	76.	J		
36.	G	77.	B		
37.	C	78.	G		
38.	J	79.	C		
39.	B	80.	F		
40.	G	81.	D		
41.	B	82.	G		

Cambridge *Essential Skills, 12th Edition*
Error Correction and Suggestion Form

Name/Location: _____ Day Phone: _____ E-mail Address: _____

Part of Materials: ☐ Student Text, Specify Subject: _____ Page: _____ Item: _____

☐ Teacher's Guide, Specify Subject: _____ Page: _____ Item: _____

Error/Suggestion: _____

_____

_____

Part of Materials: ☐ Student Text, Specify Subject: _____ Page: _____ Item: _____

☐ Teacher's Guide, Specify Subject: _____ Page: _____ Item: _____

Error/Suggestion: _____

_____

_____

Part of Materials: ☐ Student Text, Specify Subject: _____ Page: _____ Item: _____

☐ Teacher's Guide, Specify Subject: _____ Page: _____ Item: _____

Error/Suggestion: _____

_____

_____

Part of Materials: ☐ Student Text, Specify Subject: _____ Page: _____ Item: _____

☐ Teacher's Guide, Specify Subject: _____ Page: _____ Item: _____

Error/Suggestion: _____

_____

_____

Part of Materials: ☐ Student Text, Specify Subject: _____ Page: _____ Item: _____

☐ Teacher's Guide, Specify Subject: _____ Page: _____ Item: _____

Error/Suggestion: _____

_____

_____

Part of Materials: ☐ Student Text, Specify Subject: _____ Page: _____ Item: _____

☐ Teacher's Guide, Specify Subject: _____ Page: _____ Item: _____

Error/Suggestion: _____

_____

_____

Part of Materials: ☐ Student Text, Specify Subject: _____ Page: _____ Item: _____

☐ Teacher's Guide, Specify Subject: _____ Page: _____ Item: _____

Error/Suggestion: _____

_____

_____

Mail form to Cambridge Educational Services, Inc. or fax form to 1-847-299-2933. For teacher's assistance, call 1-800-444-4373 or email solutions@CambridgeEd.com. Visit our Web site at www.CambridgeEd.com.